Open and Novel Issues in XML Database Applications:
Future Directions and Advanced Technologies

Eric Pardede
La Trobe University, Australia

INFORMATION SCIENCE REFERENCE

Hershey • New York

Director of Editorial Content:	Kristin Klinger
Assistant Executive Editor:	Heather Probst
Senior Managing Editor:	Jamie Snavely
Managing Editor:	Jeff Ash
Assistant Managing Editor:	Carole Coulson
Typesetter:	Carole Coulson
Cover Design:	Lisa Tosheff
Printed at:	Yurchak Printing Inc.

Published in the United States of America by
Information Science Reference (an imprint of IGI Global)
701 E. Chocolate Avenue, Suite 200
Hershey PA 17033
Tel: 717-533-8845
Fax: 717-533-8661
E-mail: cust@igi-global.com
Web site: http://www.igi-global.com/reference

and in the United Kingdom by
Information Science Reference (an imprint of IGI Global)
3 Henrietta Street
Covent Garden
London WC2E 8LU
Tel: 44 20 7240 0856
Fax: 44 20 7379 0609
Web site: http://www.eurospanbookstore.com

Library of Congress Cataloging-in-Publication Data

Open and novel issues in XML database applications : future directions and

advanced technologies / Eric Pardede, editor.

    p. cm.

  Includes bibliographical references and index.

  Summary: "This book not only provides the current issues of XML database research, but also provides a comprehensive list of challenges

for further research in XML database and visionary ideas for future XML database research"--Provided by publisher.

  ISBN 978-1-60566-308-1 (hardcover) -- ISBN 978-1-60566-309-8 (ebook) 1.

XML (Document markup language) 2. Database management. 3. Application

software--Development. I. Pardede, Eric, 1975-

  QA76.76.H94O68 2009

  005.74--dc22

                                                2008047743

British Cataloguing in Publication Data
A Cataloguing in Publication record for this book is available from the British Library.

Table of Contents

Section I
XML Repositories and Modelling

Chapter I

Mary Ann Malloy, The MITRE Corporation, USA
Irena Mlynkova, Charles University, Czech Republic

Chapter II

Mirella M. Moro, Universidade Federal de Minas Gerais (UFMG), Belo Horizonte, Brazil
Lipyeow Lim, IBM T.J. Watson Research Center, USA
Yuan-Chi Chang, IBM T.J. Watson Research Center, USA

Chapter III

Vassiliki Koutsonikola, Aristotle University of Thessaloniki, Greece
Athena Vakali, Aristotle University of Thessaloniki, Greece

Chapter IV

Giovanna Guerrini, Università degli Studi di Genova, Italy
Marco Mesiti, Università degli Studi di Milano, Italy

Detailed Table of Contents

Section I
XML Repositories and Modelling

Chapter I

> *Mary Ann Malloy, The MITRE Corporation, USA*
> *Irena Mlynkova, Charles University, Czech Republic*

As XML technologies have become a standard for data representation, it is inevitable to propose and implement efficient techniques for managing XML data. A natural alternative is to exploit tools and functions offered by relational database systems. Unfortunately, this approach has many detractors, especially due to inefficiency caused by structural differences between XML data and relations. But, on the other hand, relational databases represent a mature, verified and reliable technology for managing any kind of data including XML documents. In this chapter, the authors provide an overview and classification of existing approaches to XML data management in relational databases. They view the problem from both state-of-the-practice and state-of-the-art perspectives, then describe the current best known solutions, their advantages and disadvantages. Finally, they discuss some open issues and their possible solutions.

Chapter II

> *Mirella M. Moro, Universidade Federal de Minas Gerais (UFMG), Belo Horizonte, Brazil*
> *Lipyeow Lim, IBM T.J. Watson Research Center, USA*
> *Yuan-Chi Chang, IBM T.J. Watson Research Center, USA*

It is well known that XML has been widely adopted for its flexible and self-describing nature. However, relational data will continue to co-exist with XML for several different reasons one of which is the high cost of transferring everything to XML. In this context, data designers face the problem of modeling both relational and XML data within an integrated environment. This chapter highlights important questions on hybrid XML-relational database design and discusses use cases, requirements, and deficiencies in existing design methodologies especially in the light of data and schema evolution. The authors' analysis results in several design guidelines and a series of challenges to be addressed by future research.

Chapter III

Nowadays, XML has become the standard for representing and exchanging data over the Web and several approaches have been proposed for efficiently managing, storing, querying, and representing XML data originating from diverse and often heterogeneous sources. The Lightweight Directory Access Protocol is a promising technology for XML data storage and retrieval since it facilitates access to information organized under a variety of frameworks and applications. As an open, vendor-neutral standard, LDAP provides an extendable architecture for centralized storage and management of information that needs to be available for today's distributed systems and services. The similarities between XML and LDAP data representation have led to the idea of processing XML data within the LDAP framework. This chapter focuses on the topic of LDAP and XML integration with emphasis on the storage and retrieval approaches implemented so far. Moreover, the chapter includes an overview and survey of the theoretical background and the adopted practices as realized in the most popular and emerging frameworks which tune XML and LDAP.

Chapter IV

The large dynamicity of XML documents on the Web has created the need to adequately support structural changes and to account for the possibility of evolving and versioning the schemas describing XML document structures. This chapter discusses and compares the support for schema evolution and versioning provided by commercial systems as well as the most relevant approaches and prototypes proposed and developed by the research community.

Section II
Querying and Processing XML

Chapter V

Stream applications bring the challenge of efficiently processing queries on sequentially accessible XML data streams. In this chapter, the authors study the current techniques and open challenges of XML stream processing. Firstly, they examine the input data semantics in XML streams and introduce the state-of-the-art of XML stream processing. Secondly, they compare and contrast the automaton-based and algebra-based techniques used in XML stream query execution. Thirdly, they study different optimization strategies that have been investigated for XML stream processing – in particular, we discuss cost-based optimization as well as schema-based optimization strategies. Lastly but not least, they list several key open challenges in XML stream processing.

Chapter VI

Sven Groppe, University of Lübeck, Germany
Jinghua Groppe, University of Lübeck, Germany
Christoph Reinke, University of Lübeck, Germany
Nils Hoeller, University of Lübeck, Germany
Volker Linnemann, University of Lübeck, Germany

The widespread usage of XML in the last few years has resulted in the development of a number of XML query languages like XSLT or the later developed XQuery language. Today, there are many products like databases in the area of XML processing that support either XSLT or XQuery, but not both of them. This may prevent users from employing their favourite XML query language. In this chapter, the authors show that both languages have comparable expression power and present a scheme for translating XQuery to XSLT and vice versa. This translation scheme enables a user to employ either XSLT or XQuery for each product which supports one of these languages. They also summarize in this chapter both current and future trends and research issues and also consider those that might emerge in the common area of XSLT and XQuery and which are particular to XSLT.

Chapter VII

Mirella M. Moro, Universidade Federal de Minas Gerais (UFMG), Belo Horizonte, Brazil
Zografoula Vagena, Microsoft Research, UK
Vassilis J. Tsotras, University of California, Riverside, USA

Content-based routing is a form of data delivery whereby the flow of messages is driven by their content rather than the IP address of their destination. With the recognition of XML as the standard for data exchange, specialized XML routing services become necessary. In this chapter, the authors first demonstrate the relevance of such systems by presenting different world application scenarios where XML routing systems are needed and/or employed. Then, they present a survey of the current state-of-the-art. Lastly, they attempt to identify issues and problems that have yet to be investigated. This discussion will help identify open problems and issues and suggest directions for further research in the context of such systems.

Chapter VIII

Philippe Poulard, The French National Institute for Research in Computer Science and
Control (INRIA), France

XML engines are usually designed to solve a single class of problems: transformations of XML structures, validations of XML instances, Web publishing, and so forth. As the relevant operations or declarations are described with XML vocabularies, their respective engines have to face similar issues such as unmarshalling, and at runtime data handling. In order to address such issues, the author proposes an innovative and reliable XPath-based framework, Active Tags, that unifies XML technologies in a coherent system where various XML languages can cooperate. In our approach, we focus on its type system that enhances the XML Data Model, specifically by allowing XPath expressions to be applied on non-XML objects, and on the ability of the engine to mix declarative languages with imperative constructs. This valuable feature is illustrated with the Active Schema Language, which allows the building of dynamic-content models.

Chapter IX

Stéphane Bressan, National University of Singapore, Singapore
Wee Hyong Tok, National University of Singapore, Singapore
Xue Zhao, National University of Singapore, Singapore

Since XML technologies have become a standard for data representation, a great amount of discussion has been generated by the persisting open issues and their possible solutions. In this chapter, the authors consider the design space for XML query processing techniques that can handle ad hoc and continuous XPath or XQuery queries over XML data streams. They present the state-of-art techniques in continuous and progressive XML query processing. They also discuss several open issues and future trends.

Section III
XML Personalization and Security

Chapter X

Fabio Grandi, Università di Bologna, Italy
Federica Mandreoli, Università di Modena e Reggio Emilia, Italy
Riccardo Martoglia, Università di Modena e Reggio Emilia, Italy

In several application fields including legal and medical domains, XML documents are "versioned" along different dimensions of interest, whose nature depends on the application needs such as time, space and security. Specifically, temporal and semantic versioning is particularly demanding in a broad range of application domains where temporal versioning can be used to maintain histories of the underlying resources along various time dimensions, and semantic versioning can then be used to model limited applicability of resources to individual cases or contexts. The selection and reconstruction of the version(s) of interest for a user means the retrieval of those fragments of documents that match both the implicit and explicit user needs, which can be formalized as what are called personalization queries. In this chapter, the authors focus on the design and implementation issues of a personalization query processor. They consider different design options and, among them, they introduce an in-depth study of a native solution by showing, also through experimental evaluation, how some of the best performing technological solutions available today for XML data management can be successfully extended and optimally combined in order to support personalization queries.

Chapter XI

In an outsourced XML database service model, organizations rely upon the premises of external service providers for the storage and retrieval management of their XML data. Since, typically, service providers are not fully trusted, this model introduces numerous interesting research challenges. Among them, the most crucial security research questions relate to data confidentiality, user and data privacy, query assurance, secure auditing, and secure and efficient storage model. Although there exists a large number of related research works on these topics, the authors are still at the initial stage and the research results are still far from practical maturity. In this chapter, they extensively discuss all potential security issues mentioned above and the existing solutions, and present open research issues relevant to security requirements in outsourced XML databases.

Section IV
XML for Advanced Applications

Chapter XII

There is a proliferation of research and industrial organizations that produce sources of huge amounts of biological data issuing from experimentation with biological systems. In order to make these heterogeneous data sources easy to use, several efforts at data integration are currently being undertaken based mainly on XML. Starting from a discussion of the main biological data types and system interactions that need to be represented, the authors discuss the main approaches proposed for their modelling through XML. Then, they show the current efforts in biological data integration and how an increasing amount of semantic information is required in terms of vocabulary control and ontologies. Finally, future research directions in biological data integration are discussed.

Chapter XIII

Current data warehouses deal for the most part with numerical data. However, decision makers need to analyze data presented in all formats which we qualify as complex data. Warehousing Complex data is a new challenge for the scientific community. Indeed, it requires revisiting the whole warehousing process in order to take into account the complex structure of data; therefore, many concepts of data warehousing will need to be redefined. In particular, modeling complex data in a unique format for analysis purposes is a challenge. In this chapter, the authors present a complex data warehouse model at both conceptual and logical levels. They show how XML is suitable for capturing the main concepts of our model, and present the main issues related to these data warehouses.

Section V
XML Benchmarking

Chapter XIV

Since XML technologies have become a standard for data representation, numerous methods for processing XML data emerge every day. Consequently, it is necessary to compare the newly proposed methods with the existing ones, as well as analyze the effect of a particular method when applied to various types of data. In this chapter, the authors provide an overview of existing approaches to XML benchmarking from the perspective of various applications and they show that to date the problem has been highly marginalized. Therefore, in the second part of the chapter they discuss persisting open issues and their possible solutions.

Foreword

There are at least two reasons why I am particularly glad to have the opportunity to write a foreword to this book. The first reason is a personal one: it has to do with my fond memory of the exchanges of ideas I had with the book's editor, Eric Pardede, in 2002, when I was visiting at LaTrobe University. Even then, it was easy to see that Eric was to become a rising star in the field of XML-related research.

The second reason has to do with the book's title, "Open and Novel Issues in XML Database Applications: Future Directions and Advanced Technologies", and contents. Indeed, reading this book, one can fully understand how much XML-related research has changed the entire database field in the last decade.

Ten years ago, XML data items were still called "tagged documents"; in the best case, they were seen as instances of nested semi-structured data (Abiteboul, S., 1997). Indeed, XML was born already equipped with a loose notion of schema, the Document Type Definition (DTD), but in the late 1990s many researchers considered DTDs as little more than patterns that XML documents should match. Some experts even forecasted that most XML data would be produced without a DTD, leaving it to extractors based on formal languages theory to infer formal languages (the DTDs) from examples (the XML documents).

It took a couple of years before a clear notion of XML data as typed, semi-structured information complying with a schema, began to emerge. The notion of an XML data model proved to be of great interest for database research, since it allowed it to finally conquer the "no man's land" between traditional database models and semi-structured information. Up until that moment, that "no man's land" had successfully resisted the combined onslaught of traditional approaches to databases and of semi-structured data processing techniques.

On the one hand, structured DBMSs (RDB or OODB) cannot easily handle flat streams or text blobs, and need additional components to do so (Abiteboul, S., Cluet, S., & Milo, T., 1998); on the other hand, traditional semi-structured data handling techniques cannot always guarantee time efficiency in answering queries and space efficiency in storing information.

The XML format, instead, could support efficient storage and fast querying of diversely structured data sets. Once this was realized, much effort went into developing XML query languages, their indexing support, and their execution algorithms. Indeed, some researchers (and a few software vendors) had, for a while, maintained the latter to be unnecessary, provided that XML storage was implemented on top of a relational databases. Early evidence, however, suggested that reconstructing XML data from relational ones could introduce a substantial overhead (e.g., from computing joins to obtain XML nested structure); also, some extra effort might be needed to translate XML queries and updates into SQL (Florescu, D., & Kossmann, D., 1999).

In the early 2000s, native XML repositories seemed the natural answer to these problems, as well as to some other issues related to the performance of concurrent access to XML data. Research into native XML repositories was aimed at identifying the right level of granularity per storage unit (an element, a sub-tree or an entire XML document) in order to support effective indexing and efficient queries. XML query languages, their syntax and semantics (Comai, S., Damiani, E., & Fraternali, P., 2001) were proposed, discussed and finally standardized.

While this work was being done, it became clear that most software applications were using XML as a format for data-in-transit rather than for data-at-rest, and the notion of XML queries and views (e.g., as ways to export XML data from relational storage) became again an important one (Fernandez, M. F., Tan, W. C., Suciu, D., 2000). Our own work (Damiani, E., Capitani di Vimercati, S. D., Paraboschi, S., & Samarati, P., 2000) focused on showing how, while these data were exported, one could apply policy-driven transformations, filtering the XML data stream according to the data owner's access control policy.

Today, more than a decade after XML was first announced, its importance as one of the core technologies of the global, service-oriented Internet cannot be underestimated. Things have progressed greatly thanks to the database research community and to the W3C standardization groups. We now have a clear notion of XML Schema and a well-specified set of query and update languages.

Still, XML is a very lively research field and a number of crucial research problems related to XML remain to be solved.

The contributions collected by Eric Pardede in this edited book successfully tackle some of these XML research issues. These chapters belong to the third and most recent generation of XML research, and are authored by leading international researchers in the XML field. They deal with new advanced topics such as XML schema evolution, personalized access to XML data, hybrid XML-relational databases, XML data integration and security issues, as well as XML query processing and optimization, benchmarking, XML warehousing, differential encryption, and XML programming.

I recommend this book, rigorous yet accessible, to non-specialists and to all those operating in the industry and in academia who are interested in XML research. The chapters in this book are also recommended reading to all young Ph.D. and post-doc researchers in computer science who look for open problems and new research challenges. Indeed, these chapters give a clear idea of why the second decade of XML research promises to be even more challenging and rewarding than the first.

Ernesto Damiani
DTI – University of Milan, Italy

REFERENCES

Abiteboul, S. (1997). Querying semi-structured data. In *ICDT*, (pp. 1-18).

Abiteboul, S., Cluet, S., & Milo, T. (1998). A logical view of structured files. In *VLDB Journal, 7*(2), 96-114.

Comai, S., Damiani, E., & Fraternali, P. (2001). Computing graphical queries over XML data. *ACM Trans. Inf. Syst. 19*(4), 371-430.

Damiani, E., Capitani di Vimercati, S. D., Paraboschi, S., & Samarati, P. (2000). Design and implementation of an access control processor for XML documents. In *Computer Networks 33*(1-6), 59-75.

Fernandez, M. F., Tan, W. C., Suciu, D. (2000). SilkRoute: trading between relations and XML. In *Computer Networks 33*(1-6), 723-745.

Florescu, D., & Kossmann, D. (1999). Storing and Querying XML Data using an RDMBS. In *IEEE Data Engineering Bulletin 22(3)*, 37-42.

Ernesto Damiani *is a professor at the Department of Information Technology, University of Milan, where he leads the Software Architectures Lab. Professor Damiani holds/has held visiting positions at several international institutions, including George Mason University (Fairfax, VA, US) and LaTrobe University (Melbourne, Australia). Professor Damiani is an adjunct professor at the Sydney University of Technology (Australia). He has written several books and filed international patents; also, he co-authored more than two hundred research papers on advanced secure service-oriented architectures, open source software and business process design, software reuse and Web data semantics. Professor Damiani is the vice chair of IFIP WG 2.12 on Web Data Semantics and the secretary of IFIP WG 2.13 on Open Source Software Development. He coordinates several research projects funded by the Italian Ministry of Research and by private companies including Siemens Mobile, Cisco Systems, ST Microelectronics, BT Exact, Engineering, Telecom Italy and others.*

Preface

OVERVIEW

XML database research has become increasingly popular with the emergence of the World Wide Web and the concept of ubiquitous computing. In the 21st Century, new research areas have emerged at a rapid pace and database communities are challenged with the demands of current technology. The utilization of XML has provided many opportunities for improvement. Future decades will see XML research reaching far beyond our current imaginings. The future research in XML database area is exciting and promising.

In response to this, in late 2007 we invited researchers, academics, and practitioners, to contribute chapters to this book by submitting manuscripts that contain various challenges, open issues, and vision in the area of XML database and applications.

The objectives of this publication can be expressed as follows. Firstly, it aims to provide a comprehensive list of open issues and challenges for further XML research in XML database. Secondly, it provides visionary ideas for future XML database research. Thirdly, it provides solid references on current research topics in XML database, which may be useful for literature survey research.

We shortlisted 24 substantial chapters from 35 proposals and after thorough reviews, we accepted 14 chapters for inclusion in this book. The authors hail from Algeria, Brazil, Czech Republic, France, Germany, Greece, Italy, Singapore, Spain, Tunisia, United States, and Vietnam. Each of them has a comprehensive knowledge of the area of XML research and applications, and their individual areas of research and interest have enabled us to put together an excellent selection of chapters, which we are confident will provide readers with comprehensive and invaluable information.

INTENDED AUDIENCES

Open and Novel Issues in XML Database Applications: Future Directions and Advanced Technologies is intended for individuals who want to learn about various challenges and new issues in the area of XML research. The information provided in this book is highly useful for:

- **Database researchers:** All chapters in this book provide a thorough discussion of challenges present in current XML database and its applications. The researchers can use chapters that are related to their particular area of research interest as a solid literature survey. Moreover, researchers can use other chapters as a starting point to familiarize themselves with other research topics.
- **Database teachers and students:** The book provides a comprehensive list of potential research topics for undergraduate and post graduate levels. Teachers and students can use the chapters as

the preliminary step of their literature survey. Teachers and students can also use the chapters as a guide to the size and significance of a potential research area.

- **Database vendors and developers:** The book provides an insight into the future direction of XML database research, thereby preparing database vendors and developers for new challenges. By including discussions of new functionalities, this book is also useful for vendors wishing to improve their products.
- **General community:** Members of the community who have an interest in the area of XML database will benefit from the discussions and descriptions of problems and the open solutions provided by this book.

ORGANIZATION OF THE BOOK

The book comprehensively deals with open issues and challenges in various XML database researches. It has entry points to different XML database topics. Each topic is written in a descriptive and analytical way, supported by solid and complete current references. Each chapter discusses the future relevance and interest of a topic and how the reader should tackle different issues. In addition, most of the authors also provide solutions based on their own research.

The book is comprised of 14 chapters organized into five sections.

Section I discusses the classical XML research topic, the selection of a repository for XML documents and the (meta-) data modeling. The decision on where to store one's XML documents is critical since it will determine the way in which the documents will be queried, the features that are available, and the way in which the data will be represented/published, in addition to many other data management issues.

Chapter I introduces the highly researched topic of using the well-established Relational Database to store XML data. In this chapter, Mary Ann Malloy and Irena Mlynkova present a concise summary of the state-of-the-practice perspective of storing XML in a Relational Database. The standard and vendor-specific practices are described in order to familiarize readers with common practices. From the research angle, the authors also discuss the state-of-the-art perspectives of storing XML in Relational Database. Various approaches such as fixed, adaptive, user-defined and schema-driven methods are described.

At the end, this chapter presents various challenges that arise when this repository is used to store XML, from both the practical and research approaches. Some simple solutions are also provided to inspire readers to investigate further.

In Chapter II, Mirella M. Moro, Lipyeow Lim, and Yuan-Chi Chang, give an insight into the storage of XML data in Hybrid XML-Relational Databases. This work is motivated by the fact that even though more organizational data can now be represented as XML documents, relational data will continue to persist. Ideally, this problem should be solved by having a database that supports both relational and XML data.

In this chapter, various design issues relating to the use of a hybrid database, and their implications, are presented. They are clearly described by use-cases in various domains. Finally, a set of trends and challenges are mentioned for future research.

Chapter III, written by Vassiliki Koutsonikola and Athena Vakali, presents an approach whereby Lightweight Directory Access Protocol (LDAP) directories are used for XML data storage and retrieval. LDAP is a prevalent standard for directory access and its representation has significant similarities to XML representation including the tree format, extensible nature, query model, open structure, and so forth. The authors discuss the integration issues of XML and LDAP, including various tools and technologies that enable the integration process. The chapter ends by noting future trends in integration, which are influenced by new network protocols and new standards.

In Chapter IV, Giovanna Guerrini and Marco Mesiti present a comprehensive survey of XML Schema Evolution and Versioning approaches. It is inevitable that XML Schema that describe XML documents on the Web will evolve and change at times due to the dynamic nature of information made available via the Web. The manner in which users handle these schema changes is a research area worthy of investigation.

The authors investigate the current approaches to handling this issue by current DBMS such as SQL Server 2008, DB2 9.5, Oracle 11g, and Tamino. Furthermore, they discuss state-of-the-art research approaches including the primitive, incremental validation and document adaptation, to mention a few. The authors also present a research result which addresses this issue.

Section II deals with an area that is highly researched in XML communities, that of XML query and processing. Two of the chapters discuss continuous XML query, which is common in XML Streams processing. The other three chapters present issues relating to XML Processing, specifically on Extensible Stylesheet Language Transformations (XSLT), XML Routing and XML Programming.

In Chapter V, Mingzhu Wei, Ming Li, Elke A. Rundensteiner, Murali Mani, and Hong Su discuss the current technologies and open challenges in the area of XML Stream Processing. The authors describe the techniques frequently used to process XML Streams, namely automaton-based and algebra-based techniques. Different optimization strategies in this research area, which are classified as either cost-based or schema-based, are also described. The chapter concludes by presenting open challenges for further research.

In Chapter VI, Sven Groppe, Jinghua Groppe, Christoph Reinke, Nils Hoeller, and Volker Linnemann focus on XSLT, as one of the languages that is commonly used for processing and publishing XML documents. This chapter is motivated by the fact that, while various methods exist for transforming XML data, currently available tools and products usually support one method only.

The authors perform extensive comparisons between XQuery language and XSLT. Their study resulted in a scheme to translate XQuery to XSLT and vice versa, thereby enabling XML users to work only with the language with which they are comfortable. Research issues are described through the translation scheme proposal. In addition, future trends in XSLT research are also noted.

In Chapter VII, Mirella M. Moro, Zografoula Vagena, and Vassilis J. Tsotras discuss an issue that has emerged with the increase in volume of XML data exchange. The use of a publish/subscribe system for exchanging data will also benefit if the system is aware of the content of the information. The authors describe how this can be achieved by using a message filtering mechanism in an XML routing system.

Through various scenarios, the authors describe recent trends in message filtering and routing. Some initial open issues are also mentioned including the textual information matching in message filtering, the heterogeneous message handling, and the scalability and extensibility of the system.

In Chapter VIII, Philippe Poulard discusses the development of an XML-based processing language called Active Tags. The language is intended to provide a framework that can unify XML technologies and promote the cooperation of multiple XML languages. The origin of native XML programming is described as are various state-of-the-practice technologies. At the end, novel issues emerging in this area are also presented.

In Chapter IX, Stéphane Bressan, Wee Hyong Tok, and Xue Zhao present a classification of XML query processing techniques that can handle ad-hoc and continuous queries over XML data streams. The current techniques are described in detail and they are categorized into progressive and continuous XML query processing. At the end of the chapter, the authors also consider future trends in the area of XML query processing.

Section III contains two chapters that discuss the research issues that have attracted significant interest in the last few years, namely XML Personalization and Security. With large volumes of XML documents being viewed, updated and exchanged, a decision needs to be made regarding those who can access the document or the subset of the documents. How to enforce some level of personalization and security for the documents is also a very interesting research area.

In Chapter X, Fabio Grandi, Federica Mandreoli, and Riccardo Martoglia describe issues of personalization access to multi-versioned XML documents. In many domains, such as legal and medical, the XML documents are prone to semantic and temporal versioning. Therefore, the query processor that handles these multi-version documents should support the selection and reconstruction of a documents' specific area of interest for a particular user. In this chapter, the authors describe a prototype that addresses the challenging area of personalization queries. They also list future trends in this new research area.

In Chapter XI, Tran Khanh Dang highlights the issue of security in outsourced XML databases. Outsourcing XML Databases will become more prevalent in the coming years when in-house database storage models can no longer cope with the size and complexity of organizational data. Together with outsourcing strategies, security maintenance has become a research area that requires further investigation.

The author describes the potential security issues including data confidentiality, user and data privacy, query assurances and quality of services, secure auditing, and secure and efficient storage. The state-of-the-art approaches to these issues are also described, including the authentic publication of XML documents, secure multi-party computation-based approach, trusted third party-based approach, hardware-based approach, hybrid tree-based approach and few other approaches. Finally, summaries of challenges and research directions conclude this chapter.

Section IV consists of two chapters that describe the use of XML technologies in advanced applications. For years, scientific data has been stored in domain-specific scientific databases or in Relational Databases. Similarly, since the emergence of the data warehouse concept, the development has mostly been done by using relational design. In this section, the use of XML technologies for biological data management and data warehouse is explored.

In Chapter XII, Marco Mesiti, Ernesto Jiménez Ruiz, Ismael Sanz, Rafael Berlanga Llavori, Giorgio Valentini, Paolo Perlasca, and David Manset discuss the issues and opportunities in Biological XML Data Management.

With the proliferation of research resources that produce a large amount of biological data, the issue of data integration in bioinformatics has become increasingly significant. The authors clearly state the advantages of using XML technologies to unify heterogeneous resources. In addition to exploring the benefits of using XML Schema, XQuery and XSL for the data management, this chapter also explores the opportunities of using XML technologies for bioinformatics semantic information. Several state-of-the-art approaches to biological data management, such as ontology-based, multi-similarity, grid-based, and other approaches are described.

In Chapter XIII, Doulkifli Boukraa, Riadh Ben Messaoud, and Omar Boussaid present the new issues of modelling an XML Data Warehouse for complex data. The authors explain the issues anticipated in this application through a step-by-step design and implementation proposal. Analysis is provided at the end of the chapter with the authors comparing their proposal with current research. Finally, directions for future research in this area are provided.

The last section, Section V consists of one chapter contributed by Irena Mlynkova and presents the current state of XML benchmarking research and the possibility of its enhancement. This work is motivated by the ongoing need for a reliable XML benchmark, especially at a time when new XML processing methods are proposed every day. XML researchers need a representative benchmark that can measure their proposed method objectively.

In this chapter, the author analyzes existing projects in terms of their features to benchmark XML parsers, validators, repositories, and query engines. Some smaller benchmark projects that are more feature-specific are also described. This chapter concludes with a concise summary of the aspects that provide scope for further investigation, in order to create a more powerful XML benchmark. The benchmark should become more widely accepted and be flexible enough to be used by various XML projects/applications.

FINAL REMARKS

The Editor anticipates that this book will respond to the need for a solid and comprehensive research source in the area of XML database and applications. We have striven to achieve a balance between descriptive and analytical content and state-of-the-art practices and approaches, and giving some direction to future research by providing open challenges. This work is considerably enriched by the authors, both academics and practitioners, all of whom have a high level of expertise and an impressive track record in this field of research.

For academics such as research students, this book provides comprehensive reading material which will assist students to decide on a specific topic of interest before they embark on future research. Since the book also covers challenges, it has the potential to influence readers to think further and investigate XML database aspects that are totally novel.

The editor hopes that readers will benefit from the information and insights provided by this book. Hopefully, the interest generated will motivate future studies and lead to exciting developments in XML research.

Melbourne, September 2008
Eric Pardede

Acknowledgment

The editor would like to acknowledge all those who have supported him during the preparation of this book. In particular:

- The authors who have trusted this project to disseminate their research works. It is with gratitude that the editor acknowledges their contributions without which this project would not have been as rewarding. Most of the authors also took on an additional role as reviewers for other chapters. Their reviews have helped to improve the chapters immensely.
- Ernesto Damiani, who has generously agreed to provide a foreword for this book despite his busy schedule. The Editor personally thanks him.
- The team at IGI Global, who have demonstrated a high level of professionalism starting from the initial consideration of this book proposal, to assisting with chapter preparation and finally to publishing the final manuscripts. A special thanks to Heather Probst, whose constant reminders have helped the editor to meet the publication schedule.
- Bruna Pomella, who has helped the editor with the proofreading of all chapters, suggesting solutions for ambiguous sentences, rectifying grammatical errors and making the chapters easier to read.
- The external reviewers and colleagues who have provided invaluable assistance during the review process of this book. The editor hopes to be able to repay them adequately in future for their unconditional support.
- The staff and administration at the Department of Computer Science and Computer Engineering, La Trobe University (the editor's employer), who have always encouraged and supported his research work, including this book project.

The editor is looking forward to collaborating with these people again in the future.

Melbourne, September 2008
Eric Pardede

Section I
XML Repositories and Modelling

Chapter I
Closing the Gap Between XML and Relational Database Technologies:
State-of-the-Practice, State-of-the-Art, and Future Directions

Mary Ann Malloy
The MITRE Corporation, USA

Irena Mlynkova
Charles University, Czech Republic

ABSTRACT

As XML technologies have become a standard for data representation, it is inevitable to propose and implement efficient techniques for managing XML data. A natural alternative is to exploit tools and functions offered by relational database systems. Unfortunately, this approach has many detractors, especially due to inefficiency caused by structural differences between XML data and relations. But, on the other hand, relational databases represent a mature, verified and reliable technology for managing any kind of data including XML documents. In this chapter, the authors provide an overview and classification of existing approaches to XML data management in relational databases. They view the problem from both state-of-the-practice and state-of-the-art perspectives. The authors describe the current best known solutions, their advantages and disadvantages. Finally, they discuss some open issues and their possible solutions.

INTRODUCTION

Without a doubt, the extensible markup language (XML) (Bray et al., 2006) is one of the most popular contemporary formats for data representation. It is well-defined, easy-to-use and involves various recommendations such as languages for structural specification, transformation, querying, updating, etc. This wide popularity naturally has evoked intense effort to propose faster and more efficient methods and tools for managing and processing XML data. Soon it became possible to distinguish several different directions. The four most popular approaches are: methods that store XML data in a classical file system; methods that store and process XML data using a relational database system; methods that exploit a pure object-oriented approach; and, native XML methods that use special indices, numbering schemes and/or data structures particularly suitable for the tree structure of XML data. Naturally, each of these approaches has both keen advocates and detractors who emphasize its particular advantages or disadvantages.

The situation is not good especially for file system-based and pure object-oriented methods. The former approach suffers from an inability to query without any additional pre-processing of the data; whereas the latter approach fails in particular in finding a corresponding efficient and comprehensive implementation. As expected, the highest-performance techniques are the native ones, since they are tailored particularly for XML processing and do not need to artificially adapt existing structures to a new purpose. Nevertheless, the most practically used methods exploit features of relational databases. Although researchers have already proven that native XML strategies perform much better, they still lack one important aspect: a robust implementation verified by years of both theoretical and practical effort.

If we consider this problem from an alternative viewpoint, we realize that considerable amounts of data in practical use are still stored in relational databases. Legacy relational stores are well-established and reliable enough that their existence is entrenched and they are unlikely to disappear anytime soon (Bruce, 2007). Developers must sustain existing investments in applications predicated on a relational architecture while, at the same time, adapting them to the heterogeneous and message-driven nature of XML. A typical use case may involve mapping Web document content from an XML representation into a relational database. Not only does this help insulate naïve Web clients from the underlying and perhaps less familiar XML technologies, it also positions the information for storage and query via the more mature technologies associated with RDBMSs. Alternatively, middleware may permit XML sophisticates to view and query relational contents as though they were XML documents, and vice versa. For the foreseeable future, some hybrid of these solutions is likely to be developed, although the major relational database vendors are already providing embedded XML support.

Consequently, currently there are many efforts focused on database-centric XML data management. The researchers focus on more efficient strategies to query evaluation, database vendors more and more support XML and even the SQL standard has been extended by SQL/XML which introduces a new XML data type and operations for XML data manipulation. But, although the amount of existing solutions is large, there are still unsolved problems, open issues and aspects to be improved.

Goals of the Chapter

The main aim of the chapter is to study the problem of XML and relational technology convergence from various points of view. Firstly we view the problem fairly generically, in terms of the various data sources, integration approaches, processing models and types of applications to be considered. Secondly, we review commercial off-the-shelf (COTS) offerings that might affect a business' strategic choices between XML and relational processing and representations, and what the major database vendors are doing.

Thirdly, we study the current trends in the research area. The main concern of these techniques is the choice of how XML data are stored into relations, so-called *XML-to-relational mapping* or *decomposition to relations*. We provide an overview of existing approaches of XML-to-relational mapping strategies and their (dis-)advantages especially with respect to the efficiency of query evaluation. We focus particularly on the most efficient and promising representatives at present: adaptive methods. Since adaptability is the ability to adapt the target relational schema to information and/or requirements which specify the future application, such methods have better performance results than the general methods designed to be reasonably efficient in all cases.

An important aim of the chapter is to identify the most striking related open issues and unsolved state-of-the-practice and state-of-the-art problems. From a practical viewpoint, we will describe areas where richer methodologies are still needed to support the coordinated exploitation of XML and RDBMS technologies. In addition, this discussion will suggest that additional engineering efforts must be invested in order to achieve acceptable results across impacted information sharing dimensions, such as Semantic, physical, size and homogeneity characteristics. Keeping these criteria in the forefront will ensure that advances on the database front do not cripple the highly touted "quick-and-easy" appeal that led developers down the XML road in the first place. From a research viewpoint, the open problems focus on issues and challenges in XML-to-relational mapping strategies. In particular, we show that although the adaptive strategies seem to be the most promising candidates, we can go even further and adapt the schema dynamically.

Roadmap

The rest of the chapter is structured as follows. First we provide some general background material to overview the problems and tradeoffs associate with mingling XML and relation data. The next section analyzes the existing approaches to XML management in relational databases from a state-of-the-practice perspective and the following one from a state-of-the-art perspective. We then describe and discuss open issues and possible solutions and, finally, offer conclusions.

GENERAL BACKGROUND

In this section, we briefly summarize the various data sources, integration approaches, processing models and applications types that comprise the problem space of XML and relational data management. This lays the foundation for the remainder of the chapter.

We also note that any meaningful discussion of XML and relational technology convergence must be grounded in some foundational topical knowledge. To fully appreciate this chapter, readers are assumed to possess a reading familiarity with the following technologies: relational databases (Codd, 1970; Date, 1999); SQL (Hare, 2007); Extensible Markup Language (XML) (Bray, 2006); XML Schema (Biron, 2004; Thompson, 2004); XQuery and XPath (Fernández, 2007); SQL/XML (Joint Technical Committee ISO/IEC JTC1, 2003); XSLT (Kay, 2007); and XQuery Update Facility (Robie, 2007). Seminal sources have been cited in the References for those readers who require more background information.

Data Sources

The data sources feeding information processing applications are many and varied. In the context of this discussion, consideration is limited to legacy relational content and XML source documents. In the former case, assume the data is stored in the tables and columns of a relational database, created and maintained by some legacy applications. Users may wish to continue processing this information in the legacy fashion, viewing and manipulating it as columnar values within tables via relational-aware applications. Or, they may wish to be provided with a virtual XML view of the relational data, presumably for accessing, querying and updating it via XML-aware applications.

There is variance in how XML is being used in industry; therefore XML source data comes in several flavours. One useful binning is to consider the degree of "structure" – or "data-centricity", versus "document-centricity" – the sources exhibit (Bourret, 2005). *Semi-structured* XML may be created for human consumption (e.g., Web pages, office documents). Such *document-centric* sources can be the realm of Web publishers or back-office residents who use content management systems that enable storing, updating and retrieving XML documents in a shared repository. Typically these systems include editors and engines that provide some or all of the following: versioning, revisions and access controls; mapping to alternative formats; collaboration; Web publishing; indexing and search. This category may also include documents that contain both freeform text and marked up content.

The other primary usage of XML is highly *structured* and *data-centric*. Here XML is used as a storage or interchange format for data that is regularly ordered and targeted for machine-processing as opposed to human-readability (e.g., SOAP messages). These documents may or may not be persisted in whole or in part, depending on their specific employments.

Integration Design Patterns

Many applications require that XML data—irrespective of its origin—be persisted in a database that allows for more sophisticated storage and retrieval. There are two fundamental approaches for accomplishing this in a relational context: CLOB (character large object) and decomposition to relations (Rys, 2005).

CLOB (Character Large Objects)

This straightforward scheme stores XML data as unstructured content, typically placing each document in its entirety into a single column in a relational table. In this way, the textual fidelity of the document and its internal relationships are preserved. A given application might store multiple types of documents in different columns or even in the same column. Supplementary information (e.g., unique identifiers, date-time stamps) might be added in other tables or columns to support document management. A disadvantage is that treating the document as "just a text file" can compromise query and search algorithms, since they cannot take advantage of structural and Semantic content exposed through XML markup. In addition, it is typical that entire documents must be read into memory one after another, parsed and searched, which poses an intimidating challenge in terms of processing overhead. This effect can be moderately improved if indices are built at insert time; yet extraction of document fragments will continue to incur expensive parsing.

Still, CLOB can be a reasonable representation choice in a number of situations; among them:

- The typical extraction is a full document and its performance is of high priority.
- Documents need to be kept intact (e.g., legal, regulatory, business requirements).
- Few attribute/element updates are expected within documents.

- Mapping the document structure into a relational schema is too complicated.
- Documents with different or evolving schemas need to be managed together.
- Documents are typically searched or identified based on "side" or "property" tables, not contents (Lapis, 2005).

Decomposition to Relations

In this approach, XML content and associated metadata are meaningfully distributed (or decomposed) across the columns of one or more relational tables. Issues and choices arise from the fact that there must be some mechanism that determines the corresponding set of tables used for this representation. The mappings can be non-trivial, and this topic continues to be discussed in the literature. Where the original input data was in XML form, the term "shredding" is used and the mapping preserves both content and structural relationships so that it should be possible to recover the original XML document in the future.

It should be noted that it can be quite difficult to define the SQL storage structure for complex XML schemas, with the attendant overhead of parsing and shredding the data for insertion and pulling them back together whenever they are retrieved. Shredding into automatically generated tables works well for fairly simple flat XML schemas, but rapidly becomes unmanageable when applying complex nested XML schemas as allowed by the standard with all the attendant overhead challenges one might expect. The State-of-the-Art section of this chapter delves into this topic in greater detail.

Decomposition is a reasonable choice when one or more of the following contingencies are met:

- The source document structure is no longer relevant once the data has been posted.
- Document content must be integrated with existing relational data.

- Document structure yields a reasonable mapping to a relational schema.
- XML source schema(s) changes are unforeseen or rare.
- Existing relational applications must be used.
- The structure of extracted XML documents is different from that of input sources.
- Anticipated queries are expressible in SQL and/or the mapping to XML-aware query language is easy or not needed.
- Few individual attribute/element updates are expected; update performance is of high importance (Lapis, 2005).

Furthermore, CLOB and decomposition can be co-mingled: part of the XML document might be shredded, while part might be maintained contiguously in a single column; or certain elements of the CLOB might be duplicated as "shredded out" columns. Relational databases that have been extended to add XML functionality may implement a native XML type. Because an automated "one-size-fits-all" transformation of arbitrary documents into the type is unlikely to be satisfactory in many contexts, hand-crafted optimization may be desirable or even required, and this must be repeated for each new document type or at any time that an existing document type changes.

If an XML-native database is available, XML source documents may be stored there, apart from any relational data. It would then be possible to use XML-aware applications to process the XML stores either separately from the relational data or in an integrated fashion. XML storage may be elected in the following circumstances:

- High performance is required whenever processing XML content.
- XML schemas are too complex, numerous, or variable to be mapped to a relational schema.

- The internal structure of the source documents must be preserved.
- The queries required are not easily expressible in SQL.
- The structure of extracted XML documents is different from that of input sources (Lapis, 2005).

A tighter integration might migrate or map the legacy relational data into the XML stores or views if practicable. These sorts of processing and application considerations are discussed in the next two sections.

Processing Models

When viewed from a high level, there are but three processing models for supporting XML-aware applications on top of a database. XML functionality may be embedded in a *custom application*. For example, "canned" XML-aware queries (expressed, e.g., in XPath or XQuery language) can be mapped a priori into SQL equivalents which are populated via a template that sits on top of a relational database. A *middleware* component may be used to provide an end application with a virtual XML view of a relational database (or vice versa). In this case, the middleware acts as a mediator, translating data and/or queries into the representations needed to interact with the user or application on the one hand, and the database on the other. Or, XML processing can be supported via functions or procedures as *extensions of the database* itself, logically co-mingling them (Draper, 2003).

Application Types

Application types (i.e., what is to be done with the data) inform the choice of processing models and which integration approaches are better than others for converging XML and relational technologies. These types also constitute a "trade space" where research and optimizations are

likely to occur: extraction, querying and updating (Draper, 2003).

The fundamental operation is *extraction*. The most basic of such applications extracts whole XML documents from a repository. In this case, it is presumed that a document would be stored contiguously in its entirety, or its constituent parts appropriately linked so that the original document could be recomposed upon extraction. Extraction of fragmentary documents additionally requires *selection*: the ability to access individual document elements, attributes and values and to evaluate predicate conditions to retrieve the desired subset. A naïve way of accomplishing this is to extract entire XML documents from the repository, and then evaluate the selection conditions as a post-processing step; but a more efficient approach is to leverage the database to perform those operations prior to—or as an integral part of—the extraction step.

The *querying* operation requires XML data navigation, selection, transformation, sorting and aggregation, and it may draw on multiple documents to create a single output. Querying is in fact a generalization of the "transformation" concept. The defining characteristic of this application type is the ability to select and combine individual pieces of data in complex ways, creating new XML constructs that may not even have existed in the source data. Querying can be accomplished as a post-processing step as discussed above; but again it is desirable to have the database do the work, either by mapping the user's query into its native language or by using an extended XML-aware query language, depending on the underlying database representation.

Finally, *updating* operations require the ability to uniquely identify nodes that need to be changed. The difference between the original document and its updated version must be translated into an appropriate set of updates against the database. In a document repository setting, the user might simply replace the entire document with the updated version! Alternatively, the application must be provided with a means of addressing selected nodes, either directly or via an application programming interface (API), to effect the changes. How complex this becomes depends on how the data were mapped into the database in the first place, as discussed earlier. Another concern is the need to coordinate with the underlying database engine regarding transactions and locking during the physical update process.

Still another perspective is accessing persisted XML documents through traditional SQL interfaces to avoid the costly conversion of legacy applications to an XML-aware query language. In this case, middleware might be leveraged to do the mediation.

STATE-OF-THE-PRACTICE PERSPECTIVES

The emergence of XML and e-commerce supported by the Internet has created new opportunities for businesses to exchange information in ways previously possible only through narrowly defined interchange formats. So, despite the dominant position of relational database management systems (RDBMSs), the growth of XML is forcing businesses to explore ways to function seamlessly in both XML and traditional relational situations. Despite the dominant position of RDBMSs, from an operational viewpoint, the growth of XML is forcing businesses to explore ways to function seamlessly in both XML and traditional relational situations.

With XML becoming the de facto standard for exchanging and querying information over the Web, new challenges have been created for persistent information storage and processing. Most contemporary enterprises need to support both XML and relational data for ease of information exchange and increased flexibility. This part of the chapter examines some ways practitioners are processing XML and relational data in parallel, co-mingling them, and migrating content to

shared representations and processing models. Our discussion assumes the enterprise that is managing data requires the following:

- To sustain or increase use of XML as a data format where appropriate;
- To administer and protect XML data;
- To archive XML data for business requirements and/or legal obligations;
- To employ existing relational applications with XML data where appropriate; and
- To integrate XML and relational data where appropriate.

Some of the typical scenarios that are motivating the need for the convergence of these technologies are: managing, querying and transforming document content for day-to-day operations as well as Web sites; integrating diverse document content from heterogeneous systems by converting them into more flexibly formatted XML documents; to represent semi-structured data, because change is occurring ever more rapidly, and XML helps mitigate some related forward- and backward compatibility problems. (Bourret, 2005) discusses many specific use cases on his Web site.

State-of-the-Practice Solutions

Users may need to extract data from a database in XML format, store XML data into a database, or both. Middleware-based solutions are available when there is a need to retrieve content from databases and return it as XML and vice versa; but there is quite a bit of variability in the functionalities they provide, whether default mappings are performed between the documents and tables, and to what degree user intervention is permitted or required to define the transformations. We discuss two popular solutions first: SQL/XML and XQuery.

SQL/XML: A Relational-Facing Solution

At one time there was no standard way to access XML data from relational databases. This changed with the development of the SQL/XML standard by the SQLX group (Eisenberg, 2002; Krishnaprasad, 2005). SQL/XML is an International Organization for Standardization (ISO) effort that integrates SQL and XML. It specifies SQL-based extensions for using XML in conjunction with SQL. It includes a definition of a native XML data type, implicit and explicit ways of generating XML from relational data, an implicit default mapping from relational data to XML, and a set of XML-generating operators that can be used to create a fixed hierarchy populated directly from a set of relational values.

The collective effect allows XML to be manipulated by SQL and relational content by an XML-aware query-language like XQuery (discussed next) once they have been appropriately rendered via the built-in mappings. It also works well in traditional SQL environments. These functions allow users to continue to think of their tasks in terms of SQL if they choose to do so, and to construct new XML elements or attributes using values from various sources including, but not limited to, relational tables. For example, SQL/XML allows the user to embed XQuery expressions in SQL expressions and return output values of type XML or as a relational table.

XQuery: An XML-Facing Solution

Middleware products have been delivering Java components or C++ programs that provide developers with options for presenting and exchanging their relational data as XML and for processing relational and XML data together. Developers can potentially replace that with a few lines of code involving XQuery. XQuery is a standardized language for combining documents, databases, Web pages and almost anything else. As stated in the World Wide Web Consortium's W3C XQuery specification, "a query language that uses the structure of XML intelligently can express queries across all these kinds of data, whether physically stored in XML or viewed as XML via middleware…XQuery…is designed to be broadly applicable across many types of XML data sources" (Fernández, 2007).

XQuery offers SQL-like functionalities to directly manipulate Web documents in the ways developers and information producers/consumers have come to expect from their RDBMS experiences. The W3C specification provides this native XML query language as a target for integration platforms and components as a replacement for proprietary middleware languages and Web application development languages. Although it was initially conceived as a query language for large collections of XML documents, it can also be used to transform them.

The XQuery language is based on a tree structure model of XML document content consisting of seven kinds of nodes: documents, elements, attributes, text, comments, processing instructions and namespaces. It uses XPath expression syntax to address specific parts of an XML document. It should be noted that this may be either a real physical document or a virtual view of database content as an XML document. (N.B., XPath is a language for selecting nodes from an XML document and for computing string, numeric or boolean values from content.) The XPath expression syntax is supplemented with the "FLWOR" (pronounced "flower") expressions FOR, LET, WHERE, ORDER BY, and RETURN, as well as syntax for constructing new XML documents using an XML-like syntax or dynamic node constructors. It is in this sense that it is a programming language that can express arbitrary XML to XML data transformations.

Although XQuery currently lacks features for full search and updating XML documents or databases, commercial RDBMSs are embedding XQuery support as a means to expose relational data as an XML data source. RDBMSs without this native XQuery support can still delegate this responsibility to middleware. In addition, as of August 2007, the W3C's XQuery Update Facility progressed to last call working draft status (Robie, 2007). This document defines an update facility that extends XQuery with expressions that can be used to make persistent document changes.

Vendor Solutions

In addition to middleware offerings, most popular databases are now *XML-enabled*. That is, they have native support for converting relational data to XML and back. In fact, every major relational database vendor has proprietary extensions for using XML with its product, but each takes a completely different approach, and there is little interoperability among them. The "Big Three" vendors (i.e., IBM, Oracle and Microsoft) are moving towards second or third generation support, which means full XML support, preserving the whole XML document; and they provide some form of XQuery support over the data. This landscape is still changing, and increasingly mature product versions are emerging with ever-improving features. The next few paragraphs provide a snapshot of current capabilities.

IBM DB2

IBM provides a truly unified XML/relational database, supporting the XML data model from the client through the database, "down to the disk and back again" through a first-class XML data type. By deeply implementing XML into a database engine that previously was purely relational, IBM offers superior flexibility and performance relative to other offerings. A high-level view of DB2 with native XML support is shown in Figure 1.

DB2 manages both conventional relational and XML data. As depicted in the Storage component of the figure, relational and XML data are stored in different formats that match their respective models: relational as traditional row-column structures; and XML as hierarchical node structures. Both types of storage are accessed via the DB2 engine which processes plain SQL, SQL/XML and XQuery in an integrated fashion.

SQL and XQuery are handled in a single modelling framework, avoiding the need to translate queries between them, via so-called bilingual queries that give developers the flexibility to use the language that matches not just application needs but also their skills. Applications can continue to use SQL to manipulate relational data or the XML store. SQL/XML extensions enable publishing relational data in XML format based on data retrieved by embedding XPath or XQuery into SQL statements. XML applications

Figure 1. IBM DB2 XML support

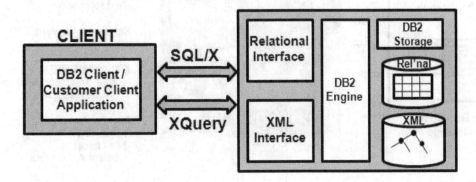

typically use XQuery to access the XML store; yet XQuery queries can optionally contain SQL to combine and correlate XML with relational data. Further details can be found in (Nicola, 2005; IBM, 2005).

Oracle XML DB

Oracle has been steadily evolving its support for XML since 1998, moving toward flexible, high-performance, scalable XML storage and processing. With new version releases every few years, they have progressed from loosely-coupled XML APIs, to XML storage and repository support, later adding XQuery then binary XML storage and indexing. Figure 2 provides a pictorial overview of XML DB's features.

XML DB implements the major W3C standards (e.g., XML, Namespace, XPath, XML Schema, XSLT). They claim the first major implementation of XQuery as well as support for SQL/XML. This hybrid database provides SQL-centric access to XML content, and XML-centric access to relational content. Multiple XML storage options allow tuning for optimal application performance. An XML DB repository is a nice addition for serving document-centric needs. Further details can be found in (Drake, 2007).

Microsoft SQL Server

A significant portion of Microsoft's SQL Server architecture is shown in Figure 3. This product features XML storage, indexing and query processing. The XML data type provides a simple mechanism for storing XML data by inserting it into an untyped XML column. The XML data type preserves document order and is useful for applications such as document management applications. Alternatively, XML Schemas may be used to define typed XML; this helps the database engine to optimize storage and query processing in addition to providing data validation. The SQL Server can also handle recursive XML Schemas as well as server-side XQuery.

Microsoft still marches to its own drummer in some respects. Their SQLXML mapping technology is used to layer an XML-centric programming model over relational data stored in tables at the server. (Note SQLXML is completely different from SQL/XML; the similarity in names can cause quite a bit of confusion.) The mapping is

Figure 2. Oracle XML DB features

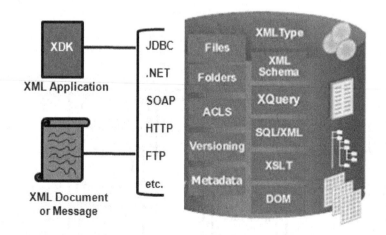

Figure 3. Microsoft SQL server architecture

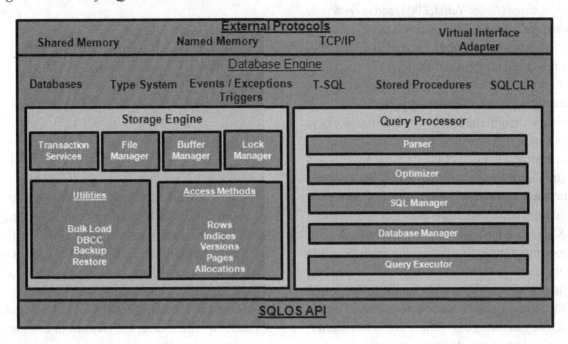

based on defining an XML schema as an XML view. This provides a bi-directional mapping of an XML Schema to relational tables. This approach can be used for bulk loading XML data into tables and for querying the tables. Document order is not preserved, however, so the mapping technology is useful for XML data processing as opposed to XML document processing. Microsoft still advocates sticking with a relational model for structured data with a known schema. Further information can be found in (Pal, 2005).

STATE-OF-THE-ART PERSPECTIVES

If we consider the problem of XML data management in RDBMSs from the research perspective, we find out that the main concern of the techniques is to find the most efficient XML-to-relational mapping, i.e., shredding the data to relations so that the respective queries can be evaluated most efficiently. An XML query (expressed in XPath

or XQuery) posed over the data stored in the database is then *translated* to a set of SQL queries (which is usually a singleton) and the resulting set of tuples is transformed to an XML document. We speak about *reconstruction* of XML fragments. The way the query can be translated is usually directly determined by the respective mapping strategy, so the key problem is to find the optimal mapping.

Based on whether they exploit or omit information from the XML schema, we can distinguish so-called *generic* (or *schema-oblivious*) (e.g., Florescu et al., 1999) and *schema-driven* (e.g., Shanmugasundaram et al., 1999; Mlynkova et al., 2004) methods. From the point of view of the input data we can distinguish so-called *fixed* methods (e.g., Florescu et al., 1999; Shanmugasundaram et al., 1999; Mlynkova et al., 2004) which store the data purely on the basis of their model, and *adaptive* methods (Ramanath et al., 2003; Klettke et al., 2000), where sample XML documents and XML queries also are taken into account. In addition, there are techniques based on user involvement. These can be divided into *user-defined* (Amer-Yahia, 2003) and *user-driven* (Amer-Yahia et al., 2004; Balmin et al., 2005). In the former case, a user is expected to define both the relational schema and the required mapping; whereas in the latter case, a user specifies just local changes to a default mapping.

But although the number of existing works is enormous, there is probably no universally efficient strategy. Each of the existing approaches is suitable for selected applications; at the same time, there can usually be found cases where it can be highly inefficient. In general, the development of XML-to-relational mapping strategies tends to exploit more and more information about the target application. It seems to be the most promising approach, since information on the future usage of the stored data can have such an impact on the efficiency of query evaluation. For better clarity, we provide several illustrative situations.

In the first simple motivating example, consider the following DTD fragment (assuming that the undeclared elements have #PCDATA data type):

```
<!ELEMENT employee (name, address)>
<!ELEMENT name (first, middle?, last)>
<!ELEMENT address (city, country, zip)>
```

the natural target relational schema (for simplicity omitting data types and obvious keys and foreign keys) would involve the relation:

```
employee1(name _ first,  name _ middle,
name _ last, address _ city, address _ coun-
try, address _ zip)
```

Suppose we know that the user always retrieves an employee's name as a whole. In other words, typical queries over the data involve queries of the form:

```
//employee/name
```

but not of the form:

```
//employee/name/first
//employee/name/middle
//employee/name/last
```

Then a more efficient relation would be:

```
employee2(name, address _ city, address _
country, address _ zip)
```

Another classical example involves updatability of the data, which can be a crucial deciding feature of database storage strategies. On the one hand, we could know that the data will not be updated too much or at all, but we need an efficient query evaluation. On the other hand, there could be a strong demand for efficient data updates; in which case, queries are of marginal importance. And there are of course cases which require efficient processing of both. Naturally, the appropriate storage strategies differ considerably. Where efficient query processing is required, various indices and numbering schemes can be exploited to speed up query evaluation, but at the cost of correspondingly expensive updates. Efficient updates, conversely, require the simplest information about mutual data relationships. And if both efficient queries and updates are required, compromise is unavoidable. And such decisions can be made correctly only if we have appropriate information.

As the last example, let us consider the question of data redundancy. Without any additional information, the optimal storage strategy is the so-called *fourth normal form (4NF) schema decomposition* into relations (Balmin et al., 2005) which can be achieved, for example, using the classical *Hybrid algorithm* (Shanmugasundaram et al., 1999), one of the fixed mapping methods. The decomposition does not involve data redundancy or violation of any normal form; i.e., it results in a database schema with the smallest number of relations and null attributes. But, similar to database design, there can be reasonable real-world cases when the data should not strictly follow the rules of normal forms and their moderation can lead to more efficient query processing.

Obviously, in general, there can hardly exist a universally efficient mapping strategy suitable for all future applications. There are reasonably efficient methods which perform well in typical cases, but we can always find a real-world application which requires different treatment. Hence, the natural solution is to exploit the idea of adaptability and automatically adapt the target schema to the current requirements.

A Look into History

If we want to exploit the idea of adaptability, we need to acquire some additional information according to which the target relational schema can be adapted. The mapping strategy in the first approaches to XML-to-relational mapping – i.e., the fixed methods – was based purely on the data model of XML documents. The methods were able to store any kind of XML data since they viewed XML documents as general labelled trees. But, the efficiency of query evaluation was quite low due to numerous join operations, and increases in efficiency were gained at the cost of increase of space overhead.

Next, researchers came up with a natural idea to exploit structural information extracted from XML schemas. The so-called schema-driven methods were based on the idea that the structure of the target relational schema is created according the structure of the source XML schema. Assuming that a user specifies the XML schema as precisely as possible with respect to the related data, we will also get a more precise relational XML schema. The problem is that DTDs are usually too general. For example, recursion or the "*" operator can in general allow infinitely deep or wide XML documents. In both cases, the respective XML documents are much simpler (Mlynkova et al., 2006) and, thus, the effort spent

on processing all the complex schema constructs is wasted.

This problem was somewhat mitigated by exploring ways by which the schema-driven approaches could leverage information extracted from XSDs (XML Schema definitions) (Mlynkova et al., 2004). The XML Schema language enables the structure of XML data to be described more precisely, especially in the case of data types. But, on the other hand, although its expressive power is higher, most of these new constructs can be considered "syntactic sugar". Hence, exploitation of XML Schema constructs does not significantly impact on XML processing efficiency and it is necessary to exploit further information.

An alternative approach to improving the fixed mapping strategies led to methods that focus on the preservation of constraints, such as key and foreign key constraints, functional dependencies or Semantic constraints, specified in the source XML schema in the target relational schema (e.g., Chen et al., 2003; Davidson et al., 2007). Such approaches reduce redundancy and improve efficiency for selected queries and, especially, update operations. But, in general, the methods suffer from the same disadvantages as do all fixed methods.

Consequently, adaptive methods emerged and they are still considered the most efficient approaches to XML-to-relational mapping. Their high performance features can be easily proven. An adaptive method starts with a fixed schema-driven mapping strategy which is modified so that the efficiency of query evaluation is enhanced. Hence, assuming that we start with the "best so far" fixed mapping strategy; the adaptive approach will provide at least an equally efficient mapping.

Overview of Adaptive Approaches

The existing representatives of adaptive methods can be divided into cost-driven and user-driven categories. Both approaches are based on the idea of exploiting additional user-provided information in order to appropriately adapt the target database schema. In the former case, it is extracted from a sample set of XML documents and/or XML queries which characterize the typical future usage. In the latter case, it is specified by user-provided annotations; i.e., the user directly specifies the required changes to a default mapping. Although there are many instantiations of the two approaches, there are still numerous weak points and open issues that should be improved and resolved.

Cost Driven Techniques

Cost-driven techniques can choose the best storage strategy for a particular application automatically, without any human intervention. Apart from various parameters of particular algorithms, the user can influence the mapping process through the provided XML schema, set of sample XML documents or data statistics, set of XML queries and eventually their weights. But after providing the input information, the algorithms cannot be influenced further by the user.

We can divide the existing cost-driven approaches into two types – *single-candidate* and *multiple-candidate*. Single-candidate approaches involve a straightforward mapping algorithm which provides a single output relational schema based on the input data. Multiple-candidate approaches also process the input data, but before providing the resulting relational schema, they evaluate multiple candidate solutions and choose the one which suits the considered application the most.

Single-Candidate Approaches

One of the first attempts at a cost-driven adaptive approach, also probably the only known representative of single-candidate approaches, was proposed in (Klettke et al., 2000). It is based on the observation that if XML documents are mostly semi-structured, a classical decomposition

of unstructured or semi-structured XML parts into relations leads to inefficient query processing caused by a surfeit of join operations. Hence, the algorithm stores well-structured parts into relations using an analogy of the Hybrid algorithm and semi-structured parts using an *XML data type*, which supports path queries and XML-aware full-text operations. The main concern is to identify the structured and semi-structured parts of the input XML schema. The process consists of the following steps:

- A schema graph G (similar to usual *DTD graph* (Shanmugasundaram et al., 1999), where nodes represent elements, attributes and operators and edges represent relationships among them) is built for a given DTD.
- For each node $v \in G$ a measure of significance ω_v (see below) is determined.
- Each node $v \in G$ which satisfies the following conditions is identified:
  - v is not a leaf node.
  - $\omega_v < \omega_{LOD}$, where ω_{LOD} is the required *level of detail*.
  - For each descendant d of v $\omega_d < \omega_{LOD}$.
  - v does not have a parent node which would satisfy the conditions too.
- Each subgraph of G consisting of a previously identified node v and its descendants is mapped to XML data type.
- The remaining parts of the graph are mapped using a fixed schema-driven mapping strategy.

The measure of significance ω_v of a node v is defined as:

$$\omega_v = \frac{1}{2}\omega_{S_v} + \frac{1}{4}\omega_{D_v} + \frac{1}{4}\omega_{Q_v}$$

$$\omega_{D_v} = \frac{card(D_v)}{card(D)}$$

$$\omega_{Q_v} = \frac{card(Q_v)}{card(Q)}$$

where D is a set of all given documents, $D_v \subseteq D$ is a set of documents containing v, Q is a set of all given queries and $Q_v \subseteq Q$ is a set of queries containing v. ω_{Sv} is derived from the DTD structure as a combination of predefined weights expressing position of v in the graph and complexity of its content model.

Multiple-Candidate Approaches

Each of the existing multiple-candidate techniques (Ramanath et al., 2003; Xiao-ling et al., 2003; Zheng et al., 2003) can be characterized by:

- An initial input XML schema S_{init},
- A set of XML schema transformations $T = \{t_1, t_2, ..., t_n\}$, where $\forall i : t_i$ transforms a given schema S into a schema S',
- A fixed XML-to-relational mapping function f_{map} which transforms a given XML schema S into a relational schema R,
- A set of input sample data D_{sample} consisting of a set of sample XML documents D

and XML queries Q which characterize the future application and

- A cost function f_{cost} which evaluates the efficiency of a given relational schema R with regard to the set D_{sample}.

The required result is an optimal relational schema R_{opt}, i.e., a schema, where $f_{cost}(R_{opt}, D_{sample})$ is minimal. A naïve, but illustrative, cost-driven storage strategy that is based on the idea of "brute force" is depicted by Algorithm 1.

The naïve algorithm first generates a set of possible XML schemas S using transformations from set T and starting from initial schema S_{init} (lines $1 - 4$). Then it searches for schema $s \in S$ with minimal cost $f_{cost}(f_{map}(s), D_{sample})$ (lines $5 - 13$) and returns the corresponding optimal relational schema $R_{opt} = f_{map}(s)$. It is obvious that the complexity of such an algorithm strongly depends on the set T. It can be proven that even a simple set of transformations causes the problem of finding the optimal schema to be NP-hard (Xiao-ling et

Algorithm 1.

Algorithm 1. A naive search algorithm

Input: $S_{init}, T, f_{map}, D_{sample}, f_{cost}$

Output: R_{opt}

1: $S \leftarrow f(S_{init})$
2: **while** $\exists\, t \in T$ & $s \in S$ s.t. $t(s) \notin S$ **do**
3:    $S \leftarrow S \cup \{t(s)\}$
4: **end while**
5: $cost_{opt} \leftarrow \infty$
6: **for all** $s \in S$ **do**
7:    $R_{tmp} \leftarrow f_{map}(s)$
8:    $cost_{tmp} \leftarrow f_{cost}(R_{tmp}, D_{sample})$
9:    **if** $cost_{tmp} < cost_{opt}$ **then**
10:       $R_{opt} \leftarrow R_{tmp}$
11:       $cost_{opt} \leftarrow cost_{tmp}$
12:   **end if**
13: **end for**
14: **return** R_{opt}

---

al., 2003). Thus, in practice, the techniques search for a suboptimal solution using various heuristics, greedy strategies, approximation algorithms, terminal conditions, etc. For instance, the *FlexMap* framework (Ramanath et al., 2003) as well as strategy proposed in (Zheng et al., 2003) optimize the naïve approach using a simple greedy strategy. On the other hand, the *Adjustable and Adaptable Method* (Xiao-ling et al., 2003) transforms the given problem to features of generic algorithms and it terminates either after a certain number of transformations or if a reasonably efficient schema is achieved.

The biggest set *T* of XML-to-XML transformations was proposed for the FlexMap framework and involves the following XSD modifications:

- **Inlining and outlining:** Mutually inverse operations which enable storing columns of a subelement or attribute either in a parent table or in a separate table
- **Splitting and merging elements:** Mutually inverse operations which enable storing columns of a shared element either in a common table or in separate tables, each for a particular sharer
- **Associativity and commutativity:** Operations which enable grouping different elements into one table
- **Union distribution and factorization:** Mutually inverse operations which enable separating out components of a union using equation $(a, (b \mid c)) = ((a, b) \mid (a, c))$
- **Splitting and merging repetitions:** Exploitation of equation $(a+) = (a, a*)$
- **Simplifying unions:** Exploitation of equation $(a \mid b) \subseteq (a?, b?)$

Note that except for commutativity and simplifying unions, the transformations generate an equivalent schema, i.e., a schema with the same set of valid XML documents. Commutativity does not preserve the order of the schema, while simplifying unions generates a more general schema, i.e., a schema with a larger set of allowed document instances.

The process of evaluating f_{cost} is, in all the approaches, significantly optimized using cost estimation. A naïve approach would require construction of a particular relational schema, loading sample XML data into the relations and cost analysis of the resulting relational structures. The *FlexMap* evaluation exploits an XML Schema-aware statistics framework *StatiX* (Freire et al., 2002) which analyzes the structure of a given XSD and XML documents and computes their statistical summary. The XML statistics are then mapped to relational statistics regarding the fixed XML-to-relational mapping and, together with sample query workload, are used as an input for a classical relational optimizer for estimating the resulting cost. The other systems use a similar strategy and estimate the cost of the query using Markov tables or various statistical approaches.

User Driven Techniques

Undoubtedly, the most flexible adaptive approach to XML-to-relational mapping is "to leave the whole process in the hands of a user" who defines both the target database schema and the required mapping. We speak about so-called user-defined mapping techniques (Amer-Yahia, 2003). Probably due to simple implementation they are especially popular and supported in most commercial database systems. At first sight the idea is correct – users can decide what suits them most and are not restricted by features or disadvantages of a particular technique. The problem is that such an approach assumes that users are skilled in two complex technologies: relational databases and XML. Furthermore, for more complex applications, the design of an optimal relational schema is generally not an easy task.

On this account, a new type of adaptive mapping strategy, so-called user-driven methods, has appeared. The main difference is that the user can influence a default fixed mapping strategy using annotations which specify the required mapping for particular schema fragments. The set of allowed mappings is naturally limited, but still powerful enough to define various mapping strategies. In other words, the user helps the mapping process, rather than performing it directly. Each of the user-driven techniques is characterized by:

- An initial XML schema S_{init},
- A set of fixed XML-to-relational mappings $f_{map}^{1}, f_{map}^{2}, ..., f_{map}^{n}$,
- A set of annotations A, each of which is specified by name, target, allowed values and function and
- A default mapping strategy f_{def} for not annotated fragments.

The existing approaches can be also divided according to the strategy used to provide the resulting relational schema. We differentiate so-called *direct* and *indirect* mappings. Most of the existing approaches belong to the first group, where the user-specified annotations are just directly applied on the annotated schema fragments. The main idea of indirect approaches is to exploit the provided information as much as possible and to use it also for those parts of the schema that are not annotated.

Direct Mapping

The approaches exploiting direct mapping are based on a straightforward algorithm. Firstly, the initial schema S_{init} is annotated with user-required mapping strategies from A. Secondly, the correctness of the annotations is checked. And finally, the XML schema is mapped. For annotated schema fragments, the specified mapping strategies f_{map}^{1}, $f_{map}^{2}, ..., f_{map}^{n}$ are used; for schema fragments that are not annotated, f_{def} is used. The existing approaches differ from one another mainly in the supported mapping strategies.

The *Mapping Definition Framework* (Amer-Yahia et al., 2004) is probably the first representative of direct user-driven mapping strategies. It allows users to specify the required mapping and it is able to check correctness and completeness of such specifications and to complete possible incompleteness. The set of annotating attributes A is listed in Table 1.

As we can see from the table, the set of allowed XML-to-relational mappings involves inlin-

Table 1. Annotation attributes for MDF

Attribute	Target	Value	Function
Outline	attribute or element	true, false	If the value is true, a separate table is created for the attribute/element. Otherwise it is inlined to parent table.
Tablename	attribute, element or group	string	The string is used as the table name.
Columnname	attribute, element or simple type	string	The string is used as the column name.
Sqltype	attribute, element or simple type	string	The string defines the SQL type of a column.
Structurescheme	root element	KFO, Interval, Dewey	Defines the way of capturing the structure of the whole schema.
Edgemapping	element	true, false	If the value is true, the element and all its subelements are mapped using Edge mapping (Florescu et al., 1999).
Maptoclob	attribute or element	true, false	If the value is true, the element/attribute is mapped to a CLOB column.

ing and outlining of an element or an attribute, Edge mapping strategy and mapping an element or attribute to a CLOB column. Furthermore, it enables specifying the required capture of the structure of the whole schema using one of the following approaches:

- **Key, Foreign Key and Ordinal Strategy (KFO):** Each node is assigned a unique ID and a foreign key pointing to parent ID; the sibling order is captured using an ordinal value
- **Interval Encoding:** A unique $\{t_{start}, t_{end}\}$ interval is assigned to each node corresponding to preorder (t_{start}) and postorder (t_{end}) traversal entering time
- **Dewey Decimal Classification:** Each node is assigned a path to the root node described using concatenation of node IDs along the path

Other attributes can be considered as side effects for specifying names of tables or columns and data types of columns. Parts that are not annotated are stored using user-predefined rules, where such a mapping is always a fixed one.

The *XCacheDB* system (Balmin et al., 2005) is the second existing representative of a direct user-driven strategy. The system also enables inlining and outlining of a node, storing a fragment into a BLOB column, specifying table names or column names and specifying column data types. The main difference is in the data redundancy allowed by attribute STORE_BLOB which enables to shred the data into table(s) and, at the same time, to store pre-parsed XML fragments into a BLOB column.

Indirect Mapping

Indirect mapping strategies try to exploit the user-provided information as much as possible. They are based on the idea that the annotations can be directly applied not only on particular schema fragments, but also for mapping the remaining schema fragments. The first and probably still the only representative of indirect user-driven strategies is system *UserMap* (Mlynkova, 2007). Its set of annotating attributes *A* covers most of the features of the previous two systems. In addition, the UserMap authors specify three types of annotation intersections – *overriding*, *redundant* and *influencing* – which define the resulting mapping strategy in case multiple annotations are specified for a single schema fragment. In case of overriding annotations, only one of the respective mapping strategies is applied on the common schema fragment. In case of redundant annotations, both the mapping strategies are applied resulting in redundant storage. And finally, if the annotations are influential, they influence each other and the respective mapping strategies are combined, resulting in a single storage strategy.

The indirect mapping proposed in the system is based on a simple observation that the user-provided schema annotations can be viewed as hints about how to store particular schema fragments. And if we know the required mapping strategy for a particular schema fragment, we can assume that structurally (or Semantically) similar schema fragments should be stored in a similar way. Hence, the system iteratively searches for similar schema fragments to find a more suitable mapping strategy.

Summary

To conclude this section, we provide an explanatory overview of the existing approaches to XML-to-relational mapping. Table 2 involves classification of the existing approaches, the key information exploited in the mapping process and respective sample representatives.

Table 2. Overview and summary of XML-to-relational mapping approaches

Approach			Exploited information	Sample representatives
Fixed (schema-oblivious)			XML data model	Florescu et al., 1999
User-defined			Purely user-specified mapping	Amer-Yahia, 2003
Schema-driven	DTD-driven		XML schema (DTD/XSD), respective constraints	Shanmugasundaram et al., 1999;
	XSD-driven			Mlynkova et al., 2004
	Constraints-preserving			Chen et al., 2003; Davidson et al., 2007
Adaptive	Cost-driven	Single-candidate	XML schema, XML documents, XML queries	Klettke et al., 2000
		Multiple-candidate		Ramanath et al., 2003; Xiao-ling et al., 2003; Zheng et al., 2003
	User-driven	Direct	XML schema, annotations	Amer-Yahia et al., 2004; Balmin et al., 2005
		Indirect		Mlynkova, 2007

OPEN ISSUES AND POSSIBLE SOLUTIONS

As we can see from the previous overview, there exist plenty of approaches to XML processing in RDBMS. But, although each of the existing approaches contributes certain interesting ideas and optimizations, there is still room for possible future improvements to the current methods. We describe and discuss them in this section and we also propose several solutions and possible enhancements.

State-of-the-Practice Challenges

A promise of XML is the smooth evolution of Web document schemas and consequently their employment by applications that are aware of and leverage them for information manipulation and transformation. Considerable progress has been made in meeting the needs of data management practitioners in the past decade; but some challenges remain.

Better Decomposition

Methodologies are needed to address the need to evolve the storage and processing of XML data, particularly when it has been decomposed (i.e., "shredded") into a relational database. Designers should note that supporting XML's ordered data model is critical in many domains (e.g., content management) where order is meaningful and exploitable. They should confirm that the automation approaches they propose include built-in order encoding methods as part of the transformations that map XML documents into relational data models. This will ensure that sufficient information is captured to reconstruct ordered XML documents as needed, and to allow exploitation of ordering during query operations.

Developers also have recognized that shredding is not a one-time event. Logical and physical mappings can rarely remain static. Data evolve through time as information exchange requirements morph. The basis of XML is that transactions will contain both data and descriptions of what the data represents, thereby reducing the degree to which applications creating or receiving data need to be customized in order to interact with each other. But the mapping into relational tables can be "lossy" of this additional metadata.

Scalability

The logical mappings from an XML schema to a relational schema are also significant, especially when a paramount requirement is to ensure efficient query execution and meaningful, relevant results. Physical data breakdown and query performance as the database grows may even make or break the solution. Similarly, the combination of potential logical and physical design considerations—such as the selection of the physical structures of the database to which the XML is shredded, its consistency with the syntax and Semantics of the original document, the degree to which the mapping is or is not "informed" by user input—produces an extremely large search space of possibilities. Choices within this space can have significant impacts on performance and efficiency and must be made with much care so that both anticipated—and reasonable though *un*anticipated—client needs can be met.

In addition, electronic commerce sites and content providers who rely on XML technologies increasingly need to deploy solutions where the data volume quickly grows to exceed "toy" size and whose content homogeneity cannot be guaranteed as stable, and which indeed changes considerably, albeit not always consistently over time. Key considerations include strategies for avoiding reloading an entire database to store evolved data, and mitigating the need to change current processing software to handle the evolved data without compromising performance.

Optimization

Many of the optimization issues associated with SQL/XML are well-known, due to its basis in SQL

which has literally decades of vendor effort behind it. Although the topic of optimizing XQuery queries is attracting much research attention, many problems are still unresolved. Because it is much younger than SQL, there is little experience as a foundational baseline. Some focus areas for optimization are element construction, user defined recursive functions, algebraic rewriting of XPath, and better cost models. A good summary of current research directions in XQuery optimization can be found in (Kader, 2007).

Standardization

Ultimately, a standards-based approach is required to ensure that solutions use XML and relational data consistently and in an interoperable manner. It should be noted that presently there is no horizontal (i.e., widely adopted) industry standard of mapping an XML document into a relational store; instead, vendors have been developing proprietary approaches to doing so, or handing mapping tools to users and leaving them to do the analysis. But pushing standardization into the access layer via XQuery and SQL/XML may obviate this concern. It would be interesting to convincingly substantiate this argument. The XQuery Update Facility (Robie, 2007) needs to come to fruition to provide applications with a flexible interface for sub-document changes.

Other Future Directions

As evidenced by the offerings of the major vendors, there are a variety of XML-enabled databases, XML query engines, XML services and native XML database that constitute a future vision, as XML documents continue to prevail as the fundamental unit of information exchange. Still there are significant, relevant and timely challenges and gaps with respect to XML and relational convergence. There are many fruitful avenues for further work, where XML and relational technologies must co-exist. These include the following:

- Strategies for mitigating the "impedance mismatch" between orderless tables and inherently ordered and hierarchically structured XML content (Tatarinov, 2002);
- Approaches for assessing the "sweet spot" where a collection of documents that are data-centric and highly amenable to relational mapping crosses over to become one that is document-centric (semi-structured or high natural language content) and therefore a less suitable mapping candidate; *and* what to do when content evolves to this point;
- Better algorithms for automated but informed schema shredding, with specific suggestions for investigation directions that may yield improvements;
- "Apples-to-apples" metrics for benchmarking performance among the various XML-enhanced relational databases and applications ala (Schmidt, 2002);
- Investigating the extent to which pushing standardization into the access layer mitigates vendor interoperability mismatches;
- Content pattern and sequence recognition techniques, which have applications for biomedical and genetic algorithms.

Just as a relational database has a row in a table as its fundamental unit, XML-native databases (e.g., Tamino, XHive, Ipedo, NeoCore, Xyleme) treat an XML document as their fundamental unit. Interesting areas to explore here include:

- State of XML-native database support across a mix of relational source data (e.g., migrating to the native store), and/or proposals for strategically accomplishing this;
- Optimization issues/challenges in the emergent XQuery Update Facility; and
- Storage/processing challenges/solutions for evolving XML Schemas and content.

State-of-the-Art Challenges

As in the realm of practice, so too in the research area are there promising and verified approaches, but we can still find various open issues and problems to be solved.

Problem of Missing Input Data

As we already know, the adaptive methods are based on the idea of exploiting various types of supplementary information. In particular, the set of input data usually consists of an XML schema S_{init}, a set of XML documents $\{d_1, d_2, ..., d_k\}$ valid against S_{init} and a set of XML queries $\{q_1, q_2, ..., q_l\}$ over S_{init}. But, naturally, not always all the data are available.

The problem of missing input XML schema has already been outlined in the introduction in connection with the advantages and disadvantages of generic and schema-driven methods. Since we assume that adaptability is the ability to adapt to a given situation, an adaptive method which does not depend on the existence of an XML schema, but which can exploit the information if it is given, is probably a natural first type of improvement. A possible solution to the problem of missing S_{init} is the exploitation of methods for automatic XML schema construction for the given set of XML documents (e.g., Moh et al., 2000; Vosta et al., 2008). These methods are able to infer corresponding content models from a given sample set of (similar) XML documents. In addition, since we can assume that XML documents are more precise sources of structural information, we can expect that a schema generated based on them will have good characteristics.

On the other hand, the problem of missing input XML documents can be solved at least partly using reasonable default settings based on general analysis of real XML data (e.g., Mignet et al., 2003; Mlynkova et al., 2006). Furthermore, the surveys show that real XML documents are surprisingly simple, so that the default mapping strategy does not have to be complex either. It should rather focus on efficient processing of frequently used XML patterns rather than all allowed constructs.

Finally, the presence of a sample query workload is crucial since there seem to be no analyses of real XML queries; i.e., there is no source of information for default settings as in the previous case. The reason is that the way to collect such real representatives is not as straightforward as in the case of XML documents, which easily can be trawled from the Internet. The best source of XML queries are currently XML benchmarking projects (e.g., Busse et al., 2003; Yao et al., 2003), but as the data and especially queries are supposed to be used for analyzing the performance of a system in various situations, they cannot be considered as an example of a real workload.

Naturally, query statistics can be gathered by the system itself and the relational schema can be adapted continuously. But, this is the problem of dynamic adaptability which we will discuss later.

Simplification of User Interaction

Another related open problem arises from the fact that both the user-driven and cost-driven approaches require a relatively well-skilled user. In the former case, the user is expected to understand and specify the required mapping strategies; whereas in the latter case, the user must be able to specify exact XML queries. Hence, a natural question is whether we can simplify the process and make the system more user-friendly. We can assume that the user does not specify exact queries and mapping strategies, but rather typical operations with the data (together with their importance), such as exploiting/omitting data updates, a need for fast reconstruction of particular fragments, etc. The problem is how to state a reasonable set of such operations, i.e., a kind of language and to what extent they can reasonably influence the target mapping.

More Efficient Search for Optional Mapping

If we consider the way the existing cost-driven multiple-candidate approaches search for the optimal mapping strategy, we can identify a significant disadvantage. All the strategies use a kind of greedy search strategy which is based on the idea of improving the current solution until there exists a possible improving step. The problem is that such an approach can easily get stuck in a local optimum. In addition, if we consider the previously stated observation that the search algorithm should begin with a locally good schema, we can even increase the probability of this problem occurring.

The natural solution is to exploit an algorithm which adds a certain randomization to the search strategy. An example of a randomized search strategy can be a meta-heuristic called Ant Colony Optimization (ACO) (Dorigo et al., 2006) which enables searching also among less efficient solutions than the suboptimal one found so far.

Combination of Cost-Driven and User-Driven Strategies

Since both the cost-driven and user-driven approaches are able to store schema fragments in various ways, another natural improvement is their combination. Although this idea requires plenty of input information in the target application (i.e., schema annotations, sample queries and sample XML documents), the resulting mapping strategy can be expected to be much more suitable. In addition, we may again assume that the query statistics, as well as sample XML data, can be gathered and exploited by the system itself while the application is running. But, once again, this is the problem of dynamic adaptability.

Theoretical Analysis of Related Problems

As we can see from the overview of the existing methods, there are various types of XML-to-XML transformations, although the cited ones certainly do not cover the whole set of possibilities. Unfortunately, there seems to be no theoretical study of these transformations, their key characteristics and possible classifications. Such a study could, among other things, focus on equivalent and generalizing transformations and as such serve as a good basis for the pattern matching strategy. Especially interesting would be the question of NP-hardness in connection with the set of allowed transformations and its complexity. Such a survey would provide useful information especially for optimizations of the search algorithm.

On the other hand, there already exist interesting theoretical studies focussing on different related problems. In particular, (Balmin et al., 2005) deal with the problem of data redundancy and related efficiency of query processing. They define and discuss four types of schema decompositions with regard to data redundancy and violations of normal forms. (Krishnamurthy et al., 2003) analyze theoretical complexity of several combinations of cost metrics and query translation algorithms. But, the analysis of the key aspect of adaptive strategies—the different storage strategies and schema transformations —is still missing.

Dynamic Adaptability

The last but not the least interesting open issue we will mention is naturally connected with the most obvious disadvantage of adaptive methods – the problem that possible changes to both XML queries and XML data can lead to an unacceptable level of degradation of efficiency. As already mentioned, related problems include missing input XML queries and ways of gathering them, as well as expecting the user to provide

plenty of information on the future application a priori. Furthermore, the question of changes in the XML data itself opens another wide research area regarding updatability – a feature that is often omitted in current approaches although its importance is critical.

The need for a solution to these issues – i.e., a system that is able to adapt dynamically – is obvious and challenging, but it is not an easy task. The first related problem is how to find the new mapping strategy efficiently. Naturally, we could repeat the whole search strategy after a certain number of operations over the current relational schema has been performed, but this naïve strategy would be quite inefficient. A better solution seems to be the exploitation of a search strategy that does not have to be restarted when the related information changes; i.e., a strategy which can be applied on dynamic systems. An example of such strategy is the above-mentioned ACO meta-heuristic.

The dynamic system should also obviate the need for total reconstructions of the whole relational schema with the corresponding necessary reinsertion of all the stored data. Alternatively, such an operation should be done only in very special cases and certainly not often. On the other hand, this "brute-force" approach can serve as a good inspiration. It is possible to suppose that changes, especially in the case of XML queries, will not be radical but will progress gradually. Thus, changes in the relational schema will be mostly local and we can apply the expensive reconstruction just locally. However, we can again exploit the idea of pattern matching and try to find the XML pattern defined by the modified schema fragment in the rest of the schema.

Another question relates to how often the relational schema should be reconstructed. The logical answer is "not too often", of course. However, on the other hand, research can be done on the idea of performing gradual minor changes. It is probable that such an approach will lead to less expensive (in terms of reconstruction) and, at the same time, more efficient (in terms of query processing) systems. The former hypothesis should be verified; the latter one can be almost certainly expected. The key issue is how to find a reasonable compromise.

CONCLUSION

In this chapter we have described and discussed current state-of-the-practice offerings, state-of-the-art progress, and open issues related to XML data management in relational databases. We have viewed the problem from two perspectives – that of practice, and that of theory. Firstly, we provided an overview of existing approaches and methodologies and outlined their advantages and disadvantages. Then, we discussed many related open issues and, where possible, also their potential solutions.

Our aim was to show that, since the idea of processing XML data using relational databases is still a valid one, it can and should be further developed and refined. Although there already exist more efficient approaches—so-called native XML databases—the world of practice still prefers less efficient, but verified and reliable XML-enabled relational databases. In addition, with so much invested in relational tools, it is still more cost-effective to map XML content into them versus migrating legacy data into an XML-native database or simultaneously maintaining both relational and XML databases.

The short-term outlook is that the data accessed by legacy applications will increasingly come from XML sources, and that XML-aware applications will continue to increase in number and popularity; hence it will become more and more desirable to store XML natively and/or to map relational source data and queries into XML counterparts. In this chapter, we discussed the ways by which this is being done at present, as well as leading-edge research into how to improve current approaches. Observable trends

suggest a transitional period where databases will contain both tables and shredded XML data, or tables and XML documents, with an increasing percentage of XML documents over time. During this transitional period, users will expect the choice of getting their results either as relational tuples or as XML, as required by consuming applications.

Web applications and XML documents will increasingly dominate the information exchange realm. Most Web applications use XML to transfer data from the databases they access and vice versa. According to (Robie, 2003), XML applications that must use relational source data will choose from these approaches: apply SQL queries to the source, then transform the results to XML; use XML extensions provided by the vendor; use SQL/XML; use XQuery. Over the long haul, legacy relational stores will be sustained for archival purposes through their legacy SQL interfaces until this becomes impractical; at which time they will either be deprecated or refitted with XQuery-mediating middleware.

Finally, it is also important to mention that while all the open issues can be studied from various points of view, they are still closely interrelated and influence each other. Thus it is always important to consider each given problem globally and not overlook important side-effects and consequences. Similarly, although we have scrutinized the problem of XML data management in relational databases from two seemingly divergent perspectives, in fact both the practical and theoretical considerations converge to a common target – efficient and user-tailored processing of XML data.

ACKNOWLEDGMENT

This work was supported in part by Czech Science Foundation (GACR), grant number 201/06/0756.

REFERENCES

Amer-Yahia, S. (2003). *Storage techniques and mapping schemas for XML*. Technical Report TD-5P4L7B, AT&T Labs-Research.

Amer-Yahia, S., Du, F., & Freire, J. (2004). A comprehensive solution to the XML-to-relational mapping problem. In *WIDM'04*, (pp. 31–38).

Balmin, A., & Papakonstantinou, Y. (2005). Storing and querying XML data using denormalized relational databases. In *VLDB Journal 14*(1), 30-49.

Biron, P. V., & Malhotra, A. (2004). *XML schema part 2: Datatypes (second edition)*. W3C Recommendation. www.w3.org/TR/xmlschema-2/

Bourret, R. (2005). Data versus documents. *XML and databases*. Retrieved March 1, 2008. htp://www.rpbourret.com/xml/XMLAndDatabases.htm

Bourret, R. (2005). Going native: Use cases for native XML databases. *XML and databases*. Retrieved March 1, 2008. http://www.rpbourret.com/xml/UseCases.htm#document

Bray, T., Paoli, J., Sperberg-McQueen, C. M., Maler, E., & Yergeau, F. (2006). *Extensible markup language (XML) 1.0 (fourth edition)*. W3C Recommendation. http://www.w3.org/TR/REC-xml/

Busse, R., Carey, M., Florescu, D., Kersten, M., Manolescu, I., Schmidt, A., & Waas, F. (2003). *XMark – An XML benchmark project*. Centrum voor Wiskunde en Informatica (CWI), Amsterdam. http://www.xml-benchmark.org/

Bruce, J. (2007). *Beyond tables: Dealing with the convergence of relational and XML data*. DevX, Jupitermedia Corporation. Retrieved March 1, 2008. http://www.devx.com/xml/Article/27975/1954

Chen, Y., Davidson, S., Hara, C., & Zheng, Y. (2003). RRXS: Redundancy reducing XML storage in relations. In *VLDB*, pages 189-200.

Codd, E. F. (1970). A relational model of data for large shared data banks. In *Communications of the ACM 13*(6), 377-387.

Date, C. J. (1999). *An introduction to database systems*. Reading, MA: Addison-Wesley Publishing Company.

Davidson, S., Fan, W., & Hara, C. (2007). Propagating XML constraints to relations. In *J. Comput. Syst. Sci., 73*(3), 316-361.

Dorigo, M., Birattari, M., & Stutzle, T. (2006). *An introduction to ant colony optimization*. Technical Report 2006-010, IRIDIA, Bruxelles, Belgium.

Drake, M. (2007). *Oracle database 11g XML DB technical overview*. Retrieved March 1, 2008. http://www.oracle.com/technology/tech/xml/xmldb/Current/11g%20new%20features.ppt.pdf

Draper, D. (2003). Mapping between XML and relational data. In H. Katz (Ed.), *XQuery from the experts: A guide to the W3C XML query language*. Reading, MA: Addison-Wesley Publishing Company.

Eisenberg, A., & Melton, J. (2002). SQL/XML is making good progress. In *SIGMOD Record 31*(2), 101-108.

Fernández, M., Florescu, D., Boag, S., Siméon, J., Chamberlin, D., Robie, J., & Kay, M. (2007). *XQuery 1.0: An XML query language*. W3C Recommendation. http://www.w3.org/TR/xquery/

Fernández, M., Siméon, J., Chamberlin, D., Berglund, A., Boag, S., Robie, J., & Kay, M. (2007). *XML path language (XPath) Version 1.0*. W3C Recommendation. http://www.w3.org/TR/xpath

Florescu, D., & Kossmann, D. (1999). Storing and querying XML data using an RDMBS. In *IEEE Data Eng. Bull. 22*(3), 27-34.

Freire, J., Haritsa, J. R., Ramanath, M., Roy, P., & Simeon, J. (2002). StatiX: Making XML count. In *SIGMOD*, (pp.181-192).

Hare, K. (2007). *JCC's SQL standards page.* JCC Consulting, Inc. Retrieved March 1, 2007. http://www.jcc.com/SQL.htm

IBM. (2005). *The IBM approach to unified XML/ relational databases.* Retrieved March 1, 2008. http://xml.coverpages.org/IBM-XML-GC34-2496.pdf

Joint Technical Committee ISO/IEC JTC 1, Information technology, Subcommittee SC 32, Data management and interchange. (2003). *ISO/IEC 9075 Part 14: XML-related specifications (SQL/ XML).* Retrieved March 1, 2008. http://www.sqlx.org/SQL-XML-documents/5FCD-14-XML-2004-07.pdf

Kader, R., & Keulen, M. (2007). Native XQuery optimization in relational database systems. In *VLDB*, (pp. 75-86).

Kay, M. (2006). Using relational data in XML applications. *Data direct technologies.* Retrieved March 1, 2008. http://www.stylusstudio.com/tutorials/relational_xml.html#

Kay, M. (Ed.). (2007). *XSL transformations (XSLT) Version 1.0.* W3C Recommendation. http://www.w3.org/TR/xslt

Klettke, M., & Meyer, H. (2000). XML and object-relational database systems – Enhancing structural mappings based on statistics. In *LNCS 1997*,(pp. 151-170).

Krishnamurthy, R., Chakaravarthy, V., & Naughton, J. (2003). On the difficulty of finding optimal relational decompositions for XML workloads: A complexity theoretic perspective. In *ICDT*, (pp. 270-284).

Krishnaprasad, M., Liu, Z., Manikutty, A., Warner, J., & Arora, V. (2005). Towards an in-

dustrial strength SQL/XML infrastructure. In *ICDE*, (pp. 991-1000).

Lapis, G. (2005). XML and relational storage—Are they mutually exclusive? In *XTech*. IDEAlliance. Retrieved March 1, 2008. http://idealliance.org/proceedings/xtech05/papers/02-05-01/

Mignet, L., Barbosa, D., & Veltri, P. (2003). The XML Web: A first study. In *WWW,2,* 500-510.

Mlynkova, I. (2007). A journey towards more efficient processing of XML data in (O)RDBMS. In *CIT*, (pp. 23-28).

Mlynkova, I., Toman, K., & Pokorny, J. (2006). Statistical analysis of real XML data collections. In *COMAD*, (pp. 20 -31).

Mlynkova, I., & Pokorny, J. (2004). From XML schema to object-relational database – an XML schema-driven mapping algorithm. In *ICWI*, (pp. 115-122).

Mlynkova, I., & Pokorny, J. (2008). UserMap – an adaptive enhancing of user-driven XML-to-relational mapping strategies. In *ADC*, pp.165 – 174.

Moh, C.-H., Lim, E.-P. & Ng, W. K. (2000). DTD-miner: A tool for mining DTD from XML documents. In *WECWIS'00*, ((pp.144-151).

Nicola, M., & van der Linden, B. (2005). Native XML support in DB2 universal database. In *VLDB*, (pp. 1164–1174.)

Pal, S., Fussell, M., & Dolobowsky, I. (2005). *XML support in Microsoft SQL Server 2005.* Microsoft Corporation. Retrieved March 1, 2008. http://msdn2.microsoft.com/en-us/library/ms345117.aspx

Ramanath, M., Freire, J., Haritsa, J., & Roy, P. (2003). Searching for efficient XML-to-relational mappings. In *XSym*, pp. 19-36.

Robie, J. (2003). SQL/XML, XQuery, and Native XML programming languages. In *XTech*.

IDEAlliance Retrieved March 1, 2008. http://www.idealliance.org/papers/dx_xml03/html/astract/05-02-01.html

Robie, J., Melton, J., Chamberlin, D., Florescu, D., & Siméon, J. (2007). *XQuery update facility 1.0.* W3C Candidate Recommendation 14 March 2008. http://www.w3.org/TR/xquery-update-10/

Rys, M., Chamberlin, D., & Florescu, D. (2005). Relational database management systems: The inside story. In *SIGMOD,* pp. 945-947.

Shanmugasundaram, J., Tufte, K., Zhang, C., He, G., DeWitt, D. J., & Naughton, J. F. (1999). Relational databases for querying XML documents: Limitations and opportunities. In *VLDB,* pp. 302-314.

Schmidt, A., Wass, F., Kersten, M., Carey, M., Manolescu, I., & Busse, R. (2002). XMark: A benchmark for XML data management. In *VLDB,* pp. 974-985.

Tatarinov, I., Viglas, S. D., Beyer, K., Shanmugasundaram, J., Shekita, E. & Zhang, C. (2002). Storing and querying ordered XML using a relational database system. In *SIGMOD,* (pp. 204-215).

Thompson, H. S., Beech, D., Maloney, M., & Mendelsohn, N. (2004). *XML schema part 1: Structures (second edition).* W3C Recommendation. www.w3.org/TR/xmlschema-1/

Vosta, O., Mlynkova, I., & Pokorny, J. (2008). Even an ant can create an XSD. In *DASFAA,* (pp. 35-50).

Xiao-ling, W., Jin-feng, L., & Yi-sheng, D. (2003). An adaptable and adjustable mapping from XML data to tables in RDB. In *LNCS 2590,* (pp. 117-130).

Yao, B. B., Ozsu, M. T., & Keenleyside, J. (2003). XBench – A family of benchmarks for XML DBMSs. In *LNCS 2590,* (pp. 162–164).

Yoshikawa, M., Amagasa, T., Shimura, T., & Uemura, S. (2001). XRel: A path-based approach to storage and retrieval of XML documents using relational databases. In *ACM Trans. Inter. Tech. 1*(1), 110-141.

Zheng, S., Wen, J., & Lu, H. (2003). Cost-driven storage schema selection for XML. In *DASFAA,* (pp. 337–344).

Chapter II
Challenges on Modeling Hybrid XML–Relational Databases

Mirella M. Moro
Universidade Federal de Minas Gerais (UFMG), Belo Horizonte, Brazil

Lipyeow Lim
IBM T.J. Watson Research Center, USA

Yuan-Chi Chang
IBM T.J. Watson Research Center, USA

ABSTRACT

It is well known that XML has been widely adopted for its flexible and self-describing nature. However, relational data will continue to co-exist with XML for several different reasons one of which is the high cost of transferring everything to XML. In this context, data designers face the problem of modeling both relational and XML data within an integrated environment. This chapter highlights important questions on hybrid XML-relational database design and discusses use cases, requirements, and deficiencies in existing design methodologies especially in the light of data and schema evolution. The authors' analysis results in several design guidelines and a series of challenges to be addressed by future research.

INTRODUCTION

Enterprise data design has become much more complex than modeling traditional data stores. The data flowing in and out of an enterprise is no longer just relational tuples, but also XML data

in the form of messages and business artifacts such as purchase orders, invoices, contracts and other documents. Moreover, regulations (such as the Sarbanes Oxley Act[1]) require much of these data (both relational and XML) to be versioned and persisted for audit trail. Last but not least, the competitiveness of enterprises is often a function of their business agility – the ability to change with the changing market. Consequently, enterprise data design needs to cope with different types of data, changing data and data schema evolution.

Relational database management systems (RDBMSs) are a dominant technology for managing enterprise data stores. Even if the enterprise data are more suitably managed as XML, the cost of migrating to XML databases may be prohibitive. Therefore, relational data will continue to persist in the database. On the other hand, the widespread use of XML data requires the ability to manage and retrieve XML information. A simple solution is to store XML data as character large objects (CLOBs) in an RDBMS, but query processing is inefficient due to per query parsing of the XML CLOBs. Another solution, adopted by most commercial RDBMSs, is shredding XML data into relational tables, for example Florescu & Kossmann (1999) and Shanmugasundaram (2001). However, shredding does not handle XML schema changes efficiently. Hence, a native XML database that stores XML data in a hierarchical format is still required. Such specialized native XML databases have been developed, for example Jagadish (2002), and some even support relational data as well, for example Halverson (2004).

Nevertheless, neither a pure relational nor a pure XML database meets all the needs of enterprise data management. Ideally, a hybrid database that supports both relational and XML is the best solution to model, persist, manage, and query both relational and XML data in a unified manner. Some commercial RDBMSs have begun to support such hybrid XML-relational data models (eg. IBM's DB2 v.9[2]). Although employing a hybrid solution seems to be a straightforward idea, in reality, it involves a complex system with a many options that may easily confuse most designers. Likewise, we noticed that most users are still uncertain about how exactly to model an XML database, not to mention a hybrid XML-relational one.

In this context, the focus of this chapter is to discuss how to design a hybrid XML-relational database. Note that we are not concerned with designing a database *system*, but rather a set of relations containing relational and XML data. The contributions and the organization of this chapter are as follows.

- We present a methodology for designing XML databases (without considering any interaction with relational data).
- We overview some of the most relevant real case scenarios that motivate the relevance of a hybrid XML-relational database.
- We present and discuss the challenges to defining a hybrid XML-relational model. We present a set of modeling ideas that serve as an initial solution for such complex modeling issues. Also, we discuss what else is needed in order to have a more complete solution – i.e., we discuss open issues on the modeling phase.

Finally, we discuss some related work and conclude this chapter with an overview of open problems.

BACKGROUND

This section presents a brief review of relational database design, which we assume is well-known in the computer science community. Traditionally, the design of relational databases is structured into three phases as follows.

- **Conceptual design** captures the Semantics of the data and provides a global description of the database independent from physical storage implementation. The conceptual model defines entities, attribute names and types, relationships between entities and Semantic constraints (e.g. relationship cardinality and participation constraints).

For relational database systems, the entity-relationship (ER) model (Chen, 1976) is usually employed in this phase.

- **Logical design** maps the entities from the Conceptual Model to relations (tables) that conform to the data model of the chosen database system. The logical design preserves all information associated with the Conceptual Model and may also include new features, such as external views and integrity constraints. The Relational Model (Codd, 1970) is usually employed in this phase, which results in a set of data definition language (DDL) statements that specify the database schema for a specific database system.

- **Physical design** focuses on implementing the logical design. It defines all database storage artifacts such as clustering structures, indexes, access paths and other optimizations. It may also require tuning the conceptual and logical designs.

This three-tiered framework is particularly suited for designing a database from scratch. In practice, however, database design is often constrained by interoperability with existing tables. Furthermore, this design framework is often an iterative process.

XML DATABASE DESIGN

This section introduces guidelines for XML database design, and summarizes them at the end. Note that for the XML case, there is no methodology that is widely accepted as are the ones for Relational design (e.g. relational model, ER diagrams). Therefore, one of the contributions of this chapter is to elaborate on a simple methodology for designing XML databases as well. These guidelines also serve as base for the hybrid XML/Relational database design proposed in the next section.

An XML database is usually modeled as a forest of unranked, node-labeled trees, one tree per document. A node corresponds to an element, attribute or value, and an edge represents element-subelement or element-value relationships (Berglund, 2007).

Designing an XML database would be easy if we could apply the ER or Relational Model concepts directly to it. However, the unstructured and flexible features of XML make the standard models unsuitable for designing an XML database. Some reasons include: XML elements are inherently ordered; XML allows different structures under the same parent and complex types as well (e.g. optional and multi-valued elements); there is no simple way of specifying many-to-many relationships because of the XML hierarchical structure; and there is no trivial mapping for other features, such as XML namespaces.

Therefore, we propose four steps for designing an XML database from scratch. These steps result from interviews with clients and XML consultants and can be regarded as initial guidelines toward a formal design methodology. Note that we do not intend to discuss how to model XML data using the entity-relationship model (ER), the relational model or even any model that employs the unified modeling language (UML), because that discussion may be found elsewhere, such as in Conrad (2000). Our discussion is independent of the language or diagram that is employed.

STEP 1: Review data and specify Semantics. After identifying data requirements, it is necessary to identify the Semantics of data elements and relationships among elements. The Semantics can be specified top-down (starting from data requirements) or bottom-up (starting from document samples). The decision depends on how well the designer knows the data and the environment. Usually, taxonomy development tools and vocabularies may assist on this phase.

For example, consider the case of defining addresses for purchase orders based on the existence of three types of addresses: the buyer's address, the billing address, and the recipient's address. Note that the values of these addresses may be different. So, step 1 defines the Semantics of addresses in purchase order that has three (possibly different) values: `permAddress`, `billToAddress`, and `sendToAddress`.

Simple *constraints* (e.g. cardinality) and *business rules* (for validating the information) may also be defined in this phase. Validation may be necessary so that the data are meaningful to the application. Note that this validation goes beyond structural constraints verification. It may range from simple rules, such as verifying the range of a numeric number, to very complex ones, such as checking cross-references between documents. The guidelines for specifying business rules are beyond the scope of this chapter, since our focus is on structural design.

STEP 2: Specify structure. Once the Semantics has been identified, the next step is to specify the data structure. For XML databases, this means specifying elements, attributes, types, values, namespaces, and containment relations (i.e. parent-child relationships).

There are three basic approaches for specifying the structure of the document, namely: (i) *uniqueness*, which defines one distinguished name for each element; (ii) *typing*, which uses attribute names to qualify elements; and (iii) *containment*, which characterizes the elements by establishing containment relationships. The main design decision here is whether to use single atomic elements with discrete names, to rely on structure qualification through containment relationships (then reducing the use of discrete names), or to employ types for qualifying the data (an intermediate solution).

This second step is correlated to the first one, and the choice of approach depends on many factors. For example, it is possible to focus on defining fewer discrete elements in the vocabulary and use the containment relationship to understand the meaning (context) of the element. We can also argue that a large vocabulary set (e.g. more than 300 words) can be hard to manage or even remember its proper usage.

Considering the addresses example, the first column on Table 1 shows the address information designed in four different ways (for clarity reasons we show the actual XML instances instead of the schema information, and we omit the address substructure, e.g. street and zipcode):

1. Defines a *unique* element for each kind of address, which results in a flat structure at the expense of more discrete names;
2. Defines a *general element* `address` with an *attribute* `type`, which results in less discrete elements, and provides a generic and more flexible schema with the structural information stored as data values;
3. Defines *containment* relationships for each type of address, which results in more nested structures with the reusability of the element `address`;
4. Defines the *containment* from `address` to each type, which is more concise than the previous design but it offers less reusability of the elements.

The choice of design impacts on the data usability. For instance, consider the query "retrieve the addresses of purchase order number 193". The second column in Table 1 illustrates the XQuery statements for each design. Note that one could consider rewriting the `let` statement of query 3 to "`let $a:=$p//address`". However, the result would be three addresses with no specification regarding whether it is permanent, billing to or send to. In other words, the result of the rewritten query would be meaningless. The results of each query also have different structures depending on the design (not shown for space constraints). Specifically, queries 1 and 3 are the same but the structures of their results are different. Likewise, queries 2 and 4 are similar with different results.

On the other hand, queries 1 and 4 are different, but their results are the same.

From this usability point of view, we can argue that designs 2 and 4 are more intuitive because the actual element names remain transparent to the user while writing the query. Nevertheless, there are other trade-offs that need to be considered when choosing an appropriate design, such as query workload and query performance. For example, if the query workload includes a considerable amount of text search queries, then modeling those queried data as elements and subelements may be more advantageous. Likewise, there may be performance problems when defining those data using attribute values.

STEP 3: Define reusable units. The previous step mentioned the problem of specifying discrete elements, which in turn increases the vocabulary size. One way of alleviating this situation is by identifying reusable portions of the vocabulary, i.e. parts of the vocabulary that can be grouped and reused throughout the model. For example, XML Schema allows defining reusable units through: type substitution, substitution group and `any` facility. It is important to note that reusability also improves readability and facilitates incremental changes and versioning. As the application evolves to include new requirements and scenarios, so does the data model in order to be synchronized with such updates. It is a common practice to iterate over steps 2 and 3 in order to map out an evolution strategy for evolving the model with minimum impact on the database.

Table 1. XML design strategies using (1) uniqueness, (2) typing, and (3,4) containment

	(a) Partial XML instances of purchase order	(b) Query: retrieve addresses from order 193
1	```<purchaseOrder number="193"> <permAddress>...</permAddress> <billToAddress>...</billToAddress> <sendToAddress>...</sendToAddress> </purchaseOrder>```	```for $p in //purchaseOrder[@number="193"] let $a:=$p/permAddress, $b:=$p/billToAddress, $c:=$p/sendToAddress return <addresses>{$a}{$b}{$c}</addresses>```
2	```<purchaseOrder number="193"> <address type="permAddress">...</address> <address type="billToAddress">...</address> <address type="sendToAddress">...</address> </purchaseOrder>```	```for $p in //purchaseOrder[@number="193"] let $a:=$p/address return <addresses>{$a}</addresses>```
3	```<purchaseOrder number="193"> <permAddress> <address>...</address> </permAddress> <billToAddress> <address>...</address> </billToAddress> <sendToAddress> <address>...</address> </sendToAddress> </purchaseOrder>```	```for $p in //purchaseOrder[@number="193"] let $a:=$p/permAddress, $b:=$p/billToAddress, $c:=$p/sendToAddress return <addresses>{$a}{$b}{$c}</addresses>```
4	```<purchaseOrder number="193"> <address> <permAddress>...</permAddress> <billToAddress>...</billToAddress> <sendToAddress>...</sendToAddress> </address> </purchaseOrder>```	```for $p in //purchaseOrder[@number="193"] let $a:=$p/address/* return <addresses>{$a}</addresses>```

Table 2 Example of schema design patterns for XML Schema

| **Russian Dolls**: defines all internal types of a component as its children (then nesting the types as Russian dolls). Each type is local to its parent and hidden from other documents. The reusability is practically non-existent but changes to a component are limited to its scope. | ```
<element name="purchaseOrder">
<complexType>
  <element name="address">
    <complexType>
      <element name="permAddress" type="string" />
      <element name="billToAddress" type="string" />
      <element name="sendToAddress" type="string" />
    </complexType>
  </element>
</complexType>
</element>
``` |
| **Salami Slices**: the opposite of Russian Dolls, defines all components connected to the root (as salami slices on a sandwich). Each element definition is global, transparent to other documents, and containment between elements is defined as references between global definitions. Now, it is possible to define reusable elements but changes to a component are reflected to all elements that reference it. | ```
<element name="permAddress" type="string" />
<element name="billToAddress" type="string" />
<element name="sendToAddress" type="string" />
<element name="address">
  <complexType>
    <element ref="permAddress" />
    <element ref="billToAddres" />
    <element ref="sendToAddress" />
  </complexType>
</element>

<element name="purchaseOrder">
  <complexType>
    <element ref="address" />
  </complexType>
</element>
``` |
| **Venetian Blinds**: a mix of the previous two designs, it keeps all elements connected to the root but defines containment through type attributes. Note that the types are named and global, but most of the elements are local. | ```
<complexType name="tAddress">
    <element name="permAddress" type="string" />
    <element name="billToAddress" type="string" />
    <element name="sendToAddress" type="string" />
</complexType>
<complexType name="tPurchase">
    <element name="address" type="tAddress" />
</complexType>
<element name="purchaseOrder" type="tPurchase"/>
``` |
| **Garden of Eden**: all elements are global and all types are named (as the biblical Adam named all creatures), such that elements and types are reusable units. | ```
<element name="permAddress" type="string" />
<element name="billToAddress" type="string" />
<element name="sendToAddress" type="string" />
<element name="address" type="tAddress" />
<complexType name="tAddress">
    <element ref="permAddress" />
    <element ref="billToAddres" />
    <element ref="sendToAddress" />
</complexType>
<element name="purchaseOrder" type="tPurchase" />
<complexType name="tPurchase">
    <element ref="address" />
</complexType>
``` |

STEP 4: Write schema, define instances. Designers need to consider the formal structures and expressiveness of schema languages such as document type definitions (DTD) and XML Schema. For example, one cannot query the total number of object instances derived from the base type in XML Schema. When using a more powerful schema language, such as XML Schema, designers also need to choose a schema design pattern. The most common patterns are as presented in Table 2. The second column illustrates the four designs for the address example, written on XML Schema. Additionally, XML Normal Forms can also be helpful for designing the database (Arenas & Libkin, 2005).

Discussion

Even though relational model and XML model are completely different, the methodologies for designing the databases have some common or related features. In summary, Table 3 presents an analogy of the main points for designing relational and XML databases following the three-phase methodology. Note that it does not consider a preparation phase of gathering the application requirements, identifying interests and functionalities.

HYBRID DATABASE USECASES

This section presents a global view of some important design challenges by describing three recent client engagements. These examples set the context and are applied more generally in later discussions.

E-Catalogs

Electronic product catalog (e-catalog) is one of the most common and successful types of e-commerce applications, where online electronic systems are in charge of distributing, buying, selling, marketing products and services. Its main functionality usually involves electronic data interchange (EDI) of information on products, their specifications, prices and delivery options. An e-catalog contains hundreds (or even tens of thousands) of products whose features may differ.

Specifically, consider a retail store (like Target, Sears or Walmart) that sells everything from clothing to electronic devices, books, jewelry, DVDs, furniture and toys. Each product has a wide range of attributes (in the context of entity properties, and not XML attributes) as for example color, size or dimensions, length, weight, material, and other specifications regarding hardware, power, capacity, and so on. Moreover, each product instance specifies values for common attributes (catalog id, price, return policy, rebate value, shipping and delivery information) and for a distinct set

Table 3. Comparing relational and XML database designs

Phase	Relational Design	XML Design
Conceptual: Semantics	Entities, attributes, types, relationships, constraints. ER diagrams	Names (taxonomy, vocabulary) and relationships – step 1.
Logical: Structure	Tables, columns, relationships, views. Normal forms, relational model, DDL.	Elements, attributes, values, relationships (containment). DTD, XML Schema – step 2.
Physical: Storage	Implementation and optimizations: storage and partitions, indexes, access paths. DDL.	Write schema, instances, and optimizations: storage and partitions, indexes, reusable units – steps 3 and 4.

of attributes. For instance, clothing items have values for type (t-shirt, skirt, blouse, pants ...), style (classic, boot-cut, low rise, relaxed ...), color, size, material, brand (Lee, Levi's, Wrangler ...), and other specific features such as the number of pockets for pants. Clearly, electronic items have completely different attributes from those of clothing.

Such *attribute diversity* is not the only problem. e-catalog information *evolves* continuously as new types of products are released every day. For example, the introduction of PDAs, mp3 players, kitchen appliances and so on, requires a continuous maintenance and possible reorganization of e-catalogs. Hence, the main challenges are how to model diverse and evolving information while retaining the system's efficiency.

Derivative Trading Community

One early adopter of the XML exchange standard is the derivative trading community, which started as privately negotiated deals in the early '80s and grew into a vibrant market of trillions, popular with institution investors and hedge funds. Since 1999, the community has been defining and evolving the financial products markup language (FpML[3]), which specifies protocols for sharing information on, and dealing in swaps, derivatives and other structured products.

FpML makes an interesting case study because of its increasing variety of derivative products on the market. Besides interest rate swaps from the early days, stocks, mortgages, corporate bonds, and foreign exchange can be part of a trade in response to the increasing demand of leverage and risk management. Then, one can create a new derivative product by changing the fixed rate amount into a rate ladder tied to a bundle of mortgage payments. The high number of variations is limited only by the creativity of trading analysts and their ability to risk price and profit. In fact, many investment banks are creating and holding contracts one or two releases ahead of the

FpML standard. It is common for a new derivative product to be released and traded every week.

Up until recently, the only choice to meet the performance requirements was to shred key fields into relational tables. According to our clients, they have tried and failed object-oriented, object-relational, XML-wrapped database systems from large and small vendors in the past. They are also not satisfied with relational database, due to frequent rebuilding of the database for schema changes in the new products. The main challenges pointed out by clients are as follows.

- **Data model updates**, as a new derivative product requires adding information to the data model. Forwards, credits and equities have been added since FpML 1.0, and commodities and weather are expected to appear in future releases.

- **Complex mapping** to the XML schema. For example, the FpML standard body employs the expressive power of the XML Schema language with type extension, substitution group, sequence, choice and other facets. The complexity makes it very hard to maintain and keep up with relational schema and SQL.

- **Proprietary extensions**, since all trading divisions in major investment banks need to add their own requirements to the standard. Hence, the transformation logic between external and internal copies needs to evolve and be synchronized with changes in both standard and extension.

- **Interoperability with relational-based applications**, as the database needs to interface and serve formatted contracts to generations of applications developed on rows and columns. Rewriting these applications at once is viewed as risky and cost prohibitive.

- **History of changes**, since a contract may exchange hands multiple times in its lifetime. The changes, often annotated and versioned, need to be kept and retrieved efficiently when requested. Therefore, delta changes and versioning are important challenges to be addressed.

- **Consistency**, as data duplication creates consistency issues and increases storage space. Minimizing the maintenance of the logic to synchronize copies of data is required.

Health Care Industry

A slightly different scenario is *evolving* XML data in the health care industry. Specifically, the Health Level 7 Clinical Document Architecture (HL7 CDA[4]) enforces a set of rules to ensure compatibility and interoperability with the version 2.X series. The rules include adding new segments and fields that can be ignored by older versions of the implementation. Data types may be enhanced by keeping the Semantic meaning of the legacy sections while adding new fields. Rules like these are meant to guide application developers to parse and interpret HL7 messages consistently and correctly. However, the backend data store still needs to store and manage messages from *different versions*. The aforementioned challenges (such as data model updates and attribute diversity) are also applied here.

Discussion

In summary, database designers seek modeling principles and guidelines to balance the trade-offs and meet the design challenges over time. The challenges of designing a hybrid XML-relational database derive from balancing the enterprise requirements with the features provided by a database management system. Specifically, based on the use cases, we can conclude that those challenges come from accommodating the following features in the hybrid database design: business artifacts, schema variability, schema evolution, data versioning, storage, redundancy, and performance. In the next sections, we approach the challenges with multiple latitudes of design considerations.

HYBRID DATABASE DESIGN

The use cases illustrated real requirements from the user's point of view. This section discusses guidelines and challenges for designing a hybrid database based on those requirements. Specifically, we focus on the following topics: business artifacts, schema variability, schema evolution, data versioning, storage, redundancy, performance, and reference system.

Conceptual Design

Conceptual modeling captures the Semantics of the data independently of the way that the data are eventually stored in the database. On the perspective of modeling a hybrid database, other aspects (besides those previously discussed) affect the Conceptual Model and are the focus of this section. Note that the decision to model the data as tables or trees is covered in the next section. We clarify our discussion with an example using an ER diagram, but similar issues also appear when designing with other languages and methodologies.

As an example, Figure 1 illustrates an ER diagram of the Conceptual Model for purchase orders. A customer can request different purchase orders with many products on a specific date, and a product can be purchased by many different customers.

Business Artifacts

Certain data are naturally grouped into documents that are artifacts of business processes. Usually, the data in these artifacts need to be processed as a single unit. These include, for example, travel expense forms, insurance claims, merchandise invoices and payments. Moreover, these artifacts often contain both structured and free text fields, and they may exist only within a single application silo.

In general, a business artifact may be modeled as an independent, atomic entity, such that its details are preserved transparently. Alternatively, a business artifact may be decomposed to avoid such transparency. However, it is important to note that some features of a semi-structured business artifact do not translate to plain Conceptual Models as, for example, the presence of ordered elements, denormalized data, and namespaces.

Challenge 1: *How to define an elegant model for data (relational or XML) and business artifacts in a unified way that captures the Semantics of business artifacts, the information within artifacts, and the relationships between entities within the artifacts to entities external to the artifacts.*

Guidelines. A direction to answer such a challenge is to extend the Conceptual Model such that an entity or a set of entities may be marked as business objects. For the individual case, an entity may become an XML document (i.e. an XML column within a relational table) whose structure is defined by the entity's attributes. For the collective case, the set of entities may become one document as well. However, mapping the respective relationships within the set of entities and with outside entities still represents a good deal of the challenge.

Suppose an enterprise is required to persist the purchase order from Figure 1 as a business artifact (these business artifacts are often encoded in industry XML standards such as FpML). The Conceptual Model in Figure 1 becomes inadequate if a customer changes his address after the purchase order was placed. Persisting the purchase order as a business artifact requires the persistence of the customer address at the time when the purchase order was placed (a problem also related to data versioning support). Since there is a one-to-many relationship between customer and purchase order, a simple solution is to model the customer `address` explicitly as an attribute of the purchase order entity. Likewise, any change to the product price should not affect the price of purchases within a purchase order. However, since purchase order and product are related via many-to-many relationships, modeling product price as an attribute of purchase order results in a very complex design. The complexity is further compounded when we consider the life-cycle of a business artifact. The first challenge summarizes the main problem.

Schema Variability

Consider that it is necessary to expand the entity `product`, from Figure 1, to include its description within an e-catalog application. In this case, `product` has a wide range of attributes (as already mentioned on the e-catalog use case), and each

Figure 1. Conceptual model for purchase order example

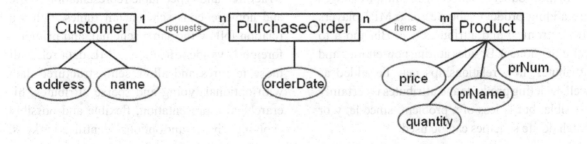

product instance specifies values for a distinct set of attributes. Hence, product is not a simple entity anymore, but it may consist of a hierarchy of product categories. Each product subtype is associated with its own set of attributes. For example, attributes for televisions are very different from attributes for T-shirts. We can model this product hierarchy explicitly in the ER diagram using "is-a" relationships (with inheritance properties), which would again result in a rather complex design. Moreover, the subsequent Logical Design phase needs to deal with this hierarchy by balancing between creating too many tables (one for each sub-product) and creating one broad, but sparse, table for the top product concept/entity.

Challenge 2: *How to design a hybrid Conceptual Model in the presence of sparse attributes and optional values.*

Guidelines. The answer to this challenge is tied to the Semantics of the data being modeled (and to the performance requirements as discussed subsequently). Ideally, optional values should be explicitly marked as so. Then, the logical design can evaluate and maybe model them as XML.

Schema Evolution

The schema evolves as changes in the modeling or in the application requirements are incorporated. Such changes include the following operations: adding and deleting entities and attributes, changing data types and names, changing relationship cardinality, composing one entity from others, and decomposing it into others.

In the product example, two common changes are adding product subtypes (e.g. MP3 players to electronics) and attributes (e.g. Bluetooth to cellular phones). Besides adding new entities and attributes, new relationships may be added as well. Deleting products and attributes is certainly possible, but is less of a problem, since lazy or batch delete schemes can be used.

Modeling the frequency of changes is also crucial, because it allows the logical design phase to pick the schema that is suited to the rate of change. Non-frequent schema changes are generally not a problem, because the changes can be incorporated when the database is re-organized. Anyhow, the main problem in this scenario is presented in the next challenge.

Challenge 3: *How to anticipate and (effectively) to capture changes in the Conceptual Model such that the work of the Logical phase is easier.*

Guidelines. An initial guideline for adding schema evolution in the Conceptual Model is to model the regular data as well as the metadata that characterize the evolution. This metadata modeling should also consider the business rules and constraints supported by the evolution (i.e. for each entity, which changes are allowed and anticipated).

Logical Design

Logical design is concerned with producing a set of table schemas (i.e., create table statements) that satisfy the conceptual requirements. In the hybrid XML-relational case (where the database management system supports both relational and XML columns), the main problem for logical design is which part of the data goes to relational columns and which goes to XML columns.

After so much work on semi-structured and unstructured data, the basic differences between relational and XML are well understood. Relational data are mostly characterized by their well structured and typed table representation, static and homogeneous schema (all tuples within a relation follow the same schema), and primary/foreign keys identification. XML data relax all those features and allow semi-structured data with optional typing and sparse attributes, hierarchical representation, flexible and possibly evolving schema, and optional identification keys.

All those features may be considered as initial guidelines when deciding which data model to use. However, what happens when designing a database for complex applications (such as those that use the FpML standard), in which parts of both sets of features are required?

Additionally, there are other features from the data or application that can be evaluated in order to answer that question. Assuming that the Conceptual Model has captured all the information requirements, then the Logical Model needs to preserve all those requirements (entities, attributes, relationships, and so on). The Logical Design can then be built by evaluating complex trade-offs among different factors as follows.

Business Artifacts

Business artifacts naturally group complex units of information that are likely to be accessed together. Hence, normalizing the data from these artifacts into multiple relations may be awkward, and retrieving these business artifacts considering such design will require joining possibly many tables.

Guidelines. In such situation, representing these groups of data as XML may be more appropriate. Moreover, existing XML formats for some of these business artifacts may already have been standardized and the use of those standards may be mandatory in some cases.

Schema Variability

When the data (or parts thereof) are inherently complex and variable, many Logical Design choices are possible. For example, Figure 2 shows four different logical designs for the `product` entity from the previous section: (a) one single relation with all possible product attributes; (b) multiple relations for each product sub-type; (c) a vertical schema; and (d) a hybrid schema with product description as an XML document. In summary, the implications of those designs are: option (a) results in a very sparse table with many NULL values; (b) results in too many tables; (c) requires many joins for query processing; and (d) is reasonable, but the problem is the next challenge.

Challenge 4: *How to determine how many XML columns should be used and which fields should be into relational columns, if any.*

Guidelines. The work in Moro (2007a) proposes an initial solution for this challenge. In summary, it establishes a measure of flexibility that considers different aspects of the schema variability. The more variable the features of an entity, the more chances for it to be modeled as an XML column.

Schema Evolution

The ability to anticipate the type and the frequency of schema changes is crucial for modeling schema

Figure 2. Logical models for purchase order example

```
(a) product(id, price, size, weight, color,
             screensize, stereo, fabric...)
(b) tshirt(id, price, size, color, fabric)
           television(id, price, weight, screensize, stereo)...
(c) product(id, attributeName, attributeValue)
(d) product(id, price, size, XMLdescription)
```

evolution on the Logical Design. Assuming that this information has been captured by the Conceptual Model, the question is how to design the Logical Model such that expensive database operations are avoided.

Guidelines. One solution would be to employ a vertical schema for the evolving data. However, the vertical schema suffers from being too generic. Another solution is to use an XML data to model the evolving part of the system, since an XML model is more flexible and adaptable to changes (mostly due to its self-describing feature). Nonetheless, it is important to establish the granularity of such division (e.g. separating relational entities from XML entities, or separating relational attributes from XML attributes). Whether the schema evolution is done using a relational or an XML data model, a related technical challenge is as follows.

Challenge 5: *How to evolve the queries on the hybrid model.*

Guidelines. Managing queries on evolving databases is usually done by employing a series of mappings and transformations. Having a hybrid database makes those mappings even more complex. Some initial guidelines for evolving queries on XML databases are presented in Moro (2007b) and Moro (2007c).

Data Versioning

Efficient versioning control is still a challenge for most commercial relational database management systems, in spite of the amount of research already published on the subject. If the database system does not have explicit support for versioning, how should the logical schema be designed? For example, suppose FpML contracts are stored as XML documents in a contract table and contracts need to be versioned at the document granularity. A possible Logical Design may consist of two tables:

```
contracts( id, fpmldoc )
contractsover( id, fpmldoc, timestamp,
editor _ id )
```

where the `contracts` table always stores the latest version, and the `contractsover` table stores all versions and the identifier of the person who created each version.

Guidelines. Some questions to guide the Logical Design are: What is the granularity of the data being versioned? Should versions be kept at the tuple level, column level, field level, XML document level, or XML fragment level? What are the query requirements? Do queries always specify a version number or timestamp?

Challenge 6: *A technical challenge presented by these last two scenarios (schema evolution and data versioning) is how to define the connection between the static data and the evolving data.*

Guidelines. An initial direction would be to keep the stable links as relational data and the dynamic ones as XML. However, how to manage such links on an evolving system is still a major challenge.

Other Features

Space. The self-describing nature of XML data does require more space (for handling descriptors). The variable space nature of XML also adds complexity to the system. However, storage media are generally inexpensive and are usually not a major concern. Therefore, we do not consider space issues as a major challenge.

Redundancy. For relational schemas, normalization is a transformation of the Logical Model for minimizing the redundancy of the information stored. Normalizing XML data has been addressed by Arenas & Libkin (2005), and we do not discuss redundancy issues any further. Note that minimizing redundancy often needs to be tempered by performance requirements, as discussed next.

Performance. While logical design is not primarily concerned with performance, performance is often a factor in logical design. For example, minimizing redundancy through normal forms can be seen as favoring update performance. On the other hand, in read intensive applications, de-normalization is applied to reduce joins for improving query performance. Hence, the desired performance criteria and characteristics of the underlying database management system need to be understood before embarking on logical design. Performance criteria generally fall into two categories: management performance (inserts, updates, deletes) and query performance (structural queries and search queries).

For hybrid databases, accessing XML data using an XPath expression is inherently more complex than accessing a single relational field. However, if XML is chosen to store complex data that might otherwise be stored in multiple relational tables, then accessing XML data is likely to be more efficient than joining multiple tables. Moreover, a portion of the data from a business artifact stored as XML may need to be accessed frequently with low latency. In such cases, the frequently accessed data may need to be replicated in relational columns for improving performance.

Challenge 7: *Other performance issues that may influence the logical design and are still technical challenges for hybrid databases include: query workload, search queries (which are perform better on XML), operation workload (XML does not support partial updates yet), indexes (on-going work on XML data).*

Reference system. In the relational model, data can reference other data using key-to-foreign key relationships. In a hybrid logical database design,

relational data need the ability to reference XML elements, and XML data need a mechanism to reference both relational and XML data. The challenge is then as follows.

Challenge 8: *How to design a more unified reference system for hybrid databases.*

Guidelines. A naive solution is to use a foreign key for relational data and the triple [primary key, column name, XPath] as a foreign key into XML data, where the [primary key, column name] pair uniquely identifies an XML document. This solution assumes freedom to design the XML schema. In cases where the XML schemas are fixed (e.g. an industry format), it is not possible to embed foreign keys or triples within the XML data itself. Hence, these referential relationships need to be persisted in a separate table.

In situations where the reference requires versioning Semantics, version identifiers or timestamps need to be added. Note also that the traditional concept of referential integrity may need to be re-defined, because XPaths are being used in keys and XPath can be much more flexible in terms of what data element(s) it matches. Whatever the case, the Logical Design phase needs to keep these referential requirements in mind, because they potentially affect the relational and XML schemas.

Physical Design

Physical database design involves choosing appropriate storage and index data structures. For hybrid databases, the main challenges are as follows.

Challenge 9: *What kind of indexing is needed for XML data and joint relational-XML data? In which columns or XML fragments to build indexes? How do indexing decisions affect performance and hence influence the logical design?*

In this chapter, we focus on the conceptual and logical aspects of the hybrid design, leaving the discussion of the physical aspects as future work.

Discussion

Business requirements evolve and no matter how evolution-friendly a database design is, a methodology is necessary for coping with unanticipated changes. Some database evolution scenarios include: Given a pure relational database, when should data be migrated to a hybrid database design? How to migrate a relational database design to a hybrid database design? Given a hybrid database and a new business requirement, how to extend the hybrid database?

The chief difference between these questions and the process of designing a database from scratch is that the methodology needs to consider migration constraints such as minimizing: downtime, changes to existing database schemas, impact to existing applications and so on. In some cases, an incremental or gradual evolution path is required in order to keep existing business applications running. Therefore, as a last challenge, we have the following.

Challenge 10: *What is the sequence of evolution steps that satisfy the business and migration constraints?*

RELATED WORK

The major commercial relational database systems (i.e. IBM DB2, Oracle and Microsoft SQL Server) provide support for storing and querying XML data in addition to relational data (Rys, 2005). While the implementation of high performance, XML-relational databases has received a great deal of attention in recent years, considerable less effort has been directed toward providing a solid

modeling methodology for designing databases on such hybrid data model.

Different approaches have been proposed to model XML data. Specifically, Conrad (2000) advocates the use of standard modeling languages such as the UML for designing XML schemas. The focus of this approach is on representing DTD concepts visually by using UML such that UML notation is extended in order to represent those concepts. Note that this work does not discuss how to model the data, but rather how to represent the data that have already been modeled.

Likewise, Bird (2000) uses the object role modeling (ORM) in order to visually model an XML Schema. The main idea is to focus on the data constraints which are represented using ORM, and to delay the definition of schema tree-structure until after the conceptual modeling phase. Also, the paper proposes some heuristics for generating the schema based on the conceptual model.

Then, Embley & Mok (2001) use a more generic conceptual model and propose the normalization rules, XML normal forms (XNF) to DTDs (not XML Schema). The idea is to produce a good conceptual model for an application and then to derive a DTD from this model. The paper proposes such derivation (transformation) by focusing on two main properties: maximum connectivity and minimal redundancy.

Finally, Embley (2004) proposes conceptual XM (C-XML) for representing each component and constraint from XML Schema (and vice-versa). Considering all previously mentioned works, this is probably the most related to XML conceptual modeling. It focuses on the abstract conceptual elements (entities and relationships), it works well for both XML Schema and DTD, it support complex structures, and it allows query specification.

Regarding the design methodology, Elmasri (2002) introduces a method for XML schema using extended entity relationship (EER) schema. The focus is on defining a methodology that allows different hierarchical views for different XML document structures. The paper then describes algorithms for generating such views from EER models, creating schemas from those views, and then creating the actual XML instance documents.

All those solutions are specific for XML and do not support both relational and XML data. Also, we are not interested in proposing yet another modeling language for XML design. Instead, our work investigates the different aspects that should be considered when designing a hybrid XML-relational database. Finally, we also discuss open questions and propose challenges that still need attention from the research community.

Challenges of evolving applications and their data models are not new. Two decades ago, Banerjee (1987) reported their attempts to enhance object-oriented data model with schema evolution, object composition, and version control, and many different proposals have emerged since then. From the document versioning perspective, Chien (2006) proposes a version model based on timestamps that enables efficient query processing over multiversion XML documents.

Another important aspect of hybrid XML-relational databases is the ability to blend text-centric with data-centric retrieval methods. While text-centric retrieval methods are inherently fuzzy and ranking-based, the traditional data-centric retrieval is exact. Some of the challenges involved in incorporating IR capabilities within database systems have been identified in Chaudhuri (2005). Clearly, as hybrid databases become more and more mainstream, relevance-based retrieval needs to be fully integrated and as optimizable as any other access method.

FUTURE TRENDS

We know that relational design is difficult, despite many years of research and experience. Having XML in the mix leads to more freedom and room for making bad choices. Being one of the first, this chapter draws up some challenges based on our experience of working with eager early adopters of the hybrid technology. As future trends, we consider that the research community will evaluate such challenges in order to establish a more complete modeling methodology for hybrid XML-relational databases.

The challenges are summarized as follows.

1. How to define an elegant model for data (relational or XML) and business artifacts in a unified way that captures the Semantics of business artifacts, the information within artifacts, and the relationships between entities within the artifacts to entities external to the artifacts.

2. How to design a hybrid Conceptual Model in the presence of sparse attributes and optional values.

3. How to anticipate and (effectively) capture changes in the Conceptual Model such that the work of the logical phase is easier.

4. How to determine the number of XML columns that should be used and which fields should be in the relational columns, if any.

5. How to evolve the queries on the hybrid model.

6. A technical challenge from these last two scenarios (schema evolution and data versioning) is how to define the connection between the static data and the evolving data.

7. Other performance issues that may influence the Logical Design and are still technical challenges for hybrid databases include: query workload, search queries (which are perform better on XML), operation workload (XML does not support partial updates yet), indexes (on-going work on XML data).

8. How to design a more unified reference system for hybrid databases.

9. What kind of indexing is needed for XML data and joint relational-XML data? In which columns or XML fragments to build indexes? How do indexing decisions affect performance and hence influence the logical design?

10. What is the sequence of evolution steps that satisfy the business and migration constraints?

CONCLUSION

The most common database modeling methodology employs a three-tier approach consisting of conceptual, logical, and physical modeling phases. This chapter discussed issues on database design for a hybrid XML-relational database. First, it introduced a methodology for designing XML databases by presenting different options for the same use case. The, it presented relevant case scenarios that motivates such hybrid modeling. Finally, this chapter proposed guidelines for modeling the hybrid XML-relational database and emphasized many challenges to such modeling. It is important to notice that the hybrid XML-relational design discipline is just in its infancy and requires more research to mature. This chapter represents just an opening step toward a more complete and well defined modeling methodology for Hybrid XML-Relational Databases.

ACKNOWLEDGMENT

We would like to thank Sharon Adler and Anders Berglund for discussions about previous versions of this chapter. This work started while Mirella M. Moro was visiting IBM T. J. Watson Research Center. She is currently supported by CNPq, Brazil.

REFERENCES

Arenas, M., & Libkin, L. (2005). An Information-Theoretic Approach to Normal Forms for Relational and XML Data. *Journal of ACM 52*(2), 246-283.

Banerjee, J., Chou, H-T., Garza, J. F., Kim, W., Woelk, D., Ballou, N., & Kim, H-J.(1987). Data Model Issues for Object-Oriented Applications. *ACM Transactions on Information Systems 5*(1), 3-26.

Berglund, A., Boag, S., Chamberlin, D., Fernández, M. F., Kay, M., Robie, J., & Siméon, J. (2007). XML Path Language (XPath) 2.0. *W3C Recommendation*. Retrieved January 26, 2008, from http://www.w3.org/TR/xpath20.

Bird, L., Goodchild, A., & T. Halpin (2000). Object Role Modelling and XML-Schema. In *ER*, (pp. 309-322).

Chaudhuri, S., Ramakrishnan, R., & Weikum, G. (2005). Integrating DB and IR Technologies: What is the Sound of One Hand Clapping? In *CIDR*, (pp. 1-12).

Chen, P. (1976). The Entity-Relationship Model - Toward a Unified View of Data. *ACM Transactions on Database Systems*, *1*(1), 9-36.

Chien, S.-Y., Tsotras, V. J., Zaniolo, C., & Zhang, D. (2006). Supporting complex queries on multiversion xml documents. *ACM Transactions on Internet Technology 6*(1), 53-84.

Codd, E. F. (1970). A Relational Model of Data for Large Shared Data Banks. *Communications of the ACM 13*(6), 377-387.

Conrad, R., Scheffner, D., & Freytag, J. C. (2000). XML conceptual modeling using UML. In *ER*, (pp. 558-571).

Elmasri, R., Wu, Y-C., Hojabri, B., Li, C., & Fu, J. (2002). Conceptual Modeling for Customized XML Schemas. In *ER*, (pp. 429-443).

Embley, D. W., Liddle, S. W., & Al-Kamha, R. (2004). Enterprise Modeling with Conceptual XML. In *ER*, (pp. 150-165).

Embley, D. W., & Mok, W. Y. (2001). Developing XML Documents with Guaranteed "Good" Properties. In *ER*, (pp. 426-441).

Florescu, D., & Kossmann, D. (1999). Storing and Querying XML Data using an RDBMS. *IEEE Data Engineering Bulletin 22*(3), 27-34 .

Halverson, A., Josifovski, V., Lohman, G. M., Pirahesh, H., & Mörschel, M. (2004). ROX: Relational Over XML. In *VLDB*, (pp. 264-275).

Jagadish, H. V, Al-Khalifa, S., Chapman, A., Lakshmanan, L.V.S., Nierman, A., Paparizos, S., Patel, J.M., Srivastava, D., Wiwatwattana, N., Wu, Y., & Yu, C. (2002). TIMBER: A Native XML Database. *VLDB Journal 11*(4), 274-291.

Moro, M. M., Lim, L., & Chang, Y.-C. (2007a). Schema Advisor for Hybrid Relational-XML DBMS. In *SIGMOD*, (pp. 959-970).

Moro, M. M., Malaika, S., & Lim, L. (2007b). Preserving XML Queries during Schema Evolution. In *WWW*, (pp. 1341-1342).

Moro, M. M., Malaika, S., & Lim, L. (2007c). Preserving XML Queries during Schema Evolution. In *IBM developerWorks*. Retrieved January 26, 2008, from http://www.ibm.com/developerworks/library/x-evolvingxquery.html.

Rys, M., Chamberlin, D., & Florescu, D. (2005). XML and Relational Database Management Systems: The Inside Story. In *SIGMOD*, (pp. 945-947).

Shanmugasundaram, J., Shekita, E. J., Kiernan, J., Krishnamurthy, R., Viglas, S., Naughton, J. F., & Tatarinov, I. (2001). A General Techniques for Querying XML Documents using a Relational Database System. *SIGMOD Record 30*(3), 20-26.

ENDNOTES

1   http://www.legalarchiver.org/soa.htm
2   http://www.ibm.com/db2
3   http://www.fpml.org
4   http://www.hl7.org

Chapter III
XML and LDAP Integration:
Issues and Trends

Vassiliki Koutsonikola
Aristotle University of Thessaloniki, Greece

Athena Vakali
Aristotle University of Thessaloniki, Greece

ABSTRACT

Nowadays, XML has become the standard for representing and exchanging data over the Web and several approaches have been proposed for efficiently managing, storing, querying and representing XML data originating from diverse and often heterogeneous sources. The Lightweight Directory Access Protocol is a promising technology for XML data storage and retrieval since it facilitates access to information organized under a variety of frameworks and applications. As an open, vendor-neutral standard, LDAP provides an extendable architecture for centralized storage and management of information that needs to be available for today's distributed systems and services. The similarities between XML and LDAP data representation have led to the idea of processing XML data within the LDAP framework. This chapter focuses on the topic of LDAP and XML integration with emphasis on the storage and retrieval approaches implemented so far. Moreover, the chapter includes an overview and survey of the theoretical background and the adopted practices as realized in the most popular and emerging frameworks which tune XML and LDAP.

INTRODUCTION

Extensible markup language (XML) has rapidly emerged as the dominant standard for representing and exchanging data over the Web. As more and more enterprises take advantage of the connectivity offered by the Internet to exchange information within and across their boundaries, XML constitutes a simple yet extensible, platform-neutral, data representation standard.

XML's simplicity and open nature has met Web data exchange requirements and nowadays the increasing amount of XML data on the Web poses the need for revising effective XML data management policies.

Among data management issues, storage and querying techniques are of particular importance, since the performance of an XML-based information system relies on them. Several approaches for storing XML data have been proposed in research literature and have been designed for various commercial tools. Apart from supporting the expected user-defined types of queries, an XML data storage system must also meet specific requirements such as:

- Supporting the management of XML schemas to define the data and the validation structures in order to map data to the predefined schemas;
- Providing mechanisms that will support effective indexing and disk space allocation methods in terms of the physical XML database storage;

- Integrating tools for content management operations (add, delete, modify) on the data organized under a specific storage framework;
- Supporting backup, replication and recovery mechanisms together with query optimization techniques based on indexing and other access paths configurations.

Although XML documents include text only and can easily be stored in files, it is worthwhile to "turn" to data management systems (e.g. databases) for their storage and retrieval, in order to apply advanced data management techniques. Figure 1 depicts the architecture of an XML-based storage and retrieval system. As depicted in this figure, appropriate storage policies are applied to the XML documents in order to store them in an XML data storage system while user applications or other application interfaces must use specific policies to retrieve the XML data. When integrating it with a database, the XML document structure has to be mapped to the database schema, which is required by every database management system. The structure of XML documents

Figure 1. XML storage and retrieval

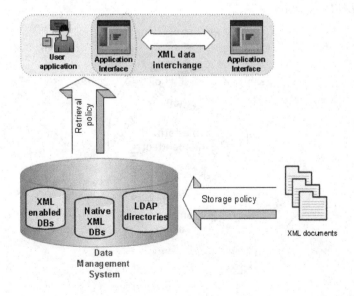

does not fit with any typical database model (e.g. relational, object-oriented, object-relational) and therefore necessary transformations are needed to enable storage of XML data in a typical database management system. Native XML databases have recently emerged as a model designed especially to store XML documents (Vakali et al., 2005; Win et al., 2003). However, the native XML databases are less mature than conventional DBMSs and have not yet become very popular, since these systems must be built from scratch.

The lightweight directory access protocol (Wahl et al., 1997) is an open industry standard that is gaining wide acceptance as a directory-access method. As the name suggests, LDAP is the lightweight version of the directory access protocol and is a direct descendant of the heavyweight X.500, the most common directory-management protocol. Many software vendors support LDAP due to its flexibility and the fact that it integrates with an increasing number of data retrieval and management applications. LDAP directories can be used for the storage of various data entries that describe data such as IT services, certificates and pictures. For example, in the case of a university, LDAP can be used for the storage of information

that describes teachers, students or workstations. Furthermore, users' certificates and revocation lists can be stored in an LDAP server and used by PKI applications. The LDAP framework also provides appropriate mechanisms for their efficient retrieval and modification, making it an effective solution as a data management system. LDAP is thus an evolving ground for research on new and existing data management practices. In this context, LDAP directories provide an efficient storage framework for XML data due to their performance in read operations and their scalability. Moreover, the use of lightweight directories as a storage medium of a variety of information has motivated the idea of processing XML data in LDAP.

The hierarchical nature and the structural similarities that XML and LDAP technologies present have motivated researchers to proceed to their integration. A significant number of common features that the two standards share, encouraged their merging. For instance, both XML and LDAP support the definition of valid entries or documents that are compliant with a predefined schema. Moreover, they both use tree structures for the data representation, they are platform-in-

Figure 2. XML and LDAP relation

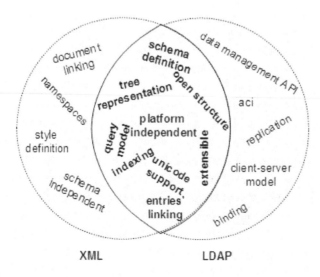

dependent, they support a similar query model and they provide a linking mechanism between entries (Xlink, referrals and aliases). On the other hand, each of the two models is characterized by specific features such as the namespaces and style definition (XSLT) supported in XML and the access control lists, replication and data management APIs provided by LDAP. An overview of the similarities and differences between the XML and LDAP standards is given in Figure 2.

Since several approaches for effective XML data storage and retrieval using LDAP servers have been proposed, we will focus on this chapter mainly on existing XML storage and retrieval methods that use LDAP as an efficient alternative to the XML data management framework. Initially, a brief background of the proposed approaches for storing XML data is given along with a discussion of the relevant retrieval methods applied for their querying. The following sections provide a detailed overview and commentary which proves that LDAP server is appropriate for the XML data storage and retrieval. The chapter concludes by highlighting the perspectives and the future trends in LDAP and XML integration.

BACKGROUND

XML Storage Policies

Various applications frameworks and technologies adopt XML in their own method for storing data, following different XML document representation models and meeting the underlying system's requirements. Current XML management systems are thus divided into XML-enabled databases and native XML databases.

XML-Enabled Databases

XML-enabled databases use typical database technologies which provide the backend for the XML documents storage. Existing approaches differentiate over the underlying storage model of the database system and fall into one of the following categories:

- **Relational databases (RDBs)**: The storing of XML documents in relational databases means describing hierarchical, tree-type structures with relations. More specifically, in order to represent XML data by using tables, it is necessary to break down the XML documents into rows and columns that sufficiently capture the parent-child and ancestor-descendant relationships between the XML nodes. This process is expected to incur some performance overhead mainly because of the continuous translation of trees to tables (and vice versa). However, due to the popularity of relational databases, the first wave of research was adopting them for storing XML and several methods have been proposed to store XML documents in relational databases. Existing approaches mainly differ in the model they use to perform the mapping between XML documents and relational tables (Florescu & Kossmann, 1999). Moreover, they may consider the XML schema as a prerequisite (Khan & Rao, 2001; Shanmugasundaram et al., 1999; Tan et al., 2005) or extract it during the mapping process (Schmidt et al., 2000). Designing efficient techniques for the tuning of XML storage schema in relational databases has also been addressed by various approaches, which provide a set of alternative storage configurations and evaluate their quality by estimating their performance on an application workload (Bohannon et al., 2002; Xu et al., 2003; Zheng et al., 2003). The configuration that minimizes the execution time (cost) of the pre-specified set of queries is ultimately applied. The strong integration between RDBs and XML is also proven by the fact that commercial DBMSs such as SQL Server (Rys et al., 2005), IBM DB2

(Beyer et al., 2006) and Oracle (Liu et al., 2005) provide native support for XML.

- **Object-oriented databases (OODBs):** In the case of Object-Oriented Databases (OODBs), the storage of the parsed XML document involves studying each component and mapping it individually to object instances, using relationships based on the object-oriented programming ideas. The advantage of using object-oriented databases is that they are the natural storage technology for the DOM since they store DOM trees without having to map the objects and their relations to other data concepts. The main drawback of the OODB systems is the factorization they cause in XML documents and the great number of joins required during the retrieval process. Moreover, the use of OODB systems is not very flexible for XML document storage since they cannot easily handle data with a dynamic structure (e.g. a new class definition is needed for a new XML document). Various approaches have been proposed to represent XML documents in terms of object-oriented data storage model which are schema-independent (Chung et al., 2001) or preserve both structure and content of XML documents (Chung & Jesurajaiah, 2005).

- **Object-relational databases (ORDBs):** Object-Relational databases are designed to bridge the gap between relational (RDBs) and object-oriented databases (OODBs). The XML documents are stored in a nested table in which each tag name in DTD (or XML schema) corresponds to an attribute name in the nested table (Pallis et al., 2003). The advantage of using ORDBs is their relational maturity and the richness of OO modeling (Pardede et al., 2004). However, as in OODB systems, the number of required joins creates costs for the retrieval process. Several approaches have been proposed in the literature which also differentiate based on whether they are schema driven requiring in advance the XML documents'

Table 1. Approaches mapping XML to conventional databases

Approach	Data model	Schema dependent	Cost driven	Content preserving
(Khan & Rao, 2001) (Tan et al., 2005)	Relational	✓		✓
(Bohannon et al., 2002) (Xu et al., 2003) (Zheng et al., 2003)	Relational	✓	✓	
(Schmidt et al. 2000)	Relational			✓
(Chung et al., 2001) (Chung & Jesurajaiah, 2005)	Object-Oriented	✓		✓
(Pardede et al., 2004) (Surjanto et al., 2000)	Object-Relational	✓		✓
(Klettke & Meyer, 2000)	Object-Relational	✓	✓	✓
(Beyer et al., 2006) (Shanmugasundaram et al., 1999) (Shanmugasundaram et al., 2001) (Rys et al., 2005) (Liu et al., 2005)	Relational	✓		

schema (Klettke & Meyer, 2000; Pardede et al., 2004; Surjanto et al., 2000) or they retain content and structural information in the obtained mapping.

A summary of the main characteristics of some indicative approaches that involve the mapping of XML documents on one of the above typical database models is given in Table 1. These approaches are categorized based on whether they need to know a priori the XML schema, or whether they can extract it during the XML documents' parsing. Moreover, there exist approaches that use a cost-based method to decide the most appropriate storage configuration or support both the logical structure and content of documents.

Native XML Databases

Native XML databases have recently emerged to satisfy the need for a more robust XML storage approach which treats XML documents and elements as the fundamental structures rather than tables, records, and fields. More specifically, a native XML database defines a logical model for an XML document and stores and retrieves documents according to that model. Native XML databases have a number of features that are useful for working with document-centric XML

such as the XML data model, which is flexible enough to model documents. Thus, documents can be stored and queried in a single location, rather than multiple locations held together by glue code. However, native XML databases have yet to become very popular since the adopted storage structure is built from scratch and is adjusted to the existing framework's needs and purposes. Typical examples of native XML databases include eXist (Meier, 2002), Timber (Jagadish et al., 2002), Sedna (Fomichev et al., 2005) and Tamino (Schoning, 2001). The main features of these systems are summarized in Table 2 and clearly indicate the different data storage policies which can be adopted and which aim to maintain the XML specific data model. As Table 2 shows, native XML databases are usually schema-independent and do not require that XML documents include schema (or DTD). Moreover, collections and trees are typically used as data organization models in the case of native XML databases while each of them adjusts to a specific storage policy.

XML Retrieval Policies

XPath[1] and XQuery[2] have been identified as the standard XML querying languages (Catania et al., 2005). XPath provides a path-like syntax for referring to nodes in an existing document.

Table 2. Native XML data stores

Native XML database	Data organization model	Schema independent	Storage policy
eXist	document collection	✓	Multiroot B+-tree
Timber	tree	✓	It is built on top of Shore, a backend store responsible for disk memory management, buffering and concurrency control
Sedna	tree	✓	Text values of xml nodes are stored in blocks while their structural part is presented in the form of node descriptors
Tamino	document collection		Document-based storage

XQuery provides flexible query facilities to extract data from XML data stores and is conceptually similar to SQL by supporting joins between multiple documents, filtering and sorting operations. Depending on the nature of the XML data store (XML-enabled or native) and the underlying XML data storage model, various approaches have been proposed for the querying of XML documents which have a query language as their basis or extend the previously mentioned query languages. Moreover, there are other research works that have been designed under a different query framework.

An enhanced index-based query processing is provided by eXist (Meier, 2002) which uses an XPath query processor with several extensions. Khan & Rao (2001) also adopt XPath queries for the querying process developed in their approach. Moreover, they present a novel mechanism for translating an XPath query into SQL statements as well as techniques which result in the construction of an XML document on the fly from an SQL statement result set. Sedna (Fomichev et al., 2006), on the other hand, implement a wide set of rule-based query optimization techniques for XQuery. The SQLGenerator presented by Cathey et al. (2004) is a scalable XML retrieval

Table 3. Information retrieval over XML databases

Approach	Data Model	Retrieval policy	Advantages
eXist	Native XML database	Supports and extends the standard XPath query mechanism	• Implements efficient index-based query processing • Supports keyword-based and proximity searches • Supports extended XPath queries
Sedna	Native XML database	Implements a wide set of rule-based XQuery optimization techniques	• Supports a locking protocol to solve synchronization protocol • Extends to support update operations
SQLGenerator	Relational database	Implements XML-QL by translating it to SQL	• Scalability • Incorporates XML documents of any schema without requiring modifications to the underlying relational schema
(Khan & Rao, 2001)	Relational database	Translates XPath queries into SQL statements	• Query performance • Efficient techniques for the construction of an XML document on the fly are proposed
(Liu et al., 2005)	Relational database	Rewrites XQuery into SQL with XML extension operators and constructs	• Enables the utilization of standard indexes and relational performance optimization techniques • Results in performance improvement
(Beyer et al., 2006)	Relational database	Provides separate parsers for SQL and XQuery and also uses an integrated query compiler for both of them	• DB2 is the first hybrid system that supports both relational and XML data • The underlying system can be extended with navigational support for XML • A visual XQuery design tool is provided
Tamino	Native XML database	Tamino extends XPath semantics to the handling of sets of documents	• Support of full text search over the content of attributes and elements
(Pal, 2005)	Relational database	XQuery expressions are compiled into an internal structure called the XML algebra tree	• Provides a good set of features that perform and scale well • The compiled query plan is optimized

engine that fully implements the XML-QL query language by translating it to SQL. An overview of the most important retrieval approaches to XML databases is given in Table 3. Considering the retrieval process that is applied on each of the described approaches, we can conclude that where an XML-enabled database is engaged for the storage of XML documents, it is necessary to use a mechanism that will translate the XML queries into SQL statements. However, in the case of native XML databases, XPath and XQuery operations are directly applicable without the need of any translation process.

XML AND DIRECTORY SERVICES

LDAP Framework: Storage and Retrieval Basics

LDAP directories have rapidly emerged as the essential framework for storing and accessing a wide range of heterogeneous information under various applications and services (Koutsonikola & Vakali, 2004). They act as searchable database repositories ensuring more efficient data retrieval mechanisms through the usage of lightweight directory access protocol (LDAP) (Wahl et al., 1997).

LDAP operations are based on the client-server model where, for example, many devices (such as printers and routers) act as clients and access data stored in a given LDAP server database. Moreover, LDAP technology has been integrated with a variety of application services and new technologies such as domain name and e-mail services. In this context, LDAP servers have been used as data stores for many heterogeneous data sources providing flexibility and meeting storage demands. For example, they have been used to store information that describes user profiles for messaging applications, configuration files of network devices and network security policies,

under the directory enabled networks (DEN) initiative (Howes & Smith, 1997), certificates and revocation lists for PKI applications (Chadwick, 2003) as well as access control lists for authentication systems (Park et al., 2001). The new H.350 standard uses LDAP to provide a uniform way to store information related to video and voice over IP (VoIP) in directories (Gemmill et al., 2003) while Grid computing has emerged as a very promising infrastructure for distributed computing, having its foundation and core in the distributed LDAP directories (Fan et al., 2005).

In addition to their support for heterogeneous data storage, the main characteristic of LDAP servers is their optimized response times in read operations, which reveal the efficient retrieval mechanisms they provide that are based on the internal LDAP data representation. LDAP also supports access control mechanisms to ensure authenticated data access as well as data replication models. An overview of the LDAP framework architecture is depicted in Figure 3 where various network devices (such as routers, printers, firewalls) and services (such as DNS, PKI, FTP) access data stored in LDAP directories through authentication mechanisms and access control policies. Moreover, as depicted in Figure 3, LDAP supports replication models between collaborating LDAP servers so as to ensure data redundancy and load balance. LDAP servers are synchronized and provide consistent information stored in the LDAP databases (directories).

The basic LDAP storage unit is the directory entry, which is where information about a particular object resides. All information within a directory entry is stored as attribute-value pairs, while the set of attributes that appear in a given entry is determined by the objectclasses that are used to describe it. The set of rules that defines the objectclasses and the attributes they contain constitutes the LDAP schema. To preserve interoperability between different vendors' LDAP servers, a well-defined standard schema exists, which is expected to be included in all LDAP servers. However, the LDAP schema is extensible, thereby allowing users to define their own object-classes and attributes to meet their applications' needs. LDAP schema also supports inheritance, meaning that one objectclass may inherit attributes from another.

LDAP directories are arranged as hierarchical information trees representing the organizations they describe. Each entry is identified by a distinguished name (DN) which declares its position in the hierarchy. The overall structure of the hierarchical organization constitutes the directory information tree (DIT) which originates from a root (RootDN). A sample DIT depicting the organization of LDAP entries that describe people and workstations that belong to the Computer Science Department of Aristotle University of Thessaloniki is given in Figure 4. In the basic core LDAP notations, *dc* stands for domain component and *o* for organizations. These two attributes belong to the core LDAP schema. The rest of the attributes i.e. the *uid, name, surname,*

domname, ipaddress and *mac* refer to the user id, name, surname, domain name, ip address and mac address of the described object, respectively.

Moreover, the hierarchical organization of LDAP entries contributes to an efficient retrieval framework since in an LDAP search operation it is possible to determine a specific subtree where the search will be executed. This is achieved by defining the level on the DIT at which searching begins and which is identified by the *dn* of the respective node (baseDN). Furthermore, in an LDAP search operation, a user can define the depth of the search which is determined by the search *scope* value. There are three types of scope. A scope of *sub* (subtree) indicates that the search will be executed to an entire subtree starting from the base object all the way down to the leaves of the tree. A scope of *onelevel* refers to a search that considers only the immediate children of the entry at the top of the search base. A scope of *base* limits the search to just the base object. This scope is used to retrieve one particular entry

Figure 3. LDAP framework

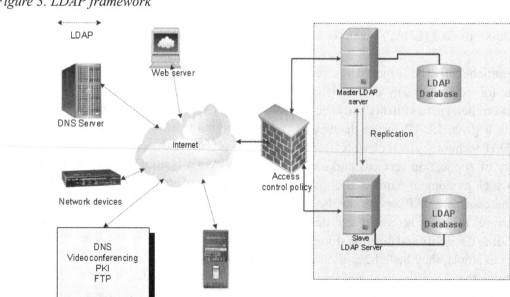

Figure 4. LDAP directory information tree hierarchy

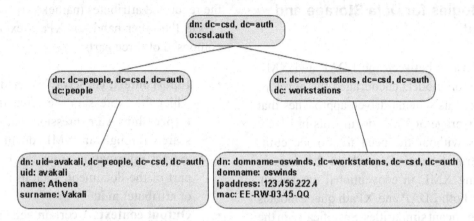

Figure 5. LDAP search operation space

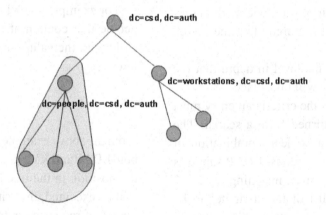

from the directory. Figure 5 depicts the search space of a query whose baseDN is *"dc=people, dc=csd, dc=auth"* and scope is *sub*.

From the above discussion it becomes evident that there is a great similarity between LDAP and XML technologies in terms of both storage and retrieval models. Specifically, as valid LDAP entries are compliant with a predefined LDAP schema, a valid and well-defined XML document must also be adjusted to an XML schema or document type definition (DTD). In addition, information regarding XML documents is stored in the form of elements-values pairs. Each element may contain

some attributes or other elements nested within, just like objectclasses contain attributes, and may inherit other objectclasses. Moreover, an LDAP entry can be both a container (superior) as well as a subordinate to another entry, in much the same way that an XML DOM node can be both a parent and a child. In terms of the retrieval process, the Lightweight Directory Access Protocol offers a querying model based on filter specification that happens to be very close in nature to that of native XPath, so that every XPath query can easily be translated into LDAP queries.

Integration of XML and LDAP Technologies for Data Storage and Retrieval

The similarities between the LDAP and XML representation models encouraged the development of various schema-driven approaches that allow the storage of XML documents in LDAP directories without the need to provide cumbersome transformations (such as the ones in representing XML in conventional databases). Moreover, both LDAP and XPath query models present significant similarities. Specifically, in the LDAP query model, a search request is composed by the following main parts:

- **baseDn**: The dn of the node in directory information tree hierarchy that the search will begin
- **Scope**: Defines the level in depth that the search operation will take place
- **Filter**: Specifies the criteria an entry must match to be returned from a search. The search filter is a boolean combination of attribute value assertions. LDAP supports exact and approximate matching
- **Attributes**: A list of the attributes to be returned from each entry, which matches the search filter.

For example, if the LDAP query described in Figure 5 (i.e. it starts from the node with "dn: dc=people, dc=csd, dc=auth" and has as scope the whole subtree) is searching for a particular entry with username='avakali', it would be expressed by the following LDAP query:

```
ldapsearch -h localhost -b "dc=people,
dc=csd, dc=auth" -s sub "uid=avakali"
name
```

Here, the parameter –h declares the host that the LDAP query will be executed, –b declares the baseDN and –s the scope. Next the search filter is declared ("uid=avakali") and the list of the requested attributes (name).

On the other hand, an XPath expression is composed of three parts:

- **Input context**: The set of XML nodes against which the expression is evaluated;
- **Expression**: An expression that is used to search through an XML document, and extract information from the nodes (any part of the document, such as an element or attribute) in it;
- **Output context**: A certain node set which results from the application of the path expression.

For example, the XPath query that returns all people that contain at least one <uid> element child with the value "avakali" would be the following:

```
people[uid="avakali"]
```

From the above examples, it becomes clear that in both LDAP and XML query models, a user defines the position in the tree hierarchy that the query will be executed, the criteria that will determine the set of requested entries and the information that the answer will contain.

Despite the wide adoption of both XML and LDAP standards and their structural similarities which can make LDAP directories an ideal medium for XML data storage and retrieval, to the best of the authors' knowledge, an XML-enabled LDAP server has not yet been designed. However, a number of approaches have been proposed in the literature to support the storage and retrieval of XML documents under and LDAP framework.

Directory services markup language[3] (DSML) is an evolving specification that has been proposed to bridge the gap between directory services and XML-enabled applications, by representing directory information in XML. It is actually an XML version of the LDAP protocol that satisfies the need for interoperability between different LDAP directories vendors' which can be achieved by adopting the XML as the standard for their data exchange. Using DSML, any XML-enabled application can manage (search, add, modify, and delete) the directory services information and take advantage of the benefits of directory services such as the scalability, replication, and security.

An XML-enabled application can retrieve directory information in DSML format by sending a request to the Web application server that hosts the DSML service. The DSML service translates the query into LDAP. Via LDAP, the data is retrieved from the directory and passed back to the DSML service, which formats the data in DSML and sends it back to the application. DSML is defined using a document content description which specifies the rules and constrains on XML documents' structure and content. A typical DSML transaction as well as the requested entry in DSML is depicted in Figure 6, where the solid arrows indicate the DSML request and the dotted arrows the DSML response. Here, the XML-enabled application executes the LDAP query described previously in this section, requesting the entry of the user with uid="avakali". The requested entry is returned in DSML format, as depicted in Figure 6.

DSML has been used in various application frameworks. For example, it was used in the implementation of a role-based authorization service for Web-based solutions (Shin et al., 2002). A Web server sends the request for the user's role in XML format to the DSML gateway server. DSML gateway server parses the request and retrieves the user's role information using the LDAP protocol. The information is then transformed to DSML and sent back to the Web server. The proposed approach enables the information handling among various servers within or beyond a single organization boundary.

Besides DSML which constitutes an important initiative to support XML in LDAP directories, and which is supported by many LDAP vendors such as IBM, Microsoft, Novell and Oracle, other approaches have been proposed that integrate XML and LDAP standards. A quite simple idea for the representation of XML documents in LDAP format, so as to make their storage in LDAP directories feasible, is one that provides two mappings (Maron & Lausen, 2001A): the first one would determine the mapping of XML DTD (or schema) to the LDAP schema definition to provide the structure, while the second one would define the mapping between XML documents and LDAP entries. However, this approach is consid-

Figure 6. A typical DSML transaction

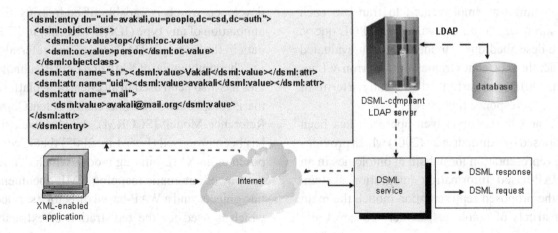

ered to have disadvantages (Marrón & Lausen, 2001A) since the LDAP schema is assumed to be static and the XML DTD's (or XML schema's) integration would involve changes. Moreover, even if the basic LDAP schema were extended to allow dynamic schema changes, it might result in illegal update operations. Therefore, in order to overcome these limitations, Marrón & Lausen (2001A) proposed the definition of three objectclasses, namely the XMLNode, XMLElement and XMLAttribute objectclasses, to combine the XML nodes, elements and attributes in the form of LDAP entries. Two algorithmic implementations, XML2LDAP and LDAP2XML, have been proposed for the transformation of XML documents to LDAP entries, and vice versa. The proposed approach has been adopted in the implementation of HLCaches (Marrón & Lausen, 2001B), a hierarchical, LDAP-based, distributed, caching system for semistructured documents and has provided an appropriate framework for efficient XML storage.

Marrón & Lausen (2001B) extended the schema proposed to support the storage of XML documents in LDAP directories by defining one more objectclass i.e. XMLQuery objectclass, that contains all relevant information about a particular query and its result set. Moreover, to fully support XPath queries, the concept of LDAPQL Query was introduced which extends the notion of scope in an LDAP query to enable the upward direction in search operations. The XPath2LDAPQL algorithm was implemented to translate each XPath query to an equivalent LDAPQL query. The described query model has been evaluated under the HLCaches framework (Marrón & Lausen, 2001B) and performed efficiently in terms of retrieval response times.

Another schema-driven approach has been proposed by Ahmedi et al. (2001) which provides the representation formalism of ontologies in an LDAP-based information integration system. In the proposed representation model, the main constructs of ontologies, namely concepts and

roles, together known as terms, are described by a corresponding objectclass definition; that is, two objectclasses, concept and role, are defined which inherit the objectclass term. Moreover, each objectclass contains a set of attributes, which can be categorized as either basic schema constructs, concept hierarchy constructs, integration constructs or interontology constructs and which are used to efficiently describe ontologies.

The LGAccess system (Ahmedi & Lausen, 2002) is a query system which combines ontologies and XML into a unified LDAP-based framework and supports querying in XPath, by deploying a slightly modified version of the XPath2LDAP translator developed as part of the HLCaches. The xml2ldap-onto component is used to provide a mapping between the conceptual entities of the internal LDAP ontology and those marked up externally in XML. Furthermore, LDAP referrals are used to implement the correspondences between the entries in the ontology and those in the source schemata.

Moreover Ahmedi (2005) identified and used another commonality between XML and LDAP standards that refers to the referral mechanism provided by LDAP and the linking concept of XLink. More specifically, LDAP referrals offer an efficient querying processing of data that may be linked internally on a local server or may be distributed across different remote servers on the network. An extended XPath processor that deploys a rich LDAP repository of links has been developed which is capable of addressing link annotation of any type (IDREF, XLink) in XML data in the form of LDAP aliases and referrals.

The combination of XML and LDAP technologies has also been used in an e-learning platform that is compliant with the Shareable Content Object Reference Model[4] (SCORM). A hybrid scheme has been proposed (Li & Lin, 2005) that is composed of an XML binding model, which defines the way of automatic mapping XML documents into objects, and a WAP-based directory service, which is used for the registration of extracted learning objects. The LDAP server acts as an intermediator and manages to provide a global view of distributed course contents in heterogeneous learning management systems (LMSs).

The tuning of LDAP and XML technologies is also accomplished in a network model to form a powerful tool for delivering dynamic database content to different network recipients' on-the-fly (Law, 2000). In the proposed framework, network devices in a multi-tier architecture ask for and receive information stored in the form of LDAP messages, which are then translated into XML by an XML parser. With this model, the information content is totally transparent to the whole hardware configuration architecture.

A summation of the described approaches is given in Table 4. From the descriptions it is shown that only the DSML can act as a standalone tool for the XML storage and retrieval over the LDAP framework. The rest of the approaches are designed according to the underlying application.

LDAP-XML Integration: Implementations and Tools

Today, many large scale software vendors such as Microsoft, Sun and Oracle support LDAP-based directory services and the directory market is becoming quite competitive. On the other hand, the wide adaptation of XML as the de facto standard for Web data representation and exchange has led many directory developers to proceed to the implementation of application interfaces that would enable the efficient storage of XML documents in LDAP servers as well as their retrieval:

- Novell's eDirectory includes DirXML[6] engine which manages the rules that govern the interpretation and transformation of directory data into XML
- The OpenDS[7] provides a special type of network daemon that is used to translate data between DSML and LDAP
- Sun ONE Directory Server[8] implements version 2 of the DSML standard allowing XML-based applications to take advantage

Table 4. XML storage and retrieval under LDAP

Approach	Storage	Retrieval	Implementation	Application
DSML	√	√	A markup language for directory information	Any DSML-compliant application
(Shin et al., 2002)	√	√	DSML	A role-based authorization service for web-based solutions
(Marrón & Lausen, 2001A) (Marrón & Lausen, 2001B)	√	√	Definition of appropriate objectclasses and transformation algorithms to support storage and retrieval	HLCaches
(Ahmedi et al., 2001) (Ahmedi & Lausen, 2002) Ahmedi (2005)	√	√	Definition of appropriate objectclasses to represent ontologies and transformation algorithms to support storage and retrieval	LGAccess
(Li & Lin, 2005)	√	√	Java XML Binding[5] defines the way of automatic mapping XML documents into objects, which are registered in the LDAP server	E-learning platform
Law (2000)		√	XML translator	3-tier network model

of directory services using HTTP while making full use of the existing Web infrastructure

- DSML Services for Windows extends the power of the Active Directory service[9]. DSML Services for Windows runs as a module on a server running Internet Information Services (IIS) version 5.0 or later. It uses SOAP over HTTP to transmit and receive directory requests from client computers. DSML Services for Windows translates the client computer's DSML *V2* requests from XML into LDAP commands. The LDAP commands are used to query the domain controllers in the Active Directory forest.

- LdapProcessor[10] is a processor for Cocoon that performs LDAP queries, translates the resultset into an XML fragment, and inserts the fragment in the original document

- The LDAPHTTP[11] consists of a set of Java classes that support the translation of XML to LDAP.

- LDAPXML[12] is a set of java classes that allow the mapping of the various LDAP objectclasses and attributes to XML namespaces, attributes and elements.

- The iPlanet XMLDAP Gateway[13] is a flexible standards-based solution which targets Web developers that need to present LDAP Directory data in multiple formats such as XML, HTML, WML, DSML, VXML etc.

- The Oracle Virtual Directory server[14] provides a standard LDAP and DSML interface to client applications.

- View500[15] XML Enabled Directory (XED) is a commercial release that extends LDAP directory search and update functions to native XML Objects.

- XML Integrator[16] is a tool for bi-directional data conversion between XML and structured data formats such as relational or LDAP data.

The above implementations differ mainly on whether they provide DSML support or they describe tools that can be used by XML-enabled applications to interact with LDAP servers for data storage and retrieval. As has already been discussed, in the case of implementations that provide DSML services (such as Active Directory, Sun ONE Directory Server and Oracle Virtual Directory server), any DSML compliant application can work with them without needing any further processing. However, there are implementations (such as LDAPHTTP and LDAPXML) which provide some tools that need to be adjusted to a specific application framework in order to produce the efficient integration of XML and LDAP. Moreover, some of the above implementations are product-tailored (such as DirXML, LdapProcessor) and demand the respective LDAP application in order to be used (Novell eDirectory, Cocoon). This can be considered as a limitation particularly in case of commercial products (e.g. Active Directory, Oracle Virtual Directory).

Future Trends

Technology keeps evolving, and networks are becoming increasingly complex in an attempt to provide better service and to satisfy the needs of an increasing number of users and more sophisticated applications. The increasing number of different types of network elements, each running a (potentially) different set of protocols and services over (possibly) different media, has resulted in an application model that requires centralized network configuration and management applications. XML, on the one hand, has been identified as the de facto standard for data representation and has dominated in distributed applications that need to exchange information. On the other hand, LDAP has without doubt undergone a rapid evolution and directories are expected to continue to proliferate. The growing number of applications that depend on directory services proves that more vendors, applications, languages, and operating

systems are supporting LDAP, and that more organizations are depending on it for management
of key information. A common framework that
will combine these two technologies seems to
be a quite promising solution for the emerging
information model that demands interoperability
between network elements, servers, applications,
and other components.

The directory enabled networks (DEN) initiative (Howes, 1997) has been taken to provide
the means for the new generation interoperable
network-enabled solutions. It provides models and schema for network-level devices and
services such as routers, switches, and virtual
private networks (VPNs). Through DEN, these
devices and services will use LDAP to implement authentication and policy services, allowing
guaranteed end-to-end quality of service (QoS)
and other features. LDAP has been established
as the standard to access, manage, and manipulate directory information under the Directory
Enabled Networks framework, which intends to
promote consistent modeling of network elements
and services across heterogeneous directories.
The ability of directories to exchange "schema"
information, data about a directory's content, in
a standard way is important for maintaining interoperability. XML is the standard that can play
a key role to this direction either in the form of
DSML or by proposing a new standard that will
render directories XML enabled.

Additionally, in the context of integrating
LDAP with XML, it appears that there have
been recorded some efforts for new application protocols that will provide a more intrinsic
framework for the storage of XML documents in
LDAP directories as well as their retrieval. The
Internet Engineering Task Force[17] (IETF) has published some Internet-drafts about XML enabled
directory[18] (XED pronounced "zed") which is
an initiative for working in XML with directory
services. XED leverages existing lightweight
directory access protocol (LDAP) and X.500
directory technology to create a directory service

that stores, manages and transmits XML data,
while maintaining interoperability with LDAP
clients and X.500 agents. XED defines a special
ASN.1 type, called the Markup type, whose abstract values can hold the content and attributes
of an XML element preserving thus the XML
renditions of directory data. Furthermore, XED
has the ability to accept at run time, user-defined
attribute syntaxes specified in a variety of XML
schema languages and to perform filter matching
on the parts of XML-format directory attribute
values. It also provides developers the flexibility
to implement XED clients using only their favored
XML schema language. XED defines an XML
version of the LDAP protocol (XLDAP) which
includes an XML form of LDAP search filters,
used to search LDAP directory data.

Moreover, the emergence of the Semantic Web
has inspired the combining of LDAP with RDF
and OWL which are built on top of XML and are
used for the publishing and sharing of ontologies
over the World Wide Web. To this direction, Dietzold (2005) presents a method to create RDF
models by mapping LDAP schema information
into OWL ontologies and LDAP objects into RDF
instances. In the same context Hu & Du (2006),
proposed a new search mechanism which extends
LDAP and can be used in the Semantic Grid
environment for Semantic searching of relative
information. The mechanism uses an ontology
learning model which maps WordNet lexicon
into OWL ontologies.

CONCLUSION

Rapid Internet growth over the past several years
has increased the need for more robust and scalable
distributed networks that are characterized by high
performance, high capacity, secure and reliable
services that can be rapidly scaled and managed.
The development of flexible and customizable
directory services can significantly contribute to
this direction. LDAP has become the standard used

throughout large companies to access directory information about users and resources and thus, directory vendors support LDAP in their products while an increasing number of LDAP-compliant products that act as clients to those directories, are appearing. Moreover, as XML becomes more widely used in the world of information processing, technologies continue to evolve in their support of the growing XML standards. Due to a close resemblance between XML and LDAP models (hierarchical, simple, flexible, extensible, etc.), and in order to allow for a seamless integration of source data and schemata discrepancies under a common framework, the idea of integrating LDAP and XML technologies has emerged as quite promising. This chapter provides an overview of a number of approaches that have been proposed and combine the XML and LDAP standards in order to provide an efficient data storage and retrieval framework. Moreover, various existing tools and implementations that couple XML and LDAP are presented while future trends of their integration are discussed. The goal of previous and ongoing research efforts is to design effective XML-enabled services that will access directory services for data storage and retrieval resulting in centralized and interoperable networks. To this end, the Directory Enabled Networks operate over a framework that integrates LDAP and XML for data storage, retrieval and exchange. Most of the existing approaches for the integration of XML and LDAP are based on mapping techniques of these two standards and thus a framework for the native support of XML in LDAP servers is indeed missing. However, the tendency towards the creation of new application protocols for the native integration between XML and LDAP is manifested by initiatives such as the XML enabled directory (XED). XED is a framework for managing objects represented using the extensible markup language (XML). XED and is built on top of X.500 and LDAP directory services technologies. The development of a framework that will support the combination of LDAP and XML

standards in a more intrinsic way could lead to more efficient storage and retrieval processes.

To sum up, both XML and LDAP have emerged and prevailed as the standards for data representation and directory access, respectively. Their similarities have motivated the idea of developing common storage and retrieval frameworks as well as new standards that combine both of them. DSML is such an initiative that aims to bridge the gap between XML and LDAP directories by providing an XML markup language for LDAP (directory) content. However, the great adaptation of both LDAP and XML seems to lead toward the development of new standards, and moreover, to the support of emerging technologies such as the Semantic Web.

REFERENCES

Ahmedi, L. (2005). Making XPath reach for the Web-wide links. In *SAC,* (pp. 1714-1721).

Ahmedi, L., & Lausen, G. (2002). Ontology-based querying of linked XML documents. In *Semantic Web Workshop.*

Ahmedi, L., Marron, P., & Lausen, G. (2001). LDAP-based Ontology for Information Integration. In *Datenbanksysteme in Buro, Technik und Wissenschaft,* (pp. 207-214).

Beyer, K., Cochrane, R., Hvizdos, M., Josifovski, V., Kleewein, J., Lapis, G., Lohman, G., Lyle, R., Nicola, M., Özcan, F., Pirahesh, H., Seemann, N., Singh, A., Truong, T., Van der Linden, R., Vickery, B., Zhang, C., & Zhang, G. (2006). DB2 goes hybrid: Integrating native XML and XQuery with relational data and SQL. In *IBM Systems Journal 45*(2), 271-298.

Bohannon, B., Freire, J., Roy, P., & Simeon, J. (2002). From XML schema to relations: A cost-based approach to XML storage. In *ICDE,* (pp. 64-75).

Catania, B., Madalena, A., Vakali, A. (2005). XML document indexes: A classification. In *IEEE Internet Computing 9*(5), 64-71.

Cathey, R., Beitzel, S., Jensen, E., Pilotto, A., & Grossman, D. (2004). Measuring the scalability of relationally mapped semistructured queries. In *ITCC, 2*, 219-223.

Chadwick, D. (2003). Deficiencies in LDAP when used to support PKI. In *Communications of the ACM 46*(3), 99-104.

Chung, S., & Jesurajaiah S. (2005). Schemaless XML document management in object-oriented databases. In *ITCC, 1*, 261–266.

Chung, T., Park, S., Han, S., & Kim, H. (2001). Extracting object-oriented database schemas from XML DTDs using inheritance. In *EC-Web*, (pp. 49-59).

Dietzold, S. (2005). Generating RDF models from LDAP directories. In *CEUR-WS, 135*.

Fan, Q., Wu, Q., He, & Y., Huang, J. (2005). Optimized strategies of grid information services. In *SKG*, (p. 90).

Florescu, D., & Kossmann, D. (1999). Storing and querying XML data using an RDBMS. In *Bulletin of the IEEE Computer Society Technical Committee on Data Engineering 22*(3), 27-34.

Fomichev, A., Grinev, M., & Kuznetsov, S. (2005). Sedna: A native XML DBMS. In *SOFSEM*, (pp. 272-281).

Gemmill, J., Chatterjee, S., Miller, T., & Verharen, E. (2003). ViDe.Net Middleware for scalable video services for research and higher education. In *ACMSE*, (pp. 463-468).

Howes, T., & Smith, M. (1997). *LDAP: Programming directory-enabled applications with lightweight directory access protoco.* PA: Macmillan Technical Publishing.

Hu, H., & Du, X. (2006). An ontology learning model in grid information services. In *ICICIC, 3*, 398-401.

Jagadish, H. V., Al-Khalifa, S., Chapman, A., Lakshmanan, L. V. S., Nierman, R., Paparizos, S., Patel, J. M., Srivastava, D., Wiwatwattana, N., Wu, Y., & Yu, C. (2002). TIMBER: A native XML database. In *VLDB Journal 11*(4), 274-291.

Khan, L., & Rao, Y. (2001). A performance evaluation of storing XML data in relational DBMS. In *WIDM*, (pp. 31-38).

Klettke, M., & Meyer, H. (2000). XML and object-relational database systems - enhancing structural mappings based on statistics. In *WebDB*, (pp. 151–170).

Koutsonikola, V., & Vakali, A. (2004). LDAP: Framework, practices, and trends. In *IEEE Internet Computing 8*(5), 66-72.

Law, K. L. E. (2000). XML on LDAP network database. In *CCECE, 1*, 469-473.

Li, S., & Lin, C. (2005). On the distributed management of SCORM-compliant course contents. In *AINA, 1*, 221-226.

Liu, Z., Krishnaprasad, M., & Arora, V. (2005). Native Xquery processing in oracle XMLDB. In *SIGMOD*, (pp. 828-833).

Marrón, P., & Lausen, G. (2001A). On processing XML in LDAP. In *VLDB*, (pp. 601-610).

Marrón, P., & Lausen, G. (2001B). *HLCaches: An LDAP-based distributed cache technology for XML.* (Tech. Rep. No. 147). Institut für Informatik, Universität Freiburg.

Meier, W. (2002). eXist: An Open Source Native XML Database. In E. R. B. Chaudri, M. Jeckle & R. Unland, (Ed.), *Web, Web-Services, and database systems*, (pp. 169-183).

Pal, S., Cseri, I., Seeliger, O., Rys, M., Schaller, G., Yu, W., Tomic, D., Baras, A., Berg, B., Churin,

D., & Kogan, E. (2005). XQuery implementation in a relational database system. In *VLDB*, (pp. 1175-1186).

Pallis, G., Stoupa, K., & Vakali, A. (2003). Storage and access control issues for XML documents. In D. Taniar and W. Rahayu (Eds), *Web information systems*, (pp. 104-140).

Pardede, E., Rahayu, J. W., & Taniar, D. (2004). On using collection for aggregation and association relationships in XML object-relational storage. In *SAC*, (pp. 703-710).

Park, J., Sandhu, R., & Ahn, G-J. (2001). Role-based access control on the Web. In *ACM Transactions on Information and System Security 4*(1), (pp. 37-71).

Rys, M., C. & Florescu, D. (2005). XML and relational database management systems: The inside story. In *SIGMOD*, (pp. 945-947).

Shanmugasundaram, J., Tufte, K., Zhang, C., He, G., DeWitt, D., & Naughton J. (1999). Relational databases for querying XML documents: Limitations and opportunities. In *VLDB*, (pp. 302-314).

Shanmugasundaram, J., Shekita, E. J., Kiernan, J., Krishnamurthy, R., Viglas, S., Naughton, J. F., & Tatarinov, I. (2001). A general techniques for querying XML documents using a relational database system. In *SIGMOD Record 30*(3), 20-26.

Shin, D., Ahn, G., & Park, J. (2002). An application of directory service markup language (DSML) for role-based access control (RBAC). In *COMPSAC*, (pp. 934-939).

Schmidt, A., Kersten, M., Windhouwer, M., & Waas, F. (2000). Efficient relational storage and retrieval of XML documents. In *WebDB 2000*, (pp. 137–150).

Schoning, H. (2001). Tamino - A DBMS designed for XML. In *ICDE*, (pp. 149).

Surjanto, B., Ritter, N., & Loeser, H. (2000). XML Content management based on object-relational database technology. In *WISE, 1*, 70-79.

Tan, Z., Xu, J., Wang, W., & Shi, B. (2005). Storing normalized XML documents in normalized relations. In *CIT*, (pp. 123-129).

Vakali, A., Catania, B., & Madalena, A. (2005). XML data stores: Emerging practices. In *IEEE Internet Computing 9*(2), 62-69.

Wahl, M., Howes, T., & Kille, S. (1997). Lightweight directory access protocol (v3). *IETF RFC 2251*, Dec. 1997; www.ietf. org/rfc/rfc2251.

Win, K.-M., Ng, W.-K., & Lim, E.-P. (2003). An architectural framework for native XML data management. In *CW*, (pp. 302-309).

Xu, Z., Guo, Z., Zhou, S., & Zhou, A. (2003). Dynamic tuning of XML storage schema in VXMLR. In *IDEAS*, (pp. 76-86).

Zheng, S., Wen, J., & Lu, H. (2003). Cost-driven storage schema relation for XML. In *DASFAA*, (pp. 55-66).

ENDNOTES

1. XPath: http://www.w3.org/TR/xpath
2. XQuery: http://www.w3.org/TR/xquery/
3. DSML: http://xml.coverpages.org/dsml.html
4. Advanced Distributed Learning: http://www.adlnet.gov/scorm/
5. Java XML Binding: http://java.sun.com/developer/technicalArticles/WebServices/jaxb/
6. Novell DirXML: http://developer.novell.com/education/tutorials/introdirxml/introDirXML.pdf
7. OpenDS: http://www.opends.org/
8. Sun ONE Directory Server: http://www.sun.com/software/products/directory_srvr_ee/dir_srvr/index.xml

9   Active Directory Server: http://www.micro-soft.com/windowsserver2003/technologies/directory/activedirectory/default.mspx

10   LdapProcessor: http://cocoon.apache.org/1.x/ldap.html

11   LDAPHTTP: http://www.onjava.com/pub/a/onjava/2003/07/16/ldaphttp.html

12   LDAPXML: http://memberwebs.com/stef/code/ldapxml/

13   iPlanet XMLLDAP Gateway: http://xml.coverpages.org/ni2001-03-02-a.html

14   Oracle Virtual Directory Server: http://www.oracle.com/technology/products/id_mgmt/ovds/index.html

15   View500: http://view500.com/v500_view500.php

16   XML Integrator: http://www.alphaworks.ibm.com/tech/XI

17   IETF: http://www.ietf.org/

18   XED: http://www.xmled.info/index.htm

Chapter IV
XML Schema Evolution and Versioning:
Current Approaches and Future Trends

Giovanna Guerrini
Università degli Studi di Genova, Italy

Marco Mesiti
Università degli Studi di Milano, Italy

ABSTRACT

The large dynamicity of XML documents on the Web has created the need to adequately support structural changes and to account for the possibility of evolving and versioning the schemas describing XML document structures. This chapter discusses and compares the support for schema evolution and versioning provided by commercial systems as well as the most relevant approaches and prototypes proposed and developed by the research community.

INTRODUCTION

XML is a markup language introduced by W3C (1998) that allows one to structure documents by means of nested tagged elements. XML is nowadays employed for the representation and exchange of information on the Web. Schema information can be represented through DTDs or XSDs (W3C, 2004). The XML Schema specification provides an extended set of data types and constraints that makes XSDs more suitable than DTDs to be used, for example, as a contract on the data types expected in a transaction, as a grammar for easily parsing application data, and as a database schema for document storing and query processing.

Both XML native (e.g., Tamino, eXist, TIMBER) and enabled (e.g., Oracle, IBM DB2, SQL Server) Database Management Systems (DBMSs) have been so far proposed (Bourret, 2007) for storing and querying XML documents. Native DBMSs rely on a data model specifically conceived for the management of XML, whereas enabled DBMSs are relational or object-relational ones that have been extended for the treatment of XML. Enabled XML DBMSs are more mature than the native ones because they are supported by big vendors and the integration of XML data with other company data is easier. Some enabled DBMSs support XML Schema for the specification of a mapping between an XSD and internal relational or object-relational representation of XML documents (Florescu & Kossman, 1999). Relevant from many points of view is the use of XSDs in data management. They can be used for the optimization of query execution, for the specification of access control policies, and indexing structures.

New requirements may arise in an application domain that lead to updating the structure of data. Moreover, the integration of heterogeneous sources may require the schema to be modified. The complex structure, size, and dynamicity of schema information require exploiting database tools for their update and management.

Given an XML database, updates to the schema information, besides modifying the schema, can lead to schema evolution or to schema versioning. Schema evolution means that the original schema is replaced by an updated schema to which some update primitives are applied, and the effects of the update on instances and applications are faced. Specifically, as far as document instances are concerned, the following issues arise for a data management system: (i) how document revalidation with respect to the evolved schema can be performed efficiently; (ii) how document adaptation to the evolved schema can be (eventually automatically) performed for documents to make them valid again. Schema versioning means that original documents and schemas should be preserved and a new updated version of the schema is created. Therefore, document revalidation and adaptation are not an issue. However, the issue of

handling different versions of the same schema needs to be addressed. Applications need to be able to handle document instances of different versions of the schema and queries, specified on a version of the schema, and also may need to be evaluated on other versions of the schema. A possible approach can rely on specifying mappings among schema versions.

In this chapter, we describe the facilities of main DBMSs to handle XML Schema and their level of support to schema evolution and versioning. Then, the chapter discusses how the research community is addressing the schema evolution and versioning issues and foresees future enhancement in the field.

The chapter starts by introducing the basics of XML documents and schemas as well as of evolution and versioning. Then, schema evolution and versioning of main XML-DBMSs are discussed. The most relevant research proposals related to schema evolution are then presented, and the X-Evolution system (Guerrini et al., 2007) is described as the most advanced approach for XML schema evolution and automatic document adaptation. Finally, schema versioning issues are considered and we conclude by discussing further research issues that still need to be addressed.

BACKGROUND

In this section, we first introduce some basic notions about XML documents and schemas and briefly present the languages for manipulating XML documents. Then, we discuss the role of schemas in XML data management systems. Finally, the concepts of schema modification, evolution, and versioning are introduced and contrasted.

XML Documents and Schemas

XML documents, as depicted in Figure 1(a), can be coupled with schema information either in the form of a DTD (document type definition) or an XML Schema (W3C, 2004) for specifying constraints on the allowed contents of documents. An XSD (that is, a schema generated according to the XML schema specification) provides the following information for each document:

- The **vocabulary** (element and attribute names)
- The **content model** (relationships and structure)
- The **data types**

Figure 1(b) contains the schema mail.xsd describing the structure of an email and presenting the main characteristics of the XML Schema specification. A schema can be viewed as a collection (vocabulary) of type definitions and element declarations contained in multiple files (named schema documents) that are connected through <include> elements. These files lead to the definition of the target namespace, that is, the vocabulary specified through the schema. When we wish to validate a document with respect to a schema, we need to check that elements/attributes specified in the documents belong to the target namespace of the schema.

Besides the XML schema language, many other languages have been proposed by the W3C for transforming XML documents (XSL), querying documents (like XPath and XQuery), and manipulating documents through APIs (SAX, DOM). Current efforts are being devoted to defining the XQuery Update language for the specification of updates on XML documents (W3C, 2008). Specifically, XQuery Update extends XQuery providing facilities to perform insert, delete, replace, or rename operations on XML document components (i.e., elements and attributes). Any one of such operations may result in invalidating the document with respect to its schema. XQuery Update allows each statement to specify whether document revalidation must be performed. Approaches for incremental document revalidation

Figure 1. XSD schema and XML document instance

(a)

```
<?xml version="1.0" ?>
<mails xmlns:xsi="http://www.w3.org/2001/XMLSchema-instance"
       xsi:noNamespaceSchemaLocation="mails.xsd">
  <mail>
    <envelope>
      <from>mesiti@dico.unimi.it</From>
      <to>guerrini@disi.unige.it</To>
      <date>2007-10-10T12:00:00-05:00</Date>
      <Subject>Xevolution: Poster</Subject>
    </envelope>
    <body>Here the poster</body>
    <attachment>
       <picture>poster.jpg</picture>
       <content>Hi Giovanna, here is the poster. Marco</content>
    </attachment>
  </mail>
  <mail>
     <envelope>
        <from>guerrini@disi.unige.it</From>
        <to>mesiti@dico.unimi.it</To>
        <date>2002-10-10T12:00:00-05:00</Date>
        <subject>tutorial</Subject>
     </envelope>
     <body>Tutorial video nd some pictures from EDBT</body>
      <attachment>
          <picture>marco-EDBT.jpg</picture>
          <content>Marco at the EDBT</content>
      </attachment>
      <attachment>
          <movie>tutorial.mov</movie>
          <content>A tutorial about XML Schema</content>
      </attachment>
   </mail>
</mails>
```

(b)

```
<xsd:schema xmlns:xsd="http://www.w3.org/2001/XMLSchema">
  <xsd:element name="mail" type="mailType" />
  <xsd:complexType name="subjectType">
    <xsd:sequence>
       <xsd:element name="address" type="addressType" />
       <xsd:element name="name" type="xsd:string"  minOccurs="0" />
    </xsd:sequence>
  </xsd:complexType>
  <xsd:complexType name="mailType">
    <xsd:sequence>
       <xsd:element name="envelope" type="envelopeType" />
       <xsd:element name="body" type="xsd:string" />
       <xsd:element ref="attachment" minOccurs="0" maxOccurs="unbounded" />
    </xsd:sequence>
  </xsd:complexType>
  <xsd:complexType name="envelopeType">
    <xsd:sequence>
       <xsd:element name="from" type="subjectType" />
       <xsd:element name="to" type="subjectType" maxOccurs="unbounded" />
       <xsd:element name="date" type="xsd:dateTime" />
       <xsd:element name="subject" type="xsd:string" />
    </xsd:sequence>
    <xsd:attribute name="header" type="xsd:string"/>
  </xsd:complexType>
  <xsd:element name="attachment">
     <xsd:complexType>
       <xsd:sequence>
          <xsd:choice minOccurs="0">
            <xsd:element name="picture" type="xsd:string" />
            <xsd:element name="audio" type="xsd:string" />
            <xsd:element name="movie" type="xsd:string" />
          </xsd:choice>
          <xsd:element name="content" type="xsd:string" minOccurs="0" />
       </xsd:sequence>
    </xsd:complexType>
 </xsd:element>
 <xsd:simpleType name="addressType">
    <xsd:restriction base="xsd:string">
       <xsd:pattern value="[^@]+@[^\.]+\..+"/>
    </xsd:restriction>
 </xsd:simpleType>
</xsd:schema>
```

of document updates have been developed and will be briefly reviewed in the XML Schema Evolution: Incremental Validation section.

XML and XML Schema in DBMSs

XML has not been specified by the database community, but its widespread use in many contexts has challenged the database research community and main DBMS vendors to deal with it. The interest of a group of DBMS vendors in extending their tools for supporting XML and related languages led to the creation in year 2000 of the INCTS (the U.S. body chartered with development of standards in IT) Task Group H2.3. This group was established "to extend SQL standard to integrate SQL and XML, supporting bidirectional movement of data and allowing SQL programmers to manage and query XML data" (Melton & Buxton, 2006) with the goal "to query SQL data and publish the results as XML, store and manage XML natively in a SQL database, query XML and publish the results as either XML or as SQL, map SQL data and identifiers to XML, and vice versa" (Melton & Buxton, 2006). Their efforts led to the inclusion in the standard specification SQL:2003 of a chapter titled "SQL part 14, XML-Related Specifications (SQL/XML)". SQL/XML allows one to query SQL data and to publish the result in XML. Moreover, it introduces the XML type as a native data type which is the basis for storing, managing, and querying XML natively in an SQL database. In the forthcoming SQL:2008 standard, the inclusion of XMLQUERY and XMLTABLE functions to query XML through XQuery and to transform XML data in relational tables, functions for the validation of data through XML Schema, and the support for XQuery Update (Michels, 2005) is expected.

The support of XML schema in native and XML-enabled DBMSs has several purposes:

- **Document validation.** Schemas can be employed for checking implicitly or explic-

itly the validity of inserted data. Implicitly means that the system considers the schema declared within the document, whereas explicitly means that a schema registered within the DBMS is employed. Depending on the system, the validation process should be explicitly required or applied on demand.

- **Shredding document instances in XML-enabled DBMSs.** XML-enabled DBMSs support XML in their relational (or object-relational) data model by introducing the XML type for the storage of XML document. Moreover, some of them provide the option of storing the document content using structured-storage techniques. Structured-storage decomposes or shreds the content of a document and stores it as a set of tables. The set of tables used to store the document is automatically derived from the XSD that is annotated for this purpose.

- **Storage optimization.** A better knowledge of the data types used in the documents can facilitate the choice of a more appropriate space for the storage. For example, an element of type integer would require less space than an element of type string.

- **Query optimization.** The internal organization of documents can be employed for the definition of query plans, thereby improving query execution time.

Schema Modification, Evolution, and Versioning

Following the terminology introduced in (Roddick, 1995) "schema modification" denotes "the introduction of changes into the schema of a populated database". Therefore, actions are applied on a schema independently of the instances associated with it. Schema modification can occur at different levels:

- At vocabulary level, by changing the names associated with elements, types, and attributes that can occur in a schema
- At content model, by changing the relationships among schema components and the structures of components
- At data types, by altering the native and user defined data types

A more general kind of modification is related to the semantics of data represented by the schema. Even if none of the previous levels is changed, the data interpretation can be altered and more sophisticated approaches are required for tracking changes. Since a schema describes in a compact way a set of admitted document structures and states the constraints on allowed document content, updates on a schema can be considerably more complex than documents' updates. Also, the impact of schema updates on documents can be greater, since several documents can be associated with a schema as instances, some of which could be still valid while some others could be invalidated.

Following the terminology introduced in (Roddick, 1995) "schema evolution" denotes the "incorporation of changes into the schema of a database without loss of data". Schema evolution also encompasses the actions to be taken in dealing with the effects of schema modification on the instances and applications developed according to the original schema. A first issue to be faced is the revalidation of documents with respect to the new schema. This document revalidation should be incremental, that is, dependent on the schema modification operation applied to the schema. Then, for the instances that are no longer valid, the issue arises of adapting them to the evolved schema. Some support should be offered to the user in (semi-)automatically adapting the invalid documents to the evolved schema, whenever possible. The terms *backward* and *forward compatibility* can be introduced, referring to the compatibility (validity) between the evolving schema and the document instances. Backward compatibility means that an instance document defined by an old schema is still valid for the new schema, whereas forward compatibility means that an instance document defined by a new schema is valid for the old schema.

Following the terminology introduced in (Roddick, 1995), by *schema versioning* we mean the "introduction of a new schema that does not alter the original schema and its instances". A DBMS supporting schema versioning should thus maintain different versions of the same schema and make available to the user appropriate interfaces for their management. The terms backward and forward compatibility can also be employed in this context (Hoylen, 2006), referring to the compatibility between schema versions and applications handling their instance documents. Specifically, backward compatibility means that an instance document defined by an old schema can be processed by an application that handles the new schema; whereas, forward compatibility means that an instance document defined by a new schema can be processed by an application that handles the old schema.

In the development of access facilities to data that are transparent to the user, typical approaches of data integration (Halevy et al., 2006) should be applied for providing a common minimal schema of the different versions (Local As View/Global As View schema in the spirit of Halevy (2000)). By contrast, in the development of access facilities that explicitly consider versions, extension of query languages should be applied for accessing a particular version or set of versions of a schema.

SCHEMA EVOLUTION AND VERSIONING IN XML DBMSS

In this section we examine the support of most relevant commercial DBMSs in the treatment of schema modification, evolution, and versioning.

For each DBMS, we briefly report the support to XML Schema and then move into the details of schema evolution and versioning. A comparison of the various systems is finally presented.

SQL Server 2008

In SQL Server (Malcolm, 2008), XML data can be generated from standard relational tables and query results by using a FOR XML clause in a SELECT statement. The converse of FOR XML is a relational rowset generator function named OpenXML; it extracts values from the XML data into columns of a rowset by evaluating XPath expressions. OpenXML is used by applications that shred incoming XML data into tables or for querying by using the Transact-SQL language. Moreover, in SQL Server, the XML type has been included for natively storing XML documents in columns of tables.

SQL Server supports a subset of W3C XML Schema specification and maintains a container of XSD files, named XML schema collection, that may be related (e.g. through <xs:import>) or unrelated to each other (Pal et al., 2006). Each schema in an XML schema collection C is identified using its target namespace. An XML schema collection C is created using the following statement for registering XSD schema documents:

```
CREATE XML SCHEMA COLLECTION C AS
    '<xs:schema>...</xs:schema>...
    <xs:schema>...</xs:schema>'
```

The schema processor identifies and stores in C the schema components supplied in the XSD files. Schema components from multiple XSD files with the same target namespace are grouped together and employed for document validation.

Columns of type XML constrained to C can be declared in the creation of tables. The constraint imposed by C is the collective set of the schema constraints imposed by the individual XSDs in C. When a value is inserted into a column of type XML constrained to C or a pre-existing value is updated, the value is validated against C.

A new version of an XSD with a new target namespace can be added to C and is treated like a new schema. Suppose that within the schema collection C, two target namespaces, named MAIL-V1 and MAIL-V2 respectively, are present. Whenever MAIL-V2 is obtained from MAIL-V1 by adding optional elements and attributes, and global elements and type definitions, no re-validation is required. An XML column of type C can store instances of both MAIL-V1 and MAIL-V2 schemas. Since queries can be posed both on documents conforming to the old and the new versions of the schema, it ensures that a search can distinguish between a <mail> element within the target namespace MAIL-V1 from one within the target namespace MAIL-V2 and thus improving the performance of query evaluation.

DB2 Version 9.5

DB2 supports the XML type for storing XML documents in columns of a table. Moreover, it allows the shredding of XML documents in relational tables, query processing through both SQL/XML and XQuery (details on the support of XML in DB2 can be found in (Steegmans et al., 2004)).

XML Schema is employed mainly for the validation of documents. DB2 has an XSD schema repository (named XSR) that maintains a copy of the schema that might be used during validation (named *object schemas*). The XSR encompasses a set of commands, stored procedures and APIs to register and manage XSD schemas. Since an object schema can be a collection of one or more XSD files, schema registration is performed through the following commands:

```
REGISTER XMLSCHEMA web resource
FROM document location AS object schema
```

```
ADD XMLSCHEMA DOCUMENT TO object schema ADD
document location' FROM webresource'
COMPLETE XMLSCHEMA logical name
```

Where "web resource" is the URI where the document is located, "document location" is the position of the document in the file system of the web resource, and the command `ADD XMLSCHEMA` is repeated as many times as the number of XSD files that should be imported in the object schema.

Once a schema has been registered, it can be used for validation. In DB2, XML Schema validation is optional and on a per-document basis, not per column. In DB2, an XSD is not assigned to a table or a column. The philosophy in schema validation is that this operation has a high cost and should be applied only when it is required (e.g. when documents come from un-trusted sources).

In DB2, XML documents are validated during insertion or using the `XMLValidate` function, which is part of the SQL/XML standard. The function can perform explicit or implicit schema validation depending on whether the XSD schema for validation is explicitly specified (i.e. the logical schema or the location of the schema to use in validation is explicitly reported in the command to insert into a table) or deduced from the document (i.e. the document contains the `xsd:schemaLocation` element).

Object schemas registered within the XSR repository can be dropped through the command `DROP XSROBJECT` *schema object*. Thus, to drop an XSR object implies deleting all schema documents associated with it.

DB2 has built-in support for a simple form of schema evolution. If the new schema is backward compatible with the old schema, then the old schema can be replaced with the new schema repository (Nicola et al. 2005). For this operation, DB2 checks that all possible elements and attributes that can exist in the old schema have the same types in the new schema. This operation

is performed through the `XSR_UPDATE` stored procedure on schemas previously registered. The procedure checks for compatibility and updates the schema only if the new schema is compatible. Retaining the old schema or dropping it once the old one has been updated is a boolean option of the procedure. Suppose `STORE.MAIL` and `STORE.NEWMAIL` are the old object schema and the new object schema registered within the XSR repository. If `STORE.NEWMAIL` is backward compatible with respect to `STORE.MAIL`, the following command can be issued:

```
CALL SYSPROC.XSR_UPDATE('STORE','MAIL','
STORE','NEWMAIL',1)
```

The contents of the XSD schema `STORE.MAIL` is updated with the contents of `STORE.NEWMAIL`, and the XSD schema `STORE.NEWMAIL` is dropped.

This form of schema evolution limits the types of changes one can make to schemas and also the effects on document validity. Indeed, since backward compatibility is required, there is no need to perform re-validation. The concepts of schema modification and schema evolution proposed by (Roddick, 1995), in the case of DB2 overlaps, only the update operations on the schema that do not alter validity are allowed.

Also, for schema versioning, DB2 offers limited facilities. It offers the possibility of maintaining the old and new versions of the schemas, under different names (in the previous example, the last parameter of the `XSR_UPDATE` procedure is set to 0).

Since validation is not performed on a column basis, in the same column of a table, a mix of documents that conform to the old schema and to the new schema can appear. Query statements can be specified on documents valid for the old, the new or both schema versions. To enable version-aware operations, DB2 supplies the function `xmlxsrobjectid` for determining the version to be used in validating a document.

Oracle 11g

Oracle supports the `XMLType` type for the representation of XML documents in columns of relational tables. Three storage models are available: *structured* (by shredding documents in object-relational tables), *unstructured* (by storing documents as CLOB files), and *binary* (by storing documents in a binary format specifically tailored for XML). Oracle supports the latest version of the W3C XQuery specification and is fully compliant with the SQL/XML standard.

In order to be useful, an XSD schema should be registered. Registration is performed through the `DBMS_XMLSCHEMA.registerschema` procedure whose main arguments are:

- `SCHEMAURL` – the XSD file URL. This is a unique identifier for the schema in the DB. It is used with Oracle XML DB to identify instance documents.
- `SCHEMADOC` – the XSD schema document.
- `CSID` – the character-set ID of the XSD file encoding.
- `OPTIONS` – to specify the storage model (structured, unstructured, binary).

After a schema has been registered, it can be used for validating XML documents through functions `isSchemaValid()` and `schemaValidate()` and for creating `XMLTYPE` tables and columns bound to the XSD.

Full and partial validation procedures are supported in Oracle. Partial validation ensures only that all of the mandatory elements and attributes are present, and that no unexpected elements or attributes occur in the document. That is, it ensures only that the structure of the XML document conforms to the SQL data type definitions that were derived from the XSD schema. Partial validation does not ensure that the instance document is fully compliant with the XSD schema. For binary XML Storage, Oracle XML DB performs a full validation whenever an XML document is inserted into an XSD schema based `XMLType` table or column. For all other models of XML storage, Oracle XML DB performs only a partial validation of the document. This is because, except for binary XML storage, complete schema validation is quite costly, in terms of performance. Full validation can always be enforced through `CHECK` constraints and PL/SQL `BEFORE INSERT` triggers. Oracle XML DB supports two kinds of schema evolution:

- **Copy-based schema evolution,** in which all instance documents that conform to the schema are copied to a temporary location in the database, the old schema is deleted, the modified schema is registered, and the instance documents are inserted into their new locations from the temporary area. The PL/SQL procedure `DBMS_XMLSCHEMA.copyEvolve` is employed for this purpose.

- **In-place schema evolution,** which does not require copying, deleting, and inserting existing data and thus is much faster than copy-based evolution, but can be applied only when there is backward compatibility of the new schema. That is, it is permitted if no changes to the storage model are required and if the changes do not invalidate existing documents. `DBMS_XMLSCHEMA.inPlaceEvolve` is the PL/SQL procedure employed for this purpose.

Table 1 reports the main parameters of the `copyEvolve` procedure. Since an XSD schema may consist of several files, the need arises to specify the XSD files in order of dependability. Notice also that it is possible to specify XSL transformation documents for adapting the documents valid for the old schema to the new one. Even if there are still many limitations in its applicability, it is a key feature of Oracle not available in the other DBMSs.

Table 1. Main parameters of the procedure DBMS_XMLSCHEMA.copyEvolve

parameter	description
schemaURLs	List of URLs of schemas to be evolved. This should also include the URLs of dependent schemas in the dependency order.
newSchemas	List of URLs of the new XSD files in the same order of old ones.
transforms	List of XSL documents that will be applied to XSD schema based documents to make them conform to the new schemas. Specify in exactly the same order as the corresponding URLs. If no transformations are required, this parameter is unspecified.
preserveOldDocs	If this is TRUE, then the temporary tables holding old data are not dropped at the end of schema evolution.

Table 2. Schema evolution and versioning support in commercial systems

DBMS	Type of schema	validation	schema modification	schema versioning	schema evolution
SQL Server	subset XML Schema	total	no	yes	no
DB2	XML Schema	total	no	partially	partially
Oracle 11g	XML Schema	partial and total	no	no	yes
Tamino	subset XML Schema	total	yes	no	partially

Procedure `inPlaceEvolve` requires only three parameters: the URL of the schema to be evolved; an XML document that conforms to the `xdiff` XSD schema, and that specifies the changes to apply and the location in the XSD schema where the changes should be applied; a bit mask that controls the behaviour of the procedure.

Tamino

Tamino (Software AG, 2008) is a DBMS developed for storing and querying XML documents directly in their native type. A database consists of multiple *collections,* that is, containers of XML documents. A collection can have an associated set of XSDs. Documents in the collection need to be validated against them.

Tamino uses a simplified version of XSD (Tamino Schema Definition —TSD) and through its schema editor it is possible to modify schemas in

different ways. Moreover, it allows the automatic conversion of DTDs, XSDs into TSDs. Schema modifications should guarantee that documents contained in a collection should remain valid against the new representation of the schema; otherwise, the schema modification operation is not permitted. To this extent, Tamino thus supports schema evolution (backward compatibility should be guaranteed). In the current version there is no support for schema versioning.

Comparison

Table 2 summarises the support of schema management from the presented commercial DBMSs. Specifically, the table reports the kind of schema specification adopted (entirely the XML Schema specification or a subset), the type of validation algorithms supported, whether they provide operators for the specification of schema modification, schema versioning, and schema evolution. We note that where the support is "partial", it means that it requires backward compatibility. Only Oracle supports schema evolution without requiring backward compatibility.

XML SCHEMA EVOLUTION APPROACHES

In this section, we present and contrast the approaches proposed by the research community for the evolution of the structural information of XML focusing on DTDs and XSDs. We first discuss approaches for expressing the updates to be performed on the schema, then approaches for efficiently revalidating the documents, and finally approaches for adapting documents to the schema. A comparison among these approaches is finally discussed.

XML Schema Evolution: Primitives

A first, basic issue is the identification of a suitable set of evolution primitives to express the changes that may occur to the schema of an XML document collection. Primitives include those for altering the internal structure of a schema (such as, insertion of new element declarations and type definitions, altering the structure of a complex type). Schema evolution was first investigated for schemas expressed by DTDs in (Kramer & Rundensteiner, 2001), who proposed and discussed in detail a set of evolution operators. The set of elementary internal operators includes: the creation of a new element, the deletion of an element, the addition and the deletion of a subelement and of an attribute to an element, the modification of quantifiers, attribute types, attribute values, and modifications to groups of elements. A notion of completeness of the proposed set of operators is provided and requirements of consistency and minimality are formulated. However, since DTDs are considerably simpler than XSDs, the proposed operators

do not cover all the kinds of schema changes that can occur on an XSD.

Tan & Goh (2004) focus on the use of XML Schema for specifying (domain-specific) standards and categorize the possible changes that may occur between revisions of standards. They identify three different categories of changes:

- **Migratory changes,** dealing with the movement of elements or attributes to other parts of the documents. Examples of changes in this category are morphing of an element to an attribute, migration of a subelement from one element to another.
- **Structural changes,** affecting the structure of the documents through the addition or removal of attributes or elements. Examples of changes in this category are additions/removals of elements, subelements, and attributes.
- **Sedentary changes,** that involve no movement and have no effect on the structure of the documents. Examples of changes in this category are renaming of elements and attributes and changes in simple data types.

Moreover, they identify one category of change that is difficult to model, i.e., semantic changes. This category may not affect the structure of the schema at all. Such changes involve a change in the interpretation or the meaning of a term or terms used within the specification. For example, the date element in the mail.xsd schema will contain the date/time of message arrival instead of message departure.

In (Guerrini et al., 2005), we have introduced the kinds of internal modifications at the vocabulary, content model, and data type levels that can be applied on an XSD classified according to the main components that can appear in a schema specification (elements, complex types, and simple types) and the main types of change (insertion, update, and deletion). Guerrini et al., (2005) also provide a set of primitives that will be discussed when presenting the X-Evolution approach, realizing the most relevant kinds of changes.

XML Schema Evolution: Incremental Validation

The incremental validation of XML documents upon schema evolution is supported only by X-Evolution. Related problems are XML document incremental validation upon document updates and XML document revalidation, briefly discussed in what follows.

Incremental validation of XML documents, represented as trees, upon document updates, has been investigated for atomic (Balmin et al., 2004; Barbosa et al., 2004; Bouchou & Ferrari Alves, 2003) and composite (Barbosa et al., 2006) XML updates. Given an update operation on a document, it is simulated, and only after verifying that the updated document is still valid for its schema, is the update executed. The key idea of these approaches is to take advantage of the knowledge of the validity of the document prior to the update, together with the update specified on the document, to avoid whole document revalidation thereby checking only the conditions that the update may invalidate.

The efficiency of those proposals is bound to the conflict-free schema property. A schema is said to be conflict-free when in type definitions subelement names appear only once. This property is assumed as well by proposals addressing revalidation and adaptation of documents upon schema evolution, concerning both the original schema and the evolved one. Most schemas employed on the Web do exhibit this property (Choi, 2002).

The problem of XML document revalidation has been investigated by Raghavachari & Shmueli (2007). They study the problem of XML documents known to conform to one schema S1 that must be validated with respect to another schema S2. They present techniques that take advantage of similarities (and differences) between the schemas S1 and S2 to avoid validating portions of the documents explicitly. At the core of the proposed techniques, there are efficient algorithms for revalidating strings known to be recognizable by a deterministic finite state automaton (DFA) according to another DFA. Note that an application mentioned for the approach is schema evolution, but the approach does not take advantage of any knowledge of the updates leading from S1 to S2 in revalidation.

XML Schema Evolution: Document Adaptation

The problem of how to adapt an XML document invalidated by a schema evolution to the new schema has been considered only in the context of X-Evolution. Related problems, which we briefly discuss below, are document correction, document adaptation to the schema upon document updates, and schema adaptation.

The issue of document corrections is addressed by the approaches proposed in (Boobna & de Rougemont, 2004; Staworko & Chomicki, 2006) for making an XML document valid to a given DTD, by applying minimal modifications detected relying on tree edit distances. A corrector (as defined in Boobna & de Rougemont, 2004) takes a DTD (or tree automaton) and an invalid XML document, and produces a valid document which is as close as possible to the DTD in terms of edit distance. Staworko & Chomicki (2006) address the problem of querying XML documents that are not valid with respect to given DTDs. Their framework measures the invalidity of the documents and compactly represents minimal repairing scenarios. No knowledge of conformance of the document to another DTD is, however, exploited by any of those approaches.

An extension of the incremental validation process to document correction is proposed in (Bouchou et al., 2006) where upon validation failure local corrections to the document are proposed to the user. This approach is not applicable for document revalidation upon schema evolution, since this would require proposing to the user, upon each schema update, the whole set of documents invalidated by the schema, together with a set of possible corrections for each document. The user should then examine these alternative corrections, and choose the most suitable for each document. Such a heavy user interaction, that might be appropriate for document revalidation after document updates, is obviously not adequate for document revalidation after schema updates.

Schema adaptation has been investigated, for schemas expressed as DTDs, by Bertino et al. (2002) and Bouchou et al. (2004), and for XML Schemas by Klettke et al. (2005). The focus is on dynamically adapting the schema to documents. In (Bouchou et al., 2004) document updates invalidating some documents can lead to changes in the DTD. Specifically, updates resulting in invalid XML documents are treated in different ways, according to the kind of user performing them. Invalid updates performed by ordinary users are rejected; whereas, invalid updates performed by administrators can be accepted, thus causing a change on the schema. The validity of a document after such an update is enforced by changing the

schema. The rationale for this approach is the increasing demand for tools specifically designed for administrators not belonging to the computer science community, but capable of making decisions on the evolution of the applicative domain, as outlined by Roddick et al. (2000). An XML document is seen as an unranked labeled tree having different kinds of nodes and the schema (DTD) as an unranked bottom-up tree automaton. Checking the validity of the document for the schema means running the automaton with the document tree as input. The correction approach focuses on insertions and results in local changes to the schema, thus producing much less ambitious results than automatic learning of automata.

Klettke et al. (2005) address the same problem in the context of XML Schema. Specifically, they distinguish four possible outcomes of update operations on documents: ignore the schema (all update operations are accepted); reject the updates that produce documents not valid for the schema; redo after an invalidating document update, request that the user explicitly modify the schema; automatically evolve the schema after an invalidating document update, which corresponds to what is proposed in (Bouchou et al., 2004).

Table 3. Main approaches for the evolution of XML structural information

	Approaches	Schema	Updates on	Validate/Adapt
Incremental validation	Balmin et al. 2004 Barbosa et al. 2004 Bouchou & Ferrari Alves 2003 Barbosa et al. 2006	DTD	document	validate
Document revalidation	Raghavachari & Shmueli 2007	XML Schema	-	validate
Document correction	Boobna & de Rougemont 2004 Staworko & Chomicki 2006	DTD	-	adapt document
Document correction upon update	Bouchou et al. 2006	DTD	document	adapt document (with user intervention)
Schema adaptation	Bertino et al. 2002 Bouchou et al. 2004 Klettke et al. 2005	DTD XML Schema	document	adapt schema
Schema evolution	X-Evolution	XML Schema	schema	validate and adapt documents

They discuss how the schema constraints can be relaxed upon deletion, insertion, renaming, and replacing of elements and attributes.

In (Bertino et al., 2002), DTD modifications are deduced by means of structure mining techniques extracting the most frequent document structures, in a context where documents are not required to exactly conform to a DTD. The focus was on obtaining the DTD that best describes the structures of a subset of documents in a collection.

Comparison

Table 3 summarizes the main approaches discussed in this section and classifies them according to a number of dimensions: whether they consider schemas expressed as DTDs or XSDs, whether they are triggered by updates on documents or on schemas, and whether they aim at (re)validating documents, at adapting them, or at adapting schemas.

X-EVOLUTION: A COMPREHENSIVE APPROACH TO XML SCHEMA EVOLUTION

X-Evolution (Mesiti et al., 2006) is a Web-based system developed on a three-tier architecture that allows the specification of schema modifications in a graphical representation of XSDs and documents stored both in the file system and in a commercial XML-enabled DBMS. It provides facilities for performing schema revalidation only when strictly needed and only on the minimal parts of documents affected by the modifications. Moreover, it supports both automatic and query-based approaches for the adaptation of original schema instances to the evolved schema. Support is provided to the user for a convenient specification of the required updates and for the specification, when required, of default values or queries on the original version of the document to populate new

Figure 2. X-Evolution Web interface

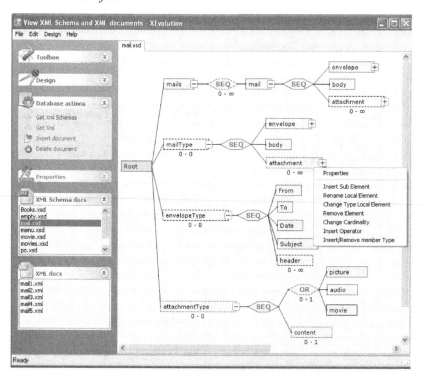

elements. This is a key feature of X-Evolution and minimizes user efforts in the passage from the original schema to the evolved one and for the adaptation of associated documents. The most relevant features are described here.

Graphical Facilities to Handle Documents and Schemas

X-Evolution connects to one or more databases in which the XSDs and documents are stored. Figure 2 shows the graphical interface in which the mail.xsd schema is drawn as a tree. The graphical representation is obtained through a Java Applet that exploits the Jgraph interface (`http://www.jgraph.com/`). Actually, a schema should be represented as a direct graph. However, for the sake of readability, we duplicate nodes of the graph with more than one incoming edge. In the schema representation, shapes representing elements have a different color from those representing types. Symbols `SEQ`, `ALL`, `OR` are employed for representing the `sequence`, `all`, and `choice` groups of elements. Cardinality constraints are reported under the corresponding shapes. The left side bar of the schema visualization facility in Figure 2 presents the identified documents and schemas. Whenever a user clicks on a schema, the system graphically represents the schema and identifies the documents that are valid for such a schema. Whenever a user clicks on a document, the system graphically represents the document and identifies the schema for which the document is an instance. The usual functionalities for loading or removing schemas/documents from the database, assigning/removing a document to/from a schema, and generating new schema and documents, are provided.

Schema Modification and Evolution Primitives

Starting from the classification of schema modification (Guerrini, 2005), corresponding primitives have been devised for updating an XSD through the graphical interface. Moreover, a schema update language, XSchemaUpdate (described in next section), has been developed for the declarative specification of the schema modification primitives (Cavalieri et al., 2008b).

Table 4 reports the evolution primitives relying on the proposed classification. For simple types, the operators are further specialized to handle the derived types restrict, list, and union. Primitives marked * in Table 4 do not alter the validity of documents. Primitives marked ° in Table 4 operate on the structure of an element. Primitives are associated with applicability conditions that must hold before their application in order to guarantee that the updated schema is still consistent. For example, global types/elements can be removed only if elements in the schema of such a type or referring to it do not exist. Moreover, when renaming an element in a complex type τ, an element with the same tag should not occur in τ. These conditions should be verified when the corresponding primitive is handled by the revalidation algorithm (detailed in Guerrini et al., 2007). Through this algorithm, X-Evolution determines whether or not documents are still valid. Intuitively, whenever a * primitive is invoked, the documents are valid without the documents having to be checked; whenever other primitives are invoked on a type, all the document elements of that type should be retrieved and checked for whether they are still valid for the new type. Depending on the primitive, different controls should be applied. For example, when renaming a global element, the algorithm extracts elements tagged with the original global name from the documents. If no element is identified, it means that the documents are still valid.

By graphically selecting a node of the tree representation of a schema, the schema evolution primitives that can be applied on such a node are visualized. For example, by clicking on the element attachment of Figure 2, the primitives for a local element are shown. When the user invokes an evolution primitive, a graphical menu for setting primitive parameters is shown to the user. For example, suppose that a sibling element is to be inserted into the attachment element in Figure 2. The menu in Figure3(a) is shown. The user can specify whether the subelement should be positioned above (i.e. before in the document order) or below (i.e. after in the document order) the element attachment, its data type, and its cardinality. Once the parameters have been inserted, X-Evolution checks whether the applicability conditions of the primitive are preserved and, in the positive case, the operation is executed and the evolved schema visualized. Moreover, the revalidation algorithm outlined above is performed. Experiments reported in (Guerrini et al., 2007)

Table 4. Evolution primitives developed within X-Evolution (Guerrini et al., 2007)

	Insertion	Modification	Deletion
Simple Type	*insert_global_simple_type*[*] *insert_new_member_type*[*]	*change_restriction* *change_base_type* *rename_type*[*] *change_member_type* *global_to_local*[*] *local_to_global*[*]	*remove_type*[*] *remove_member_type*[*]
Complex Type	*insert_glob_complex_type*[*] *insert_local_elem*^o *insert_ref_elem*^o *insert_operator*^o	*rename_local_element* *rename_type*[*] *change_type_local_element*^o *change_cardinality*^o *change_operator*^o *global_to_local*[*] *local_to_global*[*]	*remove_element*^o *remove_type*[*] *remove_substructure*^o *remove_operator*^o
Element	*insert_glob_elem*	*rename_glob_elem*[*] *change_type_glob_elem* *ref_to_local*[*] *local_to_ref*[*]	*remove_glob_elem*[*]

Figure 3. (a) Parameters of ins_elem primitive (b) Effects of change of cardinality

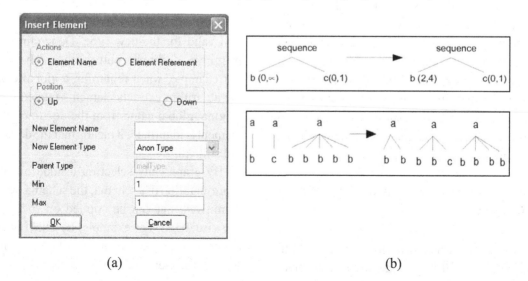

(a) (b)

shows that our revalidation algorithm outperforms standard validation algorithm when * primitives are employed and improves more than 20% the performances for the other primitives.

Document Adaptation and Population

When documents are no longer valid for the new schema, it is necessary to adapt the documents to the new schema. In X-Evolution, both automatic and query-based approaches have been devised to face this issue. The adapt algorithm, detailed in (Guerrini et al., 2007), has been developed to automatically adapt documents to the new schema by a minimal set of operations. Depending on the adopted primitives invoked on the structure of an element e, the adaptation process may require the insertion of new subelements into e, to remove subelements, or both. For example, this last case

occurs when the primitive change_cardinality is invoked and both the minimal and maximal cardinalities are updated as graphically illustrated in Figure 3(b). As another example, suppose that the OR operator in the attachmentType type is modified in the SEQ operator. In this case, new elements should be added to the elements of this type in order to be valid for the new schema. Figure 4 shows how a document is updated after the application of this evolution operation.

A key issue in the adaptation process is the determination of the values to assign when new elements should be inserted into the documents to make them valid. In X-Evolution, two approaches can be followed. Automatic approach: the user requires to assign default values for new elements depending on their types (for simple types, default primitive values are assigned, whereas, for complex types, the simplest structure of that type is extracted and associated with the element); query-based approach: a schema modification statement

Figure 4. Adaptation of a document instance

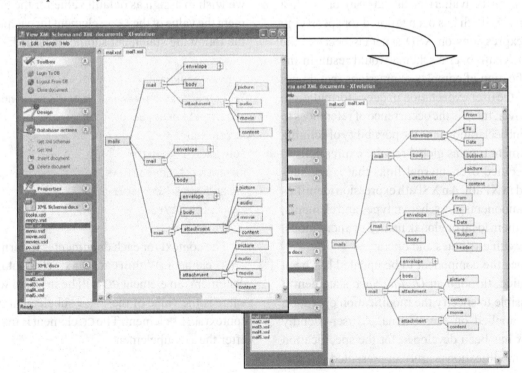

is coupled with a document update statement that specifies the new content depending on the context where it is invoked (see next section).

The user interface helps the user in the adaptation process of non-valid documents. For each non-valid document, the system points out the elements that should be removed or added and the values that will be assigned to new elements.

XSchemaUpdate Language

A statement in this language follows the pattern:

```
UPDATE SCHEMA ObjectSpec
Update Spec
AdaptSpec?
```

Where `ObjectSpec` is the specification of the *update object*, that is, the set of nodes belonging to an XSD that needs to be updated. The update operation is executed on each node belonging to the update object. An update object is specified by the location of the schema and an *XSPath* expression (Cavalieri et al., 2008a) on such a schema. XSPath has been tailored for specifying path expressions on XSD schemas because the use of XPath over a schema would result in the specification of complex expressions that do not reflect the user expectation in query formulation. Moreover, there is the occurrence of references to element declarations and the possibility of defining an element type as global require expressions to be specified over internal links that is not supported in XPath. An XSPath expression identifies the components of a schema: types and elements, being them local or global, named or anonymous, along with attributes and operators.

Once the component to be updated has been identified, through an *Update Spec* statement it is possible to specify the modification operation to be applied on the schema. A user-friendly syntax has been developed for the specification of the modification primitives presented in Table

4. The following statement specifies to insert a new optional local element `cc` (carbon copy) of type `xs:string` after the `to` element.

```
UPDATE SCHEMA
("mail.xsd")/#envelopeType!sequence
INSERT ELEMENT cc OF TYPE xs:string (0,1)
AFTER !to
```

where `/#envelopeType!sequence` is an XSPath expression identifying the `sequence` group operator in the complex type `envelopeType`.

The optional *AdaptSpec* clause allows the specification of an adaptation statement for documents that are instances of the original schema. Each node belonging to the update object has a counterpart in valid documents. Given a node *n* in the update object and a document *D*, the set of document nodes (elements, attributes or values) corresponding to *n* are identified as context for the specification of an XQuery Update expression. The expressions associated with such nodes are evaluated and the new version of the document is generated. Suppose that in the previous example, we wish to assign as default value for the `cc` element the value of the `from` element for each `mail`, the following statement should be issued:

```
UPDATE SCHEMA
    ("mail.xsd")/#envelopeType!sequence
INSERT ELEMENT cc OF TYPE xs:string (0,1)
AFTER !to
FOR EACH DOCUMENT
REFERENCES CONTEXT AS $C
INSERT NODE <CC>{$C/from}</CC>
    AFTER $C/to
```

The context for each document is in turn each `mail` element. Within each `mail` element in the document, an element `CC` will be inserted whose value is the value of the `from` subelement of the context `mail` element. The `CC` element is inserted after the `to` subelement.

XML SCHEMA VERSIONING ISSUES

Many approaches have been developed for schema versioning in the context of object-oriented DBMSs (Kim & Chou, 1988; Lautemann, 1997; Grandi et al., 2003; Liu et al., 2005) and approaches for handling XML document versions are proliferating (Chien et al., 2001; Mandreoli et al., 2006; Marian et. al., 2001). By contrast, in the context of XML Schema, there are discussions only on the issues to be faced (Costello, 2007) and the presentation of use cases (Hoylen, 2006) that systems should address.

Costello (2007) mainly provides some 'best practice' guidelines for XSD schema versioning. He distinguishes between schema updates that (may) invalidate document valid for the previous schema, and those that do not invalidate previously valid documents, and suggests using the first kind of updates only when it is unavoidable or really necessary (meaningful change). According to our terminology, the first kind of update ensures backward compatibility. The numbering of versions should reflect as much as possible whether the new version has been obtained through a major (first kind) or minor (second kind) schema update. Alternative options for identifying a new schema version, such as the (internal) schema version attribute, a new schemaVersion attribute on the root element, the target namespace, or the name/location of the schema, are discussed and contrasted for versions produced by both minor and major schema updates.

(Hoylen, 2006) is a W3C draft describing use cases where XSDs are being versioned, that is, situations when there are more than one XSD, and those schemas are related to each other in some way. The use cases describe the desired behaviour from XML Schema processors when they encounter the different versions of schemas and the documents defined by them. Different use cases are discussed according to the values taken by three orthogonal axes: which schemas are available to the processor, which kind of instance document is being processed, and the operation performed (most commonly validation). As general requirements identified for XML Schema versioning mechanisms, they must allow for multiple generations of versioning and for more than one version to be independently created. In addition, they must produce instance documents which are suitable for manual editing and viewing and must work within the framework of XML instance documents and XSDs. Among the discussed use cases, let us mention:

- **Major-minor** a schema is versioned many times, and some of those versions have insignificant changes made to them, but some others will undergo significant changes and the two types of changes need to be distinguished
- **Object-oriented** which mimics the inheritance and polymorphic behaviour of object-oriented programming languages, establishing an "is-a" relationship between the versions
- **Ignore-unknowns** schemas are written to match the expectations of the applications which process the instances, operating in a "ignore what they don't expect" mode (forward compatibility is thus achieved by deliberately ignoring extra unexpected data, allowing newer versions to add nodes without breaking older applications)
- **Comparison** schemas are compared to determine whether they can be treated as versions of each other, for instance, by testing if the set of documents described by one schema is a subset of the set described by a different schema
- **Specialization** schemas are specialized with more specific versions, and processing software needs to operate in the presence or absence of those specialized schemas (instances of the specialized schemas are always valid instances of the base schema)

- **Customization** schemas are customized for local needs, but the local version must not break validation with the original schema (customizations are extensions of the base schema thus, without any versioning mechanisms, instances of the customized schemas would not be valid instances of the base schema)

CONCLUSION AND FUTURE TRENDS

In this chapter, we have provided an overview of commercial system support and research proposals for XML Schemas evolution and versioning.

As we have seen in the discussion on commercial systems, the support for evolution and versioning in current systems is quite minimal and lacks a lot of features, leaving the opportunity for many extensions. First, the possibility of applying internal modification primitives should be considered. Indeed, as discussed in the chapter, there are modification primitives that do not alter validity and therefore there is no need to invoke a validation process. Guerrini et al. (2007) propose incremental validation approaches that reduce the cost of validation in many cases. Moreover, commercial systems mainly rely on functions/procedures for the specification of evolutions/versioning. These procedures are sometimes tricky to apply and therefore approaches based on a declarative specification of updates are required with a clear and standardized syntax and semantics. Finally, support for document adaptation should be considered, allowing both for automatic adaptation upon simple evolutions and for user-defined adaptations specified by exploiting a language providing the features available in XSchemaUpdate.

In this chapter, we have focused mostly on the impact of schema modifications on the instance documents. Schema modifications, however, also impacts applications, queries, and mappings between schemas. In (Moro et al., 2007) the im-

pact of schema evolution on queries is discussed, whereas the impact of schema evolution on mappings has been investigated by (Velegrakis et al., 2004; Andritsos et al., 2004). The issue of automatically extending applications working on the original schema when this is evolved has not been addressed in the context of XML. Interesting questions that should be faced are: is it possible to guarantee that applications return legal results on the data valid to the new version of the schema? Is there any approach for identifying the portions of the application that are affected by the schema modification? Is there any approach for automatically changing the application or introduce stubs that handle the modification? For answers to these questions, one can consider the work on "expression problems" by P. Wadler (Java Genericity mailing list, 1998) and by Torgersen (2004) for Java.

Another interesting direction is the organization of schema evolution statements in transactions. Therefore, validity checking and document adaptation can be postponed until the end of the transaction. The main issue in this direction is the presence of conflicting statements within a transaction. Conflicts can arise both at schema and instance level. At schema level, a statement can request the insertion of a subelement in the declaration of an element removed by a previous statement. At data level, an adaptation primitive can be specified considering the document at the beginning of the transaction, and not the document obtained by applying the preceding adaptation statements. Static safety conditions should thus be determined to avoid both kinds of conflicts: conditions for performing a single document adaptation at the end of the transaction; conditions under which a transaction will never commit. The same issues of (safely) composing document adaptation operations arise if the adaptation process is performed lazily, that is, when documents are accessed the first time after their schema has evolved, which is reasonable in some situations.

Concerning schema versioning, the proliferation of versions can create the need for developing approaches for handling and efficiently accessing the different versions of the same XSD. Moreover, relying on a direct graph model for representing the different versions, manipulation operations should be developed (remove old versions, delete corresponding document, move /transform documents of a version into another version, and so on).

REFERENCES

Andritsos, P., Fuxman, A., Kementsietsidis, A., Miller, R.-J., & Velegrakis, Y. (2004). Kanata: Adaptation and evolution in data sharing systems. In *SIGMOD Record 33*(4), 32-37.

Balmin, A., Papakonstantinou, Y., & Vianu, V. (2004). Incremental validation of XML documents. In *ACM Transactions on Database Systems* 29(4), 710-751.

Barbosa, D., Mendelzon, A., Libkin, L., & Mignet, L. (2004). Efficient incremental validation of XML documents. In *ICDE*, (pp. 671-682).

Barbosa, D., Leighton, G., & Smith, A. (2006). Efficient incremental validation of XML documents after composite updates. In *XSym*, (pp. 107-121).

Bertino, E., Guerrini, G., Mesiti, M., & Tosetto, L. (2002). Evolving a set of DTDs according to a dynamic set of XML documents. In *EDBT Workshops*, (pp. 45-66).

Bex, G. J., Neven, F., & Van den Bussche, J. (2004). DTDs versus XML schema: A practical study. In *WebDB*, (pp. 79-84).

Boobna, U., & de Rougemont, M. (2004). Correctors for XML data. In *XSym*, (pp. 97-111).

Bouchou, B., & Ferrari Alves, M. H. (2003). Updates and incremental validation of XML documents. In *DBPL*, (pp. 216-232).

Bouchou, B., Duarte D., Ferrari Alves, M. H., Laurent, D., & Musicante, M. A. (2004). Schema evolution for XML: A consistency-preserving approach. In *TMFCS*, (pp. 876-888).

Bouchou, B., Cheriat, A., Ferrari, M. H., &. Savary, A. (2006). XML document correction: Incremental approach activated by schema validation. In *IDEAS*, (pp. 228-238).

Bourret, R. (2007). *XML database products.* Available at http://www.rpbourret.com/xml/XMLDatabaseProds.htm

Cavalieri, F., Guerrini, G., & Mesiti, M. (2008a). *Navigational path expression on XML schemas.* Technical report. University of Genova.

Cavalieri, F., Guerrini, G., & Mesiti, M. (2008b). *XSchemaUpdate: Schema evolution and document adaptation.* Technical report. University of Genova.

Chien, S.-Y., Tsotras, V. J., & Zaniolo, C. (2001). XML document versioning. In *SIGMOD Record 30*(3), (pp. 46-53).

Choi, B. (2002).What are real DTDs like? In *WebDB*, (pp. 43-48).

Costello, R. (2007). *XML schema versioning.* http://www.xfront.com/Versioning.pdf

Florescu, D., & Kossmann, D. (1999) Storing and querying XML data using an RDMBS. In *IEEE Data Eng. Bull.*, 22(3), 27-34.

Grandi, F., & Mandreoli, F. (2003). A formal model for temporal schema versioning in object-oriented databases. In *Data and Knowledge Engineering* 46(2), 123-167.

Guerrini, G., Mesiti, M., & Rossi, D. (2005). Impact of XML schema evolution on valid documents. In *WIDM*, (pp. 39-44).

Guerrini, G., Mesiti, M., & Sorrenti, M. A. (2007). XML schema evolution: Incremental validation and efficient document adaptation. In *XSym*, (pp. 92-106).

Halevy, A. (2000) *Logic-based techniques in data integration*. In Minker, J. (Ed.), Logic-based artificial intelligence, (pp. 575-595).

Halevy, A , Rajaraman, A., & Ordille, J. (2006). Data integration: The teenage years. In *VLDB,* (pp. 9-16).

Hoylen, S. (2006). *XML Schema Versioning Use Cases*. Available at http://www.w3c.org/XML/2005/xsd-versioning-use-cases/

Kim, W., & Chou, H.-T. (1988). Versions of schema for object-oriented databases. In *VLDB*, (pp. 148-159).

Klettke, M., Meyer, H., & Hänsel, B. (2005). Evolution: The other side of the XML update Coin. In *ICDE Workshop,* (p. 1279).

Kramer, D. K., & Rundensteiner, E. A. (2001). Xem: XML evolution management. In *RIDE*, (pp. 103-110).

Lautemann, S.-E. (1997). Schema versions in object-oriented database systems. In *DASFAA*, (pp. 323-332).

Liu, X., Nelson, D., Stobart, S., & Stirk, S. (2005). Managing schema versions in object-oriented databases. In *ADBIS*, (pp. 97-108).

Malcolm, G. (2008). What's new for XML in SQL server 2008. In *Microsoft SQL Server 2008 white papers*.

Mandreoli, F., Martoglia, R., Grandi, F., & Scalas, M. R. (2006). Efficient management of multi-version XML documents for e-government applications. In *WEBIST Selected Papers*, (pp. 283-294).

Marian, A., Abiteboul, S., Cobena, G., & Mignet, M. (2001). Change-centric management of versions in an XML warehouse. In *VLDB,* (pp. 581-590).

Melton, J., & Buxton, S. (2006). *Querying XML – Xquery, XPath, and SQL/XML in context*. Morgan-Kaufmann.

Mesiti, M., Celle, R., Sorrenti, M. A., & Guerrini, G. (2006) X-Evolution: A system for XML schema evolution and document adaptation. In *EDBT*, (pp. 1143-1146).

Michels, J. E. (2005). *SQL Standard – SQL/XML functionality*. Presentation for ISO/IEC JTC 1/SC 32 N 1293.

Moro, M., Malaika, S., & Lim, L. (2007). Preserving XML queries during schema evolution. In *WWW*, (pp. 1341-1342).

Nicola, M., & van der Linden, B. (2005). Native XML support in DB2 universal database. In *VLDB*, (pp. 1164-1174).

Pal, S., Tomic, D., Berg, B., & Xavier, J. (2006). Managing collections of XML schemas in microsoft SQL server 2005. In *EDBT*, (pp. 1102-1105).

Raghavachari, M., & Shmueli, O. (2007). Efficient revalidation of XML documents. In *IEEE Transactions on Knowledge and Data Engineering 19*(4), 554-567.

Roddick, J. F. (1995). A survey of schema versioning issues for database systems. In *Information and Software Technology 37*(7), 383-393.

Roddick, J. F. et al. (2000). Evolution and change in data management: Issues and directions. In *SIGMOD Record 29*(1), 21-25.

Software AG (2008). Tamino schema editor. *Online documentation*.

Staworko, S., & Chomicki, J. (2006). Validity-sensitive querying of XML databases. In *EDBT Workshops*, (pp. 164-177).

Steegmans, B. et al. (2004). *XML for DB2 information integration*. IBM Redbook Series.

Tan, M., & Goh, A. (2004). Keeping pace with evolving XML-based specifications. In *EDBT Workshops*, (pp. 280-288).

Torgersen, M. (2004). The expression problem revisited. In *Proc. Of 18th ECOOP*, (pp. 123-143).

Velegrakis, Y., Miller, R.-J., Popa, L., & Mylopoulos, J. (2004). ToMAS: A system for adapting mappings while schemas evolve. In *ICDE*, (p. 862).

Velegrakis, Y., Miller, R.-J., & Popa, L. (2004). Preserving mapping consistency under schema changes. In *VLDB Journal 13*(3), 274-293.

W3C (1998). *Extensible markup language (XML)*.

W3C (2004). *XML schema part 0: Primer*. Second Edition

W3C (2008). *XQuery Update Facility 1.0, candidate recommendation.*

Section II
Querying and Processing XML

Chapter V
XML Stream Query Processing:
Current Technologies and Open Challenges

Mingzhu Wei
Worcester Polytechnic Institute, USA

Ming Li
Worcester Polytechnic Institute, USA

Elke A. Rundensteiner
Worcester Polytechnic Institute, USA

Murali Mani
Worcester Polytechnic Institute, USA

Hong Su
Oracle Cooperation, USA

ABSTRACT

Stream applications bring the challenge of efficiently processing queries on sequentially accessible XML data streams. In this chapter, the authors study the current techniques and open challenges of XML stream processing. Firstly, they examine the input data semantics in XML streams and introduce the state-of-the-art of XML stream processing. Secondly, they compare and contrast the automaton-based and algebra-based techniques used in XML stream query execution. Thirdly, they study different optimization strategies that have been investigated for XML stream processing – in particular, they discuss cost-based optimization as well as schema-based optimization strategies. Lastly but not least, the authors list several key open challenges in XML stream processing.

INTRODUCTION

In our increasingly fast-paced digital world all activities of humans and surrounding environments are being tagged and thus digitally accessible in real time. This opens up the novel opportunity to develop a variety of applications that monitor and make use of such data streams, typically stock, traffic and network activities (Babcock et al., 2002). Many projects, both in industry and academia, have recently sprung up to tackle newly emerging challenges related to stream processing. On the academic side, projects include Aurora (Abadi et al., 2003), Borealis (Abadi et al., 2005), STREAM (Babu & Widom, 2001), Niagara (Chen et al., 2002), TelegraphCQ (Chandrasekaran et al., 2003), and CAPE (Rundensteiner et al., 2004). On the industrial side, existing major players in database industry such as Oracle (Witkowski et al., 2007) and IBM (Amini et al., 2006) have embarked on stream projects and new startup companies have also emerged (Streambase, 2008; Coral8, 2008).

While most of these activities initially focused on simple relational data, it is apparent that XML is an established format and has been widely accepted as the standard data representation for exchanging information on the internet. Due to the proliferation of XML data in web services (Carey et al., 2002), there is also a surge in XML stream applications (Koch et al., 2004; Florescu et al., 2003; Diao & Franklin, 2003; Bose et al., 2003; Russell et al., 2003; Ludascher et al., 2002; Peng & Chawathe, 2003). For instance, a message broker routes the XML messages to interested parties (Gupta & Suciu, 2003). In addition, message brokers can also perform message restructuring or backups. For example, in an online order handling system (Carey et al., 2002), suppliers can register their available products with the broker. The broker will then match each incoming purchase order with the subscription and forward it to the corresponding suppliers, possibly in a restructured format at the request of the suppliers. Other typical applications include XML packet routing (Snoeren & Conkey, 2001), selective dissemination of information (Altinel & Franklin, 2000), and notification systems (Nguyen et al., 2001).

XML streams are often handled as a sequence of primitive tokens, such as a start tag, an end tag or a PCDATA item. To perform query evaluation over such on-the-fly XML token streams, most systems (Diao et al., 2003; Gupta & Suciu, 2003; Ludascher et al., 2002; Peng & Chawathe, 2003) propose to use automata to retrieve patterns from XML token streams. However, although automata is a suitable technique for matching expressions, how to improve and extend automata functionality in order to efficiently answer queries over XML streams has been a topic of active debate by the XML community. Further, one distinguishing feature of pattern retrieval on XML streams is that it relies solely on the token-by-token sequential traversal. It is not possible to jump to a certain portion of the stream (analogous to sequential access on magnetic tapes). Thus, the traditional index-based technologies cannot be applied for effective query optimization. In static XML processing, cost-based and schema-based optimization techniques are widely used. How to perform such optimization and other optimization techniques in the streaming XML context is a major challenge, and is thus one of the topics of this chapter.

Roadmap. XML streams can be viewed in different data granularities (i.e., different data models for XML streams), which is discussed in Section 2. In Section 3 we describe the automaton-based and algebra-based techniques used in XML stream query processing. Cost-based and schema-based optimization techniques are presented in Section 4 respectively. Section 5 lists the open challenges in XML stream processing and concludes this work.

INPUT DATA FORMATS FOR XML STREAMS

For XML streams, two granularities of input format have been primarily studied. The first type of granularity considers an XML stream that is composed of a sequence of primitive tokens, whereas the second type considers an XML stream that is composed of many XML fragments.

Token-based input streams. Here, XML streams are handled as a sequence of primitive tokens, such as a start tag, an end tag or a PCDATA item. We call it *token-based input*. In this case, a processing unit of XML streams has to be a token, which is at a lower granularity than an XML node. This processing style, i.e., a processing unit being at a lower granularity than the data model, has not received much attention in the database community as of now. This granularity difference is a specific challenge that has to be addressed in the context of XML stream processing. An example token stream is shown in Figure 1. The number in front of each token indicates the arrival order of each annotated token. For this token stream, one method would be to collect the tokens and then combine them to construct the XML documents. Then one could apply the current XML query processing techniques to generate query results. However, this method does not fit the *stream context* since query processing would commence only once the end of the document has been encountered. To process token streams "on-the-fly", many systems (Diao et al., 2003; Gupta & Suciu, 2003; Ludascher et al., 2002; Peng & Chawathe, 2003) propose to use automata to match the query patterns against the token streams.

Fragment-based input streams. In this model, an XML stream is considered to be composed of many XML fragments. For instance, in mobile devices and their data-providing applications, the server may disseminate the data in a broadcast manner and the clients are able to evaluate continuous queries on such XML data streams. In the data stream source, the stream may be fragmented into manageable chunks of information. Further, because of the network

Figure 1. Example token stream data

```
1<Open_auctions>
 2<open_auction>
  3 <annotation>
      4 <author>  5 Claude Monet   6 </author>
      7<description>  8 Representative work of
      9 <emph >10 F rench Impressionism   11 </emph >
     12 <  emph >13 w ater lilies  14 </emph >
     15 </description>
  16 <annotation>
   17 < privacy>  18 N o  19 </privacy>
  20 <initial>  21 1 30,000  22 </initial>
  23 < year>  24 1 872  25 </year>
 26 </open_auction>
 27 <open_auction>
   ...
Open_auctions Stream
```

delay, the arrival of these fragments can even be out of order. Figure 2 shows the data fragments examples (Bose et al., 2003).

QUERY EXECUTION MODELS

As indicated in Section 2, the input stream may be in the format of tokens. Many systems (Diao et al., 2003; Gupta & Suciu, 2003), when faced with such token streams, in fact use tokens as the processing unit throughout the whole evaluation process. In this case, they use automata-based methods to retrieve the patterns. The automata may be augmented with appropriate buffers to allow for further filtering or structuring. However, some systems (Diao & Franklin, 2003; Su et al., 2006; Ives et al., 2002) use the abstraction of algebra-based query plans to model the query after patterns have been retrieved in automaton. In other words, they allow for the usage of different processing units at different evaluation stages.

Using Automaton in XML Stream Processing

The concept of an automaton was originally designed for the functionality of matching expressions over strings. This functionality is similar to one of the major XML query functionalities, namely, the matching of path expressions over token streams. Such close resemblance has inspired several recent projects (Diao et al., 2003; Gupta & Suciu, 2003; Ludascher et al., 2002; Peng & Chawathe, 2003) to exclusively use automaton for XML stream query processing. Some works have studied XPath expressions. Their goals are to minimize the number of the states of the automata while handing multiple XPath expressions, such as lazy PDA and XPush model (Green et al., 2003; Gupta & Suciu, 2003). Other projects instead focus on providing more powerful automata to support advanced query capabilities, such as XSM (Ludascher et al., 2002), YFilter (Diao & Franklin, 2003), Tukwila (Ives et al., 2002) and Raindrop (Su et al., 2006). In this case, the automaton might be augmented with a stack to record state transitions

Figure 2. Three XML fragments stream data

```
<commodities
  <vendor>
    <name>  Wal-Mart </name>
    <items>
      < stream:hole id="10" tsid ="5"/>
      < stream:hole id="20" tsid ="5"/>
      ..
  </vendor>
  ..
</commodities>

              (a)
```

```
< stream:filler i  d="10" t  sid ="5">
  <item>
    <name> PDA </name>
    <make> HP </make>
    <model> PalmPilo </model>
    <price currency="USD">315.25<price>
  </item>
< stream:fille >

              (b)
```

```
< stream:filler   id="20"   tsid ="5">
  <item>
    <name> Calculator </name>
    <make> Casio </make>
    <model> FX  -100 </model>
    <price currency="USD">50.25<price>
  </item>
< stream:fille   >
              (c)
```

or a stack to record parsed tokens (Chen et al., 2004). Both directions are explained in greater detail below.

Lazy PDA (Green et al., 2003) and XPush (Gupta & Suciu, 2003) use DFA (deterministic automata) to process linear XPath expressions. The approach is to convert a query tree which includes all the XPath expressions into a DFA. If the DFA were to be built at compile time, the DFA grows exponentially with the number of expressions containing "//". To solve this problem, they propose a lazy DFA approach. The path expressions are first translated into NFA (non-deterministic automata), and this NFA is then translated into a DFA. But for the latter translation, instead of defining all the states and transitions for the NFA at compile time, the lazy DFA approach would generate states and look for transitions from the corresponding NFA table at runtime so that only the states that would actually be transitioned to are computed. In this case, the transitions and states in the lazy DFA are actually a subset of those in the standard DFA. The number of states in the lazy DFA is shown to be fairly small. It actually depends only on the structure of the XML data instead of on the number of XPath expressions. However, since the DFA has no output buffers, it cannot return the destination elements reachable via an XPath. It returns only a boolean result indicating whether or not an XPath is contained in the input stream. Lazy PDA supports only XPath expressions without filters (i.e., linear patterns) while XPush allows XPath expressions to have filters (i.e., tree patterns). XPush extends Lazy PDA by introducing additional constructs for supporting tree patterns and predicate evaluation.

Several XML query engine projects (Koch et al., 2004; Florescu et al., 2003; Ives et al., 2002; Ludascher et al., 2002; Peng & Chawathe, 2003) focus on optimizing the pattern retrieval in XML queries. XSM (Ludascher et al., 2002) and XSQ (Peng & Chawathe, 2003) use the transducer models for pattern retrieval. XSM and XSQ support XQuery and XPath respectively. XSM adopts the traditional transducer model. It translates one or more XML input streams into one output XML stream. XSM has finite sets of states and state transitions. Note that the transitions are defined based on the input content, current state and internal memory. XSM is associated with a finite set of buffers. Some buffers store the input and output content. XSM can invoke some transition operation based on an input element, or invoke storing actions by reading the pointers of the input buffer, or set up the writing pointer of the output buffer. Figure 3 gives an example of how a path expression "/a" is modeled in XSM. The automaton reads one token from the input buffer at a time.

Figure 3. XSM automaton for encoding an XPath expression "/a"

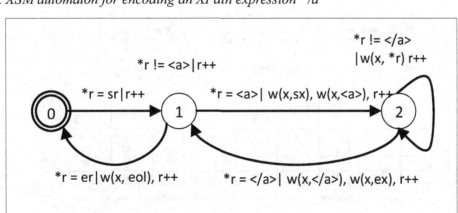

The state transition indicates that if a certain token has been read (expressed as the part before "|"), then the corresponding actions (expressed as the part after "|") will be invoked. For instance, the transition from state 1 to state 2 indicates that if a token <a> has been read, it should be copied to a certain output buffer. Given an XQuery, the XSM compiler would translate the XQuery into an XSM network, which consists of individual XSMs corresponding to the subexpressions of the XQuery.

While the transducer model embeds buffer pointers into the processing of query evaluation, some systems use the automata augmented with stack data structures to retrieve patterns, such as YFilter (Diao & Franklin, 2003) and Raindrop (Su et al., 2006). In such automata, a stack is usually used to trace the path that has been encountered. When an element corresponding to a pattern has been retrieved, it invokes the corresponding operation, like storing or predicate evaluation. Let us examine an automaton transition example using the following query.

```
Q1: FOR $a in stream("open _ auctions")/
auctions/auction[reserve]
```

```
       $b in $a/seller, $c in
$a/bidder
    WHERE $b//profile contains "frequent"
and $c//zipcode = " 01609"
    RETURN
    <auction>  { $b, $c }  </auction>
```

The augmented NFA corresponding to query Q1 is shown in Figure 4. The NFA is built based on the query. A stack is used to store the history of state transitions. The bottom of Figure 4 shows the snapshot of the stack after each token (annotated under the stack) is processed. Initially, the stack contains only the start state q0. The automaton behaves as follows:

- When an incoming token is a start tag: (a) If the stack top is not empty, the incoming token is looked up in the transition entries of every state at the stack top. The automaton pushes the states that are transitioned to onto the stack. For example, in Figure 4, when *<auctions>* is encountered, we transition q0 to q1 and push q1 onto the stack (see the second stack). If no states are transitioned to, the automaton pushes an empty set (denoted as Ø) onto the stack, e.g., when

Figure 4. Snapshots of automaton stack for Q1

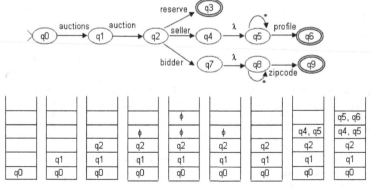

								q5, q6
				φ			q4, q5	q4, q5
			φ	φ	φ			
		q2	q2	q2	q2	q2	q2	q2
	q1	q1	q1	q1	q1	q1	q1	q1
q0	q0	q0	q0	q0	q0	q0	q0	q0

<auctions> <auction> <annotation> <emph> </emph> </annotation> <seller> <profile>

<annotation> is processed, an empty set is pushed onto the stack (see the fourth stack). (b) If the stack top is empty, the automaton directly pushes another empty set onto the stack without any lookup (see the fifth stack when *<emph>* is processed).

- When an incoming token is a PCDATA token: the automaton makes no change to the stack.

- When an incoming token is an end tag: the automaton pops off the states at the top of the stack (see the sixth stack when *</emph>* is processed).

Also, an incoming token is extracted from the stream to compose an XML element if needed. For example, in Figure 4, once q4 has been activated by a *<seller>* token, a storing flag will be raised. As long as the flag is raised, the incoming tokens will be extracted to compose the seller element nodes. When q4 is popped off the stack by a *</seller>* token, the flag is revoked. This then terminates the extraction of the seller element.

(Chen et al., 2004) do not have an explicit automaton for processing XML streams. Instead, it does, however, build stacks for the nodes in the query to record the corresponding matches. More precisely, the stacks are built based on the XPath patterns, i.e., each node in the query has a corresponding stack. When a node is encountered, if it falls into the path from root-to-leaf in the query, it will be pushed into the stack. Hence, the stacks in (Chen et al., 2004) can be regarded as an "implicit" automaton which, instead of recording history of state transitions, directly records the nodes it has encountered so far. (Chen et al., 2004) developed a query processing algorithm for twig queries on XML stream data. Similar to the automaton augmented with stack in YFilter and Raindrop, the query processing in (Chen et al., 2004) pushes matching nodes into the stack when the start of a node is encountered, or pops the nodes out of the stack when the end of a node is encountered. When a leaf node is pushed into the stack, it will

be returned as a query answer. (Chen et al., 2006) extend their work to more complex XPath queries where both predicates and descendant axes are present in queries. When an XPath includes both predicates and descendant axes, recording pattern matches can be very expensive since enumerating all pattern matches can be exponential. (Chen et al., 2006) designed a compact data structure which encodes pattern matches for the nodes in stack. It proposes the TwigM algorithm which prunes the search space by checking predicate satisfaction when processing the XML stream. TwigM achieves a complexity polynomial in the size of the data and the query.

Using Query Algebra for XML Stream Processing

The tuple-based algebraic query processing paradigm has been widely adopted by the database community for query optimization. Its success is rooted at: (1) its modularity of composing a query from individual operators; (2) its support for iterative and thus manageable optimization decisions at different abstraction levels (i.e., logical and physical levels); and (3) its efficient set-oriented processing capability. It is thus not surprising that numerous tuple-based algebras (and optimization techniques based on it) for static XML processing have been proposed (Zhang et al., 2002; Jagadish et al., 2002; Mukhopadhyay et al., 2002) in recent years. Naturally it is expected that such an algebraic paradigm could also be utilized for XML stream processing, thereby enabling us to make use of existing techniques. However, as mentioned previously, such an algebraic paradigm does not naturally handle the token input data model.

Recent work, such as Tukwila (Ives et al., 2002) and YFilter (Diao & Franklin, 2003), aims to bridge the gap between token input and the tuple input typically assumed by such an algebraic paradigm. The main idea is to split query processing into two stages. In the first stage, automata are used to handle *all* structural pattern retrieval.

XML nodes are built up from tokens and organized into tuples. These output tuples are then filtered or restructured in the second stage by a more conventional tuple-based algebraic engine. In this model, all the pattern retrieval is done in the automata. We illustrate this approach using an example below.

We again use the open auction data shown in Figure 1 and query Q1 as our running example. This query pairs sellers with bidders of a certain open auction. Figure 5 (a) shows the corresponding Tukwila query plan. While the algebraic processing is expressed as a query tree of algebra operators (skipped in the figure), the automaton processing is modeled as a single operator called X-Scan (YFilter also has a similar module called "path matching engine" (Diao & Franklin, 2003)). The X-Scan operator is an abstraction of the logic of the automaton. This automaton retrieves all patterns in the query, such as $a = auctions/auction$, $b = a/seller$, and so on. X-Scan outputs tuples containing bindings of variables such as $a and $b. The Select operator $Select_{\$f="01609"}$ then operates on these tuples, to select those tuples which

satisfy $f = "01609". Hence, the X-Scan operator would send all the pattern retrieval results to its downstream operators, namely, the bindings to all the XPath expressions in the query, as annotated beside the X-Scan operator in Figure 5 (a).

Most existing approaches in the literature assume that all the patterns in the query should be retrieved in the automaton since retrieving a pattern in an automaton is known to be rather cheap. The advantage of retrieving all patterns in the automaton is that such processing requires only one single read pass over the input; correspondingly a minimal number of element nodes is being composed. However, the Raindrop approach (Su et al., 2006) illustrated that such retrieval may not be optimal since patterns are retrieved independently when all the pattern retrieval is done in the automaton. For example, whether $a/reserve$ occurs in a binding of a does not affect whether $a/seller$ will be retrieved, and vice versa. Now consider a variation of the Tukwila plan as shown in Figure 5 (b). This plan retrieves only *auctions/auction* and $a/reserve$ in X-Scan'. In the output tuples of X-Scan', the bindings of

Figure 5. Tukwila query plan for query Q1

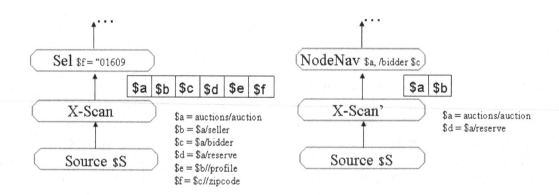

(a) Tukwila Query Plan: Retrieving All Patterns in Automaton

(b) Alternative Plan: Retrieving Subset of Patterns in Automaton

$a contain only those *auction* elements that have *reserve* children elements. These tuples are further manipulated to locate the remaining patterns. For example, $NodeNav_{\$a,/bidder}$ *$c* navigates into the *auction* element nodes to locate */bidder*. The latter plan essentially "serializes" the retrieval of *$a/reserve* and the other patterns including *$a/seller*, *$a/bidder*, *$b//profile* and *$c//zipcode*. If only a very small number of *auction* elements have *reserve* child elements, only few output tuples are generated by X-Scan'. This plan then saves the pattern retrieval of *$a/seller*, *$a/bidder*, *$b//profile* and *$c//zipcode* compared to the former plan. These savings can be significant because retrieving patterns *$b//profile* and *$c//zipcode* which contain the recursion navigation step "//" can be rather expensive (Green et al., 2003).

Raindrop (Su et al., 2006) thus proposes a paradigm that does not limit all the pattern retrieval to be conducted within the automaton. Instead, the Raindrop model allows some selected portions of pattern retrieval to be undertaken within the automaton, and other patterns may be retrieved outside the automaton. In this case, query rewriting can be applied to pull different patterns out of the automaton. This work designs a set of rewriting rules that pushes or pulls patterns into or out of the automata. The pattern matching (the computation captured most naturally by automaton processing) is modeled as a query plan composed of operators at a finer granularity than X-Scan (Ives et al., 2002). Such a model offers several benefits. First, the portion of the plan modeling automaton processing can be reasoned over in a modular fashion. That is, optimization techniques can be studied for each operator separately rather than only for the automaton as a whole. Second, since the automaton processing is expressed as an algebraic plan just like the other computations, rewriting rules can be applied to switch computations into or out of the automaton (Su et al., 2008).

Different from the other works (Ives et al., 2002; Diao & Franklin, 2003; Su et al., 2006)

which are focused on processing XML stream data, (Fernandez et al., 2007) is the first work to handle both XML stream data as well as persistent XML data. This project defines a physical data model which includes static XML and streamed XML token data. A physical algebra that supports two types of operators, operators on streamed data and static XML algebra operators, is designed. It also supports conversion between these two XML representations. In plan generation, it provides static analysis techniques for deciding which part of the plan can be streamed.

(Li & Agrawal, 2005) explore more powerful query processing capabilities on XML streams such as user-defined functions and aggregation functions. To enable the efficient evaluation of XQuery over streaming data, it proposes to execute queries using a single pass since data arrives on-the-fly. To judge whether a query can be executed in a single pass, it analyzes the dependencies in the query using a *stream data flow graph* and then applies two types of transformations, horizontal and vertical fusion. Horizontal fusion merges multiple traversals which share a common prefix in their XPath expressions into one single traversal, thus making it possible to process the query in a single pass. Vertical fusion merges multiple pipeline operations on each traversal path into a single cluster which can remove unnecessary buffering and simplify the data flow graph.

BEA/XQRL (Florescu et al., 2003) processes stored XML data where the data is stored as a sequence of tokens. The XQuery expression is compiled into a network of expressions. An expression is equivalent in functionality to an algebraic operator. BEA/XQRL adopts a pull-based processing model since they assume access back to the previous tokens is possible. In this sense, the tokens in BEA/XQRL and the tokens in XML streams are not equivalent concepts in terms of their accessibility. In BEA/XQRL, the token stream is stored (either on disk or in memory), enabling the same data to be accessed by expressions multiple times. However, in XML streams, tokens arrive on-the-fly. Only if we explicitly store the arriving tokens in XML streams into the buffer first, can we apply their pull-based processing model on XML stream data.

Most of the above works adopt a push-based query processing mechanism for XML streams. (Fegaras et al., 2006) instead propose XQPull, a pull–based query processor for XML streams. In XQPull, each single XPath step is mapped to an iterator and XQuery is mapped to a pipeline of these iterators. The idea of XQPull is to postpone caching until it is necessary. In this case, some data segments might be reduced by subsequent operators. Thus the overall buffer size is reduced by postponing caching. For instance, XPath //*/A can be split into two iterators, //* and /A. It would require caching a lot of events for the first step //*. But later on these events might be discarded because they do not satisfy the subsequence iterator /A. By allowing streamlined modules and postponing caching in the plan, it does not need to create the events for //* and the buffer size is saved. Note that, in order to support streamlined query plans without caching, each iterator in the plan must keep multiple copies of the state which is based on the document depth. But this overhead is still smaller than the input stream size.

Out-of-Order Handling in XML Stream Processing

Most XML stream systems assume that the input data is in order. However, it is possible that the input data is out of order due to network delay or some network protocol issue. When the input data is in the form of a token stream, and the tokens in a complete element are totally out of order, an intuitive method is to postpone the query processing for this element until all the tokens contained in the whole element have been received. This clearly raises many new challenges that must be tackled. How to optimize query processing in such scenarios has been little explored to date. Another scenario for out-of-order input is that the input

data is in the form of fragments. If some fragments are missing, we cannot process the query since the data is not complete. (Bose et al., 2003) propose a query algebra paradigm that works on the assumption that the fragments arrive out of order, yet all the fragments are guaranteed to be received at some point in time.

We use the query below to illustrate this query processing approach. Query Q2 returns the list of names of vendors selling HP PDAs evaluated against the fragments from the commodities stream.

```
Q2: FOR    $b in stream("commodities")//
vendor//item
       WHERE   $b/name = "PDA" and $b/make
= "HP"
       RETURN  <vendor> {$b/../../name } </
vendor>
```

Instead of reconstructing the original XML stream, the fragments are streamed through the various algebraic operators in a pipelined fashion. Fragments are discarded when the operator predicate evaluates to false. Some fragments may not contain enough information to be evaluated by a particular operator, due to the presence of holes. When an operator has insufficient information to validate a fragment, it suspends the processing of this fragment until the relevant fillers arrive. Let f1, f2, f3 denote the fragments a, b and c respectively in Figure 2. The commodities stream can be regarded as a sequence of fragments f1; f2; f3; ...; eos (end of stream). Query Q2 needs to locate the patterns $b, $b/name and $b/make. When the fragments are passed through the operators, the navigate operator which looks for pattern //vendor, suspends the fragment f1, since it encounters a hole with id = 10 during its path traversal. When the fragment f2 arrives, the suspended fragment is processed, and passed through. This fragment is then passed to the next navigation operator which looks for //vendor//item, as well as the selection operators, σ_{p_1} which evaluates whether $b/name is equal to "PDA" and σ_{p_2} which evaluates whether $b/make is equal to "HP". The result generated from fragment 2 is added to the result stream. When the fragment f3 arrives, the fragment f1, still being suspended due to another unresolved hole with id = 20, is similarly streamed through the navigate operator which looks for pattern //vendor//item. However, this desirable subpattern is filtered out in the selection stage.

QUERY OPTIMIZATION FOR XML STREAM PROCESSING

In this section, we examine different optimization strategies that have been investigated for XML stream processing – in particular, we discuss cost-based optimization and schema-based optimization techniques.

Cost-Based Optimization

Algebraic Rewriting

Cost-based algebraic rewriting is the mainstream optimization technique used in the database community. While it has been actively studied for static XML processing, this technique can also be applied in streaming XML processing. Lore (McHugh & Widom, 1999), a static XML database engine, adopts cost-based optimization techniques. They propose a set of indexes on XML. For example, a *label index* supports finding all element nodes with a certain name, e.g., finding all *seller* elements. More precisely, Lore's physical operators provide different ways for finding a path in a bottom-up, top-down or hybrid manner in the XML tree. For example, given a path *seller/phone/primary*, either we find all *seller* elements first using the label indexes (top-down), or all *primary* elements first (bottom-up) or all *phone* elements first (hybrid). Lore investigates plan enumeration algorithms to choose among different path navigation alternatives guided by

some cost model with heuristics as the search space pruning techniques.

The algebraic rewriting in Timber (Wu et al., 2003), another static XML database engine, focuses on choosing an optimal order for structural joins. Timber's search algorithm is based on the traditional dynamic programming algorithm for join ordering. The basic idea of dynamic programming for join ordering is as follows. First, all access paths to every table involved in the join are generated. Second, all partial plans with two-way joins are generated. Partial plans with three-way joins are next generated from the two-way joins and so on. Suppose in the two-way join generating phase, we have found out that join order of (table A, table B) (i.e., A is at the left of the join while B is at the right of the join) is better than the join order of (table B, table A), a three-way join in the order of (table B, table A, any other table) will not be generated since it must be worse than the join in the order of (table A, table B, any other table).

Timber eliminates some partial query plans that are guaranteed to lead to suboptimal solutions. Timber can start constructing $n+1$-way structural joins before it finishes constructing all n-way structural joins. It ranks all partial plans. It then constructs the next plans from the partial plans in the order of their ranks. The purpose of ranking is to create as early as possible complete plans that are optimal. Therefore, any partial plan that already has a higher cost than that of a best complete plan found so far can be excluded. This essentially corresponds to the classical A* search strategy. An important property that has to hold for this pruning work is that the cost of a partial plan is independent of how it is joined with the rest of the relations (we say a partial plan has independent cost). In other words, when a partial plan is expanded to a new partial plan, i.e, i-way structural joins expanded to $i+1$-way structural joins, the new partial plan must cost more than the old partial plan. This is called the *monotonically increasing cost* property in A* search. If this property does not hold, the pruning may exclude partial plans that may potentially still lead to the optimum.

Automaton-Associated Rewriting

As discussed earlier, automaton-based techniques are widely used in XML stream processing because of their similarity to one of the major XML query functionalities: namely, matching path expressions over tokens. One automaton-associated writing technique is proposed by Raindrop, which determines how much computation is performed by the automaton.

Raindrop (Su et al., 2008) allows a plan to retrieve some of the patterns in the automaton and some out of the automaton. This opens up a new optimization opportunity, called automaton-in-out. Given a query, the optimizer determines which pattern retrievals should be performed in the automaton and which should be performed out of the automaton. Raindrop uses a cost-based approach (Su et al., 2008) to explore the automaton-in-or-out opportunity. There are three key components in a cost-based approach: (1) a solution space of alternative plans; (2) a cost model for comparison of alternative plans; and (3) a search strategy for selection of a plan from the solution space. Based on these components, Raindrop derives a minimal set of statistics that need to be collected at runtime. It then enhances the algebraic operators so that they can collect statistics during query execution. It uses two types of rewrite rules to optimize the automaton-outside processing. One type of rule commutes the automaton-outside operators. The other type of rule changes the evaluation order of the input operators of structural joins. Structural joins are special joins in Raindrop that take advantage of the automaton computations to efficiently "glue" linear patterns into tree patterns. Correspondingly, Raindrop proposes both heuristics and rank functions (a cost-based technique) to optimize the plan using these rewrite rules, with a cost-model for both the token-based and tuple-based computations. For the automaton-inside computations, Raindrop observes that some cost is amortized across multiple pattern retrieval. That is to say, the cost of retrieving multiple patterns is not a simple summation of the cost of retrieving each individual pattern. Take Q1 as example. The Raindrop system collects statistics of the selectivity on reserve subelements of the auction elements. Using this runtime statistic information on the predicate selectivity on reserve, the system provides automaton pull-out (resp. push-in) for avoiding the pattern retrieval of *$a/seller*, *$a/bidder*, *$b//profile* and *$c//zipcode* when the selectivity on goes low (resp. high) in the input stream.

Compared to compile time optimization, i.e., deciding a plan before any data is processed, run-time optimization faces the additional challenge of plan migration (Zhu et al., 2004). In compile time optimization, once an optimal plan has been found, we can simply start processing the data using this plan. However, in run-time optimization, we have to consider how to migrate from a currently running plan to a new plan found by the optimizer. There are two requirements for the plan migration strategy. First, it must be correct, which means the process with the plan migration should generate exactly the same result as that without the plan migration. Second, it should be efficient. Otherwise, the benefits of run-time optimization may be outweighed by its overhead.

Raindrop designs an incremental plan migration strategy that reuses the automaton of the currently running plan (Su et al., 2008). It also proposes a *migration window*, which is a period of time in which the migration can safely be conducted without crashing the system or generating incorrect results. It further shows that another migration window cannot be defined that contains the proposed one, but still guarantees that any plan migration within it is safe. For the stream environment with stable data characteristics, Raindrop proposes both an enumerative and a greedy algorithm to search through the plan space. It expedites the search by reducing the time spent on costing each alternative plan. This is achieved by two techniques, incremental cost estimation and detection of same cost change. It also provides a greedy algorithm with pruning rules. The pruning rules exclude some alternative plans that are guaranteed not to be optimal.

Statistics Collection

Statistics are indispensable for cost-based optimization. Many studies of XML statistics focus on XML's nested structures. For example, Lore (McHugh & Widom, 1999) maintains that statistics of all paths of length up to m where m is a tunable parameter. They use these statistics to infer the selectivity of longer paths. It also proposes techniques that can more aggressively summarize the paths by pruning and aggregation to reduce the size of statistics. Their techniques do not maintain correlations between paths. Such limitations are addressed in (Chen et al., 2001) which maintains statistics for tree pattern query, as these techniques all require scanning of the whole data.

Another solution for XML statistics collection is to use query feedback (Lim et al., 2002; Lim et al., 2003). The idea is to issue a query workload on the XML data and learn information about the XML structure and PCDATA values from the query feedback (i.e., query results). Such a solution is especially suited to the scenario where XML data is either inaccessible or too large to be completely scanned.

For query evaluation over streaming XML input, two scenarios regarding the stream environment may arise. In the first scenario, the stream environment has stable data characteristics, i.e., the costs and selectivities of all operators in the query do not change over time. This means that we can start off with a plan, collect statistics for a short period, and then optimize the plan. After this optimization, we no longer have to collect statistics or perform optimization since the current plan

remains optimal for the rest of the execution. In the second scenario, the data statistics change over time. Such variation arises for instance due to the correlation between the selection predicates and the order of data delivery (Avnur & Hellerstein, 2000). Suppose a stream source about employees is clustered on *age*. A selection *salary* > 100,000 can have higher selectivity when the data of older employees are processed (older employees usually have higher salary). In such a scenario, we need to continuously monitor these statistics and constantly optimize the plan. Compared to the first scenario where the optimization needs to take place only once, the second scenario imposes a stricter time requirement on finding a new plan quickly.

Schema-Based Optimization

Semantic Query Optimization (SQO) Applicable to Both Persistent and Streaming XML

Semantic query optimization (SQO) applied in streaming XML processing has some resemblance to SQO for persistent XML. XQRL (Florescu et al., 2003) stores the XML data as a sequence of tokens. To find children of a certain type within a context element, the scan on tokens can stop early if the schema tells us that no more children are relevant for the given query once a child of a particular type has been found. Since the token sequence can be repeatedly accessed, XQRL retrieves the patterns one by one. The earlier one pattern retrieval stops, the smaller the overall cost would be.

YFilter (Diao & Franklin, 2003) and XSM (Ludascher et al., 2002) discuss SQO in the XML stream context. They use schema knowledge to decide whether results of a pattern are recursion-free and what types of children elements can be encountered respectively. These techniques in essence correspond to type inference and belong to general XML SQO.

In the automata model that XSM adopts, the transition lookup at state S is not implemented as a hash table lookup but as a linear search on all possible transitions of S. XSM uses schema knowledge to reduce the possible transitions in order to reduce the transition lookup time. For example, to find a path v/a, an XSM transducer state corresponding to v will have two transitions with conditions "next token = <a>" and "next token ≠ <a>" respectively. If it is known from the schema that a binding of v can have only a subelements, then the second transition can be eliminated.

SQO Specific for Streaming XML

The distinguishing feature of pattern retrieval on XML streams is that it relies solely on the token-by-token sequential traversal. This is similar to the sequential access manner on magnetic tapes, where there is no way to jump to a certain part of the stream. Some memory and CPU consumption caused by this access property might become unnecessary if schema constraints are considered during streaming XML processing. The goal of FluXQuery (Koch et al., 2004) uses static analysis on DTD and query to minimize the buffer size. As an illustration, let us consider the query:

```
Q3: FOR $a in stream("open _ auctions")/
auctions/auction[reserve]
      RETURN      <auction>     $a/seller,
$a/bidder   </auction>
```

This query requires that within each auction, all sellers are output before all bidders. If we are given the DTD as below:

```
<! ELEMENT auctions ((auction)*)>
<! ELEMENT auction (seller*, bidder*)>
```

Note that if there is no ordering constraint on the occurrences of seller element and bidder element, the query processing would just buffer

seller and bidder elements for each auction node. To implement the query efficiently by using the above DTD constraint, FluxQuery would immediately output all the *seller* and *bidder* children inside an *auction* node as soon as they arrive on the streams. The process will not require any data buffering. (Koch et al., 2007, Schmidt et al., 2007) have done further work on reducing main memory consumption by adopting a combination of static analysis and dynamic buffer minimization techniques during query evaluation. Once a node is irrelevant for the remaining query evaluation, it will be purged as soon as possible and the garbage collector will be triggered to minimize the buffer size.

Another class of XML stream query optimization assumes that indices are interleaved with XML streams (Green et al., 2003; Gupta & Chawathe, 2004). For instance, the stream index SIX (Green et al., 2003) uses the positions at the beginning and end of each element. If an element is found to be irrelevant, the processor can then move to its end without parsing anything in the middle. XHints (Gupta & Chawathe, 2004) extends SIX by supporting additional metadata information.

Raindrop (Su et al., 2005; Li et al., 2008) uses schema constraints to expedite traversal of the stream by skipping computations that do not contribute to the final result. They both focus on SQO specific to XML stream processing techniques. For example, given a query "*/auctions/auction[reserve][/bidder/zipcode contains "01609"]*", without schema knowledge, whether an *auction* element satisfies the two filters is known only when an end tag of auction has been seen. Query processing is composed of four computations, namely, (1) buffering the auction element, (2) retrieving pattern "*/reserve*", (3) retrieving pattern "*/bidder/zipcode*" and (4) evaluating whether a located zipcode contains "01609". Suppose instead a DTD *<!ELEMENT auction (item, reserve?, date, bidder+,...)>* is given. The pattern "*date*" can be located even though it is not specified in the query. If a start tag of date is encountered but no "*reserve*" has been located yet, we know the current "*auction*" will eventually not qualify as a match with query predicates, and therefore it will not be in the final query result. Raindrop can use this fact and then skip all remaining computations within the current "*auction*" element. This can lead to significant performance improvement when the size of the XML fragment is large (thus saving the cost of computation (1)) or there are a large number of "*bidder*" elements (saving the cost of computations (3) and (4)).

Runtime Schema Change

The SQO techniques described above assume that the XML schema is static and is available prior to the start of query execution. In real-life applications, this assumption is not always realistic and thus may render existing techniques impractical. Assume that in an online auction stream, auction items can be rather different over time. Maybe only a few core attributes, like *price* and *expiration date*, stay the same. Beyond these attributes, different sellers of items can introduce properties to describe their items at will. The stream server should be able to capture such schema refinements and provide a runtime schema to the stream receiver interleaved with the data stream. For instance, when one person or company who sells PCs happens to submit 200 laptops, the stream server can provide a refined schema to the stream receiver, valid only for the next 200 XML messages from that seller.

R-SOX system (Wang et al., 2006) is the first such system designed to tackle the above identified challenges. R-SOX efficiently evaluates XQuery expressions over highly dynamic XML streams. The schema can switch from optional to mandatory types, from potentially deep structures to shallow ones, or from recursive to non-recursive types. In R-SOX, the dynamic schema changes are embedded within the XML stream via special control messages (also called punctuations). The

stream optimizer then will exploit semantic optimization opportunities and provide the output stream in real-time using an optimized processing time and memory footprint, by shortcutting computation when possible and releasing buffer data at the earliest possible time. It designs techniques that adaptively invoke multimode operators for efficient processing of recursive pattern queries on potentially recursive data guided by run-time schema. For changes of the plan at run time, it designs techniques for safe migration by adjusting the transitions in automaton and associated plan execution controls.

SOME OPEN CHALLENGES IN XML STREAM PROCESSING

Below we sketch out a few areas that to date have received little attention in the literature in the context of XML streams, yet which are clearly of importance for reasons of practicality.

Load Shedding in XML Streams. For most monitoring applications, immediate online results often are required, yet system resources tend to be limited given the high arrival rate data streams. Therefore, sufficient memory resources may not be available to hold all incoming data and CPU processing capacity may not be adequate to always handle the full stream workload. A common technique to avoid these limitations is load shedding, which drops some data from the input to reduce the memory and CPU requirements of the given workload. Work in load shedding has been restricted to relational stream systems. We can categorize them into two main approaches (Tatbul et al., 2003; Babcock et al., 2003; Gedik et al., 2005; Gehrke et al., 2003). One, random load shedding (Tatbul et al., 2003) discards a certain percentage of randomly selected tuples. Two, semantic load shedding assigns priorities to tuples based on their utility to the output application and then sheds those with low priority first.

Both of these load shedding techniques in relational stream systems assume a "complete-tuple-granularity" drop as the basic unit of dropping is tuples. (Wei et al., 2008) propose a "structural shedding" strategy which drops subelements from an XML tree. XML query results are composed of possibly complex nested structures. Elements, extracted from different positions of the XML tree structure, may vary in their importance. Further, these subelements may consume rather different amounts of buffer space and require different CPU resources for their extraction, buffering, filtering and assembly. This provides a new opportunity for selectively shedding XML subelements in order to achieve maximum utility on output data. (Wei et al., 2008) is the first and the only work to date to address shedding in the XML stream context by incorporating this notion of the "structural utility" of XML elements into the shedding decision. They provide a preference model for XQuery to enable output consumers to specify the relative utility of preserving different sub-patterns in the query. However, many open challenges in load shedding in XML streams remain. For instance, no work has so far explored the combination of both value-based and structure-based preference models. How to address the effect of various output requirements on deciding what to shed and how to shed, such as output latency and error measure on output data, is also an open challenge.

Data Spilling in XML Streams. One viable solution to address the problem of run-time main memory shortage, while satisfying the needs of complete query results, is to push memory resident states temporarily into disk when memory overflow occurs. Such solutions have been discussed in the relational context so far, namely, XJoin (Urhan & Franklin, 2000), Hash-Merge Join (Mokbel et al., 2004), MJoin (Viglas et al., 2003) and CAPE (Liu et al., 2006). XJoin (Urhan & Franklin, 2000), Hash-Merge Join (Mokbel et al., 2004) and MJoin (Viglas et al., 2003) aim to ensure a high runtime output rate as well as the

completeness of query results for a query that contains a single operator. The processing of the disk resident states, referred to as state cleanup, is delayed until more resources become available.

CAPE (Liu et al., 2006) address the state spilling for multi-operator query plans, in particular, multi-join plans. The new problem is based on the observation that upstream operators cannot simply be locally optimized as their increased output actually clogs the query pipeline without ultimately producing results. The idea is to rank hash-based partition groups in different operators of the query plan based on their current contribution to the query results. When the memory is exhausted, the partition group with the lowest score is spilled to disk.

However, the structure-based data spilling in XML streams to date is still an open problem. For instance, since the XQuery results can be rather hierarchical, this provides the opportunity to spill some subelements to disk and then bring this data back after some time. When spilling an XML subelement, due to data dependency and query semantics, the query might need to be suspended or the query result needs to be flagged as not complete. To choose an appropriate subelement to spill, we have to consider its spilling side-effect on other elements and the reconstruction query in the clean up stage. This XML structure-based spilling problem remains unsolved to date. Further, there are additional challenges except addressing structure-based spilling. Exploring other preference models of spilling in the XML stream context is an open question. Also, no work so far has addressed the spilling problem for multiple XQueries efficiently.

Access Control in XML Streams. Access control is one of the fundamental security mechanisms in information systems, where the main concern is who can access which information under what kind of circumstances. The need of access control arises naturally when a multi-user system offers selective access to shared information. Access control has been studied extensively in a variety of contexts since it is one of the oldest problems in security, including computer networks, operating systems and databases. Due to the growing interest in XML security, various access control schemes have been proposed to limit access to stored XML data to only authorized users. Formal models for the specification of access control policies over XML data and different techniques for efficient enforcement of access control policies over XML data have been developed. For handling access control on internet data, authorizations are specified on portions of HTML files (Demers et al., 2003). For XML data, in (Damiani et al., 2000), a specific authorization sheet is associated with each XML document/DTD expressing the authorizations on the document. Its proposed model is extended by enriching the authorization types in (Damiani et al., 2002), providing a complete description of the specification and enforcement mechanism. An access control environment for XML documents and some techniques to deal with authorization priorities and conflict resolution issues are proposed in (Bouganim & Ngoc, 2004). Access control has been recently studied in the context of data stream systems (Nehme et al., 2008). However, there has been no effort to provide access control for streaming XML data. This remains an open research challenge to date.

REFERENCES

Abadi, D., Ahmad. Y., & Balazinska, M. (2005). The design of the borealis stream processing engine. In *CIDR*, (pp. 277-289).

Abadi, D., Carney, D., Cetintemel, U., Cherniack, M., Convey, C., Lee, S., Stonebraker, M., Tatbul, N., & Zdonik, S. (2003). Aurora: A new model and architecture for data stream management. In *VLDB Journal 12*(2), 120–139.

Altinel, M., & Franklin, M. (2000). Efficient Filtering of XML documents for selective dissemination. In *VLDB*, (pp. 53–64).

Avnur, R., & Hellerstein, J. M. (2000). Eddies: Continuously adaptive query processing. In *SIGMOD*, (pp. 261-272).

Babcock, B., Babu, S., Motwani, R., & Widom, J. (2002). Models and issues in data streams. In *PODS*, (pp. 1–16).

Babcock, B., Datar, M., & Motwani, R. (2003). Load shedding techniques for data stream systems. In *MPDS*.

Babu, S., & Widom, J. (2001) Continuous queries over data streams. In *SIGMOD Record 30*(3), 109-120.

Bose, S., Fegaras, L., Levine, D., & Chaluvadi, V. (2003). A query algebra for fragmented XML stream data. In *DBPL*, (pp. 195-215).

Bouganim, L., Ngoc, F. D., & Pucheral, P. (2004). Client-based access control management for XML documents. In *VLDB*, (pp. 84-95).

Carey, M. J., Blevins, M., & Takacsi-Nagy, P. (2002). Integration, Web services style. In *IEEE Data Eng. Bull. 25* (4), 17-21.

Chandrasekaran, S., Cooper, O., Deshpande, A., Franklin, M., Hellerstein, J., Hong, W., Krishnamurthy, S., Madden, S., Raman, V., Reiss, F., & Shah, M. (2003). TelegraphCQ: Continuous dataflow processing for an uncertain world. In *CIDR*.

Chen, J., DeWitt, D. J., Tian, F., & Wang, Y. (2002). NiagaraCQ: A scalable continuous query system for Internet databases. In *SIGMOD*, (pp. 379–390).

Chen, Z., Jagadish, H. V., Korn, F., Koudas, N., Muthukrishnan, S., Ng, R., & Srivastava, D. (2001). Counting twig matches in a tree. In *ICDE*, (pp. 595–604).

Coral 8 Inc. (2008). Retrieved March 1, 2008, from http://www.coral8.com/

Damiani, E., Vimercati, S. D. C. D., Paraboschi, S., & Samarati, P. (2000). Design and implementation of an access control processor for XML documents. In *Computer Networks 33*(6), 59-75.

Damiani, E., Vimercati, S. D. C. D., Paraboschi, S., & Samarati, P. (2002). A fine-grained access control system for XML documents. In *ACM TISSEC 5*(2), 169-202.

Demers, A. J., Gehrke, J., Rajaraman, R., Trigoni, A. & Yao, Y. (2003). The cougar project: A work-in-progress report. In *SIGMOD Record 32* (4), 53–59.

Diao, Y., Altinel, M., Franklin, M.J., Zhang, H.., & Fischer, P. (2003). Path sharing and predicate evaluation for high-performance XML filtering. In *ACM TODS 28*(4), 467–516.

Diao, Y., & Franklin, M. (2003, September). Query Processing for High-Volume XML Message Brokering. In *VLDB*, (pp.261-272).

Florescu, D., Hillery, C., & Kossmann, D. (2003). The BEA/XQRL Streaming XQuery Processor. In *VLDB*, (pp.997–1008).

Gedik, B., Wu, K.L., Yu, P.S., & Liu, L. (2005). Adaptive Load Shedding for Windowed Stream Joins. In *CIKM*, (pp.171–178).

Gehrke, J., Das, A., & Riedewald, M. (2003). Approximate Join Processing over Data Streams. In *SIGMOD*, (pp.40–51).

Green, T. J., Miklau, G., Onizuka, M., & Suciu, D. (2003). Processing XML Streams with Deterministic Automata. In *ICDT*, (pp.173–189).

Gupta, A., & Chawathe, S. (2004). *Skipping Streams with XHints* (Tech. Rep. No. CS-TR-4566). University of Maryland, College Park.

Gupta, A., & Suciu, D. (2003). Stream Processing of XPath Queries with Predicates. In *SIGMOD*, (pp. 419–430).

Ives, Z., Halevy, A., & Weld D. (2002). An XML Query Engine for Network-Bound Data. In *VLDB Journal 11* (4), 380–402.

Jagadish, H. V., Al-Khalifa, S., Chapman, A., Lakshmanan, L.V. S., Nierman, A., Paparizos S., Patel, J. M., Srivastava, D., Wiwatwattana, N., Wu, Y., & Yu, C. (2002). Timber: A Native XML Database. In *VLDB Journal 11*(4), 274–291.

Koch, C., Scherzinger, S., & Scheweikardt, M. (2004). FluxQuery: An Optimizing XQuery Processor for Streaming XML Data. In *VLDB*, (pp.228–239).

Li, M., Mani, M., & Rundensteiner, E.A. (2008). Semantic query optimization for processing XML streams with minimized memory footprint. In *DATAX*.

Li, X., & Agrawal, G. (2005). Efficient evaluation of XQuery over streaming data. In *VLDB*, (pp.265–276).

Lim, L., Wang, M., Padmanabhan, S., Vitter, J. S., & Parr, R. (2002). An on-line self-tuning Markov histogram for XML Path Selectivity Estimation. In *VLDB*, (pp. 442-453).

Lim, L., Wang, M., & Vitter, J. (2003). SASH: A Self-Adaptive Histograms Set for Dynamically Changing Workloads. In *VLDB*, (pp. 369-380).

Liu, B., Zhu, Y., & Rundensteiner, E.A. (2006). Run-time Operator State Spilling for Memory Intensive Long-Running Queries. In *SIGMOD*, (pp. 347–358).

Ludascher, B., Mukhopadhyay, P., & Papakonstantinou, Y. (2002). A Transducer- Based XML Query Processor. In *VLDB*, (pp. 227–238).

McHugh, J., & Widom, J. (1999). Query Optimization for XML. In *VLDB*, (pp. 315–326).

Mokbel, M. F., Lu, M., & Aref, W. G. (2004). Hash-Merge Join: A Non-Blocking Join Algorithm for Producing Fast and Early Join Results. In *ICDE*, (pp. 251–262).

Mukhopadhyay, P., & Papakonstantinou, Y. (2002). Mixing Querying and Navigation in Mix. In *ICDE*, (p. 245).

Nehme, R. V., Rundensteiner, E. A., & Bertino, E. (2008). Security Punctuation Framework for Enforcing Access Control on Streaming Data. In *ICDE*, (pp. 406-415).

Nguyen, B., Abiteboul, S., Cobena, G., & Preda, M. (2001) . Monitoring XML Data on the Web. In *SIGMOD*, (pp. 437–448).

Peng, F., & Chawathe, S. (2003). XPath Queries on Streaming Data. In *SIGMOD*, (pp. 431–442).

Russell, G., Neumuller, M., & Connor, R. (2003). Stream-based XML Processing with Tuple Filtering. In *WebDB*, (pp. 55-60).

Rundensteiner, E. A., Ding, L., Sutherland, T., Zhu, Y. , Pielech, B., & Mehta, N. (2004) . Cape: Continuous Query Engine with Heterogeneous-Grained Adaptivity. In *VLDB*, (pp. 1353–1356).

Snoeren, A., Conkey, K., & Gifford, D. (2001). Mesh-Based Content Routing using XML. In *SOSP*, (pp. 160-173).

StreamBase. (2008). Retrieved March 15, 2008, from http://www.streambase.com/

Su, H., Rundensteiner, E. A., & Mani, M. (2005) Semantic Query Optimization for XQuery over XML Streams. In *VLDB*, (pp. 277–288).

Su, H., Rundensteiner, E. A., & Mani, M. (2006). Automaton Meets Algebra: A Hybrid Paradigm for XML Stream. In *Data Knowledge Engineering 59*(3), 576–602.

Su, H., Rundensteiner, E. A. & Mani, M. (2008, March). Automaton In or Out: Run-time Plan Optimization for XML Stream Processing, In *SSPS*, (pp. 38-47).

Tatbul, N., Çetintemel, U., Zdonik, S., Cherniack, M., & Stonebraker, M. (2003). Load Shedding in a Data Stream Manager. In *VLDB*, (pp. 309–320).

Urhan, T., & Franklin, M. (2000). XJoin: A Reactively Scheduled Pipelined Join Operator. In *IEEE Data Engineering Bulletin 23*(2), 27–33.

Viglas, S., Naughton, J., & Burger, J. (2003). Maximizing the Output Rate of Multi-Way Join Queries over Streaming Information. In *VLDB*, (pp. 285–296). Morgan Kaufmann.

Wang, S., Su, H., Li, M., Wei, M., Yang, S., Ditto, D., Rundensteiner, E. A., & Mani, M. (2006). R-SOX: Runtime Semantic Query Optimization over XML Streams. In *VLDB*, (pp. 1207–1210).

Wei, M., Rundensteiner, E. A., & Mani, M. (2008). Utility-Driven Load Shedding for XML Stream Processing. In *WWW*, (pp. 855-864).

Witkowski, A., Bellamkonda, S., Li, H., Liang, V., Sheng L., Smith, W., Subramanian, S., Terry, J., & Yu, T. (2007). Continuous queries in oracle. In *VLDB*, (pp. 1173-1184).

Wu, Y., Patel, J. M., & Jagadish, H. V. (2003). Structural Join Order Selection for XML Query Optimization. In *ICDE*, (pp. 443–454).

Zhang, X., Pielech, B., & Rundensteiner, E. A. (2002, November). Honey, I Shrunk the XQuery!: An XML Algebra Optimization Approach. In *WIDM*, (pp. 15-22).

Zhu, Y., Rundensteiner, E. A., & Heineman, G. T. (2004). Dynamic Plan Migration for Continuous Queries over Data Streams. In *SIGMOD*, (pp. 431–442).

Chapter VI
XSLT:
Common Issues with XQuery and Special Issues of XSLT

Sven Groppe
University of Lübeck, Germany

Jinghua Groppe
University of Lübeck, Germany

Christoph Reinke
University of Lübeck, Germany

Nils Hoeller
University of Lübeck, Germany

Volker Linnemann
University of Lübeck, Germany

ABSTRACT

The widespread usage of XML in the last few years has resulted in the development of a number of XML query languages like XSLT or the later developed XQuery language. Today, there are many products like databases in the area of XML processing that support either XSLT or XQuery, but not both of them. This may prevent users from employing their favourite XML query language. In this chapter, the authors show that both languages have comparable expression power and present a scheme for translating XQuery to XSLT and vice versa. This translation scheme enables a user to employ either XSLT or XQuery for each product which supports one of these languages. They also summarize in this chapter both current and future trends and research issues and also consider those that might emerge in the common area of XSLT and XQuery and which are particular to XSLT.

INTRODUCTION

Today, XML is increasingly used to label the information content of diverse data sources including structured and semi-structured documents, relational databases, and object repositories. Furthermore, an increasing number of real XML databases have been developed. The World Wide Web Consortium (W3C) developed the extensible stylesheet language (XSL) (W3C, 2001; 2004b) and especially, its XSL transformations (XSLT) (W3C, 1999; 2007c) part, which is developed to express transformations of XML data. The W3C later developed the XQuery (W3C, 2007b) language, which was developed to express queries. However, many tools support either XSLT or XQuery, but not both.

This chapter clarifies which issues of XSLT are common with XQuery. For the researcher and developer, it is important to know which issues to be resolved are common for XQuery and XSLT, since they can determine which contributions for XQuery also work in principal for XSLT and vice versa. We clarify this by not only comparing the two languages XQuery and XSLT, but also by proposing translation schemes from XQuery to XSLT and vice versa. This clearly indicates which kind of contributions and solutions can be transferred from XQuery to XSLT and from XSLT to XQuery. After this has been determined, the open and novel issues of both XML querying languages XQuery and XSLT together can be considered. We also explain the differences of XSLT in comparison with XQuery, and thus we can determine which research directions apply in particular to XSLT because they are more useful for it.

Although the XSLT and XQuery languages have been developed with different aims, they have comparable expression power and similar applications. Both languages use XPath (W3C, 1999a; 2007a) as the path language for retrieving XML node sets, and have corresponding language constructs for iterations on an XML node set, definitions of variables, XML node constructors and definitions and calls of user-defined functions. Therefore, we can construct a translation from XSLT stylesheets into XQuery expressions and vice versa. A translation of an expression formulated in XSLT or XQuery into an expression formulated in the other language is correct for all input XML documents if, for each input, the results of applying the expressions are the same.

In the following, we describe application scenarios, where the applications of a translation from XQuery expressions into XSLT stylesheets and of a translation from XSLT stylesheets into XQuery expressions offer considerable benefits.

1. **Translation from XQuery expressions into XSLT stylesheets**: Using our proposed translation from XQuery expressions into XSLT stylesheets, the XQuery language can be used whenever commercially or freely available products support the processing of XSLT stylesheets, but do not support the XQuery language. Examples of such tools are BizTalk (Microsoft, 2007a), Cocoon (Apache Software Foundation, 2005a) and Xalan (Apache Software Foundation, 2005b).

2. **Translation from XSLT stylesheets into XQuery expressions**: Many commercially or freely available products support the evaluation of XQuery expressions, but do not support the XSLT language, for example Tamino XML Server (Software AG, 2007), Microsoft SQL Server 2005 Express (Microsoft, 2007b), Galax (Fernández et al., 2007) and Qizx (Axyana Software, 2007). A translation module from XSLT stylesheets into XQuery expressions can make the XSLT language available for these products. Another usage scenario is the migration of legacy systems. Legacy systems may use sub-systems which support XSLT. Further-

more, legacy systems may be migrated to sub-systems which support the new language XQuery instead of XSLT. Then a translation module can be used to translate the old XSLT stylesheets into equivalent XQuery expressions so that those expressions can be applied. Since XSLT was developed earlier than XQuery, many companies and applications use XSLT, and many XSLT stylesheets for different purposes can be found on the web. However, the new XQuery technology becomes more and more apparent in the market as the query language of XML databases and XML enabled databases. Database systems have many advantages including: support of the transaction concept, improved backup and recovery services, data consistency, improved data integrity, sharing of data, increased concurrency and improved security. If a user wants to use an XML database or an XML enabled database in order to benefit from the advantages of a database system, the user must use the XQuery language as the native language for most database systems. Again, when using our translation approach, the user can also

formulate queries in the XSLT language and afterwards apply an XSLT to XQuery translator.

The objectives of this chapter are:

- To demonstrate that XSLT stylesheets and XQuery expressions can be translated between each other in both directions;
- To clarify common issues of XSLT and XQuery; and
- To point out special issues of XSLT, which are the issues related to XSLT and not to XQuery, or which are more useful for XSLT.

XSLT AND XQUERY

We briefly introduce XSLT, XQuery and their syntax and semantics using examples. XSLT is a declarative language for the transformation of XML documents into other (XML) documents. In this process, an input XML document (see Figure 1 as an example) is transformed according to a set of transformation rules called templates,

Figure 1. Input XML document `auction.xml`

```
<site>
 <closed _ auctions>
    <closed _ auction>
            <price>35</price>
    </closed _ auction>
    <closed _ auction>
            <price>45</price>
    </closed _ auction>
 </closed _ auctions>
</site>
```

Example 1. (XSLT stylesheet): The result of the following XSLT stylesheet

```
<?xml version="1.0"?>
<xsl:stylesheet version="2.0" xmlns:
xsl='http://www.w3.org/1999/XSL/Trans-
form'>
  <xsl:template match="/">
   <xsl:for-each select="site/closed _
auctions/closed _ auction[price>='40']">
     <xsl:copy-of select="price"/>
   </xsl:for-each>
  </xsl:template>
</xsl:stylesheet>
```

which are defined in a stylesheet (see Example 1). Each template consists of an XPath-based pattern that defines to which nodes the template applies and a content that defines how the nodes are transformed.

Example 1 with input XML document `auc-tion.xml` of Figure 1 is `<price>45</price>`, which is computed as follows. First, the document node of the input XML document is selected and processed by the sole template of the XSLT stylesheet, which matches the document node. Then the XSLT processor uses a `for-each` expression to navigate through the `closed _ auc-tion` elements and selects the ones with a price greater than 40. These are returned by the `copy-of` statement.

While template rules play a central role in XSLT, SQL-alike FLWOR expressions are similar important in XQuery. FLOWR (pronounced flower) stands for `for`, `let`, `where`, `order by` and `return` and is demonstrated in the Example 2.

The `for`-clause is used to navigate through the `closed _ auction` elements, the `where`-clause applies a condition and the last line returns the appropriate elements.

Example 2. (XQuery query): The following XQuery query is equivalent to the XSLT stylesheet of Example 1

```
for     $i in doc("auction.xml")/site/
closed _ auctions/closed _ auction
where $i/price/text() >= 40
return $i/price
```

We point out the similarities and differences between XSLT and XQuery in the following sections.

Similarities of XSLT and XQuery

The data models of XQuery and XSLT have been aligned within the development of XPath 2.0 (W3C, 2007b), XQuery (W3C, 2007b) and XSLT 2.0 (W3C, 2007c), i.e., XSLT 2.0 and XQuery 1.0 are both based on the XPath data model (Fernández & Robie, 2001) and both embed XPath as the path language for determining XML node sets. Therefore, a majority of the XQuery language constructs can be translated into XSLT language constructs and vice versa. For example, `xsl:for-each` in XSLT has similar functionality as `for` in XQuery, `xsl:if` has similar functionality as `where`, and `xsl:sort` has similar functionality as `order by`. However, there are some differences between the two languages, which cannot be translated directly, and which we will discuss in the next section.

Differences of XSLT and XQuery

We present the differences between XSLT and XQuery in this section. We start by describing the template model of XSLT, then we present the differences in handling intermediate results and finally, we point out the differences between XSLT and XQuery in their language constructs.

Template Model of XSLT

XSLT uses a template model, where each template contains a pattern taking the form of an XPath expression. Whenever a current input XML node fulfills the pattern of a template, the template is executed. An XSLT processor starts the transformation of an input XML document with the document node assigned to the current input XML node. The template is called again when the XSLT processor executes the `<xsl:apply-templates select=I/>` instructions, which first select a node set `I` and then call the templates for all nodes in `I`.

In the following paragraphs, we present how the template model of XSLT can be simulated.

After initialization, the XSLT processor starts the processing of the XSLT stylesheet by applying the templates with the document node /. We simulate the status of the XSLT processor's input by using two variables. The first variable, `$n`, represents the current input XML node set of the XSLT processor and is initialized with a set containing the document root node '/'. The second variable, `$t`, represents the current input XML node of the XSLT processor. We use `$t` to iterate over the current input node set `$n`. Depending on `$t`, we start the template selection process.

We sort the templates according to their priority (either explicit priority or computed default priority) and import precedence (see W3C, 1999b; 2007c)), where the built-in templates of XSLT are the templates with the lowest priority. The selection process of the templates can be simulated by first executing the match test of the template with the highest priority and, if successful, executing the corresponding template. In the case of no success, the match test of the next template in the sorted list of templates is executed and, if successful, the corresponding template is processed.

XQuery does not support checking the XPath patterns of XSLT. Thus, we have to simulate the test of whether a *pattern* E *matches an XML node* in XQuery for a translation from XSLT stylesheets into XQuery expressions. The original definition in the XSLT specification (W3C, 1999b; 2007c) is as follows:

Definition 1 (*pattern matches XML node*): A pattern is defined to *match* a node if and only if there is a possible context such that when the pattern is evaluated as an expression with that context, the node is a member of the resulting node-set. When a node is being matched, the possible contexts have a context node that is the node being matched or any ancestor of that node, and a context node list containing just the context node.

Differences in Handling Intermediate Results

XQuery and XSLT handle intermediate results differently, which we have to consider for the translation.

- While XQuery expressions can be nested with full generality, most XSLT expressions cannot be nested. Therefore, nested XQuery expressions must be translated into a construct, where the intermediate results of the nested XQuery expression are first stored in an intermediate variable using the `<xsl:variable>` XSLT instruction. After that, the intermediate variable is referred for the result of the nested XQuery expression.
- XSLT variables, which are defined by `<xsl:variable>`, can only store element nodes. In particular, XSLT variables cannot store attribute nodes, comment nodes and text nodes. Whenever the translated XSLT stylesheets have to store XML nodes other than element nodes, the translation process can use the later described work-around.
- XQuery and XSLT both embed XPath 2.0, which contains the **is** operator. The **is** operator compares two nodes regarding their identity. In the underlying data model of XQuery and XSLT, each node has its own

identity. XQuery expressions never copy XML nodes, but always refer to the original XML nodes. Contrary to XQuery expressions, XSLT expressions can refer to original XML nodes only by using variables, which can be described by an XPath expression XP and when using the `<xsl:variable select="XP">` instruction. While computing the result of more complex XSLT expressions, which contain functionality outside the possibilities of XPath like iterating in a sorted node set retrieved by evaluating XP in `<xsl:for-each select="XP"><xsl:sort>...</xsl:for-each>`, XSLT expressions have to copy XML nodes by using `<xsl:copy>` or `<xsl:copy-of>`, where the copied XML nodes get new identities different from those of the original XML nodes or other copied XML nodes. Therefore, whenever an XQuery expression uses the **is** operator, the translation process must offer a work-around, which takes care of the identities of XML nodes to be considered in the translated XSLT stylesheet in the same way as for the identities of XML nodes in the original XQuery expression. The next section describes such a work-around.

Differences in Language Constructs

The translation process must consider the following differences in the language constructs of XQuery and XSLT:

- XSLT variables, which are defined by `<xsl:variable>`, can store only element nodes. In particular, XSLT variables cannot store attribute nodes, comment nodes and text nodes. Whenever the translated XSLT stylesheets have to store XML nodes other than element nodes, the translation process can use the later described work-around.
- The language constructs corresponding to functions in XQuery are functions or named templates in XSLT. Whereas XQuery binds parameters in function calls by positions, XSLT binds parameters of function calls and of named templates calls by parameter names.

- The **order by** construct of XQuery corresponds to `<xsl:sort>`. XQuery supports four order modifiers: **ascending, descending, empty greatest** and **empty least**. XSLT supports only **ascending** and **descending**. Therefore, **empty greatest** and **empty least** cannot yet be translated directly to native XSLT language constructs for sorting.

- Furthermore, `<xsl:sort>` has to be the first child of the corresponding `<xsl:for-each>` XSLT instruction. However, the **order by** clause can contain a variable $v, which is defined after the **for** expression. Therefore, the translated variable definition of $v occurs after the `<xsl:sort>` instruction, which must be the first child of `<xsl:for-each>`, but $v is defined later in the translated XSLT stylesheet and cannot be used in the `<xsl:sort>` instruction. In the special case of that the variable $v is defined by an XPath expression XP, we can replace the reference to $v in the translated `<xsl:sort>` XSLT instruction with XP. Furthermore, nested variables in XP must be already defined before the `<xsl:for-each>` XSLT instruction or again must be defined by an XPath expression so that the nested variables can be replaced in XP. In all other cases, the **order by** clause cannot be translated into equivalent XSLT instructions by our approach.

- There are extensions to XQuery (W3C, 2008) in order to allow expressing update queries on XML data, but there are no planned extensions for an XSLT update language.

- The XSLT instruction set is extensible with custom tag libraries, while XQuery does not have a similar feature.

TRANSLATION FROM XQUERY EXPRESSIONS INTO XSLT STYLESHEETS

In this section, we propose a translation from XQuery expressions into XSLT stylesheets. Using this translation, the XQuery language can be used in combination with commercially or freely available products that support the processing of XSLT stylesheets, but do not support the XQuery language, e.g. BizTalk (Microsoft, 2007a), Cocoon (Apache Software Foundation, 2005a) and Xalan (Apache Software Foundation, 2005b). To overcome the differences between XQuery and XSLT described in Section 4, we present additional transformation steps in this section. We also describe the cases where these additional transformation steps can be avoided, and thus the overall translation execution can be optimized. Furthermore, our translation scheme can handle intermediate results and function calls. Finally, we describe the processing of the translated XSLT stylesheets for demonstrating that XSLT is as powerful as XQuery.

Transforming Other XML Nodes into Element Nodes

Whenever XML nodes, which are not element nodes, must be stored as intermediate results, a pre-processing step of the original XML document is needed to transform these XML nodes to element nodes, as only element nodes can be stored in XSLT variables of the translated XSLT stylesheet. We use a namespace `t` in order to identify element nodes, which are transformed from non-element nodes. Tests on XML nodes, which are non-element nodes, are translated to the tests on the corresponding element nodes (see Example 3). Because the result of the translated XSLT stylesheet contains copied element nodes, which are not element nodes of the original document, a post-processing step must be applied to the

Example 3. (Translation of the attribute axis): The following reference to an attribute

```
site/people/person/@name
```

is translated into

```
site/people/person/t:name
```

result of the XSLT stylesheet, which transforms these element nodes back to the corresponding XML nodes.

The Node Identifier Insertion Approach

In the following, we summarize the work-around presented in (Lechner et al., 2001), where the identities of XML nodes are considered in the translated XSLT stylesheet in the same way as the identities of XML nodes in the original XQuery expression.

Whenever the **is** operator occurs in the XQuery expression, it is necessary to pre-process the source document in order to add a new attribute `t:id` containing an unambiguous identifier to every XML element, and post-process the result generated by the XSLT stylesheet in order to remove the attribute `t:id`. Therefore, the **is** operator can be translated to the = operator evaluated on the attribute `t:id`.

When elements are created as intermediate results, the translated XSLT stylesheet does not provide a mechanism to set the `t:id` attributes of these elements. Using the **is** operator works in these cases (see Example 4). In the case where we have to consider both intermediate results and the identity of XML nodes of the input XML document, we translate the **is** operator to two operations concatenated with the **or** operator (see Example 5). One operation compares the `t:id` attributes the results of which are `false` when there are no `t:id` attributes. The other operation uses the **is** operator the result of which is `false` if two copied XML nodes are compared.

Example 4. (Wrong translation): The result of

```
let $a:= <z/>
return $a is $a
```

is "true", but the result of the wrong translation

```
<?xml version="1.0"?>
<xsl:stylesheet xmlns:xsl='http://www.
w3.org/1999/XSL/Transform'
  version="2.0">
<xsl:template match="/">
  <xsl:variable name='let0a'>
    <xsl:element name='z'/>
  </xsl:variable>
  <xsl:copy-of select="$let0a/@t:id =
$let0a/@t:id"/>
  </xsl:template>
</xsl:stylesheet>
```

is "false".

Example 5. (Translation of the `is` *operator): The following XQuery expression*

```
. is /site[last()]
```

contains the is operator and is translated into

```
(./@t:id = /site[last()]/@t:id) or
(. is /site[last()])
```

Optimization

To reduce translation time, our proposed translation algorithm checks:

- Whether non-element nodes must be stored as intermediate results. Only in this case, we apply the first pre-and post-processing steps presented above. Otherwise, we optimize the translation by avoiding the first pre- and post-processing steps.
- Whether the **is** operator is used. Only in this case, we apply the second pre- and post-processing steps presented above. Otherwise, we optimize the translation by avoiding the second pre- and post processing steps.

Furthermore, if necessary, both pre-processing steps and post-processing steps can be applied in one step.

Handling Intermediate Results and Function Calls

XQuery supports closure by allowing nesting XQuery expressions with full generality. Due to the lack of closure in XSLT, query results must be stored in XSLT variables. The results can then be referenced by the variable names (see Example 6).

Translating parameter bindings in XQuery function calls to the XSLT representation can be solved by mapping the parameter names in the order of their occurrence in the function call to the corresponding `xsl:param` tags (see Example 7).

Example 6. (XSLT stylesheet): The following XSLT stylesheet is the translation of the XQuery expression of Example 2

```
<?xml version="1.0"?>
<xsl:stylesheet version="2.0" xmlns:xsl='http://www.w3.org/1999/XSL/Transform'>
    <xsl:variable name='rootVar1'>
        <xsl:copy-of select='document("auction.xml")'/>
    </xsl:variable>
    <xsl:template match="/">
        <xsl:variable name="for0_aux">
            <xsl:copy-of select='$rootVar1/site/closed_auctions/closed_auc-
tion'/>
        </xsl:variable>
        <xsl:for-each select="$for0_aux/*">
            <xsl:variable name="for0i" select="."/>
            <xsl:if test='$for0i/price/text()>=40'>
                <xsl:copy-of select="$for0i/price"/>
            </xsl:if>
        </xsl:for-each>
    </xsl:template>
</xsl:stylesheet>
```

Example 7. (Translation of a function): The following example shows the translation of a function. While translating a function, we store the function name, parameter names and their order in the list of parameters in a global data structure. Whenever we translate a function call, we access this global data structure in order to retrieve the necessary information of the names and order of the parameters.

```
declare function local:mult($y, $x){ $y * $x };
local:mult(10, 10)
```

is translated into

```
<xsl:template name='mult'>
    <xsl:param name='y'/>
    <xsl:param name='x'/>
    <xsl:copy-of select='$y*$x'/>
</xsl:template>
<xsl:template match="/">
    <xsl:call-template name='mult'>
        <xsl:with-param name='y' select='10'/>
        <xsl:with-param name='x' select='10'/>
    </xsl:call-template>
</xsl:template>
```

Figure 2. The abstract syntax tree of the XQuery expression of Example 2

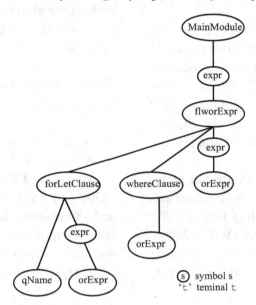

Figure 3. The abstract syntax tree including computed attributes showing the translation of the XQuery expression of Example 2 into the XSLT stylesheet of Example 6

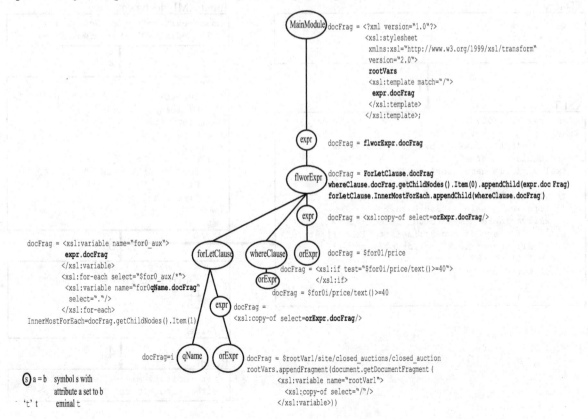

Translation of an XQuery Expression

We execute the translation from an XQuery expression to an XSLT stylesheet in two phases. In phase one, we parse the XQuery expression using the grammar given in (W3C, 2007b) in order to generate the abstract syntax tree of the XQuery expression. As an example, see the XQuery expression in Example 2 and its abstract syntax tree in Figure 2.

In phase two, we evaluate an attribute grammar on the abstract syntax tree, which describes the translation. After evaluating this, a DOM (World Wide Web Consortium (W3C), 2004a) representation of the translated XSLT stylesheet is stored in an attribute of the root node. Figure

3 presents the evaluation of attributes for every node in the abstract syntax tree of the XQuery expression in Example 2. Example 6 also presents the final result of the translation process.

Processing of the Translated XSLT Stylesheet

Our overall approach to translating XQuery expressions to XSLT stylesheets and the execution of the translated XSLT stylesheets consists of an XQuery-to-XSLT translation (Step 1 in Figure 4) and a three-step transformation process including the pre-processing step of the input XML document (Step 2), the execution of the translated XSLT stylesheet (Step 3) and the post-processing

Figure 4. The process of executing the translated XSLT stylesheet: (1) Translation from XQuery to XSLT, (2) pre-processing step of the input XML document, (3) processing of the translated XSLT stylesheet, and (4) post-processing step from the intermediate result to the final result.

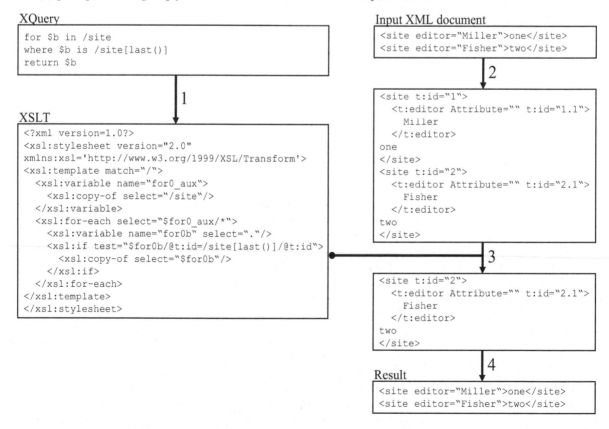

step applied to the result of the XSLT stylesheet (Step 4). In the described cases, we can avoid the pre-processing step (Step 2) and the post-processing step (Step 4).

Experimental Results

We carried out several experiments using the standard benchmark XMark (Schmidt et al., 2002) in order to compare the execution times of original queries and their translated expressions. We summarize only the experimental results here and refer the interested reader to (Klein et al., 2005) for a detailed presentation of the experimental results. In most cases, the executions of the translated expressions are somewhat slower than those of the original queries. The pre-processing and post-processing steps can be avoided in most cases, and the optimized processing without pre-processing and post-processing steps is 13% faster than with pre-processing and post-processing steps.

TRANSLATION FROM XSLT STYLESHEETS TO XQUERY EXPRESSIONS

In this section, we propose a translation from XSLT stylesheets to XQuery expressions. The translated XQuery expression has to simulate different functionalities of XSLT. Since the XQuery language does not support templates, the translated XQuery expression has to simulate the *template selection process* (see Section 4). For the template selection process, we present two different approaches: the *match node sets approach* and the *reverse pattern approach*. Furthermore, we describe how to simulate the use of parameters

Example 8. Relative and absolute part of an XPath expression

> Let I be (/a | b)/@c. The relative part of I is rp(I)= b/@c, the absolute part of I is ap(I)=/a/@c.

of XSLT templates in XQuery. Besides simple XSLT instructions that can be easily translated to an XQuery expression, some complex XSLT instructions do not have corresponding functions with the same functionality in XQuery. We outline how to use an XQuery runtime library of those functions that simulate these complex XSLT instructions. Finally, the overall translation process is described.

Match Node Sets Approach

In order to test whether a template t matches a current input XML node $c, the match node sets approach checks whether $c is contained in a pre-computed node set called the *match node set* of t. The match node set of t contains all nodes that could be matched by t.

Definition 2 (*relative and absolute part of an XPath expression*): An XPath expression I can be divided into a *relative part* rp(I) and an *absolute part* ap(I) (both of which may be empty) in such a way that rp(I) contains only relative path expressions, ap(I) contains only absolute path expressions, and the union of ap(I) and rp(I), i.e. ap(I)|rp(I), is equivalent to I. This means that applying I and applying ap(I)|rp(I) will return the same node set for all XML documents and for all context nodes in the current XML document.

Definition 3 (*match node set*): The *match node set* of a template <xsl:template match=M> are those XML nodes, which are matched by M.

Proposition 1 (*match node set*): Given a template <xsl:template match=M>. If the absolute part of M and the relative part of M are non-empty, i.e. ap(M)≠{} and rp(M)≠{}, the match node set of the template can be computed by applying the XPath query

```
ap(M)|/descendant-or-self::node()(/self::
node()|  /attribute::node()|/namespace::
node())/rp(M).
```

If `ap(M)={}` and `rp(M)≠{}`, the match node set of the template can be computed by applying the XPath query

```
/descendant-or-self::node()(
/self::node()  |  /attribute::node()|
/namespace::node())/rp(M).
```

If `ap(M)≠{}` and `rp(M)={}`, the match node set of the template can be computed by applying the XPath query `ap(M)`. If `ap(M)={}` and `rp(M)={}`, the match node set of the template is an empty set.

Proof of Proposition 1: The XPath expression

```
/descendant-or-self::node()(/
self::node()  |  /attribute::node()  |
/namespace::node())
```

returns all XML nodes of an input XML document. All XML nodes that are matched by M are the union (expressed by using the operator "|") of the absolute part of M, `ap(M)`, and of those XML nodes that are returned from the evaluation of M relative to an XML node.

In the case where we have to check only whether patterns match XML nodes of the input XML document, we declare a variable for the match node set of each template so that each match node set is computed only once in the XQuery expression. In the case where we have to check whether patterns match XML nodes of computed variables, we must compute the match node set of a variable after its assignment with a new value. Furthermore, we use the XPath expression `$t intersect $MN` to check whether a current input XML node `$t` is in a match node set `$MN`. The XPath expression `$t intersect $MN` returns the current input XML node `$t` if the current input XML node `$t` is in the given match node set `$MN`.

Example 9 (translation from XSLT to XQuery using the match node sets approach): As an example, see Figure 5 and Figure 6. The XSLT stylesheet of Figure 5 is translated to the XQuery expression of Figure 6 using the match node sets approach.

Figure 5. Example XSLT stylesheet `stringsort.xslt` *of the XSLTMark benchmark*

```
<xsl:stylesheet>
<xsl:template match="table">
  <table>
    <xsl:apply-templates select="row">
      <xsl:sort select="firstname"/>
    </xsl:apply-templates>
  </table>
</xsl:template>

<xsl:template match="*">
  <xsl:copy><xsl:apply-templates/></xsl:copy>
</xsl:template>
</xsl:stylesheet>
```

Figure 6. Translated XQuery expression of the XSLT stylesheet of Figure 7 using the match node sets approach

```
declare variable $doc_node:=fn:doc("E:/db100.xml");
declare variable $matchBuiltIn1 as node()* := $doc_node |
         $doc_node/descendant-or-self::node()/child::*;
declare variable $matchBuiltIn2 as node()* :=
  $doc_node/descendant-or-self::node()/text()|
  $doc_node/descendant-or-self::node()/attribute::node();
declare variable $match1 as node()* :=
  $doc_node/descendant-or-self::node()(/self::node()|
    /attribute::node()|/namespace::node())/table;
declare variable $match2 as node()* :=
  $doc_node/descendant-or-self::node()(/self::node()|
    /attribute::node()|/namespace::node())/*;
declare variable $noValue := <root>NOVALUE</root>;

declare function local:paramTest($name as item()*, $select as item()*) as item()* {
  if(fn:empty($name)) then $select
  else if(fn:compare(fn:string($name),xs:string
        ("NOVALUE"))= 0) then ()
      else $name
};

declare function local:copy($n as node(), $value as item()*)as item()*{
  if($n instance of element()) then element {name($n)} { $value }
else if($n instance of attribute()) then
    attribute {name($n)} {xs:string($n)}
  else if($n instance of text()) then xs:string($n)
  else if($n instance of comment()) then comment {xs:string($n)}
  else if($n instance of processing-instruction())
      then processing-instruction {name($n)} {xs:string($n)}
  else ()
};

declare function local:builtInTemplate1($t as node(), $param as item()*) as item()* {
 let $gerg:=local:apply_templates($t/child::*,$noValue)
 return $gerg
};

declare function local:builtInTemplate2($t as node(), $param as item()*) as item()* {
 let $gerg := xs:string($t) return $gerg
};
```

continued on following page

Figure 6. continued

```
declare function local:template1($t as node(), $param as item()*) as item()* {
 let $zerg1 := element table{
  let $erg1 := $t/(row)
  let $erg21 := for $t in $erg1
                order by $t/firstname ascending
                return $t
  let $zerg1:=local:apply _ templates($erg21,$noValue)
  let $gerg := ($zerg1) return $gerg }
 let $gerg := ($zerg1) return $gerg
};


declare function local:template2($t as node(), $param as item()*) as item()* {
 let $zerg1 :=
  let $erg1 := $t/(child::node())
  let $erg21 := $erg1
  let $zerg1:=local:apply _ templates($erg21,$noValue)
  let $gerg := ($zerg1)
  return local:copy($t, $gerg)
 let $gerg := ($zerg1) return $gerg
};


declare function local:apply _ templates($n as node()*, $param as item()*)as item()* {
  for $t in $n
  return if($t intersect $match1) then local:template1($t, $param)
         else if($t intersect $match2) then local:template2($t, $param)
         else if($t intersect $matchBuiltIn1)
              then local:builtInTemplate1($t, $param)
         else if($t intersect $matchBuiltIn2)
              then local:builtInTemplate2($t, $param)
         else ()
};

let $doc:=$doc _ node
return local:apply _ templates($doc,$noValue)
```

The XQuery function local:apply _ templates simulates the <xsl:apply-templates> XSLT instruction using the match node sets approach. local:apply _ templates contains the test of whether the pattern of a template matches the current input node $t in $t intersect $match1 for the first template, $t intersect $match2 for the second template, and $t intersect $matchBuiltIn1 and $t intersect $matchBuiltIn2 for the built-in templates (see bold face part of Figure 6). The functions local: builtInTemplate1 and local:builtInTemplate2 simulate the built-in templates of XSLT. local:template1 and local:template2 contain the translation of the user-defined templates of Figure 5. The translated XQuery expression does not consider different modes for the call of templates as the original XSLT stylesheet does not use different modes. In general, the function local:apply_templates must have an additional mode parameter and must consider the value of mode and the modes of the XSLT templates for calling a template. The function local:paramTest is used for the simulation of parameters in an XSLT stylesheet. The function local:copy is a function of the runtime library that simulates the <xsl:copy> XSLT instruction.

Reverse Pattern Approach

The computation of the match node sets is time consuming. With the *reverse pattern approach*,

we avoid the computation of match node sets. In order to test whether a template t with a match attribute E matches a current input XML node stored in $c, the reverse pattern approach checks whether $c[E^{-1}]\neq\emptyset, where E^{-1} is the *reverse pattern* of E.

Example 10 (translation when using the reverse pattern approach): When using the reverse pattern approach, the translated XQuery expression in Figure 6 of the XSLT stylesheet presented in Figure 5 does not contain the declaration of the variables $matchBuiltIn1, $matchBuiltIn2, $match1 and $match2 compared to the translation of the match node sets approach presented in Figure 6. Furthermore, we translate the function local:apply_templates to the one given in Figure 7 instead of the one given in Figure 6.

We present an extended variant of the approaches in (Moerkotte, 2002) and in (Fokoue et al., 2005) for a superset of the XPath patterns of XSLT. In comparison to the approaches presented in (Moerkotte, 2002) and (Fokoue et al., 2005),

Figure 7. Function local:apply_templates *when using the reverse pattern approach*

```
        declare function local:apply_templates($n as node()*, $param as
item()*)
            as item()* {
    for $t in $n
    return if($t[self::table[self instance of element()*]/parent::node()])
    then local:template1($t, $param)
    else if($t[self::*[self instance of element()*]/parent::node()])
    then local:template2($t, $param)
    else if($t is root($t) or $t/self::element())
    then local:builtInTemplate1($t, $param)
    else if($t/self::text() or $t/self::attribute())
    then local:builtInTemplate2($t, $param)
    else ()
    };
```

we present the general rules for generating the reverse patterns.

To determine the reverse pattern of a given XPath expression, we first define the reverse axes of each XPath axis as shown in Figure 4.

Definition 4 (*reverse axes of each XPath axis*): The *reverse axes* of each given XPath axis are defined in the middle column of Figure 8.

Note that the parent of an attribute node or a namespace node is its element node, but an attribute or namespace node is not a child of its element node. Therefore, attribute nodes and namespace nodes cannot be accessed by the child or descendant axes, and also not by the descendant-or-self axis if the attribute node or namespace node is not the current context node. An attribute node can be accessed only by the attribute axis and a namespace node only by the namespace axis. Thus, there is more than one reverse axis of the ancestor, ancestor-or-self or parent axes (see Figure 8).

The reverse axis of the attribute axis, the child axis and the namespace axis is the parent axis, which does not distinguish between attribute nodes, namespace nodes and other nodes (in comparison to the original axis). Therefore, we use an *additional test* (see Definition 5) in the definition of the reverse pattern (see Definition 6) to distinguish between different node types.

Definition 5 (*additional test*): The *additional test* of a given XPath axis is defined in the right column of Figure 8.

Figure 8. Reverse axes and additional test of an XPath axis

Axis A	Reverse Expressions of A	Additional Test
ancestor	1) descendant 2) descendant-or-self::node()/attribute 3) descendant-or-self::node()/namespace	[self **instance of** element()*]
ancestor-or-self	1) descendant-or-self 2) descendant-or-self::node()/attribute 3) descendant-or-self::node()/namespace	
attribute	parent	[self **instance of** attribute()*]
child	parent	[self **instance of** element()*]
descendant	ancestor	[self **instance of** element()*]
descendant-or-self	ancestor-or-self	
following	preceding	[self **instance of** element()*]
following-sibling	preceding-sibling	
namespace	parent	[**not**(self **instance of** element()*) **and not**(self **instance of** attribute()*)]
Parent	1) child 2) attribute 3) namespace	[self **instance of** element()*]
Preceding	following	[self **instance of** element()*]
preceding-sibling	following-sibling	
Self	self	

Definition 6 (*reverse pattern of an XPath expression*): The *reverse pattern* of a given XPath expression is computed as follows. At first, we transform the XPath expression into its long form. If there are disjunctions ("|") in the XPath expression, which do not occur in the scope of any filter expression, we factor out the disjunctions and reverse each expression of the disjunctions separately. Note that we do not have to consider disjunctions ("|") in filter expressions, as filter expressions remain unchanged in the reverse pattern. The whole reverse pattern is the disjunction of all separately reversed expressions. Without disjunctions, a relative XPath expression $E_{relative}$ has the form

$$\texttt{axis}_1\texttt{::test}_1\texttt{[F}_{11}\texttt{]}\ldots\texttt{[F}_{1n1}\texttt{]/axis}_2\texttt{::test}_2\texttt{[F}_{21}\texttt{]}\ldots$$
$$\texttt{[F}_{2n2}\texttt{]/}\ldots\texttt{/axis}_m\texttt{::test}_m\texttt{[F}_{m1}\texttt{]}\ldots\texttt{[F}_{mnm}\texttt{]},$$

and an absolute XPath expression $E_{absolute}$ has the form

$$\texttt{/axis}_1\texttt{::test}_1\texttt{[F}_{11}\texttt{]}\ldots\texttt{[F}_{1n1}\texttt{]/axis}_2\texttt{::test}_2\texttt{[F}_{21}\texttt{]}\ldots$$
$$\texttt{[F}_{2n2}\texttt{]/}\ldots\texttt{/axis}_m\texttt{::test}_m\texttt{[F}_{m1}\texttt{]}\ldots\texttt{[F}_{mnm}\texttt{]}$$

where $\texttt{axis}_i$ are XPath axes, $\texttt{test}_i$ are node tests and F_{ij} are filter expressions. The reverse pattern of $E_{relative}$ and of $E_{absolute}$ is

$$\texttt{self::test}_m\texttt{[F}_{m1}\texttt{]}\ldots\texttt{[F}_{mnm}\texttt{]T}_m\texttt{/}$$
$$\texttt{(raxis}_{m1}\texttt{::test}_{m-1}\texttt{|}\ldots\texttt{|raxis}_{mpm}\texttt{::test}_{m-1}\texttt{)[F}_{(m-1)1}\texttt{]}\ldots\texttt{[F}_{(m-1)nm-1}\texttt{]T}_{m-1}\texttt{/}\ldots\texttt{/}$$
$$\texttt{(raxis}_{21}\texttt{::test}_1\texttt{|}\ldots\texttt{|raxis}_{2p2}\texttt{::test}_1\texttt{)[F}_{11}\texttt{]}\ldots\texttt{[F}_{1n1}\texttt{]T}_1\texttt{/}$$
$$\texttt{(raxis}_{11}\texttt{::node()|}\ldots\texttt{|raxis}_{1p1}\texttt{::node())~T}_{root},$$

Example 11. Reverse pattern: The reverse pattern of `child::object` *is*

```
self::object[self instance of element()*]/parent::node(),
```

the reverse pattern of `/` *is*

```
self::node()[self::node() is root()],
```

and the reverse pattern of

```
/child::contains/child::object[text()='entryXY']|
ancestor::object[attribute::name='cockpit']
```

is

```
self::object[text()='entryXY'][self instance of element()*]
/parent::contains[self instance of element()*]
/parent::node()[self::node is root()]           |
self::object[attribute::name='cockpit']
[self instance of element()*]
/(descendant::node()                             |
  descendant-or-self::node()/attribute::node()   |
  descendant-or-self::node()/namespace::node()).
```

where T_{root} is [self::node() is root()] for $E_{absolute}$ and T_{root} is the empty expression for $E_{relative}$, $raxis_{i1} \ldots raxis_{ipi}$ are the reverse axes of $axis_i$, and T_i is the additional test of $axis_i$ as outlined in Figure 8, or T_i is the empty expression if there is no additional test of $axis_i$.

Simulating the Use of Parameters

While XSLT binds parameters in calls of functions and templates by parameter names, XQuery binds parameters in function calls by parameter positions. Furthermore, XQuery functions, especially the local:apply_templates function, do not support an arbitrary number of parameters. Therefore, we have to simulate named parameters using a data structure containing the names and values of the parameters. As an example, for the template call

```
<xsl:apply-templates select="*">
    <xsl:with-param  name="a1"
select="$a"/>
  <xsl:with-param name="a2">
   <xsl:copy-of select="$a"/>
  </xsl:with-param>
</xsl:apply-templates>
```

we use the following data structure for the simulation of parameters

```
<root>
  <a1> value of $a </a1>
  <a2> value of $a </a2>
</root>
```

This data structure is generated by the following translated XQuery expression:

```
let $a := $t/(*)
let $erg1 := $t/(*)
let $erg21 := $erg1
let $newParam :=  element root {
  element a1 { $a }, element a2 {
```

```
    let $erg1 := $a
    let $zerg1 := local:copy_of($erg1)
    let $gerg :=  ($zerg1) return $gerg
} }
  let $zerg1 :=(local:apply_templates($er
g21,$newParam))
  return $zerg1
```

In general, the parameters are stored in an XML tree with the root element <root>. The parameters are the children of the root element containing the values of the parameters. The data structure used is as follows

```
<root>
    <PARAM-NAME_1>PARAM_1</PARAM-
NAME_1>
      ...
    <PARAM-NAME_n>PARAM_n</PARAM-
NAME_n>
  </root>
```

where PARAM-NAME_i and PARAM_i represent the name and value, respectively, of the i-th parameter. In order to access the parameters, we use the function local:paramTest(...) given in Figure 6.

Due to the simplicity of the translation approach, the simulation of parameters for templates does not work correctly in rare cases. Let us consider the parameter a1 in the example above. In XSLT, the identities of the XML nodes of the variable $a remain the same, but the identities of the copied XML nodes in the data structure used for the translated XQuery expression differ from the ones in $a. Thus, we do not retrieve the same result when the XML nodes of the parameter a1 are compared with the XML nodes of $a by the XPath operators is, <<, or >>. In order to avoid this problem, we propose three different strategies, each of which has its own specific advantages and disadvantages. First, the function local:apply_templates could have a large list of parameters to represent all possible parameters in the XSLT stylesheet. This solution does not work if the parameter name depends on the input. Second, the function `local:apply_templates` could be inlined so that functions that simulate the templates with different numbers of parameters could be called. In general, this solution does also not work if the parameter name depends on the input. Third, the identity of an XML node can be stored in an extra attribute that is copied in the case of parameter `a1` similar to the pre-processing step and post-processing step discussed in Section 5 for the XQuery to XSLT translation. The XPath operators `is`, `<<`, or `>>` must then be replaced with operators that operate on this extra identity attribute. This solution is time consuming because of the extra pre-processing and post-processing steps.

Runtime Library

The proposed translator uses a runtime library of XQuery functions, which simulate certain XSLT instructions. The runtime library includes functions to execute the XSLT instructions `<xsl:copy>` and `<xsl:copy-of>`. The function simulating `<xsl:copy>` is given in Figure 6. See Figure 9 for the function simulating `<xsl:copy-of>`.

The complex XSLT instructions `<xsl:number>` and `<xsl:message>` are also candidates for functions of the runtime library, which have not yet been implemented in our prototype.

Translation Process

The translation process is executed in three phases as follows. In phase one, we parse the XSLT stylesheet in order to generate its abstract syntax tree. As an example, Figure 10 shows the abstract syntax tree of the XSLT stylesheet of Figure 5. In phase two, the function `local:apply_templates` is generated using the match node sets approach or using the reverse pattern

Figure 9: Function simulating `<xsl:copy-of>`

```
declare function local:copy_of($n as node()*)as item()*{
  for $t in $n return
  if($t instance of element())then
    let $next := ($t/child::node()|$t/attribute::node())
    let $new := element {name($t)}{local:copy_of($next)}
    return $new
  else if($t instance of attribute()) then
    let $new := attribute {name($t)} {xs:string($t)}
    return $new
  else if($t instance of text()) then
    let $new := xs:string($t) return $new
  else if($t instance of comment())then
    let $new := comment {xs:string($t)} return $new
  else if($t instance of processing-instruction())
  then let $new := processing-instruction {name($t)}{xs:string($t)}
      return $new
    else () };
```

approach. In phase three, we apply an attribute grammar to the abstract syntax tree of the XSLT stylesheet. This attribute grammar describes how to transform XSLT instructions to simple XQuery statements or to a call to functions of the runtime library.

Experimental Results

We carried out several experiments using the standard benchmark XSLTMark (Developer, 2005) in order to compare the execution times of original queries and their translated expressions. We summarize only the experimental results here and refer the interested reader to (Bettentrupp et al., 2006) for a detailed presentation of the experimental results. In most cases, the executions of the translated expressions are slightly slower than those of the original queries. In rare cases, the translated XQuery expressions using the reverse pattern approach with the XQuery evalu-

ator Qizx are slightly faster than the execution of the original XSLT stylesheet. Except for rare cases, the reverse pattern approach is faster than the match node sets approach for the translated XQuery expressions.

BACKGROUND OF TRANSLATIONS BETWEEN XQUERY AND XSLT

XPath 2.0 (W3C, 2007b) is known to be turing-complete (see (Gottlob et al., 2005)), i.e., XPath 2.0 is already expressive enough to simulate XQuery and XSLT. Thus, XQuery and also XSLT (2.0), which embed XPath 2.0, can simulate expressions of the other language, too.

Contributions already exist, which compare the two languages, XSLT and XQuery. Lenz (2004) shows that many XQuery constructs can easily be mapped to XSLT, but presents only examples of mappings and does not provide an

Figure 10. Abstract syntax tree of the XSLT stylesheet of Figure 5

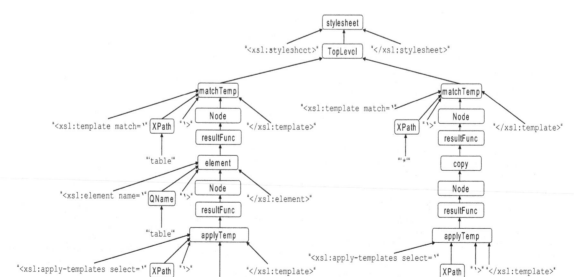

algorithm for translating XQuery expressions to XSLT stylesheets.

Lechner et al. (2001) and Klein et al. (2005) present the algorithms of translating XQuery expressions into XSLT stylesheets.

Saxon (Kay, 2007) is a processor for both XQuery expressions and XSLT stylesheets. At first, Saxon translates an XQuery expression or an XSLT stylesheet to an object model, where most but not all components are common for XQuery and XSLT. After that, Saxon executes the objects of the object model in order to retrieve the result. (Kay, 2007) does not implement a source-to-source translation as we propose. Therefore, (Kay, 2007) cannot be used in other existing tools that natively support only one of the languages, either XQuery or XSLT when the language not being supported is needed.

(Moerkotte, 2002) describes how XSL processing can efficiently be incorporated into database management systems. We extend the reverse pattern approach of (Moerkotte, 2002) by all axes of XPath. Furthermore, we introduce the match node sets approach. (Moerkotte, 2002) proposes the use of tree pattern queries, which we do not consider here.

Bettentrupp et al. (2006) and Fokoue et al. (2005) describe translations from XSLT stylesheets to XQuery expressions. In comparison with Fokoue et al. (2005), we additionally introduce the match node sets approach, which is an alternative approach to checking whether a pattern of a template matches the current XML node. Furthermore, we describe the general rules for determining the reverse pattern of an axis.

Jain et al. (2002) describes a prototype, which translates XSLT programs to SQL statements. Jain et al. (2002) does not deal with a comparison or translation between the XML transformation languages, XSLT and XQuery.

COMMON ISSUES OF XSLT AND XQUERY AND FUTURE TRENDS OF XSLT AND XQUERY

In this section, based on the experiences with translations between XQuery and XSLT, we point out the common issues of XSLT and XQuery and the kinds of transferable results. Examples include indexes, compression of XML data, streaming evaluation of queries and transformations respectively, and full text search. Saxon (Kay, 2007) uses a common core of classes for the processing of XQuery expressions and XSLT stylesheets, which is a hint for transferable results between XQuery and XSLT. Since XSLT and XQuery share XPath as underlying path expression language, many of their common issues are related to XPath.

Firstly, we address some research issues concerning XPath. (Gottlob et al., 2005) studies the complexity of XPath and states that XPath query processing is PTime-complete. For the optimization of queries, it is very important to be able to decide whether an expression is satisfiable, contains another expression, or intersects with another expression. (Benedikt et al., 2005) investigates the satisfiability problem of an XPath expression in the presence of (possibly restricted) DTDs. Considering the presence or absence of different axes, negations and recursion, it is shown that the complexity of the satisfiability problem of an XPath expression ranges from PTime to undecidable. (Genevès et al., 2007) presents an algorithm for the satisfiability problem for XPath queries with a complexity of $2^{O(n)}$ in the length of the formula while covering all XPath fragments except counting and comparisons between data values. The analysis of the containment problem and the satisfiability problem was broadened to XPath 2.0 in (Cate et al., 2007). Recently, an efficient schema-based solution was implemented to filter unsatisfiable XPath expression (Groppe J. and Groppe S., 2008). (Groppe and Linnemann, 2008) extends the approach in (Groppe J. and Groppe S., 2008) to filter the XPath queries with hidden conflicting constraints. The open issues here are to extend the existing results to detect more unsatisfiable queries or to support a larger subset of XPath and of the used schema languages.

Other approaches to optimize XPath queries include approximation, views and indexes. Approximation can be done e. g. by the use of pre-filtering techniques (Huang et al., 2006) or by the use of data summaries (Baralis et al., 2007). Optimizing queries by rewriting using materialized views, e.g. (Arion et al., 2007), is another aspect that XQuery and XSLT share. Views can be materialized to speed up evaluation of queries but there are also approaches to deal with virtual views (Shao et al., 2007) with the intention of saving memory. A formal analysis of the evaluation of XPath queries on top of materialized XPath views can be found in (Xu et al., 2005). Indexes are data structures used in databases for speeding up query evaluation. Since XQuery is usually used for querying databases, many contributions deal with optimizing the execution time of XQuery queries using XML indexes (e.g. Hammerschmidt et al., 2005; Min et al., 2005; Catania, 2005; Pettovello et al., 2006), the results of which are mostly transferable to XSLT. Furthermore, XSLT processors can speed up evaluation by the use of the built-in functions `xsl:key` and `key()` that generates and uses an index. Thus, research results concerning indexes in the area of native XML databases are typically transferable to XSLT.

Another research issue of XQuery and XSLT share is the processing of heterogeneous data. Camillo et al. (2003) propose the use of a common conceptual schema for different (but semantically similar) XML schemas and introduce the language Conceptual XPath (CXPath) for querying this conceptual schema. Camillo et al. (2003) also describe how queries posed in CXPath can be mapped to XPath. This approach is extended in dos Santos Mello and Heuser (2005) by considering a semi-automatic approach to guarantee a certain quality of the common conceptual schema.

An open issue is how these approaches can be extended from XPath to XQuery or XSLT.

Both languages, XQuery and XSLT, also benefit from research into full text search. Although both query languages provide the (same) built-in function `matches()`, there are several use cases where a more powerful full text search feature would be useful (see e.g. (Guo et al., 2003) and (Amer-Yahia et al., 2004)). Additionally, the standardization of full text search in XQuery and XPath has currently the status of a working draft at the W3C (W3C, 2007).

The motivation for compression of XML data is its verbosity. Compressors for XML data can be divided into two groups: those which produce queryable compressed XML data (see (Arion et al. 2007) for a survey) and those which do not. Many approaches (e.g. (Tolani et al., 2002; Min et al., 2003; Arion et al., 2007)) support only a subset of XPath, but there are also approaches, which support full XPath 1.0 or even extend it by constructs like union or grouping operators in the return clause like XQZip (see (Bolz, 2004)) or XCQ (see (Ng et al., 2006)).

Evaluators for streaming data evaluate queries as much as possible on the data, which the evaluator has already received. While most of the efforts concerned with streaming XML data concentrate on querying (Josifovski et al., 2005; Boettcher et al., 2007; Min et al., 2007), there are also approaches which allow streaming updates of XML data (Becker, 2003).

Compressing and streaming of XML data are areas where both languages, XSLT and XQuery, benefit from new results in research. Open issues here are to investigate how compressing and streaming XML data can further optimize the execution time of XSLT and XQuery processing.

Benchmarks provide a means of comparing XQuery and XSLT with regard to performance. While there exist several approaches comparing either XQuery or XSLT processors, there are also efforts to compare whole database implementations (Nicola et al., 2007). A comparison of different benchmarks for XML-capable database systems can be found in (Lu et al., 2005). Most benchmarks are XQuery benchmarks. Thus, an open issue is whether the XQuery benchmarks can be easily adapted to XSLT. Another open question deals with XSLT-specific aspects of benchmarks.

SPECIAL ISSUES OF XSLT AND FUTURE TRENDS OF XSLT

In this section, we point out the special issues for XSLT in program analysis and for incorporating XSLT processing in database systems like RDBMS, ORDBMS and OODBMS.

Recent research in XSLT program analysis concentrates on statically analysing the validation of XSLT results relative to given output schemas and the termination, the reachability and possible invalid calling relationships of XSLT programs. Furthermore, recent contributions focus on intersection testers for XPath expressions in order to determine possibly called templates and the optimized execution of XSLT patterns (e.g. (Moerkotte, 2002)).

XSLT has been proven to be Turing complete (Kepser, 2004), such that a precise static analysis is often impossible to decide. Program analysis therefore depends on high precision approximations of the behaviour of the XSLT program.

An approximation solution for the validation problem has been introduced in (Møller et al., 2007). The problem described here is to check whether the result of a given XSLT stylesheet and an input schema is valid relative to a given output schema. Møller et al. introduce a graph-based static validation solution. In the first step, the given stylesheet is simplified to a subset of XSLT core features, named ReducedXSLT. The static validation then relies on a former presented algorithm by (Christensen et al., 2003). The approach produces highly precise approximation results and has been generalized to handle XSLT

2.0 and XML Schema. The validation problem can be extended by trying to determine the correct output schema for a given XSLT stylesheet and an input schema. A first solution for this question has been proposed in (Groppe S. et al., 2006), which describes a static program analysis in order to determine the output schema specified in XML Schema. Future work on validation and determination of XSLT output schemas will therefore concentrate on addressing rare cases and extended XSLT features.

Another static XSLT program analysis approach has been introduced by Ce Dong and James Bailey (Dong and Bailey, 2004). This graph-based analysis solution handles four questions about the reachability, invalid calling relationships, missing templates and the termination of and in XSLT programs. For this purpose, a given schema and the stylesheet are processed to build a Refined Template and Association Graph (Refined-TAG). The Refined-TAG is then used directly or by comparing it to the former built stylesheet graph to obtain information about one of the given analysis questions. In contrast to the static validation approach, this solution limits the usable XSLT syntax.

The determination of possibly called templates is a special issue for XSLT, i.e. the determination of those templates with template head `<xsl:template match=B/>`, which may be called from an `<xsl:apply-templates select=A/>` XSLT instruction. A static test can decide, which templates are not called by proving $A \cap B = \{\}$. Based on a subset of core XPath, which is defined in (Gottlob et al., 2002), and the usage of a given DTD schema, (Böttcher, 2004) describes how to test the intersection $A \cap B = \{\}$. The presented solution generates a DTD Graph structure with filter implications on each node for the first XPath expression. Then the final algorithm searches for a filter-compatible path that can be taken by the second XPath expression, within the previous graph. If such a path does not exist, the intersection of both XPath expressions is empty for every valid XML document. In comparison to (Böttcher, 2004), (Hammerschmidt et al., 2005) presents an XPath intersection tester, which does not use schema information.

Optimization is an important query processing aspect irrespective of the examined query language. There has been recent work in the field of algebraic XQuery optimization (e.g. (May et al., 2006) and (Re et al. 2006)). For XSLT, the proposal of an appropriate algebra and further optimization techniques is still an open issue. Nevertheless, it could benefit from previous work on XQuery optimization and especially from work on XPath optimization, like the algebraic optimization of nested XPath expressions (Brantner et al. 2006).

Another special issue for XSLT is the incorporation of XSLT processing into database systems like RDBMS, ORDBMS and OODBMS. The goal is to efficiently process XSLT stylesheets on XML documents, which are stored in another data model in the database. This problem was first discussed in (Moerkotte, 2004). Existing database systems provide facilities for managing XML documents. Processing these XML documents often leads to retrieving the whole document and processing it outside the database system. Especially for incorporating XSLT stylesheet processing, it is often not necessary to retrieve the whole XML document, which is time-consuming. The approach in (Moerkotte, 2004) describes how to incorporate stylesheet processing within the database system by translating stylesheets to algebraic expressions. (Liu and Novoselsky, 2006) presents an approach for rewriting XSLT into optimised XQuery, in order to make use of existing database processing strategies for XQuery, which have been widely studied. Rewriting XSLT to optimised XQuery is based on the former work presented in (Fokoue et al., 2005). This differs from the work that has been presented in the last sections of this chapter, because only a reduced set of XSLT core features can be translated directly to XQuery (see Section 7). Neither does the presented technique handle re-

cursive XML document structures automatically, and works without the usage of XML schema. Future work needs to analyse different storage models for different kinds of XSLT stylesheets.

SUMMARY AND CONCLUSION

We show that translations between XSLT stylesheets and XQuery expressions are possible in both directions. Thus, XSLT is as powerful as XQuery, and XQuery is as powerful as XSLT. Therefore, the user can choose between XSLT and XQuery according to personal preference. In principal, scientific results can be transferred from XSLT to XQuery and from XSLT to XQuery. Thus, XQuery and XSLT have many issues in common. However, some research issues are more specific to XSLT or to XQuery, as some language constructs do not even occur in the other language like the templates of XSLT, which are simulated by translated code in XQuery. Research contributions dealing with these language constructs like optimizations or static analysis are particular to XSLT. Furthermore, some research for certain basic problems like the intersection test of XPath expressions become more important, which are parts of the research for the special language constructs like a static analysis of the templates that might be called from an `<xsl:apply-templates>` XSLT instruction. Research on basic problems as well as the research into all-embracing special constructs of these languages is still ongoing in order to deal with more cases, which are increasingly complicated.

REFERENCES

Amer-Yahia, S., Botev, C., & Shanmugasundaram, J. (2004). Texquery: A full-text search extension to xquery. In *WWW*, (pp. 583-594).

Apache Software Foundation (2005a). *Cocoon.* http://cocoon.apache.org

Apache Software Foundation (2005b). *Xalan-Java.* http://xml.apache.org/xalan-j/index.html

Arion, A., Benzaken, V., Manolescu, I. & Papakonstantinou, Y. (2007a). Structured materialized views for XML queries. In *VLDB,* (pp. 87-98).

Arion, A., Bonifati, A., Manolescu, I., & Pugliese, A. (2007b). Xquec: A query-conscious compressed xml database. In *ACM Trans. Inter. Tech., 7*(2), 10.

Axyana software (2007). Qizx/open version 1.1p7, http://www.xfra.net/qizxopen/.

Baralis, E., Garza, P., Quintarelli, E. & Tanca, L. (2007). Answering xml queries by means of data summaries. In *ACM Trans. Inf. Syst. 25*(3), 10.

Becker, O. (2003). Streaming transformations for xml-stx. In *XMIDX,* (pp. 83-88).

Benedikt, M., Fan, W., & Geerts, F. (2005). Xpath satisfiability in the presence of dtds. In *PODS,* (pp. 25-36).

Bettentrupp, R., Groppe, S., Groppe, J., Böttcher, S., & Gruenwald, L. (2006). A prototype for translating XSLT into XQuery. In *ICEIS,* (pp. 22-29).

Böttcher, S. (2004). Testing intersection of XPath expressions under DTDs, Database Engineering and Applications Symposium, In *IDEAS,* (pp. 401-406).

Böttcher, S., & Steinmetz, R. (2007). Evaluating xpath queries on XML data streams. In *BNCOD,* (pp. 101-113).

Brantner, M., Kanne, C., Moerkotte, G. & Helmer, S. (2006). Algebraic optimization of nested XPath expressions. In *ICDE,* (pp. 128-130).

Camillo, S. D., Heuser, C. A., & dos Santos Mello, R. (2003). Querying heterogeneous XML sources through a conceptual schema. In *ER,* (pp. 186-199).

Catania, B., Maddalena, A., & Vakali, A. (2005). Xml document indexes: A classification. In *IEEE Internet Computing 9*(5), 64-71.

Christensen, A. S., M, A. & Schwartzbach, M. I. (2003). Extending java for high-level Web service construction. In *ACM Trans. Program. Lang. Syst. 25*(6), 814-875.

Developer (2005). *XSLT Mark version 2.1.0,* http://www.datapower.com/xmldev/xsltmark.html

Dong, C., & Bailey, J. (2004). Static analysis of XSLT programs. In *ADC,* (pp. 151-160).

dos Santos Mello, R., & Heuser, C. A. (2005). Binxs: A process for integration of XML schemata. In *CAiSE,* (pp. 151-166).

Fernández, M., & Robie, J. (Eds) (2001). *XQuery 1.0 and XPath 2.0 Data Model.* W3C Working Draft, http://www.w3.org/TR/2001/WD-query-datamodel/

Fernández, M., Siméon, J., Chen. C., Choi, B., Dinoff, R., Gapeyev, V., Marian, A., Michiels, P., Onose, N., Petkanics, D., Radhakrishnan, M., Re, C., Resnick, L., Sur, G., Vyas, A., & Wadler, P. (2007). *Galax 0.7.2.* http://www.galaxquery.org/

Fokoue, A., Rose, K., Siméon, J., & Villard, L. (2005). Compiling XSLT 2.0 into XQuery 1.0. In *WWW,* (pp. 682-691).

Genevès, P., Layaïda, N., & Schmitt, A. (2007). Efficient static analysis of xml paths and types. In *SIGPLAN Not. 42*(6), 342-351.

Gottlob, G., Koch, C., Pichler, R., & Segoufin, L. (2005). The complexity of Xpath query evaluation and xml typing. In *J. ACM 52*(2), 284-335.

Gou, G., & Chirkova, R. (2007). Efficient algorithms for evaluating xpath over streams. In *SIGMOD,* (pp. 269-280).

Groppe, J., & Groppe, S. (2008). Filtering unsatisfiable Xpath queries. In *Data Knowl. Eng.*, *64*(1), 134-169.

Groppe, S., & Groppe, J. (2006). Determining the output schema of an XSLT stylesheet. In *ADBIS Research Communications, 215, CEUR Workshop Proceedings*.

Groppe, J., & Linnemann, V. (2008). Discovering veiled unsatisfiable XPath queries. In *ICEIS*, (pp. 149-158).

Guo, L., Shao, F., Botev, C., & Shanmugasundaram, J. (2003). Xrank: Ranked keyword search over XML documents. In *SIGMOD*, (pp. 16-27).

Gupta, A. K., & Suciu, D. (2003). Stream processing of XPath queries with predicates. In *SIGMOD*, (pp. 419-430).

Hammerschmidt, B. C., Kempa, M., & Linnemann, V. (2005). On the intersection of XPath expressions. In *IDEAS*, (pp. 49-57).

Hammerschmidt, B. C. (2005). KeyX: Selective key-oriented indexing in native XML-databases. Akademische Verlagsgesellschaft Aka GmbH, Berlin, DISDBIS 93.

Huang, C.-H., Chuang, T.-R., Lu, J. J., & Lee, H.-M. (2006). XML evolution: A two-phase XML processing model using XML prefiltering techniques. In *VLDB*, (pp. 1215-1218).

International Organization for Standardization (ISO) (1996). *ISO/IEC 14977:1996: Information technology -- Syntactic metalanguage -- Extended BNF*, http://www.iso.ch/cate/d26153.html

Jain, S., Mahajan, R., & Suciu, D. (2002). Translating XSLT programs to efficient SQL queries. In *WWW*, (pp. 616-626).

Josifovski, V., Fontoura, M., & Barta, A. (2005). Querying XML streams. In *VLDB Journal 14*(2), 197-210.

Kay, M. H. (2007). *Saxon - The XSLT and XQuery Processor*. http://saxon.sourceforge.net

Kepser, S. (2004). A simple proof for the turing-completeness of XSLT and XQuery. In *Extreme markup languages*.

Klein, N., Groppe, S., Böttcher, S., & Gruenwald, L. (2005). A prototype for translating XQuery expressions into XSLT stylesheets. In *ADBIS*, (pp. 238-253).

Lechner, S., Preuner, G., & Schrefl, M. (2001). Translating XQuery into XSLT. In *ER Workshops*, (pp. 239-252).

Lenz, E. (2004). *XQuery: Reinventing the wheel?* http://www.xmlportfolio.com/xquery.html

Liefke, H., & Suciu, D. (1999). *XMill: an Efficient Compressor for XML Data*. University of Pennsylvania, Technical Report MSCIS -99-26.

Liu, Z. H., & Novoselsky, A. (2006). Efficient XSLT processing in relational database system. In *VLDB*, pages 1106-1116.

Lu, H., Yu, J. X., Wang, G., Zheng, S., Jiang, H., Yu, G., & Zhou, A. (2005). What makes the differences: benchmarking XML database implementations. In *ACM Trans. Inter. Tech.*, *5*(1), 154-194.

May, N., Helmer, S., & Moerkotte, G. 2006. Strategies for query unnesting in XML databases. In *ACM Trans. Database Syst. 31*(3), 968-1013.

Microsoft (2007a). *Biztalk*, http://www.biztalk.org

Microsoft (2007b). *SQL Server 2005 Express*, http://www.microsoft.com/sql/express

Min, J.-K., Chung, C.-W., & Shim, K. (2005). An adaptive path index for XML data using the query workload. In *Inf. Syst. 30*(6), 467-487.

Min, J.-K., Park, M.-J., & Chung, C.-W. (2003). Xpress: A queriable compression for XML data. In *SIGMOD*, (pp. 122-133).

Min, J.-K., Park, M.-J., & Chung, C.-W. (2007). Xtream: An efficient multi-query evaluation on streaming XML data. In *Inf. Sci. 177*(17), 3519-3538.

Moerkotte, G. (2002). Incorporating XSL processing into database engines. In *VLDB*, (pp. 107-118).

M, A., Olesen, M. O., & Schwartzbach, M. I. (2007). Static validation of XSL transformations. In *ACM Trans. Program. Lang. Syst., 29*(4), 21.

Ng, W., Lam, W.-Y., Wood, P. T., & Levene, M. (2006). XCQ: A queriable XML compression system. In *Knowl. Inf. Syst. 10*(4), 421-452.

Nicola, M., Kogan, I., & Schiefer, B. (2007). An XML transaction processing benchmark. In *SIGMOD*, (pp. 937-948).

Pettovello, P. M., & Fotouhi, F. (2006). Mtree: an XML XPath graph index. In *SAC*, (pp. 474-481).

Re, C., Simeon, J., & Fernandez, M. (2006). A complete and efficient algebraic compiler for XQuery. In *ICDE,* (pp. 14-28).

Schmidt, A., Waas, F., Kersten, M., Carey, M., Manolescu, I., & Busse, R. (2002). XMark: A benchmark for XML data management. In *VLDB*, (pp. 974-985).

Shanmugasundaram, J., Shekita, E., Barr, R., Carey, M., Lindsay, B., Pirahesh, H., & Reinwald, B. (2001). Efficiently publishing relational data as XML documents. In *VLDB Journal, 10*(2-3), 133-154.

Software AG (2007). *Tamino XML server.* http://www.softwareag.com/de/products/tamino/

Tolani, P., & Haritsa, J. R. (2002). XGRIND: A query-friendly XML compressor. In *ICDE,* (pp. 225-234).

W3C (2004a). *Document object model (DOM) Level 3 Core Specification Version 1.0.* W3C Recommendation, http://www.w3.org/TR/2004/REC-DOM-Level-3-Core-20040407/

W3C (2001). *Extensible stylesheet language (XSL) Version 1.0.* W3C Recommendation, http://www.w3.org/Style/XSL/.

W3C (2004b). *Extensible stylesheet language (XSL) Version 1.1.* W3C Recommendation, http://www.w3.org/TR/xsl11/

W3C (1999a). *XML path language (XPath) Version 1.0.* W3C Recommendation, http://www.w3.org/TR/xpath/

W3C (2007a). *XML path language (XPath) Version 2.0.* W3C Recommendation, http://www.w3.org/TR/xpath20/

W3C (2007b). *XQuery 1.0: An XML Query Language.* W3C Recommendation, http://www.w3.org/TR/xquery/

W3C (2008). *XQuery Update Facility 1.0.* W3C Candidate Recommendation, http://www.w3.org/TR/xquery-update-10/

W3C (1999b). *XSL Transformations (XSLT) Version 1.0.* W3C Recommendation, http://www.w3.org/TR/1999/REC-xslt-19991116, 1999.

W3C (2007c) *XSL Transformations (XSLT) Version 2.0.* W3C Recommendation, http://www.w3.org/TR/xslt20/.

Xu, W., & Özsoyoglu, Z. M. (2005). Rewriting xpath queries using materialized views. In *VLDB*, (pp. 121-132).

Chapter VII
Recent Advances and Challenges in XML Document Routing

Mirella M. Moro
Universidade Federal de Minas Gerais (UFMG), Belo Horizonte, Brazil

Zografoula Vagena
Microsoft Research, UK

Vassilis J. Tsotras
University of California, Riverside, USA

ABSTRACT

Content-based routing is a form of data delivery whereby the flow of messages is driven by their content rather than the IP address of their destination. With the recognition of XML as the standard for data exchange, specialized XML routing services become necessary. In this chapter, the authors first demonstrate the relevance of such systems by presenting different world application scenarios where XML routing systems are needed and/or employed. Then, they present a survey of the current state of the art. Lastly, they attempt to identify issues and problems that have yet to be investigated. Their discussion will help identify open problems and issues and suggest directions for further research in the context of such systems.

INTRODUCTION

Content-based routing is a form of data delivery whereby the flow of messages is driven by their content rather than the IP address of their destination. Specifically, in *XML Routing*, there is a continuous stream of XML messages (usually, one message has one XML document) from data *producers* to *consumers*, without any of the parties having knowledge of the other (Snoeren, 2001). Message transmission is performed by a sophisticated overlay network of application-level, content-based routers (called *message brokers* or *XML routers*) that match data messages against registered client subscriptions, and forward those messages (based on such matching) to output links, i.e. other routers or clients. The task of matching incoming messages to the set of client subscriptions is called *message filtering*.

This form of communication is widely employed by content-based information dissemination services, which are usually instantiated as *publish/subscribe systems* (pub/sub for short). For example, pub/sub systems have created opportunities for new applications such as a plethora of alert and notification services that notify interested users of new products in the market, stock price changes, currency variation, better offer deals and so on. Furthermore, with the expansion of Web services, new pub/sub systems are released every week. For instance, online travel agencies such as *Priceline.com* and *Hotwire.com* inform their clients of price changes and hot deals that take into consideration the subscriber's interests. Likewise, *Ticketmaster.com* sends to its users email alerts about upcoming events and pre-sale information according to the user's signed up artists and locations.

With the recognition of XML as the standard for data exchange, specialized *XML-aware information dissemination services* become necessary (Diao, 2004). These services can be implemented as publish/subscribe systems in which the information to be routed is encoded

Figure 1. General architecture of XML routing system

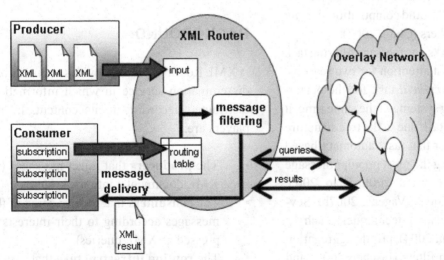

Producers inject XML messages into the system. Consumers subscribe to the system with XML query statements. A router processes the subscriptions, usually by storing and indexing them into a routing table. Then, it evaluates the set of subscriptions over the incoming messages (such processing may include parsing operations and indexing). It then filters the messages and forwards the results to the consumers. Finally, each router also interacts with the overlay network, by forwarding (receiving) queries and results to (from) other routers.

using XML, and the user subscriptions (or profiles) are expressed using XML query languages. Figure 1 illustrates the general architecture of an XML routing system.

Recent research on XML-aware information dissemination has investigated issues related to different parts of the routing system architecture. The most relevant aspects include: the discovery of Semantic communities of users with similar interests (Chand, 2007), the construction of the overlay dissemination network structure (Fenner, 2005; Diao, 2004; Snoeren, 2001), the indexing and aggregation of the profiles within a message broker (Chan, 2002; Diao, 2003; Gong, 2005; Kwon, 2005; Li, 2007; Moro, 2007a; Raj, 2007), the distribution of consumer profiles (Diao, 2004; Li, 2007; Papaemmanouil, 2005; Yoo, 2006), the encoding of the routed messages (Vagena, 2007a; Vagena, 2007b), the message filtering task (Altinel, 2000; Chan, 2002; Diao, 2003; Gong, 2005; He, 2006; Li, 2007; Kwon, 2005; Moro, 2007a; Raj, 2007; Tian, 2004; Vagena, 2007a; Vagena, 2007b), in-situ transformation of the original information (Diao, 2004), and computation sharing among message brokers (Chan, 2007).

Among those works, the message filtering task has received the most attention for two reasons. First, it is the most *critical* task for the performance of the routing system. At the same time, it is the most *complex* task due to the tree structure of the XML data. For that task, automata-based algorithms are among the most popular message matching solutions (Altinel, 2000; Diao, 2003; He, 2006; Vagena, 2007a; Vagena, 2007b). Several alternative matching techniques, such as relational joins (Tian, 2004), profile aggregation (Chan, 2002), bloom filters (Fischer, 2005) and subsequence matching (Raj, 2007; Kwon, 2005; Moro, 2007a) have also been proposed. The goal of these works is scalability with respect to the number of profiles, which is achieved by employing *multi-query processing* methods (Diao, 2003; Diao, 2004; Vagena, 2007a; Vagena, 2007b) as well as early pruning (Moro, 2007a) of irrelevant

profiles. Additionally, the proposals in (Fischer, 2005; Vagena, 2007a; Vagena, 2007b) advertise scalability on the number of messages and design matching techniques which create and operate over *batches* of messages.

In this chapter, we first review the existing work in the field of XML document routing in the context of XML-enabled publish/subscribe systems. Then, we discuss open issues and problems pertaining to the successful deployment of these types of systems. In particular, we intent to (a) present different world application scenarios where XML-enabled pub/sub systems are needed and/or are employed, in order to demonstrate the importance of such systems; (b) survey the proposals that have emerged to date and examine many aspects of pub/sub system deployment; and (c) attempt to identify issues and problems that have yet to be investigated. Our discussion will help identify open problems, relevant issues, and suggest directions for further research into such systems.

BACKGROUND

A XML Routing system provides a content-based dissemination service in which information is distributed according to its content. Its main players are:

- The **producers** that inject messages (with XML documents) into the system.
- The **consumers** that receive some of those messages according to their interests (expressed as XML queries).
- The **routing infrastructure** that forwards messages from the producers to the interested consumers, using specialized content-based routers (or *brokers*).

This kind of routing system is usually instantiated as a publish/subscribe system, where producers *publish* their content and consumers *subscribe* according to their interests using profiles. The infrastructure and flow of messages of a pub/sub system can be centralized or distributed. Figure 2a illustrates the architecture for a centralized pub/sub system, and Figure 2b shows an example of a distributed one. In both cases, each broker performs two main functions: *message filtering* (through profile/subscription matching), and *message routing* (aka. message delivery) according to the message filtering results. Moreover, in the distributed case, each broker is responsible for local clients (both producers and consumers) and is connected to other brokers through an *overlay network*.

A routing system has many design issues, and most decisions depend on the application requirements, such as: type of message content (e.g. attribute-value pairs, fixed-fields, XML messages), profile format (e.g. comparison predicates, XML query), profile storage and distribution, profile

Figure 2. General architecture for centralized and distributed pub/sub systems

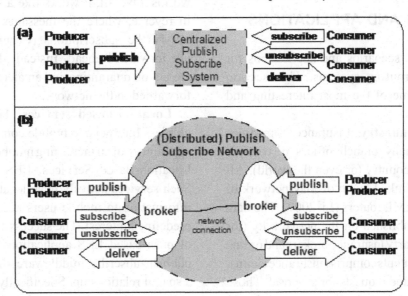

Table 1. Evolution of routing systems in the context of information dissemination

Architecture	Message	Profile	Example
Centralized	Text	Anything	Nasdaq stocks
	Topic + text	Topic	Stocks of IBM
Distributed	Fields + text	Predicates	name = IBM AND price > x
Internet	XML	XML query	//stocks[@name = "IBM" AND @day = "today"]//price[last()]

matching throughput, overlay network design and construction, latency-related metrics, bandwidth consumption constraints, and data quality. For instance, Table 1 exemplifies how routing systems evolved in the context of information dissemination: type of architecture, message content, and profile specification.

Usually, those systems are optimized for a subset of those requirements (architecture, message, profiles, and so on). In this chapter, the focus is on a system where producers inject messages with XML documents and consumers specify their profiles using XML query languages.

SCENARIOS AND APPLICATIONS

There are many scenarios and applications for content-based routing systems. This section summarizes some of the most interesting and recent ones.

Insurance industry. Insurance companies usually have many branch offices distributed throughout the country (or even the world). All offices may be linked by an overlay network of content-based XML routers (Li, 2007). The data messages are published on the network by (for example) third party insurance brokers and online clients. Their contents comprise insurance claims, insurance bids, and requests for proposal. Those data messages are routed toward a currently online, specific expert employee whose interests have been expressed by XML queries. After receiving the messages, the employee will then contact the clients and negotiate the insurance deals.

RSS feeds. (Liu, 2005) characterizes how publish-subscribe systems are used in practice by presenting an analysis of RSS as the first widely deployed publish-subscribe system. The architecture of RSS follows the basic idea of XML routing systems: clients subscribe to a feed that they are interested in and poll the feed periodically to receive updates. RSS content is encoded in XML and displayed by a feed-reader or an RSS-integrated Web browser on the client host. Many news Websites support RSS feeds. Moreover, announcements on Web sites and updates to Weblogs are typically disseminated through RSS. The paper concludes with some insights into the design of publish-subscribe systems.

Security alerts. Recent work on automatic containment of worm spread has explored network-level approaches. Such techniques analyze network traffic and derive a packet classifier that blocks or rate-limits forwarding of worm packets (Costa, 2005). In this scenario, the messages being forwarded are the network packets and the subscriptions are the presence of identifiable worms. Overall, it works like a routing system in reverse, where the messages (packets) that satisfy the subscriptions (worm features) are *not* forwarded ahead. Instead, those messages are put on quarantine and an alert is created and forwarded in the network.

Location-based services. The advance in wireless Internet and mobile computing saw the appearance of an increasing number of intelligent Location-Based Services, LBS (Chen, 2003). Such services actively push location-dependent information to mobile users according to their predefined interest. The successful development of push-based LBS applications depends on a publish/subscribe middleware that can handle a spatial relationship. Specifically, (Chen, 2003) gives two interesting examples of such services: (a) E-coupon, in which a shopping mall sends a promotion message to nearby mobile users, and (b) Mobile Buddy-List, in which a user is notified when a friend in his buddy list is nearby. In such scenarios, the messages are the stream of location of mobile users or devices, and the subscriptions are spatial predicates on location messages.

Air traffic control. (Snoeren, 2001) characterizes a routing system for air traffic control data. A traffic control system receives the aircraft situation feed that provides detailed information about the state of airspace. The messages include information on flight plans, departures, flight location, and landings. A position update is received approximately once a minute for all en route aircraft.

Stock quotes. Probably one of the most known applications of pub/sub systems is the stock market. A stock market system enables trading of company stocks, other securities, and derivatives. In such a system, the messages contain information on stock values and derivatives, and the subscriptions constrain the features that the investors are interested in dealing with. For example, (Wang, 2002) collects and analyzes real-world subscriptions from a major stock quote alert service provider. The data contains approximately 1.48 million subscriptions with 0.29 million unique subscriptions involving 21,741 stock symbols, which characterize the complexity of a real stock trading pub/sub system.

News dissemination. Another famous application for pub/sub systems is news broadcasting (Fenner, 2005). The Internet has thousands of newspapers published electronically every day. They include information of a myriad of topics and places to a variety of readers (local, national and international). Each reader is usually interested in one topic (e.g. entertainment) or a set of topics (e.g. entertainment, financial market and sports). Moreover, each reader wants to be informed of any news that is published according to his/her interests, no matter where or how the newspaper has been published.

STATE OF THE ART REVIEW

XML Routing systems provide a content-based dissemination service in which information is distributed according to its content. Two implicit tasks of XML routing are XML filtering and XML stream processing. The XML Routing problem is also related to pub/sub systems, which have received considerable attention from both the network and the data/information management communities. Hence, a plethora of work on their

efficient deployment has already appeared.

In this section, we provide an overview of some of the most relevant research efforts that surround the XML routing area. Specifically, we start by presenting early work on pub/sub systems (that did not consider XML data), XML routing systems and approaches, and follow this by summarizing routing on peer-to-peer networks.

Early Pub/Sub Systems

As previously mentioned, the requirements for pub/sub systems include the type of messages exchanged and the type of profiles evaluated. In such early systems, events (messages) are usually described as conjunctions of {attribute, value} pairs, and profiles are expressed as selection predicates over the content of events. Considering profiles formed by simple predicates (e.g. value comparison), *SIFT* (Yan, 1999) provided support for matching keyword search queries over large collections of messages. It employed the Event-Condition-Action paradigm to perform profile matching and selective dissemination of information, and since then most systems have followed this basic technique. Other early systems with such features include *Gryphon* (Aguilera, 1999), *Siena* (Carzaniga, 2001), and *LeSubscribe* (Fabret, 2001). All these systems are related to this chapter because they proposed the initial functionalities and optimizations for pub/sub systems. Compared with the XML-based pub/sub systems, the type of messages and queries supported on those systems are very simple and not as expressive.

XML Routing Systems

XML Switch (Snoeren, 2001) is recognized as the *first* XML routing system. It provided the initial definitions of an XML routing system, i.e.:

- An **XML packet** is a single independent XML document

- An **XML stream** is a sequence of XML packets, where each XML packet in a stream can have a different document type definition (DTD);
- **Clients** join the overlay network by specifying an XML query that describes the XML packets they would like to receive;
- The **overlay network** is able to configure itself to deliver the desired XML stream to a client at reasonable cost given reliability goals.

XML Switch builds a content distribution acyclic mesh in which every broker is connected to n parents, receiving duplicate packet streams from each of its parents. It focuses on in-order delivery and network resilience, rather than on efficient XML query processing (which is done using a general-purpose XML toolkit that processes one query at a time).

ONYX (Diao, 2004) establishes an overlay network of brokers that are in charge of routing XML messages sequentially (i.e. with no batching processing). It focuses on the optimization of the network by building a broadcast tree of brokers. The system performs three basic operations. The first operation is the *content-driven routing*, which builds a broadcast tree of brokers in order to avoid flooding of messages to all brokers in the

network. The second operation is an *incremental transformation*, which modifies the messages (through early projection and early restructuring) according to groups of user interests. The last operation is the *user query processing*, which uses *YFilter* (Diao, 2003) to match and transform messages against individual user profiles at their host brokers.

For the query processing, the query is decomposed into its constituent paths and each path is processed through a Finite State Machine - FSM. Starting from an initial state, each element in the query and each axis defines the transition from one state to another. The queries may be inserted in their original order, i.e. top-down as done by *YFilter*, or in their reverse order, i.e. bottom-up as done by *BUFF – Bottom-Up Filtering FSM* (Moro, 2007a). For example, Figure 3b illustrates a set of four path queries. Assume that, for simplicity, all queries consider only the ancestor/descendant axis. The respective simplified FSM for that set of queries is illustrated in Figure 3c and the reverse machine employed by *BUFF* is in Figure 3d. Note that while the regular FSM groups the queries according to their common prefixes, *BUFF* groups them according to their common suffixes.

The FSM stores partial results as the document is parsed sequentially (in document order). At each point, partial or total pattern matching

Figure 3. Top-down and bottom-up finite state machine-based approaches. An XML document, a set of queries and the respective regular simplified FSM, and reverse FSM employed by BUFF (states as circles, final states as gray circles, main transitions as arrows).

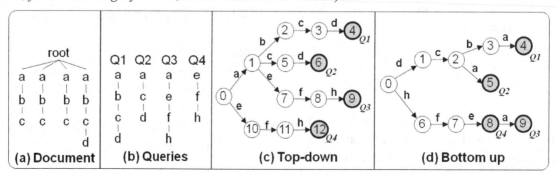

is performed, depending on the existing partial matches and the current node. Specifically, documents are parsed one tag at a time. The start-tags (reading <element>) trigger the events in the FSM, which chooses the next state according to the element read. When an end-tag is found (reading </element>), the execution backtracks to the state it was in when the corresponding start-tag was processed. A run-time stack keeps the states reached and allows such state backtracking. The intuition for the *BUFF* processing is that a bottom-up evaluation of a document should trigger fewer states than the traditional top-down approach. For example, considering the input document from Figure 3a, the top-down FSM (Figure 3c) executes transitions to states 1, 2 and 3 (after reading elements *a*, *b* and *c*) three times (once for each path -*a-b-c*) before achieving the final state 4 for query Q1 (i.e. *//a//b//c//d*). On the other hand, *BUFF* executes transitions to states 1, 2 and 3 only once (when reading the last path of the document tree, -*a-b-c-d*), then achieves the final state 4 for the same query. A similar situation occurs for query Q2.

Likewise, *XTreeNet* (Fenner, 2005) focuses on the overlay network by proposing a protocol in charge of building trees of publishers and subscribers. *XTreeNet* also enables such duplicate elimination, relevance-score based filtering, and access control to be performed in the network. However, the authors do not give any details about how XML queries are processed (message filtering task).

POX (Yoo, 2006) takes a different direction and proposes a *subscription* routing mechanism as a part of efforts to achieve scalability. It performs the XML document routing as usual, but it also routes the XML queries (subscriptions). When a query is registered with a broker, that broker determines which adjacent brokers should receive such information and transmits it to the selected brokers. Such a decision is made by comparing relationships among new and existing queries. The focus of the paper is on the query distribution,

and there is no detail about how those queries are evaluated against the XML data.

Likewise, (Li, 2007) aims at speeding up the routing computation by reducing the routing table size (where the queries or subscriptions are stored). They introduce advertisement-based routing algorithms and propose a novel data structure to maintain the queries by identifying the covering relations between them. The queries are evaluated over the advertisements.

RoXSum (Vagena, 2007a) and its counterpart *VA-RoXSum* (Vagena, 2007b) propose a data structure that aggregates the content of multiples messages, and algorithms that evaluate all queries over such aggregated content. The data structure is based on the concept of structural summary, where each node in the structure represents a set of bisimilar nodes (*extent*) from the original docum7ents. For example, Figure 4a illustrates four document trees (D1 to D4) representing the structure content of different bibliographic entries. Figure 4b illustrates the *RoXSum* structure for those documents. Note that the path instance *bib-book-title* (which appears thrice within XML document D1 and once within D2) is stored only once in the *RoXSum* structure. While the *RoXSum* aggregates the structural information of many documents, its counterpart *VA-RoXSum* also aggregates the element *values* of many documents.

In both *RoXSum* and *VA-RoXSum*, the evaluation algorithms are automata-based (similar to *ONYX*). Specifically, identifying documents (when evaluating a query) from the *RoXSum* tree is done in one in-order traversal of the tree. From each node on the *RoXSum* tree that satisfies a query, its extent and the extent of its descendants contains those, and only those, documents that satisfy the query as well. For example, consider the query */bib/book/title* on the documents of Figure 4b. There is only one path in the *RoXSum* that satisfies this query. All documents within the extent of the *RoXSum* tree node *title* (under elements *bib* and *book*), and within its descendant

Figure 4. Four documents aggregated within one RoXSum data structure

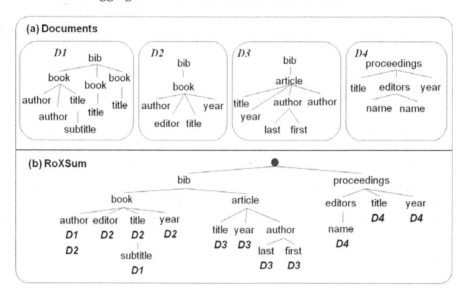

Figure 5. Profile matching on previous approaches and on RoXSum

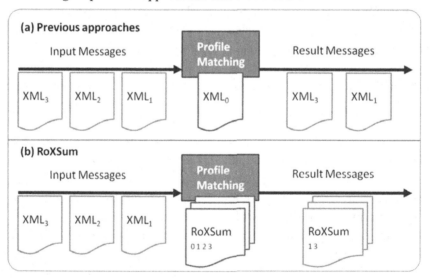

node *subtitle* satisfy the query, i.e. documents D1 and D2. Given the results of the matching phase, the next steps are: to gather the content of each document, to aggregate the contents of documents that are sent to the same broker into a new *RoXSum* structure, and to build the messages to be handed on the underlying network infrastructure. Therefore, the selected messages (i.e. those that satisfy the set of queries) are forwarded into the network within an aggregated structure as well.

In previous approaches, the profile matching on the filtering task was performed in each incoming message individually, as presented in Figure 5a. Then, the messages that satisfy the profile matching are individually routed to the respective consumers. In this example, messages numbers 1 and 3 are routed. In *RoXSum*, the input messages still come individually, but they are processed all together within the *RoXSum* structure, as illustrated in Figure 5b. Hence, the profile matching is done on the *RoXSum* structure that aggregates the content of the incoming messages (documents 0 to 3). Finally, the documents that satisfy the profiles are also aggregated into a *RoXSum* structure that is routed to the respective consumers. In summary, *RoXSum* speeds up the profile matching process because it is performed on the aggregated content of the input messages, and it also improves the transmission task because it sends the aggregate structure to the respective consumers.

Both approaches (*RoXSum* and *VA-RoXSum*) are complementary to the aforementioned works, as they target the design of a compact but directly queryable message format and can be integrated with and benefit any of the previous frameworks. For example, the system could assume that the overlay network structure is defined according to the principles proposed in (Fenner, 2005) and that the profiles are distributed over that network following the principles from (Diao, 2004). Then, *RoXSum* groups those profiles in the state machine within each broker and can start processing incoming messages.

XML Documents and Schemas

An alternative direction is to implement XML routing over peer-to-peer (P2P) networks. In this case, the architecture is different from the one employed by pub/sub systems. Specifically, the XML data are stored (and most probably indexed) over the P2P network, and the XML queries are routed through the network, looking for related content within the peers. The challenges in this type of system include indexing (summarizing) the XML data locally in the peers, locating peers with related data, processing and routing the XML queries, routing the results, and handling network updates (Koudas, 2004; Fegaras, 2006).

CURRENT AND FUTURE TRENDS

Current Research Trends

While early systems were centralized (e.g. Fabret, 2001), scalability features required the design of *distributed architectures*. *SIFT* (Yan, 1999) was one of the first systems to provide solutions for distributed message filtering and routing, being followed by systems like *Gryphon* (Aguilera, 1999) and *Siena* (Carzaniga, 2001). The main focus of those initial works was how to optimize the routing information, by merging similar profiles or indexing them. The systems have become more complex (e.g. by using XML messages) and the focus of the recent research has changed to:

- Overlay network structure (Fenner, 2005; Papaemmanouil, 2006; Snoeren, 2001)
- Profile aggregation (Aekaterinidis, 2005; Shen, 2005; Triantafillou, 2004; Yoo, 2006; Li, 2007), which builds clusters (or groups) of similar profiles such that fewer queries are evaluated
- Distribution of consumer profiles (Diao, 2004)
- Message routing policies (Papaemmanouil, 2005; Shah, 2004)

Among those, only (Diao, 2004; Fenner, 2005; Snoeren, 2001; Yoo, 2006) use XML as the encoding format for messages (which have been already covered within *XML Routing Systems* subsection).

Considering the matching task (or query evaluation process), automata-based profile algorithms are among the most popular solutions (Altinel, 2000; Diao, 2003; Gong, 2005; Green, 2003; He, 2006; Peng, 2003). Several alternative matching techniques, such as relational joins (Tian, 2004), profile aggregation (Chan, 2002), bloom filters (Gong, 2005), and subsequence matching (Kwon, 2005) have also been proposed. The goal of these works is scalability with respect to the number of profiles, which is achieved by employing *multi-query processing* methods. Additionally, the work in (Fischer, 2005) targets scalability on the number of messages and designs matching techniques which handle message *batches*.

XML *compression techniques* are also related to XML filtering scenarios. Traditional schemes compress each message before forwarding it, and decompress it either completely e.g. XMILL (Liefke, 2000) or partially e.g. XGRIND (Tolani, 2002) before performing the profile matching at each broker. A different approach is provided by *RoXSum* (Vagena, 2007a) and its counterpart *VA-RoXSum* (Vagena, 2007b). Those approaches aggregate the content of multiple messages into one summarizing structure, process the set of queries over the aggregated content, and forward the results within the aggregating structure (instead of forwarding individual messages).

Open Issues

As for the open challenges, methods for better incorporating *textual information* are still necessary. Most of the approaches focus on structural matching or value predicate evaluations. However, full-text search is needed to query large portions of text, but it must consider the structural information of the data as well. An initial study on how to evaluate full-text queries with structural features on XML streams is presented in (Vagena, 2008). Nonetheless, a more complete solution is still an open issue.

XML data and relational data will always co-exist and complement each other in enterprise data management (Moro, 2007b). Much critical, legacy data are still in relational format. However, database designers have increasingly turned to XML for storing data that do not fit into the relational model. Increasing attention is being given to how to handle relational and XML data *uniformly*. In such a context, it is natural that Internet systems will evolve for evaluating both relational and XML data at the same time.

As publish/subscribe systems have grown from topic-based systems to XML-enable systems, we believe that the next step is for them to follow the data technology and support both relational and XML data *uniformly* as well.

Content-based dissemination services have evolved following the trends and the advancements from different areas, e.g. Databases, Distributed Systems, and Networks. In Databases, more and more applications (such as Web Services, Digital Libraries, and mash-ups) are creating, manipulating and exchanging XML data. The size of such systems has also scaled to consider *large* volumes of data, and issues like distributed processing, routing, filtering, and cache operation have become critical to the data management as well. Moreover, considering all the aspects involved from other research areas (such as Distributed Systems, Information Retrieval and Data Mining), we believe that the Database technology must evolve to consider uniformly and seamlessly *any* type of data that exist with *extensible* and *Web-scalable* features. This complex scenario brings new and exciting issues to be handled by many different Computer Science communities.

CONCLUDING REMARKS

More and more applications are creating, manipulating and exchanging XML data. XML document routing is a very recent problem that has become very significant due to the wide acceptance of XML as the standard for file exchange. The importance of XML routing systems has been established by the increasing number of scenarios and applications that require disseminating XML content. Of these, pub/sub services are among the most relevant. Moreover, considering the fact that publish/subscribe applications with complex data representation and retrieval requirements emerge more and more frequently over the Internet, it is natural that XML-aware publish/subscribe systems will soon become indispensable.

Table 2. Overview of main approaches on XML Routing and pub/sub systems. The rows present the different approaches and the columns present the aspects of the system which they tackle: overlay network construction, indexing or aggregation of subscriptions, distribution of subscriptions over the network, optimizations on the message encoding, data transformations, computation sharing over the network, optimizations on the message delivery, optimizations on (and the type of) the message filtering processing, and some keywords on the novelty of ea ch approach.

Reference	Overlay network	Profile indexing/aggregation	Profile distribution	Message encoding	Data transformation	Computation sharing	Message delivery	Message filtering	Novelty
Altinel 2000		X						Automata	First XML filtering system
Chan 2002		X						Selective-based algorithms	Selective estimation of results
Chan 2007		X				X			Piggybacking annotations
Diao 2003		X						Automata	Prefix-sharing automata
Diao 2004	X		X		X			Automata (Diao 2003)	Overlay network services
Fenner 2005	X							Network building protocol	Score functions on results
Fisher 2005		X			X			Batching, indexing, post-processing	Batch processing
Gong 2005		X						Bloom-filter on queries	Bloom-filter approximate matching
He 2006								Automata	Cache-conscious automata
Kwon 2005		X		X				Subsequence matching	Sequencing twig patterns
Li 2007		X	X	X				Matching rules: advertisement, query	Advertisement-based routing
Moro 2007a			X	X				Subsequence matching	Profile early-pruning
Papaemmanouil'05									Semantic communities
Raj 2007		X		X				Subsequence matching	Results are document sub-trees
Snoeren 2001	X							General purpose XML toolkit	First XML routing system
Tian 2004								Relational engine	Relational matching
Vagena 2007a		X		X	X		X	Automata over aggregated messages	Message aggregation
Vagena 2007b		X		X	X		X	Automata + bloom filters	Message aggregation
Yoo 2006			X						Subscription partitioning

This chapter presented different scenarios for those services, including diverse and complex applications from the very popular RSS feeds to the very lucrative stock industry. It also discussed an extensive state of the art on XML routing systems, which also included early pub/sub systems as well as distributed architectures. Table 2 connects all challenges discussed and overviews the main approaches on XML Routing and pub/sub systems. Finally, as open issues on routing systems, we pointed out: how to deal with full-text search with structural features, how to handle relational and XML data uniformly, and how to evaluate uniformly and seamlessly *any* type of data there exist with *extensible* and *Web-scalable* features.

ACKNOWLEDGMENT

The work presented here was partially supported by NSF grant IIS-0705916. Mirella M. Moro was supported by CNPq, Brazil.

REFERENCES

Aekaterinidis, I., & Triantafillou, P. (2005). Internet scale string attribute publish/subscribe data networks. In *CIKM,* (pp. 44-51).

Aguilera, M. K., Strom, R.E, Sturman, D.C., Astley, M., & Chandra, T.D (1999). Matching events in a content-based subscription system. In *PODC,* (pp. 53-61).

Altinel, M., & Franklin, M. J. (2000). Efficient filtering of XML documents for selective dissemination of information. In *VLDB,* (pp. 53-64).

Carzaniga, A., Rosenblum, D. S., & Wolf, A. L. (2001). Design and evaluation of a wide-area event notification service. In *ACM Transactions on Computer Systems 9*(3), 332-383.

Chan, C. Y., Fan, W., Felber, P., Garofalakis, M. N., & Rastogi, R. (2002). Tree pattern aggregation for scalable XML data dissemination. In *VLDB,* (pp. 826-837).

Chan, C. Y., & Ni, Y. (2007). Efficient XML data dissemination with piggybacking. In *SIGMOD,* (pp. 737-748).

Chand, R., Felber, P., & Garofalakis, M. (2007). Tree-pattern similarity estimation for scalable content-based routing. In *ICDE,* (pp. 1016-1025).

Chen, X., Chen, Y., & Rao, F. (2003). An efficient spatial publish/subscribe system for intelligent location-based services. In *DEBS*.

Costa, M., Crowcroft, J., Castro, M., Rowstron, A., Zhou, L., Zhang, L., & Barham, P. (2005). Vigilante: End-to-end containment of internet worms. In *SOSP,* (pp. 133-147).

Diao, Y., Altinel, M., Franklin, M. J., Zhang, H., & Ficher, P. M. (2003). Path sharing and predicate evaluation for high-performance XML filtering. In *ACM Transactions Database Systems 28*(4), 467-516.

Diao, Y., Rizvi, S., & Franklin, M. J. (2004). Towards an Internet-scale XML dissemination service. In *VLDB,* (pp. 612-623).

Fabret, F., Jacobsen, H-A, Llirbat, F., Pereira, J., Ross, K. A., & Shasha, D. (2001). Filtering algorithms and implementation for very fast publish/subscribe. In *SIGMOD,* (pp. 115-126).

Fegaras, L., He, W., Das, G., & Levine, D. (2006). XML query routing in structured P2P systems. In *DISP2P,* (pp. 273-284).

Fenner, W., Rabinovich, M., Ramakrishnan, K. K., Srivastava, D., & Zhang, Y. (2005). XTreeNet: Scalable overlay networks for XML content dissemination and querying. In *WCW,* (pp. 4-46).

Fischer, P. M., & Kossmann, D. (2005). Batched processing for information filters. In *ICDE,* (pp. 902-913).

Gong, X., Yan, Y., Qian, W., & Zhou, A. (2005). Bloom filter-based XML packets filtering for millions of path queries. In *ICDE,* (pp. 890-901).

Green, T. J., Miklau, G., Onizuka, M., & Suciu, D (2003). Processing XML streams with deterministic automata. In *ICDT,* (pp. 173-189).

He, B., Luo, Q., & Choi, B. (2006). Cache-Conscious Automata for XML filtering. In *IEEE Transactions on Knowledge and Data Engineering 18* (12), 1629-1644.

Koudas, N., Rabinovich, M., Srivastava, D., & Yu, T. (2004). Routing XML queries. In *ICDE,* (p. 844).

Kwon, J., Rao, P., Moon, B., & Lee, S. (2005). FiST: Scalable XML document filtering by sequencing twig patterns. In *VLDB,* (pp. 217-228).

Li, G., Hou, S., & Jacobsen, H-A. (2007). XML Routing in data dissemination networks. In *ICDE,* (pp. 1400-1404).

Liefke, H., & Suciu, D. (2000) XMILL: An efficient compressor for XML data. In *SIGMOD,* (pp. 153-164).

Liu, H., Ramasubramanian, V., & Sirer, E. G. (2005). Client behavior and feed characteristics of RSS, a publish-subscribe system for Web micronews. In *Internet Measurement Conference,* (pp. 29-34).

Moro, M. M., Bakalov, P., & Tsotras, V. J. (2007a). Early profile pruning on XML-aware publish/subscribe systems. In *VLDB,* (pp. 866-877).

Moro, M. M., Lim, L., & Chang, Y-C (2007b). Schema advisor for hybrid relational XML DBMS. In *SIGMOD,* (pp. 959-970).

Papaemmanouil, O., Ahmad, Y., Çetintemel, U., & Jannotti, J. (2006). Application-aware overlay networks for data dissemination. In *ICDE Workshop,* (p.76).

Papaemmanouil, O., & Centintemel, U. (2005). SemCast: Semantic multicast for content-based data dissemination. In *ICDE,* (pp. 242-253).

Peng, F., and Chawathe, S. S. (2003). XPath queries on streaming data. In *SIGMOD,* (pp. 431-442).

Raj, A., & Kumar, P. (2007). Branch Sequencing based XML message broker. In *ICDE,* (pp. 656-665).

Shah, R., Ramzan, Z., Jain, R., Dendukuri, R., & Anjum, F. (2004). Efficient dissemination of personalized information using content-based multicast. In *IEEE Transactions on Mobile Computing 3*(4), & 394-408.

Shen, Z., Aluru, S., & Tirthapura, S. (2005). Indexing for subscription covering in publish-subscribe systems. In *ISCA PDCS,* (pp. 328-333).

Snoeren, A. C., Conley, K., & Gifford, D. K. (2001). Mesh-based content routing using XML. In *SOSP,* (pp. 160-173).

Tian, F., Reinwald, B., Pirahesh, H., Mayr T., & Myllymaki J. (2004). Implementing a scalable XML publish/subscribe system using relational database systems. In *SIGMOD,* (pp. 479-490).

Tolani, P. M., & Haritsa, J. R. (2002). XGRIND: A Query-Friendly XML Compressor. In *ICDE,* (p. 225).

Triantafillou, P., & Economides, A. A. (2004). Subscription summarization: A new paradigm for efficient publish/subscribe systems. In *ICDCS,* (pp. 562–571).

Vagena, Z., & Moro, M. M. (2008). Semantic search over XML document streams. In *DATAX.*

Vagena, Z., Moro, M. M., & Tsotras, V. J. (2007a). RoXSum: Leveraging data aggregation and batch processing for XML routing. In *ICDE,* (pp. 1466-1470).

Vagena, Z., Moro, M. M., & Tsotras, V. J. (2007b). Value-Aware RoXSum: Effective message aggregation for XML-aware information dissemination. In *WebDB*.

Wang, Y.-M., Qiu, L., Achlioptas, D., Das, G., Larson, P., & Wang, H. J. (2002). Subscription partitioning and routing in content based publish/subscribe networks. In *DiSC*.

Yan, T. W., & Garcia-Molina, H. (1999). The SIFT information dissemination system. In *ACM Transactions on Database Systems 24*(4), 529-565.

Yoo, S., Son, J. H., & Kim, M. H. (2006). An efficient subscription routing algorithm for scalable XML-based publish/subscribe systems. In *Journal of Systems and Software 79*(12), 1767-1781.

Chapter VIII
Native XML Programming:
Make Your Tags Active

Philippe Poulard
The French National Institute for Research in Computer Science and Control (INRIA), France

ABSTRACT

XML engines are usually designed to solve a single class of problems: transformations of XML structures, validations of XML instances, Web publishing, and so forth. As the relevant operations or declarations are described with XML vocabularies, their respective engines have to face similar issues such as unmarshalling, and at runtime data handling. In order to address such issues, the author proposes an innovative and reliable XPath-based framework, active tags, that unifies XML technologies in a coherent system where various XML languages can cooperate. In this chapter's approach, the authors focus on its type system that enhances the XML Data Model, specifically by allowing XPath expressions to be applied on non-XML objects, and on the ability of the engine to mix declarative languages with imperative constructs. This valuable feature is illustrated with the Active Schema Language, which allows the building of dynamic-content models.

INTRODUCTION

XML instances usually fall into one of the two following categories: XML documents and XML data structures; of course, hybrid instances that consist of a combination of these two categories can also be considered. However, a third category is worth mentioning: XML languages designed for processing purposes, such as XSLT (W3C, 1999b). Actually, since the emergence of XML technologies, numerous processing-oriented XML languages have been invented for specific purposes.

In this chapter, we will discuss native XML programming, that is to say, XML languages intended to be processed by a specific engine in order to solve a class of problem. This includes templating languages that sometimes are not strictly spoken XML languages (they are not « well-formed " according to the XML specification) but aim to reach similar objectives, and declarative-oriented languages that are certainly the most specialized languages. Among these languages, we have:

- Those that are tightly coupled to a programming language such as Java (Ant, Jelly),
- Those that are rather language-independent (SCXML, XProc),
- Those that deal only with Web problematics (JSP/JSTL/Taglib),
- Pure declarative-oriented languages (XML Catalogs, J2EE deployment descriptors, schemata),
- Those that use technologies related to XML such as XPath (XSLT, Active Tags).

In fact, apart from the capabilities of the tools mentioned above, native XML programming is fundamental to process integration, in the same way that native XML querying (XQuery) is fundamental to data extraction and remodeling. As XQuery does not address natively Web problematics (although some proprietary extension of XQuery-based systems can deal with them), native XML programming acts as the glue between the HTTP server and the XQuery query. More generally, native XML programming can stand between the different components of an XML database application.

XML programming has the following advantages.

- First of all, we agree that whatever the nature of the underlying data sources, the best method for efficient data integration is to supply them in a common format: XML. Actually, every non-XML structure only has to be mapped to an XML representation. We will see later that we are not necessarily talking about the tag representation (markups

in a file) of XML, but rather about the data model representation of XML (XDM). In any case, XML-related technologies such as XPath are likely to be used for handling these data. Conversely, tools such as Ant and Jelly that rely on the unified expression language (UEL) are very far removed from XML problematics.

- Secondly, due to its extensibility, XML is the best candidate for designing special purpose languages, including declarative languages: arbitrary complex processes can be expressed with very few tags, provided that they are backed by an appropriate implementation.
- Finally, as with XSLT, dealing with an XML language allows the designer of such a language to build XML structures by mixing XML litterals among XML instructions (the so-called « Active Tags "), as do template languages.

The objective of this chapter is to give an overview of open issues in the field of native XML programming, and demonstrate that these issues can be addressed by a unification of XML technologies that promote the cooperation of multiple XML languages.

After recalling the origins that led to the design of XML-based programs, and drawing up a comparison table between different processing-oriented XML languages, we will introduce Active Tags (Poulard 2006; 2007), a general-purpose system for native XML programming that borrows the best from many technologies and tools like those mentioned and proposes an innovative and reliable framework that can host any new processing-oriented XML language. We will show with several examples that are runnable in RefleX (the reference implementation of Active Tags in Java) how to use Active Tags within Web applications or as standalone applications in pipelines, how to use several tag libraries simultaneously, and how to expose a tag as a macro-tag.

Other examples will demonstrate Active Tags in action in XML database applications: querying various data sources with or without XQuery, relational databases, native XML databases, or LDAP directories.

Next, we discuss XML type systems and how Active Tags operate on typed data, including Semantic typed data. Unlike many similar systems, the data in Active Tags can be XML data as well as non-XML data; few of the latter are said to be « XML friendly "; that is to say, they are sensitive to XML-related operations. For example, as a file system is a hierarchical structure like XML, XPath expressions such as //* can be applied to directories to get all the files under the tree. Such objects are called « cross-operable objects ", or « X-operable objects ". We will prove that those objects are compatible with the XML data model by comparing them with typed data built from the PSVI.

One of the most outstanding features of Active Tags is its ability to host declarative languages that can combine imperative constructs. Usually, a specialized engine of a declarative language will build an abstract tree from the XML instance. As the XML instance is hard-coded, the abstract tree is static. Although declarative languages are extremely expressive, they are limited to what allows the Semantic of the language (how the tags that are representing the language can be combined). In order to overcome these limitations, we allow interweaving of imperative constructs within the declarative language: as the abstract tree is computed at runtime, it becomes dynamic, increasing dramatically the expressiveness of the language without breaking its Semantic. We will demonstrate this concept with an experimental schema language, the Active Schema Language, which is part of the Active Tags suite.

We will conclude the chapter by presenting the 'unified theory of markup'.

We begin with an acceptable rationale that leads to design programs with XML markups.

XML PROGRAMMING ISSUES: FROM THE XML ROOTS TO THE BAZAAR

It is worth mentioning the XML roots, syntactically spoken; any programming language is based primarily on syntax, and although XML was designed for data only, it has a built-in structure for declaring instructions to process, the so-called 'processing instructions'. Since they are too weak, various other means were considered and are still used today to express high-level processes, albeit in a bazaar style that we try to classify.

XML Instructions to Process

SGML and XML come with a structure called processing instruction (PI) that allows applications that read XML documents to react when such a structure is encountered. The data stored in PIs are not usually considered as content, and should not be used to store significant information: processing instructions are just for processing purposes, but with many disadvantages:

- Namespaces do not apply to PI's targets, so collisions may occur: an application could wrongly react to a PI although it may not be the legitime target of the PI;
- PIs are poorly structured, so the best effort is to consider the PI's data as attributes (conventionally called pseudo-attributes);
- PIs cannot be nested, although artifacts such as `<?start-something?>` and `<?end-some-thing?>` might be considered.

In a certain way, PIs are used to perform a specific action by a given application. Consider that, instead of using PIs, specific qualified elements are used:

- By using a qualified name, an application knows whether or not it is really for itself;

- As other elements, attributes are real attributes;
- Instructions may be nested, and complex processings that rely on the relationship between elements may be described.

Compared to tag sets, processing instructions are a very primitive means of expressing processes, given that few users, if any, would be using such instructions. One rare application that has survived and is worth mentioning is the stylesheet association supported by any Web user-agent: a browser that reads the PI `<?xml-stylesheet href="style.xsl"?>` will perform an XSLT transformation on the XML document that hosts it. Unfortunately, the XSLT process involved is in itself a very basic process: there are no means for passing parameters or resolving URIs, and browser limitations are not considered.

The Need to Combine XML Technologies

XML technologies deal with heterogeneous mechanisms all along the XML chain process. These mechanisms which are implied in a specific process or behaviour are often part of the XML instance. Examples from the bazaar:

- the `<!DOCTYPE>` **declaration**,
- the `standalone` **pseudo-attribute**,
- the `xsi:schemaLocation` **attribute**,
- the `<xi:include>` **element**,
- the `<?xml-stylesheet?>` **processing instruction**,
- etc

Another drawback is that they have to be repeated within each instance of the same class. When one of these processes evolves, for example when upgrading from DTD to W3C XML Schema, all instances of the same class that refer to the DTD have to be updated.

We do need an integrated system, a federator, that allows the homogeneous externalization of the XML chain process, and that perhaps also allows special purpose processes to be embedded in XML documents. These requirements could be fulfilled by describing processes by means of XML. In the same way that XML is the common denominator when exchanging data, it can also be the component that unifies high-level processes.

More XML Bazaar

Some tools or technologies are still dependent on the primal techniques mentioned; for example, Cocoon (the well-known publishing framework) still relies on processing instructions; it also deals with a set of custom tags and in a certain way is comparable to what we found in the XML-bazaar. Frequently, people who design tag-based systems are highly influenced by what they have already dealt with: the team that developed the Ant system perhaps focused too closely on the « Make " tools, and they apply the existing work to the XML model with the (deserved) success we observe today but without thinking deeply about XML technologies. We cannot blame them since the XML technologies were still in their infancy when Ant was being designed, and it is quite likely that if the same task were undertaken today, a very different approach would be adopted (for example, just by integrating XML namespaces). Thus, we must deal with a kind of temporal-state-of-the-art to understand how tag-based systems were designed in the early days of XML, and which lead us to the XML bazaar.

Hereinafter, some snippet codes will provide the reader with an overview of the bazaar.

Ant

Ant is an XML-based build tool for Java. In theory, it resembles Make, without Make's disadvantages. Because Make systems in general and Ant are popular, there is no need to provide an explanation of the objective of the sample below:

```
<target name="compile"
        depends="init"
        description="compile the source">
    <!-- Compile the java code from ${src}
        into ${build} -->
    <javac srcdir="${src}"
        destdir="${build}"/>
</target>


<target name="dist"
        depends="compile"
        description="generate distri
                    bution" >
    <mkdir dir="${dist}/lib"/>
    <!-- Put everything in ${build} into a
        jar file -->
    <jar jarfile="${dist}/lib/MyProject-
                  ${DSTAMP}.jar"
        basedir="${build}"/>
</target>
```

Among Ant's features, it is possible to embed some logics within a target: for example, a condition can be expressed with Ant as :

```
<condition property="cond-is-true">
  <and>
    <not>
      <equals arg1="${prop1}"
              arg2="${prop2}" />
    </not>
      <equals arg1="${prop3}"
              arg2="${prop4}" />
  </and>
</condition>
```

With an approach using XML technologies, the same condition could be written with XPath as:

```
not($prop1=$prop2) and $prop3=$prop4
```

Obviously, the latter is preferable.

JSP

JSP (JavaServer Pages) is a template language for creating Web content using Java Servlet technology. It is similar to other Web templating languages such as ASP, PHP, but in the Java world. The first versions of the language were not fully conformed to the XML specification (JSP documents were not well-formed in the XML sense), but aims to reach similar objectives. For that matter, the designers moved the language to a real XML syntax since JSP 1.2. Anyway, this is a technology tightly coupled to Web problematics and designed for Java only, but it is possible to extend the markup vocabulary with additional 'imperative statements'; this way, third-party libraries can be plugged into the system.

```
<jsp:root
    xmlns:jsp="http://java.sun.com/JSP/Page"
    xmlns:demo="/demolib"
    version="1.2">
  <jsp:directive.page
        contentType="text/html"/>
    <ul>
      <demo:myLoopTag items="myCollection"
                      var="current">
        <li>
        <jsp:getProperty
          name="current"
          property="lastName"/>,
        <jsp:getProperty
          name="current"
          property="firstName"/>
        </li>
      </demo:myLoopTag>
    </ul>
</jsp:root>
```

SCXML

SCXML is a rather well-designed XML language that allows the design of state-machines. Unlike the previous languages, it is independent of any language, platform, and runtime environment, like XSLT.

```
<scxml
    xmlns="http://www.w3.org/2005/07/scxml"
    version="1.0"
    initialstate="off">
<!--trivial microwave oven example-->
<state id="off">
   <!--off state-->
   <transition event="turn_on">
     <target next="on"/>
   </transition>
</state>
<state id="on">
   <initial>
     <transition>
        <target next="idle"/>
     </transition>
   </initial>
   <!--on/pause state-->
   <onentry>
   <!--we assume the cook_time is
                   passed
      in as a context parameter-->
   <if cond="${empty cook_time}">
     <!--default setting-->
     <var name="cook_time"
               expr="${5}"/>
   </if>
   <!--again, door_closed should be a
      part of a global context-->
   <if cond="${empty door_closed}">
     <!--default setting-->
    <var name="door_closed"
            expr="${true}"/>
   </if>
   <!--timer variable-->
   <var name="timer" expr="${0}"/>
```

```
</onentry>
<transition event="turn_off">
   <target next="off"/>
</transition>
<transition
      cond="${timer ge cook_time}">
   <target next="off"/>
</transition>
<!-- etc -->
```

XProc

XProc is the more recent one. Its lack of maturity makes its future success unable to predict. However, the use case it is intended to cover (W3C, 2006a) demonstrates the ambition of the core concepts. Unfortunately, it is intended to put all kind of steps (parsing, validation, transformation, xinclusion, etc) in a single markup language, and it is not designed to process documents other than XML, which makes the publishing process impossible to design with XProc alone.

```
<p:pipeline
    xmlns:p="http://www.w3.org/2007/03/
        xproc"
    name="pipeline">
  <p:input port-"document"/>
  <p:input port="stylesheet"/>
  <p:output port="result"/>

  <p:xinclude>
   <p:input port="source">
      <p:pipe step="pipeline"
            port="document"/>
   </p:input>
  </p:xinclude>

  <p:validate-xml-schema>
   <p:input port="schema">
    <p:document href="http://example.com/
                  path/to/schema.xsd"/>
   </p:input>
  </p:validate-xml-schema>
```

```
<p:xslt>
  <p:input port="stylesheet">
    <p:pipe step="pipeline"
          port="stylesheet"/>
  </p:input>
</p:xslt>

</p:pipeline>
```

Jelly

Jelly is a tool for turning XML into executable code. It looks like JSP but is not related to Web processing. The following Jelly script seems simple at first glance but what is missing is the heavy Java part that makes it runnable :

```
<j:jelly
    xmlns:j="jelly:core"
    xmlns:x="jelly:xml"
    xmlns:html="jelly:html"
    trim="false">

  <html>
    <head>
      <title>${name}'s Page</title>
    </head>
    <body bgcolor="${background}"
              text="#FFFFFF">
    <h1>${name}'s Homepage</h1>
    <img src="${url}"/>
    <h2>My Hobbies</h2>
    <ul>
      <j:forEach items="
              ${hobbies}" var="i">
        <li>${i}</li>
      </j:forEach>
    </ul>
    </body>
  </html>

</j:jelly>
```

There are numerous similar markup or pseudo-markup languages; we do not intend to be exhaustive, but just to give a brief overview. What is important to retain is that they are all doing more or less the same things but very differently.

Classification of Some Technologies and Tools

In the table below, we summarize some of the characteristics that we believe should belong to native XML programming systems. We classify a few of the tools taken from a (considerably large) panel of reputed tools or technologies. Below the table, we explain what each characteristic is supposed to cover[1].

- **Language independence**: The ability to be implemented in any language/platform. XSLT and XQuery (as well as most of the W3C recommendations) are such languages. Ant is not, although it has been cloned on platforms other than Java. Generally, if the language specification is not expressed in terms of another host language, it can have a rather good level of independence.

- **Target environment**: The environment where the language is intended to run; we make out those that run on a specific target: a Web server, in batch mode, or embedded in a host program. For example, JSPs are designed to run exclusively inside a Web server: it is tightly coupled to concepts such as Web cookies, Web sessions and architecturally dependent on that specific runtime environment.

- **Templates:** The ability to embed XML litterals within the code, like XSLT does. Web template languages include JSP, ASP, and PHP; although these latter have some variations with the XML syntax, they all follow the same pattern and are eligible for this feature.

- **Declarative / imperative:** In short, indicates whether the instructions are run in sequence or selected by the underlying processor. For example, when entering an XSLT stylesheet, the processor will itself select the template to run, although inside the template one might have imperative instructions. Active Tags have the ability to design declarative languages. The tags introduced in Jelly libraries or JSP libraries are imperative instructions, run in sequence. That topic will be discussed in the section titled 'Runnable declarative languages'.
- **Instruction-set extensibility:** The ability to design external libraries. JSP can import JSTL and third-party libraries as can Jelly. XSLT does not have portable tag libraries; a disputable point of view faces the EXSLT initiative, but the applicative field of XSLT prevents the design of a custom instruction set related to, say, Web problematics. Moreover, it is stated in the W3C recommendation that 'XSLT does not provide a mechanism for defining implementations of extensions'. Only systems that do define such a mecha-

nism fall into this category. 'I' indicates that the system can be extended with Imperative languages, 'D' that the system can host other Declarative languages.
- **Macro-tags:** The ability to express the implementation of a tag with other tags. That is to say, to define an active tag in terms of the XML languages considered.
- **XML type system:** When the system is able to handle W3C XML datatypes and/or similar XML type systems : `#xs:string`[2], `#xs:float` and the like.
- **XML processing:** When specific facilities are available for processing XML (parsing, validation, XInclusion, XSLT transformations, XQuery submission, etc), when XPath or XQuery are used in the language, when processing XML documents can be achieved with SAX or DOM (or similar), when the language can be used in XML pipelines. We are not saying that it is impossible to process XML documents in JSPs; we are just saying that this is not its primary intention.
- **Binary processing:** When the system can handle binary documents.

Table 1. Which feature is covered by your favorite tool?

	XSLT	JSP	Jelly	Ant	SCXML	XProc	Active Tags
language independence	x				x	x	x
target environment	*[3]	Web	*	BATCH	*	*	*
templates	x	x	x				x
declarative (D) / imperative (I)	D	I	I	D	D	D	I/D[4]
instruction-set extensibility		I	I			I[5]	I/D
macro-tags							x
xml type system	x						x
xml processing	x					x	x
binary processing		x					x
data source connectivity		x	x				x

- **Data source connectivity**: When the system is able to query various kind of data sources by its own: relational databases with SQL, LDAP repositories, native XML databases, Web services, local files, and the like.

As shown in the table above, the characteristics mentioned are not globally covered by any of the existing tools presented here. Some are language independent, others aren't. Some can run exclusively on a Web server. Some supply templating facilities, others don't. Finally, they are all doing more or less the same things but in a specific way with constraints on their runtime environment, on the nature of the data they can process, and on their extensibility. The main issues for programmers are that they have to learn different languages with different rules and walled engines not designed for cooperation.

Conversely, the support of those characteristics among others was used as the requirements for designing the Active Tags sytem that we will present hereafter.

Native XML Languages without XML

Into this category fall the languages like XQuery where XML is not the primary language. Most of these languages embed XML concrete syntax with some escaping mechanism (Schmitt,2004). Some of them are extensions to well-known languages (XJ is a Java extensions, Xtatic a C# extension), others are standalone languages. In this last case, a language like CDuce is probably closer to XQuery than to tag-based languages, and falls outside the scope of this chapter whose purpose is to discuss languages where markups themselves stand for instructions.

Here is a snippet code of a CDuce program. Don't you find it a scent of FLWOR[6] ?

```
let sel = select y
        from x in [biblio]/book ,
```

```
            y in [x]/title,
            z in [x]/author
    where ( (z = <author>[<last>['Buneman']<
first>['Peter']])
        || (z = <author>[<last>['Suciu']
<first>['Dan']]) )
```

In essence, using markup languages for programming is intrinsically weak for many reasons, essentially because the XML syntax makes programs boring to write and even more painful to read. A CDuce program or an XQuery script is less verbose and more concise than the same code that would be expressed with XML. Yet, numbers of dedicated processing languages are designed with XML: despite its verbosity, XML supplies a syntax that already exists, so that designers do not have to reinvent a specific one. They don't have to write either a parser.

Nor is XML for programming the ultimate solution. We have considered some popular technologies and tools that use XML tags as 'instructions' to perform, and pointed out that all of them are either designed to solve a single class of problems or not so close to XML technologies. Each of them has to deal with redundant low-level problematics such as how to bind the tags of the language to their implementation (which has an incidence to their extensibility); how to assign variables and refer them; and how to call functions, etc. The many drawbacks of current systems motivate and justify the Active Tags system, introduced in the next sections, that elegantly addresses these issues with a greater consistency.

ACTIVE TAGS: THE NEXT GENERATION OF XML-BASED SYSTEMS

The Active Tags system is a good candidate for XML-based systems: it is built upon the best of each current technology, and goes deeper inside XML technologies. Active Tags is not a markup language; it is a set of specifications that describe the Active Tags system and some of its libraries, called 'modules'. It is also the name of the master specification of the whole set.

In the same way that XSLT programs are called 'stylesheets', Active Tags ones are called 'active sheets'. Like XSLT, it is XPath centric, and active sheets will contain both instructions (Active Tags) and XML litterals. The main difference is that, instead of having a single instruction set, an active sheet may contain several, each bound to a namespace URI. The container that runs an active sheet and that hold the variables is called a processor instance, and an Active Tags application usually handles several processor instances. As demonstrated, XML database applications can rely advantageously on Active Tags as a post-process system after receiving querying data from various different kinds of data sources.

In this section, we do not intend to describe all of the features of Active Tags nor the foundations of the system, but rather to give an overview of a few of its features through various examples. The reader is directed to the reference specifications for further details. The next sections will clarify the data type system and the ability to combine strongly declarative languages with imperative operations.

A System with Tag-Based Scripting Languages

One of the core modules of the system is the XML control language (XCL), that supplies a set of tags that covers many common features:

- Usual control structure actions, such as alternative (`<xcl:if>` `<xcl:then>` `<xcl:else>`) or iterative actions (`<xcl:for-each>`), and logic procedure declaration and invokation
- XML oriented actions, such as XML parsing (`<xcl:parse>`) and XSLT transforming (`<xcl:parse-stylesheet>` and `<xcl:trans-form>`) ; these actions deal with entity and

URI resolving, passing parameters (`<xcl:param>`), error handling and many other options used to tune XML processes
- XML document creation (`<xcl:document>`, `<xcl:element>`, `<xcl:attribute>` etc) and high level Active Update implementation, that allow to perform update operations on XML objects and non-XML objects (`<xcl:delete>`, `<xcl:append>` etc)
- Filtering XML streams and plain-text streams (`<xcl:filter>`) by using XPath patterns (`<xcl:rule>`) and regular expressions

In this first example[7], XCL is used for parsing a document and transforming it with XSLT:

```
<xcl:active-sheet
      xmlns:xcl="http://ns.inria.org/
                        active-tags/xcl">

   <xcl:parse
       name="input"
       source="file:///path/to/
                        document.xml"/>
   <xcl:transform
       source="{$input}"
       stylesheet="file:///path/to/
                        stylesheet.xsl"
       output="file:///path/to/
                        result.html"/>

</xcl:active-sheet>
```

It is worth mentioning that to refer variables, the XPath notation called AVT (attribute value template) is used like in XSLT : `{$input}`, instead of shell-fashioned references `${input}` used in Ant, Jelly and others. Since we have an XPath expression, we can also use the XPath functions and operators: `{po:discount($price) * (1+$tax div 100)}`, and even extract a node: `{$doc//chapter[@id='glossary']/entry}`. Unlike XSLT, AVTs can appear in attributes and in text content, and the result of an XPath evaluation is never converted to a string, which allows the handling of various objects other than nodes, booleans, strings and numbers. For example, a parsed stylesheet may appear as:

```
<!--create the variable $xslt and
    store a stylesheet object within-->
<xcl:parse-stylesheet
    name="xslt"
    source="file:///path/to/
                  stylesheet.xsl"/>
```

The stylesheet object can be then referred to simply like this:

```
<xcl:transform
    source="file:///path/to/source.xml"
    stylesheet="{$xslt}"
    output="file:///path/to/result.html"/>
```

We will learn later that $xslt is a typed variable.

A System with Tag Libraries

Most programming languages have associated core libraries (or standard libraries). The core libraries of Active Tags include XCL, and other convenient modules for interactions with the underlying system, accessing to I/O functionalities, submitting SQL queries, querying native XML databases with XQuery, and dealing with Web problematics.

In the snippet code below, the I/O, System, and XCL modules combine with XSLT to transform a set of XML documents within a given directory. The modules are identified thanks to their namespace URIs, that works like an 'import' directive in other languages.

```
<xcl:active-sheet
    xmlns:io="http://ns.inria.org/
                  active-tags/io"
    xmlns:sys="http://ns.inria.org/
                  active-tags/sys"
```

```
    xmlns:xcl="http://ns.inria.org/
                  active-tags/xcl">

<!--parse XSLT ;this is preferable to
    parse it once since the same
    stylesheet will be used several
    times-->
<xcl:parse-stylesheet
    name="xslt"
    source="file:///path/to/
                  stylesheet.xsl"/>

<!--set the working directory ;
    read the environment variable
    «myDir" which has been set
    externally-->
<xcl:set
    name="dir"
    source="{io:file(string(
                  $sys:env/myDir))}"/>

<!--loop on the XML files of the
    directory ; the files are selected
    with XPath-->
<xcl:for-each
    name="file"
    select="{ $dir/*[@io:extension='
                  xml'] }">

    <!--parse each XML file à la SAX-->
    <xcl:parse
        name="document"
        source="{ $file }"
        style="stream"/>
    <!--transform it in HTML-->
    <xcl:transform
        source="{ $document }"
        stylesheet=""{ $xslt }"
        output="file:///path/to/published/{
        $file/@io:short-name }.html"/>

</xcl:for-each>
<!--job's done !-->

</xcl:active-sheet>
```

This script should be launched after setting the environment variable 'myDir' that has to point to the directory where the files needing to be transformed are located. It also reveals that in fact, there are several kinds of materials that are 'active' and that belong to the module bound to their namespace URIs[8] :

- Active tags : `<xcl:transform>`, that are operations or declarations
- Predefined properties : `$sys:env`
- XPath functions : `io:file()`
- Foreign attributes : `@xcl:version`, that are rather directives
- Data types : `#xs:float`

As every name is a QName, every kind of active material is conveniently represented as above in order to distinguish them according to their usage.

Similar scripts can be used for querying a native XML database; below, the XQuery query stands in a separate file indicated by the 'query' environment variable referred to in this active sheet:

```
<io:request
    name="result"
    connect="xmldb:exist://localhost:8181/
                              xmlrpc/db/"
    style="stream"
    type="XQueryService"
    source="{ string( $sys:env/query ) }"/>
```

In the next example, the active sheet is hosted inside a Web server; the root element consists of an HTTP service that defines a mapping for incoming URLs (thanks to a regular expression) :

```
<web:service
    xmlns:web="http://ns.inria.org/
                          active-tags/web"
    xmlns:io="http://ns.inria.org/
                          active-tags/io"
```

```
    xmlns:xcl="http://ns.inria.org/
                          active-tags/xcl">

<web:init>
  <xcl:set
      name="connexion"
      value="{ io:file('xmldb:exist://
        localhost:8181/xmlrpc/db/') }"
      scope="shared"/>
  <!--the URI scheme web:/// point to
      ressources that depend on the
      location of the Web
      application-->
  <xcl:parse-stylesheet
      name="xslt"
      source="web:///WEB-INF/
                      stylesheet.xsl"
      scope="shared"/>
</web:init>

<!--[webapp]/index.html?query=
    [file-name]the mapping is a
    regular expression-->
<web:mapping match="^/index\.html$"
              mime-type="text/html">
  <!--get the parameter from the query
      string-->
  <io:request
      name="result"
      connect="{ $connexion }"
      style="stream"
      type="XQueryService"
      source="web:///WEB-INF/{ string(
          $web:request/query ) }"/>
  <!--serialize the XML result to the
      HTTP output stream after
      transformation-->
  <xcl:transform
      source="{ $result }"
      stylesheet="{ $xslt }"
      output="{ value(
        $web:response/@web:output ) }"/>
</web:mapping>

</web:service>
```

The first sequence of the active sheet (`<web:init>`) reveals another feature of the framework: the ability to set a scope to variables ; `scope="shared"` indicates that the variables will be shared by all the threads processing the incoming URLs simultaneously.

A System with A Template Engine

Templates can be used for building complete XML documents within an active sheet:

```
<xcl:active-sheet
        xmlns:sys="http://ns.inria.org/
                    active-tags/sys"
        xmlns:xcl="http://ns.inria.org/
                    active-tags/xcl">

  <!--get the system property «who"-->
  <xcl:set name="who" value="{ string(
                    $sys:env/who ) }"/>

  <!--create an XML document with some
        litterals-->
  <xcl:document name="doc">
    <example>
      <title>Hello { $who } !</title>
    </example>
  </xcl:document>

  <!--serialize the XML document to the
        standard system output ; as the
        transformation doesn't involve a
        stylesheet, a copy is performed-->
  <xcl:transform output="{ $sys:out }"
                    source="{ $doc }"/>
</xcl:active-sheet>
```

When the templates are standalone, they are called « active documents " :

```
<!--the root element isn't an active tag,
    but a litteral element-->
<files-in-the-current-directory>
```

```
  <!--snippet active script-->
  <xcl:for-each
      xmlns:xcl="http://ns.inria.org/
                    active-tags/xcl"
      xmlns:io="http://ns.inria.org/
                    active-tags/io"
      name="file"
      select="{
              io:file('.')/*[@io:is-file] }">
    <!--another litteral element
        with a dynamic attribute and a
        dynamic content-->
    <file size="{
                string($file/@io:length) }">
      <!--the content of the element
          is the name of the file-->
      { name($file) }
    </file>
  </xcl:for-each>
</files-in-the-current-directory>
```

They are also useful for 'casting' SAX documents to DOM documents and vice versa, or for merging several documents into a single one:

```
<xcl:active-sheet
    xmlns:io="http://ns.inria.org/
                    active-tags/io"
    xmlns:sys="http://ns.inria.org/
                    active-tags/sys"
    xmlns:xcl="http://ns.inria.org/
                    active-tags/xcl">

<!--set the working directory ;
    read the environment variable «myDir"
    which has been set externally-->
<xcl:set
    name="dir"
    source="{
        io:file(string($sys:env/myDir))} «/>

<!--select the files to browse-->
<xcl:set
    name="files"
```

```
      source="{
          $dir/*[@io:extension='xml'] }"/>

<!--create the target SAX document-->
<xcl:document name="merged"
               style="stream">
  <root n="{ count($files) }">
    <!--loop on the XML files of
        the directory-->
    <xcl:for-each name="file"
                  select="{ $files }">
      <!--parse each XML file à la DOM-->
      <xcl:parse
          name="document"
          source="{ $file }"
          style="tree"/>
      <!--append it to the current
          content :as the host document
          is a SAX document, it will be
          « casted " automatically from
          DOM to SAX-->
      { $document }
    </xcl:for-each>
  </root>
</xcl:document>

<!--serialize the merged document to
    the standard system output ;as
    the transformation doesn't
    involve a stylesheet, a copy is
    performed-->
<xcl:transform
    output="{ $sys:out }"
    source="{ $merged }"/>

</xcl:active-sheet>
```

A System with XML Pipeline Facilities

Most XProc basic use cases (W3C, 2006a) are already available in Active Tags; for example, a pipeline that parse, validate, xinclude and transform a SAX or DOM input can be written simply like this:

```
<!--validate while parsing-->
<xcl:parse
    name="input"
    source="file:///path/to/input.xml"
    validate="true"
    style="stream"/>

<!--connect to an XInclude filter-->
<xcl:filter
    filter="http://www.w3.org/2001/
                          XInclude"
    name="included"
    source="{ $input }"/>

<!--connect to a stylesheet-->
<xcl:transform
    output="file:///path/to/output.xml"
    source="{ $included }"/>
```

Although specific features required by the XProc use cases such as XML signature is not yet supported in RefleX, the Active Tags system provides the mechanism revealed later for defining implementations of extensions.

A System with Macro Facilities

EXP is one of the core modules of Active Tags that allows us to 'Extend the XML Processor' by binding an active material to its implementation. When an active tag like <acme:foo> stands for an active tag in an active sheet, it means that there is moreover a module definition that supplies its implementation. In RefleX, Java classes can be bound to active materials within a module definition like this :

```
<exp:module
    xmlns:exp="http://ns.inria.org/
                   active-tags/exp"
    xmlns:acme="http://www.acme.com/
                   active-tags/foo"
```

```
    version="1.0"
    target="acme">

  <!-- definition of <acme:foo> -->
  <exp:element
      name="acme:foo"
      source="
        res:com.acme.www.foo.FooAction"/>
  <!-- definition of acme:bar() -->
  <exp:function
      name="acme:bar"
      source="
        res:com.acme.www.foo.
                      BarFunction"/>
  <!-- definition of @acme:version -->
  <exp:attribute
      name="acme:version"
      source="
        res:org.inria.ns.reflex.
        processor.core.VersionAttr"/>
</exp:module>
```

Such a module definition is available for every core module of Active Tags and every custom module. Sometimes, the `@source` attribute is missing from the definition; in this case, the implementation is not defined by a Java class, but defined inline. For example, in order to use the following active tag within an active sheet

```
<acme:say-hello
   variable-name="[name of the var
                     to create]"
   who="[name of the guy to say hello]"/>
```

that consists of creating a template XML document to store in a variable, we can simply supply its implementation with a macro; notice below how the attributes of the active tag are transmitted to the body of the macro (we will learn in the next section that it works for any object) :

```
<!--definition of <acme:say-hello>
   as a macro-->
<exp:element name="acme:say-hello">

  <!--create an XML document with some
      litterals-->
  <xcl:document name="doc">
   <example>
    <title>Hello {
      value( $exp:params/@who ) } !</title>
   </example>
  </xcl:document>

  <!--the following is used for returning
      variables in the caller processor
      instance-->
  <exp:exports>
   <exp:export
      name="{ string(
       $exp:params/@variable-name ) }"
      value="{ $doc }"/>
  </exp:exports>

</exp:element>
```

This macro mechanism makes the definition of user-defined modules straigthforward to design in most cases, without having recourse to the implementation language. RefleX is bundled with an application named XUnit which is made up entirely of macro definitions.

A System Able to Connect to Various Data Sources

We have seen how to query native XML databases with XQuery from an active sheet. Other data sources can be queried as well. An LDAP directory can be queried directly since LDAP queries are usually part of the URL:

```
<xcl:parse
   name="dsml-result"
   source="ldap://ldap.example.com:389/
```

```
        ou=Sales,o=Example,c=US?
      cn,tel,mail?scope=sub?
      (objetclass=person)"/>
```

The result is delivered in XML in the DSML v2 format (OASIS, 2002).

The RDBMS module of Active Tags can be used to query a relational database with SQL. Mapping an SQL request to an XML data structure is often performed thanks to proprietary mechanisms. Unfortunately, they are often limited if the expected XML structure is a little complex, which implies the need to post-process the result usually with XSLT. Active Tags offer a very flexible means for designing straightforward arbitrary complex XML structures. Active Tags allow one to actually:

- Choose which results have to be an attribute, and which have to be an element;
- Name elements and attributes, even if a name is taken from the value of a column;
- Decide precisely how to nest elements, particularly when an element container is wanted;
- Perform operations and use functions other than those supplied by SQL.

Here is a very simple example that illustrates a few of these features:

```
<xcl:active-sheet
    xmlns:sys="http://ns.inria.org/
                    active-tags/sys"
    xmlns:xcl="http://ns.inria.org/
                    active-tags/xcl"
    xmlns:rdbms="http://ns.inria.org/
                    active-tags/rdbms">

<!--the connexion to the database,
    set from environment variables-->
<rdbms:connect
    name="db"
    url="{ string( $sys:env/db-url ) }"
    user="{ string( $sys:env/user }"
    password="{
        string( $sys:env/password }"/>

<!--the SQL query, that accepts a
    parameter-->
<rdbms:select
    connection="{ $db }"
    name="products"
    query="SELECT
            id,product,price,currency
            FROM products
            WHERE currency = ?
            ORDER BY product">
<!--the parameter to transmit to
    the SQL query-->
<xcl:param value="{
        string($sys:env/currency) }"/>
</rdbms:select>

<!--let's build a SAX document-->
<xcl:document    name="xml"
style="stream">
    <!--a litteral element with an
        attribute which value is
        computed-->
    <products currency="{
        string($sys:env/currency) }">
    <!--browsing the result of the
        SQL query-->
    <xcl:for-each name="prod"
            select="{ $products }">
        <!--build an element, which
            name is computed in the
            context of $prod, the
            subelements are the name
            of the column involved
            in the query-->
        <xcl:element name="{ $prod/id }">
        <xcl:attribute name="price"
            value="{
            string($prod/price) }"/>
        <!--the element content-->
        { string( $prod/product ) }
```

```
        </xcl:element>
      </xcl:for-each>
    </products>
  </xcl:document>

<!--serialize to the standard output
    as the transformation doesn't involve
    a stylesheet, a copy is performed-->
<xcl:transform output="{ $sys:out }"
               source="{ $xml }"/>

</xcl:active-sheet>
```

A Multipurpose System

We have depicted the most common and comprehensive usages of Active Tags that clearly addresses efficiently and elegantly the issues reported in the previous section. The summary of the features that we arrived at is indicated by the subtitles of this section. The examples shown were unrelated use cases, but of course several of them can be judiciously selected in a complete XML database application: for example, querying the data sources and aggregating the results as XML, embedding the business logic in macros tags, and supplying Web mappings at the system frontend. At any place, Active Tags can drive XQuery and XSLT processes.

We'll see in the two next sections that Active Tags can do much more :

- It embeds a type system that allows the handling of non-XML objects as if they were XML;
- It has the outstanding ability to combine runnable declarative languages with imperative statements.

AN ADVANCED XML TYPE SYSTEM

A system that claims to be close to XML technologies ought to rely on XML data types, at least on surface. The W3C XML Schema specification establishes the basis of an XML type system (W3C, 2004b), although very disputed by Lewis (2002) who argues that it was not a real XML type system.

However, although the XML type system introduced in the W3C XML Schema specification seems pretty good, it is also limited in some points:

- It is designed to handle only text-derivative types: there is no way to handle arbitrary complex objects that do not rely on a textual representation (unlike numbers that can be represented as specified in IEEE 754), except by expressing them in a textual form, such as base64;
- It cannot be used for defining and using Semantic data types, as many other languages can.

This section will present how these topics are addressed with Active Tags and their relationship with the XML Data Model after recalling the benefits of W3C datatypes.

W3C Datatypes and Others

W3C datatypes appear basically in two flavours : those that describe XML structures, and those that apply to textual representations. We are focusing on the latter, within which we will find a large set of data types that cover common usages such as types for numbers (`#xsd:negativeInteger`, `#xsd:double`, `#xsd:float`...), types for dates (`#xsd:duration`, `#xsd:dateTime`, `#xsd:gYear`...), and a precise description of their lexical representation and value space.

The built-in data types specified by the W3C have a valuable feature: the ability to express constraints on their inherent properties, such as limiting the number of decimals on a number, the length of a string, or specifying the range within which a date is allowed:

```
<xsd:simpleType name="Salary">
    <xsd:restriction  base="xsd:decimal">
        <xsd:minExclusive  value="0"/>
        <xsd:fractionDigits  value="2"/>
    </xsd:restriction>
</xsd:simpleType>

<xs:simpleType name="Postcode">
    <xs:restriction base="xsd:string">
        <xs:length value="7" fixed="true"/>
    </xs:restriction>
</xs:simpleType>

<xsd:simpleType name="olympicDates">
    <xsd:restriction base="xsd:date">
        <xsd:minInclusive value="2008-08-08"/>
        <xsd:maxInclusive value="2008-08-24"/>
    </xsd:restriction>
</xsd:simpleType>
```

In the space of a few years, W3C datatypes have been adopted widely, and they are referred to in many other specifications. Clark and Murata (2001) wasted no time designing a specific type system for Relax NG; in fact, there is also a built-in type library in Relax NG, although it is limited to two types : `#string` and `#token`. It is obvious that Relax NG instances have to rely on foreign data type libraries, like W3C's.

Various other data types initiatives propose to cover more or less the idea of what we consider as a type: Perrad (2003) suggests patching DTDs by introducing regular expressions (DTD+RE), and Tennison (2006) designed the Datatyping Library Language that allows the user to define its data types separately from any schema technology.

At a deeper level, it is worth mentioning how XML datatypes are handled in non-XML systems such as SQL. Eisenberg and Melton (2004) describes the mappings between SQL and XML data types in the SQL/XML (ISO/IEC, 2003) specification. In the field of data binding, Sosnoski (2003) compares JAXB to Castor among other related tools. These tools are trying to create a bridge between the OO world and the XML world by 'converting' XML abstractions to objects in order to make them usable with OO languages. The opposite happens with Active Tags: as we will see, some non-XML objects are forced to behave like XML items in order to make them usable in native XML programs.

Handling Non-Text-Derivative Types

Difficulties are encountered when people have to process a non-XML structure as XML, and they try to invent some tags that are constrained by XML rules. We have seen in the past decade the proliferation of sluggish[9] XML languages, all expressed in terms of tags, with a schema for achieving an objective.

When considering a file system, there are at least two major issues when contemplating it as a markup structure:

1. Some of the directory names and file names do not conform to the XML names. Thus, the name of the file or a directory cannot be used as the name of an element;
2. When a structure such as a file system is dumped to a markup representation, we will have enough time to take a coffee before getting the XML document if we start from the root...

These issues lead to the following, adopted in Active Tags: it is much better to deal with the data model rather than to cope with the tags. We are able to relax some constraints that one dislikes for a specific usage. Markups are intolerant, the data model more flexible.

In Active Tags, a file system is an XML-friendly object: XPath expressions can be applied on it. For example, consider a given directory:

```
<xcl:set
    name="myDir"
    value="{
        io:file('file:///some/dir/')}"/>
```

Then, it is possible to retrieve a file within that directory, which is furthermore consistent with the syntax of URL paths :

- `$myDir/someDoc.xml`
- `$myDir/subdir/someDoc.xml`
- `$myDir/../../subdir/someDoc.xml`

... or to obtain a set of files (which is no longer consistent with the URL syntax) :

- `$myDir/*`
- `$myDir/*[@io:is-file]`
- `$myDir//*`
- `$myDir//*[@io:extension='xml']`
- `$myDir//*[name(..) !='WEB-INF']`
  `[@io:extension='xml']`
- `$myDir//*[@io:extension='xml' and`
  `@io:length > 1024]`

... or to obtain a file whose name is an invalid XML name (and consequently that cannot appear in an XPath step) :

- `$dir/*[name()='An illegal XML name but`
  `a valid file name']`

In Active Tags, the entire file system won't be mapped to tags, the system will access only to the directories involved in the navigation during the XPath evaluation. To those who may argue that the Unix "find" command can do the job, consider the following:

1. It works only on Unix/Linux;
2. It works only on a local file system, whereas Active Tags can also deal with ftp, Webdav, zip, tar...;
3. One does not have to learn an obscure syntax since it is XPath.

Since all seems to come from the XPath function `io:file()`, let's have a closer look at it. Usually,

an XPath function is expected to return either a node, a string, a number, or a boolean ; yet, we get something else, a typed object, actually an object that has the type `#io:x-file` (we go on with the previous notation for referring types : `#io:x-file` has the same meaning as `#xs:string` or `#xs:float`). Such objects are called cross-operable objects in Active Tags, or X-operable objects (conventionally, the type name of such objects starts with « x- "). They behave like XML objects but they aren't XML objects. An object of the type `#io:x-file` simply exposes some of its inherent properties as attributes or are available with other XML accessors ; for example, we easily understood in the previous examples that the length of a file can be get with its `@io:length` attribute, that its children are the files and directories it contains, and that its name is the name of the actual file or directory even if the name is not an XML name. In this last case, we won't be able to name the file directly in an XPath step, but we are still able to get it and display it if necessary. In the documentation of the I/O module of Active Tags, we can examine how is defined the `#io:x-file` type in terms of the XML Data Model. The user just has to look which attributes are available in this type for writing its XPath expressions.

This does not mean that all types worth to be considered XML-friendly. It is totally useless for some types that do not need to be exposed as XML objects. However, some have to be referred in the signatures of the various Active Tags materials; for this purpose, we just have to name them, such as the `#xsl:stylesheet` type which is assigned to variables created after parsing an XSLT stylesheet. These types are called 'marker types' and it means that the internals of the objects behind them are opaque to the system.

Storing Objects in XML Attributes

We can go a step further. Since we admit that the data model view can relax some constraints of the markup view, why not store objects inside, say, attributes ? It is exactly what happens when using the Web module that we introduced previously:

```
<xcl:transform
  source="{ $document }"
  stylesheet="{ $xslt }"
  output="{
  value( $web:response/@web:output ) }"/>
```

Let us consider more closely our `$web:re-sponse` predefined property; according to the Web module documentation, it is set automatically when entering the active sheet by the Web module, and is defined to be of the type `#web:x-response`. The Web module specifies precisely this data type: for example, its `@web:output` attribute refers to another object, in this case the output stream (of the type `#io:output`) where to write the HTTP response. The `value()` function is just used to extract the output stream object from the attribute.

At this stage, we learned that an object can expose another object as an attribute, that could also expose an object as an attribute. This leads to very unusual and exotic XPath expressions although syntactically legal such as `$foo/@FOO/@bar`. The important point is that those objects are not necessarily representable with XML tags: an attribute can't have an attribute in markup representation. However, this is not a drawback but on the contrary a serious advantage for several reasons:

- The (possible) high cost of round-tripping between XML and the object is avoided (for example, from binary to base64 and base64 to binary);
- Sometimes an XML representation of an object is irrelevant: the XML representation of an 'output stream' object is not of concern (we are not talking about the content of that stream, but about the object that handles it);

- Delivering the XML structure requires scanning recursively the members of the object, which is sometimes inappropriate, as we have seen before with file systems.

Compatibility with XDM

The last point to consider is the possible incompatibility of that model with the XML Data Model. As will be explained later, they are compatible.

Schema-aware applications using schema-aware parsers and APIs can make use of the types of elements and attributes. This is a concept described in W3C XML Schema and known as PSVI (Post-Schema-Validation Infoset). For example, if an attribute of an identified element is defined to be a `#xs:date`, then instead of dealing with the string value of the date, an application can handle the date as an object. This allows sorting a set of dates correctly: if a time zone is specified, sorting according to the string value of the dates would fail, but sorting according to the typed data succeeds.

In the same manner that the date object is bound to the attribute after validation, an output stream object (`#io:output`) is simply bound to the `@web:output` attribute of the `$web:response` X-operable object. The main difference is that no validation, not even parsing, has been performed previously: it is just an inherent characteristic of the host object. Notice that the attribute also has a string value, but that is totally useless in this case, thus it is implementation dependent ; in a Java implementation, it could be something that reflects the underlying object, like [`java.io.OutputStream@189c036`]. So useless.

Designing Semantic Data Types

W3C XML Schema and XML technologies in general do not offer the means to design Semantic data types. The Semantic of a data type is related to its level of abstraction. Murata (2002) defines the following 4 models with different levels of abstraction (we add a 5th at the bottom) :

- Model 4: Semantic view: 68° Fahrenheit
- Model 3: data type view: `#xs:int temp=68`
- Model 2: XML view:

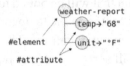

- Model 1: string view: `<?xml version="1.0"?><weather-report temp="68" unit="°F">`
- Model 0 : byte view :

```
                  3C  3F  78  6D
6C 20 76 65 72 73 69 6F 6E 3D 22 31 2E
30 22 3F 3E 3C 77 65 61 74 68 65 72 2D
72 65 70 6F 72 74 20 74 65 6D 70 3D 22
36 38 22 20 75 6E 69 74 3D 22 B0 46 22
3E
```

Model 4 is of course the closest to human concerns.

Unfortunately, XML technologies stop at Model 3. What occurs if we have to sort the following weather report by temperature?

```
<weather-report>
 <city name="Paris"temp="19" unit="°C"/>
```

```
<city name="Rome" temp="22" unit="°C"/>
<city name="Berlin" temp="32" unit="°F"/>
                    <!-- 32°F = 0°C -->
<city name="Madrid" temp="23" unit="°C"/>
<city name="London" temp="68" unit="°F"/>
                    <!-- 68°F = 20°C -->
</weather-report>
```

With XML technologies you won't be able to get the right result ; an inadmissible fact face to other technologies that are able to address this issue. Once again, Active Tags hold the solution. We have seen previously that an attribute can be bound to a typed data; why not design a skilled facility that would build a made-to-measure typed data? The Active Schema Language, further detailed in the next section, supplies the means by which to define data types. With the help of XCL, it is able to augment the amount of information of an XML document:

```
<asl:active-schema
  xmlns:xcl="http://ns.inria.org/
                        active-tags/xcl"
  xmlns:asl="http://ns.inria.org/
                        active-schema"
  xmlns:xs="http://www.w3.org/2001/
                        XMLSchema-datatypes"
  target="">
```

Figure 1.Comparison of the XML Data Model and X-operable objects

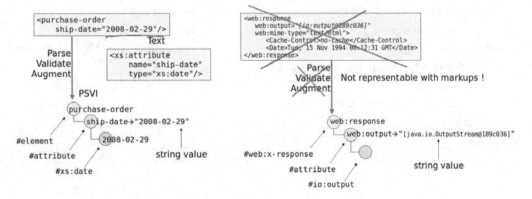

```
<!--the root element of a weather
                         report-->
<asl:element name="weather-report"
                 root="always">
  <asl:sequence>
    <asl:element
        ref-elem="city"
        min-occurs="1"
        max-occurs="unbounded"/>
  </asl:sequence>
</asl:element>


<!--a <city> contains only attributes-->
<asl:element name="city">
 <asl:attribute name="name"
              ref-type="xs:string"/>
 <asl:attribute name="temp"
            ref-type="temperature"/>

 <asl:attribute name="unit">
   <asl:text value="°C"/>
   <asl:text value="°F"/>
 </asl:attribute>
</asl:element>


<!--#temperature is our custom type
   it will build a typed data based on
   a xs:decimal-->
<asl:type name="temperature"
        base="xs:decimal"
        init="{.}">
   <xcl:if test="{
          asl:element()/@unit='°F' }">
     <xcl:then>
     <!--if @unit="°F", the typed data
          is updated-->
       <xcl:update
          referent="{ $asl:data }"
          operand="{
          (value(.) - 32) * 5 div 9 }"/>
     </xcl:then>
   </xcl:if>
```

```
    </asl:type>

</asl:active-schema>
```

The active schema language (ASL) can define content models and data types like other schema technologies (and also unlike them!). In the above instance, the typed data that will be bound to the attribute will vary according to the temperature unit used in the XML input document. The following active sheet will sort our weather report correctly:

```
<xcl:active-sheet
     xmlns:xcl="http://ns.inria.org/
                       active-tags/xcl"
     xmlns:asl="http://ns.inria.org/
                       active-schema">

   <xcl:parse
        name="wr"
        source="weather-report.xml"/>
   <asl:parse-schema
        name="wr-schema"
        source="weather-report.asl"/>
   <asl:validate
        schema="{ $wr-schema }"
        node="{ $wr }"
        augment="yes"
        deep="yes"/>
   <xcl:echo
        value="List of cities, sorted in
             temperature order:"/>
   <xcl:for-each
        name="city"
        select="{
        xcl:sort( $wr/*/city, @temp ) }">
     <xcl:echo
        value="{ $city/@temp }{
          $city/@unit } { $city/@name }"/>
   </xcl:for-each>

</xcl:active-sheet>
```

In the result, we notice that the attribute value remains the same, whereas the bound typed data was involved in this sort operation:

```
List of cities, sorted in temperature
order:
    32°F Berlin
    19°C Paris
    68°F London
    22°C Rome
    23°C Madrid
```

Furthermore, we could also imagine another Semantic data type that would handle a temperature followed immediately by its scale : `<city name="London" temp="68°F"/>`, and why not allow a combination of the two formats in the same document? A type in ASL can also be expressed in terms of a choice between several other candidate types.

The reader is invited to consult the Active Schema Language specification for further information about Semantic data types and polymorphic data types.

To summarize, the concept of X-operable objects is in essence fully compatible with XML. Various objects can be handled in Active Tags, some related to XML, others not; some X-operable, others not; some representable with markups, others not. Some with Semantics, others not. Of course, any combination of them can occur.

Trying to put XML types in OO languages with forceps is always a chore. Conversely, having an XML view of objects is extremely valuable. On the road to native XML programming, we ought to have in our repertoire XML data types like those we shown.

RUNNABLE DECLARATIVE LANGUAGES: THE DYNAMIC METHOD AND ITS NOVEL ISSUES

We mentioned several times a class of languages named « declarative languages ". This chapter discusses about how Active Tags support them.

Actually, we have seen rather imperative Active Tags : `<xcl:parse>`, `<xcl:transform>`, `<xcl:set>`, `<acme:say-hello>`... and few declarative ones that were hosting « procedures " : `<xcl:active-sheet>`, `<web:mapping>`, `<exp:element>`... Even in procedural languages, we find what we call 'declarations' in this chapter: the declaration of the name of the program, the declaration of a procedure, and in OOP, the declaration of a class or a method. Languages such as W3C XML Schema, SCXML, and XML catalogs are fully declarative, in the sense that they do not contain at all imperative operations (or very few ones in the case of SCXML). By opposition to 'procedural' or 'imperative': it will not be necessary to operate XML declarative languages sequentially since they specify 'what' rather than 'how to'; a specialized processor of such a declarative language will process it according to the intended Semantic of each tag.

In this section, we examined the way to integrate imperative statements within declarative sentences; this feature is depicted through a very inventive schema language: the active schema language (ASL).

Schema Languages and Their Issues

An XML Schema is the expression of some assertions expected in an XML document class. Assertions in XML documents ensure that applications will process them without causing faults. Expressing assertions with schemata ensure that applications developers will spend most of their time in designing data process and less of their time in controlling them. Well-known schema technologies are DTD, Relax NG, W3C XML Schema and Schematron.

Schema processors build an abstract tree from a schema instance. With a traditional grammar-based schema (DTD, W3C XML Schema, Relax NG), as the schema instance is hard-coded, the abstract tree is static, making the expressiveness of the schema limited to what is allowed by the grammar. The flaw with grammars in XML is that they only allow constraint in content models in a declarative manner, which is in essence very concise and expressive, but when the limits of the declarative syntax are reached, there is no way out; it is still possible to add a new tag to express the missing declarative tag, but the limit still exists a single step further on, at the cost of upgrading the language.

The Active Schema Language

ASL has been designed in order to be much more expressive without adding tags again and again. The immediate benefit is the avoidance of compromising a user's XML structure just because some constraints cannot be expressed by grammar-based schemata, which often happens with traditional schema languages. ASL contains constructs similar to other schema languages: an element declaration is still made of sequences or choices of element references, texts or attributes, but they are mixed with imperative constructs. As the content models are computed at runtime while validating, the result abstract tree becomes dynamic, increasing dramatically the expressiveness of the schema: the content models can adapt themselves to the incoming data to validate in an extreme flexible way (Poulard 2008). Additionally, ASL allows the dynamic computation of occurrence constraints that are, at best, hard-coded in existing schema languages.

The following document is an instance of a purchase order:

```
<purchase-order
    xmlns="http://www.example.com/
                        purchase-order"
    ship-date="2008-02-29">

  <items total="188.93">

  <item partNum="872-AA">
    <productName>Lawnmower</
                        productName>
    <quantity>1</quantity>
    <USPrice>148.95</USPrice>
  </item>

  <item partNum="926-AA">
    <productName>Baby Monitor</
                        productName>
    <quantity>1</quantity>
    <USPrice>39.98</USPrice>
  </item>

  <free-item partNum="261-ZZ">
    <productName>Kamasutra for dummies
                    </productName>
    <quantity>1</quantity>
  </free-item>

  </items>

</purchase-order>
```

It is constrained by structural rules and business rules, in the circumstances a `<free-item>` element is allowed only if the total amount exceeds $500 (which makes the above document invalid). Due to the lack of expressiveness of existing schema languages, the best we can do is to relax some constraints and ignore the business rule. The content model of the `<items>` element would be expressed like this in a DTD : `<!ELEMENT items (item+,free-item?)>`.

Unfortunately, an instance like the previous one violates our business rule although it is valid regarding the DTD. Other schema languages cannot do much better, except for Schematron (Jelliffe, 2004) that will be discussed later.

ASL allows the writing of the business rule exactly as it has been expressed:

```
<asl:active-schema
    xmlns:xcl="http://ns.inria.org/
                       active-tags/xcl"
    xmlns:asl="http://ns.inria.org/
                       active-schema"
    xmlns:xs="http://www.w3.org/2001/
                       XMLSchema"
    xmlns:po="http://www.example.com/
                       purchase-order"
    target="po"
>

    <!--the root element of a purchase
        order-->
    <asl:element name="po:purchase-order"
                 root="always">
     <asl:attribute name="ship-date"
               ref-type="xs:date"/>
     <asl:sequence>
         <asl:element ref-elem="po:items"/>
     </asl:sequence>
    </asl:element>

    <!--a dynamic content model-->
    <asl:element name="po:items"
root="never">
        <asl:attribute name="total"
               ref-type="xs:decimal"/>
        <!--a variable sequence-->
        <asl:sequence>
          <asl:element
              ref-elem="po:item"
              min-occurs="1"
              max-occurs="unbounded"/>
          <!--the test that introduces
              variability-->
          <xcl:if test="{
          asl:element()/@total &gt; 500 }">
            <xcl:then>
```

```
            <asl:element
                ref-elem="po:free-item"
                min-occurs="0"
                max-occurs="1"/>
            </xcl:then>
          </xcl:if>
        </asl:sequence>
    </asl:element>

    <asl:element name="po:item"
                 root="never">
        <!--content model here-->
    </asl:element>

    <asl:element name="po:free-item"
                 root="never">
        <!--content model here-->
    </asl:element>

    <!--other element definitions here-->

</asl:active-schema>
```

This schema demonstrates that an imperative operation is used to build the content model during the validation. The content model of the `<items>` element will vary according to the total amount found in the incoming document. Each of the 'realizations'of the element definition as illustrated by the picture below leads to a different abstract tree of the grammar. But both are expressed in a single self-adaptative schema.

Schematron is a technology that offers similar services; however, there is a fundamental difference : Schematron act outside content models whereas ASL defines them. Schematron will report constraints violations after grammar-based validation. A tool such as an editor will propose to the user to insert a `<free-item>` although it is forbidden! ASL will introduce it in the content model only when the conditions are fulfilled, and the editor will not propose it to the user.

ASL contains other innovative features. The reader is referred to the ASL specification and the RefleX Web site where other demonstrations are available.

Future Directions for Configuration Files: Moving to Declarative Languages

At the very beginning of this chapter, we intentionally cited as declarative languages, among others, the J2EE deployment descriptors, although they are the more often considered as configuration files rather than runnable declarative languages, strictly speaking. However, the borderline between XML-based configuration files and XML-based declarative languages is somewhat blurry when the configuration acts on the behaviour of the software (not on the size of the font or the background color, neither of which is our concern). Usually, a software that relies on such a configuration file will load it and sometimes instantiates some classes according to the tags encountered. It is as if the underlying software were building a plan of what to run according to how its components-objects are assembled together (this is again a very acceptable definition of what can be a declarative language). In essence, this is not really different from the way things work in Active Tags and ASL, except that with Active Tags, the software

is a general-purpose engine. The one chosen to control the interactions engine-component is, at a higher level, a matter of personal preference, but designers of applications might now consider a different architecture where they turn their configuration files to real declarative languages - dynamic declarative languages, like ASL. A configuration file that accepts injections of if-then-else statements would be more practical.

Novel Issues with Dynamic Declarative Languages: Hyperschemas

The flexibility afforded by Active Tags to runnable declarative-oriented languages leads to simplicity and efficiency. Applied to ASL, we obtain a new schema language much more powerful than traditional ones (DTD, W3C XML Schema, Relax NG, Schematron). We learned that building a dynamic execution plan is much more powerful and efficient than building a static one. By considering Active Tags while creating new declarative markup languages, a designer will be able to make them more simple and more expressive.

However, by introducing dynamicity in XML-based declarative languages, the processing engine has to defer the validation of the underlying Active Tags that are used. In fact, the system has to deal with an additional level of validation.

Figure 2.Two representations of a self-adaptive schema

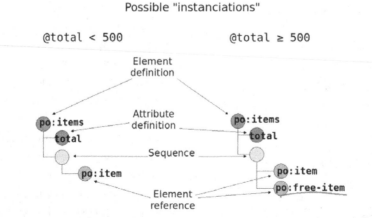

176

The former level of validation acts on XML tags and relies on classical XML validation (schema languages). The latter acts at the component level that is resolved at runtime and that might vary, as shown previously with ASL. Thus, the system might reject an invalid component during its assembly. But this can be done only at runtime, not when the Active Tags are unmarshalled. Consequently, the validation of the XML tags becomes somewhat useless, since an active tag will basically have to accept in its content any other tag. More precisely, it would have to validate those that are hard-coded, and would have to ignore those that appear to be dynamic, but this issue has not yet been addressed.

This issue is similar to systems that do not rely on static typing: at runtime, such systems raise an 'invalid cast error' or something similar. We can envisage a kind of **hyperschema** that would act at the component level rather than at the tag level, but so far, no serious solution has been considered for these novel issues in XML.

Thus, by introducing dynamicity we have boosted considerably the capability of declarative languages. The cost is that we no longer have control on their validity. This is a major drawback in active sheets that basically allow almost everything that might cause errors at runtime.

CONCLUSION AND FUTURE DIRECTIONS

The Active Tags system is so powerful simply because it relies intensively on the XML toolbox. Considered separately, each has its usefulness, but putting them all together and going deeper in the XML paradigm produces Active Tags.

We have seen with various examples how the Active Tags system neatly addressed common problems. Being XML-centric, it leverages many XML technologies like no other XML-based system has ever done. It has also the ability to limit the proliferation of runnable XML languages.

Actually, the designers of new runnable markup languages would gain considerably if they adopted Active Tags. Much effort would be saved since they would just have to choose what they need here and there and they would not have to worry about unmarshal issues, variables handling, and cooperation between languages.

We still need XML-based processing languages, and Active Tags is an innovative, consistent, coherent and solid response to what we can expect from such languages. We have seen how an enhanced type system can leverage the XML data model for handling non-XML objects with XPath or for supporting Semantic data types. The Active Schema Language demonstrates how declarative languages can be boosted by introducing dynamicity.

Throughout this chapter, we have separated Active Tags from XQuery. These two systems are not in competition since they are not serving the same purpose. Since an active sheet is full of tags and XPath expressions, we could gain in expressiveness by replacing XPath with XPath 2.0 and possibly XQuery. Another perspective is to consider that snippets of markups in XQuery are litterals, so Active Tags could possibly be allowed in some relevant places of a query. Furthermore, since XQuery has an XML syntax, XQueryX (W3C, 2007c), the injection of foreign elements other than litterals does make sense; the remaining concern would be to determine where it would be relevant. In any case, we point out that runnable markup languages and XQuery could help themselves. Fundamentally, in relation to the XML data model, they are not so distant.

This is a rough approximation to what we could call the 'unified theory of markup'.

We are witnessing a kind of Darwinian evolution in the XML eco-system: primitive processing-instructions yield their place to tag-based systems that themselves could be replaced by unified XML systems such as Active Tags. The next decade[10] will determine whether the latter 'species' has a chance to survive the 'dinosaurs' of the Industry that rule the world[11]. We have to deal with this: computer science history provides numerous anecdotal evidence where the best systems were not the systems that survived. Perhaps we will see hybrid systems becoming a trend.

REFERENCES

Apache Software Foundation. *Ant. A Java-based build tool.* http://ant.apache.org/

Apache Software Foundation. *Cocoon*, http://cocoon.apache.org

Castor. *The Castor Project.* Available at: http://www.castor.org/

CDuce. *CDuce*, http://www.cduce.org/

Clark, J., & Murata, M. (Eds.) (2001). *Relax NG specification. Organization for the advancement of structured information standards.* http://relaxng.org/spec-20011203.html

Eisenberg, A., & Melton, J. (2004). Advancements in SQL/XML. In *SIGMOD Record 33*(3), 79-86.

EXSLT. *The community extensions to XSLT.* http://www.exslt.org/

Gapeyev, V., Levin, M. Y., & Pierce, B. C. (2005). XML goes native: Run-time representations for Xtatic. In *CC*, (pp. 43–58).

Harren, M., Raghavachari, M., Shmueli, O., Burke, M. G., Bordawekar, R., Pechtchanski, I., & Sarkar, V. (2005). XJ: Facilitating XML processing in Java. In *WWW*, (pp. 278-287).

INRIA. *Active schema language.* http://ns.inria.fr/active-tags/active-schema/active-schema.html

INRIA. *Active tags technologies.* http://ns.inria.org/active-tags/

INRIA. *RefleX. An Active Tags engine in Java.* http://reflex.gforge.inria.fr/

INRIA. *XUnit. Unit tests in XML.* http://reflex.gforge.inria.fr/xunit.html

JAXB. *Java architecture for XML binding.* http://java.sun.com/xml/jaxb/.

Jelliffe, R. *The Schematron Assertion Language (Schematron).* http://www.schematron.com/spec.html

Jelly. *Executable XML. The Apache Software Foundation*, http://jakarta.apache.org/commons/jelly/

Lewis, A. (2002). *Not My Type: Sizing Up W3C XML Schema Primitives*, http://www.xml.com/pub/a/2002/07/31/wxstypes.html

Megginson, D. (2001). *Simple API for XML (SAX)*, http://www.saxproject.org/

Murata, M. (2002). Principles of Schema Languages. In H. Maruyama (Ed.), *XML and Java* (2nd ed.), (pp. 592-601).

OASIS (2002). *Directory services markup language (DSML) v2.0.* http://www.oasis-open.org/committees/dsml/docs/DSMLv2.doc

Perrad, F. (2003). *DTD+RE. XMLfr.* http://xmlfr.org/documentations/articles/ 030729-0001.

Poulard, P. (2006). Active Tags: An XML system for native XML programming, in panel Next-Generation XML APIs. In *XML*.

Poulard, P. (2007). Active tags: Mastering XML with XML. In *Extreme markup language*.

Poulard, P. (2008). Properties of schema mashups: Dynamicity, Semantic, mixins, hyperschemas. In *Balisage*.

Schmitt, A. (2004). Native XML processing in object-oriented languages: Calling XMHell from PurgatOOry. In *FOOL*.

Sosnoski, D. (2003). *Data binding, Part 1: Code generation approaches -- JAXB and more,* http://www.ibm.com/developerworks/library/x-databdopt/

ISO/IEC (2003) *SQL/XML. Database languages, SQL Part 14: XML-Related Specifications*, ISO/IEC 9075-14:2003 Information technology.

Tennison, J. (2006). Datatypes for XML: The datatyping librarylanguage (DTLL). In *Extreme markup languages*.

Sun Microsystems. *UEL. Unified expression language*, http://java.sun.com/products/jsp/reference/techart/unifiedEL.html

Sun Microsystems, *JSP. JavaServer pages technology.* http://java.sun.com/products/jsp/

Sun Microsystems *JSTL. JavaServer pages standard tag library.* http://java.sun.com/products/jsp/jstl/

Walsh, N. (2005). *XML Catalogs. Organization for the advancement of structured information standards.* http://www.oasis-open.org/committees/download.php/14809/xml-catalogs.html

Xtatic. *The Xtatic project: Native XML processing for C#.* http://www.cis.upenn.edu/~bcpierce/xtatic/

W3C (1999a). *XML path language (XPath) Version 1.0.* W3C Recommendation, http://www.w3.org/TR/xpath

W3C (1999b). *XSL transformations (XSLT).* W3C Recommendation, http://www.w3.org/TR/xslt

W3C (2000). *Document object model (DOM) level 2 core specification.* W3C Recommendation, http://www.w3.org/TR/2000/REC-DOM-Level-2-Core-20001113/

W3C (2004a). *XML Schema part 1: Structures (2nd ed.).* W3C Recommendation, http://www.w3.org/TR/xmlschema-1/

W3C (2004b). *XML Schema part 2: Datatypes Second Edition.* W3C Recommendation, http://www.w3.org/TR/xmlschema-2/

W3C (2006a). *XML processing model requirements and use cases.* W3C Working Draft, http://www.w3.org/TR/2006/WD-xproc-requirements-20060411/

W3C (2006b). *An XML pipeline language (XProc).* W3C Working Draft, http://www.w3.org/TR/2006/WD-xproc-20061117/

W3C (2007a). *XQuery/XPath data model (XDM) 1.0.* W3X Recommendation, http://www.w3.org/TR/xpath-datamodel/

W3C (2007b). *XQuery 1.0: An XML query language.* W3C Recommendation, http://www.w3.org/TR/xquery/

W3C (2007c). *XML Syntax for XQuery 1.0.* W3C Recommendation, http://www.w3.org/TR/xqueryx/

W3C (2007d). *State chart XML (SCXML): State machine notation for control abstraction.* W3C Working Draft, http://www.w3.org/TR/scxml/

ENDNOTES

[1] The author is aware that this is disputable and some readers may strongly disagree. A characteristic is reputed to be supported when it has a significant presence and is extremely well-covered by the tool mentioned.

[2] The notation `#datatype-name` is used consistently in this chapter to distinguish other usage of QNames in properties (`$property-name`), functions (`function-name()`), etc.

[3] `*` : any

[4] Active Tags can be used to design declarative languages that can be deeply interweaved with imperative statements.

[5] Once XProc has built an execution plan, the operations are run in sequence (potentially several parallel sequences); the extensibility

of XProc consists of allowing more operations, not to add composable steps.

6   The name FLWOR, pronounced "flower", is suggested by the keywords `for`, `let`, `where`, `order by`, and `return` in XQuery.

7   We do not intend to precisely describe the examples, as they are commented upon and the markup is somewhat wordy. The reader is encouraged to refer to the Active Tags and RefleX Web sites for detailed information.

8   Each module is described separately with its own specification that contains the documentation of
its active materials. Each module namespace URI conveniently points to its specification.

9   In opposition to those who define Active Tags, such XML languages are data structures.

10   From the perspective of computer sciences, a decade is a long period.

11   Which meteor could lead to their disappearance?

Chapter IX
Continuous and Progressive XML Query Processing and its Applications

Stéphane Bressan
National University of Singapore, Singapore

Wee Hyong Tok
National University of Singapore, Singapore

Xue Zhao
National University of Singapore, Singapore

ABSTRACT

Since XML technologies have become a standard for data representation, a great amount of discussion has been generated by the persisting open issues and their possible solutions. In this chapter, the authors consider the design space for XML query processing techniques that can handle ad hoc and continuous XPath or XQuery queries over XML data streams. This chapter presents the state-of-art techniques in continuous and progressive XML query processing. They also discuss several open issues and future trends.

INTRODUCTION

XML (extensible markup language) is now a standard for data dissemination and interchange. While, in most application domains, the amount of available data feeds or data streams, whether sensor or engineered data, is generally increasing, the data in particular is increasingly in XML format. To seize the opportunity created by the availability of such a wealth of network accessible timely data, modern applications need the capability to effectively and efficiently process queries to XML data streams.

From individual stock investors to large hedge fund traders, those watching the stock market are interested in monitoring activities of company stocks and derivatives in the light of other news and data related to companies and their business. An investor, considering both technical and fundamental analyses wants to know both volume and price, and sales and revenue figures of company and industry for the stocks in his portfolio of interest. For the purpose of illustration, we consider the following scenario: An investor poses a query that combines a data stream from the stock market (providing latest volume and price) with a data feed reporting fundamental data data (e.g. updated sales figures). The query is a combination of two streams, the stock market ticker (nyse.xml) and the fundamental data streams (sales.xml) as well as an XML document, the listing in the stock exchange (listing.xml) that provides the mapping of the stock ticker symbol to the company name. The XQuery below returns a set of elements resultTuple, which consists of the company name, ticker symbol, sales, last price, and volume of all the stocks in the exchange.

Reading new blogs is often disorienting as bloggers often assume that their readers are familiar with the news on which they are commenting. A possible solution is to automatically combine blog entries with headlines and provide the links to the related news. Both blogs entries and news are often available as RSS (really simple syndication) or atom feeds. Existing RSS/Atom readers provide basic keyword-based filtering and simple feed merging. Instead of relying on the limited capabilities of existing readers and their interface, and since the feeds are in XML, the desired combination can be expressed as an XQuery offering the full expressive power of a query language. Although RSS and Atom sources are more similar to Web pages being pulled than to feeds or streams pushing data, the latter can be simulated by periodic pulling. In the example at hand, the combination of blog entries and news can be achieved by the Xquery given in Figure 2.

The number and scope of possible applications is limited only by our imagination. Their effective and efficient implementation depends on the availability of algorithms, techniques and tools for the processing of continuous and progressive queries to XML data streams. Unlike the processing of queries to XML repositories, applications processing XML data streams do not have a priori access to the complete data. This makes it difficult to index and organize data. At the same time, since data is transient, only limited memory is available for immediate processing. Since data arrives continuously, these applications need XML query processors that can efficiently

Figure 1. An XQuery query combining technical and fundamental data from live feeds for market monitoring

```
( for $s in doc("nyse.xml")//symbolTuple
  for $t in doc("listing.xml")//company
  for $q in doc("sales.xml")//sales
    where $s/symbol = $t/symbol and $q/company = $t/name
    return
     <resultTuple>
        {($q/company), ($s/symbol), ($s/sales),
         ($q/lastSale), ($q/shareVolume)}
     </resultTuple>
)
```

Figure 2. An XQuery query combining blog entries with their related news from RSS/Atom feeds

```
( for $s2 in doc("news.xml")//item
    for $q in doc("blogs.xml")//entry
      where $q/tag=$s//techNews/keyword
        and contains($s/title, "CNA")
      return
      <resultTuple>
          {($s/blurb), ($s/article), ($q/entryId) }
      </resultTuple>
\
```

process queries on-the-fly. In order to ensure a good user experience, the XML query processors must deliver initial results quickly, maintain a consistently high result throughput, and ensure that the produced results are representative. Since queries are themselves long running or continuous, the XML query processors should be able to exploit the opportunities to share computation and intermediate results among queries.

The objective of this chapter is to provide a comprehensive survey of continuous and progressive XML query processing techniques. The rest of the chapter is organized as follows. We first discuss the background for XML stream processing. Next we discuss the building blocks for continuous and progressive XML query processing. We present several state-of-the-art techniques for continuous and progressive XML query processing. Finally, we conclude and discuss future trends.

BACKGROUND

Terminology

Traditional database query processing algorithms process data that is readily available as it is stored on disk. Data can be organized in ancillary data structures such as indices for supporting efficient query processing. The overhead of the construction of the ancillary data structures is amortized as several queries can reuse them. These traditional algorithms produce results only at the end of the processing. They are said to be blocking.

Algorithms that are able to produce results incrementally are called non-blocking or progressive algorithms. Such algorithms could have different granularity. They could process individual data or entire blocks before they produce results, but they do not need to wait for the whole data sets to be available.

If append-only databases data arrives continuously, it is stored and it persists. Data streams are an extension of the idea of append-only databases in which data is transient. Memory allocated to the management and processing of data is limited. Only a portion of the data is stored at any given point in time. An equivalent hypothesis is that the size of data is infinite: the stream is unbounded. For both append-only databases and data streams, the maintenance of cost-effective ancillary data structures is more challenging as it needs to be incremental.

For either append-only databases or data stream, a common scenario is one in which a user pauses a queries and expects incremental results as data arrives. Such queries are called continuous queries. We see that they must be progressive. In the case of data streams, one-pass or bounded memory algorithms for query processing emphasize the economical usage of memory:. We refer to such algorithms as streaming algorithms.

XML and XML Data Streams

XML data is commonly represented as a tree. The nodes in the trees are divided into 3 types, namely: element, attribute and value nodes. An element node consists of either open or close tags. An attribute node refers to the attributes that are defined in the start tag of an element. This is used to provide additional information regarding the element node. An important distinction between element and attribute nodes is that the later cannot be nested, and duplicated within each element node. In additional, there is no fixed order on how the attribute nodes will appear in an element node. The value nodes correspond to the data values. Figure 3 shows an sample of XML data from a stock ticker scenario. We can observe the set of start tags <StockSymbols>, <symbolTuple>, <symbol>, <description>, <market>, <industry>, and the set of end tags </StockSymbols>, </symbolTuple>, </symbol>, </description>, </market>, </industry>. Character data (i.e. PCDATA.) refers to text that is bounded by start and end tags. Some examples of PCDATA in Figure 3 include "NasdaqGS", "Software", etc.

In the XML data model, ID/IDREF attributes of elements are used to refer to other elements. In order to support the ID/IDREF, graphs are another common representation for XML data.

An XML data stream consists of either XML data that are delivered from a remote XML data repository, or a large volume of XML data that needs to be read from disk. The XML data arrives as a sequence of XML nodes. These nodes can be either an element or value node.

It is important to differentiate between the notion of an XML data stream and static XML data. For XML data streams, the query processor has sequential access to the XML nodes. Nodes arrive in document order, and the query processor has to process the nodes in one-pass. Backward traversals to older nodes are not allowed due to the limited memory that is available. This prevents the use of any labeling techniques. In contrast, query processors that handle static XML data can randomly access the complete XML data. In order to improve performance during the matching of the structural relationships (e.g. Parent/Child, Ancestor/Descendant), a labeling scheme is used to label the XML nodes.

Figure 3. Excerpt of XML stock exchange data feed

```
<root>
   <symbolTuple>
         <symbol>MSFT</symbol>
         <description>Microsoft</description>
         <market>NasdaqGS</market>
         <industry>Software</industry>
   </symbolTuple>

   <symbolTuple>
     <symbol>GOOG</symbol>
     <description>Google</description>
     <market>NasdaqGS</market>
     <industry>Internet Info Providers</industry>
   </symbolTuple>
 ...
   <root>
```

Query Languages

In this section, we discuss query languages that are used for both ad hoc and continuous queries on XML data. Concrete XML query languages, such as XPath and XQuery (W3C, 2002), express both structural and predicate constraints on the XML document/stream.

A XPath query consists of a location path expression, which specifies the path traversal from the root of the XML document to the desired element. In an XPath query, once the structural constraints have been satisfied, predicate constraints can be checked.

A XQuery query consists of FLWR (For-Let-Where-Return) clauses, and can consist of several XPath expressions. The For and Let clauses in XQuery bind the nodes that are selected by the correspond XPath expressions into user-defined node variables. The Where clause is used for specifying selection and join predicates. The Return clause is used to specify the format of the results to be returned.

One common representation of structural constraints is to make use of twig patterns. A twig pattern is a small-tree which contains information about the structural relationships between the XML nodes in the query. The edges in the Twig pattern can capture either a parent-child (P-C) or an ancestor-descendant (A-D) relationship. This is denoted as "/" and "//" respectively. In Figure 4, the Twig Query consists of three XML nodes: symbolTuple, market and industry. The edge // between the symbolTuple and market nodes denotes an ancestor-descendant (A-D) relationship. The edge / between the symbolTuple and industry nodes denotes a parent-child relationship.

In order to support window and continuous queries on XML, existing XML query languages must be extended. For relational data stream processing, the continuous query language (CQL) (Arasu et al., 2006) is used. CQL supports various sliding window Semantics. These include time-based, tuple-based and partitioned windows. In addition, CQL allows queries to be issued against a combination of data streams and stored relations. (Botan et al., 2007) noted the limitations of XQuery 1.0, which do not support window and continuous queries on XML data. Consequently, extensions to the XQuery language are proposed in (Botan et al., 2007) to support window and continuous queries. We refer to this extended XQuery language as XQueryExt.

Figure 4. An example of a twig pattern

```
          symbolTuple
           //      \
        market   industry
```

Figure 5 Extended XQuery (sliding window queries)

```
forseq $w in $stockTickerFeed tumbling window
    start curStock $first when fn:true()
    end nextStock $lookAhead when
        $first/market ne $lookAhead/market
where count ($w) ge 10
return $w[1]/market
```

In XQueryExt, the syntax and Semantics for a new FORSEQ clause is introduced. The FORSEQ clause is an extension of the XQuery FLWOR expression, and can be easily composable with other FOR, LET, and FORSEQ clauses. The main difference between the XQueryExt's FORSEQ clause and XQuery's FOR clause is that the FORSEQ clause binds the variable to a window, whereas the FOR clause binds to each item in the XML stream. Figure 5 shows an example of an extended XQuery query. In Figure 5, the query is used to find the names of all markets in the stock ticker XML feed (given in Figure 3), where there are more than 10 stock symbols in the particular market.

An example of a sliding window, continuous XML query (Botan et al., 2007) is given in Figure 6. The query in Figure 6 computes the moving averages over an infinite XML data stream. The two asterisks (i.e. (xs:int)**) are used as an annotation to represent the input. The input consists of integer values, and the XML data is continuously arriving and can be infinite. In addition, the asterisk annotation is used by the XQueryExt compiler to detect the processing of blocking operations on an infinite sequence.

Query Processing

In this section, we discuss XML query processing algorithms that are designed for processing XPath or XQuery queries. We first discuss conventional XML query processing algorithms, which assume that the algorithms have access to the entire XML data. Consequently, this allows the pre-processing of the XML data by labeling the nodes.

Twig queries form the building blocks for both XPath and XQuery query processing. Thus, query processing algorithms focused on efficiently processing twig queries. A labeling scheme (e.g. Region (Bruno et al., 2002), Dewey-based (Tatarinov et al., 2002; Lu et al., 2005), and (Lu et al., 2005) encodings) is used to encode the structural relationships inherent within the XML documents. During query processing, the algorithms rely on these labels in order to efficiently determine various structural constraints (e.g. parent/child or ancestor/descendant relationships) between XML nodes. The nodes in the XML document are labeled in a pre-processing step.

The authors of (Zhang et al., 2001; Al-Khalifa et al., 2002) propose to decompose the twig patterns into binary structural relationships. In order to identify the matching portions of the XML document, structural joins are used to combine the intermediate results. One of the key problems is that such algorithms tend to generate very large intermediate results. To address the issue of large intermediate results being generated, holistic twig join algorithms are proposed. Holistic twig join algorithms eliminate the need to decompose the twig patterns into multiple binary structural joins. Instead, a stack is used to store the results compactly.

The authors of (Bruno et al., 2002) propose the TwigStack algorithm. TwigStack uses a chain

Figure 6. Extended XQuery (sliding window continuous queries)

```
declare variable $seq as (xs:int)** external;
forseq $w in $seq sliding window
    start position $start when fn:true()
    end position $end when $end - $start eq 10
return fn:avg($w)
```

of linked stacks to store the partial results from root-to-leaf path queries. These partial results are then merge-joined to form the answers to the twig queries. While TwigStack is shown to be an I/O and CPU optimal algorithm for twig queries, TwigStack assumes that a query consists of only ancestor-descendant edges. If a query consist of ancestor-descendant and parent-child edges, the intermediate results generated by TwigStack is still significantly large.

To address this problem, (Lu et al., 2004) propose the TwigStackList algorithm. Similar to TwigStack, TwigStackList also makes use of stacks for storing the partial results. The key innovation in TwigStackList is that it performs look-ahead of the several elements and stores them into lists. This helps to reduce the size of the intermediate results. Consequently, this results in better performance for twig queries with a mixture of ancestor-descendant and parent-child edges.

TJFast (Lu et al., 2005) uses an extended Dewey-based scheme to answer queries with wild-cards in branching nodes. One of the key features of the extended Dewey labeling scheme is that it allows the names of all elements that occur from the path between the root and an element to be easily determined. This allows TJFast to evaluate twig patterns by accessing only the labels of elements in the leaf node predicate of the query. This significantly improves the performance of the twig matching algorithm.

Due to the need for prior labeling of the XML data, and the need to wait for all the intermediate results to be produced before results are available, these techniques are not suitable for continuous and progressive query processing over XML data streams.

CONTINUOUS AND PROGRESSIVE XML QUERY PROCESSING

Building Blocks

In this section, we identify the building blocks for understanding and designing continuous and progressive XML query processing algorithms over XML data streams. Next, we present several state-of-the-art continuous and progressive XML query processing algorithms that rely on one or more of these building blocks. The building blocks for continuous and progressive XML query processing are: (1) Main and Ancillary data structures used for query progressing, (2) Semantic Awareness, and (3) Memory Management

XML query processing algorithms rely on various main and ancillary data structures. Existing XML query processing algorithms rely on a main data structure for efficient and effective matching of structural relationships. Examples of main data structures include: stack (Peng and Chawathe, 2003; Chen et al., 2006), tree or array data structures (Josifovski et al., 2005), and list (Lu et al., 2004). In order to process complex XQuery queries (e.g. nested loop, recursive XQuery queries) of several XML data streams or documents, ancillary data structures are often used to partition the data space. (Tok et al., 2007b) uses hash tables for supporting value joins between multiple XML data streams.

In XML applications, the XML data are generated using a pre-defined schema. These schemas are expressed either as a DTD or XML schema. During query processing, the constraints that are expressed in the schema information can be used to determine whether an XML node needs to be buffered or whether a buffered node can be released earlier. Additional information such as XML functional dependencies can also be used. This reduces the memory requirements for the query processing algorithms. We refer to query processing algorithms which use schema-information as Semantic-Aware algorithms. In contrast,

Semantic-oblivious techniques do not make use of schema information during query processing.

In data stream applications, the amount of XML data and intermediate results that are processed is significantly larger than the available memory. Thus, it is important for the size of the main and ancillary data structures used by the query processing algorithms to be bounded. In addition, in order to support the processing of complex XQuery queries (e.g. value joins (Hong et al., 2007)), it is important to ensure that the data that are kept in the limited memory are more likely to contribute to results.

Various heuristics or statistical techniques are proposed to determine the XML fragments to discard whenever memory is full. In relational data stream processing, both heuristics and statistical techniques have been widely studied. In a heuristic-based technique, either the largest or smallest partitions of data can be discarded whenever memory is full. Alternatively, the data can be discarded in a balanced manner to ensure that there are equivalent amount of data for each of the data streams.

The insight from (Tao et al., 2005) is that while heuristic-based algorithms are shown to have a good result throughput, the algorithms cannot provide a theoretical guarantee of the expected results that are produced. To address this, the authors of (Tao et al., 2005) propose the rate-based progressive algorithm (RPJ) which uses statistics from the input data distribution to determine the data to be flushed to disk whenever memory is full. However, RPJ is limited to processing relational data due to the need for statistics on the input data distribution. In order to support various data models (e.g. relational, spatial, XML, high-dimensional), the authors of (Tok et al., 2007a) propose the result rate-based progressive algorithm (RRPJ). The key innovation in RRPJ is that it uses statistics on the result distribution. Indeed, this makes RRPJ generic and allows it to be applied to various data models.

Progressive XML Query Processing

In this section, we present progressive XML query processing algorithms for processing XML data streams. These algorithms use a combination of the building blocks discussed in the earlier section.

The XML stream machine (XSM), proposed in (Ludäscher et al., 2002), uses an extended state transducer model for processing XQuery queries on XML data streams. In XSM, the sub-expressions in an XQuery query are first mapped to a XSM network, where the output of a XSM is chained to the input of another XSM. The XSM network is represented as a directed acyclic graph (DAG). The nodes in the DAG correspond to each XSM. The labeled edges correspond to the associated output buffer for the nodes. For each pair of XSM nodes in the XSM network, a shared buffer is created. As an optimization step, in order to reduce the number of shared buffers, XSM proposes the notion of composing two XSM nodes into a single XSM node. As a result, the number of shared buffers can be significantly reduced. XSM makes use of schema information to simplify the XSM networks. This is achieved by using a type inference algorithm to infer the types of variables used in the XQuery query. The information on the type of the variable is used to determine the buffer types for the XSM network. Consequently, the buffer types can be used to optimize the structure of the XSM network. Once the XSM network has been optimized, the XSM compiler will generate a C program, which is used for processing the data stream. The XQuery to C Program compilation process is illustrated in Figure 7.

The XSQ system, proposed in (Peng and Chawathe, 2003), processes XPath queries. It supports multiple predicates, closures and aggregation. Given an XPath query, XSQ constructs several pushdown transducers. In (Peng and Chawathe, 2003), a pushdown transducer (PDT) is defined as a pushdown automation (PDA) with actions that are defined for each of the automation's transition arcs. Figure 8(a) shows an example of the state transitions for a PDA with respect to the XML stream given in Figure 3. Whenever a start tag is encountered, it is pushed onto a stack. Whenever the corresponding end tag is encountered, it is matched against the tag at the top of the stack. If the tag matches, it is removed from the stack. When the end tag does not match the tag at the top of the stack, the XML stream is not well-formed. In order to make use of the PDA for filtering XML streams, the PDA can be adapted based on the pattern to be matched. For example, if the query is //symbolTuple/symbol, then we can remove all the irrelevant branches in Figure 8(a). This results in a PDT, which is given in Figure 8(b). Whenever the filter PDA reaches state $7, the XML stream contains an element that matches the conditions specified by the query. If we output the content of the element in state $7, the filter PDA is considered to be a PDT which answers the query given earlier. To summarize, a PDT consists of a finite set of states, input symbols, and stack symbols. Based on the incoming input symbol, the pushdown transducer changes its state, and maintains the stack based on a transition function. Each of the transducers is augmented with a buffer. The key idea in XSQ is to organize the pushdown transducers in a tree structure. The position of each transducer in the tree can be used to encode the results for the predicates specified in the XPath query. Each transducer can therefore determine whether a predicate has been evaluated by determining its position in the tree.

FluXQuery, proposed in (Koch et al, 2004), processes XQuery queries over XML data streams. An XQuery query is transformed into an

Figure 7. XQuery to XSM compilation

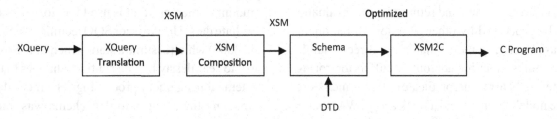

Figure 8. An example of a pushdown automation (PDA) and pushdown transducer

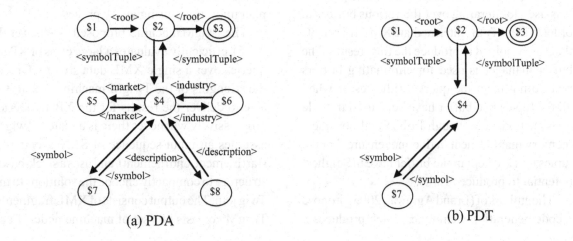

internal representation based on the FluX query language. The process-stream construct is used by the FluX query language to express the type of nodes that need are buffered in memory. This is achieved by using algebraic-based optimization based on schema information. Consequently, this allows FluXQuery to use less memory. The optimized FluX query is compiled either into an internal representation which is interpreted during execution or directly into execution Java code. One of the limitations of FluXQuery is that it does not support aggregation.

TurboXPath, proposed in (Josifovski et al., 2005), processes a subset of XQuery which consists of for-let-where clauses. TurboX processes the XML data in a single pass. It consists of four main components: expression parser, evaluator, tuple constructor and buffer manager. The expression parser is used to construct a single parse tree (PT) based on the set of path expressions specified in the query. The parse tree is used to process the set of SAX events generated from the XML data stream. Fragments that match the path expressions are extracted and returned to the evaluator to be processed by other operators in the query plan. Internally, the evaluator uses three dynamic structures which include: output buffers for storing intermediate results, predicate buffers which store the node's content, and a work array (WA) that is used for existential predicate evaluation. The tuple constructor is used to combine the intermediate results. A variant of the nested loop join algorithm was used for iterating over the various buffers in order to identify the intermediate XML fragments that can be joined to produce the final result. The buffer manager is used for eliminating buffers that do not meet the query predicates or when all the tuples in a buffer have been used in tuple construction. Even though TurboXPath considers memory management, it does not ensure that the tuples that are kept in the buffer have the highest potential to produce results.

The authors of (Li and Agrawal, 2005) propose a code generation technique, which produces a code for processing user-defined aggregates, and recursive functions. In order to support query processing and code generation, the dependencies in an XQuery query is modeled as a stream data flow graph. The graph is optimized using two techniques, namely: horizontal and vertical fusion. Horizontal fusion is used to merge traversals in the graph that share the common prefix in their XPath expressions. Vertical fusion is used to remove unnecessary buffering, and produce a simpler stream data flow graph. A generalized nested loops (GNL) technique is used to convert the final data flow graph into executable code.

The authors of (Su et al., 2005) propose Semantic-aware techniques which make use of schema constraints in order to optimize query processing. These techniques are implemented in the Raindrop system (Su et al., 2003). Various Semantic query optimization (SQO) rules are proposed to make use of the schema constraints.

R-Sox, proposed in (Wang et al., 2006), makes use of runtime schema knowledge to efficiently process the XML data streams, and to reduce the amount of memory that is used for storing intermediate data. Unlike prior SQO techniques (Su et al., 2005) which assume a static schema, R-Sox is able to seamlessly handle runtime changes to the schema during query processing. The meta-data capturing the changes to the schema was interleaved into the XML data streams, and is called runtime schema information (RSI). RSI is used for updating the system in order to facilitate a safe plan migration during query processing.

The TwigM machine, proposed in (Chen et al., 2006), efficiently evaluates a large class of XPath queries over a single XML data stream. One of the strengths of the TwigM machine is that it is able to deliver the results for the XPath queries progressively whenever there is a match. TwigM assumes an input sequence of SAX events (i.e. startElement, endElement), and uses a stack-based structure to compactly encode the solutions to the Twigjoin. The output consists of XML fragments. TwigM consists of a set of machine nodes. Each machine node is mapped to a corresponding query node in a XPath query. In addition, the machine nodes are connected by a set of edges. These edges are used to capture the structural constraints in the query. An XML node is pushed onto the corresponding stack if it satisfies the structural constraints for the edge between a machine node and its parent node. In addition, a set of possible solutions, called candidates, are identified. The candidates are then matched against the patterns specified by the query. To illustrate how TwigM works, let us consider the twig query Q given in Figure 4, and the XML stream given in Figure 3. TwigM first creates three stacks (StackS, StackM and StackI). Each stack corresponds to one of the nodes in the twig query. In addition, three TwigM machine nodes (v1, v2 and v3) are created. The edges that link the three nodes are used to capture the structural constraints (e.g. parent-child (PC) or ancestor-descendant (AD) relationships) defined by the twig query. Each stack is associated with each of the nodes, *v1* to *v3*. For a non-leaf node, its corresponding stack consists of entries. Each entry is a triple <N, C, B>, consisting of the node N, a candidate list C, and a boolean array, B. For a leaf node, the entry of the corresponding stack is just the node <N>. Figure 9 shows an example of a TwigMachine.

Static analysis techniques for identifying the streaming components of a query execution plans are introduced in (Stark et al., 2007). The key idea is the definition of a physical algebra for XQuery which allows XML streaming operators

to be intermixed with conventional XML and relational operators in a query plan. This allows pipelined plans to be easily defined. The operators defined by the physical algebra and static analysis techniques have been implemented in the Galax XQuery engine. (Stark et al., 2007) does not consider the management of stream buffers, as well as optimization issues that arise if the sample stream is accessed multiple times.

The authors of (Hong et al., 2007) propose a massively multi-query join processing (MMQJP) technique for processing value joins over multiple XML data streams. MMQJP query processing consists of two phases: XPath Evaluation and Join Processing phase. In the XPath evaluation phase, the XML data streams are matched and auxiliary information stored as relations in a commercial database management systems (DBMS) - Microsoft SQL Server. The auxiliary information is then used during the join processing phase for computing results. Thus, MMQJP can deliver results only when the entire XML documents have arrived. In addition, MMQJP has no control over the flushing policy due to its dependence on the commercial DBMS.

The authors of (Tok et al., 2007b) propose Twig'n Join (TnJ) as a practical approach for progressive processing of (FWR) XQuery queries on multiple XML streams. Twig'n Join uses TwigM for processing Twig queries and a symmetric hash join for `joining' the XML fragments (produced by the TwigM). The results are delivered progressively to the users. In TnJ, a FWR XQuery query

Figure 9. Example of a TwigMachine

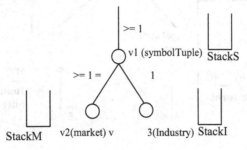

is first decomposed into three parts: (1) Structural filtering on the input streams, (2) Predicate Processing, and (3) Structural filtering on the results. Figure 10 shows an example of a TnJ query plan which consists of the input and output structural filtering and the join phases. During query processing, TnJ performs value-based filtering and the joining of the XML fragments that are produced by TwigM. As the intermediate XML fragments produced might not fit entirely into memory, TnJ needs to flush some of these XML fragments to disk so that they can be joined at a later stage. In order to maximize the number of results that are produced from the XML fragments that are retained in memory, a result-rated base flushing policy (Tok et al., 2007a) is used to determine the XML fragments to be flushed to disk whenever memory is full. TnJ supports the processing of multiple (>=2) XML data streams. This is achieved by using a novel dynamic probing technique, called Result-Oriented Probing (RoP), which determines an optimal probing sequence for the multi-way

join. This significantly reduces the amount of redundant probing for results.

Continuous Query Processing: Publish/Subscribe Systems

In XML publish/subscribe systems, there are two classes of users: data publishers and subscribers. Data publishers submit XML documents to the publish/subscribe system. Data subscribers register one or more queries with the publish/subscribe system. These queries express the type of XML documents in which they are interested. In the processing of XML data streams, the granularity of results that are produced are small fragments of the XML document which matches the XPath or XQuery queries. In contrast, the granularity of results for XML publish/subscribe systems is the entire XML document. However, we consider query processing techniques for XML publish/subscribe systems as continuous and progressive XML query processing. This is because the

Figure 10. Example of a Twig'n Join (TnJ) execution plan

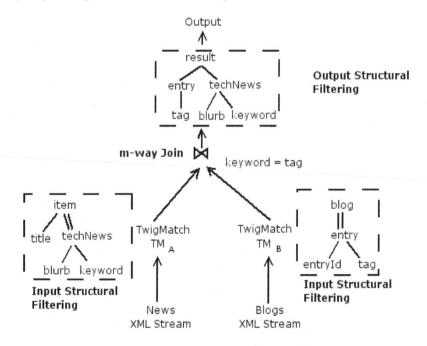

publish/subscribe system needs to continuously examine the published documents, and route the relevant documents to the subscribers based on matching the contents of the documents with the registered queries.

XFilter, proposed in (Altinel and Franklin, 2000), is a XML publish/subscribe system that is designed for efficient document filtering based on user profiles. User profiles are represented as XPath queries. Each XPath query is represented internally in XFilter as a finite state machine. A filter engine, which consists of the finite state machine, is used to filter XML documents based on user profiles. In order to efficiently match documents to queries, the filter engine also builds an inverted index, called a Query Index. Once there is a positive match between the user profile and a document, XFilter uses a unicast delivery mechanism to send the entire document to the user.

YFilter, proposed in (Diao et al., 2002), filters streaming XML documents which match the structural and predicate constraints that are expressed using XPath or XQuery queries. YFilter considers the overlap between multiples queries, and builds a single nondeterministic finite automaton (NFA) for processing them. A key advantage of using the NFA is that it significantly reduces the number of states that are used for matching the multiple queries. Consequently, this improves the overall performance of the filtering system.

The authors of (Green et al., 2003) make use of a deterministic finite automata (DFA) for processing a large number of XPath queries on XML streams. Instead of using multiple DFA for each of the XPath queries, a single DFA is built to encapsulate the processing logic for multiple queries. All the XPath queries are first converted into a nondeterministic finite automaton (NFA) in an intermediate step. Then, the NFA is converted to the DFA.

Onyx (operator network using YFilter for XML dissemination), proposed in (Diao et al., 2004), is designed for large-scale XML dissemination on the Internet. It extends the push-based YFilter algorithm for filtering large number of XML documents. Onyx is a distributed system based on an overlay network. During the routing of the XML documents, Onyx performs incremental message transformation, which performs either early projection or early restructuring. In early projection, XML messages that do not satisfy the conditions specified by the queries are removed. In early restructuring, the XML messages are modified based on the profile of the users. In addition, Onyx also organizes the various user queries into multiple partitions. This allows it to improve on the effectiveness of the content-based routing.

FiST (filtering by sequencing twigs), proposed in (Kwon et al., 2005), performs holistic matching of twig patterns with incoming XML documents. In FiST, the twig patterns that are inherent to XPath queries and XML documents are converted to sequences using the Prufer method. During query processing, FiST first performs subsequence matching to identify the XML documents that matches the queries. A refinement step is then used to verify the correctness of the matching nodes identified in the earlier subsequence matching step. In addition, FiST also makes use of a stack for storing the path from the current tag to the root of the XML document. The size of the stack is bounded by the document depth.

The authors of (Gong et al., 2005) use bloom filters for storing the path queries. Path queries of varying length are organized in using multi-level bloom filters, which is called Prefix Filters. These filters are then used for filtering the XML packets.

The authors of (Chan and Ni, 2007) consider a XML publish/subscribe system which consists of routers. These routers continuously route XML documents from the data publishers to the data subscribers. In order to reduce the processing overheads of content dissemination, (Chan and Ni, 2007) introduces the notion of piggyback optimizations. The goal of piggyback optimization is to allow upstream routers to pass information via header annotations in the XML document. This information provides downstream routers with information such as the subscriptions that have already been matched, as well as properties of the XML documents. This allows the downstream routers to reduce the computation overhead in subsequent processing of the document.

FUTURE TRENDS

In this section, we discuss future trends in XML query processing.

Synopsis Data Structures for Continuous XML data. As XQuery becomes extended with richer query Semantics (e.g. sliding window and continuous queries in (Botan et al., 2007)), synopsis data structure are needed for summarizing the underlying XML data. Synopsis data structures, such as sketches (Flajolet and Martin, 1983; Flajolet and Martin, 1985), wavelets (Graps, 1995), histograms (Kooi, 1980; Piatetsky-Shapiro and Connell, 1984, Ioannidis and Poosala, 1995; Poosala et al., 1996; Poosala and Ioannidis, 1997; Guha et al., 2004) and sampling (Cochran, 1977)), have been relatively well-studied for relational data stream processing. However, very few effective synopsis data structures for XML data streams exist. Although it can be argued that existing synopsis data structures can be used for summarizing the content of the XML tags, existing synopsis are not designed to embed structural information. Hence, they cannot be directly extended for summarizing XML data streams.

In (Aggarwal, 2007), five desirable properties for synopsis construction for relational data streams are identified. Firstly, the synopsis must be generalizable for various applications. Secondly, the algorithms used for synopsis construction and maintenance need to be one-pass algorithms. Due to the large amount of data that needs to be processed, each tuple in the data stream can be accessed once. Thirdly, the synopsis must

be compact. The size of the synopsis must be relatively smaller relative to the size of the data stream. Fourthly, the synopsis must be robust and provide guarantees for the quality of the approximation. Finally, the synopsis must be able to adapt to the changes in the data distribution. Another desirable property for synopsis data structure for XML stream is the embedding of structural information, which can be used during query processing.

Adaptive Query Processing of XML streams. The granularity and optimization of XML processing is an important issue that needs to be tackled. For instance, current algorithms assume that the XML data is arriving in its natural order and is properly nested and does not consider disassembled fragments. Many of algorithms rely on a physical query execution plan or executing generated code for processing the XML data streams. These execution plans and generated code are statically constructed. Optimization is achieved by considering schema information, as well as the cost of the various operators in the query plan. In a data stream environment, some of the XML data streams that are transmitted from remote XML repositories might block due to the unpredictable nature of the network. This necessitates the design of adaptive query processing techniques for XML data streams. Besides the adaptive framework for processing top-k queries on XML documents introduced in (Marian et al, 2005), there are relatively few works in the XML community that uses an adaptive query processing paradigm.

Approximate XML Query Processing. The continuous XML queries introduced in (Botan et al., 2007) can be used for monitoring events on XML data streams that are long-running. For long-running continuous queries, users often do not require complete answers to their queries, and are satisfied with approximate answers, with good error guarantees. Thus, approximate XML query processing techniques are necessary for delivering result subsets to the users. The result subset can then be progressively refined whenever new XML data arrives.

CONCLUSION

In this chapter, we provide a comprehensive categorization and survey of XML query processing techniques. We discuss the building blocks for designing continuous and progressive XML query processing algorithms. We presented the state-of-art techniques for progressive XML query processing, and discuss several future trends.

As illustrated with the opening examples, in order to support new application scenarios (e.g. aggregator and mash up systems), new techniques need to be developed to support the processing of complex XQuery queries over multiple XML streams. The continuous and progressive processing of multiple XML data streams still raises several open research questions. Except for (Hong et al., 2007) and (Tok et al., 2007b), existing query processing techniques have focused on the efficient processing of XPath or XQuery queries over a single XML data stream and ignored the processing of multiple streams. Even though (Hong et al., 2007) showed the processing of multiple XML documents streamed across the network, the proposed algorithm blocks until all the documents have arrived. It cannot deliver results progressively. In contrast, the algorithm proposed in (Tok et al., 2007b) is able to process XQuery queries over multiple XML streams, and deliver results progressively. Together with the XQuery extension for window and continuous queries (Botan et al., 2007), these form the essential building blocks for continuous and progressive XML query processing.

REFERENCES

Aggarwal, C. C. (2007). *Data Streams: Models and Algorithms (Advances in Database Systems)*, Springer.

Al-Khalifa, S., Jagadish, H. V., Patel, J. M., Wu, Y., Koudas, N., & Srivastava, D. (2002). Structural joins: A primitive for efficient xml query pattern matching. In *ICDE*, (p. 141).

Altinel, M., & Franklin, M. J. (2000). Efficient filtering of xml documents for selective dissemination of information. In *VLDB*, (pp. 53–64).

Arasu, A., Babu, S., & Widom, J. (2006). The CQL continuous query language: Semantic foundations and query execution. In *VLDB J.*, *15*(2), 121–142.

Botan, I., Fischer, P. M., Florescu, D., Kossmann, D., Kraska, T., & Tamosevicius, R. (2007). Extending xquery with window functions. In *VLDB*, (pp. 75–86).

Bruno, N., Koudas, N., & Srivastava, D. (2002). Holistic twig joins: optimal xml pattern matching. In *SIGMOD*, (pp. 310–321).

Chan, C. Y., & Ni, Y. (2007). Efficient xml data dissemination with piggybacking. In *SIGMOD*, (pp. 737–748).

Chen, Y., Davidson, S. B., & Zheng, Y. (2006). An efficient xpath query processor for xml streams. In *ICDE*, (p. 79).

Cochran, W. G. (1977). *Sampling Techniques*. 3rd Edition. John Wiley.

Diao, Y., Fischer, P. M., Franklin, M. J., & To, R. (2002). Yfilter: Efficient and scalable filtering of xml documents. In *ICDE*, (pp. 341).

Diao, Y., Rizvi, S., & Franklin, M. J. (2004). Towards an Internet-scale xml dissemination service. In *VLDB*, (pp. 612–623).

Fernández, M., Michiels, P., & Siméon, J., Stark, M. (2007). XQuery streaming á la carte. In *ICDE*, (pp. 2556-265).

Flajolet, P., & Martin, G. N. (1983). Probabilistic counting. In *FOCS*, (pp. 76–82).

Flajolet, P., & Martin, G. N. (1985). Probabilistic counting algorithms for data base applications. In *J. Comput. Syst. Sci. 31*(2), 182–209.

Gong, X., Yan, Y., Qian, W., & Zhou, A. (2005). Bloom filter-based xml packets filtering for millions of path queries. In *ICDE*, (pp. 890–901).

Graps, A. (1995). An introduction to wavelets. *Computational Science and Engineering, 2*(2), 50–61.

Green, T. J., Miklau, G., Onizuka, M., & Suciu, D. (2003). Processing xml streams with deterministic automata. In *ICDT*, (pp. 173–189).

Guha, S., Shim, K., & Woo, J. (2004). Rehist: Relative error histogram construction algorithms. In *VLDB*, (pp. 300-311).

Hong, M., Demers, A., Gehrke, J., Koch, C., Riedewald, M., & White, W. (2007). Massively multi-query join processing in publish/subscribe systems. In *SIGMOD*, (pp. 761-772).

Ioannidis, Y. E., & Poosala, V. (1995). Balancing histogram optimality and practicality for query result size estimation. In *SIGMOD*, (pp. 233–244).

Josifovski, V., Fontoura, M., & Barta, A. (2005). Querying xml streams. In *VLDB Journal 14*(2), 197–210.

Koch, C., Scherzinger, S., Schweikardt, N., & Stegmaier, B. (2004). Fluxquery: An optimizing xquery processor for streaming xml data. In *VLDB*, (pp. 1309–1312).

Kooi, R. P. (1980). *The optimization of queries in relational databases*. PhD thesis, Cleveland, OH, USA.

Kwon, J., Rao, P., Moon, B., & Lee, S. (2005). Fist: Scalable xml document filtering by sequencing twig patterns. In *VLDB*, (pp. 217–228).

Li, X., & Agrawal, G. (2005). Efficient evaluation of xquery over streaming data. In *VLDB*, (pp. 265–276).

Lu, J., Chen, T., & Ling, T. W. (2004). Efficient processing of xml twig patterns with parent child edges: a look-ahead approach. In *CIKM*, (pp. 533–542).

Lu, J., Ling, T. W., Chan, C. Y., & Chen, T. (2005). From region encoding to extended dewey: On efficient processing of xml twig pattern matching. In *VLDB*, (pp. 193–204).

Ludäscher, B., Mukhopadhyay, P., & Papakonstantinou, Y. (2002). A transducer-based xml query processor. In *VLDB*, (pp. 227–238).

Marian, A., Amer-Yahia, S., Koudas, N., & Srivastava, D. (2005). Adaptive processing of top-k queries in xml. In *ICDE*, (pp. 162–173).

Peng, F., & Chawathe, S. S. (2003). Xpath queries on streaming data. In *SIGMOD*, (pp. 431–442).

Piatetsky-Shapiro, G., & Connell, C. (1984). Accurate estimation of the number of tuples satisfying a condition. In *SIGMOD*, (pp. 256–276).

Poosala, V., & Ioannidis, Y. E. (1997). Selectivity estimation without the attribute value independence assumption. In *VLDB*, (pp. 486–495).

Poosala, V., Ioannidis, Y. E., Haas, P. J., & Shekita, E. J. (1996). Improved histograms for selectivity estimation of range predicates. In *SIGMOD*, (pp. 294–305).

Su, H., Jian, J., & Rundensteiner, E. A. (2003). Raindrop: a uniform and layered algebraic framework for xqueries on xml streams. In *CIKM*, (pp. 279–286).

Su, H., Rundensteiner, E. A., & Mani, M. (2005). Semantic query optimization for xquery over xml streams. In *VLDB*, (pp. 277–288).

Tao, Y., Yiu, M. L., Papadias, D., Hadjieleftheriou, M., & Mamoulis, N. (2005). RPJ: Producing fast join results on streams through rate-based optimization. In *SIGMOD*, (pp. 371–382).

Tatarinov, I., Viglas, S., Beyer, K. S., Shanmugasundaram, J., Shekita, E. J., & Zhang, C. (2002). Storing and querying ordered xml using a relational database system. In *SIGMOD*, (pp. 204–215).

Tok, W. H., Bressan, S., & Lee, M.-L. (2007a). RRPJ : Result-rate based progressive relational join. In *DASFAA*, (pp. 43–54).

Tok, W. H., Bressan, S., & Lee, M.-L. (2007b). *Twig'n join: Progressive query processing of multiple xml streams.* Technical Report TRA9/07, National University of Singapore.

W3C (2002). Xquery 1.0 and xpath 2.0 formal Semantics (W3C working draft), http://www.w3.org/tr/query-algebra.

Wang, S., Su, H., Li, M., Wei, M., Yang, S., Ditto, D., Rundensteiner, E. A., & Mani, M. (2006). R-sox: Runtime Semantic query optimization over xml streams. In *VLDB*, (pp. 1207–1210).

Zhang, C., Naughton, J. F., DeWitt, D. J., Luo, Q., & Lohman, G. M. (2001). On supporting containment queries in relational database management systems. In *SIGMOD*, (pp. 425–436).

Section III
XML Personalization and Security

Chapter X
Issues in Personalized Access to Multi–Version XML Documents

Fabio Grandi
Università di Bologna, Italy

Federica Mandreoli
Università di Modena e Reggio Emilia, Italy

Riccardo Martoglia
Università di Modena e Reggio Emilia, Italy

ABSTRACT

*In several application fields including legal and medical domains, XML documents are "versioned" along different dimensions of interest, whose nature depends on the application needs such as time, space and security. Specifically, temporal and Semantic versioning is particularly demanding in a broad range of application domains where temporal versioning can be used to maintain histories of the underlying resources along various time dimensions, and Semantic versioning can then be used to model limited applicability of resources to individual cases or contexts. The selection and reconstruction of the version(s) of interest for a user means the retrieval of those fragments of documents that match both the implicit and explicit user needs, which can be formalized as what we call **personalization queries**. In this chapter, the authors focus on the design and implementation issues of a personalization query processor. They consider different design options and, among them, they introduce an in-depth study of a native solution by showing, also through experimental evaluation, how some of the best performing technological solutions available today for XML data management can be successfully extended and optimally combined in order to support personalization queries. .*

OVERVIEW AND MOTIVATION

Nowadays, XML has become ubiquitous with an ever-increasing number of computer applications exchanging and storing information in XML format. In particular, a large number of organizations, including private companies and public institutions, place rich collections of documents at the disposal of Internet users. Generally, such collections are large XML repositories containing millions of semi-structured documents, each one containing thousands of nodes. Portals and Web-sites which allow users to access such repositories are usually equipped with classic keyword-based search engines which are not adequate to retrieve all and only the information that is relevant for the user, as the tree structure of documents must also be taken into account. As a consequence, in recent years many research efforts have been expended to support structural querying in XML repositories and discovering the occurrences of labelled trees—or **twig query**—patterns (Amer-Yahia et al., 2001) has become a core operation for XML query processing.

Moreover, in several application fields including legal and medical domains, management of bills of materials and catalogue data, accounting and finance, XML documents are "versioned" along different dimensions of interest, whose nature depends on the application needs (e.g. time, space, security). In this chapter, we consider time pertinence and applicability as versioning dimensions, which give rise to multidimensional **temporal and Semantic versioning**. Indeed, temporal and Semantic versioning is particularly demanding in a broad range of application domains where temporal versioning can be used to maintain histories of the underlying resources along various time dimensions, and Semantic versioning can then be used to model limited applicability of resources (or resource portions) to individual cases or contexts. In all these cases, while the most important version is the "current" one with respect to the temporal dimensions (and with generic applicability), past versions are also very important for applications and cannot be discarded.

For instance, in the **legal domain**, a clear example of such multi-version resources are **norm texts**, including laws, acts, decrees, provisions, regulations, etc. Norm texts are continually subject to amendments and modifications and multiple

temporal versions coexist as a consequence of the dynamics of the legislative activity. In particular, several temporal dimensions are involved in the representation and management of norm texts, including transaction, validity, efficacy, applicability, publication and enactment times (Grandi et al., 2005; Palmirani & Brighi, 2006). The most important version of a norm is the consolidated version, which is the one produced by the application of all the modifications the norm has undergone so far, as it is the one which is currently part of the regulations in force and generically applicable to all citizens. However, past versions (even with limited applicability) are also virtually needed. For instance, considering validity time and Semantic applicability to individual cases, a court might be called to judge a case involving a crime C committed at a time T on the basis of the (versions of the) laws which were valid at time T and applicable to crime C.

Another interesting example is the **medical domain**, where multi-version resources of interest are, for instance, **clinical guidelines**, which are definitions of "best practices" encoding and standardizing clinical procedures for a given disease. Clinical guidelines are also subject to continuous development and revision by committees of expert physicians and health authorities, and multiple temporal versions coexist as a consequence of the clinical and healthcare activity. Several temporal dimensions are also involved in the representation and management of clinical guidelines, including valid, transaction, event, availability, proposal and acceptance times (Combi & Montanari, 2001; Terenziani et al., 2005). Also, in the medical domain, past versions continue to be relevant, as a physician might be called upon to justify his/her actions for a given patient P at a time T on the basis on the (versions of the) clinical guidelines which were valid at time T and applicable to the pathology of patient P.

In addition to individual cases (e.g. citizens or diseases), Semantic versioning can also involve more generic applicability contexts (e.g. districts recently affected by a natural calamity or hospitals without PET diagnostic equipment), which might require the application of a particular version of the general norm or guideline, which may also no longer be part of the consolidated norm or state-of-the-art guideline. For instance, consider a norm N which in its first version v1 introduces fiscal benefits for new companies. Assume N has then been modified and fiscal benefits have been cancelled in version N.v2. However, the modifying law also stated that the benefits provided by norm N.v1 are still applicable for one year in some district D affected by a recent natural calamity. Hence, the right context must be considered in order to find out the benefits applicable, for instance, to a company resident in D. Thus, the applicable version of the norm for context D is N.v1, which is still effective though no longer valid. In a similar vein, version v1 of a clinical guideline G prescribes a biopsy to confirm a cancer diagnosis but has been superseded by a new version v2 which introduces a PET scan for the same cancer diagnosis, making in most cases the biopsy unnecessary. However, in some hospital H which is not equipped with a PET scanner, the right version of G to be followed is v1, although no longer considered valid by the medical community. Therefore, the applicable version of the guideline for context H is G.v1, with biopsy as a mandatory diagnostic means.

As far as temporal versioning is concerned, in addition to the time dimensions which model the dynamics of the considered real-world domain, transaction time (Jensen et al., 1998) plays an important role when automatic management of information through computer systems is involved and, thus, should never be neglected. For example, it might be the case that a public servant makes a wrong decision in settling an affair by following the provisions of a norm retrieved from the system when in fact the returned consolidated version is actually out-of-date; the decision was taken while a modified version of the norm was already in force, whereas the modification has been recorded

in the system only later. Hence, transaction time is needed to ascertain *a posteriori* that the correct version was stored retroactively and, thus, the public servant acted in good faith. The same applies to a physician who prescribes an obsolete therapy because the latest recommended guideline (e.g. involving the adoption of some more effective and less potentially dangerous drug) has not yet been recorded in the information system.

Semantic applicability of multi-version resources can be defined with reference to domain ontologies. *Ontologies* (Guarino, 1998; Gruber, in press), which are conceptualizations of a domain into a machine-understandable format, have recently become quite popular with the advent of the Semantic Web (Berners-Lee et al., 2001), where the introduction of common reference ontologies (OWL, 2004) becomes necessary to allow information and its interpretation to be shared by both human and automatic agents. Hence, in XML resource repositories, reference to ontology concepts can be added to the resource representation and storage as a versioning coordinate. For instance, individual applicability of norms can be defined with respect to an officially validated civic ontology, representing the position of different classes of citizens before the law (Grandi et al., in press). Appropriate applicability of clinical guidelines can be defined according to a consensual taxonomy of diseases, like the one endorsed by the World Health Organization (ICD-10, 2007).

One of the effects of versioning is an increase in the number or size of the documents to be stored, if all the different versions are arranged into a single **multi-version XML** document, owing to a uniform encoding of variant parts within the document structure. The latter solution is often unavoidable in order to keep the growth of the storage space under control, especially when different versions of the same document may differ by a few nodes only. Personalization, which has shown to be a powerful tool to cope with information overload on the Internet (Riecken, 2000), can also be particularly effective when used in the management of large XML repositories of versioned documents. In this case, the adoption of personalization techniques can prevent in most cases users to have to go through a huge amount of irrelevant information to find out the right version(s) of the one of interest and, thus, might help to make their search faster and more accurate or, in some cases, at least feasible. Hence, personalization based on Semantic versioning may improve the quality of the interaction with the user by further focusing the search on really relevant versions only. In particular, a personalization service relying on Semantic versioning is a desirable feature for norm texts and clinical guideline management. For example, a university professor could be using an e-Government portal looking for recently introduced changes in the management and fiscal treatment of research funds and could be directed by some search engine or predefined path to the latest State Budget Law. It could be the case that the norms of interest for him/her are contained in a couple of paragraphs of a few articles, but these are immersed in several hundreds of articles making up the law. Hence, the norms of interest could be quite awkward to find within the retrieved document and, thus, having to go through the whole law text would result in a very time-consuming and daunting activity. More in general, personalization of (informational and transactional) e-government services could improve the involvement of citizens and the quality of their participation in the e-Governance process. As there are many "different kinds" of citizens before the law and different applicability contexts, there should correspondingly be many different kinds of services available, which should be able to be automatically selected through a personalization service (Grandi et al., in press). In the medical domain, one of the most relevant obstacles in the use and dissemination of guidelines is the need for adapting them to constraints in local settings (e.g. concerning available hospital resources and practitioners' skills). Management

of multi-version guidelines with context-based Semantic personalization might help to overcome this problem (Cabana et al., 1999).

From the above discussion and examples, it is evident that the selection and reconstruction of the version(s) of interest for a user become a new challenging problem to support personalization in multi-versioned documents. In particular, this means the retrieval of document fragments matching with implicit and explicit user needs which can be formalized as twig queries augmented with the specification of versioning coordinates and which we will call **personalization queries**. Such document fragments must be the outcome of a correct **slicing** with respect to all the versioning dimensions. Any implementation of a system supporting personalized access to multi-versioned documents must come to terms with slicing. This has also been clearly evidenced in the temporal setting in (Gao & Snodgrass, 2003), where the authors state that "the central issue of supporting sequenced queries (in any query language) is timeslicing the input data while retaining period timestamping". For these reasons, in this chapter we will focus on the design and implementation issues of a personalization query processor.

LITERATURE REVIEW

Recently, a crop of research work addressed temporal and versioning aspects in the World Wide Web and, in particular, in the management of XML documents. Actually, more than 200 of the papers listed in the bibliography collected by Grandi (2004) could be considered related work. Also in the last years, a growing interest for the topic has been witnessed by a sustained production of papers. Therefore, we will just briefly recall some of the aspects which are somehow related to personalized access to multi-version XML databases and cite for each of the aspects a couple of references which are chosen as representatives.

As far as XML versioning is concerned, first of all we must distinguish between approaches considering monodimensional and multidimensional versioning. In fact, several authors considered multi-version XML documents, where versioning has basically a monodimensional structure. Such a structure can be a direct consequence of the update history the documents undergo, with or without an explicit representation of time. For example, a first stream of research is concerned with maintenance of versions as produced by sequences of modifications, often with the main focus on collaborative work and distributed document authoring (Vitali & Durand, 1996; Marian et al. 2001; Chien et al., 2002). Branching, leading to the coexistence of alternative versions, is also considered in this framework, whereas the implicit temporal dimension underlying the editing process (i.e. transaction time) is neglected. A second stream of research, still focusing on versions as produced by updates, explicitly considers the adoption of a temporal dimension to identify versions (Chawathe et al., 1999; Amagasa et al., 2000; Oliboni et al., 2001; Buneman et al. 2004). Alternatively, the monodimensional versioning structure coincides with the introduction of one temporal dimension —usually valid time (Jensen et al., 1998)— in XML documents which are explicitly designed to contain annotated historical information or derive from the conversion of structured historical data (Grandi & Mandreoli, 2000; Gao & Snodgrass, 2003; Wang & Zaniolo, 2003; Rizzolo & Vaisman, in press). These approaches lead to the definition of temporal XML (Dyreson & Grandi, in press), that is a timestamped instance of an XML data model. As an XML data model, instance is a graph in which nodes corresponds to elements, attributes or values and edges represent the nesting relationship of childs into the parent's content, timestamps are added to some nodes or edges in the instance in order to represent their lifetime. Timestamps can then be used by query engines to reconstruct individual temporal versions (snapshot queries) or history slices (sequenced queries) (Jensen et al. 1998; Gao & Snodgrass, 2003).

On the other hand, some research works considered multi-version XML documents with an intrinsic multidimensional structure. Some of these approaches are generalizations of temporal XML versioning with the adoption of multiple temporal dimensions, whereas other approaches also consider non-temporal versioning dimensions. The former include modelling and management of bitemporal XML documents (Manukyan & Kalinichenko, 2001; Currim et al., 2004; Wang & Zaniolo, 2004) - that is adopting valid and transaction time as proposed in temporal database research (Jensen et al., 1998) - but also other special user-defined or application-dependent temporal dimensions have been considered (Mitakos et al., 2001; Grandi et al., 2005). The latter involves modelling and management of multidimensional XML documents to be used as containers of multidimensional semi-structured data, where stored information can be equipped with multi-faceted property annotations (Dyreson et al., 1999; Wong et al., 2001; Stavrakas, et al. 2004), where time is one of these properties.

From a different perspective, also non-temporal multidimensional XML has been used to represent context-dependent Web resources, aimed at supporting for example personalization, location-based services, multi-device and multilingual presentations. Techniques have been proposed both for the design and implementation of data-intensive Web sites (Ceri et al., 1999; Grundy & Zou, 2003) and for the publishing on the Web of context-dependent non-structured documents (Stavrakas et al., 2000; Norrie & Palinginis, 2003; Giacomini Moro et al., 2004). This last stream of research includes the proposal of the so-called *intensional* Web authoring languages—including Intensional HTML and derivatives (Wadge et al., 1998; Wadge & Schraefel, 2002)—and the study of multi-dimensional techniques to implement adaptive hypermedia (Sadat & Ghorbani, 2004). Multidimensional data models used for representing context-dependent Web resources have also been enriched with a (transaction time) temporal dimension to keep track of the history of changes applied (Stavrakas & Gergatsoulis, 2002).

As far as personalization is concerned, it can be defined as the ways in which information and services can be tailored to match the unique and specific needs of an individual or a community (Callan et al., 2003). For instance, personalization is about building customer loyalty by creating a meaningful one-to-one relationship or, more in general, by understanding the needs of each individual and helping satisfy a goal that efficiently and knowledgeably addresses each individual's need in a given context (Riecken, 2000). Therefore, personalization techniques have been proposed as remedies to cope with the information overload in browsing and searching the Web, problem which is more and more emphasized by the sustained exponential growth rate of the Web. Recommender systems (Resnick & Varian, 1997; Perugini et al., 2004), Web page filtering (Godoy & Amandi, 2005), personalized search (Micarelli et al., 2007) are all proposed solutions, built upon the concept of *user profile*, which have become necessary for most Web users to cope with this problem, by increasing the quality and reducing the quantity of retrieved information and speeding-up the search task.

At the state-of-the-art level, there is a quite large bibliography on user profiles, which can be defined according to different dimensions (Rich, 1999): canonical vs. individual, explicit vs. implicit, long-term vs. short-term. Another distinction, deriving from Artificial Intelligence research, can be made between knowledge-based and behavior-based user profiling. Knowledge-based approaches adopt static user models which are dynamically matched to users in order to find the best fit. Questionnaires and interviews are often used to obtain this kind of user knowledge. Behavior-based approaches involve the analysis of the user behavior during navigation and search activities to discover useful patterns and build

individual or prototype user models, usually employing machine-learning techniques and using Web logs as data sources. Among others, Kobsa (2001), Cornelis (2003) and Frias-Martinez et al. (2006) produced good surveys on user modelling techniques and systems.

Ontologies (Guarino, 1998; Gruber, in press) had already been used both in the personalization field to represent user profiles, and in the legal and medical domains to share common terminologies and support automatic reasoning. In particular, ontologies have been diffusely exploited for either knowledge-based and behavior-based user profiling, as they can be used to model user interests and navigation contexts in a Semantically rich form, including hierarchies of concepts with various properties of interest. The ontologies used for this purpose can either be hand-made, built and maintained by domain experts or by the users themselves possibly in a collaborative fashion, or engineered using (semi-)automatic methods, like analysis and mining of domain text documents and user activity logs. Ontologies can also be built dynamically or incrementally refined starting form an initial core, with or without explicit user intervention. Pretschner (1998) presents a thorough discussion of ontology-based user profiling techniques and systems. More recent proposals include (Gauch et al., 2003; Golemati et al., 2007; Middleton et al., 2004; Razmerita et al., 2003; Trajkova et al., 2004).

In the legal domain, the introduction of ontologies as a conceptualization tool for the purpose of legal knowledge systems dates back to the studies on artificial intelligence and law in the late 'eighties. Visser & Bench-Capon (1998) review the four main proposals produced by early research in this framework. More recent proposals can be found, for instance, in (Benjamins et al., 2005; Breuker et al., 2004; Casanovas et al., 2007; Lehman et al., 2005; LKIF-Core, n.d.). Also, in the medical domain, the studies on artificial intelligence and medicine achieved in the late Eighties the introduction of ontologies as a tool for defining sharable vocabularies and representing medical knowledge aimed at developing decision-support systems. Pisanelli (2004) presents a survey of the most important contributions to the topic of formal ontology in medicine, whereas comprehensive and up-to-date references to the main initiatives concerning the development of ontologies for medical and biosciences applications can be found, for instance, in (Amies, 2006; Ontologies, n.d.).

In this chapter we focus on personalization of XML documents based on temporal and Semantic versioning. In particular, Semantic annotations consisting of references to ontology classes can be added to timestamps in the XML data model in order to represent applicability contexts of nodes and edges. Semantic annotations make up a further versioning dimension, which can be used by query engines to reconstruct individual applicable versions. This can be used as a base mechanism to support personalization of XML documents relying on user profiles or contexts. In the literature, a few approaches remarkably considered multidimensional XML versioning, where time dimensions are a subset of the adopted versioning dimensions (Dyreson et al., 1999; Mitakos et al., 2001; Wong et al. 2001), and presented general data models, query languages and implementation solutions. In particular, the proposed multidimensional XML models and query languages are expressive enough to support the temporal and Semantic personalization twig queries which are required to manage norm texts in the legal field and clinical guidelines in the medical field. However, although the proposed implementation techniques (e.g. (Stavrakas et al., 2004; Fousteris et al., 2007)) demonstrated the feasibility of personalization based on multidimensional versioning, no efficient storage and query processing techniques have been devised which can cope with the dimension and growth rate of a very large multi-version XML repository, containing thousands of documents each one composed of dozens of versions along multiple dimensions, like the ones which we encounter in the legal and medical application realms.

On the other hand, the algorithms and data structures proposed for the efficient processing of twig queries in XML databases (Bruno et al., 2002; Jiang et al. 2003; Jiang et al. 2004; Vagena et al., 2004; Chen et al., 2005; Moura Moro et al. 2005) do not behave at their best in the presence of multidimensional multi-version XML repositories, as they are not well suited to managing multidimensional selection and consistent reconstruction of personalized versions (slicing). For example, Mandreoli et al. (2006) showed how the extension of standard techniques to efficiently support twig queries even over monodimensional temporal XML documents is not straightforward and new solutions are needed to obtain reasonable performances. We remark that temporal and Semantic slicing required in processing personalization queries is a fundamental and critical issue. As Snodgrass and Gao (2003) also underlined in the first paper dealing with temporal slicing in evaluating XML queries, any implementation of temporal support in a query language must come to terms with temporal slicing. Since timestamps are distributed throughout an XML document, timeslicing a document (while retaining a compact format of the results) comes out complicated, though providing opportunities for optimization. The addition of a Semantic annotation dimension to timestamps further complicates the slicing management.

EFFICIENT PERSONALIZED ACCESSS TO MULTI-VERSION XML DOCUMENTS

In order to efficiently support the complex requirements of an XML multi-version query engine, the underlying data management infrastructure has to be carefully devised. To this end, two alternative solutions exist. One option is to rely on *traditional*

XML engines, offering XML data storage and management facilities "for free". In this case, multi-version documents are dealt with as standard XML documents and, thus, stored in the XML repository using the data structures made available by the engine. The chosen storage granularity is typically the whole document, although different options could be available. However, the problem is that those engines are not aware of the temporal and Semantic versioning aspects of the managed data. As a consequence, a software stratum has to be built on top for handling the additional features and query optimization and indexing techniques especially suited for multi-version XML documents are very difficult to apply. This introduces large overheads in performing temporal and applicability filtering on the retrieved data in order to output only the XML data portions satisfying all the user constraints. The second design option is to build a *native multi-version XML query processor* which is able to index the XML data repository and provide all the required facilities for a personalized access through appropriate data structures and querying algorithms, aware of the multi-dimensional data and query structure and employing advanced slicing techniques.

This section introduces an in-depth study of the native solution by showing how some of the best performing technological solutions avail-

able today for XML data management can be extended and optimally combined in order to support personalization queries. The underlying idea is to devise the changes that a "conventional" XML pattern matching engine needs to become able to slice multi-version XML documents. The advantage of this solution is that the processor can benefit from the XML pattern matching techniques presented in the literature, where the focus is on the structural aspects which are intrinsic also to multi-version XML documents, and that at the same time, they can be freely extended to become temporally and Semantically aware.

We begin by providing some background in Section 3.1, where the multi-version document slicing problem is defined. Then, we analyze the foundations of a native XML query processor, with particular attention to the underlying indexing and main memory structures (Section 3.2). In Section 3.3 a temporal and Semantic indexing scheme is presented, which extends the inverted list technology proposed in (Zhang et al., 2001), in order to allow the storage of multi-version XML documents. Finally, we introduce a flexible technology supporting multi-version document slicing (Sections 3.4 and 3.5). It consists of alternative solutions supporting slicing on the above storage scheme, all relying on the holistic twig join technology (Bruno et al., 2002), which is one of the most

Figure 1. An applicability class taxonomy

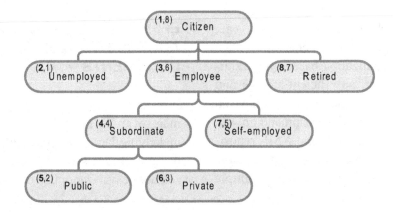

Figure 2. Reference example

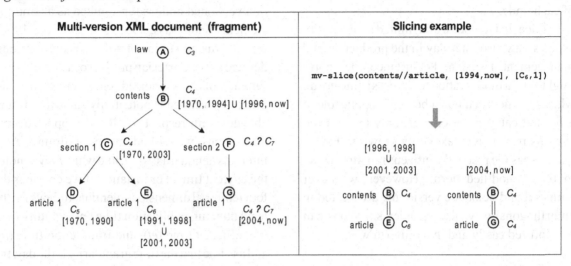

popular approaches for XML pattern matching. The proposed solutions act at the different levels of the holistic twig join architecture, with the aim of limiting main memory space requirements, I/O and CPU costs. They include the introduction of novel algorithms and the optimized exploitation of different access methods.

Preliminaries

A multi-version XML document is a tree-inner structure which records versions along with temporal and Semantic annotations.

As far as multi-dimensional temporal versioning is concerned, the timestamps of a version indicate its *lifetime* along all the supported temporal dimensions (Jensen et al., 1998). The existence of multiple versions is a consequence of the need to represent the dynamics of the modeled phenomenon and the number and types of the considered dimensions are strictly related to the phenomenon itself. For instance, in the eGovernment domain, in order to draw a complete picture and meet all the application requirements, at least four time dimensions should be considered: publication time, validity time, efficacy time, and transaction time

(Grandi et. al., 2005). Further time dimensions (e.g. enactment and applicability time) should also be considered for advanced application requirements concerning the accurate modeling of the legislative process (Palmirani & Brighi, 2006).

Semantic annotations, instead, encode the *applicability aspects* of versions. For example, going back to the eGovernment context, a given norm defining tax treatment may contain some articles which are only applicable to particular classes of citizens: one article is applicable to unemployed persons, one article to self-employed persons, one article to public servants only and so on. The applicability of a version references one or more applicability classes selected from one or more reference taxonomies (Mandreoli et al., 2005). An example of taxonomy representing a possible classification of citizens for the legal domain is shown in Figure 1. In order to distinguish the different taxonomies used to annotate a corpus of XML documents, we assume that each of these taxonomies is univocally identified through a unique name T_i and that each of its applicability classes is referenced through the pre-order rank j of the class in the taxonomy, $T_i.C_j$. The pre-order values of the applicability classes of Figure 1 are highlighted in boldface in the upper left corner of each node.

Notice that temporal and limited applicability aspects may also interplay in the production and management of versions. For instance, a new norm might state a modification to a pre-existing norm, where the modified norm becomes applicable to a limited category of citizens only (e.g. retired persons in the civic taxonomy shown in Figure 1), whereas the rest of the citizens remain subject to the unmodified norm. However, whenever temporal and Semantic versioning are treated in an orthogonal way, also complex situations can be captured easily and in a uniform way.

Document Representation

As already outlined in Section 2, the literature presents several XML data models supporting some kind of versioning. Such models are usually equipped with an XML Schema or DTD which specifies the syntax for encoding the versions and the versioning annotations in XML documents. Moreover, most of them are based on a specific Semantics, especially in the way nodes inherit annotations from their ancestors. For the sake of generality, we show how it is possible to provide a native support to personalized queries without narrowing down to a particular XML data model. On the contrary, the data model we consider here is able to capture multi-version XML documents containing timestamps defined on an arbitrary number of temporal dimensions and applicability contexts referring to arbitrary applicability class taxonomies. Moreover, it is completely independent from specific XML Schemas or DTDs.

In greater detail, the model defines a *multi-version XML database (MVXMLdb)* as a collection of XML documents, also containing multi-version documents. We denote with D^{MV} a *multi-version XML document* represented as an ordered labeled tree that contains elements and attributes (in the following denoted as nodes) versioned along either the temporal dimensions,

or Semantic dimensions, or both. The timestamp of a versioned node is represented as a temporal element (Snodgrass, 1995; Jensen et al., 1998), that is, a disjoint union of n-dimensional periods, defined as the Cartesian product of a time interval for each of the supported temporal dimensions. Since any version is potentially subject to future changes with respect to all the supported time dimensions, we will adopt right-unlimited time intervals denoted as $[t, t_\infty)$, and while *now* denotes the current time. For instance, if we consider the four temporal dimensions mentioned above for the legal domain, publication time (*pt*), validity time (*vt*), efficacy time (*et*), and transaction time (*tt*), and assume that the time granularity is the day, the temporal pertinence of a node representing a version of an article could be $[1970\text{-}01,1990\text{-}12\text{-}31]_{vt}$ x $[1970\text{-}01,1992\text{-}01\text{-}01]_{et}$ x $[1969\text{-}12\text{-}31,1990\text{-}12\text{-}31]_{tt}$ $\cup$ $[1997\text{-}06\text{-}10, now)_{vt}$ x $[1997\text{-}06\text{-}15, now)_{tt}$. It is worth noting that the adoption of timestamps made up of temporal elements instead of convex multidimensional intervals avoids the duplication of version contents in the presence of a temporal pertinence with a complex shape. Applicability contexts, instead, are represented as the conjunction of applicability classes selected from the considered taxonomies. The left part of Figure 2 depicts a multi-version XML document conforming to the reference data model. For ease of presentation, timestamps are defined on a single time dimension with a granularity of a year. From a temporal point of view, the document represents the result of a sequence of lossless updates recorded through the temporal pertinence associated with temporal nodes. For instance, nodes D and E represent two versions of the same article (Art. 1 of Sec. 1): the first version D has been introduced in 1970 and then replaced by a new version E effective from 1991. The validity of the second version E has been suspended from 1999 to 2000 and the article has been definitely cancelled effective from 2004. Applicability contexts, instead, refer to the class taxonomy shown in Figure 1; for instance, the article represented by node G is applicable to both classes of subordinate and self-employed citizens.

The tree depicted in Figure 2 represents an example of a multi-version XML document where not all nodes are versioned (e.g. node A has a single version). In order to distinguish versioned nodes from non-versioned ones, we will adopt the notation n^T to signify that node n has temporal versions and *lifetime(n^T)* to denote its timestamp, the notation n^S to signify that node n has limited applicability and *applicability(n^S)* to denote its Semantic annotation, and, finally, the notation n^{MV} when n is a multi-versioned node, i.e. when it is a temporal node with limited applicability. Sometimes it can be necessary to extend the lifetime of a node $n^{[T|MV]}$, which can be either timestamped or snapshot, to a temporal dimension not explicitly specified in its timestamp. In this case, we follow the Semantics given in (De Castro et al., 1993): If no explicit values are provided, for each newly added temporal dimension we set the default timestamp value on this dimension to the whole time-line, that is $[t_0, t_\infty)$. In the same way, when a node $n^{[S|MV]}$ must be extended to an applicability class hierarchy and no explicit Semantic reference is provided, we assume that it is applicable to the whole hierarchy and, thus, the corresponding applicability context is the most general classes in the taxonomy. Given the extensions above, in the following we can safely assume that all nodes in a multi-version document are versioned along the supported set of temporal dimensions and applicability taxonomies. For instance, the lifespan of nodes A and F of the multi-version XML document shown in Figure 2 is $[t_0, t_\infty)$.

The Slice Operator

The central issue of supporting personalization in multi-version documents is *slicing* the input data while retaining timestamping and applicability contexts. To this extent, the slice operator `mv-slice(twig,t-window,app-constraint)` is applied to a multi-version XML database and

receives in input a personalization query (`twig`, `t-window`, `app-constraint`). The twig parameter is a node-labeled twig pattern which is defined on the snapshot schema (Currim et al., 2004) of the database through any XML query languages, e.g. XPath, by specifying a pattern of selection predicates on multiple elements having some specified tree structured relationships. It defines the portion of interest in each state of the XML documents contained in the database. As far as the versioning constraints are considered, by default multi-version document slicing is applied to the whole time-lines, that is, by using every single time point contained in the time-varying documents, and to all applicability classes of the available taxonomies. The `t-window` parameter is the temporal window on which the slice operator has to be applied. With `t-window`, it is possible to restrict the set of time points by specifying a collection of periods chosen from one or more temporal dimensions. Finally, `app-constraint` specifies the applicability constraints. It is a formula in disjunctive normal form (DNF) $DNF([T_1.C_1, depth_1], ..., [T_k.C_k, depth_k])$ of taxonomy navigational patterns where each pattern $[T_j.C_i, depth_i]$ represents the applicability constraint on the taxonomy T_j given by the applicability class $T_j.C_i$ and all $T_j.C_i$'s ancestor classes up to $depth_i$ steps. Navigational patterns are particularly useful when accessing XML documents containing versions with limited applicability. Indeed, applicability class taxonomies obey to an inheritance Semantics: when a portion of a document references any applicability class, it is also applicable to all its descendant classes. For instance, the law section represented by node C in the document of Figure 2 is applicable to subordinate workers, also including public and private employees. From a querying point of view, it means that if a user is looking for norms concerning public servants (class C_5), the system should also return norms applicable to generic subordinates (class C_4), employees (class C_3) and citizens (class C_1), whose usefulness could be in some cases questionable. In order to restrict selection in order to obtain the most useful results, the query parameter $depth_i$ allows users to limit the taxonomy visit depth starting from T_jC_i. For instance, the formula $[C_5,1] \wedge [C_8,0]$ (i.e. one more step above class C_5 and no steps above C_8) translates into the formula $(C_5 \vee C_4) \wedge C_8$. It is worth noting that users are not necessarily required to explicitly specify all query parameters. For instance, in (Grandi et al., in press) it is shown how the applicability constraints can be partially derived in an implicit way by the digital identity of the citizens accessing eGov services, which represents the user profile used for Semantic personalization.

The slice operator `mv-slice(twig,t-window,app-constraint)` simultaneously retrieves the portion of each version of the multi-version XML documents in the database *MVXMLdb* which is contained in the given time period, `t-window`, refers to the given portions of applicability class taxonomies, `app-constraint`, and matches with a given XML query twig pattern, `twig`. Moreover, it is often required to combine the results back into a period-stamped (Gao & Snoodgrass, 2003) and Semantic-annotated representation. A slicing example of the multi-version XML document in the left part of Figure 2 is shown in the right part of the same figure. The personalization query represented in the top part asks for all articles descendant of a contents node (path `contents//article`) which are applicable to private employees or subordinates, i.e. $[C_6,1]$, and which refer to the period [1994,*now*]. The outcome is represented by the two portions of the document which satisfy all the constraints specified in the personalization query, where each qualifying portion is denoted as *slice*. Formally, a *slice* is a mapping from nodes in twig to nodes in *MVXMLdb*, such that:

i. Query node predicates are satisfied by the corresponding document nodes thus determining a tuple $(n_1^{MV}, \ldots, n_k^{MV})$ of all the nodes

in *MVXMLdb* that produce a distinct match with twig;

ii. $(n_1^{MV}, \ldots, n_k^{MV})$ is *structurally consistent*, i.e. they all belong to the same multi-version XML document and the parent-child and ancestor-descendant relationships between query nodes are satisfied by the corresponding document nodes;

iii. $(n_1^{MV}, \ldots, n_k^{MV})$ is *temporally consistent*, i.e. its lifetime $lifetime(n_1^{MV}, \ldots, n_k^{MV}) = lifetime(n_1^{MV}) \cap \ldots \cap lifetime(n_k^{MV})$ is not empty and it is contained in the given time period, $lifetime(n_1^{MV}, \ldots, n_k^{MV}) \subseteq$ `t-window`;

iv. $(n_1^{MV}, \ldots, n_k^{MV})$ is *Semantically consistent*, i.e. the applicability annotation of each node n_1^{MV}, *applicability*(n_1^{MV}), implies the `app-constraint` formula.

For instance, in the reference example, the tuple (B,D) is structurally consistent being B a `contents` node, D an `article` node and D a descendant of B. However, it is neither temporally consistent as $lifetime(B) \cap lifetime(D) = [1970,1990] \not\subseteq [1994,now]$ nor Semantically consistent as $applicability(D) = C_5 \not\Rightarrow C_6 \vee C_4$.

In this chapter, we focus mainly on the slicing problem, which can be formalized as follows:

Given a personalization query (`twig`,`t-window`,`app-constraint`) and a multi-version XML database *MVXMLdb*, `mv-slice(twig,t-window,app-constraint)` computes each distinct slice $(n_1^{MV}, \ldots, n_k^{MV})$ together with its temporal pertinence $lifetime(n_1^{MV}, \ldots, n_k^{MV})$.

Foundations of Native XML Query Processor

XML data is a user-designed structure which is usually modeled as an ordered tree. Queries in the W3C XML query languages, XPath and XQuery, typically specify patterns of selection predicates on multiple elements that have some specified tree structured relationships. These expressions can be represented as a node-labeled twig pattern with elements, attributes and values as node labels.

Finding all occurrences of a query twig in an XML database is thus a core operation for XML query execution. XML query processing has to go beyond relational DB query capabilities, relying on efficient ways to find all the occurrences of twig patterns in typically huge data trees. To this end, a lot of work has been done on XML query processing (see, for example, Bruno et al., 2002; Chen et al., 2005; Jiang et al., 2003; Zhang et al., 2001). They show that capturing the XML document structure using traditional indices is a good solution, on which it is possible to devise efficient structural or containment join algorithms for twig pattern matching. Early proposals in this context (e.g. Chien et al., 2002; Zhang et al., 2001) were based on the decomposition of the query into a set of binary (parent-child and ancestor-descendant) relationships between pairs of nodes. In this way, the twig query pattern can be matched by matching each of the binary relationships against the XML database and "stitching" together these basic matches. The main limitation of these approaches is that they suffer from very large intermediate result size, even when the input and the final result sizes are much more manageable. To address the problem, Bruno et al. proposed a holistic twig join approach for matching XML query twig patterns (Bruno et al., 2002).

The holistic twig join approach stores XML data by using the indexing scheme proposed in (Zhang et al., 2001). Then, a chain of linked stacks is used to compactly represent partial results of individual query root-to-leaf paths. Finally, efficient algorithms merge the sorted lists of participating element sets together and in this way avoid creating large intermediate results. In order to understand the foundations of a holistic XML query processor, in the following part of this section we will analyze these aspects in detail, while in the next one we will describe how to seamlessly extend such an architecture toward temporal and Semantic versioning management.

Position-Based Indexing Scheme

The indexing solution for XML data proposed in (Zhang et al., 2001) include

1. A numbering scheme that encodes each element and string occurrence by its positional information within the hierarchy of an XML document to which it belongs;
2. An extension of the classic inverted index data structure in Information Retrieval which maps each element or string to the inverted list of its occurrences in the XML database.

The position of a string occurrence in the XML database is represented in each inverted list as a tuple (DocId, LeftPos, LevelNum) and, analogously, the position of an element occurrence as a tuple (DocId, LeftPos:RightPos,LevelNum) where (a) DocId is the identifier of the document, (b) LeftPos and RightPos can be generated by counting word numbers from the beginning of the document DocId until the start and end of the element, respectively, and (c) LevelNum is the depth of the node in the document.

In this context, structural relationships between tree nodes can be easily determined:

- **Ancestor-descendant:** A tree node 2 encoded as 2222 is a descendent of the tree node 1 encoded as 1111 iff 12, 12, and 21;
- **Parent-child:** 2 is a child of 1 iff it is a descendant of 1 and 21.

The Holistic Twig Join Approach

The holistic twig join approach (Bruno et al., 2002) consists of stack-based algorithms which adopt the four level architecture depicted in Figure 3. In particular, both the algorithms presented in

211

(Bruno et al., 2002), one for path matching and the other for twig matching, essentially work on paths. In case of path matching, the path is the query itself (e.g. //contents/section/article); in the other case, instead, the algorithm works on each individual query root-to-leaf path.

Given a path involving n nodes, $q_1, \ldots, q_n$, associated with each node q_i there is the inverted index I_{qi} (level L0 in Figure). It is the inverted index associated with the data elements or strings that match the query predicate at node q_i. Therefore, it contains the positional representation of the matching database nodes. For instance, given the path //contents/section/article and the data tree shown in Figure 2 by ignoring versioning annotations, the inverted indices are $I_{contents}$, $I_{section}$, and $I_{article}$, where $I_{contents}$ contains one tuple encoding node B, $I_{section}$ contains two tuples encoding nodes C and F, and $I_{article}$ contains three tuples encoding nodes D, E, and G. Moreover, the algorithms associate q_i with a stack sq_i (level L2 in Figure). At each step of the algorithms, such a stack contains data nodes from I_{qi}. Each data node in the stack consists of a pair (positional representation of a node from I_{qi}, pointer to a node in $S_{[parent(qI_i)]}$). In particular, at every computation step, the data nodes in S_{qi} are guaranteed to lie on a root-to-leaf path in the XML database and the set of stacks represent in linear space a compact encoding of partial and total answers to the query twig pattern. The skeleton of the two holistic twig join algorithms (HTJ algorithms in the following) is presented in Figure 4.

At each iteration the algorithms identify the next node to be processed. To this end, for each query node q_i, level L1 contains in the main memory buffer B_{qi} the node in the inverted index I_{qi} with the smallest LeftPos value and not yet processed. Among those, step 1 chooses the node with the smallest value, let it be $n_{\bar{q}}$. Then, given knowledge of such node, the algorithms remove partial answers form the stacks that cannot be extended to total answers and push the node $n_{\bar{q}}$ into the stack $S_{\bar{q}}$. Whenever $n_{\bar{q}}$ matches a leaf node of the query path and thus it is pushed on a "leaf" stack, the set of stacks contains an encoding of total answers. Therefore, step 4 outputs these answers at SOL Level and immediately deletes $n_{\bar{q}}$. For instance, given the query //contents// section//article, let us assume that the next node to be processed is F, i.e. nodes B, C, D, and E have already been selected from level L1. At this step, $S_{contents}$ and $S_{section}$ contain B and C, respectively, while $S_{article}$ is empty. In this case, the

Figure 3. The basic four level holistic twig join architecture

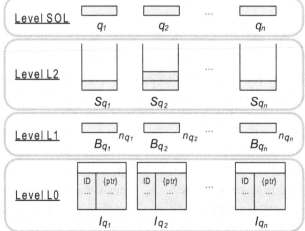

Figure 4. Skeleton of the holistic twig join algorithms (HTJ algorithms)

```
While there are nodes to be processed
(1) Choose the next node n_q̄
(2) Apply the deletion policy
(3) Push the node n_q̄ into the pertinence stack S_q̄
(4) Output solutions
```

partial answer (B,C) cannot be further extended because F belongs to a root-to-leaf path different from that of C. Therefore, C is deleted from S$_{section}$ whereas B is maintained in S$_{contents}$ because (B,F) can be extended to a total answer, as it will indeed happen when processing G.

The algorithms presented in (Bruno et al., 2002) have been further improved in (Chen et al., 2005; Jiang et al., 2003).

Indexing Scheme Extensions Towards Multi-Version Management

As multi-version XML documents are XML documents containing time-varying and Semantic annotated data, they can be indexed using the interval-based scheme described above and, thus, by indexing timestamps and applicability attributes as "standard" tuples. On the other hand, timestamped and annotated nodes have a specific Semantics which should be exploited when documents are accessed and, in particular, when the slice operation is applied. The idea is to add time and Semantic applicability to the interval-based indexing scheme by substituting the inverted indices in (Zhang et al., 2001) with multi-version inverted indices. In each multi-version inverted index, besides the position of an element occurrence in the time-varying XML database, the tuple (DocId,LeftPos:RightPos, LevelNum|SemAppl, TempPer) contains two implicit attributes, SemAppl and TempPer. The Semantic applicability attribute SemAppl consists of a Class applicability attribute, and represents a

class to which the tuple is applicable. Similarly, the temporal attribute TempPer consists of a sequence of From:To temporal attributes representing a period, one for each involved temporal dimension, and represents a period. Thus, our multi-version inverted indices are in 1NF and each multi-version node nMV, whose applicability involves multiple classes and whose lifetime is a temporal element containing a number of periods, is encoded through many tuples having the same projection on the non-implicit attributes (DocId, LeftPos:RightPos,LevelNum) but with all the different combinations of SemAppl and TempPer values, each representing a class and a period. All the multi-version inverted indices are defined on the same temporal dimensions such that tuples coming from different inverted indices are always comparable from a temporal point of view. Therefore, given the number h of the different temporal dimensions represented in the time-varying XML database, TempPer is From$_1$:To$_1$,...,From$_h$:To$_h$.

In this context, each multi-version XML document to be inserted in the database undergoes a pre-processing phase where (i) the lifetime and applicability of each node is derived from the timestamps and applicability attributes associated with it, (ii) in case, the resulting lifetime is extended to the temporal dimensions on which it has not been defined by following the approach described in Section 3.1. Figure 5 illustrates the structure of the four indices for the reference example. Notice that the snapshot node A, whose label is law, is extended to the temporal dimension

Figure 5. The temporal inverted indices for the reference example

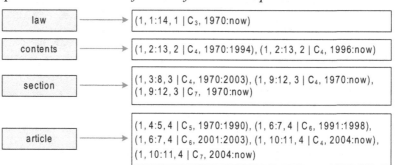

by setting the pertinence of the corresponding tuple to [1970,*now*].

A Holistic Technology for the Slice Operator: Temporal Aspects

The slice operator can be implemented by applying minimal changes to the holistic twig join architecture. The multi-version XML database is recorded in the temporal/Semantic inverted indices which substitute the "conventional" inverted index at the lower level of the architecture and thus the nodes in the stacks are represented both by the position and the temporal and Semantic attributes. Given a personalization query (`twig`,`t-window`,`app constraint`), a slice is the snapshot of any answer to `twig` which is temporally consistent and satisfies the applicability constraint. Thus, the holistic twig join algorithms continue to work as they are responsible for the structural consistency of the slices and provide the best management of the stacks from this point of view. Temporal consistency, instead, has to be managed with ad-hoc solutions. In this section, we will focus on the temporal aspects of the technology implementing the slice operator and describe in detail the solution proposed in (Mandreoli et al., 2006). Notice that for clarity of presentation, in this section we will consider only the temporal aspects and we project all tuples on their explicit and temporal attributes only. Semantic aspects

will be dealt with in the next section. Any tuple will thus be referenced as $(D,L{:}R,N|T)$.

Temporal consistency must be checked for each answer output of the overall process. In particular, for each potential slice $((D,L_j{:}R_j,N_j|T_j),\ldots,(D,L_k{:}R_k,N_k|T_k))$ it is necessary to intersect the periods represented by the values $T_j...T_k$ and then check both that such intersection is not empty and that it is contained in the temporal window of the query. In this way, we have described the "first step" towards the realization of the temporal aspects of an XML query processor. On the other hand, the performances of this first solution are strictly related to the peculiarities of the underlying database. Indeed, XML documents usually contain millions of nodes and this is absolutely true in the temporal context where documents record the history of the applied changes. Thus, the holistic twig join algorithms can produce a lot of answers which are structurally consistent but which are eventually discarded as they are not temporally consistent. This situation implies useless computations due to an uncontrolled growth of the number of tuples put on the stacks.

Temporal consistency considers two aspects: the intersection of the involved lifetimes must be non-empty (*non-empty intersection constraint* in the following) and it must be contained in the temporal window (*containment constraint* in the following). We devised alternative solutions which rely on the two different aspects of temporal consistency and act at the different levels of the architecture with the aim of limiting the number of temporally useless nodes the algorithms put in the stacks. The reference architecture is slightly different from the one presented in Figure 3. Indeed, in our context, any timestamped node whose lifetime is a temporal element is encoded into more tuples (e.g. see the encoding of the timestamped node E in the reference example). Thus, at level L1, each node n_q must be interpreted as the set of tuples encoding n_q. They are stored in buffer B_q and step 3 of the HTJ algorithms empties B_q and pushes the tuples in the stack S_q.

Non-Empty Intersection Constraint

Not all tuples which enter level L1 will at the end belong to the set of slices. In particular, some of them will be discarded due to the non-empty intersection constraint. The following Lemma characterizes this aspect. Without loss of generality, it considers paths only, as the twig matching algorithm relies on the path matching one.

Proposition 1: *Let $(D,L{:}R,N|T)$ be a tuple belonging to the temporal inverted index I_q, I_{q1},..., I_{qk} the inverted indices of the ancestors of q and $TP_{qi} = \sigma_{LeftPos<L}(I_{qi})TempPer$, for $i \in [1,k]$, the union of the temporal pertinences of all the tuples in q\s\do4(i*

having LeftPos smaller than L. Then $(D,L{:}R,N|T)$ will belong to no slice if the intersection of its temporal pertinence with TP_{q1},...,TP_{qk} is empty, i.e. $T \cap TP_{q1} \cap ... \cap TP_{qk} = \varnothing$.

Notice that, at each step of the process, the tuples having `LeftPos` smaller than L can be in the stacks, in the buffers, or still have to be read from the inverted indices. However, looking for such tuples in the three levels of the architecture would be quite computationally expensive. Thus, in the following we introduce a new approach for buffer loading which allows us to look only at the stack level. Moreover, we avoid accessing the temporal pertinence of the tuples contained in the stacks by associating a temporal pertinence to each stack (*temporal stack*). Such a temporal pertinence must therefore be updated at each push and pop operation. At each step of the process, for efficiency purposes both in the update and in the intersection phase, such a temporal pertinence is the smallest multidimensional period P_q containing the union of the temporal pertinence of the tuples in the stack S_q.

The aim of our buffer loading approach is to avoid loading the temporal tuples encoding a node $n^{[T]}$ in the pertinence buffer B_q if the inverted indices associated with the parents of q contain tuples with LeftPos smaller than that

Figure 6. Buffer loading algorithm Load

```
Input: Twig pattern twig, the last processed node n_q̄
Output: Next node n_q to be processed
Algorithm Load:

(1) if all buffers are empty
(2)     start=root(twig);
(3) else
(4)     start=↼q;
(5) for each query node q from start to leaf(twig)
(6)     get n_q;
(7)     min_q is the minimum between n_q.LeftPos and min_parent(q);
(8)     if n_q.LeftPos is equal to min_q
(9)        load n_q into B_q;
(10)return the last node inserted into the buffers
```

of q and not yet processed. Such an approach is consistent with step 1 of the HTJ algorithms as it chooses the node at level L1 with the smallest LeftPos value and ensures that when $n^{[T]}$ enters B_q all the tuples involved in Prop. 1 are in the stacks. The algorithm implementing step 1 of the HTJ algorithms is shown in Figure 6. We associate each buffer B_q with the minimum min_q among the LeftPos values of the tuples contained in the buffer itself and those of its ancestors. Assuming that all buffers are empty, the algorithm starts from the root of the twig (step 2) and, for each node q up to the leaf, it updates the minimum min_q and inserts n_q, the node in I_q with the smallest LeftPos value and not yet processed, if it is smaller than min_q. The same applies when some buffers are not empty. In this case, it starts from the query node matching with the previously processed data node and it can be easily shown that the buffers of the ancestors of such node are not empty, whereas the buffers of the subpath rooted by such node are all empty.

Lemma 1. Assume that step 1 of the HTJ algorithms depicted in Figure 4 is implemented by the algorithm Load . The tuple (D,L:R,N|T) in q will belong to no slice if the intersection of its temporal pertinence T with the multidimensional

period $P_{q1 \to qk} = P_{q1} \cap ... \cap P_{qk}$ intersecting the periods of the stacks of the ancestors $q_1,...,q_k$ of q is empty.

For instance, at the first iteration of the HTJ algorithms applied to the reference example, step 1 and step 3 produce the situation depicted in Figure 7. Notice that when the tuple (1,4:5,4|1970:1990) encoding node D (label article) enters level L1 all the tuples with LeftPos smaller than 4 are already at level L2 and due to the above Lemma we can state that it will belong to no slice.

Thus, the non-empty intersection constraint can be exploited to prevent the insertion of useless nodes into the stacks by acting at level L1 and L2 of the architecture. At level L2 we act at step 3 of the HTJ algorithms by simply avoiding pushing into the stack S_q each temporal tuple $(D,L:R,N|T)$ encoding the next node to be processed which satisfies Lemma , i.e. such that $T \cap P_{q1 \to qk} = \emptyset$. At level L1, instead, we act at step 9 of the algorithm Load by avoiding loading in any buffer B_q each temporal tuple encoding n_q which satisfies Lemma 1. More precisely, given the LeftPos value of the last processed node, say *CurLeftPos*, we only load each tuple $(D,L:R,N|T)$ such that L is the minimum value greater than *CurLeftPos* and T intersects $P_{q1 \to qk}$. To this purpose, our solution

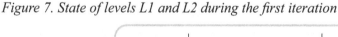

Figure 7. State of levels L1 and L2 during the first iteration

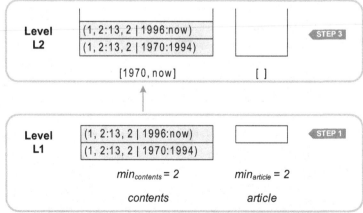

uses time-key indices combining the `LeftPos` attribute with the attributes `Fromj:Toj` in the `TempPer` implicit attribute representing one temporal dimension in order to improve the performances of range-interval selection queries on the temporal inverted indices. In particular, we considered B+-tree access.

A one-dimensional index like the B+-tree, clusters data primarily on a single attribute. Thus, we built B+-trees that cluster first on the `LeftPos` attribute and than on the interval end time To_j. In this way, we can take advantage of sequential I/O as tree leaf pages are linked and records in them are ordered. In particular, we start with the first leaf page that contains a `LeftPos` value greater than $CurLeftPos$ and a To_j value greater than or equal to $P_{q1 \to qk}|_{From_j}$, i.e. the projection of the period $P_{q1 \to qk}$ on the interval start time $From_j$. Then we proceed by loading the records until the leaf page with the next LeftPos value or with a $From_j$ value greater than $P_{q1 \to qk}|_{To_j}$ is met. This has the effect of selecting each tuple $(D,L:R,N|T)$ where L is the smallest value greater than $CurLeftPos$ and its period $T|_{From_j}:To_j$ intersect the period $P_{q1 \to qk}|_{From_j}:To_j$, as $T|_{To_j} \geq P_{q_1 \to q_k}|_{From_j}$ and $T|_{From_j} \leq P_{q_1 \to q_k}|_{To_j}$.

Containment Constraint

The following proposition is the equivalent of Prop. 1 when the containment constraint is considered.

Proposition 2. *Let $(D,L:R,N|T)$ be a tuple belonging to the temporal inverted index I_q. Then $(D,L:R,N|T)$ will belong to no slice if the intersection of its temporal pertinence with the temporal window t-window is empty.*

It allows us to act at level L1 and L2, but also between level L0 and level L1. At level L1 and L2 the approach is the same as the non-empty intersection constraint; it is sufficient to use the temporal window t-window, and thus Prop.2, instead of Lemma 1. Moreover, it is also possible to add an intermediate level between level L0 and level L1 of the architecture, which we call "under L1" (UL1), where the only tuples satisfying Prop. 2 are selected from each temporal inverted index, are ordered on the basis of their (DocId,LeftPos) values and then pushed into the buffers. Similarly to the approach explained in the previous section, to speed up the selection, we exploit B+-tree indices built on one temporal dimension. Notice that this solution deals with buffers as streams of tuples, and thus, it provides interesting efficiency improvements only when the temporal window is quite selective.

Combining Solutions

The non-empty intersection constraint and the containment constraint are orthogonal and thus, in principle, the solutions presented in the above subsections can be freely combined in order to

Table 1. Applicable computation scenarios for temporal aspects

Non-empty intersection	Containment			
	UL1	L1	L2	SOL
L1	✗	✓ L1/L1	~ L1/L2	~ L1/SOL
L2	✓ L2/UL1	~ L2/L1	✓ L2/L2	✓ L2/SOL
SOL	✓ SOL/UL1	~ SOL/L1	✓ SOL/L2	✓ SOL/SOL

decrease the number of useless tuples we put in the stacks. Table 1 shows a summary of the possible computation scenarios that can be composed by combining the solutions available for managing the above said constraints.

Each combination gives rise to a different scenario denoted as "X/Y", where "X" and "Y" are the employed solutions for the non-empty intersection constraint and for the containment constraint, respectively (e.g. scenario L1/L2 employs solution L1 for the non-empty intersection constraint and solution L2 for the containment constraint). For each scenario an applicability symbol is also reported, ranging from "fully supported" ("✓", i.e. allowed and advisable solution) to "partially supported" ("~", i.e. allowed but not particularly advisable) to "not allowed" ("×"). Some of these scenarios will be discussed in the following.

First, scenario L1/UL1 is not applicable since in solution UL1 selected data is kept and read directly from buffers, with no chance of additional indexing. Instead, in scenario L1/L1 the management of the two constraints can be easily combined by querying the indices with the intersection of the temporal pertinence of the ancestors (Proposition 1) and the required temporal window. All other combinations are straightforwardly achievable, but not necessarily advisable. In particular, when L1 is involved for any of the two constraints, the L1 indices have to be built and queried: therefore, it is best to combine the management of the two constraints as in L1/L1 discussed above. Finally, notice that the baseline scenario is the SOL/SOL one, involving none of the solutions discussed in this chapter.

A Holistic Technology for the Slice Operator: Semantic Aspects

As far as the Semantic aspects of the `slice` operator are concerned, we provide some initial solutions to the problem of computing each distinct slice obeying to the `app-constraint` formula.

Similarly to the temporal case, our ultimate goal is to introduce the changes that the holistic twig join technology should undergo in order to efficiently support Semantic aspects. Obviously, the base case is to check applicability constraints at the SOL level. However, this would mean wasting precious CPU time and main memory space for node patterns which are structurally but not Semantically consistent. In an effort to optimize the personalized access to XML documents with limited applicability, the proposed solutions will act at the different levels of the architecture shown in Figure 3 in order to limit the access to Semantically useless nodes. All these solutions will be founded on the idea of arranging the data nodes of the multi-version XML repository and the applicability constraints of the submitted query in the pre-order/post-order planes representing the reference taxonomies. Indeed, taxonomies are obedient to the inheritance Semantics and the pre-order and post-order ranks allow us to determine the ancestor-descendant relationship between any pair of applicability classes in constant time. For instance, given the (pre-order, post-order) values shown in the upper left corner of the classes depicted in Figure 1, `Employee` is an ancestor of `Private` as its pre-order is smaller than the `Private`'s pre-order while its post-order is greater than the `Private`'s post-order: 3<6 and 6>3.

In this context, each taxonomy T_i corresponds to a pre/post-order plane where nodes are arranged as follows. Each multi-version node n^{MV} whose applicability *applicability(n^{MV})* contains a class $T_i.C_j$ is represented in the T_i's plane by the point having the pre- and post-order coordinates of $T_i.C_j$. For instance, the representation of the multi-version XML document shown in Figure 2 in the pre-/post-order plane of the civic taxonomy of Figure 1 is shown in Figure 8. Notice that a multi-version node lies in more planes whenever its applicability refers to more taxonomies. At the same time, in each plane it can be represented by more points if it refers to more classes (see e.g. nodes F and G in Figure). A similar approach is followed to represent the applicability constraints app-constraint submitted to the slice operator. In particular, each navigational pattern $[T_j$. C_i, depth] is represented in the T_j's plane by the rectangle whose lower right corner corresponds to C_i and the upper left corner is the C_i's ancestor reachable in T_j in $depth_i$ steps. Figure 8 also shows a grey rectangle which corresponds to the $[C_6, 1]$ of the slicing example.

A multi-version node n^{MV} is Semantically consistent if *applicability(n^{MV})* implies at least one disjunct $[T_{j1}.C_{i1}, depth_{i1}] \wedge \ldots \wedge [T_{jk}.C_{ik}, depth_{ik}]$ of app-constraint. In the pre/post-order space this notion translates into the constraint that the encoding must be contained in each rectangle $[T_{jh}$. C_{ih}, $depth_{ih}]$. Our proposal is to efficiently select all and only the multi-version nodes that are Semantically consistent through their encoding in the pre/post-order space. The basic approach is to access each node once by sequentially scanning each plane bottom-up. In particular, we first identify the regions in each pre/post-plane encoding the applicability constraint app-constraint and then we exploit them to smartly access only the Semantically pertinent nodes.

As far as the former step is concerned, regions are non-overlapping portions of the plane. Thus,

once having represented all the app-constraint rectangles, we first detect the horizontal bounds of each region induced by the post-order values of the rectangles. For instance, in Figure 8 it is [3,4]. Notice that, for the sake of simplicity, our reference example contains only one rectangle. However, in real scenarios, rectangles can also overlap and thus the horizontal bound of each region does not necessarily coincide with the post-order values of each rectangle. Then, we detect the vertical bounds of each region as the minimum and the maximum pre-order values of the rectangles overlapping the region's horizontal bounds. Finally, regions are ordered in increasing order of their post-order values thus resulting in a sequence of non-overlapping regions: $[bpost_{R1}, epost_{R1}] \times [bpre_{R1}, epre_{R1}], \ldots, [bpost_{Rn}, epost_{Rn}] \times [bpre_{Rn}, epre_{Rn}]$.

The resulting regions could be exploited at different levels of the holistic architecture to efficiently select only the Semantically pertinent tuples. For instance, at level L1 we could act at step 9 of the algorithm Load by avoiding loading in any buffer B_q each tuple encoding n_q which is out of the region boundaries. More precisely, B+-tree indices can be built which cluster first on the LeftPos attribute and then on the post order of

Figure 8. The pre-/post-order plane of the civic taxonomy

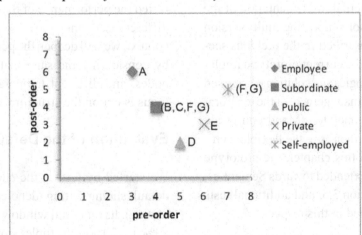

`SemAppl`. In this way, given the `LeftPos` value of the last processed node, say *CurLeftPos*, it could be possible to efficiently sequentially scan only those tuples having the smallest `LeftPos` value greater than *CurLeftPos* and lying in the regions. In particular, the access is performed firstly on (*CurLeftPos, bpost$_{R1}$*), thus allowing to load the records whose preorder values of `SemAppl` are within [*bpre$_{R1}$, epre$_{R1}$*] up to *epost$_{R1}$* and the same process is recursively applied for each region. Similarly, it could be possible to act at level L2 simply by avoiding the insertion of tuples which are out of the sequence of regions.

While the solutions proposed in Section 3.4 aim to produce temporally consistent node patterns, the ones sketched above guarantee Semantic consistency. Thus, the most trivial approach facing the problem of producing temporally and Semantically consistent solutions could be to intersect the answers returned by the two processes. However, as the two versioning aspects are dealt with in an orthogonal way, the above Semantic techniques could be freely combined with the temporal solutions at any level of the holistic architecture in order to enhance the multi-version XML engine efficiency.

EXPERIMENTAL EVALUATION

In this section, we present a selection of the results we obtained on an actual implementation of the XML query processor supporting multi-version XML documents described in the previous sections. In particular, the current prototype implements all the technologies and solutions discussed in Section 3.4 for the management of the temporal aspects of the slice operator (Mandreoli et al., 2006). In the future, thanks to the flexible architecture discussed in this chapter, the prototype capabilities will be extended towards Semantics, as described in Section 3.5, and additional tests will also be performed in this respect.

All experiments have been performed on a Pentium 4 3Ghz Windows XP Professional workstation, equipped with 1GB RAM and an 160GB EIDE HD with NT file system (NTFS).

Experimental Setting

The document collections follow the structure of the documents used in (Mandreoli et al., 2006), where three temporal dimensions are involved, and have been generated by a configurable XML generator. On average, each document contains 30-40 nodes, a depth level of 10, 10-15 of these nodes are timestamped nodes n^T, each one in 2-3 versions composed by the union of 1-2 distinct periods. We are also able to change the length of the periods and the probability that the temporal pertinence of the document nodes overlap. Finally, we investigate different kinds of probability density functions generating collections with different distributions, thus directly affecting the containment constraint.

The reference collection (C-ref) consists of 5000 documents (120 MB) generated following a uniform and lowly scattered distribution. We also employed an alternate collection (C-alt) of the same size but involving a much more scattered distribution. All the tests presented in the following sections are related to collection C-ref, while Section 4.5 will be devoted to the comparison between the C-ref and C-alt performances. We tested the performance of the slice operator with different `twig` and `t-window` parameters. In this context, we will deepen the performance analysis by considering the same path, involving three nodes, and different temporal windows as our focus is not on the structural aspects.

Evaluation of the Default Setting

We started by testing the slice operator with a default slicing setting (denoted as SS1 in the following). Its temporal window has a selectivity of 20%, i.e. 20% of the tuples stored in the temporal inverted indexes involved by the twig pattern intersect the temporal window. The returned solutions are 5584.

Table 2 shows the performance of each scenario when executing SS1. In particular, from the left: the execution time, the percentage of potential solutions at level SOL that are not temporally consistent and, in the last two columns, the percentage of tuples that are put in the buffers and in the stacks with respect to the total number of tuples involved in the evaluation. Notice that the temporal inverted indices exploited at level L1 are B+-trees.

The best result is given by the computation scenario L1/L1 whose execution time is more than 6 times faster than the execution time of the baseline scenario SOL/SOL. Such a result clearly shows that combining solutions at a low level of the architecture, such as L1, avoids I/O costs for reading unnecessary tuples and their further elaboration cost at the upper levels. The decrease of read tuples from 100% of SOL/SOL to just 7.99% of L1/L1 and the decrease of temporally inconsistent solutions from 96.51% of SOL/SOL to 23.1% of L1/L1 represent a remarkable result in terms of efficiency. Let us now have a look at the other scenarios. SS1 represents a typical querying setting where the containment constraint is much more selective than the non-empty intersection constraint. This consideration induces us to analyze the obtained performances by partitioning the scenarios in three groups, */L1, */L2 and */SOL, on the basis of the adopted containment constraint solution. The scenarios within each group show similar execution time and percentages of tuples. In group */L1, the low percentage of tuples in buffers (10%) means low I/O costs and this has a good influence on the execution time. In group */L2 the percentages of tuples in buffers are more than double those of group */L1, while the execution time is about 1.5 times higher. Finally, group */SOL is characterized by percentages of tuples in buffers and execution time approximately ten and six time higher than those in */T1, respectively. Moreover, within each group it should be noticed that raising the non-empty intersection constraint solution from level L1 to level SOL produces more and more deterioration in the overall performances.

Table 2. Evaluation of the computation scenarios with SS1

Evaluation scenarios:	Execution Time (ms)	Non-Consistent Solutions (%)	Tuples (%)	
			Buffer	Stack
L1/L1	1890	23.10 %	7.99 %	7.76 %
L2/L1	1953	23.10 %	9.23 %	7.76 %
SOL/L1	2000	39.13 %	9.43 %	9.17 %
L1/L2	2625	23.10 %	17.95 %	7.76 %
L2/L2	2797	23.10 %	23.37 %	7.76 %
SOL/L2	2835	39.13 %	23.80 %	9.17 %
L1/SOL	12125	95.74 %	88.92 %	88.85 %
L2/SOL	12334	95.74 %	99.33 %	88.85 %
SOL/SOL	12688	96.51 %	100.00 %	100.00 %

Changing the Selectivity of the Temporal Window

We are now interested in showing how the multi-version XML query processor responds to the execution of slicing with different selectivity levels; to this purpose, we considered a second slice setting (SS2) having a selectivity of 31% (lower than SS1) and returning 12873 solutions. Figure 9 shows the percentage of read tuples (Figure 9-a) and the execution time (Figure 9-b) of SS1 compared with our reference slice setting (SS1).

Notice that the trend of growth of the percentage of read tuples along the different scenarios is similar. However, for SS1, the execution time follows the same trend as the read tuples; whereas for SS2, the execution time of different scenarios are closer. In this case, the lower selectivity of the temporal window makes the benefits achievable by the L1 solutions less appreciable. Notice that, in the SOL/SOL scenario both queries have the same number of tuples in the buffers because no selectivity is applied at the lower levels; this also explains the same execution time.

Figure 9. Comparison between SS1 and SS2

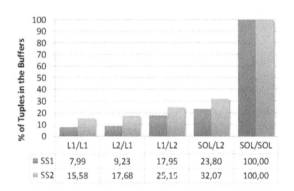

	L1/L1	L2/L1	L1/L2	SOL/L2	SOL/SOL
SS1	7,99	9,23	17,95	23,80	100,00
SS2	15,58	17,68	25,15	32,07	100,00

(a) Percentage of tuples in the buffers

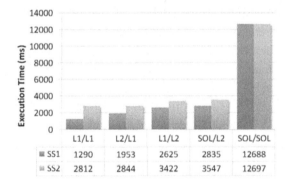

	L1/L1	L2/L1	L1/L2	SOL/L2	SOL/SOL
SS1	1290	1953	2625	2835	12688
SS2	2812	2844	3422	3547	12697

(b) Execution time (ms)

Figure 10. Comparison between the two collections C-R and C-S

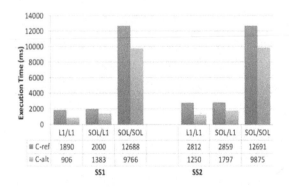

	L1/L1	SOL/L1	SOL/SOL	L1/L1	SOL/L1	SOL/SOL
C-ref	1890	2000	12688	2812	2859	12691
C-alt	906	1383	9766	1250	1797	9875
		SS1			SS2	

(a) Execution time

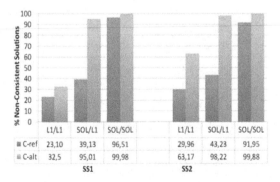

	L1/L1	SOL/L1	SOL/SOL	L1/L1	SOL/L1	SOL/SOL
C-ref	23,10	39,13	96,51	29,96	43,23	91,95
C-alt	32,5	95,01	99,98	63,17	98,22	99,88
		SS1			SS2	

(b) Percentage of non-consistent solutions

Evaluation on Differently Distributed Collections

We also considered the performance of the XML query processor on another collection (C-alt) of the same size of the reference one, but that is characterized by temporally scattered nodes. Figure 10 shows the execution time and the number of temporally inconsistent potential solutions of SS1 and SS2 on both collections. The execution time of scenarios L1/L1 and SOL/L1, depicted in Figure 10-a, shows that it is almost unchanged for collection C-ref, whereas the difference is more remarkable for both temporal slicing settings for collection C-alt. Notice also that the percentage of temporally inconsistent potential solutions when no solution is applied under level SOL is limited in the C-ref case but explodes in the C-alt case (see for instance SOL/L1 in Figure 10-b). The non-empty intersection constraint is mainly influenced by the temporal sparsity of the nodes in the collection: The more the nodes are temporally scattered the more the number of temporally inconsistent potential solutions increases. Therefore, when temporal slicing is applied to these kinds of collections, the best way to process it is to adopt a solution exploiting the non-empty intersection constraint at the lowest level, i.e. L1.

Native vs. Stratum Comparison

After having measured the behavior of the native implementation, we wanted to compare its performance to the one obtainable through a traditional "stratum" approach. In order to do that, we performed additional tests using an available implementation of a temporal-aware stratum-based XML engine (Grandi et al., 2003).

In general, as we saw in the past sections, stratum approaches require two distinct phases in order to provide the final results since they handle structural and temporal constraints in separate components. In the first phase, all of the whole documents satisfying the structural constraints are retrieved, then from a DOM representation the portions of each of these documents that do not verify the temporal constraints are pruned out in a post-processing phase. From the tests we performed, we saw that the stratum processor was able to perform the first phase of the default setting in nearly 20 seconds for the reference collection, which is more than 7 times the time required by the native XML query processor. Further, and this is typical of most stratum implementations, the post-processing phase was linear with the number of the documents retrieved; in our case, it processed nearly 10 documents per second. The stratum performances on the alternate collection (C-alt) were also significantly worse than the native ones, since, for efficiency's sake, the very large number of inconsistent solutions would require the query processor to handle non-empty intersection constraints as soon as possible, rather than in a post-processing phase as in the stratum implementation. From these and further tests we performed, we can state that a native implementation such as the one discussed in this chapter generally outperforms stratum performance in most temporal settings. Moreover, the native implementation requires less than 5% of the main memory of the DOM-based approach, typically used in stratum implementations.

Scalability

Figure 11 (notice the logarithmic scales) reports the performance of the native XML query processor in executing SS1 for the reference collection and for two collections having the same characteristics but different sizes: 10000 and 20000 documents. The execution time grew linearly in every scenario, with a proportion of approximately 0.75 with respect to the number of documents for our best scenario L1/L1. Such tests have also been performed on the other slicing settings and we measured a similar trend, thus showing the good scalability of the processor in every type of query context.

FUTURE TRENDS

As we tried to show in this chapter, personalized access is a very interesting and challenging problem, especially in a large XML repository scenario, and new technological issues arise in this context. Our claim is that equipping XML query processors with all the required technology directly from their conception, by appropriately extending the inner core structures and algorithms, appears as a superior design choice. Following the guidelines we proposed, powerful and efficient native XML engines can be built for the management of temporal and Semantic aspects of XML data.

In general, the contrast "native" versus "stratum" approach should be considered as a still open and challenging issue, which is still debated even in the context of pure temporal XML research, where two schools of thought exist. For instance, Wang & Zaniolo (2008) claim that off-the-shelf XML/XQuery technology is all that we need for efficient management of temporal and multi-version

XML data. They also discussed some indexing and clustering techniques for multi-version XML data, which could help standard XML engines to achieve efficient execution of temporal queries expressed in standard XQuery. However, they acknowledge that efficiency and optimization of temporal queries in the general XML/XQuery framework are open research issues of great importance for temporal applications. On the contrary, Noh and Gadia (2006) claim that XML and the concept of dimension are orthogonal and, as a consequence, traditional XML engines cannot behave satisfactorily when temporal management of XML data is required. They showed how an ad-hoc temporal query processor built on-top of an XML repository outperforms a standard XQuery engine when temporal queries are executed. The difference is also emphasised by the growth of the database size, as they observed that standard XQuery engines scale worse when executing temporal queries.

As far as queries involving temporal slicing are concerned, the situation is somewhat clearer,

Figure 11.Scalability results for SS1

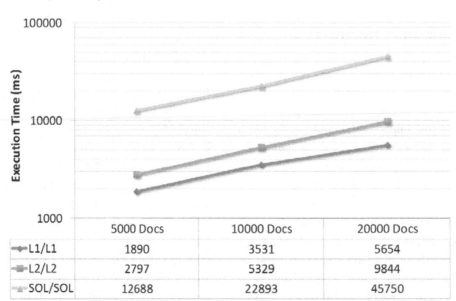

	5000 Docs	10000 Docs	20000 Docs
L1/L1	1890	3531	5654
L2/L2	2797	5329	9844
SOL/SOL	12688	22893	45750

as it has been shown that special techniques are needed to efficiently support these kinds of queries (Gao & Snodgrass, 2003; Mandreoli et al., 2006). In the case of personalization queries, involving multi-dimensional selection and slicing of XML data, the sufficiently consolidated temporal framework could be extended with the solutions sketched in Section 3.5, in order to build powerful and efficient native XML engines for the management of temporal and Semantic versioning in XML data. The experimental results we presented in this chapter show that the "native" approach outperforms the "stratum" one with the considered XML data distributions, also in the presence of large collections of multi-version XML documents. The varying document structure and version distribution we used in the experiments is apt to model text-based legal documents and medical guidelines. However, other multi-version XML data distributions and characteristics should also be considered to extend the validity of our results to a broader framework. Future research could address such an issue. Moreover, the ideas and technologies we presented in this chapter could be extended and completed in many directions.

For instance, future research directions include the ability to handle multiple taxonomies and, more generally, ontologies containing more complex hierarchies and the management of ontology evolution issues. As a matter of fact, our approach could be extended in order to fully support ontologies with generic class relationships, containing, for instance, multiple-inheritance IS-A hierarchies and equivalence relations between classes. To this end, the XML documents annotation scheme and their storage organization must be enhanced. For instance, multiple-inheritance hierarchies could be transformed into a forest of tree-shaped hierarchies, obtained by splitting classes with multiple ancestors across multiple taxonomies (preserving one of their ancestors in each taxonomy) and then connecting the split results with equivalence relations. Obviously,

this simple approach is unfeasible if multiple inheritance becomes widespread in the ontology, owing to the exponential growth of the hierarchy forest to be used.

Further, at the present stage of the research, temporally versioned taxonomies and ontologies have not been taken into account: specifically, in this chapter we considered only temporal versioning of XML resources. However, we believe that it would also be very interesting to consider ontology versioning (which would add a temporal perspective on applicability) in the general framework and, thus, to analyze in depth how proposed ontology versioning models, like the one in (Klein & Fensel, 2001), and available tools, such as t-Protégé (t-Protégé, n.d.), an extension of Protégé supporting temporal aspects, could assist in this respect.

Finally, as far as the application of our techniques to specific real-world application scenarios as the ones we described in the introductory section is concerned, other interesting research opportunities can be seen. For instance, it could be useful to consider the assessment of a prototype native XML system— such as the one we proposed —in a concrete eGovernment (eHealth) working environment, with real users and in the presence of a large repository of real legal (medical) documents. Indeed, this is exactly one of the aspects we are planning to investigate in the near future for eGovernment. Specifically, a civic ontology based on a corpus of real norms (concerning infancy schools), on which Semantic annotations could be based, is currently under development. In this way, we also plan to complement our system-oriented evaluation approach with user-oriented evaluations, measuring end-user performance and satisfaction in using our framework and pointing out the benefits of exploiting our personalization techniques. Moreover, other kinds of measures relevant for content providers (e.g. effort required for maintaining the civic ontology, for annotating the XML resources, for managing the repository contents) should also be taken into account to complete the assessment picture. Moreover, some feedback from promoting Agencies and Public Administrations willing to boost eGovernment (eHealth) services should be collected in order to rank the various metrics according to the desired priorities.

Another research direction which can be followed could also concern the adoption of other versioning dimensions in XML data modeling and querying. Examples of such dimensions could be, for instance, space (Córcoles & González, 2004), language (Stavrakas et al., 2004) or security (Dyreson et al., 2003). Each new dimension is equipped with a different Semantics which could enforce specific constraints on the document structure (e.g. constraints between annotations of nodes with an ancestor-descendant relationship), and which could thus be useful for the optimization of slicing algorithms as we have shown in Sections 3 and 4 in the case of temporal and applicability dimensions. Whereas, at first glance, spatial dimensions could be thought as having a nature more similar to temporal dimensions, also giving rise to spatio-temporal data versioning, other dimensions could give rise to new kinds of Semantic versioning more similar in nature to applicability versioning and which could be used as well for personalization based on user profiles or context-dependent information. The introduction of these elements in multi-version XML data modeling and querying and related aspects raise several challenging issues to be explored in the near future.

CONCLUSION

In this chapter, we analyzed the problem of personalized XML access, describing past, current and future trends regarding this complex issue. Starting from the holistic twig join approach (Bruno et al., 2002), which directly avoids the problem of the very large size of intermediate results by using a chain of linked stacks to

compactly represent partial results, we proposed new flexible techniques for personalized XML access consisting of alternative solutions, and extensively tested them in different experimental settings. Both temporal and Semantic applicability selection and slicing have been considered in our analysis. The resulting good efficiency of the implemented prototype is quite encouraging and testifies to the claim that designing native XML query processors with built-in personalization facilities seems to be a wise design choice.

REFERENCES

Amagasa, T., Yoshikawa, M., & Uemura, S. (2000). A Data model for temporal XML documents. In *DEXA*, (pp. 334–344).

Amer-Yahia, S., Cho, SR., Lakshmanan, L. V. S., & Srivastava, D. (2001). Minimization of tree pattern queries. In *SIGMOD*, (pp. 497–508).

Amies, A. (2006) *Introduction of OWL Web Ontology Language for Medical and Bioscience Applications*. Medical computing. Retrieved January 15, 2008, from http://medicalcomputing. net/owl1.html

Benjamins, V. R., Casanovas, P., Breuker, J., & Gangemi, A. (Eds.) (2005). *Law and the Semantic Web: Legal ontologies, methodologies, legal information retrieval, and applications*. Heidelberg, Germany: Springer-Verlag.

Berners-Lee, T., Hendler, J., & Lassila, O. (2001). The Semantic Web. In *Scientific American 284*(5), (pp. 34–43).

Breuker, J., Tiscornia, D., Winkels, R., & Gangemi, A. (Eds.) (2004). In *Journal of Artificial Intelligence and Law 12*(4), Special issue on Ontologies for Law.

Bruno, N., Koudas, N., & Srivastava, D. (2002). Holistic Twig Joins: Optimal XML pattern matching. In *SIGMOD*, (pp. 310-321).

Buneman, P., Khanna, S., Tajima, K., & Tan, W.-C. (2004) Archiving scientific data. In *ACM Transactions on Database Systems 29*(1), 2–42.

Cabana, M. D., Rand C. S. N. R., Powe, C. S., Wu, A. W., Wilson, M. H., Abboud, P. C., & Rubin, H. R. (1999). Why don't physicians follow clinical practice guidelines? A framework for improvement. In *Journal of American Medical Association 282*(15), 1458–1465.

Callan, J., Smeaton, A., Beaulieu, M., Borlund, P., Brusilovsky, P., Chalmers, M., Lynch, C., Riedl, J., Smyth, B., Straccia, U., & Toms, E. (2003). *Personalization and recommender systems in digital libraries. Joint NSF-EU DELOS Working Group Report.* Sophia Antipolis, France: ERCIM. Retrieved January 15, 2008, from http://www.ercim.org/publication/ws-proceedings/Delos-NSF/Personalisation.pdf

Casanovas, P., Biasiotti, M. A., Francesconi, E., & Sagri, M.T. (2007). *Proceedings of the Second ICAIL Legal Ontologies and Artificial Intelligence Techniques Workshop (LOAIT).* IAAIL Workshop Series. Oisterwijk, The Netherlands: Wolf Legal Publishers.

Ceri, S., Fraternali, P. & Paraboschi, S. (1999) Data-driven, one-to-one Web site generation for data-intensive applications. In *VLDB*, (pp. 615–626).

Chawathe, S. S., Abiteboul, S., & Widom, J. (1999) Managing historical semistructured data". In *Theory and Practice of Object Systems 5*(3), 143–162.

Chen, T., Lu, J., & Wang Ling, T. (2005) On Boosting holism in XML Twig pattern matching using structural indexing techniques. In *SIGMOD*, (pp. 455-466).

Chien, S.-Y., Tsotras, V. J., & Zaniolo, C. (2002). Efficient management of multiversion XML documents. In *VLDB Journal 11*(4), 332–353.

Combi, C., & Montanari, A. (2001). Data models with multiple temporal dimensions: Completing the picture. In *CAiSE*, (pp. 187–202).

Córcoles, J. E., & González, P. (2004) Studying an Approach to Query Spatial XML. In Z. Bellahsene, P. McBrien (Eds.), *DIWeb2004, 3rd International Workshop on Data Integration over the Web, Online Proceedings.* Retrieved January 15, 2008, from http://www.doc.ic.ac.uk/~pjm/diweb2004/DIWeb2004_Part3.pdf

Cornelis, B. (2003). *Personalizing search indigital libraries.* Unpublished master's thesis. The Netherlands: University of Maastricht.

Currim, F., Currim, S., Dyreson, C. E., & Snodgrass, R. T. (2004) A tale of two schemas: Creating a temporal schema from a snapshot schema with τXSchema. In *EDBT*, (pp. 348–365).

De Castro, C., Grandi, F., & Scalas, M. R. (1993). Semantic interoperability of multitemporal relational databases. In *ER*, (pp. 463-474).

Dyreson, C. E., & Grandi, F. (in press). Temporal XML. In L. Liu & M. T. Özsu (Eds.), *Encyclopedia of database systems.* Heidelberg, Germany: Springer-Verlag.

Dyreson, C. E., Böhlen, M. H., Christian S. Jensen, C. S. (1999) Capturing and querying multiple aspects of semistructured data. In *VLDB*, pages 290–301.

Fousteris, N., Gergatsoulis, M., & Stavrakas, Y. (2007) Storing multidimensional XML documents in relational databases. In *DEXA*, (pp. 23-33).

Frias-Martinez, E., Magoulas, G., Chen, S., & Macredie, R. (2006). Automated user modeling for personalized digital libraries. In *International Journal of Information Management 26*(3), 234–248.

Gao, D., & Snodgrass, R. T. (2003). Temporal slicing in the evaluation of XML queries. In *VLDB*, (pp. 632–643).

Gauch, S., Chaffee, J., & Pretschner, A. (2003). Ontology-based user profiles for search and browsing. In *Web Intelligence and Agent Systems 1*(3-4), 219–234.

Giacomini Moro, R., de Matos Galante, R., & Heuser, C. A. (2004) A version model for supporting adaptation of Web pages. In *WIDM*, (pp. 120–127).

Godoy, D., & Amandi, A. (2005). User profiling for Web page filtering. In *IEEE Internet Computing, 9*(4), 56–64.

Golemati, M., Katifori, A., Vassilakis, C., Lepouras, G., & Halatsis, C. (2007). Creating an ontology for the user profile: Method and applications. In *RCIS*, (pp. 407–412).

Grandi, F. (2004). Introducing an annotated bibliography on temporal and evolution aspects in the World Wide Web. In *SIGMOD Record 33*(2), 84-86.

Grandi, F. & Mandreoli, F. (2000) The Valid Web: An XML/XSL Infrastructure for Temporal Management of Web Documents. In *ADVIS*, (pp. 294-303).

Grandi, F., Mandreoli, F., Tiberio, P., & Bergonzini, M. (2003). A temporal data model and management system for normative texts in xml format. In *WIDM*, (pp. 29-36).

Grandi, F., Mandreoli F., & Tiberio P. (2005). Temporal Modelling and Management of Normative Documents in XML Format. In *Data & Knowledge Engineering 54*(3), 327–354.

Grandi, F., Mandreoli F., Martoglia R., Ronchetti E., Scalas M. R., & Tiberio, P. (in press). Ontology-based personalization of e-government services. In P. Germanakos & C. Mourlas (Eds.), *Intelligent user interfaces: Adaptation and personalization systems and technologies*. Information Science Reference. Hershey, PA: IGI Global.

Guarino, N. (1998). *Formal ontology in information systems*. Amsterdam: IOS Press.

Gruber, T. (in press). Ontology. In L. Liu and M. T. Özsu (Eds.), *Encyclopedia of database systems*. Heidelberg, Germany: Springer-Verlag.

Grundy, J., & Zou, W. (2003) AUIT: Adaptable user interface technology, with extended Java Server pages. In A. Seffah & H. Javahery (Eds.), *Multiple user interfaces: Cross-platform applications and context-aware interfaces,* (pp. 149-167).

ICD-10 (2007). *International Statistical Classification of Diseases and Related Health Problems - 10th Revision*. World Health Organization. Retrieved March 15, 2008, from http://www.who.int/classifications/apps/icd/icd10online/

Jensen, C. S., Dyreson, C. E., Böhlen, M. H., Clifford, J., Elmasri, R., Gadia, S. K., Grandi, F., Hayes, P., Jajodia, S., Käfer, W., Kline, N., Lorentzos, N., Mitsopoulos, Y., Montanari, A., Nonen, D., Peressi, E., Pernici, B., Roddick, J. F., Sarda, N. L., Scalas, M. R., Segev, A., Snodgrass, R. T., Soo, M. D., Tansel, A. U., Tiberio, P., & Wiederhold, G. (1998). The consensus glossary of temporal database concepts - February 1998 Version. In *LNCS 1399*, (pp. 367 – 405).

Jiang, H., Wang, W., Lu, H., & Yu, J. X. (2003). Holistic Twig Joins on indexed XML documents. In *VLDB*, (pp. 273-284).

Jiang, H., Lu, H., & Wang, W., (2004). *Efficient processing of XML Twig queries with OR-predicates*. In *SIGMOD*, (pp. 59-70).

Klein, M. C. A., & Fensel, D. (2001). *Ontology versioning on the Semantic Web*. In *SWWS*, (pp. 75–91).

Kobsa, A. (2001). Generic User Modeling Systems. In *User modeling and user-adapted interaction, 11*(1-2), 49–63.

Lehmann, J., Biasiotti, M. A., Francesconi, E., & Sagri, M. T. (Eds.) (2005). In *Proceedings of the first ICAIL legal ontologies and artificial intelligence techniques workshop (LOAIT).* IAAIL Workshop Series.

LKIF-Core (n.d.). *A core ontology of basic legal concepts.* ESTRELLA Project. Retrieved January 15, 2008, from http://www.estrellaproject.org/lkif-core/

Mandreoli, F., Martoglia, R., Ronchetti, E., Tiberio, P., Grandi, F., & Scalas, M. R. (2005). Personalized access to multi-version norm texts in an egovernment scenario. In *EGOV*, (pp. 281-290).

Mandreoli F., Martoglia R., & Ronchetti E. (2006). Supporting temporal slicing in XML databases. In *EDBT*, (pp. 295-312).

Manukyan, M. G., & Kalinichenko, L. A. (2001) Temporal XML. In *ADBIS*, (pp. 143-155).

Marian, A., Abiteboul, S., Cobena, G., & Mignet, L. (2001) Change-centric management of versions in an XML Warehouse". In *VLDB*, (pp. 581-590).

Micarelli, A., Gasparetti, F., Sciarrone, F., & Gauch, S. (2007). Personalized Search on the World Wide Web. In *LNCS 4321*, (pp. 195-230).

Middleton, S. E., Shadbolt, N., & De Roure, D. C. (2004). Ontological user profiling in recommender systems. In *ACM Transactions on Information Systems 22*(1), 54-88.

Mitakos, T., Gergatsoulis, M., Stavrakas, Y., & Ioannidis, E. V. (2001). Representing time-dependent information in multidimensional XML. In *Journal of Computing and Information Technology 9*(3), 233-238.

Moura Moro, M., Vagena, Z., & Tsotras, V. J. (2005). Tree-pattern queries on a lightweight XML processor. In *VLDB*, (pp. 205-216).

Noh, S.-Y., & Gadia, S. K. (2006). A comparison of two approaches to utilizing XML in parametric databases for temporal data. In *Information & Software Technology* 48(9), 807-819.

Norrie, M. C., & Palinginis, A. (2003). Versions for context dependent information services. In *OTM*, (pp. 503-515).

Oliboni, B., Quintarelli, E., & Tanca, L. (2001). Temporal aspects of semistructured data. In *TIME*, (pp. 119–127).

Ontologies (n.d.). Retrieved January 15, 2008, from http://openclinical.org/ontologies.html

OWL (2004). The Web ontology language home page. W3C Consortium. Retrieved January 15, 2008, from http://www.w3.org/2004/OWL/

Palmirani, M., & Brighi, R. (2006). Time model for managing the dynamic of normative system. In *EGOV*, (pp. 207–218).

Perugini, S., Gonçalves, M. A., & Fox, E. A. (2004). Recommender systems research: A connection-centric survey. In *Journal of Intelligent Information Systems 23*(2), 107–143.

Pisanelli, D. M. (Ed.) (2004) Ontologies in medicine. In *Studies in Health Technology and Informatics 102*.

Pretschner, A. (1998). *Ontology based personalized search.* Unpublished master's thesis. Lawrence, Kansas: University of Kansas.

Razmerita, L., Angehrn, A., & Maedche, A. (2003). Ontology-based user modeling for knowledge management Systems. In *UM*, (pp. 213–217).

Resnick, P., & Varian, H. R. (Eds.) (1997). *Communications of the ACM 40*(3), Special issue on Recommender systems.

Rich, E. (1999). Users are individuals: Individualizing user models. In *International Journal on Human-Computer Studies 51*(2), 323–338.

Riecken, D. (2000). Personalized views of personalization. In *Communications of the ACM, 43*(8), 27–28.

Riecken., D. (Ed.) (2000). *Communications of the ACM 43*(8), Special issue on Personalization.

Rizzolo, F., & Vaisman, A. A. (in press). Temporal XML: Modeling, indexing, and query processing. *VLDB Journal*, (pp. 1179–1212).

Sadat, H., & Ghorbani, A. A. (2004) On the Evaluation of Adaptive Web Systems. In J. Yao, V. V. Raghavan, & G. Y. Wang (Eds.), *Proceedings of the 2nd International Workshop on Web-based Support Systems*, (pp. 127-136).

Snodgrass, R. T. (Ed.) (1995). *The TSQL2 Temporal Query Language*. New York: Kluwer Academic Publishing.

Stavrakas, Y., & Gergatsoulis, M. (2002) Multidimensional semistructured data: Representing context-dependent information on the Web. In *CAiSE*, (pp. 183–199).

Stavrakas, Y., Gergatsoulis, M., Doulkeridis, C., & Zafeiris, V. (2004) Representing and querying histories of semistructured databases using multidimensional OEM. In *Information Systems 29*(6), 461-482.

Stavrakas, Y., Gergatsoulis, M., & Rondogiannis, P. (2000) Multidimensional XML. In *DCW*, (pp. 100–109).

Stavrakas, Y., Pristouris, K., Efandis, A., & Sellis, T. K. (2004) Implementing a query language for context-dependent semistructured data. In *ADBIS*, (pp. 173–188).

Terenziani, P., Montani, S., Bottrighi, A., Molino, G., & Torchio, M. (2005). Clinical guidelines adaptation: Managing authoring and versioning issues. In *AIME*, (pp. 151–155).

Trajkova, J., & Gauch, S. (2004). Improving ontology-based user profiles. In *RIAO 2004 Conference Proceedings* (pp. 380-389). Paris, France: C.I.D.

Retrieved January 15, 2008, from http://www3.riao.org/Proceedings-2004/papers/0290.pdf

t-Protégé (n.d.). *The t-Protégé Project Home Page*. University of Peloponnese. Retrieved January 15, 2008, from http://t-protege.uop.gr/

Vagena, Z., Moura Moro, M., & Tsotras, V. J. (2004) Twig query processing over graph-structured XML data. In *WebDB*, (pp. 43-48).

Visser, P. R. S., & Bench-Capon, T. J. M. (1998). A comparison of four ontologies for the design of legal knowledge systems. In *Artificial Intelligence and Law 6*(1), 27–57.

Vitali, F., & Durand, D. G. (1996). Using versioning to support collaboration on the WWW. In *WWW Journal 1*(1), 37–50.

Wadge, W. W., Brown, G. D., Schraefel, M. C., & Yildirim, T. (1998) Intensional HTML. In *PODDP*, (pp. 128–139).

Wadge, W. W., & Schraefel, M. C. (2002). A Complementary approach for adaptive and Adaptable hypermedia: Intensional hypertext. In *LNCS 2266*, 327–333.

Wang, F., & Zaniolo, C. (2003) Temporal queries in XML document archives and Web warehouses. In *TIME*, (pp. 47–55).

Wang, F., & Zaniolo, C. (2008) Temporal queries and version management in XML-based document archives. In *Data & Knowledge Engineering 65*(2), 304–324.

Wong, R. K., Lam, F., & Orgun, M. A. (2001) Modelling and manipulating multidimensional data in semistructured databases. In *WWW Journal 4*(1–2), 79–99.

Zhang, C., Naughton, J., DeWitt, D., Luo, Q., & Lohman, G. (2001) On supporting containment queries in relational database management systems. In *SIGMOD*, (pp. 425-436).

Chapter XI
Security Issues in Outsourced XML Databases

Tran Khanh Dang
National University of Ho Chi Minh City, Vietnam

ABSTRACT

In an outsourced XML database service model, organizations rely upon the premises of external service providers for the storage and retrieval management of their XML data. Since, typically, service providers are not fully trusted; this model introduces numerous interesting research challenges. Among them, the most crucial security research questions relate to data confidentiality, user and data privacy, query assurance, secure auditing, and secure and efficient storage model. Although there exists a large number of related research works on these topics, the authors are still at the initial stage and the research results are still far from practical maturity. In this chapter, they extensively discuss all potential security issues mentioned above and the existing solutions, and present open research issues relevant to security requirements in outsourced XML databases.

INTRODUCTION

In the early days of ubiquitous computing and up through the late 1990s, owning and operating a sophisticated database was a strategic advantage for an organization (Bostick, 2008). Nowadays, however, nearly every organization possesses some sort of database containing different valuable information, which is considered the lifeblood of the organization. The ability to store data is therefore no longer a strategic advantage in and of itself. Recent investigations also report that storage capacity and security requirements will soon become a big problem for organizations if they still want to manage large in-house databases (Gantz, 2007). The management of the database infrastructure and the data needs has become much more of a commodity (IBM,

2008a; DBADirect, 2008). As a result, the value is not in owning a database but in how it is used and what can be got from it.

Recently, with rapid developments of the Internet and advances in the networking technologies, outsourcing database services has been emerging as a promising trend to overcome the limitations of the in-house database storage model (Hacigümüs et.al., 2002b; Bouganim & Pucheral, 2002). Basically, there are two kinds of database outsourcing models: *housing-based* and *hosting-based*. With the *housing-based* database outsourcing model, the server and data are the property of the *outsourcer* (i.e., the data owner as illustrated in Figure 1a) and the outsourcer installs the servers. In this case, the outsourcing service provider provides the *physical* security of machines and data, and monitors (and if necessary restores) the operating condition of the server. Of course, the service provider protects the outsourced data against *physical attacks* both from **outside** and **inside**. Notwithstanding, the access rights of the

service provider depend on a particular contract with its client (i.e., the outsourcer). Basically, the service provider only gets *a special account* with the server for special managerial purposes, but the outsourcer can determine the necessary access rights of that account. As for the *hosting-based* database outsourcing model, instead of keeping data in local servers, accommodated internally inside an organization, and having a professional technical team to manage the relevant database services such as software and hardware updates, server performance tuning, or security and authorization management, etc., now all data management needs can be outsourced to outside database service providers (see Figure 1b). In this case, the service provider provides all needed facilities, such as hardware, operating system, etc. to host and manage the outsourced data. In particular, it is different from the housing-based model in that the database administrator in this hosting-based model belongs to the service provider, but not the outsourcer's. By employing this hosting-service

Figure 1. Two database-outsourcing models: Housing-based (a); and hosting-based (b)

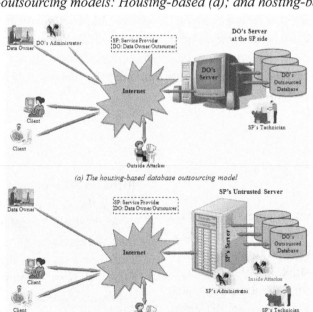

(a) The housing-based database outsourcing model

(b) The hosting-based database outsourcing model

outsourcing model, usually called the outsourced database service (ODBS) model (Dang, 2005; Hacigümüs et. al., 2002b), organizations have more freedom to concentrate on and invest in their core business activities. The ODBS model is obviously preferable to the housing-based one. In both models, however, a service provider is typically not fully trusted, and thus *they raise numerous interesting research challenges related to security issues* (Hacigümüs et.al., 2002a; Smith & Safford, 2001; Dang, 2008; Damiani et al., 2003; Dang, 2006a; Dang, 2006b; Narasimha & Tsudik, 2006; Sion, 2005; Du & Atallah, 2000; Pang & Tan, 2004; Thuraisingham, 2005; etc.). To make the outsourcing model full-fledged and practically applicable, security-related issues must be addressed radically.

Moreover, data management needs constitute the essential enabling technology for scientific, engineering, business, and social communities (Carminati & Ferrari, 2006). In order to facilitate the data exchange efficiently across heterogeneous systems, organizations should use a common standard data model/language like EDI (electronic data interchange), XML (extensible markup language), etc. Among such data models/languages, XML has been widely accepted and adopted as the basis for developing a variety of modern application domains/architectures (W3C, 2008; Brinkman et al., 2004; Bertino et.al., 2007). Emerging simultaneously with the important new database outsourcing trend above, i.e., the ODBS model, *security issues in outsourced XML databases* have been and will be among the most active topics in the research community as well as commercial world. Those security issues range from fundamental to advanced topics in the information security area, namely *data confidentiality, user and data privacy, query assurances and quality of services, secure auditing*, and *secure and efficient storage*. In this chapter, for convenience, we call the outsourced XML database service model, i.e., the XML data are outsourced to the service provider using the hosting-based model, the *OXMLDBS* model. This

chapter will discuss all known security issues and existing solutions, and will cover the open issues relevant to security requirements in outsourced XML databases. Although we will focus our discussions on the OXMLDBS (and ODBS) model, a brief discussion about potential security issues in the housing-based database outsourcing model will also be given in section 2.

The rest of this chapter is organized as follows: Section 2 presents background knowledge, security issues, and related work in the area of ensuring data outsourcing security. Most of existing approaches to security issues in outsourced XML databases are based on the proposed solutions and mechanisms in this area. Section 3 presents and discusses state-of-the-art approaches dealing with security issues in outsourced XML databases. Section 4 introduces open research issues and future trends. Finally, section 5 provides discussions of the overall coverage of the chapter and concluding remarks.

BACKGROUND

Security Issues in Outsourced Database Services

According to the two outsourcing models as illustrated in Figure 1, each of them in general consists of three entities: (1) the data owner(s)/outsourcer(s), (2) the database service provider, and (3) the client(s). The data owner creates, modifies and deletes the contents of the database. The server hosts the owner's database. At the server side, for both models, there are technicians responsible for *normal* technical maintenance tasks *except for* the database administration, which is under the control of some database administrator(s). The database administrator belongs to the outsourcer in the housing-based outsourcing model, while they are the service provider's manpower in the hosting-based one. This is the major factor that causes many security concerns in the ODBS and OXMLDBS models as we will discuss later. The clients issue queries about the database to the server (Dang, 2006b; Hacigümüs et.al., 2002b). Moreover, in many real-world cases, the data owners are also the unique clients (Du & Atallah, 2000; Dang, 2006b; Narasimha & Tsudik, 2006) (see Figure 3). Interestingly, due to its much more inherent simplicity, most of existing research works limit their focus to this special case (Hacigümüs et.al., 2002b; Damiani et al., 2003; Schrefl et. al., 2005; Li et. al., 2006; Nguyen et. al., 2007; Xie et. al., 2007; etc.). Even then, security issues of concern in the OXMLDBS model are not identical to those of the housing-based model. Below, we discuss the challenging security issues in both interested outsourcing models.

Intuitively, with the housing-based outsourcing model, the data owner is no more responsible for the server accommodation, internet connection, and other infrastructures. Data management-related tasks, however, are still their regular duties. Even then, concerning security issues in the housing service business model, **"soft"** security-related aspects are usually ignored or understood that "*the installed software or the data owner must be responsible for it*". For example, if a data owner chooses this database housing service at a company M and M gets a special account A for some special managerial activities (A was assigned very limited rights on the data owner's "outside-housed" database DB), then M is typically liable only for the so-called **physical** security of the data owner's hardware and data. It means that M is responsible only for physically securing the server containing the outsourced data (e.g., power, seamless internet connection, etc), but *not the data contents* from malicious activities (e.g., hacking, inference attacks etc). This is reasonable only if (the client believes that) the DBMS is working as expected in terms of security. In practice, *serious* problems can occur as the DBMS has some security flaws and the client may not be aware of these "soft"

flaws before they are discovered by the housing company M. In this case, M may make use of A and the found security flaws to get control (or so) of the client's DB, which is currently housed on M's premises. This is an interesting research problem and it will be very much better if M can provide the client with a means (tools/software) of detecting the database security flaws and visually monitoring the account A's real-time activities, especially with the possible DB security flaws. If M can do this, the client will be more than happy because they are assisted in detecting their DB security flaws and can control or anticipate the potential harms that may be caused by A. Although a lot of research work has been carried out to propose effective mechanisms for detecting database security breaches (Dang et al., 2008), the proposed solutions still do not satisfy users. Much more work will have to be done to secure the outsourcer's DBMSs and data in the housing-based outsourcing model. Nevertheless, in this chapter, we will not go into further detail about the security issues in this model. Next, we discuss security concerns in the ODBS (and OXMLDBS) model, a client-centric classification of the model and crucial security issues in each subclass. It is obvious that in the ODBS (and OXMLDBS) model, the data owner is no longer responsible for data management; rather, it outsources its data to one or more service providers that provide management services and query processing functionalities. Clearly, this method of data outsourcing leads to challenging security issues in that, by outsourcing its data, the data owner may potentially lose control over them. More concretely, both data and users' queries can now be exposed to the server and hackers/malicious users (corresponding to inside and outside attackers as shown in 1b, respectively). Therefore, in this ODBS model, apart from secure network communication channels and other necessary security procedures at the user side (Axelrod, 2004), efficient and effective solutions to security threats inside the server are indispensable. Consequently, a lot of research work is currently being carried out to ensure secure management of data even in the presence of an *untrusted server* (Carminati & Ferrari, 2006; Li et. al., 2006; Dang, 2008; Xie et.al., 2007; Nguyen & Dang, 2008; etc.). We discuss these server-side security-related issues below.

Security issues in the ODBS model and outsourced XML databases. First, because the lifeblood of every organization is the information stored in its databases, making outsourced data *confidential* is therefore one of the foremost challenges in this model. In addition, *privacy-related concerns* must also be taken into account due to their important role in the real-world applications (Thuraisingham, 2005). No less importantly, to make the outsourced database service viable and applicable, the system has to provide users with some means of verifying the *query assurance* claims of the service provider. Last but not least, solutions to secure auditing and efficient storage must also be addressed radically to fulfill major security requirements of concern. Overall, *most crucial* security-related research questions in the ODBS model in common, and for *outsourced XML databases* in particular, relate to the issues below (see Figure 2):

- **Data confidentiality:** Outsiders and the server's operators (database administrator-DBA) cannot see the user's outsourced data contents in any cases (even as the user's queries are performed on the server). Herein, *the user* may be the *data owner/outsourcer* or *its clients*.
- **Privacy concerns:** Although privacy-related issues have been widely investigated (PRIME Project, 2004), the question "what is the complexity of the privacy problem?" is still open in as much as the answer is quite different, depending not only on technology, but also on sociology and politics (Thuraisingham, 2005). In our context, however, user and data privacy issues are clearly identified and defined as follows (Chor et. al., 1995;

Gertner et. al., 1998; Burmester et. al., 2004; Dang, 2008):

- o **User privacy:** Users do not want the server and even the DBA to know about their queries and the results. Sometimes, user identities should also be protected from the server. Ensuring user privacy is one of the keys to the ODBS model's success.
- o **Data privacy:** Users are not allowed to access more information than what they are querying on the server. In many situations, users must pay for what they have got from the server and the data owner does not allow them to obtain more than what they have paid for; moreover, even users do not want to pay for what they do not need because of the low bandwidth connections, limited memory/storage devices and so forth. This security objective is not easy to achieve and a cost-efficient solution to this issue is still an open question.

- **Query assurance:** Users are able to verify the correctness (authenticity and data integrity), completeness, and freshness of the result set. Among all security objectives, the query assurance is *always* appealed in the ODBS model. We succinctly explain these concepts as follows and more discussions can be found in (Mykletun & Tsudik, 2006; Narasimha & Tsudik, 2006; Dang, 2008; Li et. al., 2006; Pang et. al., 2005; Nguyen & Dang, 2008):
  - o **Proof of correctness:** As a user queries outsourced data, it expects a set of tuples satisfying all query conditions and also needs assurance that data returned from the server originated from the data owner and have not been tampered with either by an outside attacker or by the server itself.

Figure 2. Security issues in outsourced (XML) databases

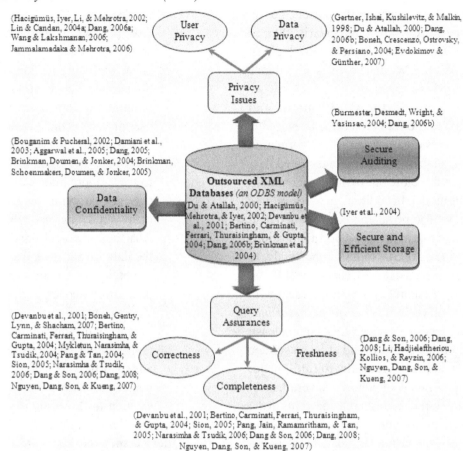

- o **Proof of completeness:** As a user queries outsourced data, completeness implies that the user can verify that the server returned *all* tuples matching all query conditions, i.e., the server did not omit any tuples satisfying the query conditions. Note that a server, which is either malicious or lazy, might not execute the query over the entire database and return no or only partial results. Ensuring the completeness of the query result aims to detect this unexpected behavior.
- o **Proof of freshness:** The user must be assured that the result set was generated with the most recent snapshot of the

database. This issue must be addressed to facilitate *dynamic* outsourced databases, which frequently have updates on their data.

- • **Secure auditing:** It is well-known that auditing and accountability play an indispensable role in e-business protocols and compliance (Jaquith, 2007; Natan, 2005). Even so, the way that the server can tackle auditing activities over encrypted databases is not a trivial matter despite recent advances in networking, data storage, and data processing. In particular, in the ODBS model, as privacy requirements are taken into account, auditing and accountability are much more difficult to achieve because their goals appear to be in contradiction (Burmester et. al., 2004).

- **Secure and efficient storage:** Although several commercial database vendors have already offered integrated solutions to provide data privacy within existing products, treating security and privacy issues as an afterthought often results in inefficient implementations (Iyer et al., 2004). Analyzing issues in current storage technologies, looking at trade-offs between security and efficiency, and proposing new secure storage models will be challenging research topics of great interest in the ODBS/OXMLDBS model.

The above security requirements differ from the traditional database security ones (Castano et. al., 1995; Umar, 2004), and will in general influence the performance, usability and scalability of the ODBS/OXMLDBS model. Although there exist a vast number of research works on the above topics, to the best of our knowledge, none of them has *radically* addressed *security issues* in *outsourced XML data*. It is well-known that XML data have their own typical characteristics, which are very much different from data stored in traditional DBMSs (W3C, 2008; Thuraisingham, 2005). In particular, XML data are tree-structured data and it has been clearly proven in the literature that tree-indexed data have played an important role in both traditional and modern database applications (Dang, 2003). Therefore, security issues with outsourced tree-indexed data need to be resolved completely in order to materialize the ODBS model. Even so, this is not a trivial task, especially as tree-based index structures are outsourced to mistrusted servers. There are many challenging and open security issues in this case (Du & Atallah, 2000; Dang, 2005; Xie et. al., 2007; Nguyen et. al., 2007) (see Figure 2). The existing solutions are still considered immature. Section 3 will focus in depth on security issues

in such XML databases, but in the outsourcing context.

Furthermore, note that the needs of the above-mentioned security requirements very much depend on particular scenarios in the ODBS model and this must be considered carefully. To identify such security enforcement needs for typical outsourcing scenarios, *a classification based on users' database access* and security requirements for each subclass are given below.

A user's remote database access-based classification. As presented in (Du & Atallah, 2000; Dang, 2006b; Mykletun et. al., 2004), there are a number of different ODBS models depending on users' database access *to the remote database*. In (Du & Atallah, 2000; Dang, 2006b), the authors distinguish four different e-commerce models that all require ensuring user privacy. Nevertheless, the two identified models are not in the context of the outsourced database because the data owner is himself the service provider. The other two are DC-UP (data confidentiality-user privacy) and DC-UP-DP (data confidentiality-user privacy-data privacy) models (Dang, 2006b). The DC-UP-DP model is exactly as illustrated in Figure 1b, where both the data owner and clients can query the outsourced database. On the contrary, in the DC-UP model, data owners are also unique clients. In this case, the data owner and clients as illustrated in Figure 1b are the same. In (Mykletun et. al., 2004), the authors distinguish between three outsourcing models: the first two, named *unified client* and *multi-querier* models, are the same as the DC-UP and DC-UP-DP ones, individually. A variant of the multi-querier model where an outsourced database is owned by a number of different owners is called the *multi-owner* model. We summarize all of these identified models, their variants and, based on system users' remote database access, classify them into *four* ODBS/OXMLDBS models *applicable in real-world application domains* as depicted in Figure 3. More details of these models are given below:

- **SS model (single user-service provider, see Figure 3a):** A single data owner is also the *unique* client, and its data is outsourced to the external server. We call both the data owner and client in this case *the user.* In this model, the data owner (also the client) is very much concerned about *data confidentiality* and *user privacy*, but *data privacy* is usually unimportant. This outsourcing model is similar to the *DC-UP* one. Again, *query assurances*, *secure auditing*, and *secure and efficient storage* are *all* required for *all* hosting-based outsourcing models.

- **MS model (multiple data owner-service provider, see Figure 3b):** There are *multiple* data owners outsourcing data to the external server similarly to the SS model; however, each data owner is also the *unique* client. As a result, security requirements are the same as those of the SS model. The main differences between these two models are the way of accessing a remote database, and the techniques for ensuring security

requirements (see section 2.2). Notably, the motivation for this model is rather straightforward. Consider the example of an outsourced insurance database. Each record in this database is created and maintained by a salesperson (of a particular branch) responsible for a particular customer. This salesperson then 'owns' the records that s/he creates.

- **SMS model (single data owner-multiple clients-service provider, see Figure 3c):** This is the most typical hosting-based outsourcing model where a single data owner outsources its database to the service provider. However, except for this data owner, multiple clients may also have access to the outsourced database on some agreement basis. This is among the most complex models in terms of security issues. The *data owner* is concerned about both *data confidentiality* and *data privacy* for both the external database server and its clients. The *client*, in turn, is apparently concerned about *user*

Figure 3. A user's database access-based classification for ODBS/OXMLDBS models

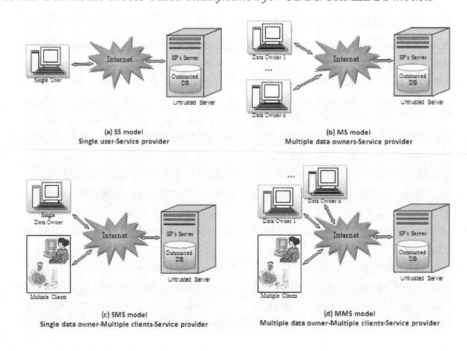

(a) SS model
Single user-Service provider

(b) MS model
Multiple data owners-Service provider

(c) SMS model
Single data owner-Multiple clients-Service provider

(d) MMS model
Multiple data owner-Multiple clients-Service provider

Table 1. Security requirements in different ODBS/OXMLDBS models

No	ODBS/OXMLDBS models	Security requirements							
		Data confidentiality	Privacy concerns		Query assurances			Secure auditing	Secure and efficient storage
			User privacy	Data privacy	Correctness	Completeness	Freshness		
1	SS	√	√	-	√	√	√	√	√
2	MS	√	√	-	√	√	√	√	√
3	SMS	√	√	x	√	√	√	√	√
4	MMS	√	√	x	√	√	√	√	√
5	Multiple service providers (SP)	- (for each SP)	- (for each SP)	- (for each SP)	√	√	√	- (for each SP)	- (for each SP)

(√: fully required, -: not required, x: not fully required)

privacy for both the *data owner* and *outsourcing server*. In some real-world cases, whose reasons may come from the data owner, service provider, or even the client itself (as discussed above), the client is also concerned about data privacy. Moreover, the data owner also takes the client role when accessing its outsourced data on the server and, in this case, the *data owner* is concerned about *user privacy* as well. This outsourcing model is similar to the *DC-UP-DP* model.

- **MMS model (multiple data owner-multiple clients-service provider, see Figure 3d):** This model is similar to the SMS one, except that there are *n* data owners owning the same outsourced database, $n \geq 2$, like the MS model. The challenging security issues for this model are the same as those for the SMS model. Besides, like the MS model, query processing and optimization are a big problem that emerges together with ensuring the security requirements. A trade-off between the two, that is, between security and performance, should be considered carefully (see section 2.2).

For the sake of clarity, in Table 1 we summarize security requirements identified for the four ODBS/OXMLDBS models above. There is a special scenario in this table, the last row, that has not been discussed before and we will clarify it shortly in the next section.

Existing Solutions to ODBS Models: An Overview

In Figure 2 we diagrammatically summarize security issues in the ODBS/OXMLDBS model, together with major references to the corresponding state-of-the-art solutions. An overview of these solutions is given below.

Ensuring Data Confidentiality

As shown in Figure 2, all crucial security objectives of the hosting-based outsourcing model have been investigated. To address the data confidentiality issue, most existing approaches opt to encrypt (outsourced) data before its being stored at the external server (Bouganim & Pucheral, 2002; Damiani et al., 2003; Dang, 2005; Evdokimov & Günther, 2007). Although an encryption scheme-based solution can protect the data from outsiders as well as the server, it introduces difficulties in the querying process, as it is hard to ensure the user and data privacy when performing queries over encrypted data. We will detail these issues later. In (Aggarwal et al., 2005), the authors argued that data encryption is unnecessary due to its negative impact on the system performance. Hence, they proposed an implementation architecture for all ODBS models where the data owner(s) outsources its data to several external database servers. Figure 4 illustrates this architecture in the MMS model.

The key idea in this implementation is to allow the client to partition its data across a number of logically independent database systems that *cannot communicate with each other.* The data partitioning is performed in such a way that it ensures that the exposure of the contents of any one database does not result in a violation of privacy objectives. The client executes queries by transmitting appropriate sub-queries to each database, and then gathering the results at the client side. Clearly, if the ODBS model is developed using this architecture, with *each service provider,* the data confidentiality, user and data privacy, secure auditing, and secure and efficient storage are unimportant (see Table 1). Nevertheless, user and data privacy would still be challenging problems in the context of the data owner and client communications concerning the *original query* and *final result.* The original query here means

the query posed by a client before it is "split" into sub-queries, which will be sent to different servers. Similarly, the final result sent to the client is a combination of results of sub-queries. In addition, a severe drawback of this outsourcing architecture is that it requires *non-collusion* between all service providers (see Figure 4), which is mostly impractical in the real-world. Thus, most existing and ongoing approaches still prefer some encryption scheme for the outsourced database confidentiality guarantee, and try to reduce related costs and complexities during the query processing.

Ensuring User and Data Privacy

In general, in order to address the issue of user and data privacy, outsourced data structures employed to manage the data storage and retrieval should be considered. Notably, the problem of user privacy has been quite well solved, even without special hardware (Smith & Safford, 2001), if the outsourced database contains only encrypted records and no tree-based indexes are used (see (Dang, 2006b) for an overview). Conversely, the research result is less incentive if such trees are employed, although some proposals have been made recently (Lin & Candan, 2004a; Dang,

Figure 4. Ensuring data confidentiality in the MMS model using multiple service providers

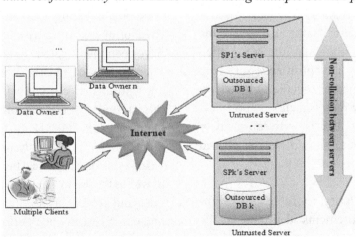

2006b). In our previous work (Dang, 2006b), we proposed an extreme protocol for the ODBS model based on private information retrieval (PIR)-like protocols (Asonov, 2001). It would, however, become prohibitively expensive if only one server were used to host the outsourced data (Chor et. al., 1995; Asonov, 2001). Damiani et al. (2003) also gave a solution to query outsourced data indexed by B+-trees, but their approach does not provide an obvious way to traverse the tree, and this may compromise security objectives (Lin & Candan, 2004a; Dang, 2006a). Lin and Candan (2004a; 2004b) introduced a computational complexity approach to solve the problem with sound experimental results reported over XML datasets. Their solution, however, supports only an obvious search on outsourced search trees, but not any insertion, deletion or modification. Hence, their solution cannot be applied to dynamic outsourced search trees where several items may be inserted and/or removed, or existing data can be modified. In our recent work (Dang, 2005; Dang, 2006a), we analyzed and introduced techniques to completely solve the problem of data confidentiality and user privacy, but query assurance, in the ODBS model with dynamic tree-indexed data supports. In (Dang & Son, 2006) (also Dang, 2008) we extended the previous work to solve all the three security objectives of query assurance as discussed in section 2.1. In particular, the extended approach can be applied to all kinds of search trees, including multidimensional index structures that have played an important role in both traditional and modern database application domains (Dang, 2003).

Contrary to user privacy, although there are initial research activities (Gertner et. al., 1998; Du & Atallah, 2000; Boneh et. al., 2004; Dang, 2006b; Evdokimov & Günther, 2007), the problem of data privacy still needs much more attention. Gertner et al. (1998) first considered the data privacy issue in the context of PIR-like protocols and proposed the symmetrical PIR

(SPIR) protocol to prevent users from knowing anything more than the answers to their queries. Unfortunately, such PIR-based approaches cannot be applied to the ODBS model because the data owners in PIR-like protocols are themselves the database service providers. Du and Atallah (2000) introduced protocols for secure remote database access with approximate matching of four different ODBS models requiring different security objectives among those presented in the previous section. Even so, their work did not support outsourced tree-indexed data. In our recent work (Dang, 2006b), we presented a solution to ensure data privacy in the ODBS model that can also be applied to tree-indexed data. Nevertheless, our proposed solution must resort to a trusted third party, which is currently uneasy to find in practice. Of late, Evdokimov and Günther (2007) proposed a new data privacy-enabling ODBS scheme. This newly proposed scheme can avoid a problem of many previous solutions: erroneous tuples that do not satisfy the select condition may be returned to the client in the result set but the probability of such an error is negligible. This capability improves the performance and simplifies the development process of a client's software. Even then, though with a small probability, data privacy is theoretically still prone to be erroneous. The only introduced scheme that allows performing search on encrypted data and does not require post-filtering is described in (Boneh et. al., 2004). This scheme, however, can hardly be applied to most ODBS models since searching an encrypted database is restricted to the search with predefined keywords. Importantly, neither of these approaches takes indexed data into account radically. Actually, a crucially challenging problem related to security in all models is to provide data privacy. This requirement is still open to the research community due to its interdisciplinary complexities.

Ensuring Query Assurance

Recently, addressing the three issues of query assurance has attracted many researchers and, as a result, a number of solutions have been proposed (e.g., Boneh et. al., 2007; Mykletun et. al., 2004; Pang & Tan, 2004; Pang et. al., 2005; Narasimha & Tsudik, 2006; Sion, 2005; Dang & Son, 2006; Li et. al., 2006). However, except for (Dang & Son, 2006; Li et. al., 2006), none of the previous work has given a solution to the problem of guaranteeing the query result freshness. To prove the correctness of a user's query results, the state-of-the-art approaches (Boneh et. al., 2007; Mykletun et. al., 2004; Pang & Tan, 2004; Sion, 2005) employed some aggregated/condensed digital signature scheme to reduce the communication and computation costs. First, Boneh et al. (2003) introduced an aggregated signature scheme that allows aggregation of multiple signers' signatures generated from different messages into one short signature based on elliptic curves and bilinear mappings. Despite the big advantage that this scheme can be applied to different ODBS models, it must bear a disadvantage related to the performance. As shown in (Mykletun et. al., 2004), the computational complexity of Boneh et al.'s (2003) scheme is quite high for practical uses in many cases. Second, Mykletun et al. (2004) introduced an RSA-based condensed digital signature scheme that can be used for providing the proof of correctness in the ODBS model. Their scheme is concisely summarized as follows.

Condensed-RSA digital signature scheme. Suppose pk=(n,e) and sk=(n,d) are the public and private keys, respectively, of the RSA signature scheme, where n is a k-bit modulus formed as the product of two k/2-bit primes p and q. Assume $\varphi(n)=(p\text{-}1)(q\text{-}1)$, both public and private exponents e, d$\in Z_n^*$ and must satisfy ed$\equiv$1 mod $\varphi(n)$. Given t different messages $\{m_1, ..., m_t\}$ and their corresponding signatures $\{s_1, ..., s_t\}$ that are generated by the *same* signer, a condensed-RSA

signature is computed as follows: $s_{1,t}=\prod_1^t s_i \bmod$ n. This signature is of the same size as a single standard RSA signature. To verify the correctness of t received messages, the user must multiply the hashes of all t messages and check that $(s_{1,t})^e\equiv \prod_1^t h(m_i) \bmod$ n.

The above scheme is possible because RSA is multiplicatively homomorphic. However, this scheme is applicable only for a single signer's signatures. In (Dang & Son, 2006; Dang, 2008) we applied this scheme to the SS model to provide correctness guarantees of the received tree nodes from the server (see section 3). Sion (2005) also employed it to address the correctness of query results in his proposed scheme for the SS model. Besides, Pang and Tan (2004) applied and modified the idea of Merkle Hash Trees (MHT) (Merkle, 1980) to provide a proof of correctness for edge computing applications, where a trusted central server outsources parts of the database to proxy servers located at the edge of the network. However, the proposed approach does not check for completeness of query results. More seriously, Narasimha and Tsudik (2006) pointed out possible security flaws in this approach.

Furthermore, there are a number of approaches to deal with the completeness of a user's query results (Sion, 2005; Pang et al., 2005; Narasimha & Tsudik, 2006; Dang & Son, 2006). First, Sion (2005) proposed a solution to provide such assurances for arbitrary queries in outsourced databases. This solution is built around a mechanism of runtime query "proofs" in a challenge-response protocol. Concretely, the data owner partitions its data into k segments {S1, ..., Sk}, computes hashes for each segment, H(Si), i= , then stores them all together at the service provider. In addition, the data owner also calculates some "challenge tokens" for Si. Actually, the challenge tokens are queries that the data owner already knows their results, which can be used for verification later. Whenever a batch of queries is sent to the server, certain challenge token(s) are also sent together. The result set is then verified using the challenge tokens for its completeness. Although this approach can be applied to different query types, query completeness cannot be guaranteed 100% because there is the chance that a malicious server can "guess" and return the correct answer to the challenge token together with fake result sets for other queries in the batch. Moreover, this approach is cost-inefficient for database updates because the challenging answers must be recalculated. Seriously, although the author did not aim to address the user privacy issue, we should note that user privacy in this approach may be compromised because the server knows what data segments are required by the user in order for inference and linking attacks to be be conducted (Dang, 2006b; Damiani et al., 2003). Second, Pang et al. (2005) introduced a solution based on aggregated signature schemes and MHT. It is an extension of their previous work (Pang & Tan, 2004), which has been proven insecure due to some possible security flaws (Narasimha & Tsudik, 2006). Last, Narasimha and Tsudik (2006) developed an approach, DSAC–digital signature aggregation and chaining, that achieves both correctness and completeness of query replies. However, in their approach, tuples must be pre-sorted in ascending order for each searchable dimension for calculation of the signature chain, and thus it does not support outsourced tree-indexed data because the order of the contents of tree nodes is undetermined. This requirement also has a tremendous negative impact on data updates, causing degeneration of the system's total performance. Recently, in (Dang & Son, 2006; Pang et. al., 2005) the authors presented comprehensive solutions to address all the three aspects of query assurance in the SS model. These approaches are considered as the vanguard ones to address dynamic outsourced databases. Notably, Dang and Son's (2006) presented approach, which is based on access redundancy and node swapping techniques (Lin & Candan, 2004a; 2004b), also supports outsourced multidimensional index structures.

Ensuring Secure Auditing

Furthermore, assume that we have a running system with the above security objectives being satisfied, then the question "How can the server conduct auditing activities in systems provided with such security guarantees?" is still left open to date. Due to the user privacy (see section 2.1), the server may not know who is accessing the system (e.g., Lin & Candan, 2004a; Dang, 2006b; Dang, 2008), what they are asking for, what the system returns to the user, and thus how it can effectively and efficiently tackle the accountability or develop intrusion detection/prevention systems. The goals of privacy-preserving and accountability appear to be in contradiction, and an efficient solution to balance the two is still open. There is just some research work on this topic. Typically, in (Burmester et. al., 2004) the authors, among the trailblazers, did investigate the problem of the conflicts existing between secure auditing/accountability and privacy in a variety of application domains. Research directions for balancing the needs of both were also highlighted. In the past, although there are some hardware-based approaches to solving security issues in ODBS models such as (Smith & Safford, 2001; Mykletun & Tsudik, 2005) and the secure auditing problem is also of their concerns no practically proven solution has been given. In section 4, we will further discuss these hardware-based approaches.

Ensuring Secure and Efficient Storage

As we can observe in Figure 2, there exists another interesting question: Is there a secure and efficient storage model for the outsourced database? However, all existing approaches for dealing with the concerned security problems do not make any assumption about the DBMS and its storage model. It is simply understood that existing commercial DBMS can be employed with some additional settings for the stored data at the server site, while the underlying storage model remains unchanged (Hacigümüs et. al., 2002; Bertino et. al., 2004; Damiani et al., 2003; Dang, 2008; etc.). In a recent research (Iyer et al., 2004), the authors carried out insightful studies on this problem, and proposed a framework for efficient storage security in RDBMS. Their approach is motivated by crucial weaknesses of today's database security solutions, namely poor efficiency, inflexibility, and non-encryption of indexes. The poor efficiency appears because the underlying model used by DBMS introduces significant computational overheads. A new solution can be possible only if the means of storing records on the disk blocks is modified. The inflexibility is manifested by the wrong encryption granularity, leading to the fact that even non-sensitive data is also encrypted in many cases. Lastly, most existing solutions offered by commercial DBMS to data encryption problem do not allow indexing techniques or must sacrifice some important functionalities (e.g., most encryption schemes are not order-preserving, thereby losing range query functionality). More concretely, Iyer et al. (2004) introduced a secure storage model and a key management architecture that enable efficient cryptographic operations while trying to maintain an acceptable level of security. The proposed approach is based on grouping sensitive data and non-encryption of non-sensitive data to minimize the number of encryption operations. Although some preliminarily sound experimental results have been reported, this model is only the first step towards a sustainable, secure and efficient storage model for ODBS/OXMLDBS models because it still assumes that the server is trusted, which typically does not exist in ODBS/OXMLDBS models.

Until now, it has been clear that dealing with security issues in ODBS models encounters many difficulties if *tree-structured data* is outsourced to untrusted servers (Du & Atallah, 2000; Dang, 2006b). On the other hand, as discussed in the literature, tree-based index structures play an indispensable role in both traditional and modern database applications (Dang, 2003). Unfortunate-ly, XML data is tree-structured inherently. Most of approaches to security issues in outsourced XML databases were inspired by, and originated from, the findings of solutions to the same issues in ODBS models with traditional numeric and text databases. In the next section, we will present and discuss the state-of-the-art approaches proposed in the most recent publications to *securely* managing the storage and retrieval of outsourced tree-indexed/XML data.

STATE-OF-THE-ART APPROACHES TO SECURITY ISSUES IN OXMLDBS MODELS

Authentic Publication of XML Documents: A Semi-OXMLDBS Model

At the very beginning, in (Devanbu et al., 2001) the authors proposed an approach for signing XML documents allowing untrusted servers to answer certain types of path and selection queries. The main research idea in this work and other similar ones is very similar to that of the SMS model (see Figure 3c). Figure 5 depicts this working model.

In this model, the XML data owner and clients play the same role as those in the SMS model. The publisher in the authentic publication of XML documents, however, is slightly different from the service provider in the SMS model: this publisher may not store the owner's encrypted data, but it can keep only the owner's plaintext XML data. Although Devanbu et al.'s (2001) solution, which is based on the MHT and a newly proposed data structure (xtrie), to provide correctness and completeness of the query results, overcomes several limitations of previous work (e.g., only one digital signature over an XML document is needed to certify answers to arbitrary selection queries over such documents, providing both

Figure 5. Authentic publication of XML documents: Document is created by owner, who uses a one-way hash function to digest it. Clients receive the digest through an authentic channel, e.g., using a public-key signature (1) and the document itself is sent to a publisher (2). In response to a query from a client (3) the publisher returns both an answer and a verification object using the MHTs and digital signatures, certifying the correctness and completeness of the answer (4).

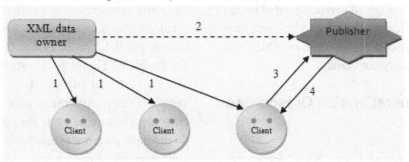

correctness and completeness of answers, etc.), not all privacy-related issues are considered (i.e., user and data privacy). Therefore, this working model is not considered as an OXMLDBS model, but a semi-OXMLDBS model. Moreover, the auxiliary structure, the xtrie, is based on the DTD, but the proposed solution works best only on non-recursive DTDs. Even then, the empirical analysis indicated that a majority of published DTDs are non-recursive, and thus this approach will be quite useful in a variety of contexts. In general, the proposed techniques for ensuring query assurance objectives in Devanbu et al.'s (2001) solution can be further explored for possible application to OXMLDBS models where a server truly stores and manages a data owner's encrypted data.

Very similarly to the above approach, in (Bertino et. al., 2004) the authors carried out extensive research in secure XML document distribution and provided a comprehensive architecture for selective, authentic, and complete third-party publication of XML documents. In the same line as Devanbu et al.'s (2001) solution, this approach also considered the publisher to be untrusted for the requirements of correctness and completeness. MHTs, digital signature schemes, and credential-based techniques have been employed to provide

correctness as well as completeness proofs for the query answers. Only one thing would be considered as being new in Devanbu et al.'s (2001) solution: that this introduced comprehensive architecture also incorporates a policy configuration that is technically a certificate issued and signed by the XML data owner containing information about access control policies that apply to the user. By utilizing this, the publisher can determine and filter out (certain portions of) XML documents before returning the query result to the client. Once again, none of these approaches is for encrypted XML databases and, consequently, data confidentiality and privacy-related issues for the publisher are not assured.

Recently, in (Bertino et. al., 2007), the authors further developed the above ideas and introduced a push-based system for distributing information through the Internet. Such systems are today becoming increasingly popular and widely used. The widespread use of such systems raises significant security concerns like those in OXMLDBS models, such as confidentiality, integrity and authenticity, and completeness of the distributed data. To cope with such issues, Bertino et al. (2007) described a system for securing push distribution of XML documents, which adopts digital signature and encryption techniques to ensure the above-mentioned security requirements and allows the specification of both signature and access control policies. The authors also described the implementation of the proposed system and presented an extensive performance evaluation of its main components. Although all privacy-related issues were still not addressed, this is a good reference for further investigations into such semi-OXMLDBS models and security concerns.

Oblivious Operations on Outsourced Search Tree

Basic settings. As we know, XML documents have tree-like structures (W3C, 2008; Lin & Candan, 2004a; Brinkman et. al., 2004) and XML has become a de facto standard for data exchange and representation over the Internet. It is also well-known that basic operations of tree-based index structures include search and updates (modify, insert, delete). To facilitate security requirements in OXMLDBS models (see section 2.1), techniques allow users to operate on their outsourced tree-structured data on untrusted servers without revealing information about the

query, and result, and outsourced data itself must be studied.

Although tree-based index structures have proven their advantages over both traditional and modern database applications, they introduce numerous research challenges as database services are outsourced to untrusted servers (Du & Atallah, 2000; Dang, 2006b). To detail the problem, Figure 6a illustrates an example of B+-tree for an attribute CustomerName with sample values. Assume a user is querying all customers whose name is Ha on this tree. If we do not have a secure mechanism for tree storage and query processing, a sequence of queries that will access in sequence nodes 0, 1, and 5 for the above query will be revealed to the server. In addition, the server also realizes that the user was accessing nodes 0, 1, and 5, which are the root, an internal node, and a leaf node, respectively, of the tree, and so the user privacy is compromised. More seriously, using such information collected gradually the server can rebuild the whole tree structure and infer sensitive information from the encrypted database. Besides, the user will also receive information showing that there are

Figure 6. An example of B+-tree (a) and the corresponding plaintext and encrypted table (b)

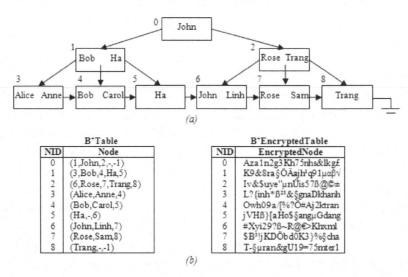

B⁺Table

NID	Node
0	(1,John,2,-,-1)
1	(3,Bob,4,Ha,5)
2	(6,Rose,7,Trang,8)
3	(Alice,Anne,4)
4	(Bob,Carol,5)
5	(Ha,-,6)
6	(John,Linh,7)
7	(Rose,Sam,8)
8	(Trang,-,-1)

B⁺EncryptedTable

NID	EncryptedNode
0	Aza1n2g3Kh75nhs&lkg£
1	K9&8ra§ÖAajh²q91µαβ√
2	Iv&$uye"µnÜis57ß@©±
3	L?{inh*ß²³&§gnaDkhanh
4	Owh09a/[%?Ö#Aj2ktran
5	jVHß}[aHo$§angµGdang
6	#Xyi29?ß~R@€>Khxml
7	$B²!jKDÖbd0K3}%§cha
8	T-§µran&gU19=75mter1

(b)

at least two other customers named John and Bob in the database.

To cope with these issues, some settings must be prepared to facilitate oblivious operations on the tree. Damiani et al. (2003) showed that encrypting each tree node as a whole to ensure the data confidentiality is preferable because protecting a tree-based index by encrypting each of its fields would disclose to the untrusted server the ordering relationship between the index values. Besides, each node is identified by a unique *node identifier* (NID) and the unit of storage and access is a tree node. The original tree is then stored at the server as a table with two attributes: *NID* and *an encrypted value* representing the node content. In our running example, Figure 6b shows the corresponding plaintext and encrypted table used to store the B$^+$-tree at the server over schema $B^+EncryptedTable = \{NID, EncryptedNode\}$.

Oblivious basic operations on outsourced XML data trees. Based on the above settings, there are some proposed approaches to facilitate basic operations on the outsourced search tree. Firstly, Damiani et al. (2003) analyzed potential inference and linking attacks, and proposed a hash-based indexing method suitable for exact match queries. To process range queries, they proposed a solution employing B+-trees with the above settings. However, Dang (2006b) indicated that this solution does not provide an oblivious way to traverse the tree and this can be exploited

by the untrusted server to carry out inference and linking attacks. Moreover, it also does not support outsourced multidimensional index structures. Later, Lin and Candan (2004a) developed an algorithm based on access redundancy and node swapping techniques to provide oblivious search on outsourced tree-indexed data.

Access redundancy and node swapping: Each time a user requests access to a node from the server, it asks for a redundancy set of m nodes consisting of at least one empty node along with the target one. The user then: (1) decrypts the target node, (2) manipulates its data, (3) swaps it with the empty node, and (4) re-encrypts all m nodes and writes them back to the server. Note that, to prevent the server from differentiating between read and write operations, a read operation is always followed by a write operation. This requires re-encryption of nodes using a different encryption scheme before they are rewritten to the server. With this technique, the possible position of the target node is randomly distributed over the data storage space at the untrusted server, and thus the probability that the server can guess the target node is 1/m.

To realize oblivious tree traversal, securely managing the root node address and empty node lists is also important: A special node called SNODE whose NID and decryption key are known to all valid users keeps pointers ROOTS pointing to the roots of all outsourced search trees; and empty nodes are stored in hidden linked lists. Based on

Box 1.

Algorithm 1: Oblivious Tree Traversal/Search
1. Lock and fetch the SNODE, let it be PARENT. Find the root and let it be CURRENT.
2. Select a redundancy set for the CURRENT, lock nodes in the set, and let the empty node in the set be EMPTY.
3. Update the PARENT's pointer to refer to the EMPTY, and release locks on the PARENT level.
4. Swap the CURRENT with the EMPTY.
5. If the CURRENT contains the needed data, return CURRENT. Otherwise:
6. Let the CURRENT be PARENT, find the child node to be traversed next, let it be CURRENT, and repeat steps 2 through 5.

---

these basic settings, Lin and Candan's (2004a) algorithm is presented as shown in Box 1.

Note that the original approach above works only with uniformly distributed data sets. In (Lin & Candan, 2004b), the authors enhanced this approach so that it can also work with non-uniformly distributed datasets, i.e., from the server's view, node accesses are always uniformly distributed. Furthermore, although the above approach supports only *oblivious* tree search operations, the two employed techniques have served as the basis for our further investigation. In (Dang, 2005; Dang, 2006a) we identified critical issues and limitations of Lin and Candan's approach and developed pragmatic algorithms for privacy-preserving search, insert, delete, and modify operations that can be applied to a variety of *dynamic* outsourced tree-based index structures and the *SS* model. Despite our previous work providing the vanguard solutions for this problem with sound empirical results, it did not consider any of the query assurance aspects.

Query assurances for outsourced tree-indexed/ XML data. In (Dang & Son, 2006; Dang, 2008) we extended our previous work and presented a full-fledged solution to the problem of ensuring the *correctness, completeness,* and *freshness* for all basic operations (insert, delete, modify, point, and range queries) on *dynamic* XML/outsourced tree-indexed data. Experimental results with real *multidimensional* datasets (R-Tree Portal, 2006)

and the kd-tree have confirmed the efficiency of our proposed solution. Figure 7 shows *core settings* in our extended approach.

Firstly, the data owner computes and signs the hash *h(m)* of each encrypted node *m*. Next, it stores the signature together with EncryptedTable at the server. The table schema stored at the server now becomes *EncryptedTable = {NID, EncryptedNode, Signature}* (see Figure 7). With this setting, users can then verify each returned node using the data owner public key, thereby ensuring *the correctness* of the result set. To minimize the costs, we adopted the condensed-RSA digital signature scheme (see section 2.2) for nodes in the redundancy set. Secondly, in order to guarantee the query completeness, in our context, as a user asks the server for a redundancy set *A* of *t* nodes $A=\{m_1, ..., m_t\}$ and the server returns him a set *R* of *t* nodes $R=\{n_1, ..., n_t\}$, the user must be able to verify that *A=R*. As presented above, a user asks for any encrypted nodes through their NIDs. Therefore, the user should be provided with a means of verifying that NID of each $m_i, i=\overline{1,t}$, equals NID of each corresponding $n_i, i=\overline{1,t}$. To ensure this, our solution is embarrassingly simple: an NID is encrypted with the corresponding node contents and this encrypted value is stored at the server side, together with its signature as described above. Users can then check if the server returned the required NIDs (*the completeness*) and verify the query result correctness all together. Lastly, in order to address the freshness issue, users must

Figure 7. Settings for verifying correctness, completeness, and freshness guarantees

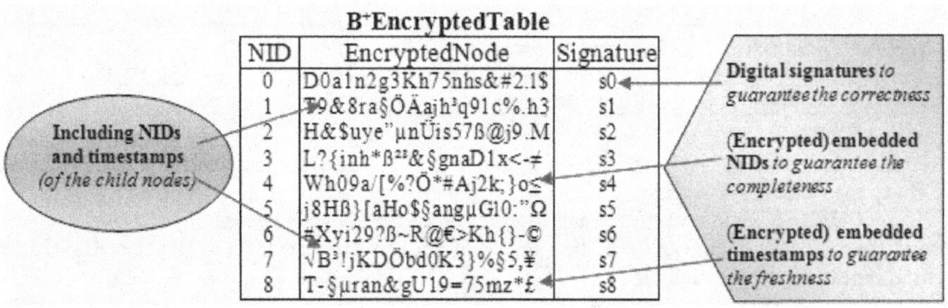

be able to verify if the server returned the most up-to-date required tree nodes. Our solution is uncomplicated but sound and complete: A time-stamp of each child node is stored at its parent node. This timestamp changes *only* as the child node *contents* (but not its address) are updated. A user can then check (from the root) if the server returned the latest version of the required node (*the freshness*). Note that, SNODE should keep the root's timestamp in addition to other information as discussed previously, and each qualified user must be informed about SNODE's timestamp (e.g., by the data owner who made the changes to the root's contents). Remarkably, to the best of our knowledge, none of the previous work has addressed all the above three security issues of query assurance in the ODBS/OXMLDBS model with regards to *dynamic multidimensional outsourced trees*. Our work therefore provides a vanguard solution for this problem.

In addition, since XML data has tree-like structures and queries can be expressed as traversal paths on these trees, the solution introduced above can be utilized for secure outsourcing of XML documents. Compared with existing PIR techniques (Asonov, 2001), this proposed solution does not need database replication and requires less communication, and is thus practical (Lin & Candan, 2004b; Dang, 2006a). However, because these solutions have been developed only for the SS model, they are not directly applicable to other OXMLDBS models due to their different security requirements.

Secure Multi-Party Computation-Based Approaches

In a multi-party computation (MPC) we have a given number of participants p1, p2, ..., pN, each having a private data, respectively d1, d2, ..., dN. The participants want to compute the value of a function F on N variables at the point (d1, d2, ..., dN). An MPC protocol is said to be secure if no participant can learn more from the description of the public function and the result of the global calculation than what s/he can learn from his/her own entry under particular conditions depending on the model used. In (Brinkman et. al., 2004), the authors, inspired by secure MPC, introduced a new approach to query outsourced XML databases. First, a plaintext XML document is transformed into an encrypted database as follows:

1. Define a mapping function $\Omega: node \rightarrow F_{p^\varepsilon}$, which maps the nodes' tag names to values of the finite field F_{p^ε}, where p^e is a prime power (p is a prime and e is a positive integer) which is larger than the total number of different tag names (see Figure 8b). Although Ω may be chosen arbitrarily, the client should keep it secret to prevent the server from seeing the query.

2. Transform the tree of tag names (see Figure 8a) into a tree of polynomials (see Figure 8c and Figure 8d) of the same structure where each node is transformed to *f(node)* where function *f: node* $\rightarrow F_{p^\varepsilon}$ *[x]/($x^{p-1}-1$)* is defined recursively: $f(node)=x-\Omega(node)$ if *node* is a leaf node, or $(x-\Omega(node))$ $\prod_{d \in child(node)} f(d)$, otherwise. Here *child(node)* returns all children of a *node*. To avoid large degree polynomials a finite ring is chosen. Two different rings have been investigated: $F_q[x]/(x^{q-1}-1)$ (where q is a prime power $q=p^e$) and $Z[x]/(r(x))$ (where *r(x)* is an irreducible polynomial). In the first case, the coefficients of the polynomials are reduced modulo q. With $Z[x]/(r(x))$, the polynomial is reduced modulo an irreducible polynomial *r(x)*. The running example as shown in Figure 8 is according to the first finite ring.

3. Split the resulting tree into a client (see Figure 8e) and a server tree (see Figure 8f). Both trees have the same structure as the original one. The polynomials in the client tree are generated by a pseudorandom gen-

erator. The polynomials of the server tree are chosen such that the sum of a client node and the corresponding server node equals the original polynomial.

4. Since the client tree is generated by a pseudo-random generator, it is sufficient to store the seed on the client. The client tree is discarded and, when necessary, it can be regenerated using the pseudorandom generator and the seed value.

Next, in the querying phase, it is simple to check whether a node N is stored somewhere in a subtree by evaluating the polynomials of both the server and the client at $\Omega(N)$. If the sum of these evaluations equals zero, this means that N can be found somewhere in the subtree N. Note that everything is calculated modulo q. To find out whether N is the root of this subtree, we have to divide the unshared polynomial by the

product of all its direct children. The result will be a monomial $(x-t)$ where t is the mapped value of the node.

The above approach, however, is only for storing and retrieving trees of tag names, but not the actual data between the tags. Later, Brinkman et al. (2005) presented an extension of their previous approach to address this problem. They proposed a representation of XML documents allowing for searching in data nodes by simply transforming all data nodes to their trie representation (Fredkin, 1960). Having translated the original XML tree into a trie, the same presented strategy can be employed to encode the document and carry out the search. Even now, clients still have to store a sheer volume of XML meta-data and tackle heavily computational tasks as does the service provider. Next, because the tree structure transformed from the XML document is in plaintext at the server, reference attacks may be launched to

Figure 8. An example for Brinkman et al.'s (2004) approach based on secure MPC

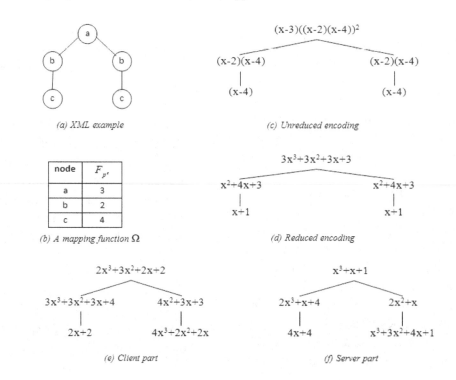

compromise data confidentiality and user privacy. In addition, data privacy has not been discussed because the proposed approach is applicable only to the SS model. More seriously, query assurances have not been investigated and they are difficult to address efficiently because no efficient multi-purpose schemes for secure MPC are known to us at the moment. Finally, dynamic outsourced XML documents have also not been studied in this approach.

Trusted Third Party-Based Approaches

As far as we know, there is no solution to the SMS/MMS models for outsourced tree-structured data for all concerned security objectives. Relying on an assumption that quite solid solutions have been developed for the SS/MS models, Dang (2006b) proposed a protocol to ensure all security requirements of the SMS/MMS models resorting to a trusted third party (TTP), namely K. The use of a TTP is to change this outsourcing model, which is very hard to address directly, to a better solved SS model. We describe five basic steps to process a query Q sent from a client A as follows (see Figure 9):

1. Client A sends Q to K for querying the data owner M's outsourced XML database DB.

2. When receiving Q, K informs M (for billing, for example) and waits for approval from M in order to access DB.

3. On receiving A's access request from K, M informs DB so that K can query DB on behalf of M. After receiving DB's acknowledgement, M informs K.

4. From this time, K takes M's role in the SS model as discussed in section 2, and it can access DB using any security protocols designed for the SS model (note that A is only capable of retrieving information from DB, but not updating M's outsourced XML data in DB).

5. Finally, K filters and returns to A only the results of Q. Obviously, K has been informed by M what A is able to get from the database, but M will not be informed what A has got regarding any Qs to ensure A's privacy wrt. M.

In practice, a TTP is difficult to find and it is also the only weakness of this protocol. With the assumption that we can establish such a TTP, it is easy to prove that the above protocol ensures all security objectives for this SMS/MMS models,

Figure 9. A secure protocol for trusted third party-based approaches

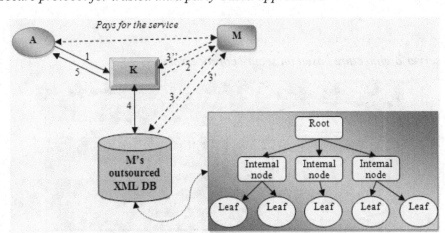

i.e. data confidentiality, user and data privacy, as well as query assurances. Eliminating K from this protocol, while still ensuring all security objectives for this ODBS/OXMLDBS model, is an open research question. In the same line as our approach but relying on special hardware equipment, IBM has developed secure co-processors acting like K (IBM, 2008b; Smith & Safford, 2001). We will elaborate on this hardware-based approach in the next section.

The above approach is a general idea to address security issues in the SMS/MMS models and it can be applied to not only outsourced XML databases, but also any general tree-indexed data outsourced. Nevertheless, even though special hardware is employed, a number of challenging problems related to improving the system performance must be taken into account (Dang, 2006b; Mykletun & Tsudik, 2005). This presents new significant research problems of great importance in the future.

Hardware-Based Approaches

Contrary to the past claims that special-purpose computers for security requirements like those of OXMLDBS models are infeasible but trivial (Goldreich & Ostrovsky, 1996), the hardware-based approach is no longer infeasible. Secure coprocessor (SC) research has advanced the state-of-the-art (IBM, 2008b), and now permits any researcher at a reasonable cost to build a private information server by taking a host machine with ample PCI slots and inserting these coprocessors. In (Smith & Safford, 2001), the authors presented an IBM secure coprocessor-based server architecture that can efficiently process a user's queries without violating security and privacy objectives, such as data confidentiality, user and data privacy. Figure 10 depicts this server architecture. This system consists of a single server that has a number of SCs, and that provides a query service to a database containing records. The stored records are encrypted and authenticated. Actually, the SCs act like the TTP as described in Figure 9, and thus this architecture could be considered as a practical implementation of the general idea presented in Dang (2006b). With the support of such special hardware, it is clear that the new server is partly capable of satisfying security objectives in OXMLDBS models.

Recently, some hardware-based solutions to security issues in OXMLDBS models have been proposed (Bouganim & Pucheral, 2002; Mykletun & Tsudik, 2005), employing IBM-like SCs, e.g., IBM 47xx SC family (IBM, 2008b). More technically, a SC is a general-purpose computer that can be trusted to carry out its computations unmolested, even if an adversary has direct physical access to the device. It is equipped with a processor, non-volatile secure memory, input devices, back-up battery and is fully enclosed in

Figure 10. A server architecture based on secure coprocessors

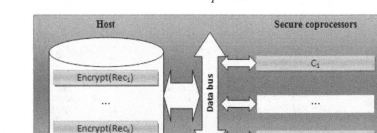

a tamper-proof container that cannot be opened without triggering sensors that alert that an attack is taking place. In the case that a penetration of the device is detected through the signaling by sensors that are monitoring possible attack venues, an alarm is triggered and all contents in the secure memory are erased, possibly by destroying the physical memory chip by leaking acid onto it (IBM, 2008b; Mykletun & Tsudik, 2005). Notwithstanding, SCs are still far away from meeting the functionalities expected by users due to the hardware-related technologies (see section 4), and thus they still do not completely solve the security issues of concern.

Hybrid Tree-Based Approaches

Although there exist approaches employing hybrid tree-based structures to address security issues in ODBS model like (Li et. al., 2006), they unfortunately have not been studied for OXMLDBS models. Very recently, in (Nguyen et. al., 2007; Nguyen & Dang, 2008), on the basis of MHTs and B+-tree, the authors introduced a new indexing structure for outsourced XML data to solve the data confidentiality and query assurances in OXMLDBS models. Even now, their approach can be extended by employing techniques presented in section 3.2 to deal with the privacy-related issues. Below, we introduce Nguyen and Dang's (2008) original approach.

Node-based XML document transformation. Each XML document has a schema tree that defines the relation between nodes and their attributes. A schema tree consists of two node types: element node (t-node) and attribute node (a-node). t-nodes and a-nodes are stored in a single table and each node has enough data to reconstruct the original XML text:

```
t-node(nodeid, xtype, datatype, nameID,
pnodeID, lmaID, value)
```

```
a-node(nodeid, xtype, datatype, nameID,
pnodeID, sibID, value)
```

where, xtype is used to distinguish t-node and a-node; datatype determines type of the data value; nameID is the node's identifier; pnodeID refers to parent node's tuple; lmaID refers to the left-most attribute of the node; sibID refers to the right-sibling attribute; value is the value of the node/attribute. For data confidentiality, each record is serialized into an encrypted binary string before outsourcing.

Nested Merkle B+-Tree. An important factor for a feasible solution to query assurance of outsourced XML databases depends on index structures. By embedding extra information into this structure, we could achieve query assurances. MHTs and digital signature schemes, as discussed in (Li et. al., 2006; Nguyen & Dang, 2008), are typically employed to provide the proof of query correctness. To obtain an effective proof for query completeness, as shown in (Narasimha & Tsudik, 2006; Nguyen & Dang, 2008), all elements must be sorted by two criteria: (path, value) and (path, parent, value), where path is the path from the tree's root to a given node. However, no existing data structures could help this. Nguyen and Dang (2008) introduced a novel Nested Merkle B+-Tree to facilitate the storage/retrieval and ensure the query assurance for outsourced XML databases.

First, all possible paths from root to leaves are listed out, and each path is associated with a unique integer called *nameid*. To maintain this, a B+-Tree, named *NameTree,* with the search key being *nameid* is employed. At each entry of a leaf node of *NameTree*, instead of the links of records, there are two links to two new B+-Trees having *value* and (*parent, value*) as their search keys, respectively. We call these trees *ValueTree* and *ParentTree*. The leaves of *ValueTree* and *ParentTree* store links to *a-node* or *t-node* records (data records). Combining these three trees, we have a Nested B⁺-Tree (NBT) as shown in Figure 11.

Second, based on the idea of the MHT, the NBT is attached with more information to facilitate the proof of query assurances. First, each node keeps hashes of its children:

a-node: $H_{a\text{-}node} = h(nodeid||xtype||...||value)$

t-node: $H_{t\text{-}node} = h(h(nodeid||\ ...||value)||\cup_i H_{attr})$

Leaf of *ValueTree, ParentTree*: $H_L = h(\cup_i H_{data\text{-}record})$

Internal node: $H_I = h(\cup_i H_{child\text{-}node})$

Leaf of *NameTree*: $H_{L\text{-}N} = h(H_{vtree}||H_{ptree})$

Root of *NameTree*: $H_R = h(\varepsilon\ ||\ \cup_i H_{child\text{-}node})$

where H_{attr} is hash value of an *a-node* of a given *t-node*; $H_{data\text{-}record}$ is either $H_{a\text{-}node}$ or $H_{t\text{-}node}$ that associated to the link; $H_{child\text{-}node}$ is one of H_L, H_I or $H_{L\text{-}N}$; H_{ptree} and H_{vtree} are hash values of *ParentTree*'s and *ValueTree*'s roots; ε denotes a timestamp value and $h()$ is a non-invertible hashing function. Additionally, *NameTree*'s root is signed by the outsourcer's private key and the corresponding public key and timestamp ε are communicated to all valid users. With these settings, the resulting tree, named the *Nested Merkle B⁺-Tree*, is capable of ensuring query assurance objectives. A concrete example below makes this clearer.

Figure 12 illustrates an example of a labeled XML schema tree, where round, rectangular and sharp corner nodes denote *elements* and *attributes*, respectively, of the XML document. The number next to a node is *nameid* value. Assume a user poses a query to the service provider: "List all sold items named 'TV'". The corresponding query in XPath is */Customer/Order/Item[@name="TV"]*. To answer this query, the server should process the mapped query (*nameid=13, value='TV'*). To do this, the server scans *NameTree* with *nameid=13* to get the *ValueTree*, then it scans on the found *ValueTree* with *value='TV'* to list out all satisfied attributes *name_13* and builds a *verification object* (VO) for authenticity. With the *pnodeid* field in each found *name_13*, it reads and appends these *Item_8* into the VO. Because there is only one *Item_8* for each *name_13*, the server does not need to provide any information to prove query assurance. For each *Item_8*, it returns two remain attributes.

Figure 11. Nested B+-Tree

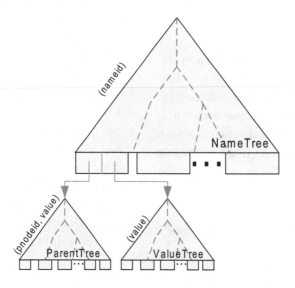

Figure 12. An example of labeled XML schema tree

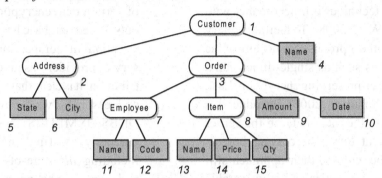

Note that, although user privacy can be incorporated into this approach by employing, for example, techniques proposed in (Lin & Candan, 2004a; Dang, 2005; Dang, 2008), this approach supports only the SS model and data privacy has not been discussed. This aspect is also typical of other hybrid tree-based approaches like (Jammalamadaka & Mehrotra, 2006). This is quite a similar approach with different auxiliary information being embedded in the outsourced XML tree to facilitate several query types. Although data confidentiality is ensured, this approach does not provide query assurances. Even so, there are two notable points of this approach: (1) the proposal of a set of encryption primitives using which a client can propose fairly complex set of security policies on XML documents; (2) the introduction of a novel multi-dimensional partitioning strategy that allows query processing to take place at the server side and overcomes the limitations of single-dimensional partitioning techniques.

Other Approaches

First of all, in (Brinkman et. al., 2004) the authors, inspired by an approach in (Song, Wagner, & Perrig, 2000), proposed a method based on the linear search algorithm to apply queries on encrypted XML documents. Basically, Song et al. (2000) introduced a way to search for the existence of a word in an encrypted textual document. How-ever, it does not scale well for large databases because the performance is linear in the document size. Based on this idea, Brinkman et al. (2004) developed a tree search algorithm applicable to encrypted XML databases. The newly proposed algorithm is more efficient in this specific context since it exploits the XML tree structure. Experiments showed that the encryption speed of the new algorithm remains linear in the input size, but that a major improvement in the search speed can be achieved. Nevertheless, this new algorithm needs to store a table containing structural information of the XML database at the server, thus compromising data confidentiality and opening a backdoor to inference attacks. Besides, it does not support flexible levels of encryption granularity.

Furthermore, there are three other previous works in the literature addressing queries over encrypted XML documents (Schrefl et. al., 2005; Yang et. al., 2006; Wang & Lakshmanan, 2006). First, Schrefl et al. (2005) proposed a technique that allows XPath selection queries to be executed at the server. Their technique supports both static and dynamic documents but it incurs two crucial limitations (Jammalamadaka & Mehrotra, 2006): (1) cannot support range queries; and (2) requires multiple rounds of communication between the client and server to answer a single query, thereby potentially undermining the performance. Next, Yang et al. (2006) presented XQEnc and XML encryption technique based on vectorization and skeleton compression of XML paths. The proposed XML encryption technique is in accordance with W3C standards (W3C, 2008). To facilitate query processing, the authors proposed using any of the existing techniques such as single-dimensional partitioning or order-preserving encryption. Last, Wang and Lakshmanan (2006) introduced a scheme for storing the meta-data on the server to support efficient query processing but, as pointed out by the authors, their approach still incurs performance penalties and is vulnerable to inference attacks. Moreover, this approach is also not cost-efficient for supporting dynamic outsourced XML databases.

We must emphasize that all the four approaches above and most of the introduced ones in previous sections belong to the SS model. Therein, security requirements are very much easier to address comparing with those of the SMS and MMS models (see Table 1). Therefore, much work still remains to be done in order to make outsourced XML databases practical. We succinctly point out major open issues and future trends in the next section.

OPEN ISSUES AND FUTURE TRENDS

Clearly, we are at the initial stage of the research for resolving security issues in outsourced XML databases. In order to apply the research results to real-world applications, we will need more time (Evdokimov et. al., 2006; Wang & Lakshmanan, 2006). Our discussions in previous sections have demonstrated that none of the existing approaches has dealt radically with all crucial security issues concerning its model. Hence, there are still a vast number of security- and privacy-related issues/ protocols that need to be solved. We introduce open research issues based on the five well-defined security problems of outsourced XML databases as follows:

- **Data confidentiality:** As discussed, the use of certain data encryption schemes for the outsourced database has drawn much more attention in comparison with a multiple service provider-based solution for data distribution. It is clear that this choice is natural and reasonable when developing a practical ODBS/OXMLDBS model. Nevertheless, currently existing encryption schemes, including *all* state-of-the-art symmetric and asymmetric encryption algorithms, create many obstacles and limitations for the querying process and for ensuring security requirements like those in in-house database services. *Is there any completely new encryption scheme that fits well with the hosting outsourcing model?* This big challenging question is now open to the research community. *This new encryption scheme should be able to facilitate both the confidentiality of the outsourced database and an effective and efficient querying method.* To the best of our knowledge, no previous or ongoing work has focused on this direction. Note that, however, if such an encryption algorithm were devised, the rest of all implementations for OXMLDBS models would be very much simpler.

- **User and data privacy:** Assuming that we are still using the state-of-the-art encryption schemes because an encryption algorithm ideal for the aforementioned OXMLDBS models does not exist, user privacy is not a big issue. The research results have shown that *user privacy* can be assured at a computationally secure level, and this is enough for most real-world applications. Notably, this problem can be solved without special hardware supports. On the other hand, current solutions to *data privacy* in OXMLDBS models have less incentive. Some of the typical existing solutions like (Dang, 2006b; Smith & Safford, 2001) must resort to special hardware or a TTP to mitigate the complexity of this very challenging issue. Therefore, there are two issues that need to be further investigated: (1) studying new protocols/techniques for ensuring data privacy in OXMLDBS models; and (2) addressing technological issues with current special hardware, say IBM SCs, in order for them to be viable and applicable. As pointed out in previous work such as (Smith & Safford, 2001; Mykletun & Tsudik, 2005), a secure coprocessor is somewhat limited in its computing resources, both in processor speed and the amount of on-board memory available. This is a consequence of a variety of factors, predominantly that of heat dissemination. For instance, an IBM 4758 SC, at the beginning, is equipped with a 99 MHz processor and 2 MB on-board memory only (IBM, 2008b). With the continued growth of the hardware technology, we are expecting a brighter future for such special hardware. Again, with the future technologies, what does a TTP looks like? If TTPs can be developed effectively, data privacy and many other challenging security issues will also be able to be resolved much easier and more cost-efficiently.

- **Query assurance:** Clearly, this problem has not been studied extensively for outsourced XML databases. Ensuring the correctness of query answers, however, has not been a big problem, but completeness- and freshness-related aspects are more challenging. Existing solutions still incur the severe limitation of having heavy computation on the client side. This reduces the benefits that the OXMLDBS models offer. Therefore, new protocols/techniques to address the completeness and freshness of query results will be of great interest in the future. Many new related problems are also foreseen (Dang, 2008), such as the *over redundancy* problem whereby the server sends the user more than what should be returned in the

answers. This may cause a user to pay more for the communication cost, to incur higher computation costs, and so this issue (and many others) needs to be investigated carefully.

- **Secure auditing:** Except for (Dang, 2006b), which must resort to a TTP to accomplish this challenging task, none of the previous research work has addressed this vital security issue, even though it is not new. Much more work will need to be done in the future to solve this issue. Moreover, the problem is exacerbated increasingly due to the new rules related to *secure auditing and compliance* such as SOX, HIPAA, PCI, etc. (Dang et. al. 2007; Jaquith, 2007). In complying with these rules, companies are forced to deal with new aspects of the expanding digital universe – since the rules set standards for record keeping, records retention, information security, and privacy protection, among other things. New rules for things like the legal discovery of documents, called "e-discovery," are driving companies to formalize new records management policies, develop archiving standards, and institute policy changes and employee training (Gantz, 2007; Dang et. al. 2007). These new requirements will significantly affect the problem with which we are concerned and will undoubtedly exacerbate it.

- **Secure and efficient storage:** This issue is totally new to outsourced XML databases. However, it is not difficult to understand because a cost-effective model for secure and efficient storage of *unencrypted* XML data has never been created.

Apart from the individual security requirement as shown above, we will also have to solve the very difficult problem of how to develop a fully-fledged solution to satisfy integrated assurances (e.g., confidentiality, privacy of access, and query assurance all together) for each concerned

OXMLDBS model. Besides, consolidating and further developing the existing research results to facilitate arbitrary operations on outsourced XML databases like those of the in-house DBMSs (Evdokimov & Günther, 2007; Mykletun & Tsudik, 2006) will also be among the most challenging of future research activities. Addressing all of these problems is the main goal because it will make the OXMLDBS models practical.

In addition, it is not difficult to guess that future trends of the data outsourcing paradigm will not only focus on outsourcing RDBMS or XML database services, but also on other large file systems like huge streaming databases, for example. This will, in turn, need new outsourcing models, new querying and security protocols to meet data management needs as effectively and efficiently as can an in-house service. The increasing importance of XML data in emerging applications, such as SOA-based systems, web services, e-business, etc., is a solid and well-grounded basis to consolidate our aforementioned prediction. Going along with this trend, it is foreseen that hardware-based solutions will become much more popular among end users because of their inherent natural simplicity.

CONCLUSION

In this chapter, we conducted an in-depth discussion of security issues in outsourced XML databases, and proposed several related future research directions. Because the outsourcing of XML databases is only a sub-problem of a very much broader field, namely the outsourcing of database services, we firstly presented background knowledge, security issues, and related work in the area of ensuring data outsourcing security. Moreover, because most existing approaches to security issues in outsourced XML databases are based on those of the broader field, we have also clearly defined and classified security issues into five major issues: data confidentiality, user and

data privacy, query assurance, secure auditing, secure and efficient storage model. On this basis, we next presented and discussed the state-of-the-art approaches to deal with security issues for outsourced XML databases in four typical OXMLDBS models. We have categorized these approaches into seven classes: (1) authentic publication of XML documents: a semi-OXMLDBS model; (2) oblivious operations on outsourced search tree; (3) secure multi-party computation-based approaches; (4) trusted third party-based approaches; (5) hardware-based approaches; (6) hybrid tree-based approaches; and (7) other approaches. With each class, technical details of the related approaches were introduced, and real-world case studies and intuitive examples were used to clarify the discussions. We have emphasized that most existing approaches focus on the SS model (see Figure 3) and none of them has radically addressed related security issues.

We introduced open research issues relevant to the problem of concern in section 4. Therein, we also provided general discussions of future trends that have been identified from the previous works, and the needs of emerging application domains. Finally, we must conclude that research results of dealing with security issues in outsourced XML databases are currently too immature for practical purposes. Many more research activities will have to be carried out to make the outsourced XML database service model viable in practice.

REFERENCES

Aggarwal, G., Bawa, M., Ganesan, P., Garcia-Mollina, H., Kenthapadi, K., Motwani, R., Srivatsava, U., Thomas, D., & Xu, Y. (2005). Two can keep a secret: A distributed architecture for secure database services. In *CIDR,* (pp. 186-199).

Asonov, D. (2001). Private information retrieval: An overview and current trends. In *ECDPvA,* (pp. 889-894).

Axelrod, C. W. (2004). *Outsourcing information security*. Norwood, MA: Artech House.

Bertino, E., Carminati, B., Ferrari, E., Thurai-singham, B., & Gupta, A. (2004). Selective and authentic third-party distribution of XML documents. In *IEEE Transactions on Knowledge and Data Engineering, 16*(10), 1263-1278.

Boneh, D., Crescenzo, G., Ostrovsky, R., & Persia-no, G. (2004). Public key encryption with keyword search. In *EUROCRYPT,* (pp. 506-522).

Brinkman, R., Doumen, J., & Jonker, W. (2004). Using secret sharing for searching in encrypted data. In *SDM,* (pp. 18-27).

Burmester, M., Desmedt, Y., Wright, R. N., & Yasinsac, A. (2004). Accountable privacy. In *International Workshop on Security Protocols,* (pp. 83-95).

Brinkman, R., Feng, L., Doumen, J., Hartel, P. H., & Jonker, W. (2004). Efficient tree search in encrypted data. In *Information System Security Journal 13*, 14-21.

Bertino, E., Ferrari, E., Paci, F., & Provenza, L.P. (2007). A system for securing push-based distribution of XML documents. In *International Journal of Information Security 6*(4), 255-284.

Boneh, D., Gentry, C., Lynn, B., & Shacham, H. (2003). Aggregate and verifiably encrypted sig¬natures from bilinear maps. In *EUROCRYPT,* (pp. 416-432).

Bouganim, L., & Pucheral, P. (2002). Chip-secured data access: Confidential data on untrusted servers. In *VLDB,* (pp. 131-142).

Bostick, J. (2008). *Why you should outsource your database infrastructure*. Retrieved February 16, 2008, from http://www.sourcingmag.com/content/c070620a.asp

Brinkman, R., Schoenmakers, B., Doumen, J., & Jonker, W. (2005). Experiments with queries over encrypted data using secret sharing. In *SDM,* (pp. 33-46).

Carminati, B., & Ferrari, E. (2006). Confidentiality enforcement for XML outsourced data. In *EDBT Workshop*, (pp. 234-249).

Castano, S., Fugini, M. G., Martella, G., & Samarati, P. (1995). *Database security*. Boston: Addison-Wesley/ACM Press.

Chor, B., Goldreich, O., Kushilevitz, E., & Sudan, M. (1995). Private information retrieval. In *FOCS*, (pp. 41-50).

Dang, T. K. (2003). *Semantic based similarity searches in database systems: Multidimensional access methods, similarity search algorithms*. PhD Thesis, FAW-Institute, University of Linz, Austria.

Dang, T. K. (2005). Privacy-preserving search and updates for outsourced tree-structured data on untrusted servers. In *iTrust,* (pp. 338-354).

Dang, T. K. (2006a). A practical solution to supporting oblivious basic operations on dynamic outsourced search trees. In *International Journal of Computer Systems Science and Engineering 21*(1), 53-64.

Dang, T. K. (2006b). Security protocols for outsourcing database services. In *Information and Security: An International Journal 18*, 85-108.

Dang, T. K. (2008). Ensuring correctness, completeness and freshness for outsourced tree-indexed data. In *Information Resources Management Journal 21*(1), 59-76.

Dang, T. K., Son, N. T. (2006). Providing query assurance for outsourced tree-indexed data. In *HPSC,* (pp. 207-224).

dbaDirect Company (2008). Retrieved from http://www.dbadirect.com

Devanbu, P. T., Gertz, M., Kwong, A., Martel, C., Nuckolls, G., & Stubblebine, S. G. (2001).

Flexible authentication of XML documents. In *CCS*, (pp. 136–145).

Dang, T. K., Le, T. T. H, & Truong, D. T. (2007). An extensible framework for database security assessment. In *iiWAS*, (pp. 419-425).

Dang, T. K., Truong, Q. C., Cu-Nguyen, P-H., & Tran-Thi, Q-N. (2008). An extensible framework for detecting database security flaws. In *ACOMP*, (pp. 68-77).

Du, W., & Atallah, M. J. (2000). Protocols for secure remote database access with approximate matching. In *ACMCCS Workshop.*

Damiani, E., Vimercati, S. D. C., Jajodia, S., Paraboschi, S., & Samarati, P. (2003). Balancing confidentiality and efficiency in untrusted relational DBMSs. In *ACMCCS*, (pp. 93-102).

Evdokimov, S., Fischmann, M., & Günther, O. (2006). Provable security for outsourcing database operations. In *ICDE*, (p. 117).

Evdokimov, S., & Günther, O. (2007). Encryption techniques for secure database outsourcing. In *ESORICS*, (pp. 327-342).

Fredkin, E. (1960). Trie memory. In *Communications of the ACM 3*(9), 490–499.

Gantz, J. F. (2007). *The expanding digital universe: A forecast of worldwide information growth through 2010.* IDC White Paper. Retrieved February 17, 2008 from http://www.emc.com

Gertner, Y., Ishai, Y., Kushilevitz, E., & Malkin, T. (1998). Protecting data privacy in private information retrieval schemes. In *STOC*, (pp. 151-160).

Goldreich, O., & Ostrovsky, R. (1996). Software protection and simulation on oblivious RAMs. In *Journal of the ACM 43*, 431–473.

Hacigümüs, H., Iyer, B.R., Li, C., & Mehrotra, S. (2002). Executing SQL over encrypted data in the database-service-provider model. In *SIGMOD*, (pp. 216-227).

Hacigümüs, H., Mehrotra, S., & Iyer, B. R. (2002). Providing database as a service. In *ICDE*, (pp. 29-40).

IBM IT Outsourcing and Hosting (2008a). Retrieved from http://www.ibm.com/services/stratout.

IBM PCI Cryptographic Coprocessor (2008b). Received from http://www-03.ibm.com/security/cryptocards/pcicc/overview.shtml on March 8, 2008

Iyer, B.R., Mehrotra, S., Mykletun, E., Tsudik, G., & Wu, Y. (2004). A framework for efficient storage security in RDBMS. In *EDBT*, (pp. 147-164).

Jammalamadaka, R. C., & Mehrotra, S. (2006). Querying encrypted XML documents. In *IDEAS*, (pp. 129-136).

Jaquith, A. (2007). *Security metrics: Replacing fear, uncertainty and doubt.* Addison-Wesley Professional.

Li, F., Hadjieleftheriou, M., Kollios, G., & Reyzin, L. (2006). Dynamic authenticated index structures for outsourced databases. In *SIGMOD*, (pp. 121-132).

Lin, P., & Candan, K. S. (2004a). Hiding traversal of tree structured data from untrusted data stores. In *ICEIS Workshop*, (pp. 314-323).

Lin, P., & Candan, K. S. (2004b). Secure and privacy preserving outsourcing of tree structured data. In *SDM*, (pp. 1-17).

Merkle, R. C. (1980). Protocols for public keys cryptosystems. In *Symposium on Research in Security and Privacy*, (pp. 122-134).

Mykletun, E., Narasimha, M., & Tsudik, G. (2004). Authentication and integrity in outsourced databases. In *NDSS*.

Mykletun, E., &Tsudik, G. (2005). Incorporating a secure coprocessor in the database-as-a-service model. In *IWIA,* (pp. 38-44).

Mykletun, E., & Tsudik, G. (2006). Aggregation queries in the database-as-a-service model. In *Data and Applications Security*, (pp. 89-103).

Natan, R. B. (2005). *Implementing database security and auditing*. Digital Press.

Narasimha, M., & Tsudik, G. (2006). Authentication of outsourced databases using signature aggregation and chaining. In *DASFAA*, (pp. 420-436).

Nguyen, V. H., Dang T. K., Son, N. T., & Kueng, J. (2007). Query assurance verification for dynamic outsourced XML databases. In *FARES*, (pp. 689-696).

Nguyen, V. H., & Dang, T. K. (2008). A novel solution to query assurance verification for dynamic outsourced XML databases. In *International Journal of Software 3*(4), 9-16.

Pang, H. H., & Tan, K-L. (2004). Authenticating query results in edge computing. In *ICDE*, (pp. 560-571).

Pang, H. H., Jain, A., Ramamritham, K., & Tan, K-L. (2005). Verifying completeness of relational query results in data publishing. In *SIGMOD*, (pp. 407-418).

PRIME Project (2004). *The PRIME Project: Privacy and identity management for Europe*. Retrieved from https://www.prime-project.eu

R-Tree Portal (2006). Received from http://www.rtreeportal.org/spatial.html

Schrefl, M., Grün, K., & Dorn, J. (2005). Sem-Crypt-Ensuring privacy of electronic documents through semantic-based encrypted query processing. In *ICDE Workshop*, (p. 1191).

Sion, R. (2005). Query execution assurance for outsourced databases. In *VLDB,* (pp. 601-612).

Smith, S. W., & Safford, D. (2001). Practical server privacy with secure coprocessors. In *IBM Systems Journal 40*(3), 683-695.

Song, D. X., Wagner, D., & Perrig, A. (2000). Practical techniques for searches on encrypted data. In *IEEE Symposium on Security and Privacy*, (pp. 44-55).

Thuraisingham, B. (2005). *Database and applications security: Integrating information security and data management*. Auerbach Publisher.

Umar, A. (2004). *Information security and auditing in the digital age: A managerial and practical perspective*. NGE Solutions.

W3C-World Wide Web Consortium (2008). Retrieved from http://www.w3c.org

Wang, H., & Lakshmanan, L. V. S. (2006). Efficient secure query evaluation over encrypted XML databases. In *VLDB*, (pp. 127-138).

Xie, M., Wang, H., Yin, J., & Meng, X. (2007). Integrity auditing in outsourced data. In *VLDB*, pages 782-793.

Yang, Y., Wilfred, N., Lau, H. L., & Cheng, J. (2006). An efficient approach to support querying secure outsourced XML information. In *CAiSE*, (pp. 157-171).

Section IV
XML for Advanced Applications

Chapter XII
Data Integration Issues and Opportunities in Biological XML Data Management

Marco Mesiti
DICO, Università di Milano, Italy

Ernesto Jiménez Ruiz
DLSI, Universitat Jaume I, Spain

Ismael Sanz
DICC, Universitat Jaume I, Spain

Rafael Berlanga Llavori
DLSI, Universitat Jaume I, Spain

Giorgio Valentini
DSI, Università di Milano, Italy

Paolo Perlasca
DICO, Università di Milano, Italy

David Manset
Maat Gknowledge, Valencia, Spain

ABSTRACT

There is a proliferation of research and industrial organizations that produce sources of huge amounts of biological data issuing from experimentation with biological systems. In order to make these heterogeneous data sources easy to use, several efforts at data integration are currently being undertaken based mainly on XML. Starting from a discussion of the main biological data types and system interactions that need to be represented, the authors deal with the main approaches proposed for their modelling through XML. Then, they show the current efforts in biological data integration and how an increasing amount of Semantic information is required in terms of vocabulary control and ontologies. Finally, future research directions in biological data integration are discussed.

INTRODUCTION

Bioinformatics is the science of storing, extracting, organizing, analyzing, interpreting, and utilizing information from biological sequences and molecules. It has been fuelled mainly by advances in DNA sequencing and genome mapping techniques. Great opportunities arise for developing novel data analysis methods. Some of the great challenges in bioinformatics include protein structure prediction, homology search, multiple alignment and phylogeny construction, genomic sequence analysis and gene finding, as well as applications in gene expression data analysis, drug discovery in the pharmaceutical industry, etc. Nowadays, there is a proliferation of research institutions that produce sources of huge amounts of biological data derived from experimentation with biological systems. These data sources can be fully exploited only if a great effort is made to integrate disparate data formats, protocols and tools. Data integration and system interoperability are currently being undertaken in order to overcome the high level of heterogeneity currently present in the available resources.

One way to expand the utility and interpretability of the individual resources would be to create a standard unified model for the description of data and, consequently, a format for their exchange and representation that is machine readable. In the literature, we can find several data formats intended to represent biological entities and systems: non XML-based, XML-based and ontology-based files. FASTA (Pearson, 1994) is an example of a non XML-based data format for the representation of sequence data. The main problem with this type of format is the lack of structure consistency, thereby leading to a possibly different interpretation of a correct file. The second group tries to overcome the problem of a consistent structure definition by using XML as the data format. Within this group, two approaches are distinguished depending on how the struc-

ture is validated, that is, whether they are using XML document type definitions (DTDs) or XML schema definitions (XSDs). The use of XSDs can be richer than DTDs since users can specify not only the structure but also the Semantics of the XML tags by defining conditions and constraints. However, the potential of XSDs is addressed in only a few proposals. Finally, ontology-based formats have emerged as a solution to the lack of Semantics and will allow the formal representation of the knowledge to be exchanged. The ontology Web language (OWL) and the open biomedical ontology (OBO) are the main languages used to represent ontologies. Unlike XML Schemas, the use of well-defined ontologies will guarantee the correct representation of the content Semantics. It must be taken into account that in the ontology-based group, we also consider the XML formats that link the content with ontologies or controlled vocabularies.

It is worth mentioning that some of the previous efforts have also defined a specific XML-like language (i.e. SBML, BioPax, PSI-MI) for the representation of biological data. The aim of these efforts is the creation of public and well-known standards, so that data source providers are able to format and externalize their biological data according to the schemas and restrictions given by the standard. This is quite an interesting approach since data source providers know how to format the data to be externalized and shared, and this data can be easily used and integrated in applications such as Taverna or Pegasys to compose complex workflows. However, as will be discussed in this chapter, other efforts are still necessary in several directions.

Another important open issue will be the selection of relevant information from XML files. Since biological data will come from heterogeneous sources, it requires the identification of approximate retrieval systems, specifically tailored for Bioinformatics, in order to extract interesting portions from XML files. The possibility of using similarity measures that can be adapted depending on the context appears to be a promising research direction.

The rest of the chapter is organized as follows. In the first part, the biological domain in which the main structures for entities and interactions exist are described. Also in this section, the main XML-like exchange standards are presented. The next section presents a survey of some XML-based systems for biological data integration, and discusses their main limitations. Finally, the last part of the chapter presents the set of new and necessary directions and trends in biological data integration.

BACKGROUND

Bio-Molecules and Bio-Molecular Data Types

In this section, we present background information on the characteristics and functions of the main bio-molecules, as well as a brief introduction to the main types of data that can be obtained from them through the application of high-throughput bio-technologies. For a detailed introduction to molecular biology, see e.g. (Lodish et al., 2000).

The main biological entities in bioinformatics and molecular biology are represented by the principal macromolecules that control the functions and constitute the structures of living cells: nucleic acids (Deoxyribonucleic acid - DNA and Ribonucleic acid - RNA) and proteins. Even if other molecules, such as lipids, sugars and other small metabolites play an important role in living cells and organisms, it is well-known that proteins, DNA and RNA are responsible for the main functionalities in biological systems.

The characteristics and properties of bio-molecules can be investigated at the "omics" level: from the study and analysis of single genes or proteins to the new bio-technologies introduced by the end of '90s allowing the analysis of the entire

set of genes (genome) or proteins (proteome) of a given species.

Specifically, the introduction of high-throughput bio-technologies produced numerous different types of bio-molecular data that need to be properly managed and processed in order to extract significant biological knowledge. The several types of data, obtained through the analysis of different bio-molecular characteristics of genes and proteins are reported in Table 1.

Significant biological knowledge can be extracted from all these different types of data, but in the following we will focus on bio-sequence data (for both nucleic acids and proteins) and on microarray data, since they are likely to be those most studied and analyzed within the bioinformatics community.

Even if macromolecules represent the main entities and are responsible for the main functions in living beings, other organizational levels also need to be considered in order to understand life and the complexity of biological functions. Indeed, cells are organized as complex systems, consisting of several organelles (e.g. ribosomes, endoplasmic reticulum, mitochondria or Golgi apparatus) that interact to realize the main biological functions. Systems Biology studies the relationships and interactions between different entities and subsystems in cells at different levels (e.g. gene networks or the metabolism of an entire cell), considering biological phenomena as the result of the integration of different processes and different interactions involving the entire genome and proteome (Kaneko, 2006; Werner, 2007).

The integration of multiple data types is one of the main topics in bioinformatics and functional genomics. Indeed, several works have shown that the integration of heterogeneous bio-molecular data sources can significantly improve the performances of data mining and computational methods for the inference of biological knowledge from the available data (Pavlidis et al., 2002; Troyanskaya et al., 2003; Lanckriet et al., 2004; Barutcuoglu et al., 2006).

Table 1. Biological data types

Data type	Description and references
DNA microarray data	They describe the gene expression level (i.e. the level of mRNA expressed in a given cell at a given time) at a genome-wide scale (Eisen et al., 1998).
Interaction data	These data denote an interaction between pairs of gene products: e.g. 2-hybrid interactions, co-immunoprecipitation, ion/protein binding, and affinity chromatography (Alfarano et al., 2005; Pellegrini et al., 2004).
Transcription Factor Binding Sites (TFBS)	Short DNA oligonucleotides to which Transcription Factors (TF) (e.g. proteins or signaling molecules) bind to regulate the transcription of genes. Known TFBS are available from databases (Matys et al., 2003), or may be inferred through computational methods (Tompa et al., 2005).
Colocalization data	Datasets that provide information about where gene products are found in the cell (Huh, 2003).
Bio-sequence data	Data related to the bio-sequences (e.g. alignments between pairs or multiple genes or proteins) (Kulikova et al., 2007).
Phylogenetic data	Data related to the evolutionary relationships of genes/gene products across multiple species (Tatusov et al., 1997).
Proteomic structural data	Data related to the structure of gene products (e.g. secondary or tertiary structure of proteins; domain structures) (Greene et al., 2007).
Protein expression data	They are usually measured by 2D gel electrophoresis, in which proteins are spatially separated in a gel according to mass and electric charge and by mass spectrometry (MS), in which the masses of protein fragments are very precisely inferred by measuring their time of flight after a defined acceleration. (Domon et al., 2006).

The representation of the basic bio-molecular entities and biological systems, their associated properties and data in a universal format interchangeable between different databases, is a key issue in bioinformatics and functional genomics, considering the exponential growth of bio-molecular data and databases (Galperin 2008).

XML Representation of Biological Data Types

Following the discussion in the previous section, in this section we report the approaches presented so far for the XML-like representation of the (1) principal bio-molecular entities and their structural properties, (2) biological expression, and (3) system biology. Table 2 summarizes some of the characteristics of a subset of existing XML languages (a further discussion on XML standards can be found in Strömbäck et al. (2007) and Brazma et al. (2006)); in particular, we note the application scope, the number and year of the current version, and comments such as the kind of

schema it relies on, or the interaction with other standards. The next subsections further discuss some of the languages summarized within Table 2; moreover, Figure 1 and Figure 2 point out the structures of the main elements of these XML-based languages. Symbols ? and * are used to denote optional and repeatable elements.

XML Representation of Bio-Molecular Entities

We now present the main works carried out for the representation of DNA, RNA, and proteins through XML. The bioinformatic sequence markup language (BSML) was one of the first attempts to develop an XML dialect to represent biological data.

BSML describes biological sequences (DNA, RNA, protein sequences) via sequence data, and sequence annotation (assertions about the properties of sequences). Sequences may be modelled at various levels ranging from complete genome and chromosomes to genes and transcripts. Each of these levels defines a class of biological objects. A BSML document consists of three major optional sections: *definitions,* encoding of genomes and sequences, data tables, sets, and networks; *research*, encoding queries, searches, analyses, and experiments; *display,* encoding of display widgets that provide graphical representations of biological objects, collected data on styles and pages.

ProXML has been proposed for the specific representation of protein sequences, structures and families. The DTD initially proposed was then replaced by a XML Schema. ProXML documents are organized in two sections: the identity section, containing the description of proteins, and the data section, containing properties of such proteins. Through properties, it is possible to represent information about primary, secondary and tertiary sequences, structural classification information, the experimentally derived distance constraints, and alignments. It is worth mentioning that ProXML belongs to the set of HOBIT (Helmholtz Open Bioinformatics Technology) XML formats (Seibel et al., 2006). The HOBIT initiative tries to group a set of XML standards to be used in data exchange. When required, new schemas are created or reused formats are extended. Currently, there exist several Web services supporting HOBIT XML formats.

RNAML has been proposed for the representation and exchange of information about RNA sequences, and their secondary and tertiary structures. The language allows the description of higher level information about the data including base pairs, base triples, and pseudoknots. A RNAML document can represent RNA molecules as a sequence along with a set of structures that describe the RNA under various conditions or modelling experiments. RNA molecules that are evolutionarily related may be further enclosed in a class element that expresses their relationship by incorporating such elements as a consensus structure and sequence alignments. Multiple tentative alignments from multiple authors can

also be represented in a single RNAML file. Furthermore, intermolecular interactions can be represented using the language, as well as many different RNAs or RNA classes can be included in a single document.

XML Representation of Biological Expressions

The first attempt to specify a language for the representation of microarray experiments was within the GeneX project (Mangalam et al., 2001). The purpose of the project was to provide a repository of gene expression data, accessible through the Internet, with an integrated toolset for analyzing the stored data. In particular, they developed a data protocol, called GeneXml, based on XML to exchange data among a variety of gene expression systems. GeneXML separates data reporting and collection from methodology and therefore stores information about data collection methodology without evaluating the measurements. This enables normalization, integration, and comparison of data across methodologies. The project is no longer active and their last goal was to shift the protocol to the one developed within the MicroArray Gene Expression (MAGE) project.

The aim of the MAGE project is to provide a standard for the representation of microarray expression data that would facilitate the exchange of microarray information between different data systems. MAGE is being sponsored by the MGED (MicroArray Gene Expression Data) Society which is responsible of the MIAME (Minimum Information About a Microarray Experiment) (Brazma et al., 2001) and MGED Ontology (Christian et al., 2003; Whetzel et al., 2006) standardization project groups. The purpose of these groups is to provide a standard for reporting microarray experiments and a common terminology for the annotation of these experiments.

MAGE project consists mainly of: a data exchange model MAGE-OM (object model) and a data exchange format MAGE-ML (markup

Table 2. XML languages for the representation of biological data types

Type of Data	Format	Concrete Scope	Version	Comments
Bio-molecular entities	BSML	Biological sequences and sequence annotation	v.3.1 / 2005	Uses DTD. Included in EMBLxml. (Spitzner et al., 1997)
	ProXML	Protein sequences, structures and families	v.1.0 / 2006	Uses XSD. Included within HOBIT formats (Hanisch et al., 2002)
	RNAML	RNA sequence, structure and experimental data	v.1.1 / 2002	Uses XSD (Waugh et al., 2002)
	AGAVE	Biological sequences and sequence annotation	2003	XSD Included in EMBLxml http://www.agavexml.org/
	Uniprot XSD	Representation of UniProt Records	2004	XSD, Successor of SP (SwissProt) ML format (Williams et al., 2004)
	EMBLxml	Biological sequences and sequence annotation	v.1.1. / 2007	Uses XSD. Currently includes BSML and AGAVE. http://www.ebi.ac.uk/embl/xml/
	GAME	Genome and Sequence	v.0.3 / 1999	Uses DTD http://xml.coverpages.org/game.html
	SequenceML	Sequence Information	v.2.1 2006	Designed to replace FASTA. Belongs to HOBIT XML formats. (Seibel et al., 2006)
Biological Expression Data	GeneXML	Gene expression data	-	Uses DTD (Mangalam et al., 2001)
	MAGE-ML	Microarray expression data	v.1.0 / 2006	Uses DTD (Spellman et al., 2002)
System Biology	CellML	Models of biochemical reaction networks	v.1.1 / 2006	Uses DTD. Available conversion to BioPAX.(Cuellar et al., 2003)
	SBML	Models of biochemical reaction networks	Level. 2. v.3.0. / 2007	Uses XSD. Available conversion to BioPAX. (Hucka et al., 2003)
	PSI-MI	Protein Interactions	v.2.5 / 2005	Uses XSD and OBO. It is linked with controlled vocabularies represented in OBO format. (Orchard & Hermjakob, 2007)
	BioPAX	Metabolic pathways, molecular interactions and protein post-translation modifications	Level. 2. v.1.0. / 2005	Uses OWL. It is linked with controlled vocabularies represented in OBO format. (Bader & Cary, 2005)
	CML	Description of Molecules and Reactions	v.2.1. / 2003	Uses XSD(Murray-Rust et al., 2003)

Figure 1. Main structures of XML-based languages

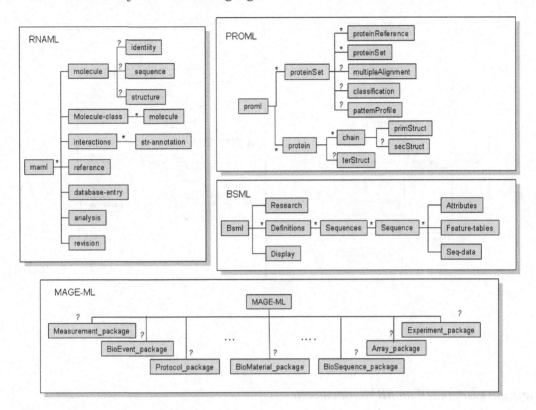

language) for microarray expression experiments. MAGE is fully MIAME compliant: all sections needed for minimum information about a published microarray gene expression experiment (experimental design, array design, samples, hybridizations, measurements, normalization controls) can be encoded in MAGE-ML. The top-level MAGE-ML schema elements refer to the MAGE-OM packages. Each of the package elements contains the lists of independent elements in that package.

XML Representation of System Biology

The need to develop XML-based languages to capture the structure and content of bio-molecular and physiological systems led to the development of SBML, the system biology markup language, CellML, the cell markup language, BioPAX, the

biological pathways exchange language and the set of HUPO-PSI (proteomics standards initiative) formats.

SBML can encode models consisting of biochemical entities (species) linked by reactions to form biochemical networks. An important principle is that models are decomposed into explicitly-labeled constituent elements, the set of which resembles a verbose rendition of chemical reaction equations; the representation deliberately does not cast the model directly into a set of differential equations or other specific interpretation of the model. This explicit modelling-framework-agnostic decomposition makes it easier for a software tool to interpret the model and translate the SBML form into whatever internal form the tool actually uses.

A CellML model consists of a number of components, each described in its own component

Figure 2. A high level comparison between CellML and SBML

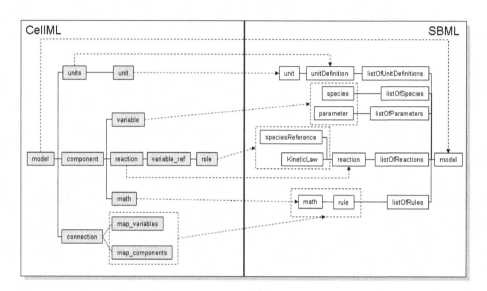

Table 3. An example of an SBML document

```
<?xml version="1.0" encoding="UTF-8"?>
<sbml xmlns="http://www.sbml.org/sbml/level2" level="2" version="1">
<model metaid="_000001" id="EPSP_Edelstein" name="EPSP_AchEvent_1996">

  <listOfSpecies>
   <species metaid="_008" id="B" name="Basal" compartment="comp1"/>
   <species metaid="_007" id="BL" name="BasalACh" compartment="comp1"/>
   (...)
  </listOfSpecies>

  <listOfParameters>
   <listOfReactions>
     <reaction metaid="_000016" id="React0" name="React0">
       <listOfReactants>
          <speciesReference species="B"/>
       </listOfReactants>
       <listOfProducts>
          <speciesReference species="BL"/>
       </listOfProducts>

     </reaction>
     (...)
   </listOfReactions>
</model>
</sbml>
```

Table 4. An example of a BioPAX document

```
<?xml version="1.0" encoding="UTF-8"?>
<rdf:RDF
      (...)
    xmlns:bp="http://www.biopax.org/release/biopax-level2.owl#"
    xmlns="http://krono.ac.uji.es/biomodles/biopax_example#"
    xml:base="http://krono.ac.uji.es/biomodels/biopax_example">

 <owl:Ontology>
    <rdfs:label>EPSP_AchEvent_1996</rdfs:label>
    <owl:imports rdf:resource="http://www.biopax.org/release/biopax-
                 level2.owl"/>

 </owl:Ontology>

<bp:openControlledVocabulary rdf:ID="comp1">
       <bp:TERM>compartment1</bp:TERM>
</bp:openControlledVocabulary>

<bp:physicalEntity rdf:ID="BL">
       <bp:NAME>BasalACh</bp:NAME>
</bp:physicalEntity>

<bp:physicalEntity rdf:ID="B">
       <bp:NAME>Basal</bp:NAME>
</bp:physicalEntity>
(...)
<bp:conversion rdf:ID="conversion_React0">
       <bp:NAME>React0</bp:NAME>
 <bp:LEFT>
       <bp:physicalEntityParticipant rdf:ID="React0_LEFT_B">
             <bp:PHYSICAL-ENTITY rdf:resource="#B"/>
             <bp:CELLULAR-LOCATION rdf:resource="#comp1"/>
       </bp:physicalEntityParticipant>
 </bp:LEFT>
 <bp:RIGHT>
       <bp:physicalEntityParticipant rdf:ID="React0_RIGHT_BL">
             <bp:PHYSICAL-ENTITY rdf:resource="#BL"/>
             <bp:CELLULAR-LOCATION rdf:resource="#comp1"/>
       </bp:physicalEntityParticipant>
 </bp:RIGHT>
</bp:conversion>

 (...)
</rdf:RDF>
```

elements. A component can be an entirely conceptual entity created for modelling convenience, or it can have some real physical interpretation (for example, it could represent the cell membrane). Each component contains a number of variables, which must be declared by placing a variable element inside the component. For example, a component representing a cell membrane may have a variable called V representing the potential difference (voltage) across the cell membrane.

The scope of CellML is broader than that of SBML, but both use almost identical mathematical expressions in MathML. Figure 2, inspired by (Schilstra et al., 2006), points out the relevant CellML and SBML elements, and gives a rough indication of a possible mapping among elements that can be obtained through an XSL transformation. As shown in (Schilstra et al., 2006), around 90% of CellML documents can be easily translated into SBML documents.

Finally, BioPAX and HUPO-PSI formats are examples of standards to represent both the structure and Semantics of biological data. These XML standards achieve this by means of controlled vocabularies and provide non-ambiguous meanings for the domain concepts. A study of these standards and the use of ontologies as controlled vocabularies are the current trends in the management of these kinds of data and will be discussed in the Future Trends section.

A fragment of SBML and BioPAX representations of a model extracted from the EMBL-EBI BioModels database are reported in Table 3 and 4. In Table 3, it can be appreciated how the SBML code follows the schema represented in Figure 2; In Table 4 the BioPAX code represents the ontology instances of the conceptual schema represented in the Bio-PAX level 2 ontology (see also Figure 6).

INTEGRATION OF BIOLOGICAL DATA: ISSUES AND CURRENT APPROACHES

Integration of Data: Basic Notions

The integration of heterogeneous data sources is a traditional research area in databases whose purpose is to facilitate uniform access to several sources of heterogeneous data, distributed through a set of connected sites that work autonomously. An integrated system provides its users with a global schema in which their views can be defined, along with the mechanisms needed to translate the elements of the global schema into the elements of the corresponding local schema, and vice versa. The heterogeneity of the integrated sources usually causes conflicts that must be resolved by the translation mechanisms in order to produce global results that are correct and complete. Heterogeneity conflicts may occur at three different levels:

- **Physical level.** The data sources to be integrated can reside in different computer platforms that run distinct database management systems (DBMSs) and operating systems, which provide different communications protocols, etc.
- **Syntactic level.** Data sources may be based on different data models, support different data types, query languages, etc.
- **Semantic level.** In different sources, different attribute names may be used for referencing the same data, the data values may be presented in different units (e.g., prices in dollars and euros), etc.

XML Technologies and Data Access

Application programming interfaces (APIs) available nowadays allow the management of the heterogeneity conflicts that appear at the physical and the syntactic levels. Currently, many of the sources export their data in XML format, and standard APIs like ODBC, JDBC or SOAP provide platform-independent interfaces for querying the data sources. Furthermore, the application of XML technologies to wrap data sources allows some of the Semantic heterogeneity problems to be solved. For example, by applying XSL transformations, the different attributes used to represent the same information at each local site, can be translated to their common representation in the global schema. However, this way of treating Semantic heterogeneity is very difficult to automate, and is also error-prone, as any small change in the local or global schemas will require the revision of the transformations made by the wrappers of the involved data sources. Furthermore, Semantic approaches are required.

Integration of Biological Data

A variety of data integration systems especially tailored to cater for bioinformatics applications have been developed (see Hernandez and Kambhampati (2004) for a general survey). The first widely cited work that recognized the importance of XML in data integration for bioinformatics is (Achard et al., 2001). Soon afterwards (Venkatesh & Harlow, 2002) noted that the "application of XML using a meta-data approach is rapidly becoming the method of choice for exchanging chemical and biological data".

In silico experiments in bioinformatics involve the integration of biological tools and information resources. Currently, the definition of biological tools made available through Web services are being widely accepted and are obviously using XML as the exchange language. In this section, we survey some of the integration applications that work around XML and integrate different services to compose biological workflows allowing domain experts to obtain complex analyses.

Pegasys

The Pegasys (Shah et al., 2005) is a workflow management system that includes and integrates numerous tools for sequence alignment, gene prediction, RNA gene detection, etc. and also filters for formatting databases and processing raw data from analysis tools. Pegasys allows the creation of sequence analysis workflows, described in XML and represented as a DAGs, and the exportation of computational results in general feature format (GFF) and GAME XML format to use them for further analyses in other tools. The server application layer receives the workflow to be executed and by means of the job execution layer, establishes the schedule of the jobs to be executed. Once the results have been collected, they are integrated in the XML format and returned to the client (as depicted in Figure 3).

Figure 3. Pegasys architecture

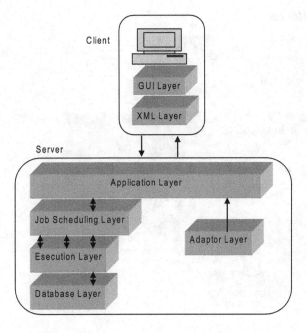

273

Automed

Automed (Zamboulis et al., 2007) targets the problem of multiple and incompatible data types and representation formats by using XML as a common representation language and providing annotations for each source. The system implements a 4-step approach:

1. Use of XML as a common representation format.
2. Use of XMLDSS as schema type. XMLDSS are DataGuide-style specifications (Goldman & Widom, 1997) derived directly from the data, though they can also be automatically generated from a DTD or an XML schema specification, if available.
3. Correspondence to available ontologies. The services inputs/outputs are annotated with correspondences between the XMLDSS schema and some existing ontology.
4. Schema and data transformation. Using this information, the output of a given service can be transformed to the format required as input by another service.

SWAMI

The goal of SWAMI (Rifaieh et al., 2007) is to provide integration of biological resources. In order to allow integration of different databases, formats and computational resources, SWAMI defines a rich middleware architecture based on two layers: the *presentation layer* which receives user requests, and the *workbench core*, which processes the request and returns the result. In these two layers, four components can be further identified: the *user* module manages presentation, while the *tool* and *data* modules abstract applications and databases, respectively; all perform their functions by orchestrating a series of *services*. A fourth component, the *broker,* serves as a coordinator, using a *registry* service that maintains information about all available services and databases, and known data formats. XML is used for the declarative specification of services. Figure 4 illustrates the SWAMI architecture.

Figure 4. SWAMI architecture

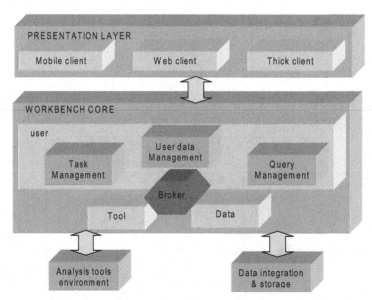

Index-Driven Integration

The work presented in (Hunt et al., 2004) and (Pankowsli & Hunt, 2005) is based on the assumption of "an explosion in specialized life science databases". In this context, researchers will need to perform queries on several databases simultaneously, whose answers "can be syntactically and Semantically heterogeneous with each other". Furthermore, "Some of them can be exact while others are approximate". The proposed solution for the integration of such sources consists of two basic procedures:

- A *key discovery* process for XML data, which can associate a unique identifier to each piece of data which needs to be integrated.
- An XML *subsumption* algorithm, used to eliminates answers which are too general or not informative.

Based on these components, and a set of partial results extracted from heterogeneous sources, the authors devise a merging algorithm that can obtain an integrated answer.

B Fabric

The goal of the B-Fabric system (Türker et al., 2007) is to serve as a workbench for experimental research in the life sciences. B-Fabric provides abstraction for *samples* (input data for experiments), which are catalogued and annotated, and *extracts*, which are prepared from samples in the laboratory and subject to measurements. B-Fabric leverages a number of existing general-purpose technologies: PostgresSQL is used as DBMS, Apache Cocoon as a Web application framework, Lucene as an engine for full text indexing, and workflow capabilities are provided with the combination of the OSWorkflow engine and OpenJMS for messaging.

XML is used extensively throughout the architecture as a medium for the specification of each component and its mapping. In particular:

- A pipelined processing model, in which the input of each step is based on the output of a previous one. Data are specified using XML.
- Workflow processes are specified using XML.

Discussion

As we have seen, the only approach which is purely for XML integration purposes is the index-driven integration approach. In all the other cases, the systems focus on computational elements, where XML is used as a sort of interfacing language. Still, XML is generally used as a common data format, but the actual data integration between heterogeneous sources is left to hand-coded implementations of ad-hoc components.

Besides this basic limitation, there are some other important issues in data integration which are not addressed by these systems:

- **Data security.** It is generally not addressed, as the focus of the reviewed systems seems to be the collaboration between localized groups. In general, the extension of the proposed architectures to support distributed teams, probably collaborating over a Grid, poses a number of challenges which are not addressed.
- **Evolution of data.** Given that, in most cases, the underlying data sources are described by hand-made specifications, any change in the structure or Semantics of the sources is inherently problematic. This is often cited as an issue.
- **Efficiency.** No attempt is made to use any technique to improve the efficiency of distributed queries, such as maintaining statistics for tuning query execution.

- As noted by (Hernandez & Kambhampati, 2004), "partially incomplete or partially correct" data can still be vital to researchers. The problem of uncertainty and high source heterogeneity are only partially addressed in the reviewed system.

- It can be noticed that conflicts at physical and syntactic levels are almost solved through Internet and XML technologies. However, conflicts at the Semantic layer are still an open issue for seamless biological data integration. In the next section, we will review the main proposals for bringing knowledge to these systems through the introduction of a series of domain ontologies.

The following section outlines several research trends addressing some of these issues.

CURRENT AND FUTURE TRENDS

In this section, we identify some technologies and experimental systems that try to address some of the shortcomings identified in the previous section. These include:

- **Ontology-based systems**, which exploit Semantic characteristics of XML sources to facilitate their integration.

- **Multi-similarity systems**, which provide advanced querying systems in the presence of complex sources.

- **Data and application evolution systems**, which provide facilities for the evolution of data structures and applications working with them.

- **Grid-based systems,** which allow the collaboration of widely distributed teams and resources.

- **Advanced security facilities** for guaranteeing the correct and safe distribution and access to sensitive personal information.

Ontology-Like Efforts

The XML-based languages described in the background section provide a representation of bio-molecular entities, biological data and the interaction of them within biomedical systems. They also provide DTD and XML Schema representations in order to define the structure and syntax of the data represented in XML files. Complete XML Schema representations could also give Semantic information about the data represented in the XML but, in most cases, they only give structural information. Ontology-like representations try to avoid the lack of Semantics of simple XML representations. OWL (ontology Web language) is an XML-based language defined by the World Wide Web Consortium[1] that has become a standard for the representation of ontologies. Ontologies try to give concise meanings to the different pieces of data by allowing the representation of domain entities (concepts, roles or properties, individuals or instances) and axioms describing and constraining the interaction between these domain entities. Moreover, OWL will enable the use of reasoning facilities to infer certain characteristics of the defined entities, that is, to classify a certain molecule as a gene if it satisfies the correspondent constraints or property restrictions.

Other relevant ontology formats have been developed by the Open Biological Ontologies (OBO) foundry[2], which provide a suite of orthogonal interoperable reference ontologies in the biomedical domain. These ontologies aim at providing a set of controlled vocabularies to be used and referenced from other representations and languages. They usually represent different kinds of hierarchies between the biological entities by means of transitive properties like is-a, part-of, develops-from, etc. From the set of OBO ontologies, we emphasize the following ones, which are mainly used in the standards we will comment below: the *"Cell Ontology"*, *"NCBI Organism Taxonomy"*, the "INOH Ontologies" (*"Molecule*

Role" and *"Event")*[3], and the *"Gene Ontology"* (GO)[4]. The latter one is widely accepted within the community and it provides three perspectives: 'molecular function', 'biological process' and 'cellular component'. It is worth mentioning that the OBO format is not XML-based, although a direct translation to XML exists.

HUPO-PSI-MI (Proteomics Standards Initiative formats)

The Protein Standard Initiative (PSI)[5] from the Human Proteome Organization (HUPO) defines standards for data representation in proteomics. These standards aim to facilitate the comparison, exchange and verification of different proteomic data sources. The following formats are currently supported: GelML (Gel Electrophoresis), mzData and analysisXML (Mass Spectrometry), spML (Sample Processing) and MIF (Molecular Interactions).

It is worth mentioning that PSI not only provides standard representations for structures, but also for content (Orchard & Hermjakob 2007; Hermjakob 2007). On one hand, it develops XML-like data exchange formats independent of the local databases. On the other hand, the use of standard controlled vocabularies (i.e.: the Gene Ontology, NCBI Taxonomy) arises as a key point in order to allow the automatic analysis, comparison and verification of proteomics datasets. These controlled vocabularies contain detailed definitions and cross references with other databases/vocabularies (i.e. UniProt[6], MetaCYC[7]) and bibliographic resources (i.e. PubMed[8]). It must be pointed out that the controlled vocabularies used by HUPO-PSI are expressed in OBO format.

One of the main HUPO-PSI efforts is the standarization of Molecular Interactions (MIF)[9]. For this purpose, an XML schema accompanied by controlled vocabularies involving more than 800 concepts, has been defined. Currently, there exist several databases providing PSI-MI for-

Figure 5. Portions of the PSI-MI vocabulary (Visualized by the OBO OLS browser)

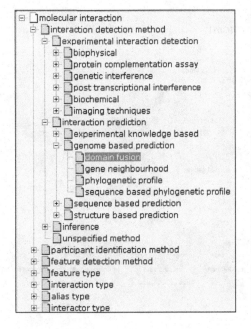
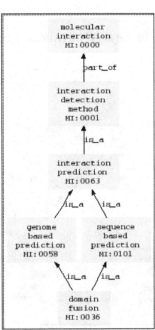

matted data: DIP, HPRD, IntAct, MINT, MIPS; Bader (2008) report a complete list of supported databases. Figure 5 represents a portion of the controlled vocabularies for PSI-MI, which can be browsed with the OBO-Ontology Lookup Service (OLS)[10].

BioPAX (Biological Pathways Exchange Language)

BioPAX[11] (Luciano & Stevens 2007) is an example of OWL-like (Ruttenberg et al., 2005) representation (the schema is defined in OWL, and the data is stored as instances/individuals of this schema) of biological entities and the interaction between them. In practical terms, BioPAX covers metabolic pathways, molecular interactions and protein post-translational modifications. This exchange language serves as a standard for the integration and exchange of data maintained in biological pathway databases. BioPAX ontology provides a conceptual framework based upon existing pathway database schemata, such as BioCyc, BIND, WIT, PATIKA, Reactome, aMAZE, KEGG,

INOH, etc. (see Bader (2008) for a complete list of supported databases).

BioPAX follows a development approach based on abstraction levels, representing a different granularity at each level. This approach is similar to the one followed by SBML. Currently, we can differentiate two levels of detail within BioPAX. Level 1 focuses on the representation of metabolic pathway data. Level 2 extends the scope of Level 1 to include the representation of molecular binding interactions and hierarchical pathways. Forthcoming BioPAX Levels will enlarge the coverage by including new pathway types (i.e. signal transduction pathways and genetic regulatory networks) and will provide better controlled vocabulary integration to make them more accessible to reasoners.

Figure 6 shows a portion of the BioPAX taxonomy in which three main concepts can be identified: *phisicalEntity*, *interaction* and *pathway*. Besides taxonomic information, the ontology contains restrictions between the interactions of concepts. The restrictions for the catalysis class can be seen, as DL axioms, in the bottom left hand side corner.

Figure 6. Portion of the BioPAX Ontology taxonomy

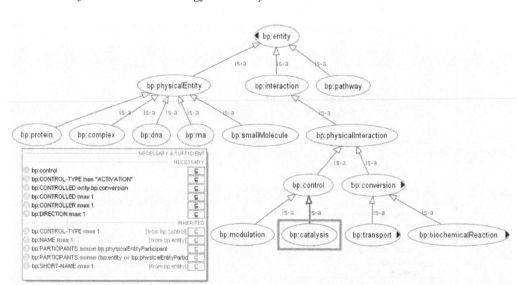

BioPax also makes use of controlled vocabularies in order to annotate the biological entities. Concretely, it references the 'Cellular location component' from GO Ontology, the Cell OBO ontology, the Organism NCBI taxonomy and the Phenotypic Quality ontology (PATO)[12]. It also incorporates other standards such as SMILES[13], CML (chemical markup language), InChI[14], etc. It is worth mentioning the high interoperability between PSI-MI and BioPAX as they use the same set of controlled vocabularies for 'protein-protein interactions'.

Figure 7 shows the coverage of all the reviewed standards for System Biology representation (BioPAX, SBML, CellML, PSI-MI). While PSI-MI is mainly focused on the protein-protein interaction domain, BioPAX is capable of representing a broader set of pathway types. On the other hand SBML and CellML are mainly focused on *biochemical reactions* and they represent mathematical models of pathways.

As stated previously, ontology-like representations will serve not only as a *static* interchange format but also as a *dynamic* classifier. The BioPAX ontology acts as a common conceptualization and the pathway datasets are stored as ontology instances of the BioPAX classes. Classes represent a set of instances which satisfy the set of restrictions involved in the class definition; therefore, classes can be used to ask questions about the instance data. In (Luciano & Stevens 2007), some experiments were carried out using the underlying reasoning characteristics of the BioPAX OWL-like ontology, in order to answer questions about Pathways: what pathways exist in a particular cell? That is, what is the set of pathways known to exist in a particular cell type? And also, what pathways involve cholesterol? That is, what is the set of pathways in which there is a step that involves cholesterol?

cPATH and Pathway Commons

cPath (Cerami et al., 2006) is an open source database software for collecting, storing and querying biological pathway data. Multiple databases can be imported and integrated into cPath via PSI-MI and BioPAX standard exchange formats. cPath data can be viewed by means of a standard Web browser or exported via an XML-based Web service API, making cPath data available to third-party applications for pathway visualization and analysis.

cPath belongs to the Pathway Commons initiative[15] in which a collection of publicly pathway databases are made available from multiple organisms (Bader, 2008). Thanks to this initiative, database providers can share their pathway data using a common language, and this data can easily be used in other applications for analysis and considerably software development costs since only a PSI-MI and BioPAX format should be in-

Figure 7. Coverage of reviewed biological exchange languages

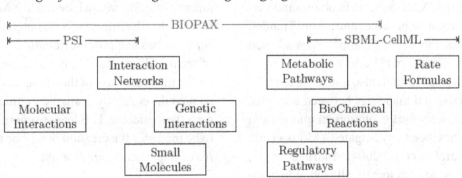

terpreted. Pathway databases providing CellML and SBML formatted data are also supported through a conversion to BioPAX format.

Another interesting feature of cPath is the interoperability with caBIG (Saltz et al., 2006) where cPath was formally tested with caBIG requirements.

Data and Application Evolution Systems

The bioinformatics application context is rapidly evolving due to the introduction of new systems for performing experiments and for the analysis of the results that are leading to the introduction of new connections for the knowledge of a given physical or chemical phenomena. The need thus arises to evolve data structures representing the results of experiments, application services working on the data, as well as the ontological elements affected by the changes. These issues can be addressed from different perspectives and we here discuss their treatment in the XML context.

The representation of biological data in the XML format might require modifying the schema (both represented through a DTD or a XML Schema) in order to meet new requirements. Moreover, the modification of the schema may lead to revalidate documents already developed according to the old schema to check whether they are still valid for the new schema. Finally, issues related to the adaptation of documents to the new schema should be addressed. These kinds of issues have been presented in the chapter of this book titled "XML Schema Evolution and Versioning: Current Approaches and Future Trends". Nevertheless, more specific approaches adapted to biological data should be addressed.

Schema modifications also impact on applications, queries, and mappings between schemas. The impact of schema evolution on queries and mappings has been investigated (Moro et al., 2007; Velegrakis et al., 2004; Andritsos et al., 2004). The issue of automatically extending ap-

plications working on the original schema when this has evolved has not been addressed in the context of XML; however, the work on "expression problems" by P. Wadler (Java Genericity mailing list, 1998) and by Torgersen (2004) for Java can be considered for this purpose.

Last, but not least, another issue to be faced is ontology evolution; that is, the issue of modifying an ontology in response to a certain change in the domain or its conceptualization. As described in the previous sections, there are many proposals for ontological representations of biological data and systems. The issues of ontology mapping, alignment, and evolution and their consequences on ontology instances should be addressed in the highly evolving context of biological data (Hasse 2004; Yildiz 2006).

Flexible Retrieval Systems for Heterogeneous Sources

The reliance of bioinformatics research in multiple, independent XML data sources is at odds with the prevailing direction of research in query languages for XML followed by the database research community, which is strongly focused on languages like XPath and XQuery, which assume a well-defined, common schema. However, in bioinformatics, there is neither a relatively regular structure that can be exploited, nor a purely textual information that is predominant as in Information Retrieval systems. We will term these collections *highly heterogeneous*. For example, bioinformatics databases contain an enormous amount of information labelled in XML, ranging from molecular information to ontologies that describe the concepts of the domain to the contents of technical articles. Many applications depend on the integrated use of those sources, but in that context the currently available techniques are not directly applicable. This leads to enormous efforts to be made for the creation of ad-hoc approaches for each particular application.

The main reason for the inadequacy of current techniques is the lack of support for heterogeneity at the structural level: techniques developed for data-oriented collections support rich XML structures, but do not tolerate a high level of variation in them; conversely, techniques developed for document-oriented collections are very good at processing complex textual content, but are limited in their support for complex structural information. This scenario implies the need for approximate retrieval techniques that are tolerant of significant variability in document structures. In most cases, there will be no exact answer to a given query, but a set of approximate results ranked according to a similarity function. A crucial issue is that a single notion of similarity that works "best" in any situation does not exist. Different users in different contexts may require different similarity functions; for instance, a biologist may wish to retrieve proteins based on a comparison with a given amino-acid sequence, while another one may issue a query asking for "malaria antigen" in the associated textual description, and a third user may combine both kinds of queries. This leads to the notion of multi-similarity systems (Adali et al., 1998), which are designed to support multiple notions of similarity simultaneously. These systems need to be able to combine different similarity measures depending on the characteristics of the data that need to be handled.

The ArHeX system (Sanz et al., 2008) provides such a multi-similarity system for XML applications. It provides a framework for defining flexible XML measures. The paper presents a literature study that shows that many existing similarity-oriented approaches for XML depend on combinations of common functions that operate at different granularity levels. For instance, a given approach may consist of a tree edit distance for computing structural similarity, which in turns relies on a *tf-idf*-based term similarity function for matching element tags. These measures are integrated into a common framework that allows the definition of new, complex measures by composition of predefined functions. An important advantage of this approach is that it can accommodate external computational modules that implement domain-specific functions, such as a protein similarity measure. In addition, it defines a query model for highly heterogeneous XML collections, based on using XML subtree patterns as flexible models for the information needs of the users. These patterns are matched to the particular fragments in the collection that maximize the similarity according to a given measure. This method has two main advantages: first, it is able to match subtrees with very high structural diversity, in which even the parent/child relation between nodes (which most other approaches depend on) is not maintained; and second, it is independent of any particular XML similarity measure.

Grid Architectures

Big research projects within Biology and Biomedicine involve massive heterogeneous and geographically dispersed resources. Such resources are generated and shared by many partners. Moreover, their research work relies on tools that require computation and data intensive methods. Apart from the traditional issues of data integration and interoperability, new issues have to be addressed in these scenarios. Most of these issues are being undertaken through the Grid technology, which provides a base technology upon which collaborative and secure applications can be built.

One of the main features provided by Grid-based approaches is that of virtual organization (VO). Through a virtual organization, temporary collaborations between researchers can be defined. A VO defines the partners and their possible groups, establishes the collaboration rules between them, and defines the privacy and security rules for all the grid resources. Notice that privacy and security is especially relevant in

Biomedicine applications, where biological data is associated to real patients, and therefore their privacy must be preserved.

Another main feature of Grid-based applications is that of distributing both intensive data and processes. One of the main objectives of a Grid infrastructure is the handling of very time-consuming processes by distributing them across a set of computer resources. For this purpose, Grid technology provides a service-based framework (e.g. Web services) to define and execute complex tasks. This framework makes it possible to define complex workflows involving a set of registered services.

Currently, there are several efforts to apply Grid technology to Biological data processing. Probably, myGRID (Globe et al., 2003) is the most outstanding project that involves both XML-based biological services and the Grid technology. Moreover, myGRID addresses the problem of composing biological services by means of the Taverna workflows (Oinn et al., 2006; 2007). Many of the standards mentioned throughout this chapter have been used within this framework. Finally, we mention that myGRID also treats Semantic heterogeneity through the inclusion of domain ontologies. These are used to annotate bioservices (i.e. their inputs and outputs) in order to discover them and to check the compatibility of combined bioservices. This kind of infrastructure that combines Semantic annotations and grid has been called Semantic Grid.

There are other big projects that are using grid technology in Biomedicine, for example the cancer Biomedical Information Grid (caBIG) (Saltz et al., 2006) and Health-e-Child (HeC) (Freund et al., 2006) projects. The former is aimed at sharing biomedical resources (i.e. data and tools) among scientists and practitioners within the cancer community. Like myGRID, there is a great effort in providing standard languages for creating and publishing biological data and services. On the other hand, Health-e-Child is aimed at developing an integrated healthcare platform for European paediatrics, providing seamless integration of traditional and emerging sources of biomedical information. Like myGRID, ontologies are used to enrich Grid resources, although Semantic annotations are more focused on clinical data than on service objects. Another relevant aspect of HeC is the vertical integration of data for knowledge discovery purposes. In other words, biological data and clinical data are intended to be integrated in order to find new evidences for the studied diseases.

Advanced Security Facilities

Several privacy and security issues arise when unauthorized subjects are able to access confidential information with the intention of using it maliciously.

Since a side-effect of the integration and management technique of heterogeneous biological data sources is the opportunity to access or to make a prediction about relevant personal data to be protected, data security and patient-privacy preservation are relevant issues to be addressed (Tavani, 2004; Spinello, 2004; Godard et al., 2003; Blatt, 2000; Meingast et al., 2006). On the other hand, data sharing is fundamental for the advancement of scientific research and should be guaranteed according to a policy protecting confidential and proprietary data.

In order to address data access, storage, and analysis, several techniques used to increase privacy and security in different context may be adopted: access control (Evered & Bogeholz, 2004) and authentication techniques can be used to limit the use of the resources and to guarantee that access requests are coming from the person it is claiming to be from, encryption can be used to ensure the security of confidential data, data obfuscation, data separation, statistical and approximate queries answers may be used to preserve privacy and security in presence of data mining techniques (Vaidya & Clifton 2002; Bertino et al., 2005).

CONCLUDING REMARKS

In this chapter, we have addressed the biological data integration issues from the perspective of using XML as a common format for the representation of biological entities, experiments and interactions in biological systems. The discussion pointed out that XML improves the possibility of integrating heterogeneous sources. XML languages like XML Schemas for the description of document structure, Xquery for querying collections of data, XSL for transforming documents from one format to another one, and other interoperability facilities (e.g., application programming interfaces, SOAP) can be profitably exploited for data integration. However, this cannot be enough. More Semantics information and more systems specifically tailored for the bioinformatics context are required. In this chapter, we have discussed how current approaches are exploiting controlled vocabulary, ontologies, and collaborative annotations in Grid environments, and also presented approaches that exploit the XML organization of data. Thus, the role of XML data management will assume more and more relevance in this interesting and continuously evolving environment in future years with a plethora of promising research issues to be faced by the database, data integration, and Information Retrieval communities.

REFERENCES

Achard, F. et al. (2001). XML, Bionformatics and data integration. In *Bioinformatics Review, 17*(2), 115-125.

Adali S. et al. (1998). A multi-similarity algebra. In *ACM SAC*, (pp. 402-413).

Alfarano, C. et al. (2005). The Biomolecular interaction network database and related tools 2005 update. In *Nucleic Acid Res.*, 33, 418—424.

Andritsos, P. et al. (2004). Kanata: Adaptation and evolution in data sharing systems. In *SIGMOD Record, 33*(4), 32-37.

Bader, G. D., & Cary, M. P. (2005). *BioPAX – Biological Pathways Exchange Language Level 2*, Version 1.0. http://www.biopax.org/release/biopax-level2-documentation.pdf

Bader, G. (2008). *Pathguide: The pathway resource list.* http://www.pathguide.org

Barutcuoglu, Z., Schapire, R. E., & Troyanskaya, O. G. (2006). Hierarchical multi-label prediction of gene function. In *Bioinformatics, 22*(7), 830-836.

Bertino, E. et al. (2005). A Framework for evaluating privacy preserving data mining algorithms. In *Data Mining and Knowledge Discovery, 11,* 121–154.

Blatt, R. J. (2000). Banking biological collections: data warehousing, data mining, and data dilemmas in genomics and global health policy. In *Community Genet., 3*, 204–211.

Brazma, A. et al. (2001). Minimum information about a microarray experiment (MIAME)—toward standards for microarray data. In *Nature Genetics, 29*, 365–371.

Brazma, A. et al. (2006). Standards for systems biology. In *Nat. Rev. Genet., 7*, 593–605.

Cerami, E. G., et al. (2006). cPath: Open source software for collecting, storing, and querying biological pathways. In *BMC Bioinformatics, 7*, 497.

Christian, J. et al. (2003). The MGED ontology: A framework for describing functional genomics experiments. In *Comparative and Functional Genomics, 4*(1), 127-132.

Cuellar, A. A., et al. (2003). CellML 1.1 for the Definition and Exchange of Biological Models. In *MCBMS,* (pp. 451-456).

Domon B. & Aebersold R. (2006). Mass spectrometry and protein analysis. In *Science, 312*(5771), 212 – 217.

Eisen, M. B., Spellman, P. T., Brown, P. O., & Botstein, D. (1998). Cluster analysis and display of genome-wide expression patterns. In *PNAS 95*(25), 14863-14868.

Evered, M., & Bogeholz, S. (2004). A Case Study in access control requirements for a health information system. In *AISW,* (pp. 53-61).

Freund, J., et al. (2006). Health-e-Child: An integrated biomedical platform for grid-based pediatrics. In *Health-Grid Conference.*

Galperin M. Y. (2008). The molecular biology database collection: 2008 update. In *Nucleic Acids Research 36,* (pp. 2-4).

Goble, C. A., et al. (2003). *Knowledge integration: in silico experiments in bioinformatics. The Grid 2: Blueprint for a New Computing Infrastructure,* Morgan Kaufmann.

Godard, B., et al. (2003) Data storage and DNA banking for biomedical research: informed consent, confidentiality, quality issues, ownership, return of benefits. A professional perspective. In *Eur. J. Hum. Genet., 11 Suppl. 2,* (pp. 88–122).

Goldman, R., & Widom, J. (1997). DataGuides: Enabling query formulation and optimization in semistructured databases. In *VLDB,* (pp. 436-445).

Greene, L. H. et al. (2007). The CATH domain structure database: new protocols and classification levels give a more comprehensive resource for exploring evolution. In *Nucleic Acid Res., 35,* 291-297.

Haase, P., & Sure, Y. (2004). D3.1.1.b State of the art on ontology evolution. http://www.aifb.uni-karlsruhe.de/WBS/ysu/publications/SEKT-D3.1.1.b.pdf

Harvey, S. C., et al. (2002). RNAML: A standard syntax for exchanging RNA information. In *RNA 8*(06), 707-717.

Hanisch, D. et al. (2002). ProML - the protein markup language for specification of protein sequences, structures and families. In *Silico Biology 2*(3), 313–324.

Hermjakob, H. (2006). The HUPO proteomics standards initiative - Overcoming the fragmentation of proteomics data. In *Proetomics Journal, 6*(S2), 34-38.

Hernandez, T., & Kambhampati, S. (2004). Integration of biological sources: Current systems and challenges ahead. In *SIGMOD Record 33*(3), 51-60.

Hucka, M. et al. (2003). The Systems biology markup language (SBML): A medium for representation and exchange of biochemical network models. In *Bioinformatics, 19*(4), 524-531.

Huh, W. K. et al. (2003). Global analysis of protein localization in budding yeast. In *Nature, 425,* 686-691.

Hunt, E. et al. (2004). Index-Driven XML data integration to support functional genomics. In *DILS,* (pp. 95-109).

Kaneko, K. (2006). *Life: An introduction to complex systems biology.* Springer

Kulikova, T. et al. (2007). EMBL nucleotide Sequence database in 2006. In *Nucleic Acid Res., 35,* 16-20.

Lanckriet, G. R. et al. (2004). A statistical framework for genomic data fusion. In *Bioinformatics, 20,* 2626-2635.

Lodish, H. et al. (2000). *Molecular cell biology.* New York: Freeman & Co.

Luciano, J. S., & Stevens, R. D (2007). e-Science and biological pathway Semantics. In *BMC Bioinformatics, 8*(S3).

Mangalam, H. et al. (2001). GeneX: An open source gene expression database and integrated tool set. In *IBM Systems Journal, 40*(2), 552-569.

Matys, V. et al. (2003). TRANSFAC: Transcriptional regulation, from patterns to profiles. In *Nucleic Acids Res., 31*(1), 374-378.

Meingast, M., et al. (2006). Security and privacy issues with health care information technology. In *Proc. IEEE Conference of Engineering in Medicine and Biology Soc.,* (pp. 5453-5458).

Moro, M., Malaika, S., & Lim, L. (2007). Preserving XML queries during schema evolution. In *WWW,* (pp. 1341-1342).

Murray-Rust, P., & Rzepa, H. S. (2003). Chemical markup, XML and the Worldwide Web. Part 4. CML Schema. In *J. Chem. Inf. comp. Sci., 43,* 757-772.

Oinn, T. et al. (2006). Taverna: Lessons in creating a workflow environment for the life sciences. In *Concurrency Comput. Pract. Exper., 18,* (pp. 1067–1100).

Oinn, T. et al. (2007). Taverna/myGrid: Aligning a workflow system with the life sciences community. In *Workflows for e-Science: Scientific Workflows for Grids*, (pp. 300-319).

Orchard, S., & Hermjakob, H. (2007). The HUPO proteomics standards initiative—easing communication and minimizing data loss in a changing world. In *Briefings in Bioinformatics 9*(2), 166-173.

Pankowski, T., & Hunt, E. (2005). Data merging in life science data integration systems. In *IIPWM,* (pp. 279-288).

Pavlidis, P. et al. (2002). Learning gene functional classification from multiple data. In *J. Comput. Biol., 9,* 401-411.

Pearson, W. R. (1994). Using the FASTA program to search protein and DNA sequence databases. In *Methods Mol Biol., 24,* 307-331.

Pellegrini, M., Haynor, D., & Johnson, J. M. (2004). Protein interaction networks. In *Expert Rev. Proteomics, 1*(2), 89-99.

Rifaieh et al. (2007). SWAMI: Integrating biological databases and analysis tools within user friendly environment. In *DILS,* (pp. 48-58).

Ruttenberg, A., et al. (2005). Experience using OWL DL for the exchange of biological pathway information. In *OWL-ED.*

Saltz, J., et al. (2006). caGrid: design and implementation of the core architecture of the cancer biomedical informatics grid. In *Bioinformatics, 22*(15), 1910-6.

Sanz, I., Mesiti, M., Guerrini, G., & Berlanga, R. (2008). Fragment-based approximate retrieval in highly heterogeneous XML collections. In *Data Knowledge Eng., 64,* 266-293.

Seibel, P. N et al. (2006). XML schemas for common bioinformatic data types and their application in workflow systems. In *BMC Bioinformatics, 7,* 490.

Shah, S. P., et al. (2005). Pegasys: Software for executing and integrating analyses of biological sequences. In *BMC Bioinformatics, 5,* 40.

Spellman, P. T. et al. (2002). Design and implementation of microarray gene expression markup language (MAGE-ML). In *Genome Biology, 3,* 0046.1–0046.9.

Spinello, R. A. (2004). Property Rights in Genetic Information. In *Ethics and Inf. Technol., 6*(1), 29-42.

Spitzner, J. et al. (1997). *Bioinformatic sequence markup language (BSML).* LabBook's BSML Sequence Tutorials.

Strömbäck, L. et al. (2007). A review of standards for data exchange within systems biology. In *Proteomics, 7,* 857–867.

Tatusov, R. L., Koonin, E. V., & Lipman, D. J. (1997). A genomic perspective on protein families. In *Science 278*, (pp. 631-637).

Tavani, H. T. (2004). Genomic research and data-mining technology: Implications for personal privacy and informed consent. In *Ethics and Inf. Technol.*, *6*(1), 15-28.

Tompa, M. et al. (2005). Assessing computational tools for the discovery of transcription factor binding sites. In *Nature Biotechnology, 1*(23), 137-144.

Torgersen, M. (2004). The expression problem revisited. In *ECOOP*, (pp. 123-143).

Troyanskaya, O. G. et al. (2003). A Bayesian framework for combining heterogeneous data sources for gene function prediction in Saccharomices cerevisiae. In *Proc. Natl Acad. Sci. USA, 100*, 8348-8353.

Türker, C. et al. (2007). B-Fabric: A data and application integration framework for life sciences research. In *DILS*, (pp. 37-47).

Vaidya, J. S., & Clifton, C. (2002). Privacy preserving association rule mining in vertically partitioned data. *SIGKDD*, (pp. 639-644).

Venkatesh, T. V., & Harlow, H. (2002). Integromics: Challenges in data integration. In *Genome Biology, 3*(8), 4027.1–4027.3

Waugh, A., et al. (2006). CellML2SBML: Conversion of CellML into SBML. In *Bioinformatics, 22*(8), 1018-1020.

Werner, E. (2007). All systems go. In *Nature, 446*, 493-494.

Whetzel, P. L. et al. (2006). The MGED Ontology: A resource for Semantics-based description of microarray experiments. In *Bioinformatics, 22*, 866–873.

Williams, A., & Runte, K. (2004). XML Format of the UniProt Knowledgbase. In *ISMB*.

Yildiz, B. (2006). *Ontology Evolution and Versioning. The state of the art.* Technical report. http://publik.tuwien.ac.at/files/pub-inf_4603.pdf

Zamboulis, L. et al. (2007). Bioinformatics service reconciliation by heterogeneous schema transformation. In *DILS*, (pp. 89-104).

ENDNOTES

[1] OWL Guide: http://www.w3.org/TR/owl-guide

[2] OBO foundry: http://www.obofoundry.org/

[3] INOH Ontologies: http://www.inoh.org/info/ontologies/

[4] GO: http://www.geneontology.org/

[5] HUPO-PSI: http://www.psidev.info/

[6] UniProt: http://beta.uniprot.org/

[7] MetaCYC: http://metacyc.org/

[8] PubMed: http://www.ncbi.nlm.nih.gov/PubMed/

[9] PSI-MI: http://www.psidev.info/index.php?q=node/60

[10] OLS: http://www.ebi.ac.uk/ontology-lookup/browse.do?ontName=MI

[11] BioPax: http://www.biopax.org and http://biopaxwiki.org/cgi-bin/moin.cgi

[12] PATO: http://www.bioontology.org/wiki/index.php/PATO:Main_Page

[13] Simplified Molecular Input Line Entry Specification: http://www.opensmiles.org/

[14] International Chemical Identifier: http://www.inchi.info/

[15] Pathway Commons: http://www.pathwaycommons.org

Chapter XIII
Modeling XML Warehouses for Complex Data:
The New Issues

Doulkifli Boukraa
University of Jijel, Algeria

Riadh Ben Messaoud
University of Nabeul, Tunisia

Omar Boussaid
University Lumière Lyon 2, France

ABSTRACT

Current data warehouses deal for the most part with numerical data. However, decision makers need to analyze data presented in all formats which one can qualify as complex data. Warehousing complex data is a new challenge for the scientific community. Indeed, it requires revisiting the whole warehousing process in order to take into account the complex structure of data; therefore, many concepts of data warehousing will need to be redefined. In particular, modeling complex data in a unique format for analysis purposes is a challenge. In this chapter, the authors present a complex data warehouse model at both conceptual and logical levels. They show how XML is suitable for capturing the main concepts of their model, and present the main issues related to these data warehouses.

INTRODUCTION

Data warehouses have proven their usefulness in the decision making process. They provide decision makers with accurate and real-time data in due course, and allow them to perform different front-end analysis tasks (Chaudhuri & Dayal, 1997). In traditional data warehouses, data are usually organized according to multidimensional schemas where numerical measures can be analyzed with discrete attributes which come from analysis axes, commonly called dimensions (Kimball & Ross, 2002). Nevertheless, such a data organization may seem inappropriate for several data structures. Thus, interesting information may remain hidden and some analysis purposes can be missed.

In fact, a lot of real world data are supported by semi-structured or unstructured documents such as emails, video-tapes and other storage devices. We generally call them 'complex data' since they have multiple formats which come from multiple sources and are managed with multiple relations.

Warehousing and exploiting complex data for the decision making process add new challenges to the data warehouse field and open new issues (Boussaid et.al., 2003). In this context, XML offers many solutions. In the one hand, it allows data to be integrated in a unique format and therefore, copes with the problem of data sources heterogeneity. In the other hand, XML makes it possible to preserve the complex internal structure of data as well as the multiple and rich relationships that may exist between them.

Recently, many researches have addressed the issue of warehousing XML data. In this context, many XML-based models for data warehouses have been proposed.

However, to the best of our knowledge, none of the current XML-based models for data warehouses allows the multidimensional analysis of data while preserving its natural complexity. In this chapter, we aim to model a complex data

warehouse. Our model is driven by a real-world case study: Digital Bibliography & Library Project (DBLP)[1]. Firstly, we present the main concepts of our model at a conceptual level using textual definitions and formal notations. Then, we show how it is possible to map these concepts at a logical level using XML. Finally, we consider the main issues raised by our model, especially XML database-related issues.

BACKGROUND

A commonly accepted definition of a data warehouse is that given by Inmon (2002) "A data warehouse is a subject-oriented, integrated, non-volatile, and time variant collection of data in support of management's decisions" (Inmon, 2002). Traditional data warehouses apply to structured data and they have gained maturity as witnessed by the number of related tools. As structured data are not the only data needed for decision making, new generations of data warehouses have emerged that take into account different structures of data. In this chapter, we focus on one kind of these data warehouses: XML warehouses. As a new research field, there is no common definition of an XML warehouse. This is due to the fact that XML is used differently in different contexts: as a format of data sources, as a means of data integration or exchange between traditional data warehouses or as a language to describe the warehouse itself. In this section, we present the research work on XML warehouses. For the sake of clarity, we propose to group the research work according to the following concepts of data warehousing: data preparation, data modeling, data storage, data exchange and data analysis.

Data Preparation

In a data warehouse, data is physically integrated from different sources. Because the sources are usually independent from each other, the integration operation may cause many problems due to data redundancy, inconsistency, etc. Thus, data needs to be cleaned before integrating it. In this context, Rusu et.al. (2005) consider XML sources and provide a method for cleaning XML data. Their method consists of four steps: correcting XML schemas, eliminating redundancy, eliminating inconsistency and eliminating errors.

Golfarelli et. al. (2001) also consider XML data sources with related DTDs. Prior to the modeling activity, the authors require DTDs to be simplified by flattening their element definitions, grouping the same-named sub-elements and reducing unary operators to single one. A similar approach is found in (Vrdoljak et.al., 2003) but it applies to XML Schemas rather than DTDs.

Data Warehouse Modeling

In order to model an XML data warehouse and derive its underlying structure, many approaches and supported models have been proposed. Pokorný (2001) defines DTD-core which describes the core data of a set of source DTDs. Then, he uses a view mechanism over DTD-cores in order to define the XMLStarSchema with explicit hierarchies. The view mechanism is also present in the work of (Baril & Bellahsène, 2003). The authors specify materialized views over multiple XML data sources. The XML warehouse is then described by an XML document with a root element "datawarehouse". The data warehouse XML document is linked to sources and materialized views by using sources' IDs and views' IDs. In (Golfarelli et al., 2001) and (Vrdoljak et al., 2003), the authors present approaches to design XML data marts or Web-houses respectively from XML DTDs and XML Schemas. These approaches include creating DTD or Schema graphs, choosing facts and defining dimensions and measures for each fact. Nassis et.al. (2004) define a Meaningful Fact named xFACT at a conceptual level using UML. The authors show how it is possible to map

UML constructs to XML Schema constructs. In addition, they express views over xFACT which they call Virtual Dimensions in order to answer analysis needs. In (Boussaïd, et.al., 2006), the authors define an XML fact as an XML element where the measures are modeled as attributes and the dimensions are modeled as nested sub-elements. Rusu et al. (2005) base their approach for constructing an XML warehouse on XQuery. They apply XQuery on XML documents and get a fact document and many dimension documents and use a linking mechanism between the fact document and dimension documents that is similar to primary and foreign keys of the relational model.

Data Warehouse Data Storage

To the best of our knowledge, there are two research works that have detailed storage techniques for an XML warehouse. The first work is the Xylème project (Xylème, 2001). This project aims at storing large volumes of XML documents, collected from the Web, and then at querying and updating them. The Xylème project is based on a specific storage system (Natix) and query performance is optimized by using a special index called XyIndex. The second work is the DAWAX system (Baril & Bellahsène, 2003). In this system, XML data is stored in a relational database. The authors map each concept of their model (fragment, view, pattern, etc.) to the relational concepts (tables, columns, etc.) and provide mechanisms for preventing data redundancy.

Data Warehouse Data Exchange

In this field of research work, data is exchanged between (possibly) heterogeneous data warehouses in XML format. Hümmer et.al. (2003) define a family of XML-based document templates called Xcube in order to exchange data warehouse data over networks. A similar work is found in (Binh et.al., 2001). The authors use XML in order to achieve interoperability between heterogeneous data warehouses.

OLAP on XML Data

Unlike structured data, online analytical processing (OLAP) of XML data is not as simple as in traditional data warehouses. In fact, given the flexible nature of XML, conventional OLAP operators are no longer appropriate; thus, XML-specific OLAP operators need to be defined. Such operators may be found in (Wang, et.al., 2005) and (Wiwatwattana, et.al., 2007).

Other techniques make use of mediators to perform OLAP operation over XML data. Niemi et.al. (2002) propose to analyze distributed XML Data of a data warehouse via a Collection Server. The Collection Server is a mediator between the data warehouses and an OLAP server based on Microsoft's MDX technology. A similar work can be found in (Jensen et. al., 2001) where the authors propose to analyze both relational and XML data using a relational-based OLAP tool. In the same context, Li & An (2005) propose to integrate XML data sources virtually by transforming their schemas into UML Diagrams through which OLAP queries are expressed.

MODELING ISSUES AND REQUIREMENTS

Regarding data preparation and integration, the main issues are caused by the flexible nature of XML. In fact, XML data are self-described and thus may be schemaless. Consequently, missing data, errors, redundancies and inconsistencies are hard to detect. On the other hand, even when XML documents are associated with schemas (DTDs or XML Schemas), these schemas remain complex to analyze with automatic tools and will always require the user's assistance (Vrdoljak et al., 2003).

Regarding XML data warehouse modeling, XML allows data to be described at a logical level and captures rich real-world Semantics using XML schema. Nevertheless, XML Schema is not suited for the warehouse conceptual design because of its complexity. Therefore, it is necessary to be able to describe an XML data warehouse at a conceptual level.

Another issue of XML warehouses is about preserving the semi-structured nature of data at the warehouse design step. In fact, few models like those of (Pokorný, 2001; Nassis et al., 2004) preserve the original structure of XML data when designing the XML data warehouse.

Moreover, an XML data warehouse requires the development of suitable OLAP tools and the enrichment of XML query languages with cube operators as stated in (Wiwatwattana, et al., 2007).

In this chapter, our aim is to model an XML data warehouse. Our model is guided by new modeling requirements which we believe have not yet been met by the current models. These requirements are drawn from a detailed analysis of the DBLP database. The new requirements can be summed up as follows:

- **Complex data as facts.** The data we need to analyze may be characterized by simple linear attributes such as numerical measures or dimension attributes like in conventional data warehouses (Kimball & Ross, 2002). However, in real life, data may have a more complex structure (tree-like or graph-like). For instance, in DBLP, *authors* may be characterized by their names and affiliations, but data about *publications* are rather semi-structured and composed of sections, paragraphs, internal and external links, etc.
- **Complex data as dimensions.** In conventional data warehouses, measures are analyzed according to structured dimensions; however, dimensions may have complex

structures. For instance, if we were to evaluate authors according to their publications, it might be necessary to go into detail for each publication and thus explore a more or less complex structure.

- **Symmetric and simultaneous facts and dimension.** In classical data warehouse modeling, facts and dimensions are treated separately. Even in symmetric models, facts and dimensions remain distinct in the context of a given analysis task. However, we may need to analyze data according to data of the same nature. For instance, we may evaluate authors according to their co-authors in publications; or we may evaluate the quality of a publication according to publications where it is cited.

- **Explicit and Semantically-rich relationships between data.** The relationships between facts and dimensions are usually implicit. For instance, when relating "sales" as facts to "departments", "products" and "time" as dimensions, we know implicitly that this schema models sales of products made by departments during periods of time. However, in real-life applications, relationships may be Semantically rich and range from simple associations to inheritance, composition, etc. For instance, in DBLP, there is an inheritance relationship between a publication and different kinds of publications (articles, inproceedings, etc). Furthermore, relationships need to be explicit in order to help distinguish one from the other in case they link the same data. For example, we can observe two relationships between authors and publications: authoring and reviewing.

- **Complex aggregations.** Conventionally, aggregation functions such as *sum* and *average* deal with numerical data, but these aggregations are not the only ones which an OLAP user needs. For example, Ravat et.al..

(2007) propose to aggregate documents using a *top_keywords* function that returns the most used keywords for documents being analyzed.

THE PROPOSED MODEL

In this section, we describe our model for a complex data warehouse at two levels: conceptual and logical.

Conceptual Model

The main concepts that comprise our model are the complex object, the complex relationship and the complex hierarchy. A complex object is a generalization of a dimension or a fact in traditional warehouse models and it captures the natural complex structure of data rather than describing it as linear attributes. Moreover, as the complex objects are autonomous, we introduce the concept of relationship to explicitly link them. Finally, the real-case study shows that hierarchies may be defined not only between attributes, but between objects as well.

Complex Object

Definition: A complex object is an abstract or physical entity that is meant to be analyzed whether as a subject (fact) or as an axis (dimension). A complex object is structured as a set of attributes. Each attribute may have one or many values within the object. A special mono-valued attribute plays the role of the object's key.

The attributes of an object may be independent from each other or linked through different kinds of relationships. We distinguish two categories of relationships:

- Hierarchical relationships where the attributes are organized hierarchically

- Non-hierarchical relationships which associate an attribute to another according to some specific Semantic.

In our model, we consider only hierarchical relationships because of their related interest to analysis. Objects that share the same structure fall into a class. In our model, we assume that each object falls into one class only.

Notations: We assume a complex object class is a three-tuple Obj = (id^{Obj}, A^{Obj}, SAH^{Obj}) where

- id^{Obj} is the key attribute of Obj
- $A^{Obj} = \{a^{Obj}_i / i = 1..N\}$ is the set of attributes
- $SAH^{Obj} = \{AH^{Obj}_i / i = 1..N\}$ is the set of attribute hierarchies of the class Obj. An attribute hierarchy AH^{Obj} is detailed in section "Complex Attribute Hierarchy".

We assume that a complex object instance is a three-tuple obj = (id^{obj}, A^{obj}, SAH^{obj}) where

- id^{obj} is the key attribute of obj
- $A^{obj} = \{a^{obj}_i / i =1..N\}$ is the set containing the sets of attribute values
- $a^{obj} = \{v(a^{Obj}) / j =1..N\}$ is the set of values of the attribute a^{Obj}. Where 'v' is a function that assigns one or many values to the attribute a^{obj} within obj

- SAH^{obj} is the set of attribute hierarchy instances of obj, which is detailed in section "Complex Attribute Hierarchy".

The set of object instances of a class is noted IO = $\{obj_i / i =1..N\}$.

Example: In the DBLP database, we identify many object classes such as *Publication, Author, Proceedings, Journal* and *Time*. The class *Publication*, for instance, is identified by the attribute *Key* and has additional attributes: *Title, Pages, URL, Keyword, Section* and *Subsection*. Figure 1 shows an instance of the class *Publication* representing the publication titled *Efficient Allocation in Distributed Object Oriented Databases*.

Complex Relationship

Definition: A complex relationship is an explicit link between two or more complex objects. In our model, we deal only with binary relationships, i.e. between pairs of objects. In fact, in a data warehouse, all relationships are binary (between facts and dimensions or between two consecutive components of a hierarchy in a snowflake schema). We believe it is preferable to decompose all non-binary relationships into binary ones to give the designer more flexibility in choosing the relationships for the purpose of analysis. A relationship class is characterized by a name and by the list

Figure 1. Example of an instance object

Key ={'conf/ISCApdcs/GrahamA03'}
Title = {Efficient Allocation in Distributed Object Oriented Databases}
Pages = {471-}
URL = {db/conf/ISCApdcs/ISCApdcs2003.html#GrahamA03}
Keyword = {object oriented database, object fragments, genetic algorithm, optimal allocation}.
Section = {Introduction, Related research, Model description and Problem Formulation ...}
Subsection = {File allocation (FAP), Database allocation (DAP), ...}

of object classes it links. Since we consider only binary relationships, we refer to the first object class as the source and to the second one as the target. A relationship instance is one that links two object instances.

Notation: A complex relationship class is a couple $R = (Obj_s^R, Obj_c^R)$ where

- Obj_s^R is the source object class of R
- Obj_c^R is the target object class of R

A complex relationship instance is denoted $r = (obj_s^R, obj_c^R)$ where

- obj_s^R is the source object instance of r
- obj_c^R is the target object instance of r

The set of a complex relationship instances is denoted IR=$\{r_i / i = 1..N \}$

Example: Publications are linked to authors via a relationship that we call *Authored_by*. Instances of *Authored_by* are of the form (p, a) where *p* refers to the object class *Publication* and *a* refers to the object class *Author*.

Figure 2 shows two instances of the relationship *Authored_by*. Here, the publication titled *Efficient Allocation in Distributed Object Oriented Databases* is authored by *Jonathan Graham* and *Jim Alves-Foss*.

Complex Attribute Hierarchy

Definition: A complex attribute hierarchy is a hierarchy defined by attributes of an object. Such a hierarchy will be useful when it belongs to a complex object that has been chosen as a fact. The analyst may observe data at different levels of the attribute hierarchy.

An attribute hierarchy class is characterized by its name and by the set of its components and may or may not include the object's key. Each component is an attribute of the complex object class. In addition, an ordering relationship < orders the hierarchy components from the finest-grained attribute up to the least fine-grained one. The last element of the hierarchy is a special attribute that we denote All^a and that is necessary for aggregation operations. An attribute hierarchy instance is then composed of many sets. Each set is ordered by < and contains at most one value per attribute. We call these sets as *instances* of the attribute hierarchy.

Notations: An attribute hierarchy class is denoted $AH^{Obj} = (\{a_i^{Obj} in A^{Obj}\} U \{id^{Obj}\}\} U \{All^a\}, <)$. Whereas an attribute hierarchy instance is denoted $ah^{Obj} = (\{w(a_i^{AH}) / a_i^{AH} in AH^{Obj}, <)$. The function *w* assigns an attribute value to the ith component of the hierarchy if it has a corresponding value within the hierarchy and assigns *null* otherwise. It also assigns a special value all^a to All^a. The set

Figure 2. Example of two complex relationship instances

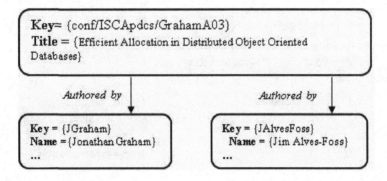

of instances of an attribute hierarchy is noted $IAH^{Obj}=\{ah^{Obj}_i / i =1..N\}$

Example: In a publication, a subsection rolls up to a section and a section rolls up to the whole document. Let's then suppose that publications contain keywords for each subsection. Then, we may define the attribute hierarchy as *H_publication* = {*Subsection* < *Section* < *All^a*}.

Figure 3 shows instances of such a hierarchy for the publication *Efficient Allocation in Distributed Object Oriented Databases*.

Complex Object Hierarchy

Definition: A complex object hierarchy is analogous to a complex attribute hierarchy with the difference that the latter is composed of attributes, whereas the former is composed of objects. An object hierarchy class is characterized by its name and by the set of its components. Each component is an object class.

In addition, an ordering relationship < orders the hierarchy components from the finest-grained up to the least fine-grained object class. The last element of the hierarchy is a special object class that we denote *All^O* and that's necessary for aggregation operations. An object hierarchy instance is then composed of many sets. Each set is ordered by < and contains at most one object instance per object class. We call such sets *instances* of the object hierarchy.

Notation: An object hierarchy class is denoted $OH = (\{Obj_i\} U\{All^{obj}\}, <)$, whereas an object hierarchy instance is noted $oh = (\{y(Obj_j)\}, <)$. The function *y* assigns an object instance to the jth component if it has a corresponding object instance within the hierarchy and assigns *null* otherwise. The set of instances of an object hierarchy is denoted $IOH=\{oh_i / i =1..N\}$.

Figure 3. Example of complex attribute hierarchy instances

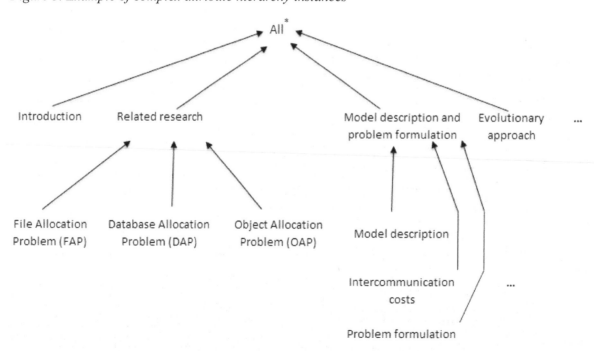

Example: In the DBLP database, we can identify many object hierarchies. For instance, the hierarchy *H_PubConf* ={*Publication* < *Proceedings* < *Conference* < *All^O*}. Figure 4 shows instances of *H_PubConf.*

Complex Multidimensional Schema

It is now argued that multidimensional modeling is best suited for data analysis of a data warehouse. Usually, in a multidimensional model, facts and dimension are separated. However, as we stated earlier, an object may be interesting as a fact in one context of analysis and as a dimension in another one. Therefore, in our model, we have only those candidate objects that are independent from any context of analysis. Our model then becomes multidimensional in this sense.

Definition: A complex multidimensional schema is composed of a set of complex objects including their attribute hierarchies. Objects are linked to each other via relationships and may be organized in object hierarchies. Since the complex multi-

dimensional schema contains only dimensions, the designer is given plenty of possibilities when selecting the objects for analysis.

A complex multidimensional class is composed of a set of complex object classes, a set of complex relationship classes and a set of object hierarchy classes. The complex multidimensional schema instance is then composed of a set of object instances per object class, a set of relationship instances per complex relationship class and a set of object hierarchy instances per object hierarchy class.

Notation: A complex multidimensional schema class is a three-tuple SCM =(SO, SR, SH) where

- SO = {Obj$_i$/ i =1..N} where Obj is a complex object class
- SR = {R$_j$ / j =1..N} where R is a complex relationship class
- SH = {OH$_k$ /k =1..N} where OH is a complex object hierarchy class

Figure 4. Example of complex object hierarchy instances

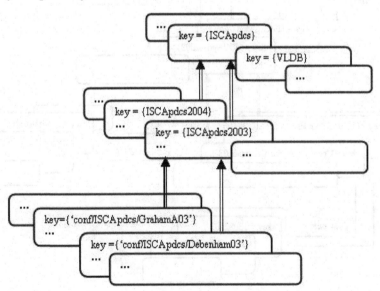

The complex multidimensional schema instance is a three-tuple scm =(SO,IR, IH) where

- so = {IO$_i$ / i =1..N} where IO is a set of object instances of a class
- sr = {IR$_j$ / j =1..N} where IR is a set of relationship instances of a class
- sh = {oh$_k$ / k =1..N}

Example: An example of a complex multidimensional schema is the schema SCM^{DBLP} = (SO^{DBLP}, SR^{DBLP}, SH^{DBLP}) where

- SO^{DBLP} = {Publication, Author, Time}
- SR^{DBLP} = {Authored_by, Date_publ} where Authored_by = (Publication, Author) and Date_publ = (Publication, Time)

- SH^{DBLP} = { H_PubConf} such that H_Pub-Conf = {Publication < Proceedings <Conference < All^{obj}}

Figure 5 shows instances of the schema. The simple arrows represent relationships and the double arrows represent hierarchies.

Complex Cube

This is a cube design step, on which the subject (fact) and axes (dimensions) of analysis are designated. The designer selects one complex object class from the available object classes to play the role of a fact object. It is also possible to add new attributes to the fact object class in order to fulfill specific analysis needs. When the fact object class is selected, all the relationships where the fact occurs—either as a source or a target—are made

Figure 5. Example of complex multidimensional schema instances

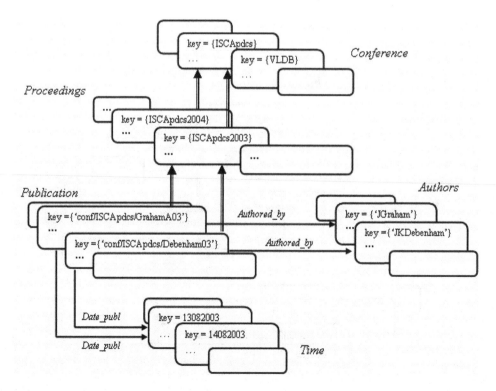

available for selection. Selecting the interesting relationships implies the selection of all related complex object classes which then play the role of dimensions. Besides, the object hierarchy classes where each dimension object occurs are made available to the designer for selection.

Definition: A complex cube class is characterized by its name and by its fact object class, the set of dimension object classes, the set of relationship classes and the set of object hierarchy classes.

A complex cube instance is composed of one fact object instance, one relationship instance per relationship class, one dimension object instance per dimension object class, and the set of object hierarchy instances per dimension object class if available.

Notation: A complex cube class is a four-tuple $CC = (F, SR^C, SD, SH^C)$ where

- $F \in SO$ is the object class selected as the fact of the cube
- $SR^C = \{R^C_i, i = 1..N\}$ is the set of relationship classes of the cube such that $SR^C \subset SR$
- $SD = \{D^C_j, j = 1..N\}$ is the set of dimensions of the cube such that $SD \subset SO$
- $SH^C = \{H^C_i, k = 1..N\}$ is the set of object hierarchies of the cube such that $SH^C \subset SH$

A complex cube instance is a four-tuple $CC = (f, r^C, d, IOH^C_d)$ where

- f is an instance of the fact object class F
- r^C is an instance of a relationship class from SR^C
- d is an instance of a dimension object class D from SD
- IOH^C_{sd} is the set of object hierarchy instances where the dimension d belongs

Example: Let us suppose that we want to analyze publication ratings in order to evaluate the authors. Then, we wish to calculate the average publica-

tion rating for each author by proceedings, by conference respectively, and finally to know the average rating for all conferences. Furthermore, we want to calculate the average rating by month, by year and by decade for each author. In addition, let us suppose that we want to analyze publication keywords for each publication's subsection and then to know the top keywords by section and finally for the whole publication. On the other hand, we want to know the number of publications for each author by month, by year and then by decade. The complex cube that corresponds to the aforementioned analysis needs is composed of the following:

- Fact object class: *Publication*
- Relationship classes of the cube: *Authored_ by* and *Date_pub*
- Dimension classes: *Author* and *Time*
- Object hierarchy classes: *H_PubConf = {Publication < Proceedings < Conference < All^O}*

Figure 6 shows instances of the complex cube. The fact objects are grey-colored.

Logical Model

In traditional data warehouses, the data structures and their formats are homogeneous. It is then possible to integrate and describe data in a unique format within the data warehouse. However, the data needed for decision making may be more or less complex. For complexity, we mean that data may have multiple formats, may be stored on different storage devices, and be in several languages and versions.

When it comes to modeling such data in a data warehouse, there is the need for a unique format that is supported by one query language, on one hand. On the other hand, companies are increasingly describing their data in XML, especially for communication purposes among heterogeneous systems.

Figure 6. Example of a complex cube instances

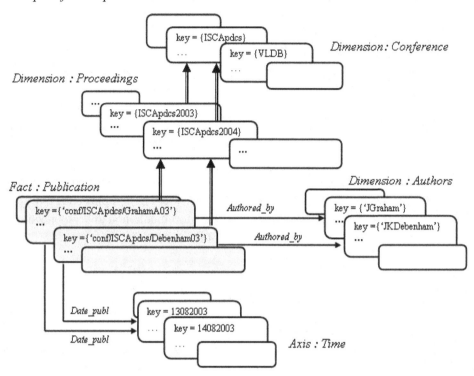

Heterogeneity is therefore the main reason for our choice of XML as a formalism to describe complex data within a data warehouse, in contrast to other research works in the same field.

We describe the main concepts of our model using XML as follows.

Complex Object

We describe a complex object class using XML schema. A complex object instance corresponds to an XML document which has to be valid against its schema. The root element of the document takes the name of the class, and has a key-typed attribute that takes the name of the object's key. Each attribute of the object corresponds to an XML element that takes the name of the attribute. Moreover, XML Schema allows defining relationships between elements, such as nesting, referencing, etc. It is worth noting that an XML

hierarchy that results from element nesting in XML does not define an attribute hierarchy as we defined it in our model. We present our modeling of an attribute hierarchy in sub-section Attribute Hierarchy. Figure 7 shows the XML document representing the publication titled *Efficient Allocation in Distributed Object Oriented*.

Complex Relationship

We describe a complex relationship class using XML schema. A relationship instance corresponds then to an XML document which has to be valid against its schema. The root element of the document takes the name of the relationship. In order to represent the source and target objects, we use a referencing mechanism. A reference is made up of two XML elements nested under the root element. Each element takes the name of its class and holds the key value of the correspond-

Figure 7. Example of an XML representation of an object instance

```
<publication key="conf/ISCApdcs/GrahamA03">
  <type>Article</type>
  <title>Efficient Allocation in Distributed Object Oriented Databases</title>
  <pages>471-</pages>
  <URL>db/conf/ISCApdcs/ISCApdcs2003.html#GrahamA03</URL>
  <sections>
  <section>Introduction</section>
  <section>Related research</section>
  <section>Model description and Problem Formulation
    <subsection>File allocation (FAP)
      <keyword>File</keyword>
    </subsection>
    <subsection>Database allocation (DAP)
      <keyword>Database</keyword>
    </subsection>
    <subsection>...</subsection>
  </section>...
</publication>
```

Figure 8. Example of two XML documents representing relationship instances

```
<Authored_by>
  <Publication>conf/ISCApdcs/GrahamA03</Publication>
  <Author>JGraham</Author>
</Authored_by>
```

```
<Authored_by>
  <Publication>conf/ISCApdcs/GrahamA03</Publication>
  <Author>JAFoss</Author>
</Authored_by>
```

ing object instance. Figure 8 shows the two XML documents corresponding to the relationship *Authored_by*.

Attribute Hierarchy

We model an attribute hierarchy as an XML element named *AttHierarchy* within the object's XML document. The element *AttHierarchy* is nested under an XML element named *Hierarchies* which is also nested under each element

that belongs to the hierarchy. *AttHierarchy* has four XML attributes:

- **Name** which contains the name of hierarchy
- **Level** which contains the object's attribute's level in the hierarchy, starting with 1 for the least fine-grained component
- **Rollsup** which contains the name of the referenced attribute of the hierarchy

Figure 9. Example of an attribute hierarchy inclusion in an XML document

```
<Publication key="conf/ISCApdcs/GrahamA03">...
 <Sections><section>Introduction</section>
 <Section>Related research
        <Hierarchies>
            <AttHierarchy Name ="h_publication" Level ="1" Rollsup="All"
        Value="all"/>
        </Hierarchies>
    <Subsection>File allocation problem (FAP)
        <Keyword>File</keyword>
        <Hierarchies>
            <AttHierarchy Name ="h_publication" Level ="2" Rollsup="Section"
                            Value ="Related research"/>
        </Hierarchies>
            </subsection>
    <Subsection>Database allocation problem(DAP)
        <Keyword>Database</keyword>
        <Hierarchies>
            <AttHierarchy Name ="h_publication" Level ="2" Rollsup="Section"
                            Value ="Related research"/>
        </Hierarchies>
    </Subsection>
 </Section>
 <Section>Model description and Problem Formulation
        <Hierarchies>
            <AttHierarchy Name ="h_publication" Level ="1" Rollsup="All"
        Value="all"/>
        </Hierarchies>
        ...
 </Section>    ...
 </Sections>
</Publication>
```

- **Value** contains a current element of the hierarchy, the value of its corresponding component at the upper level.

If the current hierarchy member is at the top of the hierarchy, *Rollsup* and *Values* contain respectively *All* and *all*. Figure 9 shows some instances of the attribute hierarchy *h_publication*.

Object Hierarchy

We model an object hierarchy as an XML element named *ObjHierarchy* within the object's XML document. The element *ObjHierarchy* is nested under the *Hirerachies* XML element described above, which is also nested under the root element. *ObjHierarchy* has four XML attributes:

- **Name** which contains the name of the hierarchy;
- **Level** which contains the object's attribute's level in the hierarchy starting with 1 for the least fine-grained component;
- **Rollsup** which contains the name of the referenced object class of the hierarchy;
- **Value** which contains for a current element of the hierarchy, the key value of its corresponding component at the upper level.

If the current hierarchy member is at the top of the hierarchy, *Rollsup* and *Values* contain respectively *All* and *all*. Figure 10 shows instances of H_PubConf hierarchy of the previous example.

Complex Multidimensional Schema

The complex multidimensional schema class is described by the set of XML Schema documents corresponding to the objects and relationships. The complex multidimensional schema instance is composed of one XML document per complex object and of one XML document per relation-

ship instance. Figure 11 shows instances of the complex multidimensional schema.

Complex Cube

The complex cube class is described by an XML schema document for the fact object class and one XML Schema document per dimension object. The complex cube instance is then composed of one XML document per fact object instance and many XML documents per dimension object class. The XML document corresponding to a fact object instance has the same structure as the

Figure 10. Example of object hierarchy instances

```
<Publication key="conf/ISCApdcs/GrahamA03">
 <Hierarchies>
    <ObjHierarchy Name ="h_PubConf" level ="3" Rollsup="Proceedings"
               Value="ISCApdcs2003"/>
 </Hierarchies>
...
</Publication>
```

```
<Publication key="conf/ISCApdcs/ Debenham03">
 <Hierarchies>
    <ObjHierarchy Name ="h_PubConf" level ="3" Rollsup="Proceedings"
               Value="ISCApdcs2003"
 </Hierarchies>
...
</publication>
```

```
<Proceedings key="ISCApdcs2003">
 <Hierarchies>
    <ObjHierarchy Name ="h_PubConf" level ="2" rollsup="Conference"
               Value =" ISCApdcs "/>
 </Hierarchies>
...
</publication>
```

```
<Conference key="ISCApdcs">
 <Hierarchies>
    <ObjHierarchy Name ="h_PubConf" level ="1" rollsup="All"
               Value ="all"/>
 </Hierarchies>...
</Publication>
```

Figure 11. Example of XML documents representing an instance of the multidimensional schema

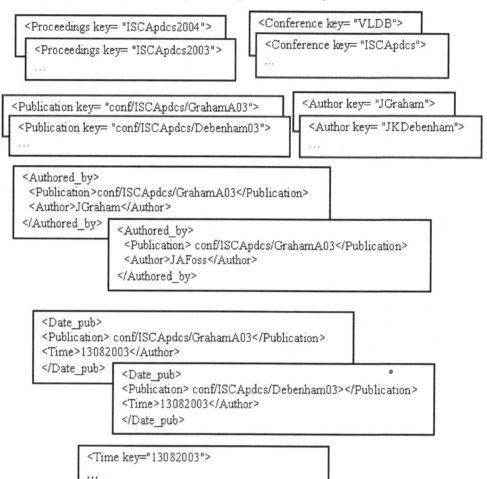

XML document of the complex objects. The only difference is that we add a new XML element named *Relationships* under the root, in order to reference the dimension objects. We nest under *Relationships* one XML element per dimension, which takes the name of the relationship. Finally, we nest the corresponding dimension object instance references as XML elements under their corresponding relationship XML elements; they take the name of the dimension object class and hold the key value of the corresponding object instance. Figure 12 shows the XML document representing a fact object instance.

DISCUSSION

Our proposed model answers the modeling requirements for a complex data warehouse that we believe have not been fully covered simultaneously by any of the existing models. In this section, we present the main features of our model and show for each feature whether it is supported by existing models. The list of selected models contains merely XML-based models described at the logical level. We use the letter Y if a feature is supported by the model and N if not. We also use the letter P if a feature may be supported by the model, but is not mentioned by the author(s).

Figure 12. Example of XML document of a fact object instance

```
<Publication key="conf/ISCApdcs/GrahamA03">
<Relationships>
        <Authored_by>
                <Author>JGraham </Author>
                <Author>JAFoss</Author>
        </Authored_by>
        <Date_publ>
                <Time>13082003</Time>
        </Date_publ>
</Relationships>

<Hierarchies>
   ...
</Hierarchies>
   ...
</Publication>
   ...
```

Finally, we use a hyphen if the feature is not considered in the model. The main features are described as follows:

1. **Preserving data structure complexity** means that the model captures and retains the complex structure of data.
2. **Explicit relationships** means that relationships between data hold names, as opposed to implicit relationships between facts and dimensions. Naming relationships makes it possible to select interesting ones for analysis purposes.
3. **Semantically rich relationships** means that the models supports various kinds of relationships ranging from simple associations to aggregations, inheritance, etc.
4. **Complex hierarchies** means that the hierarchies are defined between complex data rather than between structured data.
5. **Explicit hierarchies** means that hierarchies have names. Naming hierarchies has the same benefit as naming relationships.
6. **Symmetric treatment of facts and dimensions** means that the user may choose the same data as a fact for one analysis purpose and as a dimension for another.

7. **Simultaneous treatment of data as fact and dimensions** means that the same data may be present as either the subject or the axes of analysis.

As shown in Table 1, there are a few works that deal with the modeling of a data warehouse using XML constructs. In fact, most of the research work considers XML at the source level. This is justified by the growing popularity of XML as a formalism to describe enterprise transactional data. Furthermore, we can draw the following conclusions from Table 1:

1. In order to construct an XML data warehouse that preserves the complex nature of data, two mechanisms are used: views (Pokorný, 2001; Baril & Bellahsène, 2003) and queries (Rusu et al., 2005). In our work, we do not provide a modeling approach associated with our model. However, we believe that although views or queries are powerful for deriving a complex structure of the data

Table 1. Support of existing XML-based models of the main features of our model

Feature / Model	1	2	3	4	5	6	7
Pokorný (2001)	Y	-	-	Y	Y	N	N
Baril et al (2003)	Y	Y	-	-	-	P	P
Rusu et al (2005)	P	N	N	N	N	N	N
Boussaïd et al (2006)	N	N	N	N	Y	N	N

warehouse, they are not appropriate for a conceptual design. The approach proposed in Nassis et al. (2004) is appropriate for designing a complex data warehouse at the conceptual level. The authors use UML for this purpose but no mapping to XML is provided. Nevertheless, the authors show that UML is powerful enough to capture the main concepts of XML and to add stereotypes when no direct mapping is possible.

2. Explicit relationships between data allow the users to select interesting ones to fulfill their analysis needs. In (Rusu et al., 2005) and (Boussaid et al., 2006), relationships are defined implicitly between the fact and the dimensions in a similar way to the star schema of Kimball & Ross (2002). In contrast, the view-based model of Baril & Bellahsène (2003) allows the expression of named relationships. For instance, the authors express the relationship between authors and publications by means of an XML element authorspublications, under which they nest the title of the publication and its corresponding authors. However, according to this model, data are embedded in the relationship instances which may cause redundancy in the case where the same data is involved in different relationships. In our model, we also express named relationships as XML elements. However, we do not embed data in the relationship instances, but rather use a referencing mechanism

similar to the primary and foreign key of the relational model. Thus, we may link the same data via different relationships without causing data redundancy. Moreover, our model allows us to choose only interesting relationships and related objects for the purpose of analysis; thus, the cube construction is optimized, because we have only the data that is relevant to the analysis.

3. To the best of our knowledge, the model proposed by Nassis et al. (2004) is the only one that expresses rich relationships between data within a data warehouse. This is made possible by the rich concepts of UML used at the conceptual level. Unfortunately, as mentioned above, no mapping to XML is provided by the authors. As for our model, we can capture the relationship Semantics by naming it properly. For instance, we may use the words "is a" to name relationships of inheritance or "is composed of" to express relationships of composition, and use specific names to express association relationships, such as the relationship "authored_by".

4. Concerning complex and explicit hierarchies, Pokorný's model allows the expression of hierarchies between DTDs as opposed to conventional hierarchies that are defined between structured data. Subsequent members of a hierarchy must then satisfy the XML-referential integrity. In this way, a dimension hierarchy is organized as in a

snowflake schema. However, in Boussaid et al. (2006), the hierarchies are embedded in the XML document as nested elements under each root member of a dimension. Our approach is similar Pokorný's in the sense that we consider separate and autonomous components of a hierarchy. Furthermore, we use four attributes to associate an object with a hierarchy: hierarchy name, level, rollsup and value. The benefits we gain from this are the following:

o   The attribute name allows the associa-tion of the same data with different hierarchies simultaneously, with a different level in each hierarchy.

o   The attribute rollsup allows defining non-strict hierarchies within the same hierarchy. For instance, in DBLP, if we consider the hierarchy journal number < journal volume < journal, we can notice that some journal numbers roll up to journal volumes then to journals, whereas some other journal numbers roll up directly to journals.

o   As to Symmetric treatment of fact and dimension, this is possible within the system DAWAX (Baril & Bellahsène, 2003). Although the terms 'fact' and 'dimension' are not used by the authors, their model allows the expression of different views on the same data. In this way, the same data may occur as a subject of analysis in one view or as an axis of analysis in another one. In addition, it is possible to express views to analyze data according to data of the same nature. In our model, both of these features are possible. In fact, we use the terms 'dimension' and 'fact' only at the cube design stage. The user can choose a complex object as a fact in one analysis context and the same ob-ject as a dimension in another context.

Moreover, it is possible to select the same object as a fact and dimension. However, it is important to note that, once the cube has been generated, the dimensions and fact are distinct and stored separately.

FUTURE TRENDS

As we stated earlier, the concept of XML Data warehouses is still in its infancy and many related issues are worth investing by both research and professional communities. In fact, the whole data warehousing process needs to be revisited to cope with data complexity. For the sake of clarity, we present the main trends of XML data warehouses according to the warehousing process.

Regarding data preparation, there is a need for automatic approaches that allow the discovery of schemas for schemaless XML data sources or to define core common schema when many dif-ferent schemas are available. Furthermore, there is a need for automatic approaches that discover hidden relationships between data, especially hierarchical relationships that are necessary for multidimensional modeling. In this context, data mining techniques applied to semi-structured data, especially XML mining techniques will be of great importance for complex data preparation.

Once complex data have been extracted, they need to be modeled in multidimensional way. This is problematic because we need to preserve the complex nature of data and represent the multiple and rich relationships between them, on one hand. On the other hand, we need to consider the com-plex data warehouse design at a conceptual level that is easily manipulated by designers. The same problem occurs when we need to design cubes over a complex multidimensional schema and to filter data to meet specific analysis needs.

Another issue that researchers need to tackle is to define XML algebra for complex data warehouses. A related issue would be to enrich existing XML query languages to allow the users to perform online analysis of XML data.

The last issue is related to the complex data warehouse performance. In fact, performance is a key concept in the decision making process and solutions are provided for structured data, like materialized views, indexing and partitioning. However, such solutions are no longer applicable to complex and XML data. For instance, how is it possible to horizontally or vertically partition XML documents or cluster a set of XML documents to enhance query performance?

CONCLUSION

In this chapter, we presented a logical model for a complex data warehouse. First, we presented the main concepts of our model at a conceptual level using mathematical notations. The main innovation of our model is that it answers new modeling requirements that we believe are not met by current models. At the logical level, we showed how it is possible to capture the main concepts of our model using XML. In particular, XML Schema provides powerful constructs to capture data complexity and to model a rich set of relationships.

We also used XML to explicitly model relationships, attribute hierarchies, object hierarchies and dimensions using named tags.

Complex data warehousing and analyzing is the solution for executives who are concerned by the prospect of having to involve the whole enterprise data in the decision making process. On the other hand, it is an exciting challenge for the scientific community which needs to focus on many issues including: preparing complex data for analysis, modeling them at a conceptual level close to the designer's understanding, and analyzing them online.

REFERENCES

Baril, X., & Bellahsène, Z. (2000). A view model for XML documents. In *OOIS*, (pp. 429-441).

Binh, N. T., Tjoa, A. M., & Mangisengi, O. (2001). MetaCube-X: An XML metadata foundation for interoperability search among Web warehouses. In: *DMDW*, (p. 8).

Boussaïd, O., Ben Messaoud, R., Choquet, R., & Anthoard, S. (2006). X-Warehousing: An XML-based approach for warehousing complex data. In *ADBIS*, (pp. 39-54).

Boussaïd, O., Bentayeb, F., Darmont, J., & Rabaseda, S. (2003). Vers l'entreposage des données complexes : structuration, intégration et analyse. In *Ingénierie des Systèmes d'Information 8*(5-6), 79-107.

Chaudhuri, S., & Dayal, U. (1997). An overview of data warehousing and OLAP technology. *SIGMOD Record 26*(1), 65-74.

Golfarelli, M., Rizzi, S., & Vrdoljak, B. (2001). Data warehouse design from XML sources. In *DOLAP*, (pp. 40-47).

Hümmer, W., Bauer A., & Harde, G. (2003). XCube: XML for data warehouses. In *DOLAP*, (pp. 33-40).

Inmon, W. H. (2002). *Building the data warehouse.* NY: John Wiley and Sons.

Jensen, M. R., Møller, T. H., & Pedersen, T. B. (2001). Specifying OLAP cubes on XML data. *Journal of Intelligent Information Systems, 17*(2-3), 255–280.

Kimball, R., & Ross, M., (2002). *The data warehouse toolkit.* NY: John Wiley and Sons.

Li, Y., & An, A. (2005). Representing UML snowflake diagram from integrating XML data using XML schema. In *DEEC*, (pp. 103–111).

Nassis, V., Rajugan, R., Dillon, T. S., & Rahayu, W. (2004). Conceptual design of XML document warehouses. In *DaWaK*, (pp. 1-14).

Niemi, T., Niinimäki, M., Nummenmaa, J., & Thanisch, P. (2002). Constructing an OLAP cube from distributed XML data. In *DOLAP, 02*, 22-27.

Pokorný, J. (2001). Modelling stars using XML. In *DOLAP 2001*, (pp. 24-31).

Ravat, F., Teste, O., Tournier, R., & Zurfluh, G. (2007). A conceptual model for multidimensional analysis of documents. In *ER*, (pp. 550-565).

Rusu, L. I., Rahayu, J. W., & Taniar, D. (2004). On building XML data warehouses. In *IDEAL 2004*, (pp. 293-299).

Vrdoljak, B., Banek, M., & Rizzi, S. (2003). Designing Web warehouses from XML schemas. In *DaWaK 2003*, (pp. 89-98).

Wang, H., Li, J., He, Z., & Gao, H. (2005). OLAP for XML data. In *CIT*, (pp. 233-237).

Wiwatwattana, N., Jagadish, H., Lakshmanan Laks, V. S., & Srivastava D. (2007). X^3: A cube operator for XML OLAP. In *ICDE*, (pp. 916-925).

Xylème (2001). A dynamic warehouse for XML data of the Web. In *IEEE Data Engineering Bulletin 24*(2), 40-47.

ENDNOTE

[1] http://dblp.uni-trier.de

Section V
XML Benchmarking

Chapter XIV
XML Benchmarking:
The State of the Art and Possible Enhancements

Irena Mlynkova
Charles University, Czech Republic

ABSTRACT

Since XML technologies have become a standard for data representation, numerous methods for processing XML data emerge every day. Consequently, it is necessary to compare the newly proposed methods with the existing ones, as well as analyze the effect of a particular method when applied to various types of data. In this chapter, the auhtors provide an overview of existing approaches to XML benchmarking from the perspective of various applications and show that to date the problem has been highly marginalized. Therefore, in the second part of the chapter they discuss persisting open issues and their possible solutions.

INTRODUCTION

Since XML (Bray et al., 2006) became a de-facto standard for data representation and manipulation, numerous methods have been proposed for efficiently managing, processing, exchanging, querying, updating and compressing XML documents. And new proposals emerge every day. Naturally, each author performs various experimental tests

using the newly proposed method and describes its advantages and disadvantages. But, it can be very difficult for a future user to decide which of the existing approaches is the most suitable for his/hers particular requirements on the basis of the descriptions of methods. The problem is that various methods are usually tested on different data sets derived from diverse sources which either do not yet exist or which were created only for the testing purposes, with special requirements of particular applications etc.

An author of a new method will encounter a similar problem whenever he/she wants to compare the new proposal with an existing one. This is possible only if the source or executable files of the existing method or, at least, identical testing data sets are available. But, too often it is impossible to have access to this information. In addition, in the latter case, the performance evaluation is limited by the testing set whose characteristics are often unknown. Hence, a reader finds it difficult to obtain a clear notion of the analyzed situation.

An analogous problem occurs if we want to test the behaviour of a particular method on various types of data, or determine the correlation between the efficiency of the method and changing complexity of the input data. Not even the process of gathering the testing data sets is simple. Firstly, the real-world XML data usually contain a huge number of errors (Mlynkova et al., 2006) which need to be corrected. And what is worse, the real-world data sets are usually surprisingly simple and do not cover all constructs allowed by XML specifications.

Currently, there exist several projects which provide a set of testing XML data collections (usually together with a set of testing XML operations) that are publicly available and well-described. We can find either fixed (or gradually extended) databases of real-world XML data (e.g. project INEX (INEX, 2007)) or projects which enable us to generate synthetic XML data on the basis of user-specified characteristics (e.g. project XMark (Busse, 2003)). But, in the former case, we are limited by the characteristics of the testing set; whereas, in the latter case, the characteristics of the generated data that can be specified are trivial (such as the amount and size of the data).

Goals of the Chapter

The first aim of this chapter is to provide an overview of existing XML benchmarking projects, i.e. projects which provide a set of testing XML data collections, XML operations/scenarios etc. We will discuss their main characteristics and in particular the issues related to their versatility. We will show that the problem of sophisticated XML benchmarking has been so far highly marginalized and the number of possibilities for acquiring at least a reasonable testing set of XML data is surprisingly low.

Since the key operations of XML processing are undoubtedly parsing, validating and querying, most of the existing benchmarking projects focus mainly on them. But, there are also other popular and useful XML technologies or operations with XML data and, hence, there also exist benchmarks determined for other purposes. Nevertheless, their number is surprisingly low or the existing representatives are already obsolete.

The next aim of the chapter is to identify the most significant related open issues and unsolved problems. In particular, we will deal with a system which is able to generate synthetic XML data on the basis of a wide range of user-specified characteristics. We will focus on three aspects of the problem – automatic generation of synthetic XML documents, automatic generation of their XML schema, and automatic generation of respective XML queries. The main idea is that the author of a new method will be able to test its behaviour on any kind of data that can be described using this set of characteristics. On the other hand, any other author can use the same setting-up of characteristics, repeat the generation of the testing data sets and compare a new method with the existing results.

In general, we will describe and discuss such a system in full and focus on the related open problems as well as possible solutions. The particular implementation can then focus only on selected aspects appropriate for concrete exploitation.

Note that there already exist several analytical surveys on XML benchmarking projects (such as Nambiar et al., 2001; Bohme et al., 2003; Manegold, 2008). But, in general, most of the surveys consider only a subset of query benchmarks, often written by authors of a particular benchmarking project and, hence, the results are slightly biased or they have already become obsolete. We will mention and briefly describe them in relevant parts of our text as well.

Roadmap

The rest of the text is structured as follows: the next section classifies and briefly describes the existing approaches to XML benchmarking. The following one provides a general summary of the findings. This is followed by description and discussion of the remaining open issues and possible solutions and, finally, conclusions.

EXISTING APPROACHES AND THEIR CLASSIFICATIONS

Various XML benchmarking approaches have been proposed and can be classified as follows. From the point of view of the type of data, we can distinguish benchmarks which involve real-world data and benchmarks involving synthetic data. Though the former type seems to have more practical application, the problem is that real-world data are quite simple (Bex et al., 2004; Barbosa et al., 2005; Mlynkova et al., 2006) and do not contain most of the constructs allowed by W3C specifications, whereas benchmarks enabling the testing of all the allowed constructs are quite natural.

A different type of classification of XML benchmarks distinguishes approaches which involve a fixed set of testing data sets (e.g. XML documents, XML queries, XSL transformation etc.) and approaches which enable them to be created dynamically on the basis of user-specified parameters. While in the former case the data sets can be both real-world and synthetic, naturally in the latter case the data are purely synthetic.

On the basis of the purpose of the XML benchmark, we can further distinguish benchmarks which analyze quality and behaviour of various types of applications. The most common ones are XML parsers and validators, XML management systems, XSLT processors etc. And in particular areas, we can also establish a finer classification on, for example, the basis of exploited languages and constructs, such as DTD (Bray et al., 2006) vs. XML Schema (Thompson et al., 2004; Biron et al., 2004) benchmarks, XQuery (Boag et al., 2007) vs. XPath (Clark et al., 1999) benchmarks, XPath 1.0 (Clark et al., 1999) vs. XPath 2.0 (Berglund et al., 2007) benchmarks to name a few.

In the following sections, we briefly describe the best known representatives of particular approaches and their advantages and disadvantages. We will focus mainly on benchmarks related to the basic support of XML technologies such as parsing, validating, storing, querying and updating. Naturally, there also exist advanced XML operations and technologies which can and need to be benchmarked, such as, e.g. XSL transformations or compressing XML data, but these technologies are mostly closely related to the basic ones we will deal with. On the other hand, they may require special treatment which is outside the scope of this text.

XML Datasets

Currently, one of the most typical approaches to XML testing is exploitation of fixed sets of XML data. These sets usually involve real-world XML data that represent a particular field of XML processing. Apart from interesting rather than useful examples of XML documents, such as the Bible in XML (Fields, 1996), Shakespeare's plays (Bosak, 1997), classic novels in XML (Wendover, 2001) etc., the most common types of tested XML data are usually XML exports of various databases, such as *IMDb* (IMDb, 2008) database of movies and actors, *FreeDB* (FreeDB, 2008) database of musical CDs, *DBLP* (DBLP, 2008) database of scientific papers, *Medical Subject Headings* (MeSH, 2008) database of medical terms, *SIGMOD Record* in XML (SIGMOD, 2007) etc. or repositories of real-world XML data provided from various resources, such as project *INEX* (INEX, 2007), project *Ibiblio* (Ibiblio, 2008), *Open Directory Project* (Open Directory, 2004) etc. There also exist examples of rather special XML data, such as human genes (H-invDB, 2007), protein sequences (UniProt, 2008), RNAs (RNAdb, 2005), astronomical NASA data (XDR, 2002), linguistic trees in XML (Treebank, 1999) etc., having very uncommon structure and, hence, requiring special processing. Some of these collections were not originally created in XML format, but for the purpose of XML benchmarking they were later converted and stored in appropriate repositories, such as (XDR, 2002).

Since all these examples of XML data collections are provided without respective XML queries, XSL transformations or any other operations, they cannot be considered as true XML benchmarks.

Benchmarking Projects for XML Parsers and Validators

The first applications necessary for XML data processing are XML parsers and XML validators. Their key aim is to check the correctness of the input data, i.e. their conformance to either W3C recommendations or respective XML schemes. Hence, the benchmarks usually involve sets of both correct and incorrect data and the goal is to test whether the application being tested recognizes them correctly.

XML Conformance Test Suites

The W3C consortium has naturally provided so-called *XML Conformance Test Suites* (Martinez et al., 2008) – a set of metrics to determine how

well a particular implementation conforms to *W3C XML 1.0 (Second Edition) Recommendation*, *Extensible Markup Language (XML) 1.0 (Third Edition)*, *Extensible Markup Language (XML) 1.1 (First Edition)* and *Namespaces in XML 1.1*. It consists of a set of 2000 XML documents which can be divided into two basic types – *binary tests* and *output tests*.

Binary tests contain a set of documents from one of the following categories: valid documents, invalid documents, non-well-formed documents, well-formed errors tied to external entity and documents with optional errors. Depending on the category, the tested parser must either accept or reject the document correctly (therefore, the tests are called binary). The expected behaviour naturally differs depending on whether the tested parser is validating or non-validating.

On the other hand, the output tests determine whether the respective applications report information as required by the recommendation. Again, validating processors are required to report more information than non-validating ones.

Performance Evaluation of XML Parsers

With the arrival of various types of XML parsers as well as various implementations of parsers of the same type, it became necessary to evaluate their performance. Currently, we can distinguish so-called *event-driven parsers* and *object-model parsers*. The former ones read the document and, while reading, they return the respective structure; whereas, the latter parsers read the document and build it completely in memory. The former ones can be further divided into *push-parsers* and *pull-parsers* which differentiate in the ability to influence the reading process. In the case of push-parsers, the reading cannot be influenced; whereas pull-parsers read the next data only if they are "asked" to. Combinations of various parsers have also been considered.

Currently, there are numerous projects which

evaluate efficiency of various subsets of known XML parsers (such as, e.g., VTD-XML, 2003; Cooper, 1999; Farwick et al., 2007; Marcus, 1999; Oren, 2002), comparing either the same types of parsers or different approaches. But, they all use either a selected set of real-world XML data or a set of synthetic documents created specifically for the purpose of the benchmark. Although the authors usually make these documents available, there seems to be no true benchmarking project which enables the analysis of all the various aspects of the different types of XML parsers.

There are also various implementations of systems which enable to benchmark a selected subset of parsers (Chilingaryan, 2004; Kumar, 2002; Sosnoski, 2002). The sets of the supported applications can usually be extended; also, the data sets used for their comparison are available and often extensible. However, the problem is that these projects are not true benchmarking project which define a set of experiments testing various aspects and especially bottlenecks of XML parsing and validating.

Benchmarking Projects for XML Data Management Systems and Query Engines

Probably the biggest set of benchmarks contains projects which focus on testing XML data management systems and query engines. The aim of the benchmarks is to analyze the versatility of these tools, i.e. the number of query constructs they are able to process successfully and how efficiently they are processed. These benchmarks can be further classified on the basis of various aspects, such as the type of query language, the number of users (i.e. single user vs. multiple users), the type of the benchmark (i.e. application-level or micro-benchmarks) etc.

The authors of paper (Schmidt et al., 2001) have discussed and specified the set of challenges that a comprehensive benchmark should cover. These involve bulk loading (since at the time the paper

was published there were no recommended update operations), round-tripping (i.e. reconstruction of the original document and the price of loss-less storage), basic path traversals, casting, optional elements ordering, references, joins, construction of large results and full-text search. Most of these well-specified challenges are usually covered by the existing benchmarks.

Note that the W3C XML Query Working Group has proposed and maintains a set of so-called *XML Query Use Cases* (Chamberlin et al., 2007). But, the set of queries is not considered as a benchmark, but rather a set of examples illustrating important applications for an XML query language. On the other hand, the *XML Query Test Suite (XQTS 1.0.2)* (Rorke et al., 2007) contains over 15000 test cases, i.e. queries and expected results, which enable to test the interoperability of the W3C XML Query language. Hence, also in this case, the purpose is slightly different.

In the following text, we provide an overview of the eight best known representatives of true XML query benchmarking projects, i.e. XMark, XOO7, XMach-1, MBench, XBench, XPathMark, MemBeR and TPoX. In particular, we describe and compare their key characteristics, advantages and disadvantages.

XMark

The XML benchmarking project *XMark* (Busse, 2003) is currently one of the most popular and most commonly used XML benchmarks (Afanasiev et al., 2006). It involves a data generator called *xmlgen* which enables the creation of synthetic XML documents according to a fixed DTD of an Internet auction database. The key parameter of the required data is their size ranging from minimal document (having size of 1MB) to any arbitrary size limited only by the capacity of the particular system. The textual parts of the resulting XML documents are constructed from 17000 most frequently occurring words in Shakespeare's plays.

The XMark project also involves 20 XQuery queries which focus on various aspects of the language, such as, e.g., array look-ups ordering, casting, wildcard expressions, aggregations, references, constructors, joins, optional elements, user-defined functions, sorting etc.

Probably for the first time, the XMark benchmark has been used by its authors for analyzing the behaviour and performance of *Monet* XML framework (Schmidt et al., 2001).

X007 Benchmark

XML benchmark *XOO7* (Bressan et al., 2003) is an XML version of the original OO7 (Carey et al., 1993) benchmark for object-oriented database management systems (DBMS). Firstly, the original relational schema of OO7 was translated into the corresponding DTD using several author-defined mapping rules. The benchmark involves a generator called *genxml* which enables the generation of respective data sets on the basis of user-provided parameters of elements of the DTD. They influence the depth of the document tree (specified by the number of inclusions of a recursive element), fan-out (specified by the number of repetitions of two elements with allowed repeatable occurrence) or the amount of textual data (specified by the size in bytes of content of a textual and a mixed-content element). The authors propose three pre-defined types of data sets (small, medium and large) with pre-defined values of the parameters.

The XOO7 benchmark involves 23 XQuery queries divided into three categories – *relational queries* (involving joins, aggregation, sorting etc.), *document queries* (focussing on ordering of elements) and *navigational queries* (exploiting references and links).

Probably for the first time, the XOO7 benchmark has been used by its authors for analyzing and comparison of a semi-structured XML management system (XML MS) *Lore*, a native XML MS *Kweelt* and a commercial object-relational (OR) DBMS (see Li et al., 2001) and later

for comparison of four XML processing tools – Lore, Kweelt, an XML-enabled DBMS *XENA* and a commercial XPath implementation (see Nambiar et al., 2002).

XML Data Management Benchmark (XMach-1)

XML benchmark *XMach-1* (Bohme et al., 2001) differs from the previously mentioned ones especially in the fact that it is a multi-user benchmark. In the previous cases, the authors assumed that the tested XML MSs were run on the same machine, so that network characteristics, communication costs, numbers of users were of no importance. In this case, the benchmark is based on the idea of a web application, i.e. a typical use case of XML MS. It consists of four parts – an XML database, application servers, loaders and browser clients. The application servers support processing of XML documents and interact with the backend XML database. The loaders load and delete various XML data into/from the database via the application servers. And it is assumed that browser clients will query and retrieve the stored XML data. Therefore, the tested systems are represented via the application servers and the database. The query and upload workload is generated by virtual browsers and loaders whose number is arbitrary.

Similarly to the previous cases, the benchmark involves a data generator and a set of XQuery queries. The data generator can prepare (and store into the database) either schema-less documents or documents conforming to a pre-defined DTD. However, the schema-less documents differ only in the fact that the DTD is not maintained in the database. Also, multiple data collections can be generated, but they differ only in the element/attributes names. Similarly to the previous cases, a user can specify various characteristics of the data, such as the number of documents per a DTD, number of occurrences of four elements of the DTD, probability of occurrence of phrases and links, number of words in a sentence etc. The text values are generated from 10000 most common English words distributed according to Zipf's law.

The benchmark queries involve 8 XQuery queries and, for the first time, also 3 data manipulation operations. The queries involve similar cases as in the previous cases, such as reconstruction of the whole document, text retrieval query, navigation through document tree, counting, sorting, joining etc. The data manipulation operations involve inserting a document into the database, deleting a document from the database and updating information in the directory entry of stored documents.

The authors' experience with the benchmark and performance results of comparison of two commercial native XML DBMSs and one relational DBMS are described in paper (Bohme et al., 2003). Later, the authors of paper (Lu et al., 2005) used both XMark and XMach-1 and analyzed the performance of nine different implementations of XML DBMS involving three native and six relational approaches.

Note that since the three benchmarks, i.e. XMark, XOO7 and XMach-1, appeared almost at the same time, naturally their properties were also soon compared and contrasted (Nambiar et al., 2001). The paper focuses mainly on comparison of similar and distinct types of queries of the benchmarks with regard to generally acknowledged desired properties of an XML query language.

The Michigan Benchmark (MBench)

Contrary to the previously described *application-level* benchmarks, the *Michigan Benchmark* (Runapongsa et al., 2006) (in literature often denoted as *MBench*) is a *micro-benchmark*. The basic ideas are very similar – both types of benchmarks consist of a data set and related queries – but an application benchmark is created to help users to compare and contrast various applications, whereas a micro-benchmark should be used to evaluate the performance of a single system in various situations.

Since the aim of the benchmark is different, the data set and the set of queries also strongly differ. The data set is generated according to a synthetic XSD (XML schema definition) which consists of an element having 7 attributes (carrying information about its position in the document tree), a recursive sub-element with arbitrary occurrence and an optional element. Words of text are created synthetically and then distributed according to Zipf's law so that its characteristics are similar to a natural language and not biased by a particular language. Similarly to XMark, the generated data can be influenced by the scaling factor which expresses the size of the data.

The set of queries contains 46 queries and 7 update operations. They can be further divided into queries which reconstruct a selected structure, selection queries, join queries and aggregation queries, whereas within the groups they differ only slightly, for instance at the level of selectivity, the type of ordering, the complexity of returned data etc. The paper only describes the queries and, hence, they can be specified in any language. Nevertheless, the authors provide their SQL and XPath formulation.

Paper (Runapongsa et al., 2006) also describes performance results of the benchmark applied on two XML DBMSs and one commercial OR DBMS.

Similarly to the previous case, the four described benchmarks, i.e. XMark, XOO7, XMach-1 and MBench, were compared in paper (Bohme et al., 2003). It focuses mainly on the type of data the benchmarks include, number of involved users and servers, number of documents, schemes and element types, number of queries etc. The aim of the authors is to help users choose the most appropriate of the benchmarks, but the analysis is slightly, though naturally, biased by the fact that it is written by authors of XMach-1.

XBench

XML benchmark *XBench* (Yao et al., 2003) is denoted as a *family of benchmarks* since the authors distinguish four classes of XML applications with different requirements – text-centric/single document (TC/SD), text-centric/multiple documents (TC/MD), data-centric/single document (DC/SD) and data-centric/multiple documents (DC/MD).

For the purpose of generating XML data, the authors provide their own generator which is built on top of the ToXgene data generator (Barbosa et al., 2002) and enables the size of the generated documents to be modified – small (10MB), normal (100MB), large (1GB) and huge (10GB). The structure of the data in each of the four types of applications is based on analysis of several selected real-world XML data or XML database exports, their generalization and derivation of synthetic data on the basis of the results.

The set of XQuery queries covers functionality captured by W3C XML Query Use Cases. Similarly to the previous case the queries are specified abstractly and their XQuery specification is available. All together the authors provide 20 queries, but not all of them can be used in all the four applications. The queries involve similar cases and constructs as in the previous cases, such as exact matching ordering, function application, quantification, path expressions, joins, references, casting etc.

Using the benchmark, the authors have also performed corresponding experimental testing on three commercial DBMSs (Yao et al., 2004).

Similarly to the previous cases, paper (Manegold, 2008) provides an analysis of the five described benchmarks, that is: XMark, XOO7, XMach-1, MBench and XBench, applied on six XQuery processors.

On the other hand, paper (Afanasiev et al., 2006) analyzes the five benchmarks, but with a different aim – not to analyze the benchmarked systems, but the benchmarks themselves. Using four selected XQuery engines, the authors try to answer the following questions: How are the benchmarks currently used? What do the benchmarks measure? And what can we learn from these benchmarks? The key findings and conclusions are very interesting. In particular, the authors have discovered that only 1/3 of papers on XQuery processing use a kind of benchmark which is probably caused by the fact that 38% of benchmark queries are incorrect or outdated. In addition, 29% of the queries are XPath 1.0 queries, 61% are XPath 2.0 queries and only 10% cannot be expressed in XPath. The most popular benchmark seems to be the XMark benchmark.

It is important to note that the results of both of the papers were obtained using the project *XCheck* (Franceschet et al., 2006). It is a platform which enables the execution of multiple benchmarks on multiple query engines and helps to analyze and compare the results. The benchmarks are specified in input documents that describe the queries, the engines and the documents which should be used together. The engines can be easily added using wrapping adapters. Naturally, this is not the only representative of such an application. A very similar, but older platform facilitating XML benchmarking is system BumbleBee (BumbleBee, 2003).

XPathMark

The XML benchmark *XPathMark* (Franceschet, 2005) was designed for XML documents generated using XMark benchmark, but having the queries expressed in XPath 1.0. The benchmark has two parts consisting of a default document and a set of related queries. The former contains an XML document generated using XMark and a set of 47 XPath queries that focus on axes, node tests, Boolean operators, references and functions. The latter contains an XML document taken from a book on XML, whereas the related 12 queries focus on comments, processing instructions, namespaces and language attributes.

Paper (Franceschet, 2005) also involves results of experimental testing of two XML engines —*Saxon* and *Galax*—using XPathMark.

MemBeR:XQuery Micro-Benchmark Repository

From the above overview of the benchmarks and their various features, it is obvious that a single fixed set of queries is insufficient for the testing of various aspects of applications. Hence, the main aim of the *MemBeR repository* (Afanasiev et al., 2005) of micro-benchmarks is to allow users to add new data sets and/or queries for specific performance assessment tasks. The authors focus particularly on micro benchmarks, because of their scarcity (from the above-described best-known representatives only the MBench benchmark can be considered as a true micro-benchmark suite) and the huge amount of XML query features which need to be tested from various perspectives.

The repository has a predefined structure involving XML documents and their parameters, XML queries and their parameters, experiments and their parameters (i.e. related documents and/or queries), micro-benchmarks (i.e. sets of experiments) and micro-benchmark result sets. A new micro-benchmark or a new result set must be specified as an XML document conforming to a pre-defined DTD which describes all the related characteristics.

Currently, the repository contains three categories of benchmarks – XPath, query stability and XQuery. The benchmarks can be further classified (Afanasiev et al., 2005) into performance, consumption, correctness and completeness benchmarks on the basis of the resulting metric, type of scalability (data/query), usage of schema, query processing scenarios (e.g. persistent database, streaming etc.), query language and tested language feature.

One of the micro-benchmarks has been used in paper (Manolescu et al., 2006) for a very detailed analysis of four constructs of XQuery—XPath navigation, XPath predicates, XQuery FLWORs and XQuery node constructions—in six best-known freely available systems such as, *eXist*, Galax, MonetDB etc.

Transaction Processing over XML (TPoX)

Project *TPoX* (Nicola et al., 2007) seems to be the most recent XML query benchmark. It is an application-level benchmark simulating a financial multi-user application scenario based on the authors' real-world experience. In contrast to most of the previous cases, it does not focus on XQuery processing, but rather on other performance-relevant database features such as logging, indexing, schema validation, update operations, concurrency control, transaction processing etc. The main idea and architecture of the project are very similar to those of the XMach-1 project. The main differences are that the data set is data-centric (XMach-1 contains document-centric documents), the number of documents is several times higher than in XMach-1 and while XMach-1 enables to generate multiple synthetic DTDs, TPoX involves a single XSD consisting of multiple related subschemes all together describing the financial application.

The documents in the data set are again generated using the ToXgene data generator according to the XSD. The application can be scaled from extra small (XS) representing 3.6 millions of documents (approximately 10GB of data) and 10 users to extra-extra large representing 360 billions of documents (approximately 1PB of data) and 1 million users.

The operations over the database are divided into two stages. Stage 1 performs concurrent inserts, whereas stage 2 performs a multi-user read/write workload consisting of 70% of queries and 30% of updates. The operations are divided into 17 real-world transactions which are randomly submitted by Java threads, each representing a single user. Since most of the features of the system can be controlled via parameters, it can be even set to query-only, single-user, single-document system and, hence, compared with the other benchmarks.

Paper (Nicola et al., 2007) describes not only the TPoX project itself, but also the authors' first experience with applying the benchmark on DB2 database and its XML support.

For better clarity, we conclude this section with an overview of the main characteristics of the existing XML query benchmarks as listed in Table 1. As we have mentioned, there are also papers which compare and contrast various subsets of the benchmarks in more detail. Hence, we do not repeat the information in this paper and refer an interested reader to them.

Table 1. Main characteristics of XML query benchmarks

	XMark	XOO7	XMach-1	MBench	XBench	XPathMark	TPoX
Type of benchmark	Application-level	Application-level	Application-level	Micro	Application-level	Application-level	Application-level
Number of users	Single	Single	Multiple	Single	Single	Single	Multiple
Number of applications	1	1	1	1	4	1	1 but complex
Documents in data set	Single	Single	Multiple	Single	Single/ multiple	Single	Multiple
Data generator	✓	✓	✓	✓	✓	✓	✓
Key parameters	Size	Depth, fan-out, size of textual data	Number of documents / elements / words in a sentence, probability of phrases / links	Size	Size	Size	Size + number of users
Default data set	Single 100MB document	3 documents (small, medium, large) with pre-defined parameters	4 data sets of 10000 / 100000 / 1000000 / 10000000 documents	Single document with 728000 nodes	Small (10MB) / normal (100MB) / large (1GB) / huge (10GB) document	1 XMark document and 1 sample document from a book	XS (3.6 millions of documents, 10 users), S, M, L, XL, XXL (360 billions of documents, 1 million users)
Schema of documents	DTD of an Internet auction database	DTD derived from OO7 relational schema	DTD of an document having chapters, paragraphs and sections	DTD / XSD of the recursive element	DTD / XSD	DTD	XSD
Number of schemes	1	1	Multiple	9	1	2	1 consisting of multiple
Number of queries	20	23	8	49	19, 17, 14, 16	47 + 12	7
Query language	XQuery	XQuery	XQuery	SQL, XPath	XQuery	XPath	XQuery
Number of update queries	0	0	3	7	0	0	10

And, finally, Table 2 provides an overview of papers which describe results of analyses of testing various systems using subsets of the benchmarks. The papers usually not only analyze the systems being tested, but they also compare and contrast features of the benchmarks.

The table depicts a natural progress in papers dealing with exploitation and comparison of existing approaches. Firstly, there are papers involving tests of various selected implementations using a single, new benchmark. Later, papers emerge which perform the testing using multiple benchmarks and, hence, compare their features. As we can see, the biggest subset of compared benchmarks involves XMark, XOO7, XMach-1, MBench and XBench. For the three newest benchmarks, i.e. XPathMark, MemBerR micro benchmarks and TPoX, the respective comparison does not yet exist.

Other XML Benchmarking Projects

Since the key aspects of XML processing are undoubtedly parsing, validating and querying,

most of the existing benchmarking projects focus mainly on them. But, there are also other popular and useful XML technologies, such as, e.g. XSL transformations (Clark, 1999) and, hence, there occur also benchmarks determined for other purposes, though their number is surprisingly low or the only existing representatives are quite dated and, hence, obsolete (e.g. the XSLTMark (Kuznetsov et al., 2000) benchmark for XSLT).

From one point of view this may be caused by the fact that most of other technologies, such as, e.g., XSLT, XPointer (DeRose et al., 2002), XLink (DeRose et al., 2001) etc., are based on one of the basic ones, mostly XPath queries. Thus, an argument against new special benchmarking projects may be that projects for benchmarking XML queries in general are sufficient enough. But, on the other hand, the exploitation of, for instance, XPath in XSL can be very different from typical exploitation in XML DBMS. And, in addition, there are important aspects of XSL transformations other than the path queries which influence their correctness and efficiency. Furthermore, if we consider even more special operations on

Table 2. Subsets of benchmarks used for testing various systems

	XMark	XOO7	XMach-1	MBench	XBench	XPathMark	MemBeR	TPoX
Schmidt et al., 2001	✓	✗	✗	✗	✗	✗	✗	✗
Li et al., 2001; Nambiar et al., 2002	✗	✓	✗	✗	✗	✗	✗	✗
Bohme et al., 2003	✗	✗	✓	✗	✗	✗	✗	✗
Lu et al., 2005	✓	✗	✓	✗	✗	✗	✗	✗
Nambiar et al., 2001	✓	✓	✓	✗	✗	✗	✗	✗
Runapongsa et al., 2006	✗	✗	✗	✓	✗	✗	✗	✗
Bohme et al., 2003	✓	✓	✓	✓	✗	✗	✗	✗
Yao et al., 2004	✗	✗	✗	✗	✓	✗	✗	✗
Afanasiev et al., 2006; Manegold, 2008	✓	✓	✓	✓	✓	✗	✗	✗
Franceschet, 2005	✗	✗	✗	✗	✗	✓	✗	✗
Manolescu et al., 2006	✗	✗	✗	✗	✗	✗	✓	✗
Nicola et al., 2007	✗	✗	✗	✗	✗	✗	✗	✓

XML data, such as, e.g., XML compressing, the respective benchmark may deal with features which are for other types of XML processing marginal. Hence, the argument for special benchmarks seems to be much stronger. However, the number of these special purpose benchmarks is still low – it is difficult to find at least a single representative for each of the areas.

On the other hand, there are XML technologies that have become popular only recently and, consequently, their benchmarking projects are relatively rare. A representative of this situation is XML updating. As we can see in Table 1, some of the existing query benchmarks involve few update operations, but a true XML update benchmarking project has been proposed only recently (Phan et al., 2008).

SUMMARY

We can sum up the state of the art of existing XML benchmarking projects with the following natural, but important findings:

- Probably the most typical source of benchmarking XML data are repositories with fixed, usually real-world XML data. Their two main disadvantages are that the real-world XML data are usually too simple to cover all possible XML constructs, and they are not accompanied by respective operations, e.g., queries, updates, transformations etc.

- Since parsing and validating are two most important basic operations with XML data, the W3C consortium has defined appropriate conformance test suites which enable the testing of their correct behaviour. Hence, this area of benchmarks is well defined.

- While the conformance to W3C specifications is a natural and expected feature of XML parsers and validators, the key aspect of users' interest is their efficiency. Although

there exist several papers and projects dealing with this topic, there seems to be no true benchmark involving testing data sets and queries that would cover all or, at least, the key influencing aspects.

- The second key operation on XML data is undoubtedly querying. Not only is it the way to access stored data using various approaches, but path queries are an important part of various other XML technologies, such as XSLT, XPointer, XLink etc. Hence, the related benchmarks form the most important subset of all related benchmarking projects.

- The authors of the existing query benchmarks tried to address as many aspects of the related language (e.g. XQuery, XPath etc.) as possible. But since most of the benchmarks originated at the time when specifications of XML query languages were as yet unfinished, most of them soon became obsolete. Either the syntax of queries was no longer correct, or the respective languages now support plenty of other, at that time unknown, constructs.

- Most of the query benchmarks naturally focus on the XQuery language which involves the XPath query language. But, probably none of the benchmarks is able to test all the respective aspects. Also, there seems to be no benchmark which focuses on differences of XPath 1.0 and XPath 2.0.

- Although all the benchmarking projects involve a kind of data generator, the most popular ones seem to be those which are of simple usage (e.g. XMark), i.e. having only few parameters to specify. On the other hand, these benchmarks usually provide only very simple data, of one special type and complexity.

- In addition, most of the benchmarks are for query-only, single-user and single-document. There is only one benchmark (XBench) which takes into account several possible scenarios of applications (single vs. multiple documents and data-centric vs. document-centric documents), but it is a single-user benchmark. There are two benchmarks (XMach-1 and TPoX) which are multi-user, but, at the same time, the number of related queries is low and the data sets are quite simple.

- In general, the area of query benchmarks is relatively wide and the projects usually try to cover the key query operations. But if we consider other XML technologies which involve path queries, the typical usage can strongly differ. Hence, these technologies require special treatment and special benchmarking projects. Surprisingly, in these areas, the number of respective benchmarks is surprisingly low. Mostly, no appropriate benchmarking project exists.

OPEN ISSUES

Although each of the existing approaches contributes certain interesting ideas and optimizations, there is still room for possible future improvements. We describe and discuss them in this section.

General Requirements for Benchmarks

As mentioned in (Bohme et al., 2001), the recommended requirements for database benchmarks are that they should be domain-specific, relevant (measuring the performance of typical operations for the respective domain), portable to different platforms, scalable (applicable to small and large computer systems) and simple. But, for the purpose of XML technologies, not all of these requirements are necessary.

Portability and scalability are natural requirements which do not restrict the set of future users except for those using a selected hardware and/or operating system. Simplicity seems to be an important requirement too, although it may be sometimes be acquired only at the cost of restricted functionally. Nevertheless, as we have already mentioned, currently the most exploited benchmark seems to be XMark which involves only a fixed set of XML queries and the only parameter of the data is their size in Bytes. It confirms the importance of this requirement and indicates that since the researchers have already spent plenty of time proposing, improving and implementing their approach, they do not want to bother with a complicated benchmark system.

On the other hand, the question of domain-specificity and related relevancy is arguable. Since XML technologies have currently plenty of usages and almost every day new ones emerge, it is difficult if not impossible, to specify a benchmark which covers all of them. But, on the other hand, a benchmark which is restricted only to a single special use case cannot be very useful. We can also specify more general types of XML applications, such as the classical data-centric and document-centric, but their characteristics are still too general. Hence, a solution seems to be a versatile benchmarking project which can be highly parameterized and, at the same time, be extended to novel characteristics. On the other hand, it should involve an extensible set of pre-defined settings of the parameters which characterize particular applications.

More Sophisticated Data Generator

A natural first step towards obtaining the versatile XML benchmark is to exploit a more sophisticated data generator. The existing benchmarks use either a simple data generator, or rather, a modifier of the stored data that supports only a simple set of parameters. Sometimes they are built on top of a more complex data generator (the ToXgene generator seems to be the most popular one), but most of its characteristics are then fixed due to the fixed set of related XML queries. The generators usually deal with marginal problems such as where to get the textual data or element/attribute names to achieve as natural a result as possible; whereas, the set of characteristics which influence the structure or semantics of the data is usually trivial. For some applications (such as XML full-text operations or XML compression), it may be that the content of textual data is important, but for most of the techniques related to XML querying, these aspects are of marginal importance, whereas the structure and semantics of the data are crucial.

The structure of the data is represented by the structure and complexity of trees of XML documents or graphs of XML schemes which consist of multiple types of nodes and edges representing the relationships among them. Then the W3C recommendations specify the allowed relationships, i.e. positions of the nodes within the tree. On the other hand, the semantics of the data is specified mostly by data types, unique/key/foreign key constraints and related functional dependencies. All of these characteristics (i.e. their amount, position and complexity) can be specified by a user and, hence, the respective system can generate any kind of data. The basic characteristics of XML documents can result from characteristics analyzed in existing statistical analyses of real-world XML data (Mlynkova et al., 2006) such as, e.g., the amount and size (in bytes) of XML documents, depth of XML documents, fan-out of elements (i.e. the number of subelements and attributes), percentage of various XML constructs (such as mixed-content elements, attributes etc.) etc. More complex characteristics can be specified, such as the statistical distribution a selected aspect should have (e.g. the depth of output documents).

But, as we have mentioned, this idea is at odds with the requirement of simplicity of benchmarks, because it requires plenty of user interaction. Nevertheless, this problem can easily be solved using predefined settings of parameters which specify various applications. Furthermore, such information can be extracted from statistical analyses of real world XML data. Assuming that the set is extensible and publicly available, each user can either exploit an existing data set or specify own types of data on which the particular system was tested. Moreover, according to the parameters, a data set with the same characteristics can be generated again and, hence, a new approach can easily be compared with existing ones.

Schema Generator

A natural requirement for a generator of XML documents is to provide also the respective XML schema of the resulting data or their selected subset. This problem can be viewed from two different perspectives depending on the order of generating the data.

If the generator first creates XML documents, we can exploit and/or utilize techniques for automatic inference of an XML schema from a given set of XML documents (e.g. Vosta et al., 2008). These approaches usually start with a schema that accepts exactly the given XML documents and they generalize it using various rules (such as, e.g., "if there are more than three occurrences of an element, it is probable that it can occur an arbitrary number of times"). Since there are multiple possibilities for how to define such rules, they can be restricted by user-specified parameters as well. Furthermore, if we consider the XML Schema language which involves plenty of "syntactic sugar", i.e. sets of constructs which enable the specification of the same situation in various ways (such as, e.g., references vs. inheritance), we discover another large area of data characteristics that can be specified by a user.

On the other hand, if the generator first generates (or obtains on input) the XML schema, the characteristics of the respective instances (i.e. XML documents) are quite restricted. However, an XML schema naturally involves vague specification of the document structure – extensive examples can be * operator or recursion which allow infinitely wide or deep XML documents.

Hence, a user can specify these characteristics more precisely. A similar approach has already been exploited in the ToXgene generator, where the input XSD together with a predefined set of annotations specifies the demanded XML data. On the other hand, the annotations either only express the data characteristics more precisely (e.g. maximum length of a text value of an element, minimum and maximum value of a numeric data type etc.) or they express data features which cannot be expressed in XML schema language (e.g. the probability distributions of various numeric values – numbers of occurrences, lengths etc.). Hence, in fact, the system simply enables the schema of the target documents to be specified more precisely. In some situations, this exact specification may be useful, but for the purpose of benchmarking, this system requires information that is too precise and, hence, not user-friendly.

Similarly to the previous case, since the amount of input parameters of the data may be quite high in both cases, there should exist respective predefined settings which characterize real-world XML data or various reasonable testing sets.

Query Generator

A natural third step of data generation is the generation of XML queries. All the described and probably all the existing works involve a fixed set of queries. The problem is that a fixed set of queries highly restricts the data sets, since, naturally, the queries are expected to query over the data we are provided with and return a reasonably complex result. But, similarly to the previous case, we may assume that a user knows what characteristics the queries over the tested system should have, but their manual creation is again quite a demanding task. Hence, a system, that is able to generate a set of queries with the respective characteristics would, undoubtedly, be useful.

We can again find plenty of characteristics that a query can have. Apart from the constructs that can be used in the query (e.g. axes, predicates, con-

structors, update operations etc.), we can specify the kind of data that the query should access (e.g. attributes, keys and foreign keys, mixed-content elements, recursive elements etc.), where the data are located (e.g. at what levels), the amount of data that is required (e.g. elements with specified structure) etc. In general, this problem seems to be the most complex, least explored and most challenging open issue of XML benchmarking.

Theoretic Study of Data Characteristics

All three types of the previously specified data generators have one thing in common. If we assume that our aim is to support as much data characteristics as possible, we can find out that various subsets of the data are correlated, i.e. influence each other and, hence, not all possible settings are available. Simple examples can include the length of attribute values and/or element contents vs. size of the document in Bytes or number of elements vs. size of the document in Bytes. More complex examples may include the depth of the document vs. element fan-out vs. size of the document in Bytes. A theoretic study of the data characteristics, their classification and, in particular, a discussion of how they mutually influence each other would be a very useful source of information.

For instance, the MemBeR XML generator (Afanasiev et al., 2005) solves this problem using brute force and does not allow the specifying of depth, fan-out and size simultaneously. But, naturally, this solution seems to be too restrictive.

Analysis and Visualization of the Resulting Data

An interesting part of a benchmarking project closely related to data generators may be a statistical analyzer of the resulting synthetic data. If we assume that a user specifies general characteristics of the data, he/she may be interested in the exact metrics of the result. And, on the other hand, sometimes it may be useful to include a subset of real-world XML data and, consequently, the analysis of their complexity becomes even more crucial. As we have outlined in the introduction, without knowing the structure of the data, it is difficult to conclude whether the tested system would be useful for the future user.

A related logical part of the analyzer may be also a data visualizer designed particularly for the purpose of XML data. Most of the existing implementations which involve a kind of XML visualization support only a simple tree structure. For simple XML data such as small XML documents and non-recursive XML schemes with a low number of shared elements, this may be sufficient. However, XML documents may be relatively large or they may be separated into a huge number of smaller documents, whereas XML schemes may involve a significant portion of recursion, complete subgraphs etc.(and statistical analyses show that in real-world data these situations are quite common (Mlynkova et al., 2006)). Hence, a sophisticated visualizer which is able to parse and display such complex kinds of data in the form of a graph may be a very useful tool. A similar problem has been solved in paper (Dokulil et al., 2008) which addresses the issue of visualisation of large RDF data.

Other Areas of Exploitation

The synthetic XML data (of all kinds) can be exploited for purposes other than benchmarking of different algorithms and their implementations. One of the most promising areas is undoubtedly that of e-learning. Automatically generated data can be used for the purpose of tests and quizzes, where a huge number of distinct examples with similar, pre-defined characteristics is necessary and their manual creation is a demanding process. This general idea can be easily exploited in XML technologies as well. A similar system is proposed

in paper (Azalov et al., 2003) which enables the generation of synthetic source codes.

CONCLUSION

The main goal of this paper was to describe and discuss the current state of the art and open issues of XML benchmarking projects, i.e. projects focussing on benchmarking of various XML processing tools such as XML parsers and validators, XML data management systems etc. Firstly, we have provided several motivating examples justifying the importance of XML benchmarking as a topic. Then, we have provided an overview and classification of the existing approaches and their features and summed up the key findings. And finally, we have discussed the corresponding open issues and their possible solutions.

Our aim was to show that XML benchmarking is an up-to-date problem. From the overview of the state of the art, we can see that even though there are interesting and inspiring approaches, there is still a variety of open problems which can and need to be solved or improved to enable the development of more informative benchmarking of XML processing tools and newly proposed methods.

ACKNOWLEDGMENT

This work was supported in part by the Czech Science Foundation (GACR), grant number 201/06/0756.

REFERENCES

Aboulnaga, A., Naughton, J. F., & Zhang, C. (2001). Generating synthetic complex-structured XML data. In *WebDB'01*, (pp. 79-84).

Afanasiev, L., Manolescu, I., & Michiels, P. (2005). MemBeR: A micro-benchmark repository for XQuery. In *XSym'05*, (pp. 144-161).

Afanasiev, L., & Marx, M. (2006). An analysis of the current XQuery benchmarks. In *ExpDB*, (pp. 9-20).

Azalov, P., & Zlatarova, F. (2003). SDG – A System for Synthetic Data Generation. In *ITCC*, (pp. 69 – 75).

Barbosa, D., Mendelzon, A. O., Keenleyside, J., & Lyons, K. A. (2002). ToXgene: A template-based data generator for XML. In *SIGMOD*, (p. 616).

Barbosa, D., Mignet, L., & P. Veltri (2005). Studying the XML Web: Gathering statistics from an XML sample. In *World Wide Web 8*(4), 413-438.

Berglund, A., Boag, S., Chamberlin, D., Fernandez, M. F., Kay, M., Robie, J., & Simeon, J. (2007). *XML path language (XPath) 2.0*. W3C. http://www.w3.org/TR/xpath20/

Bex, G. J., Neven, F., & Van den Bussche, J. (2004). DTDs versus XML Schema: A practical study. In *WebDB*, (pp. 79-84).

Biron, P. V., & Malhotra, A. (2004). *XML schema part 2: Datatypes (second edition)*. W3C. www.w3.org/TR/xmlschema-2/

Boag, S., Chamberlin, D., Fernandez, M. F., Florescu, D., Robie, J., & Simeon, J. (2007). *XQuery 1.0: An XML query language*. W3C. http://www.w3.org/TR/xquery/

Bohme, T., & Rahm, E. (2001). Benchmarking XML database systems: First experiences. In *HPTS'01*.

Bohme, T., & Rahm, E. (2001). XMach-1: A benchmark for XML data management. In *BTW'01*, (pp. 264-273).

Bohme, T., & Rahm, E. (2003). Multi-user evaluation of XML data management systems with XMach-1. In *LNCS 2590*, (pp. 148-158).

Bosak, J. (2007). *Jon Bosak's XML examples*. http://www.ibiblio.org/bosak/

Bray, T., Paoli, J., Sperberg-McQueen, C. M., Maler, E., & Yergeau, F. (2006). *Extensible markup language (XML) 1.0 (fourth edition)*. W3C. http://www.w3.org/TR/REC-xml/

Bressan, S., Lee, M.-L., Li, Y. G., Lacroix, Z., & Nambiar, U. (2003). The XOO7 benchmark. In *LNCS 2590*, (pp. 146-147).

BumbleBee (2003). Clarkware Consulting, Inc. and Hunter Digital Ventures, LLC. http://www.x-query.com/bumblebee/

Busse, R., Carey, M., Florescu, D., Kersten, M., Manolescu, I., Schmidt, A., & Waas, F. (2003). *XMark – An XML benchmarking project*. Centrum voor Wiskunde en Informatica (CWI), Amsterdam. http://www.xml-benchmark.org/

Carey, M. J., DeWitt, D. J., & Naughton, J. F. (1993). The OO7 benchmark. In *SIGMOD Record 22*(2), 12-21.

Chamberlin, D., Fankhauser, P., Florescu, D., Marchiori, M., & Robie, J. (2007). *XML Query use cases*. W3C. http://www.w3.org/TR/xquery-use-cases/

Chilingaryan, S. A. (2004). *XML benchmark*. http://xmlbench.sourceforge.net/

Clark, J. (1999). *XSL Transformations (XSLT) Version 1.0*. W3C. http://www.w3.org/TR/xslt

Clark, J., & DeRose, S. (1999). *XML path language (XPath) Version 1.0*. W3C. http://www.w3.org/TR/ xpath/

Cooper, C. (1999). *Benchmarking XML parsers*. XML.com. http://www.xml.com/pub/a/Benchmark/ article.html

DBLP (2008). *Digital Bibliography & Library Project*. http://dblp.uni-trier.de/

DeRose, S., Daniel, R., Grosso, P., Maler, E., Marsh, J., & Walsh, N. (2002). *XML pointer language (XPointer)*. W3C. http://www.w3.org/TR/xptr/

DeRose, S., Maler, E., & Orchard, D. (2001). *XML linking language (XLink) Version 1.0.* W3C. http://www.w3.org/TR/xlink/.

Dokulil, J., & Katreniakova, J. (2008). Visual Exploration of RDF Data. In *SOFSEM'08*, pages 672-683.

Farwick, M. & Hafner, M. (2007). *XML Parser Benchmarks: Part 1 & 2.* XML.com. http://www.xml.com/pub/a/2007/05/09/xml-parser-benchmarks-part-1.html. http://www.xml.com/pub/a/2007/05/16/xml-parser-benchmarks-part-2.html

Fields, M. (1996). *Mark Fields's Ebooks.* http://www.assortedthoughts.com/downloads.php

Franceschet, M. (2005). XPathMark – An XPath benchmark for XMark generated data. In *XSym'05*, pages 129-143.

Franceschet, M., Zimuel, E., Afanasiev, L., & Marx, M. (2006). *XCheck.* Informatics Institute, University of Amsterdam, The Netherlands. http://ilps.science.uva.nl/Resources/XCheck/

FreeDB (2008). http://www.freedb.org/

H-InvDB (2007). *Annotated Human Genes Database.* http://www.jbirc.aist.go.jp/hinv/

Ibiblio (2008). *The Public's Library and Digital Archive.* http://www.ibiblio.org/

IMDb (2008). *The Internet Movie Database.* http://www.imdb.com/

INEX (2007). *INitiative for the Evaluation of XML Retrieval.* http://inex.is.informatik.uni-duisburg.de/

Kumar, P. (2002). *XPB4J – XML Processing Benchmark for Java.* http://www.pankaj-k.net/xpb4j/

Kuznetsov, E., & Dolph, C. (2000). *XSLT Processor Benchmarks.* XML.com. http://www.xml.com/pub/a/2001/03/28/xsltmark/index.html

Li, Y. G., Bressan, S., Dobbie, G., Lacroix, Z., Lee, M. L., Nambiar, U., & Wadhwa, B. (2001). XOO7: Applying OO7 benchmark to XML query processing tool. In *CIKM*, (pp. 167-174).

Lu, H., Yu, J. X., Wang, G., Zheng, S., Jiang, H., Yu, G., & Zhou, A. (2005). What makes the differences: Benchmarking XML database implementations. In *ACM Trans. Inter. Tech. 5*(1), 154-194.

Manegold, S. (2008). An empirical evaluation of XQuery processors. In *Inf. Syst. 33*(2), 203–220.

Manolescu, I., Miachon, C., & Michiels, P. (2006). Towards micro-benchmarking XQuery. In *ExpDB*, (pp. 28–39).

Marcus, S. (1999). *Benchmarking XML Parsers on Solaris.* XML.com. http://www.xml.com/pub/a/1999/06/benchmark/solaris.html

Martinez, S. I., Grosso, P., & Walsh, N. (2008). *Extensible Markup Language (XML) Conformance Test Suites.* W3C. http://www.w3.org/XML/Test/

MeSH (2008). *Medical Subject Headings.* http://www.nlm.nih.gov/mesh/meshhome.html

Mlynkova, I., Toman, K., & Pokorny, J. (2006). Statistical analysis of real XML data collections. In *COMAD*, (pp. 20-31).

Nambiar, U., Lacroix, Z., Bressan, S., Lee, M.-L., & Li, Y. G. (2001). XML benchmarks put to the test. In *IIWAS*.

Nambiar, U., Lacroix, Z., Bressan, S., Lee, M.-L., & Li, Y. G. (2002). Efficient XML data management: An analysis. In *EC-WEB*, (pp. 87-98).

Nicola, M., Kogan, I., & Schiefer, B. (2007). An XML transaction processing benchmark. In *SIGMOD*, (pp. 937-948).

Open Directory Project (2004). http://rdf.dmoz.org/

Oren, Y. (2002). *SAX Parser benchmarks*. Source-Forge.net. http://piccolo.sourceforge.net/bench.html

Phan, B. V., & Pardede, E. (2008). Towards the Development of XML Benchmark for XML Updates. In *ITNG*, (pp. 500-505).

RNAdb (2005). http://research.imb.uq.edu.au/rnadb/

Rorke, M., Muthiah, K., Chennoju, R., Lu, Y., Behm, A., Montanez, C., Sharma, G., & Englich, F. (2007). *XML Query Test Suite*. W3C. http://www.w3.org/XML/Query/test-suite/

Runapongsa, K., Patel, J. M., Jagadish, H. V., Chen, Y., & Al-Khalifa, S. (2006). The Michigan benchmark: Towards XML query performance diagnostics. In *Inf. Syst. 31*(2), 73-97.

Runapongsa, K., Patel, J. M., Jagadish, H. V., Chen, Y., & Al-Khalifa, S. (2006) *The Michigan benchmark: Towards XML query performance diagnostics (extended version)*. http://www.eecs.umich.edu/db/mbench/mbench.pdf

Schmidt, A. R., Waas, F., Kersten, M. L., Florescu, D., Carey, M. J., Manolescu, I., & Busse, R. (2001). Why and how to benchmark XML databases. In *SIGMOD Record 30*(3), 27-32.

Schmidt, A. R., Waas, F., Kersten, M. L., Florescu, D., Manolescu, I., Carey, M. J., & Busse, R. (2001). *The XML Benchmarking Project*. Technical Report INS-R0103, CWI, Amsterdam, The Netherlands.

SIGMOD (2007). *SIGMOD Record in XML*. http://www.sigmod.org/record/xml/

Sosnoski, D. M. (2002). *XMLBench Document Model Benchmark*. http://www.sosnoski.com/opensrc/ xmlbench/index.html

Thompson, H. S., Beech, D., Maloney, M., & Mendelsohn, N. (2004). *XML Schema Part 1: Structures (Second Edition)*. W3C. www.w3.org/TR/xmlschema-1/

Treebank (1999). *The Penn Treebank Project*. http://www.cis.upenn.edu/~treebank/

UniProt (2008). *Universal Protein Resource*. http://www.ebi.uniprot.org/index.shtml

Vosta, O., Mlynkova, I., & Pokorny, J. (2008). Even an Ant Can Create an XSD. In *DASFAA*, (pp. 35-50).

VTD-XML (2003). *Benchmark report for version 2.0*. XimpleWare. http://www.ximpleware.com/2.0/ benchmark_2.0_indexing.html

Wendover, A. (2001). *Arthur's classic novels*. http://arthursclassicnovels.com/

XDR (2002). *XML data repository*. www.cs.washington.edu/research/xmldatasets/www/repository.html

Yao, B. B., Ozsu, M. T., & Keenleyside, J. (2003). XBench – A Family of Benchmarks for XML DBMSs. In *LNCS 2590*, (pp. 162-164).

Yao, B. B., Ozsu, M. T., & Khandelwal, N. (2004). XBench benchmark and performance testing of XML DBMSs. In *ICDE'04*, (pp. 621-632).

Compilation of References

Abadi, D., Ahmad. Y., & Balazinska, M. (2005). The Design of the Borealis Stream Processing Engine. In *CIDR*, (pp. 277-289).

Abadi, D., Carney, D., Cetintemel, U., Cherniack, M., Convey, C., Lee, S., Stonebraker, M., Tatbul, N., & Zdonik, S. (2003). Aurora: A New Model and Architecture for Data Stream Management. In *VLDB Journal 12*(2), 120–139.

Aboulnaga, A., Naughton, J. F., & Zhang, C. (2001). Generating Synthetic Complex-Structured XML Data. In *WebDB'01*, (pp. 79–84).

Achard, F. et al. (2001). XML, Bionformatics and data integration. In *Bioinformatics Review, 17*(2), 115-125.

Adali S. et al. (1998). A multi-similarity algebra. In *ACM SAC*, (pp. 402-413).

Aekaterinidis, I., & Triantafillou, P. (2005). Internet scale string attribute publish/subscribe data networks. In *CIKM*, (pp. 44-51).

Afanasiev, L., & Marx, M. (2006). An Analysis of the Current XQuery Benchmarks. In *ExpDB*, (pp. 9 – 20).

Afanasiev, L., Manolescu, I., & Michiels, P. (2005). MemBeR: A Micro-Benchmark Repository for XQuery. In *XSym'05*, (pp. 144-161).

Aggarwal, C. C. (2007). *Data Streams: Models and Algorithms (Advances in Database Systems)*, Springer.

Aggarwal, G., Bawa, M., Ganesan, P., Garcia-Mollina, H., Kenthapadi, K., Motwani, R., Srivatsava, U., Thomas, D., & Xu, Y. (2005). Two can keep a secret: A distributed architecture for secure database services. In *CIDR*, (pp. 186-199).

Aguilera, M. K., Strom, R.E, Sturman, D.C., Astley, M., & Chandra, T.D (1999). Matching events in a content-based subscription system. In *PODC*, (pp. 53-61).

Ahmedi, L. (2005). Making XPath reach for the Web-wide links. In *SAC*, (pp. 1714-1721).

Ahmedi, L., & Lausen, G. (2002). Ontology-based querying of linked XML documents. In *Semantic Web Workshop*.

Ahmedi, L., Marron, P., & Lausen, G. (2001). LDAP-based Ontology for Information Integration. In *Datenbanksysteme in Buro, Technik und Wissenschaft*, (pp. 207-214).

Alfarano, C. et al. (2005). The Biomolecular interaction network database and related tools 2005 update. In *Nucleic Acid Res.*, 33, 418—424.

Al-Khalifa, S., Jagadish, H. V., Patel, J. M., Wu, Y., Koudas, N., & Srivastava, D. (2002). Structural joins: A primitive for efficient xml query pattern matching. In *ICDE*, (p. 141).

Altinel, M., & Franklin, M. J. (2000). Efficient filtering of XML documents for selective dissemination of information. In *VLDB*, (pp. 53-64).

Amagasa, T., Yoshikawa, M., & Uemura, S. (2000). A Data model for temporal XML documents. In *DEXA*, (pp. 334–344).

Amer-Yahia, S. (2003). *Storage techniques and mapping schemas for XML*. Technical Report TD-5P4L7B, AT&T Labs-Research.

Amer-Yahia, S., Botev, C., & Shanmugasundaram, J. (2004). Texquery: A full-text search extension to xquery. In *WWW*, (pp. 583-594).

Amer-Yahia, S., Cho, SR., Lakshmanan, L. V. S., & Srivastava, D. (2001). Minimization of tree pattern queries. In *SIGMOD*, (pp. 497-508).

Amer-Yahia, S., Du, F., & Freire, J. (2004). A comprehensive solution to the XML-to-relational mapping problem. In *WIDM'04*, (pp. 31–38).

Amies, A. (2006) *Introduction of OWL Web Ontology Language for Medical and Bioscience Applications*. Medical computing. Retrieved January 15, 2008, from http://medicalcomputing.net/owl1.html

Andritsos, P., Fuxman, A., Kementsietsidis, A., Miller, R.-J., & Velegrakis, Y. (2004). Kanata: Adaptation and evolution in data sharing systems. In *SIGMOD Record 33*(4), 32-37.

Apache Software Foundation (2005). *Cocoon*. http://cocoon.apache.org

Apache Software Foundation (2005). *Xalan-Java*. http://xml.apache.org/xalan-j/index.html

Apache Software Foundation. *Ant. A Java-based build tool*. http://ant.apache.org/

Apache Software Foundation. *Cocoon*, http://cocoon.apache.org

Arasu, A., Babu, S., & Widom, J. (2006). The CQL continuous query language: Semantic foundations and query execution. In *VLDB J.*, *15*(2), 121–142.

Arenas, M., & Libkin, L. (2005). An Information-Theoretic Approach to Normal Forms for Relational and XML Data. *Journal of ACM 52*(2), 246-283.

Arion, A., Benzaken, V., Manolescu, I. & Papakonstantinou, Y. (2007a). Structured materialized views for XML queries. In *VLDB*, (pp. 87-98).

Arion, A., Bonifati, A., Manolescu, I., & Pugliese, A. (2007b). Xquec: A query-conscious compressed xml database. In *ACM Trans. Inter. Tech.*, *7*(2), 10.

Asonov, D. (2001). Private information retrieval: An overview and current trends. In *ECDPvA*, (pp. 889-894).

Avnur, R., & Hellerstein, J. M. (2000). Eddies: Continuously adaptive query processing. In *SIGMOD*, (pp. 261–272).

Axelrod, C. W. (2004). *Outsourcing information security*. Norwood, MA: Artech House.

Axyana software (2007). Qizx/open version 1.1p7, http://www.xfra.net/qizxopen/.

Azalov, P., & Zlatarova, F. (2003). SDG – A System for Synthetic Data Generation. In *ITCC*, (pp. 69 – 75).

Babcock, B., Babu, S., Motwani, R., & Widom, J. (2002). Models and Issues in Data Streams. In *PODS*, (pp. 1–16).

Babcock, B., Datar, M., & Motwani, R. (2003). Load Shedding Techniques for Data Stream Systems. In *MPDS*.

Babu, S., & Widom, J. (2001) Continuous Queries over Data Streams. In *SIGMOD Record 30*(3), 109-120.

Bader, G. (2008). *Pathguide: The pathway resource list*. http://www.pathguide.org

Bader, G. D., & Cary, M. P. (2005). *BioPAX – Biological Pathways Exchange Language Level 2*, Version 1.0. http://www.biopax.org/release/biopax-level2-documentation.pdf

Balmin, A., & Papakonstantinou, Y. (2005). Storing and querying XML data using denormalized relational databases. In *VLDB Journal 14*(1), 30-49.

Balmin, A., Papakonstantinou, Y., & Vianu, V. (2004). Incremental validation of XML documents. In *ACM Transactions on Database System*s 29(4), 710-751.

Banerjee, J., Chou, H-T., Garza, J. F., Kim, W., Woelk, D., Ballou, N., & Kim, H-J.(1987). Data Model Issues for Object-Oriented Applications. *ACM Transactions on Information Systems 5*(1), 3-26.

Baralis, E., Garza, P., Quintarelli, E. & Tanca, L. (2007). Answering xml queries by means of data summaries. In *ACM Trans. Inf. Syst. 25*(3), 10.

Barbosa, D., Leighton, G., & Smith, A. (2006). Efficient incremental validation of XML documents after composite updates. In *XSym*, (pp. 107-121).

Barbosa, D., Mendelzon, A. O., Keenleyside, J., & Lyons, K. A. (2002). ToXgene: A Template-Based Data Generator for XML. In *SIGMOD*, (p. 616).

Barbosa, D., Mendelzon, A., Libkin, L., & Mignet, L. (2004). Efficient incremental validation of XML documents. In *ICDE*, (pp. 671-682).

Barbosa, D., Mignet, L., & P. Veltri (2005). Studying the XML Web: Gathering Statistics from an XML Sample. In *World Wide Web 8*(4), 413 – 438.

Baril, X., & Bellahsène, Z. (2000). A view model for XML documents. In *OOIS*, (pp. 429-441).

Barutcuoglu, Z., Schapire, R. E., & Troyanskaya, O. G. (2006). Hierarchical multi-label prediction of gene function. In *Bioinformatics, 22*(7), 830-836.

Becker, O. (2003). Streaming transformations for xml-stx. In *XMIDX*, (pp. 83-88).

Benedikt, M., Fan, W., & Geerts, F. (2005). Xpath satisfiability in the presence of dtds. In *PODS*, (pp. 25-36).

Benjamins, V. R., Casanovas, P., Breuker, J., & Gangemi, A. (Eds.) (2005). *Law and the Semantic Web: Legal ontologies, methodologies, legal information retrieval, and applications*. Heidelberg, Germany: Springer-Verlag.

Berglund, A., Boag, S., Chamberlin, D., Fernández, M. F., Kay, M., Robie, J., & Siméon, J. (2007). XML Path Language (XPath) 2.0. *W3C Recommendation*. Retrieved January 26, 2008, from http://www.w3.org/TR/xpath20

Berners-Lee, T., Hendler, J., & Lassila, O. (2001). The Semantic Web. In *Scientific American 284*(5), (pp. 34-43).

Bertino, E. et al. (2005). A Framework for evaluating privacy preserving data mining algorithms. In *Data Mining and Knowledge Discovery, 11,* 121–154.

Bertino, E., Carminati, B., Ferrari, E., Thuraisingham, B., & Gupta, A. (2004). Selective and authentic third-party distribution of XML documents. In *IEEE Transactions on Knowledge and Data Engineering, 16*(10), 1263-1278.

Bertino, E., Ferrari, E., Paci, F., & Provenza, L.P. (2007). A system for securing push-based distribution of XML documents. In *International Journal of Information Security 6*(4), 255-284.

Bertino, E., Guerrini, G., Mesiti, M., & Tosetto, L. (2002). Evolving a set of DTDs according to a dynamic set of XML documents. In *EDBT Workshops*, (pp. 45-66).

Bettentrupp, R., Groppe, S., Groppe, J., Böttcher, S., & Gruenwald, L. (2006). A prototype for translating XSLT into XQuery. In *ICEIS*, (pp. 22-29).

Bex, G. J., Neven, F., & Van den Bussche, J. (2004). DTDs versus XML schema: A practical study. In *WebDB*, (pp. 79-84).

Beyer, K., Cochrane, R., Hvizdos, M., Josifovski, V., Kleewein, J., Lapis, G., Lohman, G., Lyle, R., Nicola, M., Özcan, F., Pirahesh, H., Seemann, N., Singh, A., Truong, T., Van der Linden, R., Vickery, B., Zhang, C., & Zhang, G. (2006). DB2 goes hybrid: Integrating native XML and XQuery with relational data and SQL. In *IBM Systems Journal 45*(2), 271-298.

Binh, N. T., Tjoa, A. M., & Mangisengi, O. (2001). Meta-Cube-X: An XML metadata foundation for interoperability search among Web warehouses. In: *DMDW*, (p. 8).

Bird, L., Goodchild, A., & T. Halpin (2000). Object Role Modelling and XML-Schema. In *ER,* (pp. 309-322).

Biron, P. V., & Malhotra, A. (2004). *XML Schema Part 2: Datatypes (Second Edition).* W3C Recommendation. www.w3.org/TR/xmlschema-2/

Blatt, R. J. (2000). Banking biological collections: data warehousing, data mining, and data dilemmas in genomics and global health policy. In *Community Genet., 3,* 204–211.

Boag, S., Chamberlin, D., Fernandez, M. F., Florescu, D., Robie, J., & Simeon, J. (2007). *XQuery 1.0: An XML Query Language.* W3C. http://www.w3.org/TR/xquery/.

Bohannon, B., Freire, J., Roy, P., & Simeon, J. (2002). From XML schema to relations: A cost-based approach to XML storage. In *ICDE,* (pp. 64-75).

Bohme, T., & Rahm, E. (2001). Benchmarking XML database systems – First experiences. In *HPTS'01.*

Bohme, T., & Rahm, E. (2001). XMach-1: A benchmark for XML data management. In *BTW'01,* (pp. 264–273).

Bohme, T., & Rahm, E. (2003). Multi-user evaluation of XML data management systems with XMach-1. In *LNCS 2590,* (pp. 148 – 158).

Boneh, D., Crescenzo, G., Ostrovsky, R., & Persiano, G. (2004). Public key encryption with keyword search. In *EUROCRYPT,* (pp. 506-522).

Boneh, D., Gentry, C., Lynn, B., & Shacham, H. (2003). Aggregate and verifiably encrypted sig¬natures from bilinear maps. In *EUROCRYPT,* (pp. 416-432).

Boobna, U., & de Rougemont, M. (2004). Correctors for XML data. In *XSym,* (pp. 97-111).

Bosak, J. (2007). *Jon Bosak's XML examples.* http://www.ibiblio.org/bosak/.

Bose, S., Fegaras, L., Levine, D., & Chaluvadi, V. (2003). A query algebra for fragmented XML stream data. In *DBPL,* (pp. 195-215).

Bostick, J. (2008). *Why you should outsource your database infrastructure.* Retrieved February 16, 2008, from http://www.sourcingmag.com/content/c070620a.asp

Botan, I., Fischer, P. M., Florescu, D., Kossmann, D., Kraska, T., & Tamosevicius, R. (2007). Extending XQuery with window functions. In *VLDB,* (pp. 75–86).

Böttcher, S. (2004). Testing intersection of XPath expressions under DTDs, database engineering and applications symposium, In *IDEAS,* (pp. 401-406).

Böttcher, S., & Steinmetz, R. (2007). Evaluating XPath queries on XML data streams. In *BNCOD,* (pp. 101-113).

Bouchou, B., & Ferrari Alves, M. H. (2003). Updates and incremental validation of XML documents. In *DBPL,* (pp. 216-232).

Bouchou, B., Cheriat, A., Ferrari, M. H., &. Savary, A. (2006). XML document correction: Incremental approach activated by schema validation. In *IDEAS,* (pp. 228-238).

Bouchou, B., Duarte D., Ferrari Alves, M. H., Laurent, D., & Musicante, M. A. (2004). Schema evolution for XML: A consistency-preserving approach. In *TMFCS,* (pp. 876-888).

Bouganim, L., & Pucheral, P. (2002). Chip-secured data access: Confidential data on untrusted servers. In *VLDB,* (pp. 131-142).

Bouganim, L., Ngoc, F. D., & Pucheral, P. (2004). Client-based access control management for XML documents. In *VLDB,* (pp. 84-95).

Bourret, R. (2005). Data versus documents. *XML and Databases.* Retrieved March 1, 2008. htp://www.rpbourret.com/xml/XMLAndDatabases.htm

Bourret, R. (2005). Going native: Use cases for native XML databases. *XML and Databases.* Retrieved March 1, 2008. http://www.rpbourret.com/xml/UseCases. htm#document

Bourret, R. (2007). *XML database products.* Available at http://www.rpbourret.com/xml/ XMLDatabaseProds. htm

Boussaïd, O., Ben Messaoud, R., Choquet, R., & Anthoard, S. (2006). X-Warehousing: An XML-based approach for warehousing complex data. In *ADBIS,* (pp. 39-54).

Boussaid, O., Bentayeb, F., Darmont, J., & Rabaseda, S. (2003). Vers l'entreposage des données complexes : structuration, intégration et analyse. In *Ingénierie des Systèmes d'Information 8*(5-6), 79-107.

Brantner, M., Kanne, C., Moerkotte, G. & Helmer, S. (2006). Algebraic optimization of nested XPath expressions. In *ICDE,* (pp. 128-130).

Bray, T., Paoli, J., Sperberg-McQueen, C. M., Maler, E., & Yergeau, F. (2006). *Extensible Markup Language (XML) 1.0 (Fourth Edition)*. W3C Recommendation. http://www.w3.org/TR/REC-xml/

Brazma, A. et al. (2001). Minimum information about a microarray experiment (MIAME)—toward standards for microarray data. In *Nature Genetics, 29,* 365–371.

Brazma, A. et al. (2006). Standards for systems biology. In *Nat. Rev. Genet., 7,* 593–605.

Bressan, S., Lee, M.-L., Li, Y. G., Lacroix, Z., & Nambiar, U. (2003). The XOO7 Benchmark. In *LNCS 2590,* (pp. 146–147).

Breuker, J., Tiscornia, D., Winkels, R., & Gangemi, A. (Eds.) (2004). In *Journal of Artificial Intelligence and Law 12*(4), Special issue on Ontologies for Law.

Brinkman, R., Doumen, J., & Jonker, W. (2004). Using secret sharing for searching in encrypted data. In *SDM,* (pp. 18-27).

Brinkman, R., Feng, L., Doumen, J., Hartel, P. H., & Jonker, W. (2004). Efficient tree search in encrypted data. In *Information System Security Journal 13,* 14-21.

Brinkman, R., Schoenmakers, B., Doumen, J., & Jonker, W. (2005). Experiments with queries over encrypted data using secret sharing. In *SDM,* (pp. 33-46).

Bruce, J. (2007). *Beyond tables: Dealing with the convergence of relational and XML data*. DevX, Jupitermedia Corporation. Retrieved March 1, 2008. http://www.devx.com/xml/Article/27975/1954

Bruno, N., Koudas, N., & Srivastava, D. (2002). Holistic twig joins: optimal xml pattern matching. In *SIGMOD,* (pp. 310-321).

BumbleBee (2003). Clarkware Consulting, Inc. and Hunter Digital Ventures, LLC. http://www.x-query.com/bumblebee/

Buneman, P., Khanna, S., Tajima, K., & Tan, W.-C. (2004) Archiving scientific data. In *ACM Transactions on Database Systems 29*(1), 2-42.

Burmester, M., Desmedt, Y., Wright, R. N., & Yasinsac, A. (2004). Accountable privacy. In *International Workshop on Security Protocols,* (pp. 83-95).

Busse, R., Carey, M., Florescu, D., Kersten, M., Manolescu, I., Schmidt, A., & Waas, F. (2003). *XMark – An XML benchmark project*. Centrum voor Wiskunde en Informatica (CWI), Amsterdam. http://www.xml-benchmark.org/

Busse, R., Carey, M., Florescu, D., Kersten, M., Manolescu, I., Schmidt, A., & Waas, F. (2003). *XMark – An XML Benchmarking project*. Centrum voor Wiskunde en Informatica (CWI), Amsterdam. http://www.xml-benchmark.org/.

Cabana, M. D., Rand C. S. N. R., Powe, C. S., Wu, A. W., Wilson, M. H., Abboud, P. C., & Rubin, H. R. (1999). Why don't physicians follow clinical practice guidelines? A framework for improvement. In *Journal of American Medical Association 282*(15), 1458-1465.

Callan, J., Smeaton, A., Beaulieu, M., Borlund, P., Brusilovsky, P., Chalmers, M., Lynch, C., Riedl, J., Smyth, B., Straccia, U., & Toms, E. (2003). *Personalization and recommender systems in digital libraries. Joint NSF-EU DELOS Working Group Report*. Sophia Antipolis, France: ERCIM. Retrieved January 15, 2008, from http://www.ercim.org/publication/ws-proceedings/Delos-NSF/Personalisation.pdf

Camillo, S. D., Heuser, C. A., & dos Santos Mello, R. (2003). Querying heterogeneous XML sources through a conceptual schema. In *ER,* (pp. 186-199).

Carey, M. J., Blevins, M., & Takacsi-Nagy, P. (2002). Integration, Web services style. In *IEEE Data Eng. Bull. 25* (4), 17-21.

Carey, M. J., DeWitt, D. J., & Naughton, J. F. (1993). The OO7 benchmark. In *SIGMOD Record 22*(2), 12–21.

Carminati, B., & Ferrari, E. (2006). Confidentiality enforcement for XML outsourced data. In *EDBT Workshop*, (pp. 234-249).

Carzaniga, A., Rosenblum, D. S., & Wolf, A. L. (2001). Design and evaluation of a wide-area event notification service. In *ACM Transactions on Computer Systems 9*(3), 332-383.

Casanovas, P., Biasiotti, M. A., Francesconi, E., & Sagri, M.T. (2007). *Proceedings of the Second ICAIL Legal Ontologies and Artificial Intelligence Techniques Workshop (LOAIT)*. IAAIL Workshop Series. Oisterwijk, The Netherlands: Wolf Legal Publishers.

Castano, S., Fugini, M. G., Martella, G., & Samarati, P. (1995). *Database security*. Boston: Addison-Wesley/ACM Press.

Castor. *The Castor Project*. Available at: http://www.castor.org/

Catania, B., Madalena, A., Vakali, A. (2005). XML document indexes: A classification. In *IEEE Internet Computing 9*(5), 64-71.

Catania, B., Maddalena, A., & Vakali, A. (2005). XML document indexes: A classification. In *IEEE Internet Computing 9*(5), 64-71.

Cathey, R., Beitzel, S., Jensen, E., Pilotto, A., & Grossman, D. (2004). Measuring the scalability of relationally mapped semistructured queries. In ITCC, 2, 219-223.

Cavalieri, F., Guerrini, G., & Mesiti, M. (2008). *Navigational path expression on XML schemas*. Technical report. University of Genova.

Cavalieri, F., Guerrini, G., & Mesiti, M. (2008). *XSchemaUpdate: Schema evolution and document adaptation*. Technical report. University of Genova.

CDuce. *CDuce*, http://www.cduce.org/

Cerami, E. G., et al. (2006). cPath: Open source software for collecting, storing, and querying biological pathways. In *BMC Bioinformatics, 7*, 497.

Ceri, S., Fraternali, P. & Paraboschi, S. (1999) Data-driven, one-to-one Web site generation for data-intensive applications. In *VLDB*, (pp. 615-626).

Chadwick, D. (2003). Deficiencies in LDAP when used to support PKI. In *Communications of the ACM 46*(3), 99-104.

Chamberlin, D., Fankhauser, P., Florescu, D., Marchiori, M., & Robie, J. (2007). *XML Query Use Cases*. W3C. http://www.w3.org/TR/xquery-use-cases/

Chan, C. Y., & Ni, Y. (2007). Efficient XML data dissemination with piggybacking. In *SIGMOD*, (pp. 737-748).

Chan, C. Y., & Ni, Y. (2007). Efficient XML data dissemination with piggybacking. In *SIGMOD*, (pp. 737–748).

Chan, C. Y., Fan, W., Felber, P., Garofalakis, M. N., & Rastogi, R. (2002). Tree pattern aggregation for scalable XML data dissemination. In *VLDB*, (pp. 826-837).

Chand, R., Felber, P., & Garofalakis, M. (2007). Tree-pattern similarity estimation for scalable content-based routing. In *ICDE*, (pp. 1016-1025).

Chandrasekaran, S., Cooper, O., Deshpande, A., Franklin, M., Hellerstein, J., Hong, W., Krishnamurthy, S., Madden, S., Raman, V., Reiss, F., & Shah, M. (2003). TelegraphCQ: Continuous Dataflow Processing for an Uncertain World. In *CIDR*.

Chaudhuri, S., & Dayal, U. (1997). An overview of data warehousing and OLAP technology. *SIGMOD Record 26*(1), 65-74.

Chaudhuri, S., Ramakrishnan, R., & Weikum, G. (2005). Integrating DB and IR Technologies: What is the Sound of One Hand Clapping? In *CIDR*, (pp. 1-12).

Chawathe, S. S., Abiteboul, S., & Widom, J. (1999) Managing historical semistructured data". In *Theory and Practice of Object Systems 5*(3), 143–162.

Chen, J., DeWitt, D. J., Tian, F., & Wang, Y. (2002). NiagaraCQ: A Scalable Continuous Query System for Internet Databases. In *SIGMOD*, (pp. 379-390).

Chen, P. (1976). The Entity-Relationship Model - Toward a unified view of data. *ACM Transactions on Database Systems, 1*(1), 9-36.

Chen, T., Lu, J., & Wang Ling, T. (2005) On boosting holism in XML twig pattern matching using structural indexing techniques. In *SIGMOD*, (pp. 455-466).

Chen, X., Chen, Y., & Rao, F. (2003). An efficient spatial publish/subscribe system for intelligent location-based services. In *DEBS*.

Chen, Y., Davidson, S. B., & Zheng, Y. (2006). An efficient XPath query processor for xml streams. In *ICDE*, (p. 79).

Chen, Y., Davidson, S., Hara, C., & Zheng, Y. (2003). RRXS: Redundancy reducing XML storage in relations. In *VLDB*, pages 189-200.

Chen, Z., Jagadish, H. V., Korn, F., Koudas, N., Muthukrishnan, S., Ng, R., & Srivastava, D. (2001). Counting Twig Matches in a Tree. In *ICDE*, (pp. 595–604).

Chien, S.-Y., Tsotras, V. J., & Zaniolo, C. (2001). XML document versioning. In *SIGMOD Record 30*(3), (pp. 46-53).

Chien, S.-Y., Tsotras, V. J., & Zaniolo, C. (2002). Efficient management of multiversion XML documents. In *VLDB Journal 11*(4), 332-353.

Chien, S.-Y., Tsotras, V. J., Zaniolo, C., & Zhang, D. (2006). Supporting complex queries on multiversion XML documents. *ACM Transactions on Internet Technology 6*(1), 53-84.

Chilingaryan, S. A. (2004). *XML Benchmark*. http://xmlbench.sourceforge.net/

Choi, B. (2002).What are real DTDs like? In *WebDB*, (pp. 43-48).

Chor, B., Goldreich, O., Kushilevitz, E., & Sudan, M. (1995). Private information retrieval. In *FOCS*, (pp. 41-50).

Christensen, A. S., M, A. & Schwartzbach, M. I. (2003). Extending Java for high-level Web service construction. In *ACM Trans. Program. Lang. Syst. 25*(6), 814-875.

Christian, J. et al. (2003). The MGED ontology: A framework for describing functional genomics experiments. In *Comparative and Functional Genomics, 4*(1), 127-132.

Chung, S., & Jesurajaiah S. (2005). Schemaless XML document management in object-oriented databases. In *ITCC, 1*, 261–266.

Chung, T., Park, S., Han, S., & Kim, H. (2001). Extracting object-oriented database schemas from XML DTDs using inheritance. In *EC-Web, (pp. 49-59)*.

Clark, J. (1999). *XSL Transformations (XSLT) Version 1.0*. W3C. http://www.w3.org/TR/xslt.

Clark, J., & DeRose, S. (1999). *XML Path Language (XPath) Version 1.0*. W3C. http://www.w3.org/TR/xpath/.

Clark, J., & Murata, M. (Eds.) (2001). *Relax NG specification. Organization for the advancement of structured information standards*. http://relaxng.org/spec-20011203.html

Cochran, W. G. (1977). *Sampling Techniques*. 3rd Edition. John Wiley.

Codd, E. F. (1970). A relational model of data for large shared data banks. In *Communications of the ACM 13*(6), 377 – 387.

Combi, C., & Montanari, A. (2001). Data models with multiple temporal dimensions: Completing the picture. In *CAiSE*, (pp. 187-202).

Conrad, R., Scheffner, D., & Freytag, J. C. (2000). XML conceptual modeling using UML. In *ER,* (pp. 558-571).

Cooper, C. (1999). *Benchmarking XML Parsers*. XML.com. http://www.xml.com/pub/a/Benchmark/ article.html

Coral 8 Inc. (2008). Retrieved March 1, 2008, from http://www.coral8.com/

Córcoles, J. E., & González, P. (2004) Studying an approach to query spatial XML. In Z. Bellahsene, P. McBrien (Eds.), *DIWeb2004, 3rd International Workshop on Data Integration over the Web, Online Proceedings*.

Retrieved January 15, 2008, from http://www.doc.ic.ac. uk/~pjm/diweb2004/DIWeb2004_Part3.pdf

Cornelis, B. (2003). *Personalizing search indigital libraries*. Unpublished master's thesis. The Netherlands: University of Maastricht.

Costa, M., Crowcroft, J., Castro, M., Rowstron, A., Zhou, L., Zhang, L., & Barham, P. (2005). Vigilante: End-to-end containment of internet worms. In *SOSP*, (pp. 133-147).

Costello, R. (2007). *XML schema versioning*. http://www. xfront.com/Versioning.pdf

Cuellar, A. A., et al. (2003). CellML 1.1 for the definition and exchange of biological models. In *MCBMS*, (pp. 451-456).

Currim, F., Currim, S., Dyreson, C. E., & Snodgrass, R. T. (2004) A tale of two schemas: Creating a temporal schema from a snapshot schema with τXSchema. In *EDBT*, (pp. 348–365).

Damiani, E., Vimercati, S. D. C. D., Paraboschi, S., & Samarati, P. (2000). Design and implementation of an access control processor for XML documents. In *Computer Networks 33*(6), 59–75.

Damiani, E., Vimercati, S. D. C. D., Paraboschi, S., & Samarati, P. (2002). A fine-grained access control system for XML documents. In *ACM TISSEC 5*(2), 169–202.

Damiani, E., Vimercati, S. D. C., Jajodia, S., Paraboschi, S., & Samarati, P. (2003). Balancing confidentiality and efficiency in untrusted relational DBMSs. In *ACMCCS*, (pp. 93-102).

Dang, T. K. (2003). *Semantic based similarity searches in database systems: Multidimensional access methods, similarity search algorithms*. PhD Thesis, FAW-Institute, University of Linz, Austria.

Dang, T. K. (2005). Privacy-preserving search and updates for outsourced tree-structured data on untrusted servers. In *iTrust*, (pp. 338-354).

Dang, T. K. (2006). A practical solution to supporting oblivious basic operations on dynamic outsourced search trees. In *International Journal of Computer Systems Science and Engineering 21*(1), 53-64.

Dang, T. K. (2006). Security protocols for outsourcing database services. In *Information and Security: An International Journal 18*, 85-108.

Dang, T. K. (2008). Ensuring correctness, completeness and freshness for outsourced tree-indexed data. In *Information Resources Management Journal 21*(1), 59-76.

Dang, T. K., Le, T. T. H, & Truong, D. T. (2007). An extensible framework for database security assessment. In *iiWAS*, (pp. 419-425).

Dang, T. K., Son, N. T. (2006). Providing query assurance for outsourced tree-indexed data. In *HPSC*, (pp. 207-224).

Dang, T. K., Truong, Q. C., Cu-Nguyen, P-H., & Tran-Thi, Q-N. (2008). An extensible framework for detecting database security flaws. In *ACOMP*, (pp. 68-77).

Date, C. J. (1999). *An introduction to database systems*. Reading, MA: Addison-Wesley Publishing Company.

Davidson, S., Fan, W., & Hara, C. (2007). Propagating XML Constraints to Relations. In *J. Comput. Syst. Sci., 73*(3), 316-361.

dbaDirect Company (2008). Retrieved from http://www. dbadirect.com

DBLP (2008). *Digital Bibliography & Library Project*. http://dblp.uni-trier.de/

De Castro, C., Grandi, F., & Scalas, M. R. (1993). Semantic interoperability of multitemporal relational databases. In *ER*, (pp. 463-474).

Demers, A. J., Gehrke, J., Rajaraman, R., Trigoni, A. & Yao, Y. (2003). The Cougar Project: A work-in-progress report. In *SIGMOD Record 32* (4), 53-59.

DeRose, S., Daniel, R., Grosso, P., Maler, E., Marsh, J., & Walsh, N. (2002). *XML pointer language (XPointer)*. W3C. http://www.w3.org/TR/xptr/

DeRose, S., Maler, E., & Orchard, D. (2001). *XML Linking Language (XLink) Version 1.0*. W3C. http://www. w3.org/TR/xlink/

Devanbu, P. T., Gertz, M., Kwong, A., Martel, C., Nuckolls, G., & Stubblebine, S. G. (2001). Flexible authentication of XML documents. In *CCS*, (pp. 136-145).

Developer (2005). *XSLT Mark version 2.1.0*, http://www.datapower.com/xmldev/xsltmark.html

Diao, Y., & Franklin, M. (2003, September). Query processing for high-volume XML message brokering. In *VLDB*, (pp.261-272).

Diao, Y., Altinel, M., Franklin, M. J., Zhang, H., & Ficher, P. M. (2003). Path sharing and predicate evaluation for high-performance XML filtering. In *ACM Transactions Database Systems 28*(4), 467-516.

Diao, Y., Fischer, P. M., Franklin, M. J., & To, R. (2002). Yfilter: Efficient and scalable filtering of xml documents. In *ICDE*, (pp. 341).

Diao, Y., Rizvi, S., & Franklin, M. J. (2004). Towards an Internet-scale XML dissemination service. In *VLDB*, (pp. 612-623).

Dietzold, S. (2005). Generating RDF models from LDAP directories. In *CEUR-WS, 135*.

Dokulil, J., & Katreniakova, J. (2008). Visual Exploration of RDF Data. In *SOFSEM'08*, pages 672 – 683.

Domon B. & Aebersold R. (2006). Mass spectrometry and protein analysis. In *Science, 312*(5771), 212 – 217.

Dong, C., & Bailey, J. (2004). Static analysis of XSLT programs. In *ADC*, (pp. 151-160).

Dorigo, M., Birattari, M., & Stutzle, T. (2006). *An introduction to ant colony optimization*. Technical Report 2006-010, IRIDIA, Bruxelles, Belgium.

dos Santos Mello, R., & Heuser, C. A. (2005). Binxs: A process for integration of XML schemata. In *CAiSE*, (pp. 151-166).

Drake, M. (2007). *Oracle database 11g XML DB technical overview*. Retrieved March 1, 2008. http://www.oracle.com/technology/tech/xml/xmldb/Current/11g%20new%20features.ppt.pdf

Draper, D. (2003). Mapping between XML and relational data. In H. Katz (Ed.), *XQuery from the experts: A guide to the W3C XML query language*. Reading, MA: Addison-Wesley Publishing Company.

Du, W., & Atallah, M. J. (2000). Protocols for secure remote database access with approximate matching. In *ACMCCS Workshop*.

Dyreson, C. E., & Grandi, F. (in press). Temporal XML. In L. Liu & M. T. Özsu (Eds.), *Encyclopedia of database systems*. Heidelberg, Germany: Springer-Verlag.

Dyreson, C. E., Böhlen, M. H., Christian S. Jensen, C. S. (1999) Capturing and querying multiple aspects of semistructured data. In *VLDB*, pages 290–301.

Eisen, M. B., Spellman, P. T., Brown, P. O., & Botstein, D. (1998). Cluster analysis and display of genome-wide expression patterns. In *PNAS 95*(25), 14863-14868.

Eisenberg, A., & Melton, J. (2002). SQL/XML is Making Good Progress. In *SIGMOD Record 31*(2), 101-108.

Eisenberg, A., & Melton, J. (2004). Advancements in SQL/XML. In *SIGMOD Record 33*(3), 79-86.

Elmasri, R., Wu, Y-C., Hojabri, B., Li, C., & Fu, J. (2002). Conceptual Modeling for Customized XML Schemas. In *ER*, (pp. 429-443).

Embley, D. W., & Mok, W. Y. (2001). Developing XML Documents with Guaranteed "Good" Properties. In *ER*, (pp. 426-441).

Embley, D. W., Liddle, S. W., & Al-Kamha, R. (2004). Enterprise Modeling with Conceptual XML. In *ER*, (pp. 150-165).

Evdokimov, S., & Günther, O. (2007). Encryption techniques for secure database outsourcing. In *ESORICS*, (pp. 327-342).

Evdokimov, S., Fischmann, M., & Günther, O. (2006). Provable security for outsourcing database operations. In *ICDE*, (p. 117).

Evered, M., & Bogeholz, S. (2004). A Case Study in access control requirements for a health information system. In *AISW*, (pp. 53-61).

EXSLT. *The community extensions to XSLT*. http://www.exslt.org/

Fabret, F., Jacobsen, H-A, Llirbat, F., Pereira, J., Ross, K. A., & Shasha, D. (2001). Filtering algorithms and implementation for very fast publish/subscribe. In *SIGMOD*, (pp. 115-126).

Fan, Q., Wu, Q., He, & Y., Huang, J. (2005). Optimized strategies of grid information services. In *SKG*, (p. 90).

Farwick, M. & Hafner, M. (2007). *XML Parser Benchmarks: Part 1 & 2*. XML.com. http://www.xml.com/pub/a/2007/05/09/xml-parser-benchmarks-part-1.html. http://www.xml.com/pub/a/2007/05/16/xml-parser-benchmarks-part-2.html.

Fegaras, L., He, W., Das, G., & Levine, D. (2006). XML query routing in structured P2P systems. In *DISP2P*, (pp. 273-284).

Fenner, W., Rabinovich, M., Ramakrishnan, K. K., Srivastava, D., & Zhang, Y. (2005). XTreeNet: Scalable overlay networks for XML content dissemination and querying. In *WCW*, (pp. 4-46).

Fernández, M., & Robie, J. (Eds) (2001). *XQuery 1.0 and XPath 2.0 Data Model*. W3C Working Draft, http://www.w3.org/TR/2001/WD-query-datamodel/

Fernández, M., Florescu, D., Boag, S., Siméon, J., Chamberlin, D., Robie, J., & Kay, M. (2007). *XQuery 1.0: An XML query language*. W3C Recommendation. http://www.w3.org/TR/xquery/

Fernández, M., Michiels, P., & Siméon, J., Stark, M. (2007). XQuery streaming á la carte. In *ICDE*, (pp. 2556-265).

Fernández, M., Siméon, J., Chamberlin, D., Berglund, A., Boag, S., Robie, J., & Kay, M. (2007). *XML path language (XPath) Version 1.0*. W3C Recommendation. http://www.w3.org/TR/xpath

Fernández, M., Siméon, J., Chen. C., Choi, B., Dinoff, R., Gapeyev, V., Marian, A., Michiels, P., Onose, N., Petkanics, D., Radhakrishnan, M., Re, C., Resnick, L., Sur, G., Vyas, A., & Wadler, P. (2007). *Galax 0.7.2*. http://www.galaxquery.org/

Fields, M. (1996). *Mark Fields's Ebooks*. http://www.assortedthoughts.com/downloads.php.

Fischer, P. M., & Kossmann, D. (2005). Batched processing for information filters. In *ICDE*, (pp. 902-913).

Flajolet, P., & Martin, G. N. (1983). Probabilistic counting. In *FOCS*, (pp. 76–82).

Flajolet, P., & Martin, G. N. (1985). Probabilistic counting algorithms for data base applications. In *J. Comput. Syst. Sci. 31*(2), 182–209.

Florescu, D., & Kossmann, D. (1999). Storing and querying XML data using an RDBMS. In *Bulletin of the IEEE Computer Society Technical Committee on Data Engineering 22*(3), 27-34.

Florescu, D., Hillery, C., & Kossmann, D. (2003). The BEA/XQRL Streaming XQuery Processor. In *VLDB*, (pp.997–1008).

Fokoue, A., Rose, K., Siméon, J., & Villard, L. (2005). Compiling XSLT 2.0 into XQuery 1.0. In *WWW*, (pp. 682-691).

Fomichev, A., Grinev, M., & Kuznetsov, S. (2005). Sedna: A native XML DBMS. In *SOFSEM*, (pp. 272-281).

Fousteris, N., Gergatsoulis, M., & Stavrakas, Y. (2007) Storing multidimensional XML documents in relational databases. In *DEXA*, (pp. 23-33).

Franceschet, M. (2005). XPathMark – An XPath Benchmark for XMark Generated Data. In *XSym'05*, pages 129-143.

Franceschet, M., Zimuel, E., Afanasiev, L., & Marx, M. (2006). *XCheck*. Informatics Institute, University of Amsterdam, The Netherlands. http://ilps.science.uva.nl/Resources/XCheck/.

Fredkin, E. (1960). Trie memory. In *Communications of the ACM 3*(9), 490–499.

FreeDB (2008). http://www.freedb.org/.

Freire, J., Haritsa, J. R., Ramanath, M., Roy, P., & Simeon, J. (2002). StatiX: Making XML count. In *SIGMOD*, (pp.181-192).

Freund, J., et al. (2006). Health-e-Child: An integrated biomedical platform for grid-based pediatrics. In *Health-Grid Conference*.

Frias-Martinez, E., Magoulas, G., Chen, S., & Macredie, R. (2006). Automated user modeling for personalized digital libraries. In *International Journal of Information Management 26*(3), 234–248.

Galperin M. Y. (2008). The molecular biology database collection: 2008 update. In *Nucleic Acids Research 36*, (pp. 2-4).

Gantz, J. F. (2007). *The expanding digital universe: A forecast of worldwide information growth through 2010.* IDC White Paper. Retrieved February 17, 2008 from http://www.emc.com

Gao, D., & Snodgrass, R. T. (2003). Temporal slicing in the evaluation of XML queries. In *VLDB*, (pp. 632–643).

Gapeyev, V., Levin, M. Y., & Pierce, B. C. (2005). XML goes native: Run-time representations for Xtatic. In *CC*, (pp. 43–58).

Gauch, S., Chaffee, J., & Pretschner, A. (2003). Ontology-based user profiles for search and browsing. In *Web Intelligence and Agent Systems 1*(3-4), 219–234.

Gedik, B., Wu, K.L., Yu, P.S., & Liu, L. (2005). Adaptive Load Shedding for Windowed Stream Joins. In *CIKM*, (pp.171–178).

Gehrke, J., Das, A., & Riedewald, M. (2003). Approximate Join Processing over Data Streams. In *SIGMOD*, (pp.40–51).

Gemmill, J., Chatterjee, S., Miller, T., & Verharen, E. (2003). ViDe.Net Middleware for scalable video services for research and higher education. In *ACMSE*, (pp. 463-468).

Genevès, P., Layaïda, N., & Schmitt, A. (2007). Efficient static analysis of xml paths and types. In *SIGPLAN Not. 42*(6), 342-351.

Gertner, Y., Ishai, Y., Kushilevitz, E., & Malkin, T. (1998). Protecting data privacy in private information retrieval schemes. In *STOC*, (pp. 151-160).

Giacomini Moro, R., de Matos Galante, R., & Heuser, C. A. (2004) A version model for supporting adaptation of Web pages. In *WIDM*, (pp. 120–127).

Goble, C. A., et al. (2003). *Knowledge integration: in silico experiments in bioinformatics. The Grid 2: Blueprint for a New Computing Infrastructure*, Morgan Kaufmann.

Godard, B., et al. (2003) Data storage and DNA banking for biomedical research: informed consent, confidentiality, quality issues, ownership, return of benefits. A professional perspective. In *Eur. J. Hum. Genet., 11 Suppl. 2*, (pp. 88–122).

Godoy, D., & Amandi, A. (2005). User profiling for Web page filtering. In *IEEE Internet Computing, 9*(4), 56–64.

Goldman, R., & Widom, J. (1997). DataGuides: Enabling query formulation and optimization in semistructured databases. In *VLDB*, (pp. 436-445).

Goldreich, O., & Ostrovsky, R. (1996). Software protection and simulation on oblivious RAMs. In *Journal of the ACM 43*, 431–473.

Golemati, M., Katifori, A., Vassilakis, C., Lepouras, G., & Halatsis, C. (2007). Creating an ontology for the user profile: Method and applications. In *RCIS*, (pp. 407–412).

Golfarelli, M., Rizzi, S., & Vrdoljak, B. (2001). Data warehouse design from XML sources. In *DOLAP*, (pp. 40-47).

Gong, X., Yan, Y., Qian, W., & Zhou, A. (2005). Bloom filter-based XML packets filtering for millions of path queries. In *ICDE*, (pp. 890-901).

Gottlob, G., Koch, C., Pichler, R., & Segoufin, L. (2005). The complexity of XPath query evaluation and xml typing. In *J. ACM 52*(2), 284-335.

Gou, G., & Chirkova, R. (2007). Efficient algorithms for evaluating xpath over streams. In *SIGMOD*, (pp. 269-280).

Grandi, F. & Mandreoli, F. (2000) The valid Web: An XML/XSL infrastructure for temporal management of Web documents. In *ADVIS*, (pp. 294-303).

Grandi, F. (2004). Introducing an annotated bibliography on temporal and evolution aspects in the World Wide Web. In *SIGMOD Record 33*(2), 84-86.

Grandi, F., & Mandreoli, F. (2003). A formal model for temporal schema versioning in object-oriented databases. In *Data and Knowledge Engineering 46*(2), 123-167.

Grandi, F., Mandreoli F., & Tiberio P. (2005). Temporal modelling and management of normative documents in XML format. In *Data & Knowledge Engineering 54*(3), 327–354.

Grandi, F., Mandreoli F., Martoglia R., Ronchetti E., Scalas M. R., & Tiberio, P. (in press). Ontology-based personalization of e-government services. In P. Germanakos & C. Mourlas (Eds.), *Intelligent user interfaces: Adaptation and personalization systems and technologies*. Information Science Reference. Hershey, PA: IGI Global.

Grandi, F., Mandreoli, F., Tiberio, P., & Bergonzini, M. (2003). A temporal data model and management system for normative texts in xml format. In *WIDM*, (pp. 29-36).

Graps, A. (1995). An introduction to wavelets. *Computational Science and Engineering, 2*(2), 50–61.

Green, T. J., Miklau, G., Onizuka, M., & Suciu, D (2003). Processing XML streams with deterministic automata. In *ICDT*, (pp. 173-189).

Greene, L. H. et al. (2007). The CATH domain structure database: new protocols and classification levels give a more comprehensive resource for exploring evolution. In *Nucleic Acid Res., 35,* 291-297.

Groppe, J., & Groppe, S. (2008). Filtering unsatisfiable Xpath queries. In *Data Knowl. Eng., 64*(1), 134-169.

Groppe, J., & Linnemann, V. (2008). Discovering veiled unsatisfiable XPath queries. In *ICEIS*, (pp. 149-158).

Groppe, S., & Groppe, J. (2006). Determining the output schema of an XSLT stylesheet. In *ADBIS Research Communications, 215, CEUR Workshop Proceedings*.

Gruber, T. (in press). Ontology. In L. Liu and M. T. Özsu (Eds.), *Encyclopedia of database systems*. Heidelberg, Germany: Springer-Verlag.

Grundy, J., & Zou, W. (2003) AUIT: Adaptable user interface technology, with extended Java Server pages. In A. Seffah & H. Javahery (Eds.), *Multiple user interfaces: Cross-platform applications and context-aware interfaces,* (pp. 149-167).

Guarino, N. (1998). *Formal ontology in information systems*. Amsterdam: IOS Press.

Guerrini, G., Mesiti, M., & Rossi, D. (2005). Impact of XML schema evolution on valid documents. In *WIDM*, (pp. 39-44).

Guerrini, G., Mesiti, M., & Sorrenti, M. A. (2007). XML schema evolution: Incremental validation and efficient document adaptation. In *XSym*, (pp. 92-106).

Guha, S., Shim, K., & Woo, J. (2004). Rehist: Relative error histogram construction algorithms. In *VLDB*, (pp. 300-311).

Guo, L., Shao, F., Botev, C., & Shanmugasundaram, J. (2003). Xrank: Ranked keyword search over XML documents. In *SIGMOD*, (pp. 16-27).

Gupta, A. K., & Suciu, D. (2003). Stream processing of XPath queries with predicates. In *SIGMOD,* (pp. 419-430).

Gupta, A., & Chawathe, S. (2004). *Skipping Streams with XHints* (Tech. Rep. No. CS-TR-4566). University of Maryland, College Park.

Gupta, A., & Suciu, D. (2003). Stream Processing of XPath Queries with Predicates. In *SIGMOD*, (pp. 419-430).

Haase, P., & Sure, Y. (2004). D3.1.1.b State of the art on ontology evolution. http://www.aifb.uni-karlsruhe.de/WBS/ysu/publications/SEKT-D3.1.1.b.pdf

Hacigümüs, H., Iyer, B.R., Li, C., & Mehrotra, S. (2002). Executing SQL over encrypted data in the database-service-provider model. In *SIGMOD*, (pp. 216-227).

Hacigümüs, H., Mehrotra, S., & Iyer, B. R. (2002). Providing database as a service. In *ICDE*, (pp. 29-40).

Halevy, A , Rajaraman, A., & Ordille, J. (2006). Data integration: The teenage years. In *VLDB,* (pp. 9-16).

Halevy, A. (2000) *Logic-based techniques in data integration.* In Minker, J. (Ed.), Logic-based artificial intelligence, (pp. 575-595).

Halverson, A., Josifovski, V., Lohman, G. M., Pirahesh, H., & Mörschel, M. (2004). ROX: Relational Over XML. In *VLDB,* (pp. 264-275).

Hammerschmidt, B. C. (2005). KeyX: Selective key-oriented indexing in native XML-databases. Akademische Verlagsgesellschaft Aka GmbH, Berlin, DISDBIS 93.

Hammerschmidt, B. C., Kempa, M., & Linnemann, V. (2005). On the intersection of XPath expressions. In *IDEAS,* (pp. 49-57).

Hanisch, D. et al. (2002). ProML - the protein markup language for specification of protein sequences, structures and families. In *Silico Biology 2*(3), 313–324.

Hare, K. (2007). *JCC's SQL standards page.* JCC Consulting, Inc. Retrieved March 1, 2007. http://www.jcc.com/SQL.htm

Harren, M., Raghavachari, M., Shmueli, O., Burke, M. G., Bordawekar, R., Pechtchanski, I., & Sarkar, V. (2005). XJ: Facilitating XML processing in Java. In *WWW,* (pp. 278-287).

Harvey, S. C., et al. (2002). RNAML: A standard syntax for exchanging RNA information. In *RNA 8*(06), 707-717.

He, B., Luo, Q., & Choi, B. (2006). Cache-Conscious Automata for XML filtering. In *IEEE Transactions on Knowledge and Data Engineering 18* (12), 1629-1644.

Hermjakob, H. (2006). The HUPO proteomics standards initiative - Overcoming the fragmentation of proteomics data. In *Proetomics Journal, 6*(S2), 34-38.

Hernandez, T., & Kambhampati, S. (2004). Integration of biological sources: Current systems and challenges ahead. In *SIGMOD Record 33*(3), 51-60.

H-InvDB (2007). *Annotated Human Genes Database.* http://www.jbirc.aist.go.jp/hinv/

Hong, M., Demers, A., Gehrke, J., Koch, C., Riedewald, M., & White, W. (2007). Massively multi-query join processing in publish/subscribe systems. In *SIGMOD,* (pp. 761-772).

Howes, T., & Smith, M. (1997). *LDAP: Programming directory-enabled applications with lightweight directory access protoco.* PA: Macmillan Technical Publishing.

Hoylen, S. (2006). *XML Schema Versioning Use Cases.* Available at http://www.w3c.org/XML/ 2005/xsd-versioning-use-cases/

Hu, H., & Du, X. (2006). An ontology learning model in grid information services. In *ICICIC, 3,* 398-401.

Huang, C.-H., Chuang, T.-R., Lu, J. J., & Lee, H.-M. (2006). XML evolution: A two-phase XML processing model using XML prefiltering techniques. In *VLDB,* (pp. 1215-1218).

Hucka, M. et al. (2003). The Systems biology markup language (SBML): A medium for representation and exchange of biochemical network models. In *Bioinformatics, 19*(4), 524-531.

Huh, W. K. et al. (2003). Global analysis of protein localization in budding yeast. In *Nature, 425,* 686-691.

Hümmer, W., Bauer A., & Harde, G. (2003). XCube: XML for data warehouses. In *DOLAP,* (pp. 33-40).

Hunt, E. et al. (2004). Index-Driven XML data integration to support functional genomics. In *DILS,* (pp. 95-109).

Ibiblio (2008). *The Public's Library and Digital Archive.* http://www.ibiblio.org/.

IBM IT Outsourcing and Hosting (2008a). Retrieved from http://www.ibm.com/services/stratout.

IBM PCI Cryptographic Coprocessor (2008). Received from http://www-03.ibm.com/security/cryptocards/pc-icc/overview.shtml on March 8, 2008

IBM. (2005). *The IBM approach to unified XML/relational databases.* Retrieved March 1, 2008. http://xml.coverpages.org/IBM-XML-GC34-2496.pdf

ICD-10 (2007). *International Statistical Classification of Diseases and Related Health Problems - 10th Revision*. World Health Organization. Retrieved March 15, 2008, from http://www.who.int/classifications/apps/icd/icd10online/

IMDb (2008). *The Internet Movie Database*. http://www.imdb.com/.

INEX (2007). *INitiative for the Evaluation of XML Retrieval*. http://inex.is.informatik.uni-duisburg.de/.

Inmon, W. H. (2002). *Building the data warehouse*. NY: John Wiley and Sons.

INRIA. *Active schema language*. http://ns.inria.fr/active-tags/active-schema/active-schema.html

INRIA. *Active tags technologies*. http://ns.inria.org/active-tags/

INRIA. *RefleX. An active tags engine in Java*. http://reflex.gforge.inria.fr/

INRIA. *XUnit. Unit tests in XML*. http://reflex.gforge.inria.fr/xunit.html

International Organization for Standardization (ISO) (1996). *ISO/IEC 14977:1996: Information technology -- Syntactic metalanguage -- Extended BNF*, http://www.iso.ch/cate/d26153.html

Ioannidis, Y. E., & Poosala, V. (1995). Balancing histogram optimality and practicality for query result size estimation. In *SIGMOD*, (pp. 233–244).

ISO/IEC (2003) *SQL/XML. Database languages, SQL Part 14: XML-Related Specifications*, ISO/IEC 9075-14:2003 Information technology.

Ives, Z., Halevy, A., & Weld D. (2002). An XML Query Engine for Network-Bound Data. In *VLDB Journal 11* (4), 380–402.

Iyer, B.R., Mehrotra, S., Mykletun, E., Tsudik, G., & Wu, Y. (2004). A framework for efficient storage security in RDBMS. In *EDBT*, (pp. 147-164).

Jagadish, H. V, Al-Khalifa, S., Chapman, A., Lakshmanan, L.V.S., Nierman, A., Paparizos, S., Patel, J.M.,

Srivastava, D., Wiwatwattana, N., Wu, Y., & Yu, C. (2002). TIMBER: A Native XML Database. *VLDB Journal 11*(4), 274-291.

Jain, S., Mahajan, R., & Suciu, D. (2002). Translating XSLT programs to efficient SQL queries. In *WWW*, (pp. 616-626).

Jammalamadaka, R. C., & Mehrotra, S. (2006). Querying encrypted XML documents. In *IDEAS*, (pp. 129-136).

Jaquith, A. (2007). *Security metrics: Replacing fear, uncertainty and doubt*. Addison-Wesley Professional.

JAXB. *Java architecture for XML binding*. http://java.sun.com/xml/jaxb/.

Jelliffe, R. *The Schematron Assertion Language (Schematron)*. http://www.schematron.com/spec.html

Jelly. *Executable XML. The Apache Software Foundation*, http://jakarta.apache.org/commons/jelly/

Jensen, C. S., Dyreson, C. E., Böhlen, M. H., Clifford, J., Elmasri, R., Gadia, S. K., Grandi, F., Hayes, P., Jajodia, S., Käfer, W., Kline, N., Lorentzos, N., Mitsopoulos, Y., Montanari, A., Nonen, D., Peressi, E., Pernici, B., Roddick, J. F., Sarda, N. L., Scalas, M. R., Segev, A., Snodgrass, R. T., Soo, M. D., Tansel, A. U., Tiberio, P., & Wiederhold, G. (1998). The consensus glossary of temporal database concepts - February 1998 Version. In *LNCS 1399*, (pp. 367 – 405).

Jensen, M. R., Møller, T. H., & Pedersen, T. B. (2001). Specifying OLAP cubes on XML data. *Journal of Intelligent Information Systems, 17*(2-3), 255-280.

Jiang, H., Lu, H., & Wang, W., (2004). *Efficient processing of XML Twig queries with OR-predicates*. In *SIGMOD*, (pp. 59-70).

Jiang, H., Wang, W., Lu, H., & Yu, J. X. (2003). Holistic Twig Joins on indexed XML documents. In *VLDB*, (pp. 273-284).

Joint Technical Committee ISO/IEC JTC 1, Information technology, Subcommittee SC 32, Data management and interchange. (2003). *ISO/IEC 9075 Part 14: XML-related specifications (SQL/XML)*. Retrieved March 1, 2008.

http://www.sqlx.org/SQL-XML-documents/5FCD-14-XML-2004-07.pdf

Josifovski, V., Fontoura, M., & Barta, A. (2005). Querying XML streams. In *VLDB Journal 14*(2), 197-210.

Kader, R., & Keulen, M. (2007). Native XQuery optimization in relational database systems. In *VLDB*, (pp. 75-86).

Kaneko, K. (2006). *Life: An introduction to complex systems biology.* Springer

Kay, M. (2006). Using relational data in XML applications. *Data Direct Technologies.* Retrieved March 1, 2008. http://www.stylusstudio.com/tutorials/relational_xml.html#

Kay, M. (Ed.). (2007). *XSL transformations (XSLT) Version 1.0.* W3C Recommendation. http://www.w3.org/TR/xslt

Kay, M. H. (2007). *Saxon - The XSLT and XQuery Processor.* http://saxon.sourceforge.net

Kepser, S. (2004). A simple proof for the turing-completeness of XSLT and XQuery. In *Extreme markup languages.*

Khan, L., & Rao, Y. (2001). A performance evaluation of storing XML data in relational DBMS. In *WIDM*, (pp. 31-38).

Kim, W., & Chou, H.-T. (1988). Versions of schema for object-oriented databases. In *VLDB*, (pp. 148-159).

Kimball, R., & Ross, M., (2002). *The data warehouse toolkit.* NY: John Wiley and Sons.

Klein, M. C. A., & Fensel, D. (2001). *Ontology versioning on the Semantic Web.* In *SWWS*, (pp. 75–91).

Klein, N., Groppe, S., Böttcher, S., & Gruenwald, L. (2005). A prototype for translating XQuery expressions into XSLT stylesheets. In *ADBIS*, (pp. 238-253).

Klettke, M., & Meyer, H. (2000). XML and object-relational database systems – Enhancing structural mappings based on statistics. In *LNCS 1997,*(pp. 151- 170).

Klettke, M., Meyer, H., & Hänsel, B. (2005). Evolution: The other side of the XML update coin. In *ICDE Workshop,* (p. 1279).

Kobsa, A. (2001). Generic user modeling systems. In *User modeling and user-adapted interaction,* *11*(1-2), 49–63.

Koch, C., Scherzinger, S., & Scheweikardt, M. (2004). FluxQuery: An optimizing XQuery processor for streaming XML data. In *VLDB*, (pp.228-239).

Koch, C., Scherzinger, S., Schweikardt, N., & Stegmaier, B. (2004). Fluxquery: An optimizing xquery processor for streaming xml data. In *VLDB*, (pp. 1309–1312).

Kooi, R. P. (1980). *The optimization of queries in relational databases.* PhD thesis, Cleveland, OH, USA.

Koudas, N., Rabinovich, M., Srivastava, D., & Yu, T. (2004). Routing XML queries. In *ICDE*, (p. 844).

Koutsonikola, V., & Vakali, A. (2004). LDAP: Framework, practices, and trends. In *IEEE Internet Computing* *8*(5), 66-72.

Kramer, D. K., & Rundensteiner, E. A. (2001). Xem: XML evolution management. In *RIDE*, (pp. 103-110).

Krishnamurthy, R., Chakaravarthy, V., & Naughton, J. (2003). On the difficulty of finding optimal relational decompositions for XML workloads: A complexity theoretic perspective. In *ICDT*, (pp. 270-284).

Krishnaprasad, M., Liu, Z., Manikutty, A., Warner, J., & Arora, V. (2005). Towards an industrial strength SQL/XML infrastructure. In *ICDE*, (pp. 991-1000).

Kulikova, T. et al. (2007). EMBL nucleotide Sequence database in 2006. In *Nucleic Acid Res., 35*, 16-20.

Kumar, P. (2002). *XPB4J – XML Processing Benchmark for Java.* http://www.pankaj-k.net/xpb4j/.

Kuznetsov, E., & Dolph, C. (2000). *XSLT Processor Benchmarks.* XML.com. http://www.xml.com/pub/a/2001/03/ 28/xsltmark/index.html.

Kwon, J., Rao, P., Moon, B., & Lee, S. (2005). FiST: Scalable XML document filtering by sequencing twig patterns. In *VLDB,* (pp. 217-228).

Kwon, J., Rao, P., Moon, B., & Lee, S. (2005). Fist: Scalable xml document filtering by sequencing twig patterns. In *VLDB*, (pp. 217–228).

Lanckriet, G. R. et al. (2004). A statistical framework for genomic data fusion. In *Bioinformatics*, *20*, 2626-2635.

Lapis, G. (2005). XML and relational storage—Are they mutually exclusive? In *XTech*. IDEAlliance. Retrieved March 1, 2008. http://idealliance.org/proceedings/xtech05/papers/02-05-01/

Lautemann, S.-E. (1997). Schema versions in object-oriented database systems. In *DASFAA*, (pp. 323-332).

Law, K. L. E. (2000). XML on LDAP network database. In *CCECE, 1*, 469-473.

Lechner, S., Preuner, G., & Schrefl, M. (2001). Translating XQuery into XSLT. In *ER Workshops*, (pp. 239-252).

Lehmann, J., Biasiotti, M. A., Francesconi, E., & Sagri, M. T. (Eds.) (2005). In *Proceedings of the first ICAIL legal ontologies and artificial intelligence techniques workshop (LOAIT)*. IAAIL Workshop Series.

Lenz, E. (2004). *XQuery: Reinventing the wheel?* http://www.xmlportfolio.com/xquery.html

Lewis, A. (2002). *Not My Type: Sizing Up W3C XML Schema Primitives*, http://www.xml.com/pub/a/2002/07/31/wxstypes.html

Li, F., Hadjieleftheriou, M., Kollios, G., & Reyzin, L. (2006). Dynamic authenticated index structures for outsourced databases. In *SIGMOD*, (pp. 121-132).

Li, G., Hou, S., & Jacobsen, H-A. (2007). XML Routing in data dissemination networks. In *ICDE,* (pp. 1400-1404).

Li, M., Mani, M., & Rundensteiner, E.A. (2008). Semantic Query Optimization for Processing XML Streams with Minimized Memory Footprint. In *DATAX.*

Li, S., & Lin, C. (2005). On the distributed management of SCORM-compliant course contents. In *AINA, 1*, 221-226.

Li, X., & Agrawal, G. (2005). Efficient Evaluation of XQuery over Streaming Data. In *VLDB*, (pp.265–276).

Li, Y. G., Bressan, S., Dobbie, G., Lacroix, Z., Lee, M. L., Nambiar, U., & Wadhwa, B. (2001). XOO7: Applying OO7 Benchmark to XML Query Processing Tool. In *CIKM*, (pp. 167–174).

Li, Y., & An, A. (2005). Representing UML snowflake diagram from integrating XML data using XML schema. In *DEEC*, (pp. 103–111).

Liefke, H., & Suciu, D. (1999). *XMill: an Efficient Compressor for XML Data*. University of Pennsylvania, Technical Report MSCIS -99-26.

Liefke, H., & Suciu, D. (2000) XMILL: An efficient compressor for XML data. In *SIGMOD*, (pp. 153-164).

Lim, L., Wang, M., & Vitter, J. (2003). SASH: A Self-Adaptive Histograms Set for Dynamically Changing Workloads. In *VLDB*, (pp. 369-380).

Lim, L., Wang, M., Padmanabhan, S., Vitter, J. S., & Parr, R. (2002). An On-line Self-Tuning Markov Histogram for XML Path Selectivity Estimation. In *VLDB*, (pp. 442-453).

Lin, P., & Candan, K. S. (2004). Hiding traversal of tree structured data from untrusted data stores. In *ICEIS Workshop*, (pp. 314-323).

Lin, P., & Candan, K. S. (2004). Secure and privacy preserving outsourcing of tree structured data. In *SDM*, (pp. 1-17).

Liu, B., Zhu, Y., & Rundensteiner, E.A. (2006). Run-time Operator State Spilling for Memory Intensive Long-Running Queries. In *SIGMOD*, (pp. 347–358).

Liu, H., Ramasubramanian, V., & Sirer, E. G. (2005). Client behavior and feed characteristics of RSS, a publish-subscribe system for Web micronews. In *Internet Measurement Conference,* (pp. 29-34).

Liu, X., Nelson, D., Stobart, S., & Stirk, S. (2005). Managing schema versions in object-oriented databases. In *ADBIS*, (pp. 97-108).

Liu, Z. H., & Novoselsky, A. (2006). Efficient XSLT processing in relational database system. In *VLDB*, pages 1106-1116.

Liu, Z., Krishnaprasad, M., & Arora, V. (2005). Native Xquery processing in oracle XMLDB. In *SIGMOD*, (pp. 828-833).

LKIF-Core (n.d.). *A core ontology of basic legal concepts*. ESTRELLA Project. Retrieved January 15, 2008, from http://www.estrellaproject.org/lkif-core/

Lodish, H. et al. (2000). *Molecular cell biology*. New York: Freeman & Co.

Lu, H., Yu, J. X., Wang, G., Zheng, S., Jiang, H., Yu, G., & Zhou, A. (2005). What makes the differences: benchmarking XML database implementations. In *ACM Trans. Inter. Tech.*, *5*(1), 154-194.

Lu, J., Chen, T., & Ling, T. W. (2004). Efficient processing of xml twig patterns with parent child edges: a look-ahead approach. In *CIKM*, (pp. 533–542).

Lu, J., Ling, T. W., Chan, C. Y., & Chen, T. (2005). From region encoding to extended dewey: On efficient processing of xml twig pattern matching. In *VLDB*, (pp. 193–204).

Luciano, J. S., & Stevens, R. D (2007). e-Science and biological pathway Semantics. In *BMC Bioinformatics*, *8*(S3).

Ludäscher, B., Mukhopadhyay, P., & Papakonstantinou, Y. (2002). A transducer-based xml query processor. In *VLDB*, (pp. 227–238).

Moller, A., Olesen, M. O., & Schwartzbach, M. I. (2007). Article 21 - Static Validation of XSL Transformations. *ACM Transactions on Programming Languages and Systems*. 29 (4), 21.

Malcolm, G. (2008). What's new for XML in SQL server 2008. In *Microsoft SQL Server 2008 white papers*.

Mandreoli F., Martoglia R., & Ronchetti E. (2006). Supporting temporal slicing in XML databases. In *EDBT*, (pp. 295-312).

Mandreoli, F., Martoglia, R., Grandi, F., & Scalas, M. R. (2006). Efficient management of multi-version XML documents for e-government applications. In *WEBIST Selected Papers*, (pp. 283-294).

Mandreoli, F., Martoglia, R., Ronchetti, E., Tiberio, P., Grandi, F., & Scalas, M. R. (2005). Personalized access to multi-version norm texts in an egovernment scenario. In *EGOV*, (pp. 281-290).

Manegold, S. (2008). An Empirical Evaluation of XQuery Processors. In *Inf. Syst. 33*(2), 203–220.

Mangalam, H. et al. (2001). GeneX: An open source gene expression database and integrated tool set. In *IBM Systems Journal, 40*(2), 552-569.

Manolescu, I., Miachon, C., & Michiels, P. (2006). Towards Micro-Benchmarking XQuery. In *ExpDB*, (pp. 28–39).

Manukyan, M. G., & Kalinichenko, L. A. (2001) Temporal XML. In *ADBIS*, (pp. 143–155).

Marcus, S. (1999). *Benchmarking XML Parsers on Solaris*. XML.com. http://www.xml.com/ pub/a/1999/06/ benchmark/solaris.html.

Marian, A., Abiteboul, S., Cobena, G., & Mignet, L. (2001) Change-centric management of versions in an XML Warehouse". In *VLDB*, (pp. 581-590).

Marian, A., Amer-Yahia, S., Koudas, N., & Srivastava, D. (2005). Adaptive processing of top-k queries in xml. In *ICDE*, (pp. 162–173).

Marrón, P., & Lausen, G. (2001A). On processing XML in LDAP. In *VLDB*, (pp. 601-610).

Marrón, P., & Lausen, G. (2001B). *HLCaches: An LDAP-based distributed cache technology for XML*. (Tech. Rep. No. 147). Institut für Informatik, Universität Freiburg.

Martinez, S. I., Grosso, P., & Walsh, N. (2008). *Extensible Markup Language (XML) Conformance Test Suites*. W3C. http://www.w3.org/XML/Test/.

Matys, V. et al. (2003). TRANSFAC: Transcriptional regulation, from patterns to profiles. In *Nucleic Acids Res., 31*(1), 374-378.

May, N., Helmer, S., & Moerkotte, G. 2006. Strategies for query unnesting in XML databases. In *ACM Trans. Database Syst. 31*(3), 968-1013.

McHugh, J., & Widom, J. (1999). Query Optimization for XML. In *VLDB*, (pp. 315–326).

Megginson, D. (2001). *Simple API for XML (SAX)*, http://www.saxproject.org/

Meier, W. (2002). eXist: An Open Source Native XML Database. In E. R. B. Chaudri, M. Jeckle & R. Unland, (Ed.), *Web, Web-Services, and database systems,* (pp. 169-183).

Meingast, M., et al. (2006). Security and privacy issues with health care information technology. In *Proc. IEEE Conference of Engineering in Medicine and Biology Soc.*, (pp. 5453-5458).

Melton, J., & Buxton, S. (2006). *Querying XML – Xquery, XPath, and SQL/XML in context.* Morgan-Kaufmann.

Merkle, R. C. (1980). Protocols for public keys cryptosystems. In *Symposium on Research in Security and Privacy*, (pp. 122-134).

MeSH (2008). *Medical Subject Headings.* http://www.nlm.nih.gov/mesh/meshhome.html.

Mesiti, M., Celle, R., Sorrenti, M. A., & Guerrini, G. (2006) X-Evolution: A system for XML schema evolution and document adaptation. In *EDBT*, (pp. 1143-1146).

Micarelli, A., Gasparetti, F., Sciarrone, F., & Gauch, S. (2007). Personalized Search on the World Wide Web. In *LNCS 4321*, (pp. 195-230).

Michels, J. E. (2005). *SQL Standard – SQL/XML functionality.* Presentation for ISO/IEC JTC 1/SC 32 N 1293.

Microsoft (2007). *Biztalk,* http://www.biztalk.org

Microsoft (2007). *SQL Server 2005 Express*, http://www.microsoft.com/sql/express

Middleton, S. E., Shadbolt, N., & De Roure, D. C. (2004). Ontological user profiling in recommender systems. In *ACM Transactions on Information Systems 22*(1), 54-88.

Mignet, L., Barbosa, D., & Veltri, P. (2003). The XML Web: A first study. In *WWW,2,* 500-510.

Min, J.-K., Chung, C.-W., & Shim, K. (2005). An adaptive path index for XML data using the query workload. In *Inf. Syst. 30*(6), 467-487.

Min, J.-K., Park, M.-J., & Chung, C.-W. (2003). Xpress: A queriable compression for XML data. In *SIGMOD*, (pp. 122-133).

Min, J.-K., Park, M.-J., & Chung, C.-W. (2007). Xtream: An efficient multi-query evaluation on streaming XML data. In *Inf. Sci. 177*(17), 3519-3538.

Mitakos, T., Gergatsoulis, M., Stavrakas, Y., & Ioannidis, E. V. (2001). Representing time-dependent information in multidimensional XML. In *Journal of Computing and Information Technology 9*(3), 233-238.

Mlynkova, I. (2007). A journey towards more efficient processing of XML data in (O)RDBMS. In *CIT*, (pp. 23-28).

Mlynkova, I., & Pokorny, J. (2004). From XML schema to object-relational database – an XML schema-driven mapping algorithm. In *ICWI*, (pp. 115-122).

Mlynkova, I., & Pokorny, J. (2008). UserMap – an adaptive enhancing of user-driven XML-to-relational mapping strategies. In *ADC*, pp. 165 – 174.

Mlynkova, I., Toman, K., & Pokorny, J. (2006). Statistical analysis of real XML data collections. In *COMAD*, (pp. 20 -31).

Moerkotte, G. (2002). Incorporating XSL processing into database engines. In *VLDB*, (pp. 107-118).

Moh, C.-H., Lim, E.-P. & Ng, W. K. (2000). DTD-miner: A tool for mining DTD from XML documents. In *WECWIS'00*, ((pp.144-151).

Mokbel, M. F., Lu, M., & Aref, W. G. (2004). Hash-Merge Join: A Non-Blocking Join Algorithm for Producing Fast and Early Join Results. In *ICDE*, (pp. 251–262).

Moro, M. M., Bakalov, P., & Tsotras, V. J. (2007). Early profile pruning on XML-aware publish/subscribe systems. In *VLDB*, (pp. 866-877).

Moro, M. M., Lim, L., & Chang, Y.-C. (2007). Schema Advisor for Hybrid Relational-XML DBMS. In *SIGMOD*, (pp. 959-970).

Moro, M. M., Malaika, S., & Lim, L. (2007). Preserving XML Queries during Schema Evolution. In *WWW*, (pp. 1341-1342).

Moro, M., Malaika, S., & Lim, L. (2007). Preserving XML queries during schema evolution. In *WWW*, (pp. 1341-1342).

Moura Moro, M., Vagena, Z., & Tsotras, V. J. (2005). Tree-pattern queries on a lightweight XML processor. In *VLDB*, (pp. 205-216).

Mukhopadhyay, P., & Papakonstantinou, Y. (2002). Mixing Querying and Navigation in Mix. In *ICDE*, (p. 245).

Murata, M. (2002). Principles of Schema Languages. In H. Maruyama (Ed.), *XML and Java* (2nd ed.), (pp. 592-601).

Murray-Rust, P., & Rzepa, H. S. (2003). Chemical markup, XML and the Worldwide Web. Part 4. CML Schema. In *J. Chem. Inf. comp. Sci., 43*, 757-772.

Mykletun, E., & Tsudik, G. (2006). Aggregation queries in the database-as-a-service model. In *Data and Applications Security*, (pp. 89-103).

Mykletun, E., &Tsudik, G. (2005). Incorporating a secure coprocessor in the database-as-a-service model. In *IWIA*, (pp. 38-44).

Mykletun, E., Narasimha, M., & Tsudik, G. (2004). Authentication and integrity in outsourced databases. In *NDSS*.

Nambiar, U., Lacroix, Z., Bressan, S., Lee, M.-L., & Li, Y. G. (2001). XML Benchmarks Put To The Test. In *IIWAS*.

Nambiar, U., Lacroix, Z., Bressan, S., Lee, M.-L., & Li, Y. G. (2002). Efficient XML data management: An analysis. In *EC-WEB*, (pp. 87-98).

Narasimha, M., & Tsudik, G. (2006). Authentication of outsourced databases using signature aggregation and chaining. In *DASFAA*, (pp. 420-436).

Nassis, V., Rajugan, R., Dillon, T. S., & Rahayu, W. (2004). Conceptual design of XML document warehouses. In *DaWaK*, (pp. 1-14).

Natan, R. B. (2005). *Implementing database security and auditing*. Digital Press.

Nehme, R. V., Rundensteiner, E. A., & Bertino, E. (2008). Security punctuation framework for enforcing access control on streaming data. In *ICDE*, (pp. 406-415).

Ng, W., Lam, W.-Y., Wood, P. T., & Levene, M. (2006). XCQ: A queriable XML compression system. In *Knowl. Inf. Syst. 10*(4), 421-452.

Nguyen, B., Abiteboul, S., Cobena, G., & Preda, M. (2001) . Monitoring XML data on the Web. In *SIGMOD*, (pp. 437-448).

Nguyen, V. H., & Dang, T. K. (2008). A novel solution to query assurance verification for dynamic outsourced XML databases. In *International Journal of Software 3*(4), 9-16.

Nguyen, V. H., Dang T. K., Son, N. T., & Kueng, J. (2007). Query assurance verification for dynamic outsourced XML databases. In *FARES*, (pp. 689-696).

Nicola, M., & van der Linden, B. (2005). Native XML support in DB2 universal database. In *VLDB*, (pp. 1164–1174.)

Nicola, M., Kogan, I., & Schiefer, B. (2007). An XML transaction processing benchmark. In *SIGMOD*, (pp. 937-948).

Niemi, T., Niinimäki, M., Nummenmaa, J., & Thanisch, P. (2002). Constructing an OLAP cube from distributed XML data. In *DOLAP, 02*, 22-27.

Noh, S.-Y., & Gadia, S. K. (2006). A comparison of two approaches to utilizing XML in parametric databases for temporal data. In *Information & Software Technology 48*(9), 807-819.

Norrie, M. C., & Palinginis, A. (2003). Versions for context dependent information services. In *OTM*, (pp. 503-515).

OASIS (2002). *Directory services markup language (DSML) v2.0.* http://www.oasis-open.org/committees/dsml/docs/DSMLv2.doc

Oinn, T. et al. (2006). Taverna: Lessons in creating a workflow environment for the life sciences. In *Concurrency Comput. Pract. Exper., 18,* (pp. 1067-1100).

Oinn, T. et al. (2007). Taverna/myGrid: Aligning a workflow system with the life sciences community. In *Workflows for e-Science: Scientific Workflows for Grids,* (pp. 300-319).

Oliboni, B., Quintarelli, E., & Tanca, L. (2001). Temporal aspects of semistructured data. In *TIME,* (pp. 119-127).

Ontologies (n.d.). Retrieved January 15, 2008, from http://openclinical.org/ontologies.html

Open Directory Project (2004). http://rdf.dmoz.org/

Orchard, S., & Hermjakob, H. (2007). The HUPO proteomics standards initiative—easing communication and minimizing data loss in a changing world. In *Briefings in Bioinformatics 9*(2), 166-173.

Oren, Y. (2002). *SAX Parser Benchmarks.* SourceForge.net. http://piccolo.sourceforge.net/bench.html.

OWL (2004). The Web ontology language home page. W3C Consortium. Retrieved January 15, 2008, from http://www.w3.org/2004/OWL/

Pal, S., Cseri, I., Seeliger, O., Rys, M., Schaller, G., Yu, W., Tomic, D., Baras, A., Berg, B., Churin, D., & Kogan, E. (2005). XQuery implementation in a relational database system. In *VLDB,* (pp. 1175-1186).

Pal, S., Fussell, M., & Dolobowsky, I. (2005). *XML support in Microsoft SQL Server 2005.* Microsoft Corporation. Retrieved March 1, 2008. http://msdn2.microsoft.com/en-us/library/ms345117.aspx

Pal, S., Tomic, D., Berg, B., & Xavier, J. (2006). Managing collections of XML schemas in microsoft SQL server 2005. In *EDBT,* (pp. 1102-1105).

Pallis, G., Stoupa, K., & Vakali, A. (2003). Storage and access control issues for XML documents. In D. Taniar and W. Rahayu (Eds), *Web information systems,* (pp. 104-140).

Palmirani, M., & Brighi, R. (2006). Time model for managing the dynamic of normative system. In *EGOV,* (pp. 207-218).

Pang, H. H., & Tan, K-L. (2004). Authenticating query results in edge computing. In *ICDE,* (pp. 560-571).

Pang, H. H., Jain, A., Ramamritham, K., & Tan, K-L. (2005). Verifying completeness of relational query results in data publishing. In *SIGMOD,* (pp. 407-418).

Pankowski, T., & Hunt, E. (2005). Data merging in life science data integration systems. In *IIPWM,* (pp. 279-288).

Papaemmanouil, O., & Centintemel, U. (2005). SemCast: Semantic multicast for content-based data dissemination. In *ICDE,* (pp. 242-253).

Papaemmanouil, O., Ahmad, Y., Çetintemel, U., & Jannotti, J. (2006). Application-aware overlay networks for data dissemination. In *ICDE Workshop,* (p.76).

Pardede, E., Rahayu, J. W., & Taniar, D. (2004). On using collection for aggregation and association relationships in XML object-relational storage. In *SAC,* (pp. 703-710).

Park, J., Sandhu, R., & Ahn, G-J. (2001). Role-based access control on the Web. In *ACM Transactions on Information and System Security 4*(1), (pp. 37-71).

Pavlidis, P. et al. (2002). Learning gene functional classification from multiple data. In *J. Comput. Biol., 9,* 401-411.

Pearson, W. R. (1994). Using the FASTA program to search protein and DNA sequence databases. In *Methods Mol Biol., 24,* 307-331.

Pellegrini, M., Haynor, D., & Johnson, J. M. (2004). Protein interaction networks. In *Expert Rev. Proteomics, 1*(2), 89-99.

Peng, F., & Chawathe, S. (2003). XPath queries on streaming data. In *SIGMOD,* (pp. 431–442).

Perrad, F. (2003). *DTD+RE. XMLfr.* http://xmlfr.org/documentations/articles/ 030729-0001.

Perugini, S., Gonçalves, M. A., & Fox, E. A. (2004). Recommender systems research: A connection-centric survey. In *Journal of Intelligent Information Systems 23*(2), 107-143.

Pettovello, P. M., & Fotouhi, F. (2006). Mtree: An XML XPath graph index. In *SAC*, (pp. 474-481).

Phan, B. V., & Pardede, E. (2008). Towards the Development of XML Benchmark for XML Updates. In *ITNG*, (pp. 500-505).

Piatetsky-Shapiro, G., & Connell, C. (1984). Accurate estimation of the number of tuples satisfying a condition. In *SIGMOD*, (pp. 256-276).

Pisanelli, D. M. (Ed.) (2004) Ontologies in medicine. In *Studies in Health Technology and Informatics 102*.

Pokorný, J. (2001). Modelling stars using XML. In *DOLAP 2001*, (pp. 24-31).

Poosala, V., & Ioannidis, Y. E. (1997). Selectivity estimation without the attribute value independence assumption. In *VLDB*, (pp. 486-495).

Poosala, V., Ioannidis, Y. E., Haas, P. J., & Shekita, E. J. (1996). Improved histograms for selectivity estimation of range predicates. In *SIGMOD*, (pp. 294-305).

Poulard, P. (2006). active tags: An XML system for native XML programming, in panel Next-Generation XML APIs. In *XML*.

Poulard, P. (2007). Active tags: Mastering XML with XML. In *Extreme markup language*.

Poulard, P. (2008). Properties of schema mashups: Dynamicity, Semantic, mixins, hyperschemas. In *Balisage*.

Pretschner, A. (1998). *Ontology based personalized search*. Unpublished master's thesis. Lawrence, Kansas: University of Kansas.

PRIME Project (2004). *The PRIME Project: Privacy and identity management for Europe*. Retrieved from https://www.prime-project.eu

Raghavachari, M., & Shmueli, O. (2007). Efficient revalidation of XML documents. In *IEEE Transactions on Knowledge and Data Engineering 19*(4), 554-567.

Raj, A., & Kumar, P. (2007). Branch sequencing based XML message broker. In *ICDE*, (pp. 656-665).

Ramanath, M., Freire, J., Haritsa, J., & Roy, P. (2003). Searching for efficient XML-to-relational mappings. In *XSym*, pp. 19-36.

Ravat, F., Teste, O., Tournier, R., & Zurfluh, G. (2007). A conceptual model for multidimensional analysis of documents. In *ER*, (pp. 550-565).

Razmerita, L., Angehrn, A., & Maedche, A. (2003). Ontology-based user modeling for knowledge management systems. In *UM*, (pp. 213-217).

Re, C., Simeon, J., & Fernandez, M. (2006). A complete and efficient algebraic compiler for XQuery. In *ICDE*, (pp. 14-28).

Resnick, P., & Varian, H. R. (Eds.) (1997). *Communications of the ACM 40*(3), Special issue on Recommender systems.

Rich, E. (1999). Users are individuals: Individualizing user models. In *International Journal on Human-Computer Studies 51*(2), 323-338.

Riecken, D. (2000). Personalized views of personalization. In *Communications of the ACM, 43*(8), 27–28.

Riecken., D. (Ed.) (2000). *Communications of the ACM 43*(8), Special issue on Personalization.

Rifaieh et al. (2007). SWAMI: Integrating biological databases and analysis tools within user friendly environment. In *DILS*, (pp. 48-58).

Rizzolo, F., & Vaisman, A. A. (in press). Temporal XML: Modeling, indexing, and query processing. *VLDB Journal*, (pp. 1179–1212).

RNAdb (2005). http://research.imb.uq.edu.au/rnadb/.

Robie, J. (2003). SQL/XML, XQuery, and Native XML programming languages. In *XTech*. IDEAlliance Retrieved March 1, 2008. http://www.idealliance.org/papers/dx_xml03/html/ astract/05-02-01.html

Robie, J., Melton, J., Chamberlin, D., Florescu, D., & Siméon, J. (2007). *XQuery update facility 1.0.* W3C Candidate Recommendation 14 March 2008. http://www.w3.org/TR/xquery-update-10/

Roddick, J. F. (1995). A survey of schema versioning issues for database systems. In *Information and Software Technology 37*(7), 383-393.

Roddick, J. F. et al. (2000). Evolution and change in data management: Issues and directions. In *SIGMOD Record 29*(1), 21-25.

Rorke, M., Muthiah, K., Chennoju, R., Lu, Y., Behm, A., Montanez, C., Sharma, G., & Englich, F. (2007). *XML Query Test Suite.* W3C. http://www.w3.org/XML/Query/test-suite/.

R-Tree Portal (2006). Received from http://www.rtree-portal.org/spatial.html

Runapongsa, K., Patel, J. M., Jagadish, H. V., Chen, Y., & Al-Khalifa, S. (2006). The Michigan benchmark: towards XML Query Performance Diagnostics. In *Inf. Syst. 31*(2), 73-97.

Rundensteiner, E. A., Ding, L., Sutherland, T., Zhu, Y. , Pielech, B., & Mehta, N. (2004). Cape: Continuous query engine with heterogeneous-grained adaptivity. In *VLDB*, (pp. 1353–1356).

Russell, G., Neumuller, M., & Connor, R. (2003). Stream-based XML Processing with Tuple Filtering. In *WebDB*, (pp. 55-60).

Rusu, L. I., Rahayu, J. W., & Taniar, D. (2004). On building XML data warehouses. In *IDEAL 2004*, (pp. 293-299).

Ruttenberg, A., et al. (2005). Experience using OWL DL for the exchange of biological pathway information. In *OWL-ED*.

Rys, M., C. & Florescu, D. (2005). XML and relational database management systems: The inside story. In *SIGMOD*, (pp. 945-947).

Rys, M., Chamberlin, D., & Florescu, D. (2005). Relational database management systems: The inside story. In *SIGMOD*, pp. 945-947.

Sadat, H., & Ghorbani, A. A. (2004) On the Evaluation of Adaptive Web Systems. In J. Yao, V. V. Raghavan, & G. Y. Wang (Eds.), *Proceedings of the 2nd International Workshop on Web-based Support Systems*, (pp. 127-136).

Saltz, J., et al. (2006). caGrid: Design and implementation of the core architecture of the cancer biomedical informatics grid. In *Bioinformatics, 22*(15), 1910-6.

Sanz, I., Mesiti, M., Guerrini, G., & Berlanga, R. (2008). Fragment-based approximate retrieval in highly heterogeneous XML collections. In *Data Knowledge Eng., 64*, 266-293.

Schmidt, A. R., Waas, F., Kersten, M. L., Florescu, D., Carey, M. J., Manolescu, I., & Busse, R. (2001). Why and how to benchmark XML databases. In *SIGMOD Record 30*(3), 27- 32.

Schmidt, A. R., Waas, F., Kersten, M. L., Florescu, D., Manolescu, I., Carey, M. J., & Busse, R. (2001). *The XML Benchmarking project.* Technical Report INS-R0103, CWI, Amsterdam, The Netherlands.

Schmidt, A., Kersten, M., Windhouwer, M., & Waas, F. (2000). Efficient relational storage and retrieval of XML documents. In *WebDB 2000,* (pp. 137-150).

Schmidt, A., Wass, F., Kersten, M., Carey, M., Manolescu, I., & Busse, R. (2002). XMark: A benchmark for XML data management. In *VLDB*, pp. 974-985.

Schmitt, A. (2004). Native XML processing in object-oriented languages: Calling XMHell from PurgatOOry. In *FOOL*.

Schoning, H. (2001). Tamino - A DBMS designed for XML. In *ICDE,* (pp. 149).

Schrefl, M., Grün, K., & Dorn, J. (2005). SemCrypt-Ensuring privacy of electronic documents through semantic-based encrypted query processing. In *ICDE Workshop*, (p. 1191).

Seibel, P. N et al. (2006). XML schemas for common bioinformatic data types and their application in workflow systems. In *BMC Bioinformatics, 7*, 490.

Shah, R., Ramzan, Z., Jain, R., Dendukuri, R., & Anjum, F. (2004). Efficient dissemination of personalized information using content-based multicast. In *IEEE Transactions on Mobile Computing 3*(4), & 394-408.

Shah, S. P., et al. (2005). Pegasys: Software for executing and integrating analyses of biological sequences. In *BMC Bioinformatics, 5*, 40.

Shanmugasundaram, J., Shekita, E. J., Kiernan, J., Krishnamurthy, R., Viglas, S., Naughton, J. F., & Tatarinov, I. (2001). A general techniques for querying XML documents using a relational database system. In *SIGMOD Record 30*(3), 20-26.

Shanmugasundaram, J., Shekita, E., Barr, R., Carey, M., Lindsay, B., Pirahesh, H., & Reinwald, B. (2001). Efficiently publishing relational data as XML documents. In *VLDB Journal, 10*(2-3), 133-154.

Shanmugasundaram, J., Tufte, K., Zhang, C., He, G., DeWitt, D., & Naughton J. (1999). Relational databases for querying XML documents: Limitations and opportunities. In *VLDB,* (pp. 302-314).

Shen, Z., Aluru, S., & Tirthapura, S. (2005). Indexing for subscription covering in publish-subscribe systems. In *ISCA PDCS,* (pp. 328-333).

Shin, D., Ahn, G., & Park, J. (2002). An application of directory service markup language (DSML) for role-based access control (RBAC). In *COMPSAC,* (pp. 934-939).

SIGMOD (2007). *SIGMOD Record in XML.* http://www.sigmod.org/record/xml/

Sion, R. (2005). Query execution assurance for outsourced databases. In *VLDB,* (pp. 601-612).

Smith, S. W., & Safford, D. (2001). Practical server privacy with secure coprocessors. In *IBM Systems Journal 40*(3), 683-695.

Snodgrass, R. T. (Ed.) (1995). *The TSQL2 Temporal Query Language.* New York: Kluwer Academic Publishing.

Snoeren, A. C., Conley, K., & Gifford, D. K. (2001). Mesh-based content routing using XML. In *SOSP,* (pp. 160-173).

Software AG (2008). Tamino schema editor. *On-line documentation.*

Song, D. X., Wagner, D., & Perrig, A. (2000). Practical techniques for searches on encrypted data. In *IEEE Symposium on Security and Privacy,* (pp. 44-55).

Sosnoski, D. (2003). *Data binding, Part 1: Code generation approaches -- JAXB and more,* http://www.ibm.com/developerworks/library/x-databdopt/

Sosnoski, D. M. (2002). *XMLBench Document Model Benchmark.* http://www.sosnoski.com/opensrc/ xml-bench/index.html

Spellman, P. T. et al. (2002). Design and implementation of microarray gene expression markup language (MAGE-ML). In *Genome Biology, 3*, 0046.1–0046.9.

Spinello, R. A. (2004). Property Rights in Genetic Information. In *Ethics and Inf. Technol., 6*(1), 29-42.

Spitzner, J. et al. (1997). *Bioinformatic sequence markup language (BSML).* LabBook's BSML Sequence Tutorials.

Stavrakas, Y., & Gergatsoulis, M. (2002) Multidimensional semistructured data: Representing context-dependent information on the Web. In *CAiSE,* (pp. 183–199).

Stavrakas, Y., Gergatsoulis, M., & Rondogiannis, P. (2000) Multidimensional XML. In *DCW,* (pp. 100–109).

Stavrakas, Y., Gergatsoulis, M., Doulkeridis, C., & Zafeiris, V. (2004) Representing and querying histories of semistructured databases using multidimensional OEM. In *Information Systems 29*(6), 461-482.

Stavrakas, Y., Pristouris, K., Efandis, A., & Sellis, T. K. (2004) Implementing a query language for context-dependent semistructured data. In *ADBIS,* (pp. 173–188).

Staworko, S., & Chomicki, J. (2006). Validity-sensitive querying of XML databases. In *EDBT Workshops,* (pp. 164-177).

Steegmans, B. et al. (2004). *XML for DB2 information integration.* IBM Redbook Series.

StreamBase. (2008). Retrieved March 15, 2008, from http://www.streambase.com/

Strömbäck, L. et al. (2007). A review of standards for data exchange within systems biology. In *Proteomics, 7*, 857–867.

Su, H., Jian, J., & Rundensteiner, E. A. (2003). Raindrop: a uniform and layered algebraic framework for xqueries on xml streams. In *CIKM*, (pp. 279–286).

Su, H., Rundensteiner, E. A. & Mani, M. (2008, March). Automaton In or Out: Run-time Plan Optimization for XML Stream Processing, In *SSPS*, (pp. 38-47).

Su, H., Rundensteiner, E. A., & Mani, M. (2005). Semantic query optimization for xquery over xml streams. In *VLDB*, (pp. 277–288).

Su, H., Rundensteiner, E. A., & Mani, M. (2006). Automaton Meets Algebra: A Hybrid Paradigm for XML Stream. In *Data Knowledge Engineering 59*(3), 576–602.

Sun Microsystems *JSTL. JavaServer pages standard tag library*. http://java.sun.com/products/jsp/jstl/

Sun Microsystems, *JSP. JavaServer pages technology*. http://java.sun.com/products/jsp/

Sun Microsystems. *UEL. Unified expression language*, http://java.sun.com/products/jsp/reference/techart/unifiedEL.html

Surjanto, B., Ritter, N., & Loeser, H. (2000). XML content management based on object-relational database technology. In *WISE, 1*, 70-79.

Tan, M., & Goh, A. (2004). Keeping pace with evolving XML-based specifications. In *EDBT Workshops*, (pp. 280-288).

Tan, Z., Xu, J., Wang, W., & Shi, B. (2005). Storing normalized XML documents in normalized relations. In *CIT* , (pp. 123-129).

Tao, Y., Yiu, M. L., Papadias, D., Hadjieleftheriou, M., & Mamoulis, N. (2005). RPJ: Producing fast join results on streams through rate-based optimization. In *SIGMOD*, (pp. 371–382).

Tatarinov, I., Viglas, S. D., Beyer, K., Shanmugasundaram, J., Shekita, E. & Zhang, C. (2002). Storing and querying ordered XML using a relational database system. In *SIGMOD*, (pp. 204-215).

Tatbul, N., Çetintemel, U., Zdonik, S., Cherniack, M., & Stonebraker, M. (2003). Load Shedding in a Data Stream Manager. In *VLDB*, (pp. 309–320).

Tatusov, R. L., Koonin, E. V., & Lipman, D. J. (1997). A genomic perspective on protein families. In *Science 278*, (pp. 631-637).

Tavani, H. T. (2004). Genomic research and data-mining technology: Implications for personal privacy and informed consent. In *Ethics and Inf. Technol., 6*(1), 15-28.

Tennison, J. (2006). Datatypes for XML: The datatyping librarylanguage (DTLL). In *Extreme markup languages.*

Terenziani, P., Montani, S., Bottrighi, A., Molino, G., & Torchio, M. (2005). Clinical guidelines adaptation: Managing authoring and versioning issues. In *AIME*, (pp. 151–155).

Thompson, H. S., Beech, D., Maloney, M., & Mendelsohn, N. (2004). *XML Schema Part 1: Structures (Second Edition)*. W3C. www.w3.org/TR/xmlschema-1/

Thuraisingham, B. (2005). *Database and applications security: Integrating information security and data management.* Auerbach Publisher.

Tian, F., Reinwald, B., Pirahesh, H., Mayr T., & Myllymaki J. (2004). Implementing a scalable XML publish/subscribe system using relational database systems. In *SIGMOD*, (pp. 479-490).

Tok, W. H., Bressan, S., & Lee, M.-L. (2007). RRPJ : Result-rate based progressive relational join. In *DASFAA*, (pp. 43–54).

Tok, W. H., Bressan, S., & Lee, M.-L. (2007). *Twig'n join: Progressive query processing of multiple xml streams.* Technical Report TRA9/07, National University of Singapore.

Tolani, P. M., & Haritsa, J. R. (2002). XGRIND: A Query-Friendly XML Compressor. In *ICDE*, (p. 225).

Tompa, M. et al. (2005). Assessing computational tools for the discovery of transcription factor binding sites. In *Nature Biotechnology, 1*(23), 137-144.

Torgersen, M. (2004). The expression problem revisited. In *Proc. Of 18th ECOOP*, (pp. 123-143).

t-Protégé (n.d.). *The t-Protégé Project Home Page*. University of Peloponnese. Retrieved January 15, 2008, from http://t-protege.uop.gr/

Trajkova, J., & Gauch, S. (2004). Improving ontology-based user profiles. In *RIAO 2004 Conference Proceedings* (pp. 380-389). Paris, France: C.I.D. Retrieved January 15, 2008, from http://www3.riao.org/Proceedings-2004/papers/0290.pdf

Treebank (1999). *The Penn Treebank Project*. http://www.cis.upenn.edu/~treebank/

Triantafillou, P., & Economides, A. A. (2004). Subscription summarization: A new paradigm for efficient publish/subscribe systems. In *ICDCS*, (pp. 562–571).

Troyanskaya, O. G. et al. (2003). A Bayesian framework for combining heterogeneous data sources for gene function prediction in Saccharomices cerevisiae. In *Proc. Natl Acad. Sci. USA, 100*, 8348-8353.

Türker, C. et al. (2007). B-Fabric: A data and application integration framework for life sciences research. In *DILS*, (pp. 37-47).

Umar, A. (2004). *Information security and auditing in the digital age: A managerial and practical perspective*. NGE Solutions.

UniProt (2008). *Universal Protein Resource*. http://www.ebi.uniprot.org/index.shtml.

Urhan, T., & Franklin, M. (2000). XJoin: A Reactively Scheduled Pipelined Join Operator. In *IEEE Data Engineering Bulletin 23*(2), 27–33.

Vagena, Z., & Moro, M. M. (2008). Semantic search over XML document streams. In *DATAX*.

Vagena, Z., Moro, M. M., & Tsotras, V. J. (2007). RoXSum: Leveraging data aggregation and batch processing for XML routing. In *ICDE*, (pp. 1466-1470).

Vagena, Z., Moro, M. M., & Tsotras, V. J. (2007). Value-Aware RoXSum: Effective message aggregation for XML-aware information dissemination. In *WebDB*.

Vagena, Z., Moura Moro, M., & Tsotras, V. J. (2004) Twig query processing over graph-structured XML data. In *WebDB*, (pp. 43-48).

Vaidya, J. S., & Clifton, C. (2002). Privacy preserving association rule mining in vertically partitioned data. *SIGKDD*, (pp. 639-644).

Vakali, A., Catania, B., & Madalena, A. (2005). XML data stores: Emerging practices. In *IEEE Internet Computing 9*(2), 62-69.

Velegrakis, Y., Miller, R.-J., & Popa, L. (2004). Preserving mapping consistency under schema changes. In *VLDB Journal 13*(3), 274-293.

Velegrakis, Y., Miller, R.-J., Popa, L., & Mylopoulos, J. (2004). ToMAS: A system for adapting mappings while schemas evolve. In *ICDE*, (p. 862).

Venkatesh, T. V., & Harlow, H. (2002). Integromics: Challenges in data integration. In *Genome Biology, 3*(8), 4027.1–4027.3

Viglas, S., Naughton, J., & Burger, J. (2003). Maximizing the Output Rate of Multi-Way Join Queries over Streaming Information. In *VLDB*, (pp. 285–296). Morgan Kaufmann.

Visser, P. R. S., & Bench-Capon, T. J. M. (1998). A comparison of four ontologies for the design of legal knowledge systems. In *Artificial Intelligence and Law 6*(1), 27–57.

Vitali, F., & Durand, D. G. (1996). Using versioning to support collaboration on the WWW. In *WWW Journal 1*(1), 37–50.

Vosta, O., Mlynkova, I., & Pokorny, J. (2008). Even an ant can create an XSD. In *DASFAA*, (pp. 35-50).

Vrdoljak, B., Banek, M., & Rizzi, S. (2003). Designing Web warehouses from XML schemas. In *DaWaK 2003*, (pp. 89-98).

VTD-XML (2003). *Benchmark Report for Version 2.0.* XimpleWare. http://www.ximpleware.com/2.0/ benchmark_2.0_indexing.html

W3C (1998). *Extensible markup language (XML).*

W3C (1999). *XML path language (XPath) Version 1.0.* W3C Recommendation, http://www.w3.org/TR/xpath

W3C (1999). *XSL Transformations (XSLT) Version 1.0.* W3C Recommendation, http://www.w3.org/TR/1999/REC-xslt-19991116, 1999.

W3C (2000). *Document object model (DOM) level 2 core specification.* W3C Recommendation, http://www.w3.org/TR/2000/REC-DOM-Level-2-Core-20001113/

W3C (2001). *Extensible stylesheet language (XSL) Version 1.0.* W3C Recommendation, http://www.w3.org/Style/XSL/.

W3C (2002). Xquery 1.0 and xpath 2.0 formal Semantics (W3C working draft), http://www.w3.org/tr/query-algebra.

W3C (2004). *XML schema part 0: Primer.* Second Edition

W3C (2004). *Document object model (DOM) Level 3 Core Specification Version 1.0.* W3C Recommendation, http://www.w3.org/TR/2004/REC-DOM-Level-3-Core-20040407/

W3C (2004). *XML Schema part 1: Structures (2nd ed.).* W3C Recommendation, http://www.w3.org/TR/xmlschema-1/

W3C (2004). *Extensible stylesheet language (XSL) Version 1.1.* W3C Recommendation, http://www.w3.org/TR/xsl11/

W3C (2004). *XML Schema part 2: Datatypes Second Edition.* W3C Recommendation, http://www.w3.org/TR/xmlschema-2/

W3C (2006). *XML processing model requirements and use cases.* W3C Working Draft, http://www.w3.org/TR/2006/WD-xproc-requirements-20060411/

W3C (2006). *An XML pipeline language (XProc).* W3C Working Draft, http://www.w3.org/TR/2006/WD-xproc-20061117/

W3C (2007). *XML path language (XPath) Version 2.0.* W3C Recommendation, http://www.w3.org/TR/xpath20/

W3C (2007). *XQuery/XPath data model (XDM) 1.0.* W3X Recommendation, http://www.w3.org/TR/xpath-datamodel/

W3C (2007). *XQuery 1.0: An XML Query Language.* W3C Recommendation, http://www.w3.org/TR/xquery/

W3C (2007). *XQuery 1.0: An XML query language.* W3C Recommendation, http://www.w3.org/TR/xquery/

W3C (2007) *XSL Transformations (XSLT) Version 2.0.* W3C Recommendation, http://www.w3.org/TR/xslt20/.

W3C (2007). *XML Syntax for XQuery 1.0.* W3C Recommendation, http://www.w3.org/TR/xqueryx/

W3C (2007). *State chart XML (SCXML): State machine notation for control abstraction.* W3C Working Draft, http://www.w3.org/TR/scxml/

W3C (2008). *XQuery Update Facility 1.0.* W3C Candidate Recommendation, http://www.w3.org/TR/xquery-update-10/

W3C-World Wide Web Consortium (2008). Retrieved from http://www.w3c.org

Wadge, W. W., & Schraefel, M. C. (2002). A Complementary approach for adaptive and Adaptable hypermedia: Intensional hypertext. In *LNCS 2266*, 327–333.

Wadge, W. W., Brown, G. D., Schraefel, M. C., & Yildirim, T. (1998) Intensional HTML. In *PODDP*, (pp. 128–139).

Wahl, M., Howes, T., & Kille, S. (1997). Lightweight directory access protocol (v3). *IETF RFC 2251*, Dec. 1997; www.ietf. org/rfc/rfc2251

Walsh, N. (2005). *XML Catalogs. Organization for the advancement of structured information standards.* http://www.oasis-open.org/committees/download.php/14809/xml-catalogs.html

Wang, F., & Zaniolo, C. (2003) Temporal queries in XML document archives and Web warehouses. In *TIME*, (pp. 47–55).

Wang, F., & Zaniolo, C. (2008) Temporal queries and version management in XML-based document archives. In *Data & Knowledge Engineering* 65(2), 304–324.

Wang, H., & Lakshmanan, L. V. S. (2006). Efficient secure query evaluation over encrypted XML databases. In *VLDB*, (pp. 127-138).

Wang, H., Li, J., He, Z., & Gao, H. (2005). OLAP for XML data. In *CIT*, (pp. 233-237).

Wang, S., Su, H., Li, M., Wei, M., Yang, S., Ditto, D., Rundensteiner, E. A., & Mani, M. (2006). R-SOX: Runtime Semantic Query Optimization over XML Streams. In *VLDB*, (pp. 1207–1210).

Wang, Y.-M., Qiu, L., Achlioptas, D., Das, G., Larson, P., & Wang, H. J. (2002). Subscription partitioning and routing in content based publish/subscribe networks. In *DiSC*.

Waugh, A., et al. (2006). CellML2SBML: Conversion of CellML into SBML. In *Bioinformatics, 22*(8), 1018-1020.

Wei, M., Rundensteiner, E. A., & Mani, M. (2008). Utility-Driven Load Shedding for XML Stream Processing. In *WWW*, (pp. 855-864).

Wendover, A. (2001). *Arthur's Classic Novels.* http://arthursclassicnovels.com/

Werner, E. (2007). All systems go. In *Nature, 446*, 493-494.

Whetzel, P. L. et al. (2006). The MGED Ontology: A resource for Semantics-based description of microarray experiments. In *Bioinformatics, 22,* 866–873.

Williams, A., & Runte, K. (2004). XML Format of the UniProt Knowledgbase. In *ISMB*.

Win, K.-M., Ng, W.-K., & Lim, E.-P. (2003). An architectural framework for native XML data management. In CW, (pp. 302-309).

Witkowski, A., Bellamkonda, S., Li, H., Liang, V., Sheng L., Smith, W., Subramanian, S., Terry, J., & Yu, T. (2007). Continuous queries in oracle. In *VLDB*, (pp. 1173-1184).

Wiwatwattana, N., Jagadish, H., Lakshmanan Laks, V. S., & Srivastava D. (2007). X^3: A cube operator for XML OLAP. In *ICDE*, (pp. 916-925).

Wong, R. K., Lam, F., & Orgun, M. A. (2001) Modelling and manipulating multidimensional data in semistructured databases. In *WWW Journal 4*(1–2), 79–99.

Wu, Y., Patel, J. M., & Jagadish, H. V. (2003). Structural Join Order Selection for XML Query Optimization. In *ICDE*, (pp. 443–454).

XDR (2002). *XML Data Repository.* www.cs.washington.edu/research/xmldatasets/www/repository.html.

Xiao-ling, W., Jin-feng, L., & Yi-sheng, D. (2003). An adaptable and adjustable mapping from XML data to tables in RDB. In *LNCS 2590*, (pp. 117-130).

Xie, M., Wang, H., Yin, J., & Meng, X. (2007). Integrity auditing in outsourced data. In *VLDB*, pages 782-793.

Xtatic. *The Xtatic project: Native XML processing for C#.* http://www.cis.upenn.edu/~bcpierce/xtatic/

Xu, W., & Özsoyoglu, Z. M. (2005). Rewriting XPath queries using materialized views. In *VLDB*, (pp. 121-132).

Xu, Z., Guo, Z., Zhou, S., & Zhou, A. (2003). Dynamic tuning of XML storage schema in VXMLR. In *IDEAS*, (pp. 76-86).

Xylème (2001). A dynamic warehouse for XML data of the Web. In *IEEE Data Engineering Bulletin 24*(2), 40-47.

Yan, T. W., & Garcia-Molina, H. (1999). The SIFT information dissemination system. In *ACM Transactions on Database Systems 24*(4), 529-565.

Yang, Y., Wilfred, N., Lau, H. L., & Cheng, J. (2006). An efficient approach to support querying secure outsourced XML information. In *CAiSE*, (pp. 157-171).

Yao, B. B., Ozsu, M. T., & Keenleyside, J. (2003). XBench – A family of benchmarks for XML DBMSs. In *LNCS 2590*, (pp. 162–164).

Yao, B. B., Ozsu, M. T., & Khandelwal, N. (2004). XBench Benchmark and Performance Testing of XML DBMSs. In *ICDE'04*, (pp. 621–632).

Yildiz, B. (2006). *Ontology Evolution and Versioning. The state of the art.* Technical report. http://publik.tuwien.ac.at/files/pub-inf_4603.pdf

Yoo, S., Son, J. H., & Kim, M. H. (2006). An efficient subscription routing algorithm for scalable XML-based publish/subscribe systems. In *Journal of Systems and Software 79*(12), 1767-1781.

Yoshikawa, M., Amagasa, T., Shimura, T., & Uemura, S. (2001). XRel: A Path-Based Approach to Storage and Retrieval of XML Documents Using Relational Databases. In *ACM Trans. Inter. Tech. 1*(1), 110-141.

Zamboulis, L. et al. (2007). Bioinformatics service reconciliation by heterogeneous schema transformation. In *DILS*, (pp. 89-104).

Zhang, C., Naughton, J. F., DeWitt, D. J., Luo, Q., & Lohman, G. M. (2001). On supporting containment queries in relational database management systems. In *SIGMOD*, (pp. 425–436).

Zhang, C., Naughton, J., DeWitt, D., Luo, Q., & Lohman, G. (2001) On supporting containment queries in relational database management systems. In *SIGMOD*, (pp. 425-436).

Zhang, X., Pielech, B., & Rundensteiner, E. A. (2002, November). Honey, I Shrunk the XQuery!: An XML Algebra Optimization Approach. In *WIDM*, (pp. 15-22).

Zheng, S., Wen, J., & Lu, H. (2003). Cost-driven storage schema relation for XML. In *DASFAA*, (pp. 55-66).

Zhu, Y., Rundensteiner, E. A., & Heineman, G. T. (2004). Dynamic Plan Migration for Continuous Queries over Data Streams. In *SIGMOD*, (pp. 431–442).

About the Contributors

Eric Pardede is a lecturer at La Trobe University, Melbourne. He completed his Master of Information Technology and Doctor of Philosophy in Computer Science at La Trobe University He also holds a Master of Quality Management degree from University of Wollongong and a Bachelor of Engineering degree from Bandung Institute of Technology. He has co-authored a book and several research papers appeared in international journals and conference proceedings. He is an active scholar that has chairing several international conferences and workshops. His current research area is in XML database, data modeling, query optimization, and health informatics.

* * *

Riadh Ben Messaoud is an associate professor, since 2007, in computer science at the School of Economics and Management of Nabeul which belongs to the University of Carthage, Tunisia. He received his PhD degree in the Decision Support Databases Research Group of the ERIC Laboratory in the School of Economics and Management of the University of Lyon 2, France in 2006. Since 2002, he is an engineer on "Statistics and Data Analysis" from the School of Computer Sciences of Tunis, Tunisia. He received a Research Master's degree on "knowledge discovery in databases" from the University of Lyon 2, France in 2003. His research interests are data warehousing, OLAP, complex data, and data mining. Since January 2004, he has actively published his work on several national and international conferences and journals.

Stéphane Bressan is an associate professor in the Computer Science department of the School of Computing (SoC) at the National University of Singapore (NUS). He received his PhD in Computer Science in 1992 from the University of Lille. Stéphane was a researcher at the European Computer-industry Research Centre (ECRC) of Bull, ICL, and Siemens in Munich, Germany. From 1996 to 1998, he was a research associate at the Sloan School of Management of the Massachusetts Institute of Technology (MIT). Stéphane's research interest is the integration and management of information from heterogeneous, distributed and autonomous information sources.

Doulkifli Boukraa has received his Master's degree in computer science in 2005 from the National Computer Science Institute (INI) of Algiers, Algeria. In 2003, He becames an Oracle certified developer (version 9i). He got his engineering degree in computer science in 1998 from the National Computer Science Institute (INI) of Algiers, Algeria. Since 2006, he has been working on XML warehouses within the context of his PhD thesis preparation. His research interests include modeling XML data warehouses and optimizing their performance.

Omar Boussaid is a full professor in computer science at the School of Economics and Management of the University of Lyon 2, France. He received his PhD degree in computer science from the University of Lyon 1, France in 1988. Since 1995, he is the director of the Master Computer Science Engineering for Decision and Economic Evaluation of the University of Lyon 2. He is a head of the Decision Support Databases Research Group within the ERIC Laboratory. His main research subjects are data warehousing, multidimensional databases and OLAP. His current research concerns complex data warehousing and mining, XML warehousing, combining OLAP and data mining, and the use of ontologies within complex data warehousing.

Yuan-Chi Chang is a research staff member and manager of the database research group at IBM Thomas J. Watson Research Centre in Hawthorne, New York, USA. Dr. Chang and his group have been conducting research and development in data management topics including content-based retrieval, e-commerce search, data warehouse, XML data modeling and design as well as business performance monitoring. He received his PhD in 1991 from National Taiwan University. Dr. Chang holds over a dozen patents in the US and worldwide.

Tran Khanh Dang received his BEng degree from the Faculty of Computer Science & Engineering in HCMC University of Technology-HCMUT (Vietnam) in 1998. He achieved the medal awarded for the best graduation student. From 1998-2000, he had been working as a lecturer and researcher in the same faculty. Then, he received a PhD scholarship from the Austrian Exchange Service (OeAD) in 2000-2003, and finished his PhD degree (Dr.techn.) in May 2003 at FAW Institute, University of Linz (Austria). He has worked as a lecturer and researcher at the School of Computing Science, Middlesex University in London (UK) since August 2003. In October 2005, he returned home and has continued working for the Faculty of Computer Science & Engineering in HCMUT. Dr. Dang's research interests include database and information security, information retrieval, location-based services, and grid data management. He has published more than 40 scientific papers in international journals & conferences. Dr. Dang has also participated in and managed many research as well as commercial projects.

Fabio Grandi is currently an associate professor in the Faculty of Engineering of the University of Bologna, Italy. Since 1989 he has worked at the CSITE center of the Italian National Research Council (CNR) in Bologna, initially supported by a CNR fellowship. In 1993 and 1994 he was an adjunct professor at the Universities of Ferrara, Italy, and Bologna. He joined his current department (Dept. of Electronics, Computer Science and Systems) as a research associate in 1994. His scientific interests include temporal databases, version management, Web information systems, knowledge representation. He is a member of the TSQL2 language design committee. He received a Laurea degree cum laude in electronics engineering and a PhD in electronics engineering and computer science from the University of Bologna.

Sven Groppe earned his diploma degree in informatik (computer science) from the University of Paderborn in 2002 and his Doctor degree from the University of Paderborn in 2005. From 2005 to 2007, he worked as postdoc in the University of Innsbruck. He is currently working as postdoc in the University of Lübeck. In 2001/2002, he worked in the project B2B-ECOM, which dealt with distributed internet market places for the electrical industry. From 2002 to 2004, he worked in the project MEMPHIS in the area of premium services. From 2005 to 2006, he worked in the projects ASG and TripCom in the areas of Semantic Web Services. All projects were funded by the European Union. He was a member of the DAWG W3C Working Group, which developed SPARQL. He is currently the project leader of LUPOSDATE, a German national project funded by the DFG, which deals with Semantic Web data streams.

Jinghua Groppe earned her Bachelor's degree in computer science and applications from the Beijing Polytechnic University in 1989 and her Master's degree in computer science from the University of Amsterdam in 2001. She worked as software engineer in the Chinese Academy of Launch Vehicle Technology/China Aerospace Corporation from 1989 to 1999. She was a scientific employee in the Department of Computer Science/University of Paderborn from 2001 to 2005 and in the Institute of Computer Science/University of Innsbruck from 2005 to 2006. She is currently a scientific employee in the Univeristy of Lübeck Germany, and has recently submitted her doctoral thesis. She worked in the projects EUQOS, UBISEC, E-Colleg, VHE and ASG. All projects were funded by the European Union. She is currently working in the project LUPOSDATE, a German national project funded by the DFG, which deals with Semantic Web data streams.

Giovanna Guerrini is associate professor at the Department of Computer and Information Sciences of the University of Genova, Italy. She received the MS and PhD degrees in computer science from the University of Genova, Italy, in 1993 and 1998, respectively. She had been assistant professor at the University of Genova (1996-2001) and associate professor at the University of Pisa (2001-2005). Her research interests include object-oriented, active, and temporal databases as well as semi-structured and XML data handling. She served as program committee member of international conferences, like EDBT, ECOOP, ACM OOPSLA, ACM CIKM and she is currently serving as Conference Co-chair for ECOOP 2009.

Nils Hoeller studied computer science at the University of Luebeck where he received his diploma degree in March 2007. Since April 2007 he is a scientific employee in the Institute of Information Systems/ University of Luebeck. His main research focus is XML data management and continuous XML query languages. His special research interests cover the integration of XML data handling and XML query processing in mobile ad-hoc networks like sensor networks, whereby a motivation is the adaptation of the service-oriented paradigm to sensor network engineering.

Vassiliki Koutsonikola received the BS degree in computer science from Aristotle University of Thessaloniki, Greece in 2001, and the MS degree in information systems from the University of Macedonia, Greece in 2003. Currently, she is a PhD student at Aristotle University of Thessaloniki. Her research interests include clustering, directory services and network-based data organization.

Ming Li is a PhD student in the Computer Science Department at Worcester Polytechnic Institute. He received his BS degree in computer science from Fudan University and his MS degree in computer science from Worcester Polytechnic Institute. His main area of interest is in database systems, especially query processing and optimization in XML streams and complex event processing.

Lipyeow Lim is a research staff member in the event-based systems group at IBM Thomas J. Watson Research Centre in Hawthorne, New York, USA. Dr. Lim obtained his PhD in 2004 from Duke University,

North Carolina, USA, and his MSc and BSc in 1999 and 1998 respectively from the National University of Singapore. His research interests lie in the area of data management technology – in particular, XML database, statistics collection, query optimization, data stream systems and data warehousing.

Volker Linnemann earned his PhD (Dr. rer. nat.) from the Technical University Carolo-Wilhelmina zu Braunschweig in 1979. He was a PostDoc at the University of Toronto from 1979 to 1980. He was working at Nixdorf Computer AG in Paderborn from 1981 to 1982. He was an assistant professor at the Johann Wolfgang Goethe-University Frankfurt am Main from 1982 to 1986. He joined the IBM Scientific Center Heidelberg in the AIM-Project from 1986 to 1991. He was associate professor at the Julius-Maximilians-University of Würzburg (1991-1993). Since December 1993, he has been a full professor at the University of Lübeck and the head of the Institute of Information Systems (IFIS). His research interests cover persistent data in sensor networks, programming languages for XML-based applications, data base programming languages for XML data, indices for XML databases, software tools for WWW applications, Web services, data modelling for advanced applications, non-standard-databases, heterogeneous information systems, description of data types by grammar, relationships between programming languages and databases, media archives and recursion in databases.

Rafael Berlanga Llavori is an associate professor of computer science at Universitat Jaume I, Spain. He received the BS degree from Universidad de Valencia in Physics, and the PhD degree in computer science in 1996 from the same university. He is the author of several articles in international journals, such as *Information Processing & Management, Concurrency: Practice and Experience, Applied Intelligence*, among others, and numerous communications in international conferences such as DEXA, ECIR, CIARP, etc. His current research interests are knowledge bases, information retrieval, and temporal reasoning.

Mary Ann Malloy is a principal information systems engineer for MITRE, a federally-funded research and development corporation in the USA. She completed her PhD (1995) with a concentration in software reliability modeling at Old Dominion University in Norfolk, Virginia, USA, where she remains an adjunct faculty member. Dr. Malloy is an internationally recognized expert in information interoperability, operational constraints management and digital culture. She has nearly 30 years of hands-on experience in software design and development for defense applications. Dr. Malloy is a sought-after speaker on technology topics including, but not limited to, information and knowledge management, business process and rules management, XML technologies and service-oriented architecture. She has authored more than 40 technical papers. Recent publications include *A Model for Successful Engineering Internship, "Wicked" Project Management, A Lightweight Approach to Building the Department of Defense's Semantic Web* and *Online Reputation Management.*

Federica Mandreoli is a research associate at the Department of Information Engineering of the University of Modena and Reggio Emilia, Italy. She holds a Laurea degree in computer science and a PhD in electronics engineering and computer science from the University of Bologna. Her scientific interests are in the field of information and knowledge management and, currently, mainly concerns data sharing in P2P networks and personalized access to great quantity of graph-based information. As to those research themes, she is author of publications and book chapters dealing with query processing in P2P networks, structural disambiguation for Semantic-aware applications and personalized accesses to XML data and ontologies.

Murali Mani is an assistant professor in the Department of Computer Sciece at Worcester Polytechnic Insitute, where he joined in 2003. Before that, he finished his MS and PhD from University of California, Los Angeles, and his BTech from Indian Institute of Technology, Madras. His research interests are in database systems, where he focuses on data integration, web and XML systems, and data management for health informatics.

David Manset holds a PhD from the University of Bristol. He is the director of Biomedical Applications at Maat Gknowledge and the owner at Maat Gknowledge France. His research interests include service-oriented architectures and grid technology.

Riccardo Martoglia is a research associate at the Faculty of Mathematical, Physical and Natural Sciences of the University of Modena e Reggio Emilia. He received his Laurea degree (*cum Laude*) and his PhD in computer engineering from the same University. He teaches a number of subjects in the area of databases, information systems, information retrieval and Semantic Web. His current research is about studying new methodologies for efficiently and effectively querying and managing large amounts of semi-structured and multi-version data. He is author of many publications and book chapters about the above mentioned topics. He is a member of ACM and IEEE Computer Society.

Marco Mesiti is an assistant professor at University of Milan, Italy. He received the MS and PhD degrees in computer science from the University of Genova, Italy, in 1998 and 2003, respectively. His main research interests include the management of XML documents, XML schema evolution, and access control mechanisms for XML. He has been a visiting researcher at the applied research center of Telcordia Technologies, Morristown, New Jersey. He co-organized the three editions of the EDBT DataX workshop and served as PC member of EDBT PhD workshop 2006 and 2008, ADBIS Conference 2006, IEEE SAINT 2005 and 2006, EDBT Workshop ClustWeb 2004, and as reviewer for international conferences and journals.

Irena Mlynkova has received her Master and PhD degrees in computer science at the Charles University in Prague, Czech Republic, where she currently works at the Department of Software Engineering as an assistant professor. Her research areas involve XML data management in (O)RDBMSs, similarity of XML data and its exploitation, analysis of real-world XML data, synthesis of XML data and XML benchmarking. She publishes her results at international conferences, in journals, as well as in refereed books. Some of them gained significant awards. During her teaching career she has co-authored and currently teaches lectures "*XML Technologies*" and "*Advanced XML Technologies*" for the Charles University and in the same area she supervises master and bachelor theses as well as student projects.

Mirella M. Moro is assistant professor at the Computer Science Department of UFMG (Federal University of Minas Gerais, Brazil). She holds a PhD in computer science (University of California Riverside - UCR), and MSc and BSc in computer science as well (UFRGS, Brazil). After her PhD, she spent a year as posdoc at UFRGS, funded by a CNPq (Brazilian Research Foundation). She has previously worked as intern at IBM T. J. Watson Research Center and IBM Silicon Valley Lab. She is part of the Education Board of the Brazilian Computer Society - SBC, and is also a member of ACM, ACM SIGMOD, and IEEE. She also serves/ed as program committee member of ICDE Demo'09, CIKM'08, ACM DocEng'08, EDBT Demo'08, SBBD'08, XSym'07, and is the publicity chair of ER'2009 and proceedings chair of ICDE 2010. Her current research areas of interest include XML query optimization and content-based dissemination systems.

Paolo Perlasca is assistant professor at University of Milan, Italy. He received the MS and PhD degrees in computer science from the University of Milan. His main research interests include access control, database security, integrity and protection. Current research focuses on XML schema and security policy evolution, integration and management of heterogeneous biological data sources, data security and patient-privacy preservation.

Philippe Poulard is a software engineer at INRIA (French national institute for research in computer science and control) where he is involved in Web-oriented problematics. He has been specialized in XML technologies and e-documentation for 10 years. During this period, he has developed XML and SGML-based solutions and prototypes on behalf of the French Army and INRIA. More recently he has designed and implemented a set of XML technologies named "Active Tags". He also teaches XML and Java at Nice/Sophia-Antipolis University and Aix/Marseille University. He has an engineer degree (MSc) from the Conservatoire National des Arts et Metiers.

Christoph Reinke has been a research assistant at the Institute of Information Systems in Luebeck since June 2007. He received his Diploma degree in computer science at the University of Luebeck in May 2007 and is currently working on his dissertation in the area of database management systems in sensor networks. His particular research interests are the integration of XML processing into wireless sensor networks combined with the development of self-organizing service-oriented sensor networks. As a major issue for enabling self-organization in service-oriented sensor networks, he investigates concepts for the transactional replication and migration of services.

Ernesto Jiménez Ruiz joined the Temporal Knowledge Bases Group (TKBG) at University Jaume I of Castellón as a PhD Student in 2004. In 2006 he got a FPI Doctoral Grant, Valencian Autonomous Government. His main research tasks are being focused on the topics related to the Semantic Web where the management-representation of knowledge (mainly ontologies) arises as a key point. He is mainly interested in the application of the Semantic Web techniques within the biomedical domain, in which huge amounts of data, information and knowledge is required to be managed. Within his doctoral education he maintains an active collaboration with the Text Mining Group at European Bioinformatics Group (Cambridge), the Information Management Group at University of Manchester, the Information Systems Group at Oxford University and the company Maat GKnowledge.

Elke Rundensteiner is full professor in the Department of Computer Science at Worcester Polytechnic Institute. Professor Rundensteiner is a well-known expert in databases and information systems, having spent 20 years of her career focusing on the development of scalable data management technology in support of advanced applications including business, engineering, and sciences. Her current research interests include data integration, Web database management, stream processing, and visual analytics. She has over 300 publications in these areas and related areas. Her research has been funded by government agencies including NSF, NIH, DOE and by industry including IBM, Verizon Labs, GTE, HP, NEC, Mitre Corporation. She has been a recipient of numerous honors, including NSF Young Investigator, Sigma Xi Outstanding Senior Faculty Researcher, and WPI Trustees' Outstanding Research and Creative Scholarship awards. She is on program committees of prestigious database conferences and associate editor of *IEEE Transactions on Data and Knowledge Engineering Journal.*

Ismael Sanz is a lecturer at the Department of Computer Science and Engineering at Universitat Jaume I (UJI) in Spain. After receiving a BSc in computer science from UJI in 1997 he worked at STARLab in the Free University of Brussels and in the private sector as a software engineer. He holds a M.Sc. and a PhD in computer science from UJI. His current research interests include flexible query processing for complex and heterogeneous data, and approximate retrieval of XML. He co-organized last edition of the EDBT DataX workshop and served as reviewer for international conferences and journals.

Hong Su received her bachelor and master degree in computer science from Central South University in Changsha, P.R.China. She received her PhD in computer science from Worcester Polytechnic Institute, Worcester, USA. She has received IBM Cooperative fellowship for three consecutive years during her PhD study. Her research interests are in the areas of databases, information and software systems. She now works in the optimizer group at Oracle Corporation in Redwood Shores, CA.

Wee Hyong, Tok is a PhD candidate at the Department of Computer Science of the School of Computing (SoC) at the National University of Singapore (NUS). He graduated with a Master and Bachelor degree in computer science from NUS in 2002 and 2000 respectively. From 2003 to 2008, he worked as a teaching assistant at SoC. His research focuses on the design of progressive and adaptive query processing algorithms for different data models.

Vassilis J. Tsotras is a professor at the Department of Computer Science and Engineering, University of California, Riverside (UCR). His research interests include access methods, temporal and spatiotemporal databases, XML query processing and data dissemination. He received the NSF Research Initiation Award (1991) and the Teaching Excellence Award from the Bourns College of Engineering at UCR (1999). He has served as program committee member at numerous database conferences including: VLDB, SIGMOD, ICDE and EDBT. Dr. Tsotras was the program co-chair of the MIS'99 conference, the general chair of the SSTD'01 and the program chair (Database Track) of the ACM CIKM'06. He serves as Demos co-Chair for ICDE 2009. He is the general co-chair for ICDE 2010. He was a keynote speaker at SSTD'07 and MobiDE'08. He is co-editor in chief of the *International Journal of Cooperative Information Systems* and serves/ed on the editorial board of the *VLDB Journal* and *IEEE TKDE.* He has co-authored a book on *Advanced Database Indexing* (1999).

Zografoula Vagena (PhD, University of California, Riverside, 2005) is part of the Systems and Networking Group of Microsoft Research in Cambridge, UK. Before that she was a postdoctoral research associate at the IBM Almaden Research Center (CA, USA). She has also spent research internships at IBM Almaden Research (CA, USA), AT&T Labs (NJ, USA) and Microsoft Research Redmond (WA, USA). Her primary research interests include query processing and optimization, text indexing and retrieval and XML data management. She is a member of ACM.

Athena Vakali received her PhD in informatics from the Aristotle University, her MS in computer science from Purdue University and her BS in mathematics from the Aristotle University. She is currently an associate professor in the Department of Informatics at the Aristotle University, Thessaloniki. She is the head of the Operating Systems Web/INternet Data Storage and management research group. Her research activities are on various aspects and topics of the Web information systems, including Web data management, content delivery on the Web, Web data clustering, Web caching, XML-based authorization models, text mining and multimedia data management. She is a member of the editorial board of the *Computers and Electrical Engineering Journal* (Elsevier), the *International Journal of Grid and High Performance Computing* (IGI) and since March 2007, she is the coordinator of the IEEE TCSC technical area of Content Management and Delivery Networks. Prof. Vakali has leaded many research projects in the area of Web data management and Web Information Systems.

Giorgio Valentini received the degree in biological sciences and in computer science from the University of Genova, Italy in 1981 and 1999, and the PhD degree in computer science from the same University in 2003. He is currently assistant professor at DSI, Computer Science Department of the University of Milano, Italy. His main research focuses on bioinformatics and machine learning. He is author of about 60 papers published in international peer-reviewed journals and conference proceedings. He is member of the International Neural Network Society and of the International Society of Computational Biology.

Mingzhu Wei is a PhD student in the Computer Science Department, at Worcester Polytechnic Institute. She has received her BS degree and MS degree in computer science from University of Science and Technology Beijing, China. Her main area of interest is in database systems, especially continuous query processing in XML streams and complex event processing.

Xue Zhao graduated from the School of Computing at the National University of Singapore with a Bachelor degree in computing. Her honours year project was on the continuous query processing of XML. She is a system engineer in SingTel, a telecommunications company, headquartered in Singapore.

Index